Published by

THE BIBLE FOR TODAY PRESS
900 Park Avenue
Collingswood, New Jersey 08108
U.S.A.

Church Phone: 856-854-4747
BFT Phone: 856-854-4452
Orders: 1-800-John 10:9
e-mail: BFT@BibleForToday.org
Website: www.BibleForToday.org
fax: 856-854-2464

We Use and Defend
the King James Bible

October, 2005
BFT2906BK

ISBN #1-56848-047-4

Acknowledgments

**I wish to thank and to acknowledge the assistance
of the following people:**

- **The Congregation** of the **Bible For Today Baptist Church**, for whom these messages were prepared, to whom they were delivered, and by whom they were published. They listened attentively and encouraged their Pastor as he preached;

- **Yvonne Sanborn Waite**, my wife, who encouraged the publication of these sermons, read the manuscript several times, suggested the various boxes, and gave other helpful suggestions and comments;

- **Dianne W. Cosby**, for typing these messages from the original cassette tapes and put them in computer format;

- **Dr. Edward L. Smith**, for editing the messages in the computer format, inserting the texts of various Bible verses used, and paragraphing the exposition;

- **Daniel S. Waite**, the Assistant to the Bible For Today Director, who kept my computer working, guided the book through the printing process, and made important suggestions;

- **Barbara Egan**, our Bible For Today secretary who proofread the manuscript and, as usual, offered valuable suggestions and comments.

- **Joann Nawracki**, one of our **Bible For Today Baptist Church** friends who read some of the manuscript and gave some helpful suggestions.

- **Loretta Smith**, a former attender of our **Bible For Today Baptist Church**, having moved out of state, volunteered to continue reading the manuscript and offered her valuable suggestions chapter by chapter throughout the book.

𝕱oreword

- **The Beginning**. This book is the **sixth** in a planned series of books based on expository preaching from various books of the Bible. It is an attempt to bring to the minds of the readers two things: (1) the **meaning** of the words in the verses and (2) the practical **application** of those words to the lives of both saved and lost people. The book of Romans was written by Paul before he ever visited that city. Though this verse-by-verse book is four times longer than our former books, because of Romans' valuable theological message, I decided these teachings should be published.

- **Preached Sermons**. These are messages that have been preached to our **𝕭ible 𝕱or 𝕿oday 𝕭aptist 𝕮hurch** in Collingswood, New Jersey, broadcast over audio and video, and placed on our Website as follows:

    http://www.BibleForToday.org

This site is for people all over the world to listen to and view, should they wish. As the messages were originally preached, they are on the pages before you. I took half a chapter during our Sunday morning services, spending about forty-five minutes on each message.

- **Other Verses**. In connection with both the meaning and application of the verses in this book, there are many verses from other places in the Bible that have been quoted for further elaboration of Paul's discussion. One of the unique features of this study is that all of the various verses of Scripture used to illustrate further truth are written out in full for easy reference.

- **A Transcription**. It should be noted that this book is made up largely from the transcription of the tape recordings of the messages as they were preached. These recordings are available in audio, VHS or DVD formats **(BFT#2906/1-16; BFT #2906VC1-8, or BFT #2906DV1-8)**. Though there has been some editing, the words are basically the same as in the sermons.

- **The Audience**. The audience intended is the same as the audience that listened to the messages in the first place. These studies are not meant to be overly scholarly, though there is some reference to various Greek words used by Paul. My aim is to help lay people to understand the Words of God. It is my hope that I can get as many as possible of my expositions in print, as time and funds permit, so that my children, grandchildren, and all children in the faith may be able to rejoice with me in the things the Lord has brought to my attention as I have preached verse by verse from the Bible.

Yours For God's Words,

𝒟. 𝒶. 𝒲aite

Pastor D. A. Waite, Th.D., Ph.D.
𝕭ible 𝕱or 𝕿oday 𝕭aptist 𝕮hurch

Table of Contents

Romans
Chapter One

Romans 1:1

"Paul, a servant of Jesus Christ, called *to be* an apostle, separated unto the gospel of God,"

"Paul, a servant of Jesus Christ" Paul was a *"servant"* of Jesus Christ. The Greek word for *"servant"* is DOULOS. It means:

"one who gives himself up to another's will, those whose service is used by Christ in extending and advancing His cause among men; devoted to another to the disregard of one's own interests."

This word is the strongest Greek word for *"servant."* It is literally a *"slave"* or a *"bond slave."* I believe in being a *"slave"* to the Lord Jesus Christ. This is very strong language, I realize, but I believe we need to know what being a *"slave"* means. I believe that everyone who trusts Christ as Saviour should be totally committed to the Saviour and Master of our souls. The Lord Jesus Christ showed this attitude toward His Father when he prayed in the Garden of Gethsemane, *"Not my will, but thine be done"* (Luke 22:42b).

I think we have too few Christians who are *"slaves"* to the Lord Jesus Christ. *"Slavery"* means servitude! Paul was a *"servant."* He did not use the lesser word, DIAKONOS. It means:

"to be a servant, attendant, domestic, to serve, wait upon; to minister to one, render ministering offices to; to be served, ministered unto; to wait at a table and offer food and drink to the guests; of women preparing food; to minister i.e. supply food and necessities of life; to relieve one's necessities (e.g. by collecting alms), to provide take care of, distribute, the things necessary to sustain life; to take care of the poor and the sick, who administer the office of a deacon; in Christian churches to serve as deacons; to minister; to attend to anything, that may serve another's interests; to minister a thing to one, to serve one or by supplying any thing."

We get our word, "*deacon,*" from this term. He used, instead, DOULOS. This is the strongest word possible for "*servant.*" It means:

> "*a slave, bondman, man of servile condition; a slave; metaph., one who gives himself up to another's will those whose service is used by Christ in extending and advancing His cause among men; devoted to another to the disregard of one's own interests; a servant, attendant.*"

What sort of attitude should a person have when he or she gets yoked to the Lord Jesus Christ by genuine saving faith? Should he or she say? "*Well, I did not really care too much. I'll do my own will. I'll do what I want to do.*" This should not be his attitude. Paul wasn't that kind of a "*servant.*" He was a "*bond slave,*" who through his life "*gave himself up to another's will.*" He was "*devoted to another to the disregard of one's own interests.*" The Apostle was a true "*slave*" in every sense of that word to the One Who had saved his soul, forgiven all his sins, and given him eternal life by genuine faith.

- **Ephesians 2:8-9**

  For **by grace are ye saved through faith**; and that not of yourselves: *it is* the gift of God: Not of works, lest any man should boast.

"called *to be* an apostle" Paul was also "*called to be an apostle.*" His selection to be an "*apostle*" was his "*call.*" He did not make himself an "*apostle*" on his own. The Lord Jesus Christ met him and blinded him. He fell to the ground. He was blinded (Acts 9:8), not because of the sun, though it was about "*noon*" (Acts 22:6) when the sun is the brightest. He saw a Light that was brighter than the sun (Acts 9:3). When Paul heard a "voice" from Heaven, he asked, "*Who art thou, Lord?*" (Acts 9:4-5). The Lord said, "*I am Jesus whom thou persecutest*" (Acts 9:5). After he knew it was the Lord Jesus Christ, the first question Paul asked was, "*Lord what wilt thou have me to do?*" (Acts 9:6). He was completely open to service for Christ. Paul was no longer looking to kill Christians (Acts 9:1). He was no longer on his own. He was "*called to be an apostle.*" The Greek word for "*apostle*" is APOSTOLOS. It means: "*a delegate, messenger, one sent forth with orders.*" It comes from two Greek words, APO ("*from or forth*") and the verb STELLO ("*to send.*") An "*apostle*" is one who has been "*sent forth*" by the Lord. In the strict sense, there are no more "*apostles*" today, but every Christian has been "*sent forth*" with the gospel to tell others about the Lord Jesus Christ and His salvation (Mark 16:15).

"separated unto the gospel of God" Paul was also "*separated unto the gospel of God.*" This phrase, "*the gospel of God*" is the theme of the entire book of Romans. Paul was an "*apostle*" who was also "*separated unto the gospel of God.*" The Greek word translated "*separated*" is APHORIZO. It means:

"to mark off from others by boundaries, to limit, to separate; in a good sense: to appoint, set apart for some purpose."
It comes from two Greek words, APO (*"from"*) and HORIZO which means:
"to mark out the boundaries or limits (of any place or thing)."
We get the English word, *"horizon"* from this term. The *"horizon"* separates the land from the sky. Paul was *"separated."* This is the way Paul was. We also need to be *"separated unto the gospel of God."*

Two Phases of Separation

Separation has two phases: Phase #1: separation UNTO the Lord and all of His will. Phase #2: separation FROM the Devil and all of his will.

Romans 1:2

"Which he had promised afore by his prophets in the Holy Scriptures." The *"Holy Scriptures"* refer to the Old Testament. In them is the *"promise"* of the *"gospel of God."* This might be a reference to Genesis 3:15. It refers to the Lord Jesus Christ. Theologians call it the *PROTO EVANGELIUM* or the *"first gospel."* God spoke to Satan who had taken the form of a serpent in the Garden of Eden.

● **Genesis 3:15**
And I will put enmity between thee and the woman, and between thy Seed and **her seed; it shall bruise thy head**, and thou shalt bruise his heel.

There was to be a battle between the *"seed"* of the serpent and the *"Seed"* of the woman. This is the first gospel message because it promises victory for the virgin-born Seed of the woman, the Saviour, the Lord Jesus Christ.

● **Deuteronomy 18:15-18**
The LORD thy God will raise up unto thee **a Prophet** from the midst of thee, of thy brethren, like unto me; unto him ye shall hearken; According to all that thou desiredst of the LORD thy God in Horeb in the day of the assembly, saying, Let me not hear again the voice of the LORD my God, neither let me see this great fire any more, that I die not. And the LORD said unto me, They have well spoken that which they have spoken. I will raise them up **a Prophet** from among their brethren, like unto thee, **and will put my words in his mouth; and he shall**

speak unto them all that I shall command him.
The Lord Jesus Christ is that *"Prophet."*

● **Isaiah 7:14**
Therefore the Lord himself shall give you a sign; Behold, a virgin shall conceive, and bear a son, and shall call his name Immanuel.

This is another prophecy of the Lord Jesus Christ in the Old Testament spoken of *"afore by his prophets."*

● **Jeremiah 31:22**
How long wilt thou go about, O thou backsliding daughter? for the LORD hath created a new thing in the earth, A woman shall compass a man.

This verse also predicted the virgin birth of the Lord Jesus Christ. It speaks about the miracle of the Virgin birth right there in Jeremiah, who was speaking of the Lord Jesus Christ. He is the very heart of the *"gospel of God."* He is the *"Good news."*

● **Isaiah 53:6**
All we like sheep have gone astray; we have turned every one to his own way; and the LORD hath laid on him the iniquity of us all.

This is a prediction of the substitutionary sufferings and death on Calvary of our Saviour, the Lord Jesus Christ.

● **Genesis 22:18**
And in thy Seed shall all the nations of the earth be blessed; because thou hast obeyed my voice.

It was the Lord Jesus Christ Who was Abraham's *"Seed."* The gospel was predicted and prophesied in all the Old Testament by the prophets.

Romans 1:3

"Concerning his Son Jesus Christ our Lord, which was made of the Seed of David according to the flesh;"

"Concerning his Son Jesus Christ our Lord" What was the *"gospel of God"* about? We find this in Romans 1:3. The gospel, the good news, must be *"concerning His Son."* *"Gospel"* means *"good news."* It means *"glad tidings."* It is something that is happy. It is *"concerning His Son."* The Lord Jesus Christ is God's Son.

"which was made of the Seed of David according to the flesh" The Lord Jesus Christ had to have a true and sinless human nature in order for Him to be our Saviour. He had to be one of us, yet perfect, not sinful like we are. If we are saved by grace through faith, we are still sinners.

We have the old sin nature which loves to sin. Though saved people have this old sin nature, God has given them His Holy Spirit to help them walk in God's power rather than the flesh. The Lord Jesus Christ possessed a perfect and sinless humanity which was *"made of the Seed of David."*

Two Genealogies--Matthew & Luke

There are two genealogies in Scripture, one in Matthew, and the other in Luke. Matthew gives us the genealogy from Joseph, the foster father of the Lord Jesus. The Lord God of Heaven and earth is the Father of the Lord Jesus Christ. So this genealogy in Matthew 1 goes through a cursed line. Luke gives us Mary's line. The Lord Jesus Christ had to be in that line, the line of David. Matthew goes through Solomon, Josias, and Jechonias (which is Jehoiachin). Another name for Jechonias is Coniah. He was under a curse (Jeremiah 22:24, 28).

- **Jeremiah 22:24**
  As I live, saith the LORD, though **Coniah** the son of Jehoiakim king of Judah were the signet upon my right hand, **yet would I pluck thee thence;**

It was Jehoiakim, the father of Coniah (or Jechonias), who, when the Word of God was being read, ripped apart those Words with his pen knife and threw the scroll into the fire on the hearth. God never forgot that man's hatred and destruction of His Words. So his son, Coniah (or Jechonias) the son of Jehoiakim, was cursed.

- **Jeremiah 22:28-30**
  Is this man Coniah a despised broken idol? is he a vessel wherein is no pleasure? wherefore are they cast out, he and his seed, and are cast into a land which they know not? O earth, earth, earth, hear the word of the LORD. Thus saith the LORD, **Write ye this man childless, a man that shall not prosper in his days: for no man of his seed shall prosper, sitting upon the throne of David, and ruling any more in Judah.**

This is a very clear curse on Joseph's line in Matthew. If the line in Matthew were Mary's line, it would be under Coniah's curse.

The whole curse of Jechonias was bypassed in Mary's line in Luke Chapter 3. That is why the Virgin birth was so important. The Lord Jesus was *"made of the seed of David,"* but made according to the right genealogy, without any cursed line.

● **1 Timothy 3:16**
And without controversy great is the mystery of godliness: **God was manifest in the flesh,** justified in the Spirit, seen of angels, preached unto the Gentiles, believed on in the world, received up into glory.

That is the *"mystery of Godliness,"* that *"God was manifest in the flesh."* The Lord Jesus Christ had to be of *"the seed of David"* Who was *"manifest in the flesh,"* but He was, and is, absolute Deity.

1 Timothy 3:16 is translated incorrectly in almost all of the new versions. This is because they have a corrupted Greek text in this verse. Here is the correct rendering of the important part of 1 Timothy 3:16 in the King James Bible:

---

1 Timothy 3:16--Six False Readings

"<u>God</u> was manifest in the flesh." (King James Bible)

"<u>He who</u> was manifested in the flesh" (American Standard Version, 1901)

"<u>He </u>was manifested in the flesh" (Revised Standard Version, 1950's)

"<u>He who</u> was revealed in the flesh" (New American Standard Version)

"<u>He</u> appeared in a body" (New International Version)

"<u>He </u>was revealed in the flesh" (New Revised Standard Version)

"<u>He</u> was shown to us in a human body" (New Century Version)

You will notice that the **ONLY** correct reading that has "**<u>GOD</u>**" being manifested in the flesh is the King James Bible. That is the true reading. The other versions made use of the false Westcott and Hort type of Greek text. Our King James Bible has it right. We have the very essence of the incarnation of the Lord Jesus Christ in this verse. Almighty God became Perfect Man in the Person of our Saviour. He had to be *"made of the seed of David according to the flesh"* in order for God to inherit the likeness of man.

Romans 1:4

"And declared *to be* the Son of God with power, according to the spirit of holiness, by the resurrection from the dead:"

"declared *to be* the Son of God with power" In this present verse, Paul continues his explanation of the Person of the Lord Jesus Christ. He was not only *"the seed of David"* as to His humanity, but He was also *"the Son of God"* as to His Deity. The Lord Jesus had to be both perfect Man and perfect God. This He was. Some heretical teachers in the early churches denied His true humanity. They thought the Lord Jesus Christ was just a ghost or spirit. Other early heretics denied His Deity, saying He was just a human being as all of us are. We have many apostate Unitarians, Modernists, and Liberals today who believe that the Lord Jesus was only a man.

The leaders and those who espouse the program of the *National Council of Christian Churches* are leaders in these heresies. The cults, such as Christian Science, deny Christ's Deity. Jesus was *"declared the Son of God with power."* He had *"power,"* which is a translation of the Greek word, DUNAMIS. We get the word, *"dynamite"* from this term. God has manifested His *"power"* in many ways. He manifested His power in miracles, for example.

- **Romans 9:17**
  For the scripture saith unto Pharaoh, Even for this same purpose have I raised thee up, **that I might shew my power in thee**, and that my name might be declared throughout all the earth.

This verse talks about Pharaoh and about the *"power"* of the miracles in Egypt. That was a great *"power"*--ten plagues. There were a number of miracles that God used to show His *"power."*

1. The First Demonstration of God's "Power."

During the tenth plague (the death of the firstborn) Pharaoh let Israel go free.

- **Exodus 12:31-33**
  And he called for Moses and Aaron by night, and said, Rise up, and get you forth from among my people, both ye and the children of Israel; and go, serve the LORD, as ye have said. Also take your flocks and your herds, as ye have said, and be gone; and bless me also. And the Egyptians were urgent upon the people, that they might send them out of the land in haste; for they said, We be all dead men.

Pharaoh was finally impressed with God's mighty *"power."* Then Pharaoh changed his mind and tried to bring the children of Israel back. He probably wondered what he would do for his slave laborers. They had been building all of his treasure cities. So, the *"power"* of God was seen all through those ten plagues.

2. The Second Demonstration of God's "Power."

Then there was the *"power"* of God manifested as the Egyptians followed the Israelites. The opening up of the Red Sea was absolutely miraculous. That was *"power"*!

3. The Third Demonstration of God's "Power."

The Lord not only opened up the Red Sea so that the Israelites could walk through (600,000 men plus women and children probably about 2 or 3 million people), but also the Lord had a cloud (Exodus 13:21) that caused a darkness to the Egyptians so that they could not see anything (Exodus 14:20). There was light in the front of the cloud for the Israelites. This was a miracle and a further evidence of God's *"power."*

4. The Fourth Demonstration of God's "Power."

When the Israelites got through the Red Sea and the Egyptians tried to do this, God closed up the water. All the liberals and modernists say that this was just a *"reed"* sea and not a part of the Red sea at all. They say this is why the Israelites could walk across. They have a serious problem with this, however. Because if this were a *"reed"* sea with only six or seven inches of water, how could that sea drown the Egyptians? (Exodus 15:4). The unbelievers have an explanation of the one miracle, but they will have to work out a miracle to drown the host of Pharaoh in a few inches of water. It was the real Red sea and not a *"reed"* sea.

"according to the spirit of holiness, by the resurrection from the dead"

4. The Fifth Demonstration of God's "Power."

In this part of the verse, the greatest *"power"* of all is mentioned. This *"power"* was manifested *"by the resurrection from the dead"* of the Lord Jesus Christ. Man has never been able to do that, has he? Man talks about cryobiology, freezing bodies, and maybe later on attempting to bring them back to life. I doubt its success greatly. God has the *"power"* of life, the *"power"* of death, and the *"power"* of resurrection.

Some people have been resuscitated and have had near-death experiences, but resurrection is impossible as far as I am concerned. These unsaved people have what they describe as a beautiful and wonderful experience. That is a strong delusion. The unsaved do not want to worry about where they will spend eternity so they make up stories about near-death. It is a terrible delusion from the Devil--the master-delusionist.

The power of resurrection was manifested when God the Son was raised from the dead after suffering and dying in our place for the sins of the world.

This is the ultimate *"power"* that God manifested.

Romans 1:5

"By whom we have received grace and apostleship, for obedience to the faith among all nations, for his name:"

"By whom we have received grace" The reference of the words, *"by whom"* go back to verse 3, *"concerning His Son, Jesus Christ our Lord."* Paul said those who were saved had *"received grace."* If we have been born-again, we *also "received grace."* Grace and mercy are two opposite words.

I remember Dr. M. R. DeHaan, founder of the Radio Bible Class. He was my teacher in the Detroit Bible Class every Friday night when I was a student at the University of Michigan in Ann Arbor during the years from 1945 to 1948. The cook at the University hospital, Brother David McRoberts, used to take us young fellows over to Detroit, Michigan every Friday night. That was where Dr. M. R. DeHaan held his Detroit Bible Class. He taught the Words of God from the book of Hebrews week by week. It was through his faithful ministry that I gave my life to surrender to be a preacher of the Words and go into training for the Lord's work. He always gave these two definitions that I shall never forget concerning *"mercy"* and *"grace." "Grace"* is positive. *"Getting something we don't deserve."* That is receiving Heaven's blessings for all eternity. *"Mercy"* is negative. *"Not getting something that we do deserve."* That is an escape from Hell and damnation. Paul said that *"we,"* meaning he and his comrades, *"received grace."*

"and apostleship, for obedience to the faith among all nations, for his name" Paul also said that he received *"apostleship."* By the way, if we are saved here today we also receive grace. The same grace of the Lord Jesus Christ. For what was *"apostleship"* meant? It wasn't just to represent his country, but *"for obedience to the faith among all nations, for his name."* Paul was an *"apostle,"* which is *"one sent forth," "for obedience to the faith."* The office of *"apostles"* is no longer in the church today. All nations, everywhere in the world, should be *"obedient to the faith"* which is in Christ Jesus. That is why he was an *"apostle."* That is why you and I ought to go and send forth the gospel wherever we are so that many might be given to the *"obedience to the faith."*

Romans 1:6

"Among whom are ye also the called of Jesus Christ:"
Notice in verse 6 Paul was writing to the Christians at Rome saying that they also were *"the called."* A *"call"* is an invitation. Everyone in the world is invited to come to obedient faith in the Lord Jesus Christ and be saved. We read in our Bible this morning Matthew 11:28-29. My wife and I read through the Scriptures together, 85 verses each day. We listen to it on the cassette, and Mrs. Waite follows, sometimes in a different version to see what the various differences are that might be found there. One year she used the *"Tyndale New Testament."*

- **Matthew 11:28-29**
  Come unto me, all ye that labour and are heavy laden, and I will give you rest. Take my yoke upon you, and learn of me; for I am meek and lowly in heart: and ye shall find rest unto your souls.

There is the Lord Jesus Christ's kind invitation to all sinners in the world. When you accept that invitation, you are *"called."* You are invited. Not everyone accepts that *"call"* to believe. Not everyone says *"yes"* to the Lord Jesus Christ. Is that not right? Maybe you are here this morning and you haven't said yes to the Lord Jesus Christ, but that is the call.

Romans 1:7

"To all that be in Rome, beloved of God, called *to be* saints: Grace to you and peace from God our Father, and the Lord Jesus Christ."

"To all that be in Rome, beloved of God, called *to be* saints" In verse 6, these believers in Rome were "called." In this verse, they were not only *"called,"* but *"called to be saints"* People in the Roman Catholic Church wait until people are canonized before they call them *"saints,"* even though most, if not all of them, were lost souls. Paul did not wait. He was writing to Rome, the very seat of the papacy and the Vatican. He said in effect, *"Do not wait until you are canonized. You who are saved are saints right now."* That is why the new Bible versions use the word *"saint"* or *"saints"* less frequently than our King James Bible. Perhaps these versions feel they must placate the Roman Catholic Church in some way. All of the born-again Christians who ever believed have been *"called to be saints."* That is their name.

Here are the totals for the use of *"saint"* or *"saints"* in the New Testament for some of the Bible versions.

Frequency of "Saint" or "Saints"

KJB--King James Bible	68 times
NRSV--New Revised Standard Version	63 times
ASV--American Standard Version	62 times
RSV--Revised Standard Version	62 times
NKJV--New King James Version	62 times
NASV--New American Standard Version	61 times
NIV--New International Version	45 times
NCV--New Century Version	1 time

"Grace to you and peace from God our Father, and the Lord Jesus Christ." *"Grace"* or CHARIS was the greeting used by the Greeks. *"Peace"* or SHALOM was the greeting used by the Hebrews. It is still used by them today. Paul combined these two greetings. *"Grace"* to those of the readers who are Greeks and not Jews. *"Peace from God our Father"* to those who are saved. The source of *"grace"* is from *"God our Father and the Lord Jesus Christ."* The source of *"peace"* is also from *"God our Father and the Lord Jesus Christ"* as well. You cannot get *"grace"* or *"peace"* apart from the Lord. He is the grace and peace-giver.

- Romans 5:1
  Therefore being justified by faith, **we have peace with God** through our Lord Jesus Christ:
That peace comes from *"our Lord Jesus Christ"* and from God the Father. The false Greek text of Westcott and Hort changed one word in this verse which completely changes the sense. The KJB and the true Greek text rightly read: *"Being justified by faith we have peace with God."* The verb *"we have"* comes from the Greek word ECHOMEN (εχομεν) with an omicron, small "o." The translation of the false Greek text reads *"let us have peace with God."* The translators are not certain whether or not saved people really have *"peace."* It is just a wish. Their Greek text reads ECHOMEN (εχωμεν) with an omega, large "O." This latter reading does not mean *"we have peace"* (indicative mood), but *"let us have peace with God"* (subjunctive mood). We do not have it, we're not sure of it but *"let us have peace with God."* No, it is not *"let us."* *"We HAVE"* it if we're saved and justified by faith. *"We have peace with God."* The Greek word for *"peace,"* is EIRENE.

Definition of God's "Peace"

"of Christianity, the tranquil state of a soul assured of its salvation through Christ, and so fearing nothing from God and content with its earthly lot, of whatsoever sort that is."

There is no question about it. Our God, through being *"justified by faith,"* gives us peace. We are no longer at war with the righteous God in Heaven.

Romans 1:8

"First, I thank my God through Jesus Christ for you all, that your faith is spoken of throughout the whole world."

"First, I thank my God through Jesus Christ for you all" That word, *"I thank,"* in the Greek language is a continuous present action. It means that Paul *"continues to thank"* his *"God through Jesus Christ."* It is through the Lord Jesus that these people have become saints and have become saved. At this point in time, Paul apparently had never yet seen the Roman Christians. He had never been to Rome. But, apparently through the testimony of the Roman soldiers that Paul had led to Christ, the gospel was taken to these people and they were saved. Paul heard about them and wrote this letter to these believers.

Paul did not continuously thank his God for only one or two people in the congregation. He was thankful for *"all"* of the people. He did not single- out the handsome or the beautiful ones. He did not single-out the skinny ones rather than the fat ones. He did not single-out the rich ones rather than the poor ones. He did not single-out the short ones, rather than the tall ones. That is a pastor's heart. That is an apostle's heart. I thank God for all of you who are here, by the way, in this, our first service of our Bible For Today Baptist Church. I did not know I had so many friends.

"that your faith is spoken of throughout the whole world" Others had heard about the church at Rome. It was not the Roman Catholic Church. These believers probably met in homes, in caves, or in dark places. They were more interested in hearing the Words of God preached than to be entertained. How times have changed today! I am sure the Christians there were being persecuted as this book was being written. Paul was thankful that their *"faith was spoken of throughout the whole world."* That was their testimony.

Churches have testimonies. Do you know that? When churches break up, that bad news gets around. Churches that have pastors who are unfaithful--that gets around. Churches that have treasurers who steal money--that gets around. Churches that do not like this one or that one or have fights and battles and corruption--that gets around. Churches where you have one side of people sit on one side of the church because they do not speak to the people on the other side of the church--that gets around. Am I right? You cannot stop news traveling about what goes on in churches.

In the case of this church in Rome, their *"faith"* was *"spoken of throughout the whole world."* It was spoken of, I am sure in a good way, not in a bad way.

Romans 1:9

"For God is my witness, whom I serve with my spirit in the gospel of his Son, that without ceasing I make mention of you always in my prayers;"

"For God is my witness, whom I serve with my spirit in the gospel of his Son" Paul prayed for these Roman Christians. No one on earth could testify of Paul's *"prayers"* for them. He said: *"God is my witness."* Only the Lord knows about our prayers.

I suppose you get letters from pastors and church leaders--maybe radio preachers, or T.V. preachers--who say they are praying for you. How do you know who they are? You do not know. How do you know that Paul was praying continuously for these Christian believers in Rome? Well, he said *"God is my witness"* That is all we can say.

Sometimes we do not have any people who believe us. Nobody knows what we do, but God is our *"witness."* He's the One Who sees us, hears us, and knows what we do, whether it be good or bad. We cannot get away from Him. We cannot run from Him. There is nowhere we can go--North, South, East, or West. Our God is there watching. As the song goes,

---

Our God Is Omnipresent

"My Lord is writing all the time.
He sees all you do,
He hears all you say.
My Lord is writing all the time."

He is our *"witness"* and He alone.

Notice also Paul's relationship to his God. Paul said, about Him, *"whom I serve with my spirit in the gospel of his Son."* Paul *"served"*! The Greek word for *"serve"* here is LATREUO. It means:

"to perform sacred services, to offer gifts, to worship God in the observance of the rites instituted for his worship; of priests, to officiate, to discharge the sacred office."

Paul performed this kind of *"service"* with his *"spirit in the gospel of his Son."* If you *"serve"* in your body, I guess that would be all right. But what about your *"spirit"*? Our *"spirit"* is on the inside of us. If you are saved, you must *"serve"* the Lord, not only with your body, but also with your *"spirit."* The Lord wants us to "serve" Him with our spirit, soul, and body--all three parts of our human nature. Paul wrote:

- **1 Thessalonians 5:23**
  And the very God of peace sanctify you wholly; and I pray God **your whole spirit and soul and body be preserved blameless** unto the coming of our Lord Jesus Christ.

The Lord is interested in our *"spirits"* as well as our bodies. The Lord wants our spirits, souls and bodies. The Devil also wants our spirits, souls, and bodies. We must give all that we are to the Lord, not the Devil.

Paul *"served"* his God *"in the gospel of his Son."* That is the good news about the Lord Jesus Christ. That is the area where Paul was *"serving."* That is the area of his witness, and the type of his *"service."* The highest *"service"* that any saved person could render is the *"service"* for the Lord Jesus Christ, the Son of God and our Saviour. You may have a secular business, but I hope you *"serve"* the Lord Jesus Christ, whatever that business is. I hope that you give Him honor and glory, and wherever possible, bear witness to His saving grace.

"that without ceasing I make mention of you always in my prayers" God was a *"witness"* about Paul's prayers for the Christians there in Rome. It is commendable. Praying seems to be a lost art today. If any of us were honest with ourselves, we would stand up and say that we do not pray as often, or as much, or as earnestly as we should.

A Prayer of Concern

I did not read God's Words today,
Nor did I take the time to pray;
I busy went upon my way,
And thus betrayed my Lord.

I did not lean upon His might
When new day cares came with the light;
I tried to walk by my own sight,
And thus I grieved my Lord.

I did not raise my voice in praise
But murmured oft' on many days,
And did not to myself say 'nay,'
And thus denied my Lord.

Dear Lord, I yearn to be so bent
Unto Thy will and be content
To trust Thee for each day and hour,
And draw from Thee Thy grace and power.

By Gertrude Grace Sanborn

Romans 1:10

"Making request, if by any means now at length I might have a prosperous journey by the will of God to come unto you." After Paul mentions his "*prayers*" for the believers in Rome, he lists what he has been praying about. He wants to have a "*prosperous journey*" to visit them. Paul wants to see them. He had never been there. If you remember, Paul was taken as a prisoner from Caesarea to Rome. A very rough storm (Acts 27:14) came up while Paul's ship was in Crete. They were blown to the island of Melita which is now called Malta. While there, Paul healed the father of Publius who was sick of a fever (Acts 28:8). Did he have a "*prosperous journey*"? How would you answer this? Paul mentioned the words, *"by the will of God."* The shipwreck was part of God's "will" for Paul. God spared his life and all those on board that boat. Paul did, in the Lord's *"will,"* have a *"prosperous journey."*

It was a rough journey. During that storm the prisoners were going to be killed in one way or another, but Paul told the officer in charge not to do that. The guards thought that the prisoners would escape on planks or in some other way. Paul said, *"Sirs, . . . I believe God, that it shall be even as it was told me"*(Acts 27:25). He assured them that there would be no loss of life to anyone on the vessel. Paul took assertive control of that shipwreck. God broke up the ship. There was nothing left of it, but all the prisoners escaped to the island of Melita.

Look For the Bright Side

Look for the bright side of your life, even though it may not seem *"prosperous"* to you. If God is in it, and if it is God's *"will,"* put a different interpretation on it. Was it the *"will"* of God for Paul to go to Rome? I believe it was. Was it the will of God that he go as a prisoner? I believe it was also.

In the book of Acts Paul went before Felix and Festus and Agrippa. Three different Roman officials. He was his own attorney, PRO SE, as we call it. He did not have any lawyer. Finally he said, *"I appeal unto Caesar"* (Acts 25:11b). Paul knew his rights. He took his case all the way to Rome. So the Roman soldiers took Paul to Rome. The Lord worked it out for Paul to see His Christian friends. When he was locked up in the Roman prison, the Christians at Rome came to visit him. I am sure they were overjoyed to meet Paul for the first time. Wouldn't you have been? They had never met each other previously. Paul wanted to come to them because of his missionary heart. Do you have a missionary heart?

Romans 1:11

"For I long to see you, that I may impart unto you some spiritual gift, to the end ye may be established;" Notice why Paul wanted the *"will of God."* He had a strong desire to see these believers so that he could *"impart unto them some spiritual gift, to the end they may be established."* Notice, Paul did not want to get an offering from them, as some preachers and missionaries sometimes request. He did not try to fleece them. He did not request them to put him up in a very nice home for the rest of his life. Instead of receiving from them, Paul wanted to give them something, a "spiritual gift." That was his great joy. The Lord Jesus said, "*It is more blessed to give than to receive*" (Acts 20:35). He wanted to give them some "*spiritual gift.*"

Paul did not have much money. Maybe some of you do not have much money to leave to your children, but I hope that you give them a spiritual heritage, the things of the Lord Jesus Christ. May your "*light so shine*" before them that they may "*see your good works, and glorify your Father which is in Heaven*" (Matthew 5:16).

Notice the reason that Paul wanted the born-again saints in Rome to have a "*spiritual gift.*" He wanted them to "*be established.*" The goal of all of Paul's preaching was the "*establishment*" of the believers. This should be the goal of every preacher in the world today! The Greek word for "*established*" is STERIZO. It means:

> "*to make stable, place firmly, set fast, fix; to strengthen, make firm; to render constant, confirm one's mind.*"

The Lord wants all of his saved believers to be "*stable.*" A sailboat in a storm is not "*stable.*" Any boat in a storm is not "*stable.*" In fact, even a boat in calm water is not "*stable,*" because you can rock it very easily. Paul wanted the believers in Rome to be "*stable, confirmed, constant, firm, and placed firmly.*" He did not want them up one day and down the next. He did not want them to be carried away with the winds of change.

There is an old saying, "*Rolling stones, gather no moss.*" People are rolling around all about us. They do not know what to believe. As Paul wrote in the book of Ephesians, some people were "*like children, tossed to and fro, and carried about with every wind of doctrine, by the slight of men*" (Ephesians 4:14). Paul wanted to come to the Christians in Rome in order to "*establish*" them, settle them, and stabilize them in the Faith.

Stick to the Bible!

We do not have to move all around in our beliefs and doctrines. Every time a new doctrine comes out, we do not have to say, "*Oh, I'd better believe that and change my ways.*" No. Stick to what the Bible says. Make sure it is Biblical, and then stick to it. Be "*established*" in it. Be firm in it. Do not let anybody push you away from Biblical truth.

People might say to you, "*Oh you have to change. You have to have new music, new Bibles, new churches, new methodology. You have to have all these new gimmicks.*" No! You do not need these "*new*" things. Once some truth has been "*established,*" it is true forever. Truth does not change. Truth is as eternal as God. The *establishment* in the Faith is a very important thing.

Romans 1:12

"That is, that I may be comforted together with you by the mutual faith both of you and me." Paul needed *"comfort"* also. Paul was alone as an apostle. I was in the Naval Chaplain Corps for five years on active duty. I observed that the commander of the troops had to be alone to be effective. He could not fraternize with his troops. If he did, he would lose his *"command presence."* He could not even fraternize too closely with his junior officers. There is a little bit more flexibility with the officers, but they speak of the status of the commanding officer as *"the loneliness of command."*

Pastors often experience this *"loneliness."* Other pastors do fraternize with their people. Where is the balance that should be maintained? This doesn't mean that a pastor should be a boss over his people. The Lord cautions this in 1 Peter 5:3, *"Neither as being lords over God's heritage, but being ensamples to the flock."*

Respect the Pastoral Office

There is a place for respect of the pastoral office, yet there should be a friendliness on the part of the pastor. There should also be a respectable distance to maintain the proper relationship between pastor and people.

Though Paul was an apostle, he was friendly. I am sure that pastors, if they are doing their job, should be as friendly as possible.

Paul wanted to be *"comforted together"* with the believers, as he wrote: *"by the mutual faith both of you and me."* Paul needed fellowship. You and I also need fellowship with fellow believers, and with the Words of God. Our *"mutual faith"* encourages and *"comforts"* us, does it not? As you hear brother Dick Carroll play the hymns of the faith so skillfully, and as we sing those hymns, that is a sharing of our *"mutual faith."* We believe these words, do we not? I hope we sing the hymns with the joy that God can give us because of the Scriptural words.

Romans 1:13

"Now I would not have you ignorant, brethren, that oftentimes I purposed to come unto you, (but was let hitherto,) that I might have some fruit among you also, even as among other Gentiles." In verse 11, Paul *"longed to see them."* In verse 12, he wanted to be *"comforted together."* In this verse 13, he said that he often *"purposed to come unto them,"* but he was *"let"* or *"hindered."*

Paul's purpose in *"longing to see them"* was not for money, nor reward. It was that he *"might have some fruit among them even as among other Gentiles."* This was Paul's goal. That was his ministry. He wanted to come to them, even though he had never seen them. Is it not strange that the Lord would allow him to come to Rome at government expense? That is interesting is it not? I have traveled to many places in the world while in the Navy. It was all at government expense. I did not have to pay for it.

Paul did not have to pay for his trip to Rome, even though it began with a shipwreck. It was a terrible ride. It was almost a disaster. Paul wanted to come to Rome, and he got there. The Lord took care of that. Just think of God's miraculous power that resulted in the lives of all the men on that little fragile ship, which broke apart on the stormy sea, being spared. Every single soul was saved from drowning.

Romans 1:14

"I am debtor both to the Greeks, and to the Barbarians; both to the wise, and to the unwise." Have you ever been in debt? I think, if you are like most of us, there is some type of debt hanging over your head. I do not know what it is. Maybe you do not have one. At present, we do not have any debt on this house. We've lived here since 1965, and, although the debt has been paid off, the present taxes are more than our original payments were. That is a kind of debt is it not? As the bumper sticker says, and most people can say it too, *"I owe, I owe, its off to work I go."*

Paul had a *"debt."* He was a *"debtor"* in terms of a spiritual *"debt."* I do not know whether we feel like we are spiritually indebted to anybody. We must come to them and bring them the gospel of the Lord Jesus Christ. Paul was a *"debtor."* He was a *"debtor"* not only to the *"Greeks"* but also to the *"Barbarians,"* both *"to the wise, and to the unwise."* The *"Barbarians"* could not even read Greek. That was the measure of intelligence in those days.

Paul Was A Debtor

If you could not read Greek you were a "*Barbarian.*" Paul was a debtor to the "*wise*" and also to the "*Barbarians.*" He was a "*debtor*" both to those who had been to the colleges, seminaries, and universities, and, to those on the streets who never had the privilege (sometimes it is a curse) of higher learning.

Romans 1:15

"So, as much as in me is, I am ready to preach the gospel to you that are at Rome also." Paul said he was not only a "*debtor,*" but he was also "*ready to preach the gospel*" to those in "Rome also." How do you get "*ready to preach the gospel*"?

1. <u>First of all you have to be saved</u>. No person, lost in sin, can ever be "*ready*" to "*preach the gospel*" and lead someone to saving faith in the Lord Jesus Christ.

2. <u>Second, you have to be walking with, and living for, the Lord</u>. You cannot "*preach the gospel*" if your life does not "*preach the gospel*" as well. Your life has to "*preach the gospel*" before your mouth even opens up. People have to believe what you are saying. You have to be "*ready.*"

3. <u>Third, you have to open the Book, the Scriptures, from Genesis through Revelation.</u> You have to read your King James Bible daily, asking God to help you, and give you wisdom to understand what you are reading.

4. <u>Fourth, ask the Holy Spirit to guide and direct you as to where, when, how, and to whom you should "*preach the gospel.*"</u>

Women Preachers Are Unscriptural

Who should "*preach the gospel*"? Though women can evangelize one on one with their personal witness, the Scriptures do not permit women to be "*preachers.*" Many churches today believe in woman preachers, but this is not Scriptural. It is amazing how many women preachers there are. Even the Southern Baptists have opened up to women preachers. The Methodists, and Episcopalians, and many other denominations have always had women preachers.

Paul had been all over the then-known world. He took three missionary journeys and then had a voyage to Rome as a prisoner. He had *"preached the gospel"* to many people of all different nations, languages, and cultures. He still wanted to *"preach"* at Rome also. He was *"ready."* He had prepared himself.

Romans 1:16

"For I am not ashamed of the gospel of Christ: for it is the power of God unto salvation to every one that believeth; to the Jew first, and also to the Greek."

"For I am not ashamed of the gospel of Christ" Are you *"ashamed of the gospel of Christ"*? Paul was not. The Lord Jesus Christ was not *"ashamed"* of His Father, was He? When Pilate asked Jesus, *"Art thou the King of the Jews?"* The Lord answered: *"Thou sayest it"* (Luke 23:3).

Paul was not ashamed either to escape death, or to escape judgment from the Roman procreators. Look how Paul responded in the book of Acts before Felix (Acts 24), or Festus (Acts 25), or Agrippa (Acts 26). He preached the *"gospel of Christ"* faithfully. Some people wanted to do away with Paul, put him in prison, stone him, or kill him. To all these threats and more, Paul said, *"I am not ashamed of the gospel of Christ."*

Delivered From Cancer

In 1985, the Lord permitted cancer to come into my body. The cancer was Hodgkins Disease, which attacks the lymph glands. It caused the left side of my neck to swell up. I started to combat this with Vitamin B-17 or Laetrile, then finally used chemotherapy. The Lord worked through all of this and delivered me from that cancer. I am still free.

I have been going to my doctor once each year for the last few years for a check-up. The cancer has not yet come back. What is there for me to be ashamed of after this? I was ready to go Home to be with the Lord. There was no question on that. My body was as good as dead, but not my spirit. While in Nevada to get the intravenous Laetrile, a fundamental Baptist pastor asked me to preach for him. I preached on:

● **Romans 12:1-2**

I beseech you therefore, brethren, by the mercies of God, that ye **present your bodies a living sacrifice, holy, acceptable unto God**, which is your reasonable service. And be not conformed to this world: but be ye transformed by the renewing of your mind, that ye may prove what is that good, and acceptable, and perfect, will of God.

After I returned from Nevada, I preached on those verses for several months in different churches. After coming back from what I considered certain death, it has been my goal to preach truly, straight, and unashamed. I do not care if people differ with me as long as I am doctrinally and Biblically correct. Not that I am going to be obnoxious. But our The Bible For Today ministry has sought to be faithful to the Lord Jesus Christ and His gospel.

"Christ" Removed From the Gospel

I want you to notice that the words *"of Christ"* in Romans 1:16 have been removed from the false Westcott and Hort Greek text, as well as the modern versions of that text--the Nestle-Aland text and the United Bible Society text. These false Greek texts do not read, *"the gospel of Christ."* They just have *"the gospel."* The same is true of the New International Version, the New American Standard Version, the New King James (in the footnotes of the study edition), the Revised Standard Version, the New Revised Standard Version, and most other modern versions. They take out *"of Christ."* What good news is it if you leave out Christ?

The King James Bible and the *Textus Receptus* Greek Text underlying it have it right. It is the *"gospel"* concerning the Lord Jesus Christ. *"Good news"* could be about your new hat, your new house, your new car, your new job, your raise, or some other *"good news."* This is the good news about "Christ," and the *"gospel"* is incomplete if He is left out.

"for it is the power of God unto salvation to every one that believeth; to the Jew first, and also to the Greek" This is the wonderful soul-changing *"gospel"* that Paul preached. This is also the *"gospel"* that he is going to talk about. The *"gospel of God"* (Romans 1:1); the *"gospel of His Son"* (Romans 1:9); and the *"gospel of Christ"* (Romans 1:16). Three times he refers to this gospel. The gospel of God, of His Son, and of Christ.

The Good News About Christ

The whole book of Romans is going to be about this good news about Christ. This *"good news"* is that, though all men are sinners (Romans 3:23), God the Father sent God the Son (John 3:16) to pay for the sins of the entire world (John 1:29b) by shedding of His blood on the cross (Romans 3:25), so that whosoever trusts him and receives Him (John 1:12) should not go to Hell (John 3:15), but have everlasting life (John 5:24).

Romans 1:17

"For therein is the righteousness of God revealed from faith to faith: as it is written, The just shall live by faith."

In the gospel of the Lord Jesus Christ *"the righteousness of God"* is revealed. Sinners are down here in this wicked world. The Lord Jesus Christ came down for the purpose of redeeming all the sinners of the world who would trust in Him. The *"righteousness of God"* is revealed in that gospel. Because God is righteous, He had to send His sinless Son, the Lord Jesus Christ, to pay the penalty for and *"take away the sin of the world"* (John 1:29b).

That is the *"righteousness of God"* which was *"revealed from faith to faith"* in this gospel. *"The just shall live by faith."* This is quoted in three other places in the Bible:

- Habakkuk 2:4
  Behold, his soul which is lifted up is not upright in him: but **the just** shall live by his faith.
- Galatians 3:11
  But that no man is justified by the law in the sight of God, it is evident: for, The just **shall live** by faith.
- Hebrews 10:38
  Now **the just shall live by faith**: but if any man draw back, my soul shall have no pleasure in him.

Some have said in one place the emphasis is on the *"JUST,"* that is, those who are righteous. In another place, the emphasis is on *"SHALL LIVE,"* that is, how we should live. In still another place, the emphasis is on *"BY FAITH,"* that is, by the principle of trust. In Hebrews it is *"by faith."* We must be living *"by faith."*

I was reading Dean John William Burgon's work, *Inspiration and Interpretation*. Remember, he was the great defender of the Traditional Greek text and the King James Bible in the late 1800's. Burgon said that we must realize the difference between when it is we are to walk by faith, and when we are to walk by sight. Occasionally, you have to walk by sight or you will stumble in this physical world. There are things physical and there are also things spiritual. We do not always understand. Paul says in this passage that we do walk by faith and not by sight.

Romans 1:18

"For the wrath of God is revealed from heaven against all ungodliness and unrighteousness of men, who hold the truth in unrighteousness:" This portion of the chapter is a message that I would not select to preach about ordinarily. It contains some very controversial and sensitive subjects. But it is in this book of Romans, so I am going to preach it.

Paul talked about the *"wrath of God."* The religious liberals and modernists are always stressing the *"love of God."* Though one of God's attributes is love, He also possesses the attributes of righteousness, holiness, and wrath. Who is this *"wrath"* against? It is *"revealed from Heaven against all ungodliness and unrighteousness of men."* There is a Scripture verse in John:

● **John 3:36**
   He that believeth on the Son hath everlasting life: and he that believeth not the Son shall not see life; but **the wrath of God abideth on him.**

God is a God of *"love,"* but He is also a God of *"wrath"* against those who reject the penalty and remedy of their sin and mine. Notice this *"wrath"* is *"revealed."* The Greek word for this is APOKALUPTO. It means:

   "to uncover, lay open what has been veiled or covered up; disclose, make bare; to make known, make manifest, disclose what before was unknown."

The *"wrath of God"* was *"manifest,"* was it not, in the days of Noah? The whole earth perished except eight souls: Noah, his wife, his three sons, and their wives. That is all who survived the flood. The wrath of God was *"revealed"* completely.

Then was not the *"wrath of God"* also *"revealed"* against Sodom and Gomorrah (Genesis 19:24)? God judged the terrible wickedness, the Sodomites, and the sins of that wicked nation. God's *"wrath"* was completely exposed against all ungodliness and unrighteousness. Notice what these people do to God's *"truth."*

"Who hold the truth in unrighteousness:" The word for *"hold"* is KATECHO. It means: *"to restrain, hinder (the course or progress of); that which hinders."* These people are holding back the truth. Being the present tense, it is a progressive and continuous action. They continue "*to hold back, restrain, and hinder*" God's "*truth*."

Holding Back the Truth

God's "*truth*" should not be held back. It should be let loose. This is why I believe in exposing these modern versions and perversions of our Bibles. They are "*holding back*" the Words of God, and the Truth of God. I would hate to be in their position or in their shoes. The wrath of God is against them too. They "*hold down*" much of the truth of God by omission of Words, by addition of words, and by use of false Hebrew, Aramaic, or Greek texts. They leave out important words.

- **Romans 1:16**
  For I am not ashamed of the gospel **of Christ**: for it is the power of God unto salvation to every one that believeth; to the Jew first, and also to the Greek.

The modern versions, such as the NIV, TNIV, NASV, RSV, NRSV, and others "*hold back and hold down*" the truth by removing the Words, "*of Christ*" out of that verse. Because of their false Greek text underlying them, they read, "*I am not ashamed of the gospel*," rather than "*the gospel of Christ*."

Romans 1:19

"Because that which may be known of God is manifest in them; for God hath shewed *it* unto them." The heathen world is responsible to God for the sins they have committed. God has made "*manifest*" to them many things. The Greek word for "*manifest*" is PHONEROS. It means: "*apparent, manifest, evident, or known*." God's knowledge is opened to these heathen people. I am talking here about the heathen who live in foreign lands. But the verse applies equally to the heathen in this country. They are just as wicked and corrupt as any African, Chinese, Russian, Latin American, or a resident of any nation in the world. The unsaved heathen in this country are under the same condemnation of the Lord. God "*hath shewed*" it unto them in a complete manner.

Romans 1:20

"For the invisible things of him from the creation of the world are clearly seen, being understood by the things that are made, *even* his eternal power and Godhead; so that they are without excuse:" Notice the types of things that are "*clearly seen*" in this verse. They are "*the invisible things.*" These are the unseen things "*from the creation of the world*" that are "*clearly seen.*" At first glance, there seems to be a contradiction. How can things be "*invisible*" and yet be "*clearly seen*"? The Lord is "*invisible*"; and yet, through the Scriptures, He can be "*clearly seen.*"

Can you see this pulpit up here? It is made of wood. Can you see this light, or this microphone? You can see me, and I can see you.

Visible Made Up of the Invisible

But we are made up of "*invisible things.*" We are made up of atoms, molecules, protons, neutrons, and electrons which are "*invisible*" to the naked eye. "*The invisible things are clearly seen.*" That's interesting, is it not?

I suppose that physics has not changed too much through the years. Atoms, neutrons, protons, and electrons are still unable to be seen by the naked eye. They can be seen only by powerful microscopes.

Just think of the moon. Think of the stars. Think of the earth. Things that God has created are "*clearly seen*" by the heathen all over the world. There is no excuse. I looked up today in an encyclopedia about our Milky Way. Scientists estimate, though they cannot count them, that there are about one hundred billion stars in that Milky Way galaxy. Then they say that there are over a billion other galaxies of a similar size. Can you imagine the things which are "*clearly seen*"?

Things Clearly Seen by Heathen

The heathen people in this country and the heathen people in foreign countries all over the world can clearly see God's creation as His handiwork. There is no question about that. The sun, the moon, the stars being *"understood by the things that are made."*

Notice specifically what God says is *"understood by the thing that are made."* The first thing that God has shown in nature and in His creation, is His *"eternal power."* This power has been in evidence *"eternally."* There is no *"time"* with the Lord. Like all of the other of His Divine attributes, His *"power"* is from all eternity. Only God's *"power"* could create all of these things such as the sun, moon, stars, planets, earth, and even our bodies.

The second thing that God has shown in nature and in His creation is His *"Godhead."* The Greek word for this is THEIOTES. It refers to God's *"Divinity"* and *"Divine nature."* His *"Godhead"* is revealed by His mighty power and miracles.

The Heathen Are "Without Excuse"

The result of this revelation is that the entire heathen world is *"without excuse."* Are the heathen lost? Yes, they are lost. They are *"without excuse."* God says this clearly in this verse. Are the heathen in this country lost? Yes, they are without excuse until they come to Christ and receive Him as their Saviour from sin.

Missionaries are sent out either to this country or to foreign lands to bring these heathen the gospel of Christ. They do not even live up to what God has shown them in nature and in the things He has created. To be *"without excuse"* is from the Greek word ANAPOLOGETOS. It means: *"without defense or excuse; that which cannot be defended, inexcusable."*

In a later portion of this book, Paul talked about a time when *"every mouth"* would be *"stopped."*

- **Romans 3:19**
  Now we know that what things soever the law saith, it saith to them who are under the law: **that every mouth may be stopped, and all the world may become guilty before God**.

The judgment referred to here is God's Great White Throne Judgment where the unbelievers of all the ages will be judged (Revelation 20:11-15). These people cannot say a word. God will have them *"dead to rights,"* as we say. If we human beings are able to know so much with our computers, and computer chips that can follow cars all over the countryside, think of what an omniscient God can know. God knows everything that everyone of us has done. There will also be a judgment of the saved people at the Judgment Seat of Christ (2 Corinthians 5:10). This will be a judgment for what the believers have done for the Lord Jesus Christ after they were saved. Why are the unbelievers without excuse? The next verse will give us that answer.

Romans 1:21

"Because that, when they knew God, they glorified *him* not as God, neither were thankful; but became vain in their imaginations, and their foolish heart was darkened." This present verse tells us that there was a time when the heathen of the world *"knew God."* They knew Him through revelation of His creation and His mighty power. But *"they glorified him not as God."* They did not give Him the honor due Him. Neither were they *"thankful"* to the Lord for anything that He had done. They *"knew"* Him, but they did not *"glorify"* Him. Instead, these heathen *"became vain in their imaginations."* The Greek verb for *"vain"* is MATAIOO. It means *"to make empty, vain, or foolish."* This vanity was in relation to their *"imaginations."* The Greek word for this is DIALOGISMOS. It means:

> *"the thinking of a man deliberating with himself; a thought, inward reasoning; purpose, design; a deliberating, questioning about what is true; hesitation, doubting; disputing, arguing."*

In their *"vain imaginations,"* the heathen thought up in their minds all the things that were contrary to God.

Paul also said that *"their foolish heart was darkened."* There are things about the *"heart"* in this passage. There are things about the body in this passage. And there are things about the mind in this passage. All three of these things are involved here: the heart, the body, and the mind. With a *"heart"* that is *"darkened,"* everything else goes wrong. This is what happened with the heathen world--*"their foolish heart was darkened."* The Greek word for *"foolish"* is ASUNETOS. It means *"unintelligent, without understanding, stupid."* These heathen were *"stupid."* They were without any proper reasoning or understanding. Their *"heart was darkened"* because they did not want to have the Lord's Words and will in their lives. They rejected His truth.

Romans 1:22

"Professing themselves to be wise, they became fools"

This is true of many people in the United States of America. The Greek word for *"professing"* is PHASKO. It means: *"to affirm, allege, portend or profess."* These heathen people *"affirm or allege"* that they are *"wise."* If people are *"wise"* in their own strength, without the wisdom of God, they are fools. There are some other verses that deal with this.

- **Psalm 53:1**
  The fool hath said in his heart, There is no God. Corrupt are they, and have done abominable iniquity: there is none that doeth good.

- **1 Corinthians 1:21**
  For after that in the wisdom of God **the world by wisdom knew not God**, it pleased God by the foolishness of preaching to save them that believe.

- **1 Corinthians 2:8**
  Which none of the princes of this world knew: for had they known it, they would not have crucified the Lord of glory.

This verse talks about the *"wisdom of God."* It says that these *"princes of this world"* took the Lord of Glory, the wisdom of God, and put Him on a cross in open shame. They crucified Him. Though it does have some advantages, education is one of the most dangerous things in the world.

Education is the seat and source of all kinds of unbelief. It always has been. Someone has said the following, and I agree with the sentiment:

"Satan, in the garden of Eden, camped under the tree of knowledge
(Genesis 2:17) *and he has been camping there ever since."*

Consider the source of apostasy and unbelief. It has originated in either the theological seminaries, the colleges, or the universities. But such apostasy goes right down to the people. It continues with the people who accept the false theology at these institutions.

"Professing themselves to be wise, they became fools." They became *"fools"* because they rejected God's wisdom. Think of Harvard. Think of Yale. Think of Princeton. Think of Temple University. Consider all these different schools. Look at Fuller Seminary. Look at the decline of the schools affiliated with the General Association of Regular Baptist Churches (GARBC). I think of the Grand Rapids school. It used to be called *Grand Rapids Baptist Bible College.* First they took away "Bible." They did not want it to have the word "Bible" in the title. They thought that was too foolish. They changed it to *Grand Rapids Baptist College.* Then they did not like the word *"Baptist,"* so they removed it, making it *Grand Rapids College.* As of my last information,

the school is now called *Cornerstone College.* That is all it is.

We are right now, in our own day, among many people who are rejecting the wisdom of God. People do not just transform themselves into fools. They become fools by rejecting God's revealed truth, that is, by rejecting real wisdom and by rejecting the Words of God.

Romans 1:23

"And changed the glory of the uncorruptible God into an image made like to corruptible man, and to birds, and fourfooted beasts, and creeping things."

"And changed the glory of the uncorruptible God into an image" All these things were true of the heathen in foreign lands, but it is also true of the heathen in this country too. The Greek word for *"uncorruptible"* is APHTHARTOS. It means: " *uncorrupted, not liable to corruption or decay, imperishable."* God is *"uncorruptible."* It means He cannot corrupt. He cannot corrode. He cannot decay. All things around us corrupt, corrode, and decay. They corrupt and corrode gradually at different levels depending on what we are talking about. Our bodies decay and corrupt in a relatively short period of time. Some live even into the 100's of years, but this is unusual. A tree lasts many more years. Some trees are over 1,000 years old.

Our house should outlast us by many years. This house was built by the Reams family in about 1927, the same year that Mrs. Waite and I were born. We bought the house from Mrs. Smith in 1965. So far as we know, the first two owners are dead and buried. Now we are living in this house. After we have died and been buried (unless the Lord Jesus should return and take us Home before that time), or unless something unforeseen should happen, this house will go on standing. We and our house are the same age. It is a strong and sturdy brick house.

"made like to corruptible man, and to birds, and fourfooted beasts, and creeping things" God, however, is uncorruptible and unbreakable. He will never pass away. The people in heathendom all over the world, as well as those in heathendom who live in civilized nations today, have also exchanged the *"uncorruptible God"* for an image or icon which was. Though these can be seen, they soon pass away. They believe the images that they made, made them. Is not that stupid when you think of it?

We have a network chain of five or six computers in our Bible For Today ministry here. They occasionally get broken. We take them, on occasion, to a Japanese company who have very good mechanics. I noticed, the last time I went into their shop, that they had a *"God-shelf"* with candles burning to

Buddha. We have heathenism right here in this country. You do not have to go over to Africa, or Asia, or Europe to find people who want to make the *"uncorruptible God"* into an image that you can see. People always want to see.

- **John 4:24**
  God is a Spirit: and **they that worship him must worship him in spirit** and in truth.

Notice this verse in Romans 1:27 says, *"made like."* Who made this image? Did God make it? No, man made those things. Men changed what God made into what they made, so they could sit down and worship it. Now, is not that silly? Here they are worshiping a "god" which they have made. They are believing that the "god" which they have made (whether it is an image of man, birds, or creeping things) made them. They are thinking that those snakes or birds are the things that made them. If that is not ridiculous. God holds that to them. They are without excuse, whether they are in this country or in other countries all over the world.

"made like to corruptible man" There are two passages that I especially like concerning idols in the Old Testament.

- **Psalm 115:4-8**
  Not unto us, O LORD, not unto us, but unto thy name give glory, for thy mercy, and for thy truth's sake. Wherefore should the heathen say, Where is now their God? But our God is in the heavens: he hath done whatsoever he hath pleased. **Their idols are silver and gold, the work of men's hands. They have mouths, but they speak not: eyes have they, but they see not: They have ears, but they hear not: noses have they, but they smell not: They have hands, but they handle not: feet have they, but they walk not: neither speak they through their throat. They that make them are like unto them; so is every one that trusteth in them.**

- **Psalm 135:15-18**
  The idols of the heathen are silver and gold, the work of men's hands. They have mouths, but they speak not; eyes have they, but they see not; They have ears, but they hear not; neither is there any breath in their mouths. They that make them are like unto them: so is every one that trusteth in them.

These idols are man's idols. They are made of corruptible things, including silver and gold. Those are two of the materials that will appear at the Judgment Seat of Christ.

- 1 Corinthians 3:12-13
  Now if any man build upon this foundation **gold, silver, precious stones**, wood, hay, stubble; Every man's work shall be made manifest: for the day shall declare it, because it shall be revealed by fire; and **the fire shall try every man's work of what sort it is.**

The gold, silver, and precious stones last long in the fire, but the wood, hay, and stubble get burned up. Even gold, silver, and precious stones one day will pass away and corrupt. These are corruptible things.

Romans 1:24

"Wherefore God also gave them up to uncleanness through the lusts of their own hearts, to dishonour their own bodies between themselves:"

"Wherefore God also gave them up to uncleanness" The words *"gave them up"* or *"gave them over"* are used three times in this passage (verses 24, 26, 28). It is the same Greek word exactly (PARA-DIDOMI), and in the same order of Greek words. The order in which God gives it to us in the Greek language is *"gave up them God."*

In the Greek language, the first thing that you put in the sentence is the thing that you are emphasizing. The emphasis here is *"gave them up."* Because of their *"foolishness,"* God would have nothing to do with these people. That Greek word PARADIDOMI means:

"to give over into (one's) power or use; to deliver to one something to keep, use; to deliver up one to custody, to be judged, condemned, punished, scourged, tormented, put to death"

Why God "Gave Them Up"

God *"gave them up"* for at least seven reasons:

(1) because of rejecting truth;

(2) because of holding down the truth;

(3) because of professing themselves wise, yet becoming fools;

(4) because of making images;

(5) because of not retaining God in their knowledge;

(6) because of making themselves vain in their imaginations; and

(7) because of darkening of their foolish hearts.

That is what that word *"wherefore"* signifies. It is because of these previous seven things that God decided to *"give them up."* God does not do things without a reason. He is very patient before He cuts these heathen off. He just let them have their own way. God permitted and allowed them to do just what they wanted to do.

This is illustrated in what happened with Pharaoh. The Lord dealt with him by sending him ten different plagues. Finally, because his heart was hardened, he would not let Israel go out of Egypt. It took the death of his first- born son to get his attention.

Giving Up on People

I do not know how many times the Lord dealt with you before you were almost ready to give up on Him. The Lord does not give up on you if you are saved. He just keeps on with His own. With the unsaved people, there is a time when it becomes the end of the line. God will just let them alone. It is just like Judas. Judas was lost. He was never saved. Satan took over his life.

Notice that God gave up these people *"to uncleanness."* The Greek word for this is AKATHARSIA. It means: *"in a moral sense: the impurity of lustful, luxurious, profligate living; of impure motives."* This type of living was what these heathen wanted, and this is what they lived for.

"through the lusts of their own hearts, to dishonour their own bodies between themselves" The means of this *"uncleanness"* is *"through the lusts of their own hearts."* The *"hearts"* of the heathen are affected. The Greek word for *"lust"* is EPITHUMIA. It means: *"desire, craving, longing, desire for what is forbidden, lust."* It is from the root word, THUMOS. This root word means:

> *"passion, angry, heat, anger forthwith boiling up and soon subsiding again; glow, ardour, the wine of passion, inflaming wine (which either drives the drinker mad or kills him with its strength)."*

This *"lust"* is a *"craving"* that burns like a fire in order to do what is evil, what is wrong, and what is filthy. It is that which is *"forbidden,"* which is *"boiling up"* in the heart.

Filthy Hearts Led to Filthy Bodies

Notice this *"lust"* of their *"hearts"* led these heathen *"to dishonour their own bodies."* The *"heart"* attitude led to the dishonoring of their *"bodies."* When you give up on the Lord, the heart becomes filthy with lust. Then the body gets involved. When you have a *"heart"* that is filthy, it effects the body.

It comes out in what you do. It comes out in your life. In the next couple of verses we'll see some of the bodily activities that are filthy, wicked, and wrong, but it starts with the heart.

"My son," says the book of Proverbs 23:26, *"give me thine heart."* Matthew 12:34b says, *"for out of the abundance of the heart the mouth speaketh."* The *"heart"* is the center of our life. That is why the Lord wants our heart. Let me suggest again, He wants our hearts. If He has them, He will also have our heads, our hands, our feet, our mouths, and all the rest of us.

I like what some have said about our Bibles.

Where is Your Bible?

"The Bible in the hand is <u>good</u>.
The Bible in the head is <u>better</u>.
The Bible in the heart is <u>best</u>.
Good, better, best--
Never let it rest.
Till your good is better,
And your better's best."

The heart that is wicked will manifest itself in wicked and filthy activities of the body.

Romans 1:25

"Who changed the truth of God into a lie, and worshipped and served the creature more than the Creator, who is blessed for ever. Amen."

"Who changed the truth of God into a lie" These heathen people "change" and exchange *"the truth of God into a lie."* God has showed to them many things in nature that He has created. They turned the visible things of God's creation *"into a lie."* They said, in effect, *"We are not going to worship the God who made all these things. Instead, we are going to make our own idols to worship."* When we make our own things, plans, and idols to worship (whether cars, houses, idols, money etc.) we will be in trouble.

The new versions and perversions of our New Testament and Old Testament are guilty of changing in many places *"the truth of God into a lie."* They insist on adding words, which is sin; subtracting words, which is sin; and changing words in some other way, which is also sin. I have studied those new versions.

Some of these new versions have been revised. I used the original versions as they first came out to do my tabulations. I went through carefully the entire New King James Version, verse by verse, and compared it to the Hebrew, Aramaic, and Greek Words. I found over 2,000 examples that either added to the Hebrew, Aramaic, or Greek Words, subtracted from these Words, or changed these Words in some other way. That is not quite as bad as the New American Standard Version. I looked at that version from Genesis to Revelation and found over 4,000 examples of adding, subtracting, or changing in some other ways the Words of God.

That is not quite as bad as the New International Version. I went through that also from Genesis to Revelation, and found 6,653 specific examples of either adding, subtracting, or changing in some other ways the Words of God. I quit counting after two years and eight months. My computer was filling up. These are perversions. They have over 356 doctrinal passages that are involved. It is a terrible situation. They are *"changing the truth of God into a lie."* If you do not have the whole truth, you've got a lie somewhere.

"and worshipped and served the creature more than the Creator" How can we *"worship and serve a creature"*? A creature is something that is made by a Creator. We human beings are creatures. God made us. You should not want to worship men. Look at Hirohito who was worshipped in Japan during the second World War. How silly that was, we thought, when Japanese people were falling down before that emperor and worshiping him during the second World War. Japanese Kamikaze pilots committed suicide killing themselves for the sake of their emperor so that they could go home to their brand of "Heaven." These pilots would aim their planes at our United States warships for the sake of their Emperor whom they worshipped.

Caesar was a man that the Romans worshipped. The early Christians did not bow down to Caesar. They were often given a choice. Christians who were solid in their faith would not bow down to Caesar. Because of this, they were put to death. The Romans worshipped the "*creature more than the Creator.*" The Creator was the One Who made everything. He Who created all is the One we should worship.

The Lord Jesus Christ--Creator

Remember, the Lord Jesus Christ is One of the Creators of this world in addition to God the Father and God the Holy Spirit. The entire Trinity was involved. The new versions leave the Lord Jesus Christ out as the Creator:

- **Ephesians 3:9**
  And to make all men see what is the fellowship of the mystery, which from the beginning of the world hath been hid in God, who created all things **by Jesus Christ**

Because of the false Westcott and Hort Greek text, most of the new versions omit the words, "*by Jesus Christ*" in this verse. This includes the New International Version, the Today's New International Version, the New American Standard Version, the Revised Standard Version, the New Revised Standard Version, and even in the footnotes of the study edition of the New King James Version. Our Saviour was active in the creation of all things. We must worship Him Who is blessed forever.

Romans 1:26

"For this cause God gave them up unto vile affections: for even their women did change the natural use into that which is against nature:" Here is the second time Paul mentioned that "*God gave them up.*" God never does anything without a reason. The first time Paul mentioned it was because of "*uncleanness*" (Romans 1:24). Now He "*gave them up unto vile affections.*" The Greek word for "*affections*" is PATHOS. It means:

"*whatever befalls one, whether it be sad or joyous; specifically. a calamity, mishap, evil, affliction; a feeling which the mind suffers; an*

*affliction of the mind, emotion, passion; passionate deed; in the NT in
a bad sense, depraved passion, vile passions."*

Here is a picture of lesbianism, the female homosexuals in this verse. *"for
even their women did change the natural use into that which is against nature:"*
These evil, sinful women *"change the natural use"* of a woman into something
that is *"against nature."* The Greek word for *"natural"* is PHUSIKOS. It
means: *"produced by nature, inborn; agreeable to nature; governed by (the
instincts of) nature."*

Homosexuality Learned, Not Inborn

Though modern homosexuals deny it, homosexuality, whether it
is female or male, is not *"produced by nature or inborn."* It is a
learned activity. Those homosexuals who try to tell us differently
are absolutely wrong. Medical men and various others have
proved this as well. The Lord himself would not condemn the
"homosexual lifestyle," as they call it, if it were inborn. It is a sin
that is learned at some time in life. Whether it is early in life, or
late in life, it is a lifestyle. It is a "change" of the "natural" sexual
use of a woman into *"that which is against nature."*

There are lesbians all over our country, including Washington D.C. Some
are in political power like a former attorney general. It is even alleged, whether
true or false, that a former first lady has had lesbian activities with other women,
as well as with other men as a *"bisexual."* The sin of lesbianism and male
homosexuality is being taught in many public schools as an *"alternate lifestyle."*
God condemns homosexuality right here in this verse.

Romans 1:27

**"And likewise also the men, leaving the natural use of
the woman, burned in their lust one toward another; men
with men working that which is unseemly, and receiving
in themselves that recompence of their error which was
meet."**

**"And likewise also the men, leaving the natural use of
the woman, burned in their lust one toward another; men
with men working that which is unseemly"** In this verse, God
condemns the male homosexuals. The Greek word for "leaving" is APHIEMI.
It means, among other things: *"to desert wrongfully; to go away leaving*

something behind; abandon, leave destitute"

Here are *"men with men working that which is unseemly."* These men are doing that which is evil, sinful, and vile. They *"burned in their lust one toward another."* This *"lust"* is a *"burning"* fire in the homosexual males. This does not make it any less wicked and sinful, but even more so. It stems from the fallen Adamic nature inherited from our first parent. The word for "lust" is OREXIS. It means: *"desire, longing, craving for; eager desire, lust, appetite."*

The homosexuals form one of the strongest lobbies in Washington today. Various Presidents, whether Democrats or Republicans, have placated the homosexuals in many ways. There is voting power with the homosexuals and their friends. How many of them are there? Who knows? There are some that are hidden, and some that are out of the closet. The Kinsey Report (which has been shown to contain many errors) stated that ten percent of all males are homosexuals. There is a new report that says the figure is one percent. Either way, there are many of them, and they are multiplying rapidly.

In the school districts, such as Philadelphia, they are now teaching lesbianism, and male homosexual activity as an alternate lifestyle. God calls it sin, wickedness, and evil. Though this sin began in heathenism, it has been brought over into so-called civilized countries all over the world. They say that everyone is doing it and because of this, it is all right. You have the lesbian, Ellen on the TV, who is glorified. There is another woman who had a TV program who is also a lesbian. There are whole churches that are homosexual churches. You have this woman, Dr. Virginia Molenkott, who was on the editorial board of the New International Version (NIV), who is a lesbian. She has come out of the closet recently, but I have known she was a lesbian since the 1960's. There are homosexual movie stars like Rock Hudson and Richard Chamberlain. There was the pianist, Liberace, who was also a homosexual, and many, many others who were prominent in their field.

"receiving in themselves that recompence of their error which was meet" Since the word, *"receiving"* is in the present tense, these sinful people continue *"to receive in themselves their recompense."* The Greek word for *"recompense"* is ANTIMISTHIA. It means: *"a reward given in compensation, requital, recompence."* In this case, it is a negative *"reward"* for sin. God says that *"the wages of sin is death, but the gift of God is eternal life through Jesus Christ our Lord"* (Romans 6:23). These *"wages"* are also a recompense or a payback because of sin. Notice that they receive a *"recompence of their error which was meet."* This fitting *"recompence"* is *"in themselves."* It is part of their bodies.

This *"error,"* or wickedness, or sin was *"meet."* The Greek word for *"was meet"* is DEI. It means:

"it is necessary, there is need of, it behooves, is right and proper;

necessity lying in the nature of the case; necessity brought on by circumstances or by the conduct of others toward us."

The word, *"was meet,"* is in the imperfect tense which is a past action that is continuous. It was a necessity. If these homosexuals are going to play with the devil and continue in this filthy and sinful lifestyle, they will get a *"recompense"* wages in their own bodies which are deserved and necessary for their crimes against nature and their own bodies. Many of these people receive AIDS as well as all kinds of venereal diseases that have been begun and are continued by the homosexual community.

God Says Homosexuality Is Sin

God says clearly in God's Words that homosexuality is sin. Many people disagree with God and say that it is all right.

- Leviticus 18:22
  Thou shalt not lie with mankind, as with womankind: it is abomination.

- Leviticus 20:13
  If a man also lie with mankind, as he lieth with a woman, both of them have committed an abomination: they shall surely be put to death; their blood shall be upon them.

In the Old Testament homosexuals were to be killed.

- 1 Corinthians 6:9
  Know ye not that the unrighteous shall not inherit the kingdom of God? Be not deceived: neither fornicators, nor idolaters, nor adulterers, **nor effeminate, nor abusers of themselves with mankind.**

- 1 Timothy 1:10
  For whoremongers, for **them that defile themselves with mankind**, for menstealers, for liars, for perjured persons, and if there be any other thing that is contrary to sound doctrine.

This is speaking of the homosexuals. God is against the homosexual sin and we should be against it. The Bible is against it. One of these days we will be told that we cannot even preach out against the sin of homosexuality or we will be put out of commission. They will tell us that speaking against the sin of homosexuality is a flagrant crime against a nation of people.

This will be called genocide, or speaking out against a group of people. You will not be able to speak against the Jews, against Negroes, against White people, against Chinese, or against Homosexuals. Governments will make laws one of these days preventing free speech even when the Bible is clear on a subject. Laws are already made in Canada and in some other parts of the world. Preachers there are not able to preach out against homosexuals anymore without being penalized or put in jail.

In fact, I was told that there was a law suit several years ago against *Oxford University Press* because they produce The King James Bible which speaks out against sodomites and homosexuals. I do not know how that lawsuit will turn out or has turned out. I am sure they are not going to win it. If they can put the King James Bible out of commission from *Oxford University Press* they will try to do the same to us for speaking out for what the Scriptures clearly teach.

Facts About Homosexuals

The Berean Call for September, 2003, had an article on "Homosexual Facts." Among other things, they mentioned the following:

"In 1988--74.9% of Americans thought sex between two members of the same sex was wrong. In 1998--only 54.6% felt that it was wrong.

The Cathedral of Hope in Dallas, Texas, claims to be the world's largest homosexual church with 3,000 members.

Harvey Milk High School will open this fall in New York as the first homosexual public school.

The median age of death for heterosexual males is 75. The median age of death for gay males is 42, and with gay males with AIDS is 39.

The median age of death for heterosexual females is 79. The median age of death for gay females is 45."

The various Scripture passages given in this article against homosexuality are: "Leviticus 18:22; Leviticus 20:13; Deuteronomy 23:17; 1 Kings 14:24; Matthew 15:19; Romans 1:18-32; 1 Corinthians 6:9-10; Galatians 5:19-21; and 1 Timothy 1:9-10."

Romans 1:28

"And even as they do not like to retain God in *their* knowledge, God gave them over to a reprobate mind, to do those things which are not convenient" Here is that phrase again, *"God gave them over."* Because these heathen did not *"like to retain God in their knowledge,"* He *"gave them over to a reprobate mind."* Earlier in the chapter, Paul mentioned the heathen's *"heart"* (vv. 21 and 24); their *"bodies"* (v. 24); and here is their *"mind."* You had the heart, the body, and now the mind.

The things that are *"not convenient"* are listed in the following verses. The heathen did these things because of their *"reprobate mind."* There is nothing more devastating than a *"reprobate."* The Greek word for "reprobate" is ADOKIMOS. It means:

> *"not standing the test, not approved; properly used of metals and coins; that which does not prove itself such as it ought; unfit for, unproved, spurious, reprobate."*

The *"reprobate mind"* continues to do that which is evil and wrong.

Romans 1:29

"Being filled with all unrighteousness, fornication, wickedness, covetousness, maliciousness; full of envy, murder, debate, deceit, malignity; whisperers" That verb for *"being filled"* is a Greek present tense. As such, it means a continuous action. These heathen are *"continuing to be filled up."* The Greek word for *"filled"* is PLEROO. It means:

> *"to make full, to fill up, i.e. to fill to the full; to cause to abound, to furnish or supply liberally; to fill to the top: so that nothing shall be wanting to; full measure, fill to the brim."*

It implies that these heathen have the full measure of *"unrighteousness."*
Though *"fornication"* usually is contrasted with *"adultery,"* meaning sexual intercourse on the part of the unmarried person, the meaning of PORNEIA also includes, on occasion, any

> *"illicit sexual intercourse; adultery, fornication, homosexuality, lesbianism, intercourse with animals etc.; sexual intercourse with close relatives; Lev. 18; sexual intercourse with a divorced man or woman; Mk. 10:11,12"*

This is part of the *"recompense"* that God has brought upon them because of their *"reprobate minds."*

The term, *"wickedness,"* includes all kinds of evil.

Decent People Don't Understand

Decent human beings cannot understand how low-down men and women can be. Decent people do not parade around the porn shops. They do not see the wicked devices that these wicked people are using and so on and so forth. They do not read about all the things that they do with their bodies.

These heathen are from the devil's own workshop because of their *"reprobate mind."* They are thinking only of themselves and how they can get filthier and filthier and dirtier and dirtier.

The Greek word for *"covetousness"* is PLEONEXIA. It means: *"greedy desire to have more, covetousness, avarice."* "Malignity" means a desire to have more. Malignity is malicious craftiness and depravity in heart and life. *"Whispers"* in Greek is PISOTHURISTES. Do you hear the *"whisper"* in the pronunciation? Just like "MOO" is an onomatopoeia word. The noun says what it means. Like the serpent's "hissssss." *"Whispers"* means *"secret slanderers who whisper and lie about people."* This is something that they do because they do not know the Lord.

Romans 1:30

"Backbiters, haters of God, despiteful, proud, boasters, inventors of evil things, disobedient to parents,"

A *"backbiter"* is an evil speaker. The Greek word is KATALALOS. It means: *"a defamer, evil speaker."* It is one who talks evilly and against the truth, defaming other people's character.

These heathen were *"haters of God"* Who created them and Who created the beautiful world around them.

The Greek word for *"despiteful"* is HUBRISTES. It means:
"an insolent man; one who, uplifted with pride, either heaps insulting language upon others or does them some shameful act of wrong."
The Greek word for *"proud"* is HUPEREPHANOS. It means:
"showing one's self above others, overtopping, conspicuous above others, pre-eminent; with an overweening estimate of one's means or merits, despising others or even treating them with contempt, haughty."
In other words, Mr. and Mrs. Big. This is pride. It comes from the craftiness of the evil heart and the evil mind that is disapproved. This is what sin leads to, pride.

The Greek word for "*boasters*" is ALAZON. It means: "*an empty pretender, a boaster.*" His "*boasts*" are "*empty*" and not real. We all know such people.

In the expression of "*inventors of evil things,*" the Greek word for "*evil*" is KAKOS. It means:

> "*of a bad nature; not such as it ought to be; of a mode of thinking, feeling, acting; base, wrong, wicked; troublesome, injurious, pernicious, destructive, baneful.*"

This would include porn shops of all kinds. It would include the wicked pornography that is sent, totally unsolicited, via e-mail to multiplied thousands of homes.

- **Micah 7:2b-3a**

  they all lie in wait for blood; they hunt every man his brother with a net. **That they may do evil with both hands earnestly. . .**"

This "*evil*" with "*both hands earnestly*" is a picture of these heathen and of the heathen around us today as well. There does not seem to be any bounds for the "*evil*" that is thought up and practiced.

The Greek word for "*disobedient*" in the expression "*disobedient to parents*" is APEITHES. It means: "*Not persuadable, not compliant, disobedient, contumacious.*" We have this on every hand. It is not just the heathen in foreign lands that are this way. We have that also with the heathen right here in this country. The children are disobedient to their parents. It is a disgrace. No wonder they are disobedient to teachers in schools. I can testify to that having been a teacher in Language Arts (English) for nineteen years in the School District of Philadelphia, Pennsylvania.

I remember a pastor told us in a sermon that if he would do something wrong in school his teacher would take a hold of his neck and shake it. I wish I could have done something like that in my nineteen years of school teaching in Philadelphia. I could not touch those little kids unless they attacked me. Only then I could protect myself. If they are disobedient to parents, they are certainly going to be disobedient to teachers. A terrible disgrace for the heathen on the foreign field or here at home as well.

Someone has said because of our electronics and all of our gadgets that everything around the home seems to be run with a flick of the switch, except the kids. That is entirely neglected is it not? This is a grievous situation. They are in the place of the Lord as far as teaching young people to honor authority. If they will not honor authority in the home, they certainly will not honor it with the Lord as well.

Romans 1:31

"Without understanding, covenantbreakers, without natural affection, implacable, unmerciful:"

The Greek word for *"without understanding"* is ASUNETOS. It means: *"unintelligent, without understanding, stupid."* Sin brings stupidity. That is what this phrase means. It is without any grasp of intelligence. God calls it stupidity. Some people may think they are wise, but they are fools. They think they are right--but they are wrong! So with people today.

The Greek word for *"covenantbreakers"* is ASUNTHETOS. It means: *"uncompounded, simple covenant breaking, faithless."* One who is faithless does not want to have any agreement. A young man called last night and talked about an agreement he had with a man to deliver papers. This man was supposed to pay this boy so many thousands of dollars a week. The man owes this boy over $4,000. I said to the young man,

"You must crack down on that man. Just throw his papers out. Do something. This man must sit up and take notice."

What about the covenant of marriage? We have divorces and remarriages on every hand. People do not even want to stand up to their agreements. It used to be that one-third of our marriages end up in divorce. Now it is one-half or even 60 percent of all marriages end up in divorce.

The Greek word for the phrase *"without natural affection"* is ASTORGOS. It means: *"without natural affection, unsociable, inhuman, unloving.* It comes from A ("not") and STORGOS *"to cherish affectionately."* Consider all the abortions that are performed daily. Killing an unborn baby is certainly *"unnatural affection."* *"Late-term abortion"* is when you take the baby's head when it comes out and crack it open in order to kill him. It is truly amazing that President Clinton refused to sign the bill preventing partial-birth abortion. This is a terrible disgrace. President Bush said he would sign that bill. It is certainly *"without natural affection."*

God gives us *"affection"* for our children. People have *"affection"* for dogs, cats, snakes, and everything else in the world, but often not their children. This is a sin not only in the heathen in the foreign field, but the heathen in "civilized" countries as well.

The Greek word for *"implacable"* is ASPONDOS. It means: *"without a treaty or covenant; of things not mutually agreed upon e.g. abstinences from hostilities; that cannot be persuaded to enter into a covenant, implacable."*

It refers to those who can not be persuaded to enter into either a treaty or a covenant.

Those who are *"unmerciful"* are without any mercy whatsoever.

We have so many atrocities. They are all around us. Hitler killed millions of Jews and many others in Germany. Stalin and the communists in Russia and other slave states slaughtered millions upon millions of people. Castro slaughtered many in Cuba. He is made out to be some kind of great Saviour in the press and in TV interviews. On the contrary, Castro was *"unmerciful"* in his communist killings.

Romans 1:32

"Who knowing the judgment of God, that they which commit such things are worthy of death, not only do the same, but have pleasure in them that do them."

The heathen know *"the judgment of God"* very well. God's judgments are always fair. He will never make a mistake in *"judgment."* The Greek word for *"commit"* is in the present tense. It signifies continuous action. It speaks of the heathen who continuously "commit" the things mentioned in the previous verses. They know that they are *"worthy of death"* because of their actions. "The wages of sin is death" (Romans 3:23a). That is the judgment. These unsaved heathen, whether in foreign lands or in our own land, will face the Great White Throne Judgment (Revelation 20:11-15) where all the unsaved will appear before God. They will be cast into the Lake of Fire which is the second death. They that do these things and are godless with impure minds, are guilty of death. They <u>know</u> that this is true.

"not only do the same, but have pleasure in them that do them." The ones who are evil want to get others to do the same things. Sinners delight and have *"pleasure"* in other sinners who are committing the same sins they are doing. The Greek verb for *"commit"* is in the present tense. It teaches that these people are continuously *"committing"* these sins. The Greek word for *"have pleasure"* is SUNEUDOKEO. It means:

"to be pleased together with, to approve together (with others); to be pleased at the same time with, consent, agree to; to applaud."

Since this is also a Greek present tense, it means that there is a continuous action going on, a continual *"pleasure"* in the sinners who live in these wayward ways. You get one sinner together with another sinner and they enjoy each other's company. They love what they are doing. They have great *"pleasure"* in their wickedness and great *"pleasure"* in their sin. That is why these terrible marches by these homosexuals in Washington and all these other places are so rowdy, corrupt, and brazen.

Corruption has no bounds. I hope that you and I will have *"pleasure"* in those who love the Lord Jesus Christ and not in those who are wicked. These verses in Romans show us the state of the heathen. God has pronounced a judgment against all of heathenism, whether they are in this country and in foreign countries.

𝕽𝖔𝖒𝖆𝖓𝖘 𝕮𝖍𝖆𝖕𝖙𝖊𝖗 𝕿𝖜𝖔

Romans 2:1

"Therefore thou art inexcusable, O man, whosoever thou art that judgest: for wherein thou judgest another, thou condemnest thyself; for thou that judgest doest the same things."

Paul now changes the focus from the lost heathen to the religious hypocrites. They are also under the judgment of God. As Paul will show, there are four principles of God's judgment.

God's Four Principles of Judgment

1. Judgment is according to truth.
2. Judgment is according to righteousness.
3. Judgment is according to deeds.
4. Judgment is without respect of persons.

We know what religious hypocrisy is. There is nothing wrong with judging and analyzing. The Lord Jesus said that *"by their fruits ye shall know them"* (Matthew 7:20). Doing the same things you are judging others for is hypocrisy.

- Job 8:13
  So are the paths of all that forget God; and the **hypocrite's hope shall perish**:

- **Job 20:5**
  That the triumphing of the wicked is short, and **the joy of the hypocrite but for a moment**?

The Lord Jesus Christ talked about those who say one thing and do another in Matthew. What about the destiny of hypocrites, those who say one thing and then do another? I believe the Scriptures tell us they are going to end up in Hell. Let me give you some verses on that. You may be thinking just because you are a hypocrite, you say one thing and then do another, you will go to Hell?

- **Matthew 15:7-8**
  Ye **hypocrites**, well did Esaias prophesy of you, saying, This people draweth nigh unto me with their mouth, and honoureth me with their lips; but their heart is far from me.

- **Matthew 23:14**
  Woe unto you, scribes and Pharisees, **hypocrites**! for ye devour widows' houses, and for a pretence make long prayer: therefore ye shall receive the greater damnation.

- **Matthew 23:15**
  Woe unto you, scribes and Pharisees, **hypocrites**! for ye compass sea and land to make one proselyte, and when he is made, ye make him twofold more the **child of Hell** than yourselves.

Here is a hypocrite, a Pharisee, who pretends to obey the law and yet does not obey it and fulfill it. The Lord Jesus says he is a "*child of Hell.*"

- **Matthew 23:27**
  Woe unto you, scribes and Pharisees, **hypocrites**! for ye are like unto whited sepulchres, which indeed appear beautiful outward, but are within full of dead men's bones, and of all uncleanness.

- **Matthew 24:51**
  And shall cut him asunder, and appoint him his portion with the **hypocrites**: there shall be weeping and gnashing of teeth.

- **Matthew 7:5**
  Thou **hypocrite**, first cast out the beam out of thine own eye; and then shalt thou see clearly to cast out the mote out of thy brother's eye.

Hypocrites say one thing and do another. Their heart is far from it, but their mouth is there. We have religious hypocrites all over the world today. You know the Jim Bakers, the Jimmy Swaggarts. What does God say about them? They are in serious trouble.

- Matthew 7:20
  Wherefore **by their fruits ye shall know them**.

When Paul said *"thou art inexcusable"* it means that hypocrites are without excuse. If you judge one that is dangerous, and problematic, yet you are doing the same things, you are going to be in trouble too.

"Therefore thou art inexcusable" That word *"inexcusable"* is the same word that we found in Chapter 1 where the heathen were *"without excuse."* The Greek word for this is ANAPOLOGETOS. It means: *"without defense or excuse; that which cannot be defended, inexcusable."* They had seen all the creation of the world and they are *"without excuse."* Here the religious people are *"without excuse"* as well.

Romans 2:2

"But we are sure that the judgment of God is according to truth against them which commit such things."

1. God's Judgment Is According to Truth

The first principle of God's judgment is *"according to truth."* God knows the end from the beginning. He is not like we are when we have half truth. Not like our judges who know just part, but He knows everything. God's omniscience allows Him to know the truth. We do not have omniscience. Judgments, whether they be in the O. J. Simpson case or other cases, all the truth is not brought out. I have heard it said: *"There is your truth, my truth, and God's truth."* This is something to think about.

The rules of argument, the rules of government, and the rules of law forbid you to bring out certain truths in some court cases. Not so with the Lord. When judgment comes, whether for the Great White Throne for those who are lost, or the Judgment Seat of Christ for those who are saved, all the truth will be brought to bear.

Hypocrisy Is Amazing

In Romans 1:29-33 Paul lists twenty-three sins that the heathen have committed, and these religious people are doing the same twenty-three sins. They say how horrible these heathen people are who do these twenty-three sins, and here they are doing the same things. The exposure of the hypocrisy is amazing. We have people today naming the name of Christ, maybe even going to church and putting on their Sunday best, but their heart is far from the Lord.

Romans 2:3

"And thinkest thou this, O man, that judgest them which do such things, and doest the same, that thou shalt escape the judgment of God?"

There is no way to escape God's judgment. It is final. It is clear.

- **Hebrews 9:27**
  And as it is appointed unto men once to die, **but after this the judgment**:

If we are saved people, that will be the Judgment Seat of Christ where we will be judged according to our works. We will get either rewards or lack of rewards. For people who are unsaved and have never genuinely trusted the Lord Jesus Christ as Redeemer, The Great White Throne Judgment will be their fate. God will judge and send those people to Hell according to truth.

A lot of people think that they will escape the judgment of God. They say they have a nice neat plan. They will get cremated. They will get their body burned up to ashes. I am against cremation. I think burial is Scriptural. Cremation will not help you to escape God's judgment.

One of the ladies had a brother who was cremated against her will and against the brother's will, but the wife wanted to save a few dollars so she cremated her husband. The woman was afraid for this man. She wondered if he would be able to be resurrected. I told her that if he is saved, a professing Christian, born-again, waiting for the Lord's return ,then the Lord will take care of that.

The Lord will take the bodies that have been lost in the sea where sharks have eaten, and He will some how put them together and transform them into resurrection bodies. That is up to the Lord who made the Milky Way and the other billions of galaxies. The Lord can take care of small things like the resurrection of our bodies. No, we cannot escape the judgment of God: it is according to truth. Hypocrites can't escape the judgment of God.

Romans 2:4

"Or despisest thou the riches of his goodness and forbearance and longsuffering; not knowing that the goodness of God leadeth thee to repentance?"

These religious hypocrites, I think, would look at the heathen and say, "*Oh I am so glad they are going to Hell.*" May that not be our desire. May that not be our heart. We must realize that God is good and the "*goodness*" and "*long-suffering*" of God has lead us, if we are saved, to repentance and faith in Christ.

We should not say that we hope that they get theirs. Those hypocrites will get that same kind of treatment. Just because they say one thing, if they do the same things as the heathen they are lost and will be judged the same.

The Riches of God's Goodness

We should not "*despise the riches of his goodness.*" He gave us His Son, the Lord Jesus Christ. The riches that He gave us are indelible. He is "*longsuffering not willing that any should perish, but that all should come to repentance*" (2 Peter 3:9). We should realize that the "*goodness*" of God leads us to "*repentance.*"

Romans 2:5

"But after thy hardness and impenitent heart treasurest up unto thyself wrath against the day of wrath and revelation of the righteous judgment of God."

2. God's Judgment Is Righteous

This is the second principle of judgment in this Chapter. The first was in verse 2, "*according to truth.*" God will never judge a man, woman, or child contrary to truth. He will have the evidence and it will be clear.

Secondly, it is "*the righteous judgment of God.*" The Lord Jesus Christ talked about judging.

● **John 7:24**

Judge not according to the appearance, but **judge righteous judgment.**

● **John 5:22**
For the Father judgeth no man, but **hath committed all judgment** unto the Son:

God's Son the Sole Judge of All

The Father has placed His Son as the sole Judge of all mankind.

Remember Abraham asked the question in the Old Testament, "*Shall not the judge of all the earth do right?*" This was when He was about to judge Sodom and Gomorrah and rain fire and brimstone on that whole civilization. Abraham was told by the Lord what He was going to say. The Lord said, "*Shall I hide from Abraham that thing which I do?*" God told Abraham about the judgment of Sodom and Gomorrah. That is where Abraham plead on the mercy and goodness and long suffering of the Lord. Abraham said, "*Oh Lord may not that be.*" That is what our attitude should be.

May it not be to the heathen and lost people. Maybe there are fifty righteous. Would you destroy the righteous with the wicked? No, if there were fifty righteous, or forty, or thirty, or twenty or even ten righteous God would not destroy the city. He couldn't find even ten righteous people.

Abraham said, "*Shall not the judge of all the earth do right?*"

Righteous Judgment For All

There is not a single person in this world who is going to be judged by God who is not going to have a righteous judgment. He is going to make sure it is absolutely right.

You and I may not think that it is right, but that is not up to us. God is the God who is the judge and the justice, and He will make it right. He certainly will be fair in His judgments of all mankind whoever they may be.

People may ask, "*will He be fair at the Judgment Seat of Christ when the saved people will be judged*"? You who are born-again believers might wonder if He will be fair toward you. Yes, He will be right and righteous in that judgment. The Foundation for all saved people is the Lord Jesus Christ.

● **1 Corinthians 3:11**
For **other foundation can no man lay than that is laid, which is Jesus Christ.**

The two kind of materials are either (1) hay, wood, and stubble which will be burned up (*"The fire shall try every man's work"*) or (2) gold, silver, and precious stones which will be purified by the fire.

Some Believers' Works Burned Up

Many believers will be appearing before the Judgment Seat of Christ and will watch their works burn up in the fire. Their works are nothing more than to be seen of man.

The large works are made of wood, hay, and stubble which everyone can see. Gold, silver, and precious stones are in a small amount. Some of you ladies with precious stones such as diamonds know what we mean.

God will judge believers in a righteous way. *"Shall every man have the praise of God..."*

Romans 2:6

"Who will render to every man according to his deeds."

3. God's Judgment Is According to Deeds

In this verse Paul lays down the third principle of God's judgment. It is *"according to his deeds."* The first principle is *"according to truth"* (verse 2). The second principle is *"righteous judgment"* (verse 5). This verse gives us the third principle *"according to his deeds."* This is not that we are saved by our works or our deeds.

● **Matthew 10:14-15**
And whosoever shall not receive you, nor hear your words, when ye depart out of that house or city, shake off the dust of your feet. Verily I say unto you, **It shall be more tolerable for the land of Sodom and Gomorrha in the day of judgment, than for that city.**

Various Degrees of Judgment

In this verse the Lord tells that there are various degrees of judgment for those who go to Hell, just like there are various degrees of judgment for those who go to Heaven.

Some will have rewards or crowns which shall be laid at the feet of Christ.

Some will enter into the joy of the Lord. Some will be in Heaven as but by fire:

- **1 Corinthians 3:15**
  If any man's work shall be burned, **he shall suffer loss: but he himself shall be saved**; yet so as by fire.

So it will be with the wicked. There seems to be a differential. They will all be in Hell, but it will be different.

- **Matthew 11:22**
  But I say unto you, **It shall be more tolerable for Tyre and Sidon at the day of judgment, than for you**.

Apparently there is a gradation. They will all go to Hell because they have rejected Christ, but there is a gradation. I do not know if the fire is hotter. I do not know whether the suffering is greater, but something is different. They will be judged according to their works. In fact, it says in the book of Revelation:

- **Revelation 20:12-15**
  And I saw the dead, small and great, stand before God; and the books were opened: and another book was opened, which is the book of life: and **the dead were judged out of those things which were written in the books, according to their works.** And the sea gave up the dead which were in it; and death and Hell delivered up the dead which were in them: and they were **judged every man according to their works**. And death and Hell were cast into the Lake of Fire. This is the second death. And whosoever was not found written in the book of life was cast into the Lake of Fire.

Judgment According to Works

The Great White Throne Judgment will be according to their works and their deeds as well. Not that they will escape Hell, but they certainly will not be judged as harshly as others who have more light.

Verse 5 seems to indicate that the hypocrites will have wrath in the day of judgment. They will be going to Hell because they are not doing what should be done.

Romans 2:7

"To them who by patient continuance in well doing seek for glory and honour and immortality, eternal life:"

Some have thought there is a contradiction here in the book of Romans that salvation is by works. No, it is not by *"works,"* it is *"by grace through faith"* as Paul will bring out very clearly in Romans Chapter three through Chapter six. Some are seeking *"for glory and honour."*

- **Romans 3:11**
  There is none that understandeth, there is **none that seeketh after God**.

- **Isaiah 55:6**
  Seek ye the LORD while he may be found, call ye upon him while he is near:

The Lord wants us to *"seek"* Him. He wants us to trust the Lord whatever that may entail.

- **Jeremiah 29:13**
  And ye shall seek me, and find me, when ye shall search for me with all your heart.

God wants us to seek Him.

- **Lamentations 3:25**
  The LORD is good unto them that wait for him, to **the soul that seeketh him**.

There is nothing wrong with seeking Him.

- **Amos 5:4**
  For thus saith the LORD unto the house of Israel, **Seek ye me**, and ye shall live:

- **Amos 5:8**
  Seek him that maketh the seven stars and Orion, and turneth the shadow of death into the morning, and maketh the day dark with night: that calleth for the waters of the sea, and poureth them out upon the face of the earth: **The LORD is his name**:

Nothing Wrong In Seeking

Let me say it again. The Lord Jesus Christ said, *"Seek ye first the kingdom of God."* There is nothing wrong with seeking. The best *"seeking"* that we can do is to *"seek"* the Lord Jesus Christ as Saviour and Redeemer.

The two angels at the Lord's tomb asked the women who came to anoint His body, *"Why seek ye the living among the dead?"* (Luke 24:4-5). This is what was said to the woman who came to anoint the body of the Lord. The wise men also came to seek the Lord. *"Seek and ye shall find, knock and it shall be opened"* (Matthew 7:7; Luke 11:9).

I believe that the *"seekers"* are the ones who continuously seek for eternal life that He provides by His grace through our genuine faith in His Son. These will be honored and glorified by the Lord.

Romans 2:8

"But unto them that are contentious, and do not obey the truth, but obey unrighteousness, indignation and wrath"

This verse speaks of the opposite of those who seek the Lord. This seems to be those who are listed as unbelievers and hypocrites. They will not be honored by the Lord. They will be condemned. They are *"contentious and do not obey the truth."* Those will be receiving *"indignation and wrath."* The Greek word for *"contentious"* is ERITHEIA. It means:

> *"electioneering or intriguing for office; apparently, in the NT a courting distinction, a desire to put one's self forward, a partisan and fractious spirit which does not disdain low arts; partisanship, fractiousness."* Wayne Steury comments on this word as follows: *"This word is found before NT times only in Aristotle where it denotes a self-seeking pursuit of political office by unfair means. (A&G) Paul exhorts to be one in the mind of Christ not putting self forward or being selfish (Phil 2:3). James 3:14 speaks against having selfishness or self-promoting in your heart."*

The Lord Jesus is the Way, the Truth, and the Life, and hypocrites are headed for Hell. The heathen in Chapter one have not even obeyed the truth of creation. God wants us to seek Him, not be *"contentious,"* and not disobey the truth. He wants us to obey that which is right.

Romans 2:9

"Tribulation and anguish, upon every soul of man that doeth evil, of the Jew first, and also of the Gentile;"

Those that do *"evil,"* do wrong, there is nothing but Hell that will await them. And of course this practice of evil, this great evil that they do, is going to be judged by the Lord. It will be according to His righteous judgments, according to His righteous principles mentioned in Chapter one.

● **Ezekiel 18:4**
Behold, all souls are mine; as the soul of the father, so also the soul of the son is mine: **the soul that sinneth, it shall die.**

Certainly that is God's judgment. We're not judged because our parents have sinned. We're not judged because our friends have sinned. We're not judged because our spouses have sinned, but we are judged because we have sinned. *"All have sinned and come short of the glory of God."*

Hell Not Pleasant

Hell is not a pleasant place.

I know that there are many people today who are preaching that Hell is not real. They believe that Hell is just a feeling of unbelief, and Hell is a feeling of disappointment. I think Evangelist Billy Graham, several years ago, said that Hell was just a place, not of fire, but just simply a place where we would be sorry that we did not do right to start with. Then there are some, so-called, Bible-believing Christians who are taking the fire out of Hell. Some are taking the judgment and the eternality out of Hell. They are saying that Hell is not eternal. You just have a little bit of punishment and then you are free. It is as if you get a lenient sentence, but the Lord talks about the eternal fires of Hell.

Hell Is Everlasting

Everlasting damnation is just as everlasting as everlasting life. The greatest *"evil"* one can commit is the *"evil"* of rejecting the Lord Jesus Christ and His salvation which will send a person to Hell.

Notice God says *"of the Jew first, and also of the Gentile."* Saved Jews and saved Gentiles will go to Heaven, and unsaved Jews and unsaved Gentiles will go to Hell. God gives equal opportunity to both groups and is fair in His judgment.

Romans 2:10

"But glory, honour, and peace, to every man that worketh good, to the Jew first, and also to the Gentile:"

At first thought, this sounds, again, that it is salvation by works, but I do not believe that this is the teaching of Scripture. There is a rule of interpretation of Scripture. *"Never interpret a difficult passage when you have plain passages that are very clear and evident. Always look at the plain passages."* When it speaks of *"worketh good,"* there is a verse I like to use to clarify the only *"work"* on the part of the unsaved that pleases the Lord is found in the Gospel of John.

- John 6:28-29
  Then said they unto him, What shall we do, that we might work the works of God? Jesus answered and said unto them, **This is the work of God, that ye believe on him whom he hath sent.**

That is the most important *"work of God,"* that is, *"that ye believe on Him Whom He hath sent."* Faith is one of the most important *"works of God"* as mentioned in John 6:28-29.

In other words, if they have faith in the Lord Jesus Christ and *"believe in Him Whom He has sent,"* they can have eternal life and salvation by faith.

Romans 2:11

"For there is no respect of persons with God."

4. God's Judgment Does Not Respect Persons

The Greek word for *"respect of persons"* is PROSOPOLEPSIA. It means:
"respect of persons; partiality; the fault of one who when called on to give judgment has respect of the outward circumstances of man and not to their intrinsic merits, and so prefers, as the more worthy, one who is rich, high born, or powerful, to another who does not have these qualities"
There are many references against *"respecting persons."*

- James 2:1
  My brethren, have not the faith of our Lord Jesus Christ, the Lord of glory, with **respect of persons**.

- **James 2:3**
  And ye have **respect to him** that weareth the gay clothing, and say unto him, Sit thou here in a good place; and say to the poor, Stand thou there, or sit here under my footstool:

- **James 2:9**
  But if ye have **respect to persons**, ye commit sin, and are convinced of the law as transgressors.

- **Proverbs 24:23**
  These things also belong to the wise. It is not good to have **respect of persons** in judgment.

If you respect persons, you cater to the one who is the most beautiful or handsome, the one that is the most rich or well-to-do. This is a terrible thing.

The Lord is blind to who they are or who we are. He doesn't care if you are the President of the United States, the governor of the state, or the mayor of the city, rich or poor, a great teacher at a great university, or whether you are a Sunday School teacher in a local church. God has *"no respect of persons."* His judgment is *"according to truth,"* not according to respect of persons.

- **Proverbs 28:21**
  To have **respect of persons is not good**: for for a piece of bread that man will transgress.

Bribes and "Respect of Persons"

If you have *"respect of persons,"* you can be bribed with just a piece of bread and will do what that person wants you to do.

We have bribery going on all the time in our courts do we not. Occasionally a person will be slipped a thousand dollar bill if he will simply wave a traffic ticket or something else. There is *"no respect of persons with God."*

- **Ephesians 6:9**
  And, ye masters, do the same things unto them, forbearing threatening: knowing that your Master also is in Heaven; **neither is there respect of persons with him**.

The Master in Heaven has no respect of persons.

- **Colossians 3:25**
  But he that doeth wrong shall receive for the wrong which he hath done: **and there is no respect of persons**.

- **James 2:1**
  My brethren, have not the faith of our Lord Jesus Christ, the

Lord of glory, **with respect of persons**.

- 1 Peter 1:17
  And if ye call on the Father, **who without respect of persons** judgeth according to every man's work, pass the time of your sojourning here in fear:

God's Four Principles of Judgment

1. Judgment is according to truth.
2. Judgment is according to righteousness.
3. Judgment is according to deeds.
4. Judgment is without respect of persons.

This is very important to understand that God is not a man as we are seeing the difference between persons. He does not respect them. That does not mean that He does not like the people, but it means you do not play one against another.

Romans 2:12

"For as many as have sinned without law shall also perish without law: and as many as have sinned in the law shall be judged by the law;"

Those that are heathen people are without the law of Moses. If they had not lived up to what God had given to them, as evidenced by their worship of images, beasts, and four-footed things, they were going to perish. On the other hand, those Jews had the law, but had not followed it would be judged by that law.

The blood sacrifices under the law of Moses are not what saved the Jews. It was genuine and personal faith in the one sacrifice of God's Lamb, the Lord Jesus Christ to which the sacrifices pointed that would save these Jews. They shall be judged by the law. The heathen shall *"perish"* without the law.

"Perish" Speaks of Eternal Hell

The word *"perish"* speaks of the everlasting fires of Hell and eternal damnation.

● John 3:16

For God so loved the world, that he gave his only begotten Son, that **whosoever believeth in him should not perish**, but have everlasting life.

Rejecting Christ Leads to Hell

That is an important verse. Trusting Christ we have everlasting life. If people reject that Savour, they will *"perish"* or go to Hell.

● John 3:15

That **whosoever believeth in him should not perish**, but have eternal life.

The Lord Jesus Christ was explaining to Nicodemus about Moses' lifting up the serpent in the wilderness (Numbers 21:8-9).

The words *"should not perish"* are removed by the false Westcott and Hort Greek Text (plus the Nestle/Aland, United Bible Societies, Vatican, and Sinai texts). It is also removed from the modern versions of our day. The New International Version in John 3:15 leaves off *"should not perish."* New American Standard Version leaves off *"should not perish"* in John 3:15. The New King James in the study edition footnotes leaves off *"should not perish"* in John 3:15. The Revised Standard Version and the New Revised Version both leave off *"should not perish"* in John 3:15.

"Perishing" is important. The Devil doesn't want to remind people that there is a *"perishing"* when we reject Christ and reject Truth. We praise the Lord for the New Testament in the King James Bible which is clear on *"perishing"* as well as eternal life.

Romans 2:13

"(For not the hearers of the law *are* just before God, but the doers of the law shall be justified."

It is the *"doers of the law"* who *"shall be justified,"* not only the *"hearers of the law."* At first glance this might sound like salvation by works. This is not true. Paul clarifies this in other places in Romans. James talked about *"doers."*

● James 1:22

But be ye **doers of the** , and not hearers only, deceiving your own selves.

It is not the hearing only, but the doing. The doers of the law, I maintain, are not saved by the works of the laws, but the doers are those who practice properly the Old Testament sacrifices as they pertain to the Lamb of God Who would "*take away the sin of the world*" (John 1:29b).

The Old Testament sacrifices that were made many, many times cannot save as it says in the book of Hebrews. They did point to the Lamb of God, the Lord Jesus Christ, who did one day come to take away the sins of the world for those who believe. I believe the doers of the law here are those who, not only did, but also had faith.

In Isaiah Chapter 1 the remnant of Israel, the ones who lived by faith, and knew what that sacrifice meant looking forward in faith to the Messiah, I maintain, is what Paul means here when he talks about the "*doers*" of the law being "*justified.*"

- **Romans 3:24**
  Being justified freely by his grace through the redemption that is in Christ Jesus:

His grace is what justifies us or declares us righteous before the Lord. That is a wonderful state to be in, righteous and just before the Lord.

Romans 2:14

"For when the Gentiles, which have not the law, do by nature the things contained in the law, these, having not the law, are a law unto themselves:"

I believe that these "*Gentiles*" are the heathen from back in Chapter one who worshiped the idols and the images and the four-footed beasts that cannot save. If they "*do by nature the things contained in the law, these, having not the law, are a law unto themselves.*" God will pardon and judge justly.

Heathen Looking for the Saviour

Many have said that they have not seen many heathen who are looking for the things of the Lord. Missionaries have gone to foreign fields and are amazed when they see some people who immediately accept Christ as their Saviour when the Gospel if Preached. Their hearts are looking for the ones who come to give the truth. I believe that this is why we have to have foreign missions as well as home missions to take the good news, the gospel, to those who will receive it and trust Christ as their Saviour.

Those who are heathen out there without Christ, it is hard sometimes to minister to them, but God wants us to go into all the world and preach the gospel to every creature.

Romans 2:15

"Which shew the work of the law written in their hearts, their conscience also bearing witness, and *their* thoughts the mean while accusing or else excusing one another;)"

You cannot depend upon a *"conscience."*

- **1 Timothy 4:2**
Speaking lies in hypocrisy; **having their conscience seared** with a hot iron;

Seared so that they cannot feel anymore. Seared so they do not know what sin is. They do not have any *"conscience."*

The Greek word for "conscience" is SUNEIDESIS. It means:
"the consciousness of anything; the soul as distinguishing between what is morally good and bad, prompting to do the former and shun the latter, commending one, condemning the other; the conscience."

Conscience means knowing within ourselves. God has given us a conscience if we know and study the Words of God. When we sin, our conscience says this is wrong. This is true if we have a conscience that is functioning.

If a conscience is seared with a hot iron, sin has no affect. To believers, when God the Holy Spirit is living in our bodies, we have a conscience. Paul says:

- **Acts 24:16**
And herein do I exercise myself, to have always a **conscience** void of offence toward God, and toward men.

The thoughts are spoken about in Isaiah:

- **Isaiah 55:7-8**
Let the wicked forsake his way, and the unrighteous man **his thoughts**: and let him return unto the LORD, and he will have mercy upon him; and to our God, for he will abundantly pardon. **For my thoughts are not your thoughts**, neither are your ways my ways, saith the LORD.

The thoughts of people either do two things. They either accuse them or excuse them. If the thoughts are based upon the Scripture, the Words of God, the thoughts of people can accuse them as sin.

The Bible Accuses Us

If we are saved, as we read the Words of God, the Bible accuses us. Our thoughts accuse us of wickedness and sin, and so we will repent, confess that sin unto the Lord (1 John 1:9), get back in fellowship with Him, and do what is right.

Some thoughts of unbelievers, and I am sorry to say the thoughts of some Christians excuse one another. You have heard of rationalization. Rationalization is a very clever thought process which gets us out of trouble and sin. It calls black *"white,"* and white *"black,"* and rationalizes our way out of a difficult situation if we can make a good reason why we did this.

The man on television whose excuse is, *"the Devil made me do it,"* is rationalization. Eve was the one who blamed the serpent, *"the serpent made me do that,"* the sin of taking the forbidden fruit.

Our thoughts excuse many times, but God knows no excuse for sin. Our thoughts cannot excuse us; the Words of God are clear, yet sometimes people's thoughts will excuse them from doing what is right. God does not accept excuses. He judges according to truth. When He judges us, it is going to be a true picture and not a false picture.

Romans 2:16

"In the day when God shall judge the secrets of men by Jesus Christ according to my gospel."

5. God's Judgment Is According to the Gospel

In this verse, God adds a fifth principle of His judgment. There are now a total of five principles that Paul has laid down in this book of Romans.

God's Five Principles of Judgment

1. Judgment is according to truth.
2. Judgment is according to righteousness.
3. Judgment is according to deeds.
4. Judgment is without respect of persons.
5. Judgment is according to Paul's gospel.

Notice that this verse speaks about a time *"when God shall judge the secrets of men."* Does God know our *"secrets"*? He certainly does. His Omniscience penetrates right down into the recesses of the heart, not just the superficial, but the heart. Right down into the depths of where we live. He is going to be judging those secrets. We hope that we will have our sins confessed and are walking right with the Lord and in fellowship with Him.

There is another verse which talks about God's judging our secrets and that is in 1 Corinthians.

● **1 Corinthians 4:5**
Therefore judge nothing before the time, until the Lord come, who both will bring to light **the hidden things of darkness**, and will make manifest the counsels of the hearts: and then shall every man have praise of God.

The *"hidden things of darkness"* God will bring to *"light."*

I taught that at a Baptist Church years ago in a large adult Sunday School class. One of the Christian ladies came up afterwards and asked about all the things which we confessed. She wondered if God will bring those things up. She said that we may as well not confess them if He is going to bring them up again. I told her that, *"If we confess our sins, He is faithful and just to forgive us our sins and to cleanse us from all unrighteousness"* (1 John 1:9). She was worried about that. She did not want to confess her sins and then have them brought back up again. The Lord is faithful. He is going to be judging these things by Jesus Christ.

There are many verses which tell us it is the Lord Jesus Himself, God's Son, Who will be the judge. It won't be the Father, it won't be the Holy Spirit, but it will be the Son.

● **John 5:22**
For the Father judgeth no man, but **hath committed all judgment unto the Son**:

● **John 5:30**
I can of mine own self do nothing: as I hear, I judge: and my judgment is just; because I seek not mine own will, but the will of the Father which hath sent me.

● **John 7:24**
Judge not according to the appearance, but judge righteous judgment.

Two Important Judgments

There are at least two important judgments. The first for the born-again believers. The second is for the lost of all ages. The judgment of the believers is called the Judgment Seat of Christ. The judgment of the unsaved is called the Great White Throne Judgment.

In both those instances there will be righteous judgments handed out. The saved will be judged according to what we have done to the Lord. The "*hay, wood, and stubble*" (1 Corinthians 3:12) will be burned up. The "*gold, silver, and precious stones*" (1 Corinthians 3:12) will be refined, and God will say, "*Well done thou good and faithful servant*" (Matthew 25:21a).

All of us, if we are saved, will go to Heaven, but there will be differences as far as rewards. The unsaved, at the Great White Throne Judgment, will all go to Hell, but there are degrees of punishment in Hell apparently (Matthew 10:15; 11:23-24; Mark 6:11; Luke 10:12).

- **John 12:47**
  And if any man hear my words, and believe not, I judge him not: for **I came not to judge the world, but to save the world**.

Christ Came to Save the World

The Lord Jesus Christ did not come at His first coming to "*judge the world.*" He came to "*save the world.*"

One day He's coming in His second coming, and He will be a judge. Without His salvation, without His death, burial, and resurrection, the shedding of His blood for the forgiveness of sins, nobody could be saved. He came to save the world the first time.

- **2 Timothy 4:1**
  I charge thee therefore before God, and the **Lord Jesus Christ, who shall judge the quick and the dead at his appearing and his kingdom;**

Judging the Saved and the Lost

The Lord Jesus Christ will be the *"judge."* The *"quick"* are the living people or those who are saved. The *"dead"* are the unsaved people at the Great White Throne Judgment. I believe that these are the two most important judgments of the many in Scripture. He will judge the *"quick"* at the rapture of the saved. Those of us who are saved will be raptured up before the tribulation period on this earth takes place. This is the Judgment Seat of Christ. He will judge the *"dead,"* those who are lost, at the Great White Throne Judgment at the end of the thousand year Millennial reign of Christ on this earth.

- 2 Timothy 4:8
  Henceforth there is laid up for me a crown of righteousness, which **the Lord, the righteous judge**, shall give me at that day: and not to me only, but unto all them also that love his appearing.

- Hebrews 10:30
  For we know him that hath said, Vengeance belongeth unto me, I will recompense, saith the Lord. And again, **The Lord shall judge his people**.

- Revelation 20:12-13
  And I saw the dead, small and great, stand before God; and the books were opened: and another book was opened, which is the book of life: and **the dead were judged** out of those things which were written in the books, according to their works. And the sea gave up the dead which were in it; and death and Hell delivered up the dead which were in them: and **they were judged every man according to their works**.

Paul says, *"...in the day when God will judge the secrets of men by Jesus Christ according to my gospel."* Romans 1:16 gives the gospel.

- Romans 1:16
  For **I am not ashamed of the gospel of Christ: for it is the power of God unto salvation** to every one that believeth; to the Jew first, and also to the Greek.

The *"gospel of Christ"* is the *"power of God unto salvation."* What is this good news about? There is some bad news about our condition as people. We are all sinners in God's sight.

- Romans 3:23
  For all have sinned, and come short of the glory of God;

Good News for All Eternity

Yet there is also some good news. There is a *"gift of God"* which can bring *"eternal life"* for those who repent of their sins and have genuine faith in the Lord Jesus Christ. They will receive God's eternal salvation in Heaven for all eternity.

- Romans 6:23
  For the wages of sin *is* death; but **the gift of God *is* eternal life** through Jesus Christ our Lord.

The *"gospel"* will be the measure of God's judgment.

What have we done with the Lord Jesus Christ? What have we done with the *"gospel"*? This is the judgment that the Lord Jesus will have.

Romans 2:17

"Behold, thou art called a Jew, and restest in the law, and makest thy boast of God,"

Here he is talking to the Jews in the church in Rome, Italy. Paul is writing from Corinth which is a city in Greece. He is talking to the Jews in Rome. In the earlier part of Chapter two he talked about moralists in general. In Chapter one he talked about the lost, the heathen and the idol worshipers. Now he is talking to the Jews, and he is going to get right down to brass tacks as it were. He is talking to his own people.

Paul addresses those who *"rest in the law, and make thy boast of God."* Boasting is one of the sins mentioned in Romans 1:30.

- Ephesians 2:8-9
  For by grace are ye saved through faith; and that not of yourselves: it is the gift of God: Not of works, **lest any man should boast**.

God does not want us to boast.

These Jews were resting in the law of Moses because they are Jews. They are trusting peacefully and quietly in their religion. They boast and are boasters.

We, if we are saved, may be resting in whatever we are. Whether we are Baptists or whatever, and we may boast also. Look at our failures. We may have a fine doctrinal statement. We may have a lot of things, but we ought not to boast. We ought to be humble, and put away any boasting. Just because we are saved, just because we are Baptists, just because we are born-again, just because we have what the Lord has given us, we should not boast.

We must be careful that we are not like these Jews who rest in the law, "*and makest thy boast of God.*" Their mouth is big, but their life is not so big. It is small. We hope that our life may be strong and big, and not small like these Jews Paul is talking about.

Romans 2:18

"And knowest *his* will, and approvest the things that are more excellent, being instructed out of the law;"

Notice these Jews were not just ordinary Jews. They knew God's will and approved "*the things that are more excellent.*" These were high on the ladder of information about the Old Testament. They were an "*instructed*" people.

One of the old-time Bible teachers used to say:

God's Will Is Found in God's Words

"*Full knowledge of God's will is found in a full knowledge of God's Words.*"

That is very important. These Jews had a full knowledge of God's will. They must have known His Words. We must keep on studying "*to show ourselves approved unto God a workman that needeth not to be ashamed, rightly dividing the Word of Truth*" (2 Timothy 2:15). Only in this way can we know God's will, "*approve the things that are more excellent being instructed out of the law*" and from the complete Words of God.

Now, if we are instructed and we have much knowledge that could be dangerous. Let me tell you why.

- Luke 12:48

  But he that knew not, and did commit things worthy of stripes, shall be beaten with few stripes. For **unto whomsoever much is given, of him shall be much required:** and to whom men have committed much, of him they will ask the more.

More Given--More Required

The more knowledge that we have of the Words of God, the more God expects from us. If we are saved we cannot say at the Judgment Seat of Christ that we did not know any better. God says that, *"unto whomsoever much is given, of him shall be much required."*

God is going to require more of those of us who know things. These Jews that knew the law of Moses and just knew things backwards and forwards and could quote Scripture and knew everything about it were in serious trouble because much was going to be required of them. Does that mean that it is better to be ignorant of God's Words so that you do not get so much judgment? No, we must know God's Words. He said, *"Study to shew thyself approved unto God"* (2 Timothy 2:15a). Not unto men, but unto God.

Be diligent and study the Words of God to show yourself approved. The Greek word for *"workman"* is ERGATES. It means:

"a workman, a labourer; usually one who works for hire esp. an agricultural worker; one who does, a worker, perpetrator."

This *"workman"* would know how to work with his tools, the Scriptures. He or she is one *"that needeth not to be ashamed, rightly dividing the Word of truth"* (2 Timothy 2:15b). These Jews in this verse new very well God's *"will"* and were *"instructed out of the law."*

Romans 2:19

"And art confident that thou thyself art a guide of the blind, a light of them which are in darkness,"

These religious Jews were *"confident."* They thought that they were even a *"guide of the blind."* That is fine, if it is true.

Across the street every Saturday night there is a meeting of blind folks in this city. They come with their canes. They come with their dogs. They go into the church. I saw yesterday either a friend, a mother, a sister, or a relative carrying a big long cane guiding a blind man.

We have a blind lady on our street. She has a dog and goes out walking. She is a younger lady. It is good to have *"guides to the blind."* These Jews thought that they were *"guides to the blind"* and a *"light of them which are in darkness,"* but they were not. What did the Lord Jesus say of these Pharisees of the Jews in His day?

- Matthew 15:14

  Let them alone: they be **blind leaders of the blind**. And if the **blind lead the blind**, both shall fall into the ditch.

That is a far cry to being *"a guide to the blind."* These are blind themselves.

- Matthew 23:16

  Woe unto you, **ye blind guides**, which say, Whosoever shall swear by the temple, it is nothing; but whosoever shall swear by the gold of the temple, he is a debtor!

Can you imagine a blind person leading you anywhere? I do not know where I would want to go with a blind man leading me. How can a blind person lead anybody? It is true that during the 9/11 disaster in New York City in 2001 a blind person did lead some out of the building.

Dean Burgon has written many books on the King James Bible and the Traditional Greek Text, and he said of one of the Greek men who forsook the *Textus Receptus* and went along with the false Greek text of Westcott and Hort, *"It is like a man putting out both his eyes and then going to a strange place and seeing how it is."* He rejected truth and knowledge.

We should not be blind in what we do. We ought to be having the light of truth and not be like these Pharisees. As far as being confident, we must be careful of being confident. We have to be careful of arrogance, of pride, of pomposity, of being pompous.

- Philippians 3:3

  For we are the circumcision, which worship God in the spirit, and rejoice in Christ Jesus, and **have no confidence in the flesh**.

They are pushing themselves upwards, but we have to *"have no confidence in the flesh."* Paul said,

- Romans 7:18

  For I know that **in me (that is, in my flesh,) dwelleth no good thing:** for to will is present with me; but how to perform that which is good I find not.

We must have the light of God's Words. We must have the Words of God and the Spirit of God, if we are saved, to guide us in all that we do.

Romans 2:20

"An instructor of the foolish, a teacher of babes, which hast the form of knowledge and of the truth in the law." In addition to the foregoing attributes, Paul said that these Jews were *"instructors of the foolish."* As I said before, God says that *"unto whomsoever much is given, of him shall be much required."*

They also claimed to be *"a teacher of babes."* The Greek word for "*babe*s" is BREPHOS. It means: "*an infant, little child; a minor, not of age; metaph. childish, untaught, unskilled.*"

That word for "*instructor*" is like a disciplinarian who takes care of the "*babes*" and children. Be careful with only a "*form of knowledge.*" We should be glad that we are able to read our Bibles and are able to read English. We should not be boastful. We should be humble, but these people were not humble.

Is there a difference between an instructor and a pupil? Yes, there certainly is. An instructor is one who knows, one who studies, one who has the knowledge. A pupil is one who is learning. I hope that all of us will be pupils all the rest of our lives and learn from God's Words.

We Have Never "Arrived"

We must never say "*I have arrived.*" There is no plateau in the Christian life. There is no saying, "*I have reached* it." Every single day of our lives there are new things that we can find in the Words of God.

I was lead to the Lord by my high school janitor. They call them "*custodians*" now. His name was Uncle Charlie Allen. That was back in 1944. I had just entered my senior year. This is a long time ago.

Shortly after I was saved our pastor (Pastor Earl Willetts from Berea, Ohio) on New Years Eve said it is a very good idea to read the Bible through in the coming year. I thought that was a good idea because I was a new Christian and newly saved. I thought I would go ahead and read my Bible.

Yearly Bible Reading

I asked my future father-in-law, Mr. R. O. Sanborn, how to do this? I wondered how many chapters or verses I had to read each day to finish in a year. The King James Bible that Uncle Charlie gave me had the number of chapters, verses and words in every book of the Bible. I came up with the total number of verses and I divided it by 365 and 1/4th days. This averages 85 verses per day. I began reading at that point 85 verses per day. I then made up my YEARLY BIBLE READING SCHEDULE with each day's reading on it. This schedule has been printed into the thousands since 1945 when I first made it up.

In the Preface of our *Defined King James Bible* published by the Bible For Today, we have every book introduced briefly. Then we have the number of Chapters, verses, and words in every book and Chapter of the Bible. That is copied from the Bible that Uncle Charlie gave me when he led me to Christ back in 1944. Throughout this *Defined King James Bible* there is a little diamond at the end of each one of those 85 verse sections. I have made it my purpose, at least once a year, to finish the Words of God from Genesis to Revelation. When I was newly saved I would read it through two and sometimes three times per year. I would get up at 4 o'clock in the morning to read the Bible because I was a new Christian.

God wants us to know His will. We can never say *"we have arrived."* We should always be learning daily from the Words of God. That will take away all our boasting. Every time I read the Bible I find something new. It probably was not new, but maybe it was fresh to me. Praise the Lord for being able to grow in the things of the Lord Jesus Christ.

Romans 2:21

"Thou therefore which teachest another, teachest thou not thyself? thou that preachest a man should not steal, dost thou steal?" Paul is still speaking to the Jews. Here is Jewish hypocrisy at its very worst. We who are Gentiles can be just as hypocritical. We can teach somebody else not to do something, and then we do it ourself. We have to be very careful. Paul was very serious:

- **1 Corinthians 9:27**
  But I keep under my body, and bring it into subjection: **lest that by any means, when I have preached to others, I myself should be a castaway.**

Don't Be A "Castaway"

Paul did not want to be *"put on the shelf,"* to be no good, no longer used by the Lord, a *"castaway."* We must be very careful that when we preach to others, and when we teach to others, that our lives might be shipwrecked. Only by guarding our lives can the Lord honor and bless us and others through us.

I remember one of our friends that we went to school with. There were rumors, and I suppose true rumors because many had witnessed it, that the wife of this friend who was a theologian and a preacher was a kleptomaniac. She would steal, and steal, and steal. I do not know what would hit the lady. Every time she'd get in a new place she would steal. I was told that the poor pastor had to be moving from place to place every time she got caught. It was a terrible stench to the nostrils of God, and also to the people who were around her. This pastor would teach that you shouldn't steal, and here his wife stole. That is hypocrisy.

Jim Baaker of the PTL was put in jail because, among other things, his organization was not handling funds in a proper manner. I do not know how many televangelists are guilty of that. They preach not to steal, yet when they divert funds and use them for wrong purposes, they become thieves. This is a crookedness. You've heard the expression perhaps, "*Crooked as a dog's hind leg.*" That is the way some of these preachers are, and this is a terrible thing. I believe we must be very careful when we preach to others that we do not do those things that we preach against.

Romans 2:22

"Thou that sayest a man should not commit adultery, dost thou commit adultery? thou that abhorrest idols, dost thou commit sacrilege?" Here is the question of adultery, whether sexual or spiritual (which is idolatry). Now, we are getting into all sorts of definitions. Our former President has used all different definitions. God's Words do not change. "*Thou shall not commit adultery*" (Exodus 20:14; Deuteronomy 5:18). We have problems.

In a church in New Jersey, a former pastor had unwise counseling practices with a woman. Because of this, he was asked to leave that church. Some believed he had committed adultery, but that was never proved conclusively. Others were convinced that there was no adultery. I first heard about this ugly rumor from my unsaved principal where I was a teacher in Philadelphia. He asked me if I had heard about the "Elmer Gantry" of that city. At that time I had not heard anything about this rumor, or whether it was true or false. Elmer Gantry is from a movie. He is a man who preaches wonderfully and then lives for the Devil. Adulterous rumors, whether true or false, have a way of leaking out to the unsaved world around us do they not? Good things have a way of leaking out as well.

Another church that I know about had a wave of adultery. First the assistant pastor of youth committed adultery with the choir leader. Then a new preacher came on staff and he became an adulterer with one of the women attending his church. One after another. I do not know what is going to become of that church. I was told that the church came within just a few votes of having the pastor remain in the pulpit after his adultery. They were willing to forget the whole thing and have him be a pastor again. I do not know how the vote came out, but I understood that just a few votes would have put that adulterer right back in preaching to the others. It is a sad thing indeed, is it not? We have problems even today with various televangelists. As I think of Jewish hypocrisy, or any hypocrisy, I think of the verses in Isaiah Chapter one as God looks down into the hypocrisy of His people.

- Isaiah 1:2

  Hear, O Heavens, and give ear, O earth: for the LORD hath spoken, **I have nourished and brought up children, and they have rebelled against me.**

- Isaiah 1:4

  Ah sinful nation, a people laden with iniquity, a seed of evildoers, children that are corrupters: they have forsaken the LORD, they have provoked the Holy One of Israel unto anger, they are gone away backward.

- Isaiah 1:6

  From the sole of the foot even unto the head there is no soundness in it; but wounds, and bruises, and putrifying sores: they have not been closed, neither bound up, neither mollified with ointment.

- Isaiah 1:11

  To what purpose is the multitude of your sacrifices unto me? saith the LORD: I am full of the burnt offerings of rams, and the fat of fed beasts; and I delight not in the blood of bullocks, or of lambs, or of he goats.

The blood of bulls and lambs were not offered in faith.

- Isaiah 1:13

  Bring no more vain oblations; incense is an abomination unto me; the new moons and sabbaths, the calling of assemblies, I cannot away with; it is iniquity, even the solemn meeting.

- Isaiah 1:15

  And when ye spread forth your hands, I will hide mine eyes from you: yea, **when ye make many prayers, I will not hear: your hands are full of blood**.

- Isaiah 1:16

  Wash you, make you clean; **put away the evil of your doings** from before mine eyes; cease to do evil;

- Isaiah 1:18

  Come now, and let us reason together, saith the LORD: **though your sins be as scarlet, they shall be as white as**

snow; though they be red like crimson, they shall be as wool.
The hypocrisy of the Jews was the same thing here as Paul was pointing out.

Romans 2:23

"Thou that makest thy boast of the law, through breaking the law dishonourest thou God?" These Jews were making a *"boast of the law"* and yet they were *"breaking"* it and *"dishonouring"* God.

We Must Not Dishonour the Lord

When we say that we are believers, and do not live like we are supposed to live, it *"dishonors"* the Lord.

- Proverbs 6:33

A wound and **dishonour** shall he get; and his reproach shall not be wiped away.

The Greek word for *"dishonour"* is ATIMAZO. It means: *"to dishonour, insult, treat with contempt; whether in word, deed or thought."* This is what Israel did and this is what saved people do who do not live for the Lord and follow the Bible. They treat the Lord with *"contempt and insult."*

Men and Women of Our Word

It is better not to say anything than to say something and to break what we have said. We should be men and woman of our word.

Romans 2:24

"For the name of God is blasphemed among the Gentiles through you, as it is written." The name of God was being *"blasphemed"* because these Jews were disobedient people. The Greek word for *"blasphemed"* is BLASPHEMEO. It means: *"to speak reproachfully, rail at, revile, calumniate, blaspheme; to be evil spoken of, reviled, railed at."*

Dishonoring Christ is Blasphemy

When a preacher, or a deacon, any Christian, or anybody else dishonors the name of God, this is a form of *"blasphemy."* It is a disgrace to the Lord Jesus Christ.

- 1 Timothy 6:1

  Let as many servants as are under the yoke count their own masters worthy of all honour, **that the name of God and his doctrine be not blasphemed.**

In Paul's day Christian servants were to be obedient to their masters, so that God's Name and doctrine *"be not blasphemed."* The servants should do what they are told as long as it is not contrary to God's Words.

- Titus 2:5

  To be discreet, chaste, keepers at home, good, obedient to their own husbands, **that the word of God be not blasphemed**.

That phrase, *"it is written,"* occurs 63 times in the Bible. The Greek word for this is GEGRAPTAI. It is the perfect tense of the verb GRAPHO. It means various things:

> *"to write, with reference to the form of the letters; to delineate (or form) letters on a tablet, parchment, paper, or other material; to write, with reference to the contents of the writing; to express in written characters; to commit to writing (things not to be forgotten), write down, record; used of those things which stand written in the sacred books (of the OT); to write to one, i.e. by writing (in a written epistle) to give information, directions; to fill with writing; to draw up in writing, compose."*

Bible Preservation of God's Words

GEGRAPTAI was used 26 times by the Lord Jesus Christ Himself. The force of the perfect tense is that something was written in the past, has been preserved as it was written down to the present, and it will continue to be preserved on into the future. This is proof of Bible preservation of the Words of Hebrew, Aramaic, and Greek Old and New Testaments. God has preserved His Words. It applies equally to Old Testament Words and New Testament Words. Those Words are going to be preserved right into the future. It has been written in the past. It stands written in the present. And it will continue to be written and preserved into the future.

We have in our fundamentalist circles many people who deny the preservation of the Words of God. They deny that He preserved His original Hebrew, Aramaic, and Greek Words. In fact, many of these fundamentalist schools and colleges do not even believe God has PROMISED to preserve His Words. The four leading schools that teach this unbelief are as follows: (1) Bob Jones University in Greenville, South Carolina; (2) Detroit Baptist Seminary in Detroit, Michigan; (3) Central Baptist Seminary in the Minneapolis, Minnesota area; and (4) Calvary Baptist Seminary in Lansdale, Pennsylvania. If this were true (and it is not) our Bible translations today would be worthless.

The Only Accurate English Bible

I believe that our King James Bible is the only accurately translated English Bible. It has been based upon the verbally preserved Hebrew, Aramaic, and Greek Words.

Romans 2:25

"For circumcision verily profiteth, if thou keep the law: but if thou be a breaker of the law, thy circumcision is made uncircumcision." This rite of circumcision was first found in Genesis.

- **Genesis 17:10**
  This is my covenant, which ye shall keep, between me and
  you and thy seed after thee; **Every man child among you
  shall be circumcised**.

Circumcision was given to the nation of Israel (Genesis 17:11; John 7:22;
Romans 4:11). It was not given to the Gentiles. That was a sign to Israel.
People today circumcise their male children for health reasons, but for Jews, it
is an Israelitish bond and seal. It is a part of their covenant. That is why all the
way through these verses which follow, "*circumcision*" is referring to the Jews,
and "*uncircumcision*" is referring to the Gentiles (Galatians 3:11). It is an
outward sign which could not save a person's soul. It identified that person with
a covenant people.

For instance, believers' baptism is an outward sign (not that baptism is
similar to circumcision, but that is what some churches teach). Here is a person
who professes faith in Christ, and in obedience to Him is immersed (buried with
Christ and risen with Christ in order to walk in newness of life). That is an
outward sign. That in itself is worthless unless this life fulfills the will of the
Lord after the baptism. Some Southern Baptists baptize those who go down
into the water a dry sinner, and come up out of the water a wet sinner. Neither
baptism nor circumcision can save us. It is important that we have, not only an
outward sign, but also an inward reality.

Romans 2:26

**"Therefore if the uncircumcision keep the
righteousness of the law, shall not his uncircumcision be
counted for circumcision?"** In other words, here you have a case of
the Old Testament Jews who did not keep the law and a Gentile who keeps the
law. Paul makes a point that the keeping of the law should be "*counted*" as
"*circumcision*" if an "*uncircumcised*" Gentile kept it. He is putting the
emphasis on the inner compliance with God's requirements rather than merely
on an outer condition of the body, even though the law could never save
anyone's soul. That could be accomplished in the Old Testament only by the
person's looking forward in faith to God's Lamb Who would one day come to
take away the "*sin of the world*" (John 1:29b) and to save those who received
and trusted Him (John 1:12).

Romans 2:27

**"And shall not uncircumcision which is by nature, if it
fulfil the law, judge thee, who by the letter and
circumcision dost transgress the law?"** The Gentiles who
fulfilled the law of Moses could rightly "*judge*" the Jews who were wayward

and "*transgressed the law.*"

God Judges Disobedience

In the Old Testament time the ten northern tribes of Israel were taken into the Assyrian captivity by the Lord. The two Southern tribes were taken into Babylon for seventy years. The whole Gentile world could see what disobedient people the Israelites were. They were corrupt, and wicked. Because of this God took them away from their land. The Gentiles were judges of the Jews. It is the same way today. The unsaved world judges the professing Christians who profess to know the Lord Jesus Christ as their Saviour. Sometimes their standards for the Christians are higher than their own.

I remember when I was a pastor of Immanuel Baptist Church in Newton, Massachusetts. I had just been released from the Navy after five years of active duty as a Naval Chaplain. The church had a parsonage where our family lived while at that church. Our boys used to play outside in the back yard on Sundays. Across the street lived, as far as I knew, an unsaved person. She called me and asked me if I knew that my boys were outside on the swing set on a Sunday. After that those boys stayed in the house. They kept their clothes clean for a testimony to the neighbors. Not that there is anything wrong with playing on the swing set on Sunday, but my position after that was to tell my four sons and one daughter:

"*You must stay clean so that you can go to the young peoples' meeting tonight. In this way, you do not have to take another bath or shower before the evening services.*"

They were to stay in the house and do what they could do.

Some lost people have higher standards than some Christians. In fact some of their lives are more moral than some professing Christians. It is a sad thing and a terrible disgrace. My father-in-law (my wife's father) used to say when you take your car to be worked on, be careful if they are Christians. He was a man who was a saved man, a godly man, a wonderful Baptist. He was a deacon in many churches. Dad Sanborn was a prince of a fellow, but he had found in his experience (he died at the age of eighty-four) that he could not completely trust Christians. Not that all of them are that way, but he had enough of experience with this one and that one that he came to this conclusion. He started to go to the unsaved. At least when you complained they may do something about it. If you complain about the Christians they get mad and say

"Aren't you a Christian?"

One of the churches in this area had their carpet laid poorly. In fact, I know a carpet layer who works in a carpet store and he told me one day that he would rather lay a carpet in a home of an unsaved person than for Christians. The reason is that some of the Christians who he has laid carpets for have complaints about little things. That was his testimony. We have to be careful that we are not this way. Christians should strive to have a good testimony!

Romans 2:28

"For he is not a Jew, which is one outwardly; neither *is that* **circumcision, which is outward in the flesh."** Paul makes an interesting comparison here. It is the *"outward"* versus the *"inward."* God prefers the *"inward."* We need the *"outward"* as well, but not the *"outward"* only. Just as God looks at the Jews from an *"inward"* perspective, He looks at us.

Remember when Israel was going to have a king. Saul was head and shoulders above all the others in Israel (1 Samuel 9:2). A tall giant of a man. The Lord did not want him because he was a fleshly, carnal man. Then when another king was to be picked, Samuel went into Jesse's household and looked at the sons that were in the house at the time (1 Samuel 16:10). Samuel asked Jesse if he had any other sons. Jesse said that he had one son, but he was out tending the sheep. Samuel asked for this son, David, to be brought in. This, of course, was God's choice to be king of Israel. Samuel explained the choice. He said:

- **1 Samuel 16:7**
  But the LORD said unto Samuel, Look not on his countenance, or on the height of his stature; because I have refused him: for *the LORD seeth* not as man seeth; **for man looketh on the outward appearance, but the LORD looketh on the heart**

God looked on the heart of all the sons of Jesse. The other sons were warriors and fighters, but none was the one for God. God looks on our hearts as well.

- **Proverbs 3:1**
  My son, forget not my law; but **let thine heart keep my commandments:**

- **Proverbs 4:23**
  Keep thy heart with all diligence; for out of it are the issues of life.

- **Proverbs 23:26**
  My son, give me thine heart, and let thine eyes observe my ways.

God wants our hearts.

There is a phrase in the Psalms which occurs frequently, *"an instrument of ten strings"* (Psalms 33:2; 92:3; 144:9). This verse refers to the Old Testament harp or the lyre. When I was first saved there was a book written, back in 1944. This book was called, *An Instrument of Ten Strings*, by William Pettingill who was one of the editors of the Old Scofield Reference Bible. He took that phrase and gave illustrations of how we can praise the Lord on our ten strings.

Our Ten-String Instruments

We do not have a harp, but we do have two eyes, two ears, two hands, two feet, one mouth, and one heart. If you count those up you have ten strings with which you can praise and serve the Lord. We should praise the Lord with all that we have and with all that we are if we are saved, and have the Lord Jesus Christ living within us. That is what we need to do.

Romans 2:29

"But he *is* a Jew, which is one inwardly; and circumcision *is that* of the heart, in the spirit, *and* not in the letter; whose praise *is* not of men, but of God." God pierces down among all of our externals and He asks us what we have *"inwardly."* This verse shows the Lord's emphasis on the *"heart"* and *"spirit"* more than merely on that which is on the outside of us.

It is good to be dressed up on the outside also. There is nothing wrong with taking care of the external, but God looks right inside. He says that *"circumcision"* is both external as well as internal. It works both ways.

Separation of the Heart

Those who have an *"inward"* aspect of separation to the Lord, or *"circumcision"* which is of the *"heart"* and *"spirit'* rather than the *"letter,"* do not have *"praise"* from *"men"* but from *"God."* We have people all the time wanting to be praised by men. They will placate men for *"praise."* What about God's *"praise"*?

- **2 Timothy 2:15**
  Study to **shew thyself approved unto God**, a workman that needeth not to be ashamed, rightly dividing the of truth.

That is the praise of the Lord.

- **John 12:42-43**
  Nevertheless among the chief rulers also many believed on him; but because of the Pharisees they did not confess him, lest they should be put out of the synagogue: **For they loved the praise of men more than the praise of God.**

It is a very frightening thing *"to love the praise of men rather than the praise of God."* That does not mean that we need to be mean and ugly so that people will not like us. That is not what the Scriptures are talking about.

A person must choose between living a godly, spiritual, straight-forward life of following the Scriptures, or between living a debauched life, living to please the worldly crowd. We must choose living a godly life. We must never choose the *"praise of men"* at the expense of the *"praise of God."*

In our Bible reading the other day, the Lord Jesus Christ talked about the Old Testament false prophets.

- **Luke 6:26**
  Woe unto you, **when all men shall speak well of you! for so did their fathers to the false prophets.**

That is interesting. I hope that some people *"speak well of you."* I hope that some people *"speak well"* of me. I know for sure that there are many who do not *"speak well"* of me because I stand for the King James Bible and the Hebrew, Aramaic, and Greek Words that underlie it, among other things.

Does God "Speak Well" of Us?

I am a fundamentalist Christian. I am a separatist Christian. I am a Baptist Christian. Many people do not agree with these positions. We should be sure that we stand where the Lord wants us to stand, and that He *"speaks well"* of us.

There is going to be a judgment day for every born-again Christian at the Judgment Seat of Christ (2 Corinthians 5:10). The Lord Jesus Christ is going to pierce right into the hidden things of our heart. Everything is going to be open before Him. He is not going to be fooled like you can fool people. You can fool a lot of people. The Lord Jesus Christ, the Righteous Judge (2 Timothy 4:8), is not going to fooled. As the gospel song goes, we must live to please our Lord and Saviour:

"I'll live for today, nor anxious be, Jesus, my Lord, I soon shall see,
Glad day, glad day! Is it the crowning day?"

𝕽𝖔𝖒𝖆𝖓𝖘 𝕮𝖍𝖆𝖕𝖙𝖊𝖗 𝕿𝖍𝖗𝖊𝖊

Romans 3:1

"What advantage then hath the Jew? or what profit *is there* of circumcision?" Paul inquires as to the *"advantage"* and *"profit"* that the *"Jew"* or *"circumcision"* might have. The Greek word for *"advantage"* is PERISSOS. It has various meanings, such as:

"exceeding some number or measure or rank or need; over and above, more than is necessary, superadded; exceeding abundantly, supremely; something further, more, much more than all, more plainly; superior, extraordinary, surpassing, uncommon; pre-eminence, superiority, advantage, more eminent, more remarkable, more excellent."

Jude warns of false teachers who carry on their lives for the sake of *"advantage"* to them.

- **Jude 16**
  These are murmurers, complainers, walking after their own lusts; and their mouth speaketh great swelling *words*, having men's persons in admiration **because of advantage**.

The *"advantage"* in Romans 3:1 speaks of the blessings of God's choosing the Jews as His earthly people.

- **Genesis 22:18**
  And **in thy Seed shall all the nations of the earth be blessed**; because thou hast obeyed my voice.

The Jews were chosen by God. The *"Seed"* here speaks of the Lord Jesus Christ. He came through the line of Abraham, Isaac, and Jacob.

- **Galatians 3:16**
  Now to Abraham and his Seed were **the promises** made. He saith not, **And to seeds, as of many; but as of one, And to thy Seed, which is Christ**.

The Jews have a promise. Most of us in our church are of Gentile rather than

Jewish background and stock. It was through the Jews that our Lord Jesus Christ came.

There are many people in this world who hate them. We should not hate the Jews. God promises to "*bless them that bless*" Abraham's Seed (Genesis 12:3). We should love the Jews and try to win them to Christ. Paul was a Jew before he became a Christian.

There are presently only three classes of people in this world.

- **I Corinthians 10:32**
  Give none offence, neither to the **Jews**, nor to the **Gentiles**, nor to the **church of God**:

According to this verse, everyone in the world is either (1) a Jew, (2) a Gentile, or (3) a member of the "*Church of God*," that is a Christian. When you become a Christian, God no longer considers you either a Jew or a Gentile, regardless of your racial stock. You are a Christian.

- **Romans 1:3**
  Concerning his Son **Jesus Christ our Lord, which was made of the seed of David according to the flesh**;

These Jews had much "*profit*." They had "*advantage*" because the Lord blessed them in the past, and he is going to prosper them greatly in the future one day when they turn to Christ. "*For I say unto you, Ye shall not see me henceforth, till ye shall say, Blessed is he that cometh in the name of the Lord.*" (Matthew 23:39

Romans 3:2

"Much every way: chiefly, because that unto them were committed the oracles of God." In this verse, Paul specifies a clear "*advantage*" and "*profit*" for the Jew. Unto them were "*committed the oracles of God.*" The Greek word for "oracles" is LOGION. It means: "*a brief utterance, a divine oracle (doubtless because oracles were generally brief); in the NT, the words or utterances of God; of the contents of the Mosaic law.*"

The Jews Guarded God's Words

The Jews were given by God a special privilege and charge to care for and keep accurately the very Words of God, both Old Testament Hebrew and Aramaic Words and New Testament Greek Words.

Some people believe that one of the New Testament writers was a Gentile. I believe all of the writers of Bible books were Jews. I think there is evidence to this. Brother Mike McCubbins, an ex-Jew who became a Christian, has written a book where he points out that even the one writer that was thought to be a Gentile was, in reality, a Jew. I believe he made a convincing case for this position.

Let us take a look at how the Jews fulfilled this Biblical promise by their strict rules in copying the Hebrew Old Testament. The Jews took meticulous care of the Old Testament Hebrew text. Here are some of the methods they used as found in my book, *Defending the King James Bible*, pages 24-26:

This information was taken from *General Biblical Introduction* by H. S. Miller written in 1960, pages 184-185. Miller lists eight rules the Jews used in the copying of the Synagogue Rolls of the Old Testament Scriptures. These rules are mentioned in the Talmud.

Eight Copying Rules by the Jews

"1.   The parchment must be made from the skin of clean animals; must be prepared by a Jew only, and the skins must be fastened together by strings taken from clean animals.

2.   Each column must have no less than 48 nor more than 60 lines. The entire copy must be first lined.

3.   The ink must be of no other color than black, and it must be prepared according to a special recipe.

4.   No word nor letter could be written from memory; the scribe must have an authentic copy before him, and he must read and pronounce aloud each word before writing it.

5.   He must reverently wipe his pen each time before writing the word for "God" [which is *Elohim*] *and he must wash his whole body before writing the name "Jehovah"* [which is translated "LORD" in our KING JAMES BIBLE] *lest the Holy Name be contaminated.*

6.   Strict rules were given concerning forms of the letters, spaces between letters, words, and sections, the use of the pen, the color of the parchment, etc.

7.   The revision of a roll must be made within 30 days after the work was finished; otherwise it was worthless. One mistake on a sheet condemned the sheet; if three mistakes were found on any page, the entire manuscript was condemned.

8.   Every word and every letter was counted, [Notice that the words and letters were counted. Think of counting all the letters on every page of the Hebrew Old Testament. Talk about exactness. Yet that was the method God used to preserve the Old Testament.] *and if a letter were omitted, an extra letter inserted, or if one letter touched another, the manuscript was condemned and destroyed at once."* *[Miller, op. cit., pp. 184-185]* [My comments in brackets.]"

The Greek word for "*committed*" is PISTEUO. It has various meanings, including "*to believe.*" It also means: "*to entrust a thing to one, i.e. his fidelity; to be intrusted with a thing.*" The Words of God were "*entrusted*" to the Jews by God Himself. There are other uses of the word, "*commit*," though a different Greek term:

- **2 Timothy 2:2**
  And the things that thou hast heard of me among many witnesses, the same **commit thou to faithful men**, who shall be able to teach others also.

- **2 Timothy 1:12**
  For the which cause I also suffer these things: nevertheless I am not ashamed: for I know whom I have believed, and am persuaded that he is able to keep **that which I have committed unto him** against that day.

- **1 Timothy 1:11**
  According to the glorious gospel of the blessed God, **which was committed to my trust**.

- **2 Corinthians 5:19**
  To wit, that God was in Christ, reconciling the world unto himself, not imputing their trespasses unto them; and **hath committed unto us the word of reconciliation.**

God has "*committed*" to us and given to our care the gospel message and the "*Word of reconciliation*" by faith, so that people can come to Christ to be saved. The Greek word for "*reconciliation*" is KATALLAGE. It means:

"*exchange; of the business of money changers, exchanging equivalent values; adjustment of a difference, reconciliation, restoration to favour; in the NT of the restoration of the favour of God to sinners that repent and put their trust in the expiatory death of Christ.*"

The Jews had a great "*commission.*" We talk about the Lord Jesus Christ's Great Commission, "*And he said unto them, Go ye into all the world, and preach the gospel to every creature*" (Mark 16:15). The Jews had a "*commission*" given by the Lord also. They were "*committed*" to preserve, copy accurately, and **guard** the Words of God in the original languages in which God spoke them.

There are some so-called Fundamentalist people, and even institutions of higher learning, that do not believe that God has even PROMISED to preserve His original Words, much less fulfilled such a PROMISE. They say this in their tapes and books, and they teach it in their classrooms and chapels.

False Bible Preservation in Four Schools

The four major Fundamentalist institutions that teach falsely on the subject of Bible Preservation are:

(1) Bob Jones University, Greenville, SC;

(2) Detroit Baptist Theological Seminary, Detroit, MI;

(3) Central Baptist Theological Seminary, Minneapolis, MN;

(4) Calvary Baptist Theological Seminary, Lansdale, PA

I can illustrate this from a book published years ago by the Central Baptist Theological Seminary in the Minneapolis, Minnesota, area. Some chapters in that book are written by their Hebrew professor. I have answered his arguments on my radio broadcast and also in my book entitled *Central Baptist Seminary Refuted on Bible Versions*. It is **BFT #2926** for a gift of **$10.00 + $4.00 S&H**. This Hebrew teacher at Central Seminary wrote that there are errors in the Hebrew Words that underlie our King James Bible. He believes that none of these Hebrew Words can be trusted completely. He is teaching this to his students in a so-called Fundamentalist school. Can you believe it? Similar doubts have been expressed in the books, speeches, and writings of various teachers in the other three institutions named above. This is a serious situation in Fundamentalism today.

The Original Words Are Preserved

I believe that God entrusted to the Jews the Words of God. I believe that God has protected and preserved His Old Testament Hebrew, Aramaic, and Greek Words which underlie our King James Bible. I believe by the same token that He has preserved the Greek Words which underlie our King James Bible.

We have a battle in this vital area with four main groups: (1) the Roman Catholics; (2) the modernists, liberals, and apostate Protestants; (3) the neo-evangelicals; and (4) some leading Fundamentalists.

There was an article several years ago that appeared in the *Baptist Bible College Journal* which is connected with the General Association of Regular Baptist Churches (GARBC). The article was written by a teacher from Pillsbury Baptist College. This article questioned the New Testament Greek Text. They mentioned my name and some of the things that I have been writing in this area.

They mentioned the Dean Burgon Society where I am President. They mentioned Dean John William Burgon. They ripped to shreds the idea that God has preserved His Greek Words of the New Testament.

We are living in terrible days. We must have our eyes open, our ears open, and our hearts open to receive the truth. I have been a Baptist ever since I was saved. When Baptists start to depart from the Words of God and from the Words of Truth (as they have been departing), I am going to be against that brand of Baptists. We must stick with the truth!

Romans 3:3

"For what if some did not believe? shall their unbelief make the faith of God without effect?" The preceding verse spoke of the Jews who were guarding the Scriptures. Some of these, no doubt, were not saved. That is, they did not believe in God's promise of a coming Messiah, but they still were used of God to guard the Words of the Scriptures. *"Shall their unbelief make the Word of God without effect"*? The answer to this rhetorical question is *"No."* They still protected God's Words faithfully even though they were unsaved Jews that guarded the Scriptures. God superintended this entire process to fulfill His promise.

We who are saved Christians should be thankful for the Jewish guardians of God's Words, even though some of them were unbelievers. It did not make the Words of God and *"the faith of God"* without effect. We can see that we are dependent upon the Jews who were committed to guarding the *"oracles of God."* We are in the debt of the Old Testament Jews who guarded the Words of God.

Romans 3:4

"God forbid: yea, let God be true, but every man a liar; as it is written, That thou mightest be justified in thy sayings, and mightest overcome when thou art judged." The words, *"God forbid,"* have been criticized because the word, *"God,"* is not found in the Greek text. The Greek words are ME GENOITO. They literally mean:

"May it not . . . become, i.e. to come into existence, begin to be, receive being; to become, i.e. to come to pass, happen; of events, to arise, appear in history, come upon the stage."

Though *"God"* is not in the text, the expression *"God forbid"* was, in 1611, a very accurate expression of ME GENOITO and the readers understood it as we today understand it.

Let God Be True!

It is important that *"God be true, but every man a liar."* I think about that truth when I preach from God's Words and write things about the Scriptures. I know there are some people who do not like some of the things I speak about and write. When they object, I often quote this phrase, *"Let God be true, but every man a liar."* That word, *"liar,"* is not used too much in the Bible. It occurs only 13 times in the King James Bible. People don't like to be called *"liars."*

Here are a few verses about lying.

- **Psalm 116:11**
  I said in my haste, **All men *are* liars.**

The Psalmist concluded that all men and woman are *"liars"* without exception.

- **Proverbs 30:6**
  Add thou not unto his words, lest he reprove thee, **and thou be found a liar.**

That is what these new Bible versions and perversions are doing. They are adding to the Words of God, subtracting from the Words of God, and changing the Words of God. God says he is going to call those who do these things *"liars."*

- **John 8:44**
  Ye are of *your* father the devil, and the lusts of your father ye will do. He was a murderer from the beginning, and abode not in the truth, because there is no truth in him. When he speaketh a lie, he speaketh of his own: **for he is a liar, and the father of it.**

From this verse, we see that if a person *"lies,"* he or she *"abides not in the truth"* and is linked to the *"devil."* It would appear from this verse that all the lies of all the ancient times and present times, and future times are from Satan. He is the *"father"* of all of them.

- **1 John 1:10**
  If we say that we have not sinned, **we make him a liar**, and his word is not in us.

There is no sinless perfection in any person on earth. Even though we might be saved and with a new nature, we with our old nature do sin. But there is an antidote, *"If we confess our sins, he is faithful and just to forgive us our sins, and to cleanse us from all unrighteousness"* (1 John 1:9).

- **1 John 2:4**
  He that saith, I know him, and keepeth not his commandments, **is a liar**, and the truth is not in him.

Those are strong words. If you say you know Him and then go out and live like the Devil, you are a *"liar."* That is straight talk, is it not?

- **1 John 2:22**
  Who is a liar but he that denieth that Jesus is the Christ? He
  is Antichrist, that denieth the Father and the Son.

From this verse, we would have to say that every modernist, and every unbeliever, and every Christian Science person, and all followers of the cults are *"liars,"* because they deny that *"Jesus is the Christ,"* the Messiah of God, Who has come in the flesh by His incarnation.

- **Revelation 21:8**
  But the fearful, and unbelieving, and the abominable, and
  murderers, and whoremongers, and sorcerers, and idolaters,
  and all liars, shall have their part in the lake which burneth
  with fire and brimstone: which is the second death.

What is involved in *"all liars"* in this verse? Not that we have never lied in our life, but to have this term applied to you, you would be a continual, perpetual, and all-the-time *"liar."* That is their lifestyle, a falsification of truth. I would not want to be in their shoes.

- **Titus 1:2**
  In hope of eternal life, which God, **that cannot lie**, promised
  before the world began;

- **Hebrews 6:18**
  That by two immutable things, **in which *it was* impossible for
  God to lie**, we might have a strong consolation, who have fled
  for refuge to lay hold upon the hope set before us:

It is *"impossible for God to lie."* God is not a *"liar."* But *"every man"* is a *"liar."*

I want you to notice another term used in this verse, *"it is written."* The Greek word for this is GEGRAPTAI which is the perfect tense of GRAPHO. The perfect indicates an action that was begun in the past, has been carried into the present, and on into the future. This is Bible preservation of the Words of Hebrew, Aramaic, and Greek. GRAPHO means:

> *"to write, with reference to the form of the letters; to delineate (or form) letters on a tablet, parchment, paper, or other material; to write, with reference to the contents of the writing; to express in written characters; to commit to writing (things not to be forgotten), write down, record"*

"It Is Written"=Bible Preservation

As I said before, the perfect tense shows us that God's Words have been preserved through the centuries. The Lord Jesus Christ used this *"it is written"* perfect tense twenty-six times. Altogether in the New Testament there are sixty-three instances of this expression. Every time this is used, it means that the Words of God were written in the past, they stand written today, and they will be continuously preserved by God in the future. *"It is written,"* is a wonderful proof for the Bible's preservation of its Hebrew, Aramaic, and Greek Words.

- Job 40:8
  Wilt thou also disannul my judgment? wilt thou condemn me, that thou mayest be righteous?

God is always *"justified in His sayings"* regardless of how many seek to *"judge"* Him. People *"judge"* the Lord all the time. They think that He is not doing things right, but He will overcome all such erroneous *"judgment"* against Him. He is always right.

Our Just Lord

The Lord is always just!

Romans 3:5

"But if our unrighteousness commend the righteousness of God, what shall we say? *Is* God unrighteous who taketh vengeance? (I speak as a man)"

The first part of this verse is somewhat difficult to understand at first glance when Paul wrote, *"if our unrighteousness commend the righteousness of God."* In other words, we who are *"unrighteous"* can be saved and made *"righteous"* by God's grace. God can save us through genuine faith in His Son, and *"commend"* us so that we can become partakers of the very *"righteousness of God."* God can forgive and pardon our *"unrighteousness."*

Does this pardoning of sinners because of their genuine faith and trust in the Lord Jesus Christ make God *"unrighteous"*? How can a *"righteous"* God pardon those of us who are *"unrighteous?"* That is the issue. God is not "*unrighteous.*" God the Father's judgment of our sins, yours and mine, as well as the sins of the entire world, was meted out on the cross of Calvary upon His only begotten and beloved Son, the Lamb of God Who "*taketh away the sin of the world*" (John 1:29b). It is said of the Lord Jesus Christ that "*His own self bare our sins in His own body on the tree*" (1 Peter 2:24). That righteousness, that judgment of sins, made God able to pardon sinners by simple, yet genuine, faith in the Lord Jesus Christ.

The question is asked by Paul, "*is God unrighteous who taketh vengeance?*" No, He is not "*unrighteous.*" People in a foreign country had a mud slide some time ago. A volcano collapsed and lava and earth came down from that mountain. One thousand homes were destroyed. They did not know how many were dead. Think of the horrible fires in California recently. Some people died. Tens of thousands of acres of trees were destroyed. Two or three thousand homes went up in smoke. Some people blame God for that. They think God is "*unrighteous.*" They shake their fist at God every time death comes. Their spouse is taken. Their child is taken. They are sick or attacked by disease. They shake their fist in the face of God. They believe God is "*unrighteous*" in these things. Is God "*unrighteous*"? No. He is not "*unrighteous.*" He is forever "*righteous*" in all of His actions, as well as in the things He might permit to happen.

- **Genesis 18:25**
  That be far from thee to do after this manner, to slay the righteous with the wicked: and that the righteous should be as the wicked, that be far from thee: **Shall not the Judge of all the earth do right?**

God Always Does Right

There is never any of us at any time who will ever be able to shake our fist in the face of God and say that God had done wrong. We're the ones who have done wrong. He has never done anything wrong. He has done "*right*" and He will always "*do right.*"

- **Romans 9:14**
  What shall we say then? *Is there* unrighteousness with God? God forbid.

- **Hebrews 6:10**
  For **God *is* not unrighteous** to forget your work and labour of love, which ye have shewed toward his name, in that ye have ministered to the saints, and do minister.
- **1 John 1:9**
  If we confess our sins, **he is faithful and just** to forgive us *our* sins, and to cleanse us from all unrighteousness.

God is the Cleanser of all *"unrighteousness"* for the born-again Christians if they follow this verse in all that it means.

As far as *"vengeance"* is concerned, God is a Judge, and as such He must take *"vengeance"* on sin. The Greek word used here for *"vengeance"* is ORGE. It means:

*"anger, the natural disposition, temper, character; movement or agitation of the soul, impulse, desire, any violent emotion, but esp. anger; anger, wrath, indignation; **anger exhibited in punishment, hence used for punishment itself;** of punishments inflicted by magistrates."*

The flood of Noah is certainly an indication of God's "vengeance" on a world of unrepentant sinners. The judgment of Sodom and Gomorrah is certainly another illustration of this. Hell itself, the Lake of Fire, is a further example of how a righteous God must exercise His just and righteous *"vengeance"* on those who have refused to receive His pardon by faith in His Son.

- **Deuteronomy 32:35**
  To me *belongeth* vengeance, and recompence; their foot shall slide in *due* time: for the day of their calamity *is* at hand, and the things that shall come upon them make haste.

What Is God's "Vengeance"?

"Vengeance" is a *"recompense"* for evil.

- **Deuteronomy 32:41**
  If I whet my glittering sword, and mine hand take hold on judgment; **I will render vengeance to mine enemies,** and will reward them that hate me.
- **Deuteronomy 32:43**
  Rejoice, O ye nations, *with* his people: for he will avenge the blood of his servants, **and will render vengeance to his adversaries**, and will be merciful unto his land, *and* to his people.

God is One Who does takes "*vengeance*" for the sake of His holy and righteous justice.

God's Attribute of Holiness

- **Nahum 1:2**

  God *is* jealous, and the LORD revengeth; the LORD revengeth, and *is* furious; the LORD will take vengeance on his adversaries, and he reserveth *wrath* for his enemies.

  God is a God of love, that is true, but that is not the only attribute of God. He has other attributes, including judgment and justice, righteousness, and holiness. This is what makes it necessary for Him to render judgment to those who deserve it.

- **Romans 12:19**

  Dearly beloved, avenge not yourselves, but *rather* give place unto wrath: for it is written, **Vengeance *is* mine; I will repay, saith the Lord.**

- **2 Thessalonians 1:7-8**

  And to you who are troubled rest with us, when the Lord Jesus shall be revealed from Heaven with his mighty angels, **In flaming fire taking vengeance on them that know not God,** and that obey not the gospel of our Lord Jesus Christ:

  Just think of it. This verse is speaking of the Lord Jesus Christ Himself when He comes back to earth in glory. This is the second phase of His second coming after the seven-year Tribulation period. His feet will touch down upon this earth and split the Mount of Olives north and south. All changes in His millennial reign will take place. It is our Saviour who is going to take vengeance "*in flaming fire.*" This is the same Lord Jesus Christ who bids sinners come to Him with the words: "*Come unto me, all ye that labour and are heavy laden, and I will give you rest*" (Matthew 11:28). At the same time He is just, and He must judge wickedness.

- **Hebrews 10:30**

  For we know him that hath said, **Vengeance *belongeth* unto me, I will recompense,** saith the Lord. And again, The Lord shall judge his people.

The Mark of the Beast

The people in the seven-year Tribulation period who are loyal to the anti-Christ will take *"the mark of the beast"* (Revelation 16:2). It will be a *"mark in their right hand, or in their foreheads"* (Revelation 13:16).

One of the things Mrs. Waite and I heard about in one of the recent Southwest Radio Conferences concerned this *"mark."* One of the speakers believed it would be a chip. He explained what he meant. He said in one state all cats must have chips underneath their skin to tell where they are at all times. In one state it is a rule for dogs. In another state the rule applies to horses. Soon it might apply to human beings. If we are saved, we will be taken up to Heaven in the rapture of our Saviour before any part of Daniel's Seventieth Week, or the tribulation comes to pass. We will not witness the *"mark of the beast."* That speaker showed us the chip itself. He got it from the dog pound somewhere. He also showed us an injector gun to inject this chip under the skin. He told us we could examine it after his talk. Anywhere a person might try to hide from the anti-Christ will be found. It is amazing the computer skills that men have now developed. There will not be a place on earth that a person will be able to hide safely because of the chip in his hand or forehead.

● **Revelation 6:16**
   And said to the mountains and rocks, **Fall on us, and hide us** from the face of him that sitteth on the throne, and from the wrath of the Lamb:

This is not the Antichrist here, but no one can hide from the Lord. He knows everything.

Romans 3:6

"God forbid: for then how shall God judge the world?"

God is *"not unrighteous who taketh vengeance."* If that were the case, how could He judge the world? He is the Judge of all the world and He will *"do right."*

Seven Major Judgments

I can think of at least seven major events concerning God's judgments in Scripture.

1. The judgment of death. I start with the physical and spiritual death of Adams race. *"Wherefore, as by one man sin entered into the world, and death by sin; and so death passed upon all men, for that all have sinned"* (Romans 5:12). Because Adam and Eve sinned in the garden of Eden, physical and spiritual death passed to us all.

2. The flood of Noah. The wickedness was so great on all the earth He had to slaughter all of them except eight.

3. The destruction of Sodom and Gomorrah. The sins of these cities were so widespread that there could not be found even ten righteous people. Rather than perpetuate that evil of sodomy and other sins, God destroyed these cities and the people who lived and sinned there. I wonder when God will judge the United States of America for its tolerance to sodomy.

4. The ten plagues of Egypt. There was such evil that God poured out these plagues against Egypt and her false gods.

5. The destruction of the Canaanites in the land of Palestine. Joshua and the Israelites were to destroy them all, but they failed to do this.

6. The judgments in the book of Revelation. This includes the seven seal judgments, the seven trumpet judgments, the seven vial judgments and all the rest. These are judgments from the Lord God of Heaven and earth.

7. The judgment of the Lake of Fire. At the great White Throne Judgment (Revelation 20:11), God will judge the lost world in righteousness and then send the lost to Hell where the beast and the false prophet and the Devil will also be cast (Revelation 19:30). GOD IS A GOD OF RIGHTEOUS JUDGMENT!

Romans 3:7

"For if the truth of God hath more abounded through my lie unto his glory; why yet am I also judged as a sinner?" This verse is also somewhat difficult to understand at first. Paul was considered by the people in Rome and by others to be a *"liar"* when he told them about *"the gospel of Christ"* (Romans 1:16). He preached *"the Truth of God"* which *"abounded"* and increased unto God's *"glory."* These people thought Paul was a liar because he said that unrighteous people could be made righteous by faith in the Person and Work of the Lord Jesus Christ.

God's truth of justification by faith through Paul's alleged *"lie"* *"abounded"* to God's *"glory."* God had prospered and saved many sinners there in Rome. If this were true, then why was Paul *"judged as a sinner?"* God has vindicated Paul's message of *"the truth of God"* and He should not be considered to be a *"liar"* in any way.

Romans 3:8

"And not *rather*, (as we be slanderously reported, and as some affirm that we say,) Let us do evil, that good may come? whose damnation is just." Here again Paul was misjudged and was *"slanderously reported"* of. Have you ever been *"slandered"*? It is interesting. *"Slander"* is to be accused of something that you have not done. Slander is verbal. A libel is in writing. Some of us have been the recipients of both verbal and written falsehoods. Paul never said, nor would he ever say: *"Let us do evil, that good may come."* It is true that evil sinners can be justified by genuine faith in the Lord Jesus Christ. God's grace comes into the lives of sinners and can save them, but that does not mean that we should do evil so that God's grace can come into us again, or do evil so that God will make it good. That is foolish.

Slander Versus Libel

Let me read you a definition of *"slander."* It has been defined briefly as *"the utterance in the presence of another person of a false statement or statements damaging to a third person's character or reputation."* This is distinguished from libel, which is written. So, in the presence of someone else, speaking a false statement that damages someone else's character or reputation would be *"slander."*

Paul was certainly "*damaged.*" The Lord Jesus Christ was "*damaged*" as well. He had all kinds of things heaped up against Him. People said that He was "*born of fornication*" (John 8:41) and many other false charges. People said that He was not a proper prophet (Matthew 14:5), but He just took it anyway, and went on about His business. This is what we have to do as well.

Romans 3:9

"What then? are we better *than they*? No, in no wise: for we have before proved both Jews and Gentiles, that they are all under sin" Paul included himself, a former Jew, in the universal declaration by God that "*both Jews and Gentiles*" are "*all under sin.*" We today are not better than these people Paul wrote about, whether they are Jews or Gentiles in Rome, or wherever they might be. They are "*all under sin.*" There is not a single person in the world who ever lived (except the Lord Jesus Christ) who has escaped God's assessment in this area.

In Romans Chapter One, all the heathen, with their idols, their four-footed beasts, and creeping things have all been judged by God. The hypocrites, the moralists, and the faithless Jews were judged in Chapter Two. The Jews said "*Do not commit adultery,*" yet they themselves committed adultery. They said "*Do not steal,*" yet they stole.

When Paul wrote that he had "*before proved*" that both "*Jews and Gentiles*" were "*all under sin,*" he used the Greek word, PROAITIAOMAI. It means: "*to bring a charge against previously (i.e. in what has previously been said).*" It establishes or demonstrates something to be a fact. There is not a single one that has escaped God's judgment on sin.

This is an important thing, because if any of us can say that we are free from sin, there would not have been the need for the Lord Jesus Christ to come into the world to die for sinners. The Lord Jesus Christ would not have had to come to this earth, if we could save ourselves. If we could save ourselves and could make ourselves righteous before God, we would not have needed a Redeemer.

We All Need a Saviour

The Lord Jesus Christ did come because we are sinners, and because we needed a Saviour and Redeemer.

Romans 3:10

"As it is written, There is none righteous, no, not one:"

Notice again, Paul used the phrase, *"as it is written."* The Greek word is GEGRAPTAI. It is the perfect tense. The meaning is that these Words were written down in the past (possibly in Psalm 14:3; or 53:1-3) in the Old Testament. These Words have been preserved to Paul's day, and they will be preserved into the future up to our own day.

The Four Protestant "Nones"

Here is the first in a series of what we humorously call, the four Protestant *"nones."* This is the first one in verse 10.

1. There is none righteous (verse 10).

2. There is none that understandeth (verse 11).

3. There is none that seeketh after God (verse 11).

4. There is none that doeth good (verse 12).

So if you want to say something to your Catholic friends tell them that we have some **Protestant "nones."** We are sinners right from our conception.

- **Psalm 51:5**
  Behold, **I was shapen in iniquity; and in sin did my mother conceive me.**

This does not mean that conception is *"sin,"* but that right from the conception of the baby, the sin nature is there.

- **Psalm 58:3**
  The wicked are **estranged from the womb: they go astray as soon as they be born, speaking lies**.

Right from the start, the wicked *"from the womb . . . go astray"* as soon as they are born, *"speaking lies."* The Pharisees thought they were pretty good. They thought they had all kinds of things that were right. The Lord Jesus Christ said of their *"righteousness"*: *"For I say unto you, That except your righteousness shall exceed the righteousness of the scribes and Pharisees, ye shall in no case enter into the kingdom of Heaven"* (Matthew 5:20).

What does God say? *"There is none righteous, no, not one:"*

- **Ecclesiastes 7:20**
  For *there is* not a just man upon earth, that doeth good, and sinneth not.

Sinners All

We are all sinners.

- Genesis 6:5
And GOD saw that the **wickedness of man** *was* **great** in the earth, and *that* every imagination of the thoughts of his heart *was* only evil continually.
- Jeremiah 17:9
The heart *is* **deceitful** above all *things*, **and desperately wicked**: who can know it?
- Romans 7:18
For I know that in me (that is, in my flesh,) **dwelleth no good thing**: for to will is present with me; but *how* to perform that which is good I find not.
- Romans 3:23
For **all have sinned**, and come short of the glory of God;

Romans 3:11

"There is none that understandeth, there is none that seeketh after God." There is a beautiful gospel song called, *"God Understands."* Humans do not understand many things in life, but God the Father, Who is omniscience, understands us in all of our thoughts and ways. The Lord Jesus Christ, God the Son, also understands us. That is why He can be a faithful and merciful High Priest to intercede for us because He was not a High Priest Who *"could not be touched with the feeling of our infirmities"* (Hebrews 4:15). He knew our temptations.

Though God understands, but, as far as men and women *"there is none that understandeth."* That is the second Protestant *"none"--"none that understandeth."* Human beings do not understand the Lord. They do not understand what salvation is. They do not understand anything about Heaven and Hell. In fact they do not even understand anything about the age of the earth.

We listened yesterday to the Southwest Radio Church Ministries broadcast. There were several speakers who spoke on prophecy. They were against evolution and in favor of creationism. There are many proofs, from physical evidence, of a young earth. The earth is perhaps 6,000 years old, which puts it right in the time frame of the book of Genesis. The flood was maybe 5,000 years ago. These men who put the age of the earth at millions and billions of years ago do not understand the meaning of the evidence. They do not want to believe that there is anything such as a God. All the various evidences, such as the fossils, prove that our earth is a young earth, and not an earth that is billions or even millions of years-old. These men who talked yesterday were scientists and gave many proofs for the young earth.

The third Protestant *"none"* is also in this verse; *"there is none that seeketh after God."* God has sought us. We are not the ones who first have sought Him. God made the first move toward seeking us.

- **John 3:16**
  For **God so loved the world, that he gave his only begotten Son,** that whosoever believeth in him should not perish, but have everlasting life.

- **Luke 19:10**
  For **the Son of man is come to seek and to save** that which was lost.

Some modernist theologians teach that there is so much good in the worst of us, and so much bad in the best of us. They say that everyone has light within us, a little spark of *"the Divine."* That is foolishness!

On the contrary, the Bible states clearly that *"There is none that understandeth, there is none that seeketh after God."* People think that they can gain salvation by themselves. No they cannot! There is no such thing as *"bootstrap religion,"* that is, picking yourself up by your own bootstraps. People say that they are going to take themselves to Heaven. Try it sometime. You will not succeed. All the ones who have ever died on this earth have found only to their dismay that they did not get the proper way to do it. They were depending on their works. They wanted to do, do, and do. God says it is *"done."* It is finished. By faith in the finished work of Christ we can have everlasting life.

Romans 3:12

"They are all gone out of the way, they are together become unprofitable; there is none that doeth good, no, not one." Proverbs speaks of various *"ways."*

- **Proverbs 16:25**
  There is a way that seemeth right unto a man, but the end thereof *are* **the ways of death**.

The Lord Jesus is the right *"Way."*

- **John 14:6**
  Jesus saith unto him, **I am the way**, the truth, and the life: no man cometh unto the Father, but by me.

Everyone in the world has *"gone out of the way."* There is not a single one who has not. They have left God's perfect way to walk. The Lord Jesus Christ the

Way is the One all sinners must go to and receive as Saviour and Lord.

* **Isaiah 53:5-7**

  But he *was* wounded for our transgressions, *he was* bruised for our iniquities: the chastisement of our peace *was* upon him; and with his stripes we are healed. **All we like sheep have gone astray**; we have turned every one to his own way; and the LORD hath laid on him the iniquity of us all. He was oppressed, and he was afflicted, yet he opened not his mouth: he is brought as a lamb to the slaughter, and as a sheep before her shearers is dumb, so he openeth not his mouth.

Everyone has *"gone out of the way"* according to this verse.

* **Psalm 14:1**

  To the chief Musician, *A Psalm* of David. The fool hath said in his heart, *There is* no God. **They are corrupt, they have done abominable works,** *there is* none that doeth good.

That is what I like about our King James Bible. The Old Testament corroborates and agrees with the New Testament. In many of the new versions, the Old Testament wording does not agree with the New Testament quotation of the verse. You have a completely different wording. In the King James Bible, however, the Old and New Testaments dovetail together.

* **Psalm 14:3**

  They are all gone aside, they are *all* together become filthy: ***there is* none that doeth good, no, not one.**

This is almost a direct quotation in Romans 3:12.

* **Psalm 53:3**

  Every one of them is gone back: they are altogether become filthy; ***there is* none that doeth good, no, not one.**

Paul knew his Bible did he not?

Read Eighty-Five Verses per Day

I hope that we know our Bibles well and read our Bibles daily. One of the things in our *Defined King James Bible* which we have built into it is the eighty-five verses-a-day Bible-reading section. We have the schedule in the front, but we also have a little diamond in the verse that marks the end of each eighty-five-verse daily reading section. I hope in this present new year everyone of us will read God's Words from Genesis through Revelation at least once. If you read eighty-five verses a day, you will be able to read your Bible through one time in a year. If you don't want to stop at eighty-five verses-a-day, you can read more.

As far as the phrase, "*they are all gone out of the way,*" there was a popular singer who died recently who used to sing about "*My Way.*" That was one of his hit-songs. *Burger King* tells us, in their ads, to "*Have it your way.*" I remember that *Roy Rogers* used to have a "*fixing bar*" where you could fix your meal "*your way.*" That is the way with people. They have all "*gone out of the way*" rather than going in God's way. They want their own "*way.*"

Remember what the Lord Jesus Christ said,

- **Matthew 7:13-14**
  Enter ye in at the strait gate: for wide is the gate, and broad is the way, that leadeth to destruction, and many there be which go in thereat: Because strait is the gate, and **narrow is the way**, which leadeth unto life, and few there be that find it.

The Only "Way" to Heaven

The Lord Jesus Christ is the "*Way*" and if you have trusted in Him you have found God's "*Way*" to Heaven. Let us not go "*out of the way*" but stay on God's perfect pathway as given us in the Bible.

That is one thing that Christians fail with so often. They have left the "*Way.*" They know the path. They know the "*Truth.*" They are informed, intelligent, Bible-led Christians, but they take a notion to go "*out of the way.*" Just like a horse who is frightened and goes off the path and into a ditch. We must guard ourselves in order to stay on that "*Way.*" When people are "*out of the way,*" they also "*become unprofitable.*"

Romans 3:13

"Their throat *is* an open sepulchre; with their tongues they have used deceit; the poison of asps *is* under their lips:" This verse begins the Great Physician's detailed examination of every part of sinful people. The first thing the Lord looks at is the *"throat."* The *"tongues"* and the *"lips"* are also mentioned in this verse. In verse 14, the *"mouth"* is examined. In verse 15, the *"feet"* are mentioned. The Lord compares the wickedness of the *"throat"* to an *"open sepulchre."* The *"sepulchre"* is a tomb where dead people are buried. We bury people normally in caskets. When a person dies, usually the undertaker takes the blood out of the body and replaces it with embalming fluid in the veins. This keeps the smell of death to a minimum so that people can visit the funeral parlor to pay their last respects. When you go to a funeral parlor, you do not smell any bad odor from the dead body because the body has been treated.

Our Mouths--Open Graves

The Lord's inspection shows that our *"mouths"* are filled with an untreated corpse that have been placed in an *"open"* grave.

The smell of death is foul and unbearable. I have never been to a home where a person had just died, but I did talk to an undertaker who lives close by. He told us that he came upon a body recently that had been in a house for two or three days. He said that the smell and the stench was absolutely indescribable. He has been an undertaker for many years, but he has never had such a bad situation. Normally, he is called immediately to come and remove the body, but this was not done in that case. He said that the house will never be the same. You can never get that smell of death out of those walls, according to the undertaker. Pardon me for talking about death like this, but God talks about it when He says that the *"throat"* of sinners is like an *"open sepulchre."* Every person in the world, before they repent of their sins and come to genuine faith in the Lord Jesus Christ, has one of those *"mouths"* like *"open tombs"* which are wicked, evil, and smelly.

After looking at the *"throat,"* the Great Physician looks at both the *"tongues"* and the *"lips"* of the lost people.

- Job 27:4
  My **lips** shall not speak wickedness, nor my **tongue** utter deceit.

Watch Our Tongues!

We must be careful with our tongues.

- **Psalm 10:7**
  His **mouth** is full of cursing and deceit and fraud: under his **tongue** *is* mischief and vanity.
- **Psalm 36:3**
  The words of his **mouth** *are* iniquity and deceit: he hath left off to be wise, *and* to do good.

These are the ungodly people. If the Lord Jesus Christ has saved us, let us not be like these ungodly people.

- **Psalm 120:2**
  Deliver my soul, O LORD, from **lying lips**, *and* from a **deceitful tongue**.
- **Proverbs 27:6**
  Faithful *are* the wounds of a friend; but the **kisses** of an enemy *are* deceitful.
- **Isaiah 53:9**
  And he made his grave with the wicked, and with the rich in his death; because he had done no violence, neither *was any* deceit in his **mouth**.
- **Jeremiah 17:9**
  The **heart** *is* deceitful above all *things*, and desperately wicked: who can know it?
- **Micah 6:12**
  For the rich men thereof are full of violence, and the inhabitants thereof have spoken lies, and their **tongue** *is* deceitful in their mouth.

The unsaved, unregenerate individuals have problems in the areas of the "*throat,*" the "*tongue*" and the "*lips.*" Sad to say, some Christians have the same problems!

Romans 3:14

"Whose mouth *is* full of cursing and bitterness" This is just a short verse, but my mind goes back to the five years I was on active military duty as a Navy Chaplain. I was with the U. S. Marine Corps for three years and the U. S. Navy for two years. All too often, the unsaved men and even women of both branches of these services illustrated the truth of this verse. Their "*mouth*" was truly "*full of cursing and bitterness.*" They would sometimes stop their *"cursing"* when the Chaplain came around, but not always.

I also think of my nineteen years of teaching Language Arts (English) in the Philadelphia school district. I taught eighteen years in a Junior High School and one year in a Senior High School. There was much *"cursing"* and filth in the *"mouths"* of those unsaved students. I would not permit it in my classroom. I would say many times, *"Shut your filthy mouth."* I got called down to the Vice Principal one time. He said, *"Why are you using that word, 'filthy'"*? He was a Spanish-speaking man from one of the Spanish countries. I said, *"Sir, 'filthy' is a very good word."* I said *"It is good English."* Coming from a Spanish world, he probably thought it was a bad word. The Vice Principal said, *"You can't put your religion on these people."* I replied, *"I am not trying to put my religion on them, Sir. They are disrupting my class by talking."* Sometimes they would swear and curse God's Name. I would tell them to be quiet. The principal said that I couldn't stop them from swearing. I said that I could stop them from disrupting my class. When they swear, or when they *"curse,"* they are disrupting my class. It was within my rights to stop them for such disruption. I did not have to say that this was because of my faith. Underneath it all, that was part of it, but I wanted to stop the disruption in a proper manner.

Incidentally, this same Vice Principal, many years later contacted me on another matter. He has been born-again and saved by personal faith in the Lord Jesus Christ. He is now part of the teaching faculty at a theological seminary in Pennsylvania. Praise the Lord!

- **James 3:10**
  Out of the same mouth proceedeth blessing and cursing.
  My brethren, these things ought not so to be.

- **Psalm 10:7**
  His mouth is full of cursing and deceit and fraud: under his tongue *is* mischief and vanity.

The Evil Garment of Cursing

Our present verse was taken from Psalm 10:7. Some people put on *"cursing"* as a garment. They seem to wrap themselves up with filthy, cursing talk, and blasphemy against the Lord Jesus Christ and God the Father.

And then, these unsaved people have much *"bitterness"* as well.

- **Isaiah 38:17**
  Behold, for peace **I had great bitterness**: but thou hast in love
  to my soul *delivered it* from the pit of corruption: for thou hast
  cast all my sins behind thy back.

Before we were saved, all we had was *"bitterness."* What was there left?
We were bitter about almost everything. I hope that it is not true of us today.
I hope the Lord has sweetened us up a little. The Greek word for *"bitterness"*
is PIKRIA. Picric acid is bitter. It comes from this Greek word which means:
*"bitter gall; extreme wickedness; a bitter root, and so producing a bitter fruit;
metaphor; bitterness, bitter hatred."*

There is *"bitter"* chocolate and there is sweet chocolate. My wife likes the
"bitter" chocolate, and I like the sweet chocolate. Some people have an
expression on their face as if they have just bitten into a lemon. I realize that we
can put on a false face, and smile, and still be *"bitter."* May the Lord Jesus
Christ give His own children His sweetness.

- **Zechariah 12:10**
  And I will pour upon the house of David, and upon the
  inhabitants of Jerusalem, the spirit of grace and of
  supplications: and they shall look upon me whom they have
  pierced, and they shall mourn for him, as one mourneth for *his*
  only *son*, **and shall be in bitterness for him, as one that is
  in bitterness for *his* firstborn**.

The Lord is going to make Israel recognize His Son and come to Him in great
numbers one day.

- **Ephesians 4:31**
  Let all bitterness, and wrath, and anger, and clamour, and
  evil speaking, be put away from you, with all malice:

If we are born-again believers, we must let the Holy Spirit guide us, lead us, fill
us, and control us, so that the *"bitterness and wrath,"* and all the other things
that come from the flesh will be put away.

- **Hebrews 12:15**
  Looking diligently lest any man fail of the grace of God; **lest
  any root of bitterness springing up trouble *you***, and
  thereby many be defiled;

"Bitterness" is contagious. Beware of it. We must get rid of the *"root of
bitterness."* That can spoil many.

O Bitterness

O Bitterness!
Thou doest lie in wait, to do thy work in Christians
And with great activity spring to life
At sound of strife or strain,

Calling forth each carnal impulse,
Urging, luring, leading on
To conclude that life is vain.
Dark thou art, and cruel and so unloving.

Nor forgives, forgets--art blind, 'tho ever hears.
Troubles all who bow before thy scepter,
Giving freely days and nights of scalding tears;
Ne'er content thou art to trouble only one heart.

By Gertrude Grace Sanborn

Romans 3:15

"Their feet *are* swift to shed blood:" Here are the
"murderous" feet of the evil flesh. The *"feet"* in this verse, instead of being
peaceful and bringing the gospel message, are *"swift to shed blood."* This
means these unsaved people are murderers. I believe in capital punishment for
genuine first-degree murder. I believe it is Biblical. It is Biblical in the Old
Testament. It is Biblical in the New Testament. Take for example:

- **Numbers 35:16**
  And if he smite him with an instrument of iron, so that he die,
  he *is* a murderer: **the murderer shall surely be put to death.**

This is Old Testament law, I realize, but I will give some New Testament verses
on it as well.

- **Numbers 35:18**
  Or *if* he smite him with an hand weapon of wood, wherewith he
  may die, and he die, he *is* a murderer: **the murderer shall
  surely be put to death.**

- **Numbers 35:20**
  But **if he thrust him of hatred**, or hurl at him by laying of wait,
  that he die;

- Numbers 35:30
  Whoso killeth any person, **the murderer shall be put to death** by the mouth of witnesses: but one witness shall not testify against any person *to cause him* to die.

What about capital punishment in the age of grace? Romans 13 speaks about the "*rulers*" being all on your side if you do that which is good, but if you do that which is evil be careful.

- Romans 13:4
  For he is the minister of God to thee for good. But **if thou do that which is evil, be afraid; for he beareth not the sword in vain: for he is the minister of God, a revenger to *execute* wrath upon him that doeth evil.**

In the phrase, "*He beareth not the sword in vain,*" there is a reference to capital punishment taught in the New Testament. The Greek word for "sword" is MACHAIRA. It means: "*a large knife, used for killing animals and cutting up flesh; a small sword, as distinguished from a large sword; curved sword, for a cutting stroke; a straight sword, for thrusting.*" This "sword" was about eighteen inches in length. It was used by the Roman government to decapitate those who merited capital punishment.

Regarding capital punishment, consider the treatment of the Lord Jesus Christ. He was ordered by the Jewish leaders and the Roman authorities to receive the sentence of capital punishment by means of crucifixion. He did no sin. The sentence, from the standpoint of human fairness, was a miscarriage of justice. From God the Father's standpoint, however, it was the only way He could forgive repentant sinners who received His Son as their Saviour by personal faith. Though He was wrongfully crucified, He did not resist. In fact, He said to Simon Peter:

Capital Punishment Defended

- Matthew 26:52
  Then said Jesus unto him, Put up again thy sword into his place: for all <u>they that take the sword shall perish with the sword</u>.

This is a clear defended capital punishment by the Lord Jesus Christ Himself. What He was saying was if someone takes a "*sword*" to kill someone, the "*sword,*" in the hand of the government, will cause you to "*perish with the sword.*"

Paul defended capital punishment in the book of Acts.

- **Acts 25:11**

  For **if I be an offender, or have committed any thing worthy of death, I refuse not to die**: but if there be none of these things whereof these accuse me, no man may deliver me unto them. I appeal unto Caesar.

Paul was for capital punishment, even for himself if he deserved it.

- **Numbers 35:31**

  Moreover ye shall **take no satisfaction for the life of a murderer, which** *is* **guilty of death: but he shall be surely put to death.**

In the Old Testament, there could be *"no satisfaction for the life of a murderer which is guilty of death."* God does not want our *"feet swift to shed blood."* On the contrary, He wants our *"feet"* to be *"shod with the preparation of the gospel of peace."*

Romans 3:16

"Destruction and misery *are* **in their ways:"** These two terms, *"destruction and misery"* illustrate the plight and fate of all the unsaved in the world. I have mentioned about God's detailed inspection of those sinners. Like a Heavenly Doctor, God looked at their *"mouth,"* *"tongue,"* and *"lips."* In doing this, the Lord beheld many sins and much wickedness. Looking at their *"feet,"* God saw that they were *"swift to shed blood."*

In this verse, the Lord focuses on the results of their sins. *"Destruction and misery are in their ways."* The Lord Jesus said in Matthew 7:13, *"broad is the way, that leadeth to destruction."* Peter talks about *"swift destruction."*

- **2 Peter 2:1**

  But there were false prophets also among the people, even as there shall be false teachers among you, who privily shall bring in damnable heresies, even denying the Lord that bought them, and bring upon themselves **swift destruction.**

Talk about *"misery."* The ones who are lost have *"misery."* Do you remember the time when you were lost before you were born-again? Do you remember how miserable it was? There was not peace, happiness, nor joy, but a *"misery"* that was in our lives. In the book of Judges, the Lord looked down on His poor Israelites.

- **Judges 10:16**

  And they put away the strange gods from among them, and served the LORD: and **his soul was grieved for the misery of Israel.**

They had sinned. They had left the Words of God. They had left faith in the Lord.

Leaving the Lord's Will

Whenever you leave the Lord's will, leave the Lord's Words, and do your own way, you are in "*misery.*"

- **Ecclesiastes 8:6**
  Because to every purpose there is time and judgment, therefore the **misery of man** *is* great upon him.

You look at all the unsaved men and women all over the world there is great "*misery.*" They do not have peace. They do not have anything. It is a sad thing. In the "ways" of the sinners, there is also "*misery.*"

- **Proverbs 2:13**
  Who leave the paths of uprightness, to walk in the **ways of darkness;**

Certainly unsaved people have "*darkness*" in their "*ways.*"

- **Proverbs 2:15**
  Whose **ways** *are* **crooked**, and *they* froward in their paths:
- **Proverbs 14:12**
  There is a **way** which seemeth right unto a man, but **the end thereof** *are* **the ways of death.**

Christ the Only Way to Heaven

The "*ways*" of the wicked are "*destruction and misery.*" The Lord said, "*I am the Way, the Truth, and the Life.*" The Lord Jesus Christ is the Way. He is the only Way to take us to Heaven by genuine faith in Him. We should not walk in our own "*way.*"

Isaiah paints the picture clearly:

- **Isaiah 53:6**
  All we like sheep have gone astray; **we have turned every one to his own way**; and the LORD hath laid on him the iniquity of us all.

Even those of us who are saved often want our "*own way.*" But "*destruction and misery*" are in the "*ways*" of those who are lost, apart from saving faith in Christ, and without peace with God.

Romans 3:17

"And the way of peace have they not known:" The Lord
Jesus Christ had much to say about *"peace."*

- **Matthew 10:34**
  Think not that I am come to send peace on earth: I came
  not to send peace, but a sword.

That applies to unsaved men and women, but on the other hand He said
something else to His followers who trusted in Him.

- **John 14:27**
  Peace I leave with you, my peace I give unto you: not as
  the world giveth, give I unto you. **Let not your heart be
  troubled**, neither let it be afraid.

The peace of the Lord Jesus Christ makes us have trouble-free hearts. It is His
peace.

- **Romans 5:1**
  Therefore being justified by faith, we have peace with God
  through our Lord Jesus Christ:

The greatest thing that this world needs is *"peace with God."* *"How beautiful
are the feet of them that preach the gospel of peace"* (Romans 10:15).

- **Philippians 4:7**
  And **the peace of God**, which passeth all understanding, shall
  keep your hearts and minds through Christ Jesus.

The *"peace of God"* is something that these unsaved people do not have. Here
is an interesting definition of what peace is. *"The tranquil state of a soul
assured of its salvation through Christ, and so fearing nothing of God and
content with its earthly lot of whatever sort it is."* That is a definition of peace.
It is certainly *"contentment with great gain"* (1 Timothy 6:6).

You have people all around you where you live. There are people you see
every day. Maybe you have friends or loved ones who have no *"peace."* It says
in Isaiah:

- **Isaiah 57:20-21**
  But the wicked *are* like the troubled sea, when it cannot rest,
  whose waters cast up mire and dirt. *There is* **no peace, saith
  my God, to the wicked.**

You know what a raging sea is like. It pounds and pounds with big breakers ten
or fifteen feet high. Often there are tidal waves. This is what the *"wicked"* are
like. They have *"no peace."*

Romans 3:18

"There is no fear of God before their eyes." We have the expression *"God-fearing."* It can be used either of men or women. It means that they have a *"fear of God."* Because of this, they try to please Him.

The unsaved of whom this verse speaks have *"no fear of God."* They shake their fist in the face of God. They are like those who allegedly went up in the Russian Sputnik. They claimed they went up into space and did not see God up there. Therefore, they concluded that there is no God.

Do you think God is going to reveal Himself by faith to these unbelievers in this way? He has already revealed Himself to us who believe in the Lord Jesus Christ. We know that He is there, because we have been redeemed by saving faith in Him. But, there is *"no fear of God before the eyes"* of the unsaved. One of David's Psalms speaks of this same thing.

- **Psalm 36:1**
  To the chief Musician, *A Psalm* of David the servant of the LORD. The transgression of the wicked saith within my heart, *that* **there** *is* **no fear of God before his eyes**.

- **2 Samuel 23:3**
  The God of Israel said, the Rock of Israel spake to me, **He that ruleth over men** *must be* **just, ruling in the fear of God.**

Godly leaders should *"rule in the fear of God."* We know that very few of them do. Yet, this is what God wants--*"just men,"* not unsaved men who are wicked and corrupt. The Lord Jesus Christ talked about proper *"fear."*

- **Matthew 10:28**
  And fear not them which kill the body, but are not able to kill the soul: but rather **fear him which is able to destroy both soul and body in Hell.**

We should fear the Lord of all the earth.

Fear, I know a lot of people say means *"reverential trust."* Well, that is true. There is much of *"reverential trust"* in it. There is trust in the Lord. We want to trust in Him. There is no question about that. This word PHOBOS, which is the Greek word for *"fear,"* really means *"to be afraid."* You have to have a *"fear"* of the Lord otherwise you will not respect Him and most certainly you will not trust Him for your eternal life.

The Bible's Hell Is Real

Some people say that we should not *"fear"* God. They say that God is love. That is true, but God is also a God of justice. He is One Who will send men and women to Hell if they reject His salvation provided by His Son, the Lord Jesus Christ. We need to be God-fearing men and women who honestly want to please Him.

We do not want to please people because we fear them. This is often done. Sometimes you do fear people and because of this you will do something for them. I know of a man who does not have much ability to say *"no"* to anybody. Because of this, he permits some punk to twist his arm, threaten to knock his block off, to smack him, or something worse unless this man does what he is told. I cannot understand it.

There are some people who have *"fear."* *"Fear"* does many things to people. We do not want to live in fear, but we must *"fear"* God. He is a just God who loves the entire world. He sent His Son to be our Saviour. We must be mindful that we are **not** dealing with another human being. Some people refer to the Lord as *"the man upstairs."* That is very disrespectful. In fact, it is blasphemous. We must respect our God. He's a great God. He made the Heavens, the earth, the stars, all the animals, human beings, and everything else. He is a powerful God. We should not treat Him like He is some neighbor that lives next to us. He's a powerful God. We must respect Him and have a fear of God.

"No fear of God before their eyes" is manifested in the unsaved people by their swearing, cursing, and taking the name of the Lord Jesus Christ and God the Father in vain (Exodus 20:7). In fact, the British people have a way of swearing that we do not perhaps understand. They say *"zounds."* That word does not mean anything to us, but it stands for "God's wounds," referring to the wounds of Christ. When the British say *"bloody this"* or *"bloody that"* they are referring to the blood of Christ. That is blasphemous swearing. These people do not care if they live or die. They live for self and sin come what may.

Romans 3:19

"Now we know that what things soever the law saith, it saith to them who are under the law: that every mouth may be stopped, and all the world may become guilty before God." Just pretend that you are in a court of law. Normally, you can speak for yourself, especially if you are *"pro se,"* that is, without an attorney and defending yourself. If you are up for charges for murder, theft, or whatever it may be. Either you can talk in your own defense, or your lawyer can talk. However, when God's judgment of the lost takes place, the Great White Throne Judgment (Revelation 20:11-15), these people will appear before God, *"every mouth will be stopped."* They will be speechless. They will be just like the deaf and dumb who cannot speak. The Lord Jesus Christ will be their judge (John 5:22). They are unable to speak because they know that the Lord Jesus Christ is right about every sin that is brought against them. He is perfectly just in condemning them to Hell because they have rejected Him as their Saviour.

The Judgment Seat of Christ

For those of us who are saved, and genuinely trusting the Lord Jesus Christ as our Saviour, there is also a judgment. It is called the "Judgment Seat of Christ" (Romans 14:10; 2 Corinthians 5:10). Every born-again Christian will appear at this judgment. All their *"mouths will be stopped"* as well. The Lord Jesus Christ will ask us what we did for Him while we were on this earth after we were saved. He will ask, *"Why did you do this? Why did you say that?"* If it is known unconfessed sin (1 John 1:9), we are going to be held accountable, and our *"mouths will be stopped."*

In the case referred to in this verse, it is a reference to the Great White Throne Judgment (Revelation 20:11-15). At that judgment, *"every mouth will be stopped, and the whole world will become guilty before God."* God is just. He is righteous. His judgments are just.

- **James 3:10**
  Out of the same mouth proceedeth blessing and cursing.
  My brethren, these things ought not so to be.

These cursing *"mouths"* must be stopped. The Greek word for "stopped" is PHRASSO. It means: *"to fence in, block up, stop up, close up; to put to silence."* God is going to do something that would have the effect of taking a big wad of gauze or tape and "*closing up the mouths*" of the lost on that occasion. This is at the Great White Throne Judgment (Revelation 20:11-15). The reason for this is that they will not have any answers to the charges against them that will satisfy the Lord.

All the lost world is "*guilty before God.*" They will be "*guilty*" because they have rejected the eternal salvation that has been offered by the Lord Jesus Christ. They will be "*guilty*," not because these people have or have not done various works or deeds. This will be based solely on their rejection of the Saviour. In any event, "*every mouth will be stopped.*" What a silence!

Romans 3:20

"Therefore by the deeds of the law there shall no flesh be justified in his sight: for by the law *is* the knowledge of sin." The" *law*" gives us "*the knowledge*" of what's right and wrong. If you have a speed-limit sign, it tells you the upper limit of your speed. The new speed limits in some areas in New Jersey have been raised to 65-miles per hour. I have noticed as you go into New Jersey that the fines are doubled if you exceed the speed.

The "*law*" gives the "*knowledge of sin.*" You know that you have broken the "*law*" when it has been made clear to you. The "*law*" cannot save any of us. As it says, "*by the deeds of the law there shall no flesh be justified.*"

- **Acts 13:39**
  And by him all that believe are justified from all things, from which **ye could not be justified by the law of Moses**.
- **Romans 3:28**
  Therefore we conclude that a man **is justified by faith without the deeds of the law**.

"*Deeds*" will not justify us. They will not make us righteous.

- **Galatians 2:16**
  Knowing that **a man is not justified by the works of the law, but by the faith of Jesus Christ**, even we have believed in Jesus Christ, that we might be justified by the faith of Christ, and not by the works of the law: for by the works of the law shall no flesh be justified.
- **Galatians 3:11**
  But that **no man is justified by the law in the sight of God**, *it is* evident: for, The just shall live by faith.

Notice, "*in the sight of God.*" He does not care about our works that cannot save us. Faith alone, genuine belief in the Lord Jesus Christ saves us.

To be justified in the sight of man, James has a different picture.

- **James 2:21**
  Was not Abraham our father justified by works, when he had offered Isaac his son upon the altar?

Faith Is Invisible--Works Are Not

You cannot see my faith. You can just see what I do, and what I say. You can see my "*works.*" So, in the sight of man, we are justified, or declared righteous or unrighteous, by what we do. But not with God. He does not care about our deeds as far as salvation is concerned. After we are saved, He does care about our deeds and works (Ephesians 2:8-10). Abraham proved that he believed in God by what he did.

- **Genesis 22:2**
  And he said, **Take now thy son, thine only *son* Isaac, whom thou lovest,** and get thee into the land of Moriah; **and offer him there for a burnt offering** upon one of the mountains which I will tell thee of.

You might talk about faith. Abraham had faith in God. He had so much faith that he obeyed God's strange command. The knife was raised and the Angel of the Lord said,

- **Genesis 22:12**
  And he said, **Lay not thine hand upon the lad,** neither do thou any thing unto him: for **now I know that thou fearest God, seeing thou hast not withheld thy son, thine only *son* from me.**

A ram was caught in a thicket to be killed in the place of Isaac. Abraham was justified by people because they saw what he did and how he relied totally on the Lord.

Man Can See Our Works

God does not need to see what we do. He sees our hearts. But man must see our works to believe that we have genuine faith.

Romans 3:21

"But now the righteousness of God without the law is manifested, being witnessed by the law and the prophets"

We are now introduced to *"the righteousness of God."* This is a *"righteousness"* that is apart from the *"law"* of Moses. A person can get God's *"righteousness"* without doing any deeds. Such *"righteousness"* was manifested both in the *"law and the prophets."*

- **2 Corinthians 5:21**
  For he hath made him *to be* sin for us, who knew no sin; **that we might be made the righteousness of God in him.**

By means of the Lord Jesus Christ, if we trust in Him genuinely, we are *"made the righteousness of God in Him."*

That is an amazing thing. Receiving God's *"righteousness"* is not by what we do. It is not by our works. It is by what the Lord Jesus Christ did.

Righteousness Only In Christ

"Righteousness" was made possible to the born-again believer without anything to do with the law of Moses.

- **Genesis 15:6**
  And he believed in the LORD; and he counted it to him for **righteousness.**

This was a *"righteousness"* apart from deeds, apart from works, and apart from the law of Moses.

- **Galatians 3:6**
  Even as Abraham **believed God, and it was accounted to him for righteousness.**

Proper belief makes *"righteousness"* count.

I do not understand it. It would seem to have *"righteousness"* you would have to be righteous. In the sight of man that's true. In the sight of God it is received by personal, saving faith in the Lord Jesus Christ.

- **James 2:23**
  And the scripture was fulfilled which saith, **Abraham believed God, and it was imputed unto him for righteousness**: and he was called the Friend of God.

"Imputed" means it was *"reckoned to his account."* It is just like on a ledger. You have pluses and minuses. When you put money into a bank account that is *"imputation"* to your account. How we understand it, who knows? God does

it. That is His mathematics. It is very difficult for us human beings to understand fully how God can justify and make righteous, lost and undone sinners when they repent of their sins and receive as their Saviour the Lord Jesus Christ. But He said in His Words that He does it. We must believe it.

Romans 3:22

"Even the righteousness of God *which is* by faith of Jesus Christ unto all and upon all them that believe: for there is no difference" Notice this *"righteousness of God"* is possible alone by personal *"faith of Jesus Christ."* I believe this *"of"* is the translation of the Greek objective genitive. It is not a subjective genitive. As an objective genitive it has the meaning in English of *"faith in Jesus Christ."*

- **Acts 26:18**

  To open their eyes, *and* to turn *them* from darkness to light, and *from* the power of Satan unto God, **that they may receive forgiveness of sins, and inheritance among them which are sanctified by faith that is in me.**

When Paul was first saved this was his mission. It is *"by faith"* that is in the Lord Jesus Christ by which sinners can get *"forgiveness of sins"* and be *"sanctified."*

- **Galatians 3:22**

  But the scripture hath concluded all under sin, **that the promise by faith of Jesus Christ might be given to them that believe.**

Again, it is clear that, in the sight of God, *"righteousness"* is by faith. Look at the words showing the recipients of this *"righteousness."* This offer is *"unto all and upon all them that believe."* Notice the difference between the two prepositions, *"unto"* and *"upon."*

- **John 1:29**

  The next day John seeth Jesus coming **unto him**, and saith, Behold the Lamb of God, which taketh away the sin of the world.

When John the Baptist saw Jesus coming, he said that the Lamb of God, the Lord Jesus Christ, *"taketh away the sin of the world."* This forgiveness is offered *"unto all."* All the *"sin of the world"* has been removed by Christ's work on the cross. There is not one sin that has not been atoned for by His blood sacrifice for all the sinners of the world. However, these sinners of the world cannot take advantage of this remission of sins unless they repent of their sins and receive this Saviour by personal and genuine faith. This forgiveness is offered *"unto all,"* but, unless they believe in and receive the Lord Jesus Christ as their Saviour, it is not *"upon all."* That is the difference.

- **John 3:16**
  For God so loved the world, that he gave his only begotten Son, that **whosoever believeth in him** should not perish, but have everlasting life.

This is an offer "*unto all*" and for all, but it is "*upon those*" who genuinely "*believe*" in the Lord Jesus Christ.

I can offer "*unto you*" the coat on my back, but it will not be "*upon you*" until you take it off of me and put it on you. Only then could it be correct to say that is "*upon you*."

The same is true of God's universal offer of His eternal salvation. I do not agree with the "*limited atonement*" view of the "*hyper-Calvinist*" people. They teach wrongfully that the offer of salvation is limited only to what they term "*the elect*." They do not teach that the Lord Jesus Christ died for the sins of the whole world, but rather only for the sins of the "*elect*." They wrongly teach that if you are not elect, you do not have the opportunity to be saved at all. This is a serious false doctrine.

Salvation Offered to All

God's salvation is offered to every lost person in the world. It is a bona fide offer to every boy and girl, every man and woman, no matter their age, all over the world. This is regardless of the amount they might have in their bank account. God's salvation is "*unto all*."

The Lord Jesus said, "*Come unto me, all ye that labour and are heavy laden, and I will give you rest*" (Matthew 11:28). This is an open door. It is a legitimate summons.

- **Revelation 22:17**
  And **the Spirit and the bride say, Come.** And **let him that heareth say, Come.** And **let him that is athirst come.** And **whosoever will, let him take the water of life freely**.

These are indeed words of universal invitation "*unto all*" to receive God's salvation so that it is "*upon them*" who genuinely believe in His Son.

Romans 3:23

"For all have sinned, and come short of the glory of God" Many of us have memorized this verse. There are no exceptions! "*ALL*" means everybody. You might say, "*Well, does this include even the little baby, or the child of five or six?*" Yes. It includes "*all*" who have ever lived or who will ever live in the future. The only exception to this is the Lord Jesus Christ.

- **Psalm 58:3**
  The wicked are estranged from the womb: **they go astray as soon as they be born, speaking lies.**

These little ones and children all need the Lord Jesus Christ and His salvation. Though they may be safe for a little while should they die in infancy, as soon as they come to what we call the *"age of accountability,"* they must either accept or reject God's provision of salvation.

Only Christ Was Perfect

As I said before, there is only One Person on the face of this earth Who has never sinned (nor could He ever sin) and *"come short of the glory of God."* That One is the Lord Jesus Christ. He combined in One Person the nature of perfect God and the nature of perfect Man. All the rest of us *"have come short"* of God's glory. God's glory involves Heavenly bliss, a Heavenly position, eternal life, and the forgiveness of our sins. We have *"come short"* of all of that *"glory."* None of us, in our own selves, by our own works, could ever attain God's *"glory."*

When you *"come short"* of something, it is like jumping from one roof to the other roof of two adjacent tall buildings that are separated by a gap of six or eight feet. As you attempt to leap between these two buildings, it does not matter if you miss the other roof by one or two feet, or by one or two inches. You would still *"come short"* and fall to your death. All of us are sinners in the eyes of God and have *"come short"* of His glory.

We often classify people as either the *"down and outers,"* or the *"up and outers,"* but both groups are *"outers"* and are lost. You may have been *"up"* but still *"out"* before you were saved. You might have thought you were "hot stuff," as they say--the best that the world has to offer. But your best in God's eyes is the worst. Then, there are the *"down and outers"* such as the bums on Skid Row. They are *"out"* also. Both of these groups need the Lord Jesus Christ and His salvation. Salvation is truly a wonderful thing.

Romans 3:24

"Being justified freely by his grace through the redemption that is in Christ Jesus" Notice in the last verse we saw that *"all have sinned."* This includes the Jews, the moralist Gentiles, and the heathen who live in darkness and idolatry.

Justification Defined

This verse speaks about *"being justified freely."* God's term for *"justified"* and *"justification"* has been defined as *"the judicial act of Almighty God by which He declares a sinner absolutely and perfectly righteous in His sight."* *"Being justified"* brings us a righteous standing before God and makes us *"saved."*

What does the word *"freely"* mean in this verse? The same Greek word (DOREAN) has been translated in an interesting way in John 15:25.

* **John 15:25**
  But *this cometh to pass*, that the word might be fulfilled that is written in their law, They hated me **without a cause**.

Dr. Lewis Sperry Chafer, my teacher for four years at *Dallas Theological Seminary* (1948-1952), often referred to this verse to explain God's salvation and justification. As I mentioned, *"without a cause"* in this verse is the same word translated *"freely"* in Romans 3:24. The Greek word used is DOREAN. It means *"undeservedly"* or *"without any cause."*

Saved Without Any Cause

If we are saved, we have been *"justified"* by God *"without any cause"* in us. There is not a single cause in us. In us who are sinners and who have *"come short of the glory of God,"* there is not a shred of evidence that would cause God to declare us just and righteous in His sight.

This declaration can be made by the Lord only *"by His grace through the redemption that is in Christ Jesus."*

First of all, this *"justification"* by God is *"by His grace."* Grace was defined by Dr. M. R. DeHaan many years ago as *"getting something that we don't deserve.*" It is contrasted to God's mercy which is "*not getting something that we do deserve.*"

Second of all, this "*justification*" by God is only "*through the redemption that is in Christ Jesus.*" The Greek word for "*redemption*" is APOLUTROSIS. It means: "*a releasing effected by payment of ransom; a redemption, a deliverance; a liberation procured by the payment of a ransom.*" It is like somebody who has been kidnaped and who has been ransomed for $100,000, $200,000, or even $1,000,000. In this event, the victim cannot be set free until someone "*redeems*" him or "*pays his ransom money.*"

Ransomed By Christ's Blood

Likewise, no one can get set free from sin and the bondage of his soul until someone pays the ransom. The only Person in the world Who can "*pay the ransom*" for our sin and for the sins of the whole world is the Lord Jesus Christ. He has done this by the shedding of His precious blood in His death on Calvary's cross.

We are set free "*without any cause*" in ourselves by God's grace completely "*through the redemption that is in Christ Jesus.*" That next verse is going to tell us about the price that was paid.

Romans 3:25

"Whom God hath set forth *to be* a propitiation through faith in his blood, to declare his righteousness for the remission of sins that are past, through the forbearance of God" Here we learn that the Lord Jesus Christ was "*set forth*" by God the Father "*to be a propitiation through faith in His blood.*" The Greek word for "*propitiation*" is HILASTERION. It has various meanings, such as:

"*relating to an appeasing or expiating, having placating or expiating force, expiatory; a means of appeasing or expiating, a propitiation; used of the cover of the ark of the covenant in the Holy of Holies, which was sprinkled with the blood of the expiatory victim on the annual day of atonement (this rite signifying that the life of the people, the loss of which they had merited by their sins, was offered to God in the blood as the life of the victim, and that God by this ceremony was appeased and their sins expiated); hence the lid of expiation, the propitiatory; an expiatory sacrifice; a expiatory*"

victim."

God the Father Was Satisfied

The net result of the Lord Jesus Christ's propitiatory sacrifice was that God the Father was satisfied with the finished work of His Son. It is through *"faith in His blood"* that applies this *"propitiation"* to the sinner.

The word, *"propitiation,"* no longer occurs in The New International Version. They just wiped it out. *"Propitiation"* simply means *"satisfaction."* God is satisfied with the substitutionary death of His Son on the cross. This *"propitiation"* also was *"to declare His righteousness for the remission of sins that are past, through the forbearance of God."* In Christ's redemptive sacrifice on the cross, God declared *"His righteousness"* and also provided *"remission of sins that are past."* All the Old Testament saints looked forward in genuine faith to Calvary. They looked forward to the blood of the Lord Jesus Christ that was shed for the sins of the whole world. They looked forward to the sacrifice of the Lamb of God that *"taketh away the sin of the world"* (John 1:29b).

The Meaning of Remission

Those sins have been *"remitted"* or forgiven *"through the forbearance of God."* The debt has been paid for the repentant sinner who comes to God's Son in genuine faith. The Greek word for *"remission"* is PARESIS. It means: *"passing over, letting pass, neglecting, disregarding."*

"Faith in His blood" is the ransom that was paid for us sinners. It was the blood of the Lord Jesus Christ. I would like to have all of my readers to have my book entitled *John MacArthur's Heresy on the Blood of Christ* (BFT #2185). MacArthur thinks that *"blood"* is merely a metonym or figure of speech for *"death"* rather than meaning literal *"blood."*

I would like to go over some of the verses on the blood of Christ. *"Blood"* means *"blood."* *"Death means death."* The Greek word for *"blood"* is HAIMA. From this Greek word, we get the term, *"hematology"* which is the study of blood and its diseases. *"Anemia"* literally means, *"no blood."* The Greek word for *"death"* is THANATOS. These are two different words. When

John MacArthur and others say that "*blood*" is just a "*metonym*" or just a symbol, the true importance of the "*blood*" of Christ is minimized. Let me read a few verses on the "*blood*" of Christ.

- **Acts 20:28**
  Take heed therefore unto yourselves, and to all the flock, over the which the Holy Ghost hath made you overseers, to feed the church of God, which he hath **purchased with his own blood**.

The Lord Jesus Christ "*purchased*" the "*church of God*" with "*His own blood,*" not with His own "*death.*" It is true He died for our sins, but it is the shedding of His "*blood*" that was the price of redemption. It is not simply His death.

One staff member of Charles Swindoll wrote a letter to one of my friends to the effect that the Lord Jesus Christ could have died by electrocution or some other means of death without the shedding of his "*blood.*" That idea would have been all right for this man, so long as Jesus died, but this is not correct theologically.

Blood Does Not Mean Death

"*Blood*" means "*blood.*" Let no one say that "*blood*" means "*death*" or something else, as John MacArthur and others have taken and done.

- **Ephesians 2:13**
  But now in Christ Jesus ye who sometimes were far off are **made nigh by the blood of Christ.**

We who are Gentiles who have been saved are made "*nigh*" by His "*blood.*"

- **Colossians 1:20**
  And, **having made peace through the blood of his cross**, by him to reconcile all things unto himself; by him, *I say*, whether *they be* things in earth, or things in Heaven.

The "*blood*" of Christ brings peace.

- **Hebrews 9:12**
  Neither by the blood of goats and calves, but **by his own blood he entered in once into the holy place**, having obtained eternal redemption *for us*.

- Hebrews 9:14
  How much more shall **the blood of Christ,** who through the eternal Spirit offered himself without spot to God, purge your conscience from dead works to serve the living God?

Christ's *"blood"* is a purging substance.

- Hebrews 9:22
  And almost all things are by the law purged with blood; and **without shedding of blood is no remission.**

- Hebrews 10:19
  Having therefore, brethren, **boldness to enter into the holiest by the blood of Jesus,**

Christ's shed *"blood"* opened up the mercy seat in Heaven.

- 1 Peter 1:18-19
  Forasmuch as ye know that ye were not **redeemed** with corruptible things, *as* silver and gold, from your vain conversation *received* by tradition from your fathers; But with **the precious blood of Christ**, as of a lamb without blemish and without spot: (KJV)

The *"blood"* of Christ *redeems*.

- Hebrews 10:29
  Of how much sorer punishment, suppose ye, shall he be thought worthy, who hath trodden under foot the Son of God, and **hath counted the blood of the covenant**, wherewith he was sanctified, **an unholy thing**, and hath done despite unto the Spirit of grace?

The phrase, "*an unholy thing*" means "*a common thing*," therefore possessed by most people. That is what John MacArthur thinks about the blood of the Lord Jesus Christ. He believes that Christ's blood is the same as your blood and mine. It is merely "*human blood*" to John MacArthur. If the blood of the Lord Jesus Christ was just like your blood or my blood, then we could shed blood for each other and be saved. This position is blasphemous! It is a terrible and a despiteful doctrine. I believe that John MacArthur and others will be the recipient of the "*much sorer punishment*." I believe strongly that the judgment spelled out in Hebrews 10:29 applies to John MacArthur and all others whom he has influenced to hold this false doctrine and heresy.

There are many people who are beginning to agree openly with John MacArthur on his heretical belief on the blood of Christ. He is not the only one. There are many important people who share this false view. MacArthur opened the floodgates, and now his followers are coming out of the woodwork. Some of them are theologians. Some of them teach in Bible institutes, colleges, universities, and even theological seminaries.

Be Careful of Dangers in Schools

Sometimes the most dangerous place to be is in a Bible Institute, a College, or a Theological Seminary. This is why some call such seminaries, "*cemeteries.*" They kill many of their students spiritually. It is a terrible thing when teachers teach students the wrong things. They are teaching them against the King James Bible in many of these schools.

- Hebrews 12:22-24
  But **ye are come unto mount Sion**, and unto [1] the city of the living God, [2] **the Heavenly Jerusalem**, and to [3] an innumerable company of angels,[4] To the general assembly and church of the firstborn, which are written in Heaven, and [5] to God the Judge of all, and [6] to the spirits of just men made perfect, And [7] **to Jesus** the mediator of the new covenant, and [8] **to the blood of sprinkling**, that speaketh better things than *that of* Abel.

These verses tell us clearly that eight things are in Heaven.

These Eight Things Are in Heaven

1. "*The city of God*" is in Heaven.
2. The "*Heavenly Jerusalem*" is in Heaven.
3. The "*angels*" are in Heaven.
4. The "*church of the firstborn*" is in Heaven.
5. "*God*" is in Heaven.
6. The "*spirits of just men*" are in Heaven.
7. "*Jesus*" is in Heaven.
8. "*blood of sprinkling*" is in Heaven.

Many theologians and preachers deny that the blood of Christ is on the Mercy Seat in Heaven. This verse makes it clear that it is there, along with the other seven specific things mentioned clearly.

Christ's blood is in Heaven.

- Hebrews 13:12
Wherefore Jesus also, **that he might sanctify the people with his own blood,** suffered without the gate.

Christ's blood is "*sanctifying*" blood.

- Hebrews 13:20-21
Now the God of peace, that brought again from the dead our Lord Jesus, that great shepherd of the sheep, **through the blood of the everlasting covenant, Make you perfect** in every good work to do his will, working in you that which is wellpleasing in his sight, through Jesus Christ; to whom *be* glory for ever and ever. Amen.

Christ's blood is "*perfecting*" blood.

- 1 Peter 1:18-19
Forasmuch as ye know that ye were **not redeemed** with corruptible things, *as* silver and gold, from your vain conversation *received* by tradition from your fathers; **But with the precious blood of Christ**, as of a lamb without blemish and without spot:

Christ's blood is "*precious blood.*"

- 1 John 1:7
But if we walk in the light, as he is in the light, we have fellowship one with another, **and the blood of Jesus Christ his Son cleanseth us from all sin.**

Christ's blood is "*cleansing*" blood.

- Revelation 1:5
And from Jesus Christ, *who is* the faithful witness, *and* the first begotten of the dead, and the prince of the kings of the earth. Unto him that loved us, **and washed us from our sins in his own blood,**

Christ's blood can "*wash us from our sins.*" It is cleansing

- Revelation 5:9
And they sung a new song, saying, Thou art worthy to take the book, and to open the seals thereof: for **thou wast slain, and hast redeemed us to God by thy blood** out of every kindred, and tongue, and people, and nation;

Christ's blood is "*redeeming*" blood.

John MacArthur is in deep heresy by his views on the blood of Christ. He says "*slain*" ("*death*") and "*blood*" are the same. He erroneously teaches that the word, "*blood*" is just a metonym or a figure of speech for "*death*." No! This is very clear. In this very verse, God makes a distinction between "*slain*" and "*blood*."

In the same way, the Passover lamb was "*slain*" so that the Israelites could be spared, but the "*blood*" had to be applied (in a separate and distinct action) to the top and side posts of the door. These actions are two separate entities. They are not combined. They are not one in the same.

* **Revelation 12:9-11**
  And the great dragon was cast out, that old serpent, called the Devil, and Satan, which deceiveth the whole world: he was cast out into the earth, and his angels were cast out with him. And I heard a loud voice saying in Heaven, Now is come salvation, and strength, and the kingdom of our God, and the power of his Christ: for the accuser of our brethren is cast down, which accused them before our God day and night. **And they overcame him by the blood of the Lamb**, and by the word of their testimony; and they loved not their lives unto the death.

Christ's blood is also "*overcoming*" blood.

God has sent forth His Son to be our "*propitiation through faith in His blood.*" Blood is blood. These preceding verses show very clearly that God has redeemed us by His precious "*blood*" as He died on the cross of Calvary.

* **Hebrews 10:5**
  Wherefore when he cometh into the world, he saith, Sacrifice and offering thou wouldest not, **but a body hast thou prepared me**:

In this verse, the Lord Jesus Christ is speaking to God the Father. He says that "*a body hast thou prepared me.*"

I believe that God the Father prepared the Lord Jesus Christ's "*body*" in fulfillment of this verse. It included every part of His "*body.*" Among many other parts of His perfect human "*body*" included His blood, His muscles, His hands, His nerves, His feet, and all of the many other parts of that "*body.*" All were "*prepared*" by God. That was made possible by His miraculous Virgin Birth. Through this miracle birth, the *blood* of the Lord Jesus Christ was special "blood." It was "*incorruptible*" and was and is able to redeem sinners who sincerely trust in Him.

Romans 3:26

"**To declare, *I say*, at this time his righteousness: that he might be just, and the justifier of him which believeth in Jesus**" In this verse, God is "*declaring*" His "*righteousness*" in forgiving the "*sins that are past, through the forbearance of God.*" The Lord had to perform this feat by being both "*just, and the justifier*" of the one who "*believeth in Jesus.*" God was offended by sin and had to punish sin to defend

His holiness. To perform this, God Himself, in the Person of God the Son, the Lord Jesus Christ, paid the penalty for those sins by His death and shed blood on Calvary's cross. In this was, God could be "*just*" and yet also the "*justifier*" of those who have a genuine faith in the Lord Jesus Christ.

It is almost like a judge that would condemn a criminal to death, and then that same judge would take the place of the criminal and die in his place. That is what God did for us who are sinners.

I think of the man that was accused on the news this morning. He killed one woman, raped her, and threw her body in the river. He confessed that he had murdered three other women as well. Now he is a murderer four times. The judge assigned that man to death on death row. I believe in capital punishment for first-degree murder if there is solid evidence involved. The Scriptures teach this. The judge is just who sentenced that man to death-row to die, whether by lethal injection or the electric chair.

What if the judge came off the bench, took the place of the condemned man, and went to the death-row himself. That is what the Lord Jesus Christ did for you and for me. We were condemned to spend eternity in Hell's Lake of Fire. The Lord Jesus Christ paid the price that we should have paid. In this way, God was "*just*" in demanding a penalty for our sins, yet He was also the "*Justifier*" of those who receive Christ as their own Saviour.

To Heaven Only By God's Airplane

The kind of people that God "*justifies*" are not those who are good, or beautiful, or rich. The only requirement is personal and genuine faith. It is for those who "*believeth in Jesus.*" That is the way God justifies. We cannot do it ourself. He is the One who has to do it for us. We can no more "*justify*" ourselves than we can "*fly.*" We must get into an airplane in order to "*fly*" from Philadelphia to New York City. If we try to get to Heaven by ourselves, without the "Airplane" of the Lord Jesus Christ by faith in Him, we will never make it. God the Father is both "*just*," and the "*Justifier*" of those who genuinely and sincerely "*believeth in Jesus.*"

Romans 3:27

"Where *is* boasting then? It is excluded. By what law? of works? Nay: but by the law of faith."

- Ephesians 2:9
Not of works, **lest any man should boast.**

If we worked our way to Heaven, we would boast about it. I have never seen a *"self-made man"* that does not *"boast"* about it. A friend of ours has many rich people living in the large Philadelphia hotel where he works. It is the fourteenth luxury hotel in the country, and the seventy-first in the world. There are many in his hotel who are *"self-made men."* They are millionaires. Sometimes they *"boast"* about how they got all their money. Sam says that even though these people are rich and boastful, many of them are miserable and grumpy. There is not a one of us when we get to Heaven that will be able to boast about it. We will not get there because of our own merits, but because we trusted in the Lord Jesus Christ Who alone can save sinners.

If your dad or mom gave you an inheritance of a million dollars, how can you boast about it that you have done it? You did not earn it. You received it by the grace of your parents. We can never boast of our salvation. We just have to say, *"Thank you, Lord for giving me the wings to fly to Heaven."* It is only by God's grace, and not by works lest any man should boast.

Romans 3:28

"Therefore we conclude that a man is justified by faith without the deeds of the law." There are many verses that teach this same principle of *"justification by faith"* without any of our *"deeds"* or *"works."*

- Romans 4:6
Even as David also describeth the blessedness of the man, **unto whom God imputeth righteousness without works,**
- Galatians 2:16
Knowing that a **man is not justified by the works of the law, but by the faith of Jesus Christ,** even we have believed in Jesus Christ, that we might be **justified by the faith of Christ,** and not by the works of the law: for by the works of the law shall no flesh be justified.
- 2 Timothy 1:9
Who hath saved us, and called *us* with an holy calling, **not according to our works, but according to his own purpose and grace,** which was given us in Christ Jesus before the world began,

- Titus 3:5
Not by works of righteousness which we have done, but according to his mercy he saved us, by the washing of regeneration, and renewing of the Holy Ghost;

Put the Horse Before the Cart

We're not saved by our good "*works.*" Once you are "*justified by faith,*" good "*works*" should follow your saving faith. You should not put the cart before the horse. You cannot pull the horse with a cart. You must get the horse in front of the cart. Let the horse do its job. "*Faith*" must pull our cart of works. If we have not saving "*faith,*" our "*works*" will do us no good.

But once we are saved, God expects us to live for Him, to love Him, to serve Him, and to do "*good works*" for Him. "*Works*" are not to get us saved, but they should occur after we have been saved because we want to please our Saviour.

- Ephesians 2:10
For we are his workmanship, created in Christ Jesus unto good works, which God hath before ordained that we should walk in them.

Romans 3:29

"*Is he* the God of the Jews only? *is he* not also of the Gentiles? Yes, of the Gentiles also" Is God limited as to the objects of His salvation? That is the question here. He is the God of everybody who will come to His Son as Saviour and receive Him by faith, whether they be Jews, Gentiles, Mormons, or anyone else.

- Psalm 18:31
For **who *is* God save the LORD?** or who *is* a rock save our God?

- Psalm 46:10
Be still, and know that I *am* God: I will be exalted among the heathen, I will be exalted in the earth.

- Psalm 96:5
For all the gods of the nations *are* idols: but **the LORD made the Heavens**.

Our God is the only real One there is in the universe. He is exclusive as God; yet He wants to include everyone in the world who will trust His Son for salvation.

In the Old Testament, the ten tribes of the northern kingdom of Israel were removed into Assyria. The two tribes of the southern kingdom of Judah were taken into Babylon. When they were removed into captivity, they had some people come back into Jerusalem to take care of the crops. These people did not know "*the manner of the God of the land*" (2 Kings 17:26-27). So they asked the Jews to teach them so lions would not attack them. They thought the Lord was only the "God of the land."

The Lord is the Lord of the universe. He is not simply a provincial God. Many heathen people have little god-shelves where they have placed their false gods.

The God of All the Earth

The Bible's God is the God of all the earth and wants all the earth to worship Him and Him alone through saving faith in His beloved Son, the Lord Jesus Christ.

Romans 3:30-31

"Seeing *it is* one God, which shall justify the circumcision by faith, and uncircumcision through faith. Do we then make void the law through faith? God forbid: yea, we establish the law." No one can keep the "*law*" of the God of Heaven and earth. No one can attain unto His righteousness. We cannot do it by ourselves. The Lord Jesus Christ fulfilled the law completely.

- **Romans 10:4**
  For **Christ *is* the end of the law for righteousness** to every one that believeth.
- **Romans 8:4**
  That the righteousness of the law might be fulfilled in us, who walk not after the flesh, but after the Spirit.

God is the One Who fulfills the "*law*" in us when we trust Christ as our Saviour.

"God Forbid" Is Clear

Because the King James Bible uses the phase, *"God forbid,"* many people say that it favors dynamic equivalency. The word, *"God"* is not in this phrase. It is ME GENOITA which means *"may it not be."* In 1611, this was the strongest statement for Paul to use. It may be a colloquialism or something along that line, but that is exactly what it conveys to the English reader. This is very clearly what Paul meant.

If you think that this is dynamic equivalency in the King James Bible (and I do not necessarily agree that it is), it is a very rare occurrence there. When compared to the almost 800,000 words in the King James Bible, you can find very few examples of anything like that. This compares to the over 2,000 examples of dynamic equivalency I found in the New King James Version; over 4,000 examples I found in the New American Standard Version; and over 6,653 examples I found in the New International Version. The King James Bible translators wanted to get it across to the people that they were writing to in 1611, and that was the way they did it. *"God forbid"* occurs twenty-four times in the King James Bible (9 in the Old Testament and 15 in the New Testament). It is not swearing. It means, *"may it never come to pass."* Do not fault the King James Bible because it uses *"God forbid."*

We who are saved are saved by the promise concerning Abraham's Seed, the Lord Jesus Christ (Galatians 3:16). The Lord Jesus Christ was the Seed (Genesis 22:18). It was promised to Abraham. By genuine faith in that Seed, the Lord Jesus Christ, we are saved.

- **John 3:16**

  For God so loved the world, that he gave his only begotten Son, that **whosoever believeth in him should not perish, but have everlasting life**.

So, it wasn't written only for Abraham's sake, but it was for us too! God can *"justify"* both the *"circumcision"* (the Jews) and the *"uncircumcision"* (Gentiles) by faith.

The *"law"* is *"established"* by *"faith"* because by personal faith in the Lord Jesus Christ the *"righteousness of the law"* is *"fulfilled in us."*

Romans
Chapter Four

Romans 4:1

"What shall we say then that Abraham our father, as pertaining to the flesh, hath found?" Abraham is called *"our father, as pertaining to the flesh."* He is the *"father"* of the Jews certainly, but as far as his *"faith,"* he is *"father"* of the saved Gentiles as well. This does not mean, however, that Israel is the Church, or the Church is Israel. It only means that in terms of Abraham's *"faith,"* he is a true spiritual *"father"* of all those who have genuine *"faith"* in the Lord Jesus Christ. There are those of the Jewish people who are still lost and need the Lord Jesus Christ. Paul was a Jew. He was lost and Christ saved Him. God can save the Jews today.

Abraham was the *"father"* of the faith before the law ever came along. We will see this as we proceed through this chapter. Abraham was a man of *"faith."* He is a picture and an illustration of faith for us today.

Romans 4:2

"For if Abraham were justified by works, he hath whereof to glory; but not before God." It is important that we define what it means to be *"justified"* by God. The Greek verb for "justify" is DIKAOIOO. It means various things, such as:

> *"to render righteous or such he ought to be; to show, exhibit, evince, one to be righteous, such as he is and wishes himself to be considered;* **to declare, pronounce, one to be just, righteous,** *or such as he ought to be."*

What Is Justification?

In a theological sense, *"justification"* is:

"God's Divine and immutable declaration that the one who has been redeemed by genuine faith in His Son is absolutely righteous on His books, and in His eyes."

That does not mean that saved people are perfectly righteous here on earth in our earthly bodies, though that should be their goal and aim. When we come to Christ and trust Him as our Saviour and Redeemer, He imputes to us His *"righteousness."* We are *"justified"* by saving faith in the Lord Jesus Christ, not by our *"works"* or good deeds of any kind.

If Abraham were *"justified"* by his *"works"* he could *"glory"* and boast. He could say, "Look what I did." He could say he was a self-made man, as many people say. We like to boast of what we do. He could not *"glory"* before God, because God does not look at our works before we are saved. He does not say that our works are the things that make us saved.

Here are a few verses on the theme of *"justification."*

- **Job 25:4**
  How then can man be **justified** with God? or how can he be clean *that is* born of a woman?

Job had a question, and the New Testament has the answer. A person is *"justified"* by genuine faith in the Lord Jesus Christ, the Redeemer. That is the only way we who are *"born of a woman"* can be made just, righteous, and *"clean."*

- **Psalm 143:2**
  And enter not into judgment with thy servant: for **in thy sight shall no man living be justified**.

This was true in the Old Testament time before Christ had come.

Righteousness Needed for Heaven

No man or woman could possibly be declared righteous, absolutely holy, in God's *"sight."* If a person does not possess perfect righteousness before God, he or she cannot go to God's Heaven.

That is a fact. It is not by our righteousness, but only by Christ's righteousness can we get to Heaven, because He "*justifies*" repentant sinners who trust in Him by faith.

- **Romans 3:20**
  Therefore by the deeds of the law there shall no flesh be **justified in his sight**: for by the law *is* the knowledge of sin.
- **Romans 3:24**
  Being **justified freely by his grace** through the redemption that is in Christ Jesus:
- **Romans 3:28**
  Therefore we conclude that a **man is justified by faith** without the deeds of the law.
- **Romans 5:1**
  Therefore being **justified by faith**, we have peace with God through our Lord Jesus Christ:
- **Romans 5:9**
  Much more then, being now **justified by his blood**, we shall be saved from wrath through him.
- **Galatians 2:16**
  Knowing that a man is **not justified by the works of the law**, but by the faith of Jesus Christ, even we have believed in Jesus Christ, that we might be **justified by the faith of Christ**, and not by the works of the law: **for by the works of the law shall no flesh be justified**.
- **Galatians 3:11**
  But that **no man is justified by the law in the sight of God**, *it is* evident: for, **The just shall live by faith**.
- **Titus 3:7**
  That being justified by his grace, we should be made heirs according to the hope of eternal life.

There is another book in the Bible which speaks about this, not just the books of Romans and Galatians. The book of James has a different picture of justification. In fact, Martin Luther wanted to throw out the book of James. He said that book is a "a right strawy epistle," meaning it was a worthless thing book. James is talking about "*justification*" before men. Men cannot see our faith, only our works. The only thing that can justify us before men is what we do--our works.

- **James 2:21**
  Was not Abraham our father **justified by works**, when he had offered Isaac his son upon the altar?

People could see Abraham's "*works.*" They could not see Abraham's faith in God's ability to raise his son up from death if he were actually slain upon that altar. They could only see his "*works.*"

Abraham believed God and was "*justified*" in His sight. He was also "*justified*" in front of men by his "*works.*" God did not need to see Abraham's "*works*" in order to see his faith. He can see the faith, but we need deeds in order to see for ourselves whether or not a person is declared righteous before the Lord.

- **James 2:24**

  Ye see then how that **by works a man is justified**, and not by faith only.

That is "*justification*" before men, not before God. There is not a contradiction. It is just an expansion of this whole idea of "*justification*" before man and before God.

- **James 2:25**

  Likewise also **was not Rahab the harlot justified by works**, when she had received the messengers, and had sent *them* out another way?

They could not see her faith. Rahab was a harlot woman down in the dumps. She was a down-and-outer woman. Who would want to believe her? She believed that the God of Israel would make the walls of Jericho fall down. Nobody would believe a harlot, a prostitute, a woman of the street, but they saw her "*works.*" They saw how she hid those "*messengers*" and spies. She saved these men's lives.

In front of people, we are justified by what we do, not by our faith. The trouble with many Christians is that when the world looks at them, they do not "*justify*" them because of unrighteous deeds that are seen and heard.

People See What We Do

God wants to see our faith, but people want to see what we do. They want to see that we are really "*righteous*" before God because they see we are living for the Lord Jesus a life that is true. Justification before God is not by our works. Justification before men is by our works that they behold, whether for good or for ill. The apostle Paul wrote, "*Ye are our epistle written in our hearts, known and read of all men*" (2 Corinthians 3:2).

Romans 4:3

"For what saith the scripture? Abraham believed God, and it was counted unto him for righteousness."

"For what saith the scripture" The Greek word for *"Scripture"* is GRAPHE. It is used in 2 Timothy 3:16 in the phrase, PASA GRAPHE, *"all Scripture."* These words occur fifty-two times in the King James New Testament. In all but one of these times (2 Timothy 3:15 where GRAMMA is used), the Greek word, GRAPHE, is used. It means: *"a writing, thing written; the Scripture, used to denote either the book itself, or its contents; a certain portion or section of the Holy Scripture."* It refers to the Words and writings of the Almighty God of the Bible. It does not refer to or mean the "message, thought, idea, concept, message, or voice" of the Bible, as is currently being proclaimed by teachers, graduates, and books from Fundamentalist schools such as Bob Jones University, Detroit Baptist Seminary, Central Baptist Seminary, Calvary Baptist Seminary, Maranatha Baptist Bible College and others. GRAPHE **always** refers to the **Words** of the Bible.

GRAPHE Refers to Words

I repeat again, GRAPHE, *"Scripture"* or *"Scriptures"* do not refer to or mean the Bible's "message, thought, idea, concept, message, or voice" but exclusively its Words. These important definitions and distinctions form the basis for the most important and major battlefield in the Fundamentalist world today. If wrongly determined and defined, I predict it has led, is leading, and will continue to lead the Fundamentalist world first into neo-evangelicalism, and finally into apostasy.

I believe the original Words of both the Old Testament Hebrew/Aramaic and the New Testament Greek were *"God-breathed,"* that is, *"inspired"* Words. This is taught by the use of THEOPNEUSTOS (*"given by inspiration of God,"* or "inspired of God," or "God-Breathed") in 2 Timothy 3:16. As such, these Words were inerrant, infallible, and absolutely perfect.

I also believe that God has promised to keep, guard, and preserve those original Hebrew/Aramaic and Greek Words of the Old and the New Testament. I further believe that God has kept that promise, and has preserved the Old Testament Hebrew/Aramaic Words in the *Masoretic Text* underlying the King James Bible, and in the New Testament *Textus Receptus* Greek Words underlying the King James Bible. This is a matter of my personal faith, which is based on many undeniable facts, after studying this subject intensely since 1971. I am well aware, sad to say, that these views and beliefs are not popular among many Fundamentalist "*leaders*" today.

KJB--God's Words in English

God has not left us without a witness. God has preserved for us His Hebrew/Aramaic and Greek Words in the English language. I believe the King James Bible gives us an accurate translation of those preserved Hebrew/Aramaic and Greek Words. I believe, therefore, that in the *King James Bible*, we have the Words of God in English.

The news this week about the Iraq situation is an interesting parallel with Bible translation. I heard on the news that the Iraqis wrote a letter and sent it to the United Nations. They wrote it in Arabic. The interpreters worked very hard as they translated it from Arabic into English. You can rest assured that such an important event which involves attacking the capital of Iraq necessitated that every Arabic word be carefully and precisely translated into English. The understanding of the letter concerned the possibility of dropping bombs on Iraq because of their possible possession or use of nuclear war heads and germ warfare. The translators of that document did not use "*dynamic equivalence*" in their important letter like the New International Version, or the New American Standard Version, and other versions do for the Bible. They wanted to use exactly the right and correct English word for every Arabic word. There could be no misunderstanding.

That is what our King James Bible has given to us. They have placed the Hebrew, Aramaic, and Greek Words accurately into our English language. They did not add. They did not subtract. They did not change in other ways. They felt that the Scriptures were important. It had to be translated accurately and properly.

If we are English, the Bible should be translated accurately in English, as we have it in our King James Bible. If you speak Spanish, French, German, or any other language, the Bible should be accurately translated into that language.

"Abraham believed God, and it was counted unto him for righteousness." This statement about Abraham is found in Genesis 15.

* **Genesis 15:6**
  And **he believed in the LORD; and he counted it to him for righteousness**.

This is important because in Genesis 17 Abraham was given the sign and *"covenant"* of circumcision.

- **Genesis 17:9-12**
  And God said unto Abraham, Thou shalt keep my covenant therefore, thou, and thy seed after thee in their generations. **This *is* my covenant**, which ye shall keep, between me and you and thy seed after thee; **Every man child among you shall be circumcised.** And ye shall circumcise the flesh of your foreskin; and it shall be a token of the covenant betwixt me and you. And **he that is eight days old shall be circumcised among you**, every man child in your generations, he that is born in the house, or bought with money of any stranger, which *is* not of thy seed.

Circumcision Could Not Save

Abraham's faith preceded the covenant of circumcision. It is clear that circumcision had nothing to do with Abraham being justified before God. That was by his faith.

What did Abraham believe God about? What was his faith that was *"counted unto him for righteousness"*? God told Abraham that He was going to give him a *"seed."* Abraham said he did not have any *"seed."* He told the Lord, in effect, *"I do not have any children. This man, my servant, Eliezer, is he going to be the one that you can bless?"*

The Lord did not agree with Abraham. He said: *"And, behold, the word of the LORD came unto him, saying, This shall not be thine heir; but he that shall come forth out of thine own bowels shall be thine heir"* (Genesis 15:4). After this, God explained to Abraham what He was about to do. *"And He brought him forth abroad, and said, Look now toward Heaven, and tell the stars, if thou be able to number them: and he said unto him, So shall thy seed be"* (Genesis 15:5).

We cannot count the stars. We must just guess at them. Scientists have estimated that there are billions upon billions upon billions of them. God put them all there. God said to Abraham, *"So shall thy seed be."* That is what Abraham believed God about. Talk about faith. There it is. Right after that statement, it is written of Abraham: *"And he believed in the LORD; and He counted it to him for righteousness"* (Genesis 15:6).

If the Lord would tell us some of these things, I am wondering about our faith. Do you see why Abraham is called the *"father"* of those that believe

(Romans 4:1; James 2:21)? This is true not only of the Jews, but also of the Gentiles. It includes anybody who genuinely believes. He is the *"father"* because of his faith.

- **Galatians 3:6**
  Even as Abraham believed God, and it was **accounted** to him for righteousness.

The Greek word for *"accounted"* is LOGIZOMAI. That Greek word for *"accounted"* occurs no less than eight times in these twelve verses. Notice in verse 3, *"it was **counted**."* That's the same word.

Verse 4, *"not reckoned"* is the same word. Verse 5, *"is **counted** for righteousness"* is the same word. Verse 6, *"**imputeth**,"* Verse 8, *"**impute** sin,"* Verse 10, *"How was it then **reckoned**?"* and Verse 11, *"might be **imputed** unto them,"* are all the same word for *"accounted."* LOGIZOMAI has a number of meanings:

> *"to reckon, count, compute, calculate, count over; to take into account, to make an account of; metaph. to pass to one's account, to impute; a thing is reckoned as or to be something, i.e. as availing for or equivalent to something, as having the like force and weight; to number among, reckon with; to reckon or account; to reckon inward, count up or weigh the reasons, to deliberate; by reckoning up all the reasons, to gather or infer; to consider, take into account, weigh, meditate on; to suppose, deem, judge; to determine, purpose, decide."*

Another way to understand this is as follows:

> *"This word deals with reality. If I 'logizomai' or reckon that my bank book has $25 in it, it has $25 in it. Otherwise I am deceiving myself. **This word refers to facts not suppositions**."*

Paul wrote in Galatians, *"Even as Abraham believed God, and it was **accounted** to him for righteousness."* This means that *"righteousness"* has been put on his account. It is just like when you have a million dollars and you put it into your bank. That money is there. It is in your account. It has been reckoned. It has been imputed to you. It is on the books of your bank.

When Abraham had no children and God told him he would have children like the stars in Heaven and the sand on the seashore, Abraham believed God. God said to Abraham in effect, *"That is good enough for Me. You have righteousness. You have a righteous standing before me. You are going to be the sample of believers all through the ages."* So Abraham has been this sample. That is what it means to be reckoned righteous by faith. It was reckoned unto Abraham by *"faith,"* not by what he did. That was the story in Genesis 15.

Genuine Faith Produced Works

In Genesis 22, Abraham's faith produced works. That is when he took his promised son to a mountain as a sacrifice.

- **Genesis 22:2**
  And he said, **Take now thy son**, thine only *son* Isaac, whom thou lovest, and get thee into the land of Moriah; **and offer him there for a burnt offering** upon one of the mountains which I will tell thee of.

Human sacrifice was revealed by God as not acceptable. It was condemned as murder. God was testing Abraham when He told him to offer up his son Isaac. It was a test of his faith. God had told him his children would be into the millions, as the sand of the sea. Both believing Jews and believing Gentiles are all part of Abraham's "*seed.*"

- **Galatians 3:16**
  Now **to Abraham and his Seed were the promises made. He saith not, And to seeds, as of many; but as of one, And to thy Seed, which is Christ.**

"*Christ*" is the answer to the Jew. He is the answer to the Gentiles. He is the answer to the whole world. Abraham believed God and it was counted and reckoned unto him for righteousness when he actually took his son up to Mount Moriah in the 22nd chapter of Genesis and obeyed God. It showed by what he did, that he believed the Lord. His works showed that his faith was genuine. He believed God when He told him that he would have millions and millions of children.

Abraham's Tremendous Faith

Abraham believed God meant it, and was not going to back down one inch. Abraham believed so strongly in the Lord's promise that if Isaac died, God would raise him up, which he did "*in a figure*" (Hebrews 11:19). That is tremendous "*faith.*"

We who are saved must have that kind of faith. When we trust in the Lord Jesus Christ, we might not be able to understand things completely. We do not understand how sinners such as all of us are can be declared to be absolutely righteous before God by simple, yet genuine faith in the Saviour, Who shed His blood as a payment for the sins of the world. This is something we cannot fully comprehend. We have to by faith believe that this is what has happened to us who are born-again. We walk by faith and not by sight.

Romans 4:4

"Now to him that worketh is the reward not reckoned of grace, but of debt" If you work for somebody, you get a salary. You get paid. Your employer owes you a *"debt."* If it is so much an hour, or so much a week, or so much a month, whatever your salary is, he owes you something. It is not *"reckoned of grace."* It is not because he likes you and therefore wants to give you some money.

This is not what happened to Abraham. If he worked for this righteousness, then God would owe him something. Since he did not work for it, God is not indebted to Abraham or to any of us. Our *"reward"* of salvation and eternal life is by God's grace, and not by our works.

What if you get some gifts for Christmas, or your birthday, or New Years, or some other occasion? What if someone gives you a new car, a new hat, or a new coat? You did not work for it. That would be grace, getting something you did not deserve or work for.

Suppose, however, you put in eight hours of work and you get so many dollars per hour. At the end of your week, you expect your employer to pay you what he owes you. That is a *"debt."* God is not indebted to anybody. We cannot say, *"I worked for your salvation, Lord, so now you must take me to Heaven."*

Works Cannot Take Us to Heaven

If we got what we deserved, every one of us would be sent to the Lake of Fire for sure (Revelation 20:15). Nobody can work hard enough to get to Heaven.

It is the Lord Jesus Christ Who did all that was required by God the Father to make possible the salvation of the world.

Two Types of Religions

There are two basic types of religions in this world. The first type speaks of various works for their adherents and says "Do." The Christian faith speaks to all the sinners of the world concerning Christ's finished work on the cross of Calvary and says "Done."

Romans 4:5

"But to him that worketh not, but believeth on him that justifieth the ungodly, his faith is counted for righteousness"   Here is this word *"counted"* again.   It is the Greek word, LOGIZOMAI. This does not mean that after we are saved God does not want us to *"work"* for Him.   When Paul speaks of *"worketh not,"* he is not talking about working in order to receive our salvation.   After we are saved it is certain that we ought to work for the Lord.   As the hymn writer has penned:

> *"Let us labor for the Master from the dawn till setting sun,*
> *Let us talk of all His wondrous love and care;*
> *Then when all of life is over and our work on earth is done,*
> *And the roll is called up yonder, I'll be there."*

After we have been regenerated by God's Holy Spirit, we must *"labor for the Master."*

"but believeth on him that justifieth the ungodly"

Only God Can Justify

God is in the *"justifying"* business. Remember, *"justification"* is *"a judicial declaration whereby God declares the saved sinners to be absolutely righteous in His eyes"*--just as righteous, just as clean, just as perfect, just as pure, and just as sinless as God's own Son. God is in the business of *"justifying the ungodly."*

Being *"ungodly"* is the condition of everyone who has never been redeemed by genuine faith in the Lord Jesus Christ.

- **Psalm 1:1**
  Blessed *is* the man that walketh not in the **counsel of the ungodly**, nor standeth in the way of sinners, nor sitteth in the seat of the scornful.

We have *"ungodly"* people all around us.

- **Psalm 1:4**
  The ungodly *are* not so: but *are* like the chaff which the wind driveth away.

They are like *"chaff."* They have no roots.

- **Psalm 1:5**
  Therefore **the ungodly shall not stand in the judgment**, nor sinners in the congregation of the righteous.

They are going to fall down. They will be sent to the burning fires of Hell.

- **Psalm 1:6**
  For the LORD knoweth the way of the righteous: but **the way of the ungodly shall perish**.

- **Romans 5:6**
  For when we were yet without strength, **in due time Christ died for the ungodly**.

If people do not recognize themselves to be *"ungodly,"* then, according to this verse, you would not think Christ *"died"* for you, because He *"died for the ungodly."*

Righteous or Ungodly?

Some people think they are righteous, not *"ungodly."* If this is the case, they do not think they have a need for a Saviour.

If we are not willing to assume the status of lost sheep, then He did not come to save us. He came to save sinners and *"ungodly."* One of the things about being saved is that we recognize we are sinners--lost, Hell-bound, and ungodly. Only those who recognize that they are sinners, lost, and undone, can have a Saviour. The righteous do not think they have a need of a Saviour, so they do not turn to Him in repentance and genuine faith.

The Lord Jesus gave us this principle. *"When Jesus heard it, he saith unto them, They that are whole have no need of the physician, but they that are sick: I came not to call the righteous, but sinners to repentance"* (Mark 2:17). If you come to the Great Physician, He will make you well. If you say, *"I am not sick, I do not need any physician. I do not need to go to the doctor,"* then you will stay lost because you have not come to the Saviour Who can redeem your soul.

There is a verse in Jude that has that word, *"ungodly,"* no less than 4 times.

- **Jude 15**

  To execute judgment upon all, and to convince all that are **ungodly** among them of all their **ungodly** deeds which they have **ungodly** committed, and of all their hard *speeches* which **ungodly** sinners have spoken against him.

  I tell you it's a terrible thing.

"His faith is counted for righteousness" The person who has saving *"faith"* in the Lord Jesus Christ, it is their *"faith"* that is *"counted"* or reckoned, for *"righteousness"* in the sight of God. This *"righteousness"* is recorded in the books of Heaven. Through this transaction, the Lord Jesus Christ as our Saviour can make us just before God and fit for Heaven.

Romans 4:6

"Even as David also describeth the blessedness of the man, unto whom God imputeth righteousness without works"

"Even as David also describeth the blessedness of the man" Paul was quoting from Psalm 32.

- **Psalm 32:1**

  A *Psalm* of David, Maschil. **Blessed** *is* *he* whose transgression *is* forgiven, *whose* sin *is* covered.

"Blessed" is the word for *"happy."* This is a truly wonderful condition with our sins both *"forgiven"* and *"covered"* by the blood of the Lord Jesus Christ.

- **Psalm 32:2**

  Blessed *is* **the man** unto whom the LORD imputeth not iniquity, and in whose spirit *there is* no guile.

It is a tremendous thing to be forgiven, saved, and set apart.

"Unto whom God imputeth righteousness without works," It is a blessing. The gospel song says: *"O happy day that fixed my choice On Thee, my Saviour and my God!"* David writes of this also in the Psalms.

Romans 4:7

"Saying, Blessed are they whose iniquities are forgiven, and whose sins are covered" The Greek word for *"forgiveness"* is APHIEMI. It has many meanings, such as:

> *"to send away; to bid going away or depart; of a husband divorcing his wife; to send forth, yield up, to expire; to let go, let alone, let be; to disregard; to leave, not to discuss now, (a topic); of teachers, writers and speakers; to omit, neglect; to let go, give up a debt, forgive, to remit; to give up, keep no longer; to permit, allow, not to hinder, to give up a thing to a person; to leave, go away from one; in order to go to another place; to depart from any one; to depart from one and leave him to himself so that all mutual claims are abandoned; to desert wrongfully; to go away leaving something behind; to leave one by not taking him as a companion; to leave on dying, leave behind one; to leave so that what is left may remain, leave remaining; abandon, leave destitute."*

The basic meaning is from APO (*"from,"* or *"away"*) and HIEMI (*"to send."*)

Do You Have God's Forgiveness?

If we have God's *"forgiveness"* by personal faith in His Son, all of our sins are *"sent away,"* never to be returned against us. Our sins are placed upon Christ. He has borne them on His own body on the cross of Calvary. That is a tremendously important truth.

- Matthew 9:2

  And, behold, they brought to him a man sick of the palsy, lying on a bed: and Jesus seeing their faith said unto the sick of the palsy; Son, be of good cheer; **thy sins be forgiven thee**.

This palsied man was in need of a physical healing, but the Lord Jesus Christ saw his spiritual need first and forgave his sins. That is what we need to see in those with whom we live.

- Luke 7:47

  Wherefore I say unto thee, Her sins, which are many, **are forgiven**; for she loved much: but to whom little is **forgiven**, *the same* loveth little.

The woman in this passage was a wicked woman, probably a woman of the street. She came to the Lord Jesus Christ, then she washed His feet with her tears in her eyes, and dried them with the hairs of her head. The Lord Jesus said to these who were gathered around that *"her sins, which are many, are forgiven."* That is wonderful. The evangelist who led one of our former pastors to Christ had just this one word on his tombstone, *"forgiven."* It is wonderful when God can forgive our sins through His Son's redemption.

- **Ephesians 4:32**
  And be ye kind one to another, tenderhearted, **forgiving one another,** even as God for Christ's sake **hath forgiven you.**

It is for *"Christ's sake"* that we have forgiveness because of His death on Calvary for us.

- **Colossians 2:13**
  And you, being dead in your sins and the uncircumcision of your flesh, hath he quickened together with him, **having forgiven you all trespasses;**

All Trespasses Forgiven

For the born-again Christian, *"all trespasses"* have been *"forgiven,"* whether past, present, or future. This is illustrated with Mephibosheth.

- **2 Samuel 9:13**
  So Mephibosheth dwelt in Jerusalem: for **he did eat continually at the king's table; and was lame on both his feet.**

Mephibosheth was the son of Jonathan, King David's friend. When Mephibosheth was five years old, he was being carried by his nurse (2 Samuel 4:4). As they were fleeing, after receiving some bad news, his nurse dropped him. That is when he became *"lame on both his feet."* Yet, even though *"lame,"* he did *"eat continually at the king's table."* This is a picture of pure grace and love.

Though David was King Saul's enemy, David loved Jonathan, Saul's son. David made a covenant with Jonathan that he would be kind to Jonathan and his seed. Jonathan should have been king after Saul, but God chose David. So David, in his grace, took this crippled boy, Mephibosheth, morning, noon, and night, and fed him at his table. He did not mind his crippled legs.

This is an illustration of what the Lord Jesus Christ has done to those who have trusted Him as Saviour. Think of the table cloth that covered the crippled feet of Mephibosheth. That is like the covering that God has given to us who are *"in Christ."* When we are saved and *"in Christ,"* our sins are covered just as Mephibosheth's poor lame feet were covered.   David's grace toward Mephibosheth is like God's grace toward us.

- **Psalm 85:2**
  Thou hast **forgiven** the iniquity of thy people, thou hast covered all their sin. Selah.
- **Psalm 140:7**
  O GOD the Lord, the strength of my salvation, thou hast **covered my head** in the day of battle.

Our Heads Must Be Covered

It is very important that our *"heads"* are covered when we are in *"battle."* The *"head"* is very important. A wound to the *"head"* usually kills instantly.

- **Isaiah 61:10**
  I will greatly rejoice in the LORD, my soul shall be joyful in my God; for he hath clothed me with the garments of salvation, **he hath covered me with the robe of righteousness**, as a bridegroom decketh *himself* with ornaments, and as a bride adorneth *herself* with her jewels.

There are many different pictures of God's dealing with sin. In the Old Testament it is often spoken of as a *"covering."* It is also spoken of as a *"removal."* *"As far as the east is from the west, so far hath he **removed** our transgressions from us"* (Psalm 103:12).

In the New Testament, however, when the Lord Jesus Christ came, we see that He is the *"Lamb of God which **taketh away** the sin of the world"* (John 1:29b). The Greek word for *"taketh away"* is AIRO. It has many meanings:

> *"to raise up, elevate, lift up; to raise from the ground, take up stones; to raise upwards, elevate, lift up the hand; to draw up: a fish; to take upon one's self and carry what has been raised up, to bear; to bear away what has been raised, carry off; to move from its place; to take off or away what is attached to anything; to remove; to carry off, carry away with one; to appropriate what is taken; to take away from another what is his or what is committed to him, to take by force; to take and apply to any use; to take from among the living, either by a natural death, or by violence; cause to cease."*

If a person has been born-again by saving faith in the Lord Jesus Christ, He has *"taken away, carried off, removed, and moved from their place"* all of his sins. He no longer has to bear these sins himself. He no longer has to endure them.

He no longer has to spend an eternity in the Lake of Fire (Revelation 20:14-15). The Lord Jesus Christ, the *"Lamb of God"* has forgiven him all his sins. Praise God for the *"Lamb"*!

Romans 4:8

"Blessed *is* the man to whom the Lord will not impute

sin" This is a quotation from David in the Psalms.

- **Psalm 32:2**
  Blessed *is* the man unto whom the LORD imputeth not iniquity, and in whose spirit *there is* no guile.

The apostle Paul also talked about the Lord not *"imputing"* sins.

- **2 Corinthians 5:19**
  To wit, that God was in Christ, reconciling the world unto himself, **not imputing their trespasses unto them**; and hath committed unto us the word of reconciliation.

Trespasses Not Imputed

Because the Lord Jesus Christ died for us, if we have trusted Him as our Saviour, our *"trespasses"* are not *"imputed"* or reckoned against us.

- **James 2:23**
  And the scripture was fulfilled which saith, Abraham believed God, **and it was imputed unto him for righteousness**: and he was called the Friend of God.

It is a *"blessed"* man *"to whom the Lord will not impute sin."* The Greek word, MAKARIOS, *"blessed"* means *"happy."*

Are you sad? If you are sad, remember what the Lord Jesus Christ has done for you. Be happy if God has not *"imputed"* sin anymore to you. If you trust Him, your sins have been placed upon Him. The Lord Jesus Christ is your sin-bearer if you are trusting in Him as your personal Saviour. You no longer have your sin, He is the one Who bore your sins *"in His own body, on the tree"* (1 Peter 2:24).

Romans 4:9

"*Cometh* this blessedness then upon the circumcision *only,* or upon the uncircumcision also? for we say that faith was reckoned to Abraham for righteousness" The "*circumcision*" would refer to the Jews. Is this "*blessedness*" of faith, like Abraham's, only to the Jews? If this is only to the Jews, we who were Gentiles would be ruled out of it.

You see, Abraham was before the law of Moses. Moses is first spoken of in the book of Exodus, the second book of our Bible.

Justification Before Circumcision

Abraham was mentioned in Genesis, the first book of our Bible. This reckoning of "*blessedness*," or "*happiness*" in faith with the imputation of righteousness and justification of the ungodly, was performed on Abraham even before he had been "*circumcised.*"

Romans 4:10

"How was it then reckoned? when he was in circumcision, or in uncircumcision? Not in circumcision, but in uncircumcision" Here again, the faith of Abraham was exercised when he was "*in uncircumcision,*" not when he was "*in circumcision.*" This is an important point.

Abraham--Father of the Faithful

"*Abraham believed in the Lord; and He counted it to him for righteousness*" (Genesis 15:6). The "*token of the covenant*" of circumcision was given to Abraham and to his seed in Genesis 17:11, two chapters later. So, the faith exemplified in Abraham is for all, whether circumcised or uncircumcised, whether Jew or Gentile, whether bond or free. This is why Abraham can be considered as "*our father*" (Romans 4:12) even if we are Gentiles who have trusted in the Lord Jesus Christ.

That is not to say that the covenant theologians are right. They are wrong. I believe that the Scriptures teach what is called "*dispensationalism.*" The Bible is clear that Israel is separate from the church. Covenant theology, however, teaches that all the promises of Israel are fulfilled in the church. Therefore the "*church*" is identified with "*Israel.*" Harold Camping, president of Family Radio, heard on our local station WKDN, believes that there is no future for literal physical Israel. I believe that this teaching is wrong and unscriptural. The Bible teaches that there is a future for Israel. We will be seeing this clearly in Romans 9, 10, and 11. Romans 9 speaks of Israel's past. Romans 10 speaks of Israel's present. Romans 11 speaks of Israel's future.

The covenant theology teaches that Israel has now become the church. No. All the Old Testament promises that God made to Israel will be fulfilled by the children of Israel in the millennium. When God speaks about a King Who will sit on Mount Zion (Psalm 2:6) to reign for a thousand years in the Millennium, that will also be fulfilled. When God states in the Old Testament that the desert shall "*blossom as the rose*" (Isaiah 35:1) , that will be fulfilled in the Millennial reign of Christ. All these promises will be fulfilled.

Covenant Theology Is Unscriptural

Covenant theology twists the Scriptures. They teach that saved people today are "spiritual Israel." This means that there is no longer any national Israel. There are no longer any promises for national Israel. All the promises of Israel will be fulfilled by the church. These views are not Scriptural.

Abraham is the "*father*" (Romans 4:16) of all believers, both Old Testament and New Testament, in that he had absolute and genuine faith in the promises and the Words of God. He had faith in all the Lord had promised him. He believed that his seed would be as many as the stars in Heaven and the sands on the shore, even after he was told to sacrifice his own son. That is `why Abraham is "*father of us all*" (Romans 4:16). It is not that we all of a sudden become Jews. It was before his circumcision that his "*faith was reckoned*" to him "*for righteousness.*"

Romans 4:11

"And he received the sign of circumcision, a seal of the righteousness of the faith which *he had yet* **being uncircumcised: that he might be the father of all them that believe, though they be not circumcised; that righteousness might be imputed unto them also"**

Abraham received "*the sign of circumcision*" in Genesis 17:11. It is here called "*a seal of the righteousness of the faith.*" Notice that Abraham had the "*faith*" before he was "*circumcised.*" The "*faith*" of Abraham is found in Genesis 15:6. His "*circumcision*" was not mentioned until Genesis 17:11.

Abraham--Father of the Believers

If you are trusting in Christ as your Saviour, if you are a born-again believer today, Abraham is your "*father.*" He is the "*father of all them that believe,*" whether Jews or Gentiles. Not that we are Jews, but he is the "*father*" of the faithful.

This does not refer to the physical line of Israel. Even though people were Gentiles, "*righteousness might be imputed unto them also*" by "*faith.*" God was very specific and exact. He wanted to make it plain that salvation in the Old Testament was by "*faith*" and salvation in the New Testament was also by "*faith.*"

Many people get confused about the law of Moses and its required sacrifices. They wonder if salvation was by works. No!

O.T. Salvation Also by Faith

Salvation in the Old Testament was still by "*faith,*" looking forward to the death of Christ on the cross as the "*Lamb of God*" (John 1:29). That "*Lamb*" would come one day and shed His blood for the forgiveness of the sins of the world.

That is what it said back in Romans chapter 3.

- **Romans 3:25**
  Whom God hath set forth to be a propitiation through faith in his blood, to declare his righteousness for **the remission of sins that are past, through the forbearance of God;**
  The Lord Jesus was the sacrifice for the sins of the Old Testament saints as well as the New Testament saints. The Old Testament saints looked forward. The New Testament saints look backward.

- **Genesis 17:10**
  This is my covenant, which ye shall keep, between me and you and thy seed after thee; **Every man child among you shall be circumcised.**
  That is referring to physical Israel, not Christians.

- **Exodus 31:13**
  Speak thou also unto the children of **Israel,** saying, **Verily my sabbaths ye shall keep: for it is a sign between me** and you throughout your generations; that ye may know that I am the LORD that doth sanctify you.
  This was for physical Israel.

  The Seventh Day Adventist are wrong by teaching that we should worship the Lord on Saturday during the church age. I had one of the callers come into our office of the "80" that called after the recent WKDN Halloween interview that I had. One of the ladies who called said she could not come in to pick up something because it was Saturday, the Sabbath day. She was a Seventh Day Adventist. I did not argue with her on the phone.

The Sabbath Was for Israel

The sign of the Sabbath, which is Saturday, was given to Israel. That day of worship was not given to the New Testament church. It was the New Testament practice to worship the Lord on Sunday, the first day of the week, which was the day of our Lord's resurrection (Matthew 28:1; Mark 16:2; Luke 24:1; John 20:1; John 20:19; Acts 20:7; 1 Corinthians 16:2).

The Saturday Sabbath, the 7th day of the week was a sign, like circumcision, to physical Israel. It has absolutely nothing to do with the church today.

- **Exodus 31:17**
  It is a sign between me and the children of Israel for ever: for in six days the LORD made Heaven and earth, and on the seventh day he rested, and was refreshed.
- **Isaiah 7:14**
  Therefore **the Lord himself shall give you a sign**; Behold, a virgin shall conceive, and bear a son, and shall call his name Immanuel.

The Jews seek after a sign, and that was what they are looking for.

- **Matthew 12:39**
  But he answered and said unto them, **An evil and adulterous generation seeketh after a sign**; and there shall no sign be given to it, but the sign of the prophet Jonas:
- **Matthew 26:48**
  Now **he that betrayed him gave them a sign**, saying, Whomsoever I shall kiss, that same is he: hold him fast.
- **1 Corinthians 1:22**
  For **the Jews require a sign**, and the Greeks seek after wisdom:

I believe that the sign of Jonas was that the Lord Jesus Christ would be in the tomb a literal *"three days and three nights"* (Matthew 12:40).

Wednesday, not Friday, Crucifixion

I believe the Lord Jesus Christ was crucified on Wednesday, not Friday. I believe that the Lord Jesus Christ was in the tomb for 72 hours. Most people say that *"three days and three nights"* means only a part of three days and nights. Our day begins at 12:00 midnight one day and goes to 12:00 midnight the next day. The Jewish day began at 6:00 p.m. one day and goes to 6:00 p.m. the next day.

The full 72 hours would be figured this way:

(1) The Lord was crucified on Wednesday, 9:00 a.m. to at least 3:00 p.m.

(2) He was buried Wednesday at about 6:00 p.m. which was really the end of Wednesday and the beginning of Thursday.

(3) Thursday was the Sabbath feast of Passover. This is why the dead bodies of those crucified had to be buried before 6:00 p.m. the end of Wednesday, which was the beginning of Thursday.

(4) Saturday was the weekly Sabbath that began at 6:00 p.m. Friday

evening and ended at 6:00 p.m. Saturday evening which was also Sunday morning.

(5) The Lord Jesus Christ arose at around 6:00 p.m. Saturday evening which was also considered to be Sunday morning, the first day of the week. In this way, *"three days and three nights"* (72 hours) were fulfilled literally.

In interpreting "three days and three nights," as in all Bible interpretation, we must make use of *"The Golden Rule of Bible Interpretation:"*

The Golden Rule of Bible Interpretation

"When the PLAIN SENSE of Scripture makes COMMON SENSE, SEEK NO OTHER SENSE. Therefore, take EVERY WORD at its primary, ordinary, usual, literal meaning, UNLESS the facts of the immediate context, studied in the light of related passages, and axiomatic and fundamental truths, indicate CLEARLY otherwise. God, in revealing His Word, neither intends nor permits the reader to be confused. He wants His children to understand." [Author Unknown]

Romans 4:12

"And the father of circumcision to them who are not of the circumcision only, but who also walk in the steps of that faith of our father Abraham, which *he had* being *yet* uncircumcised"

Abraham--Father of All Believers

Abraham is the *"father of all them that believe"* (Romans 4:11), whether they are Jews or Gentiles.

God is also the Father of the saved ones. But there is another fatherhood mentioned in the Scriptures by the Lord Jesus Christ Himself.

- **John 8:44**
  Ye are of *your* father the devil, and the lusts of your father ye will do. He was a murderer from the beginning, and abode not in the truth, because there is no truth in him. When he speaketh a lie, he speaketh of his own: for he is a liar, and the father of it.

The eternal Son of God; the eternal Saviour; He knew Abraham, and He held him up as a man of faith.

- **John 8:58**
  Jesus said unto them, Verily, verily, I say unto you, **Before Abraham was, I am**.

- **Galatians 3:8**
  And the scripture, foreseeing that **God** would justify the heathen through faith, **preached before the gospel unto Abraham,** *saying*, In thee shall all nations be blessed.

In this verse, it is clear that God "*preached before the gospel unto Abraham.*" God told Abraham about His Son, the Lord Jesus Christ our Saviour. When this "*gospel*" was presented, Abraham believed God. God told him about the "*Seed*" Who was the Lord Jesus Christ.

- **Genesis 22:18**
  And in thy Seed shall all the nations of the earth be blessed; because thou hast obeyed my voice.

- **Galatians 3:16**
  Now to Abraham and his Seed were the promises made. **He saith not, And to seeds, as of many; but as of one, And to thy Seed, which is Christ**.

The Gospel Unto Abraham

God preached the "*gospel*" unto Abraham. Abraham believed it just like you and I believe it today. It is the same "*gospel.*"

Notice, Abraham was not only the "*father*" of the Gentiles because he was a man of faith, but also the father of the Jews. It is not because they are Jews by flesh. They are going to be lost and bound for Hell, just as the Gentiles, unless they come to Abraham's Saviour, the Lord Jesus Christ.

Those who are of the "*circumcision,*" the Jews, can come to Christ. They can be saved if they walk in the steps of that faith of our father Abraham. That is why in Isaiah Chapter One, and in other places, God is ready to vomit out the Israelites because they just go through rituals. They offer blood offerings and sacrifices because it is a show and a sham (Isaiah 1:11-16).

It reminds me of so much of religion today. So much, even of Bible-believing Christianity, is sometimes just a show and a sham. It is not a greater church membership that God is looking for. It is our faith that is most important. God wants us to walk in the steps of Abraham who was a man of faith. He was a man who believed God's Words and walked therein.

That Greek word for "*steps*" is ICHNOS. It means: "*a footprint, track, footstep; in the NT, metaph. of imitating the example of any one.*" Normally, the Greek word for "*walk*" is PARIPATEO, "*to walk around.*" The Greek word used here, however, is STOICHEO. It means: "*to proceed in a row as the march of a soldier, go in order; metaph. to go on prosperously, to turn out well; to walk; to direct one's life, to live.*" We must walk "*in order*" in the steps of the faith of Abraham, step by step by step. It includes everything that comes our way. "*The just shall live by faith*" (Romans 1:17; Galatians 3:11; Hebrews 10:38). That is the kind of faith that saves.

As I said before, Abraham had two kinds of faith. (1) He had faith to believe that he was going to have as many children as the stars in Heaven and as the sand on the sea shore (Genesis 22:17), even before his son Isaac was married. (2) He had faith to believe that even if he sacrificed his son, in order to fulfill His promise, God would raise him up from the dead.

Righteousness By Genuine Faith

It is only God Who can justify us and declare us righteous by genuine faith in the Lord Jesus Christ. I am glad to have Abraham as my "*father*" in the faith. I do not mean a literal Jewish father because I am not a Jew. It is wonderful to be identified with a man of faith. He was not perfect. God did not say he was perfect. God points to that one event of how Abraham "*believed in the Lord and He counted it to him for righteousness*" (Genesis 15:6).

This is a transaction by the Lord and you if you are saved. You will never lose His salvation once you have received it. That is another thing that some people are afraid of. They think they have to hang on to something. No! It is the Lord Who hangs on to us once we are saved. It is a transaction that is on the books of Heaven. When our faith is planted firmly and clearly in the Lord Jesus Christ, it will never be taken off God's books. We are saved for eternity.

Romans 4:13

"For the promise, that he should be the heir of the world, *was* not to Abraham, or to his seed, through the law, but through the righteousness of faith" The promise to Abraham and the law of Moses are completely different. There is a vast distinction between the dispensation of promise and the dispensation of the law. There are also differences between the dispensations of law, grace, and the millennial kingdom. This whole idea of dispensationalism must be understood by us. God has different obediences and different things that He expected mankind to do in the various dispensations.

- **John 1:17**
  For the law was given by Moses, *but* grace and truth came by Jesus Christ.

The Biblical Dispensations

These are what we call dispensations or periods of testing of man. We have the dispensation of the law of Moses. We have the dispensation of the church or grace, which is the period we are in right now. Then there is the dispensation of the millennial kingdom age, the one-thousand-year reign of the Lord Jesus Christ on this earth. Those are three of the longest dispensations (law, grace, and kingdom). There are four other ones: innocence, conscience, human government, and promise.

Starting in the Garden of Eden with the dispensation of innocence, each of the dispensations ended with failure on the part of man. God gave Adam and Eve certain tasks and responsibilities to do, and they refused to do them. Because they sinned, they were expelled from the Garden of Eden. That was the end of the dispensation of innocence. The second dispensation is the age of conscience. The age of conscience ended with the flood in Chapter 6 of Genesis. After the flood came the dispensation of human government. That was ended at the Tower of Babel when God dispersed the nations. After that, God said I am going to select one man, Abraham. That began the dispensation of promise. That ended in the dispersion into Egypt and the slavery of the children of Israel. Then God raised up Moses. The dispensation of the law was then initiated. The final two dispensations are grace and the millennial kingdom. These are the seven dispensations only briefly listed. This is the best way to consider the entire Bible. It is called the dispensational approach.

When this verse says that "*the promise*" to Abraham was not "*through the law*," this refers to the law of Moses.

Three Parts of the Law of Moses

The Mosaic law had three parts: (1) the Ten Commandments; (2) the civil judgments; and (3) the sacrificial system.

The *"promise"* is not *"through the law, but through the righteousness of faith."* There is no exception. God keeps His promises. The promises were that Abraham should be heir.

- **2 Chronicles 6:15**
  Thou which hast kept with thy servant David my father that **which thou hast promised him**; and spakest with thy mouth, and hast fulfilled *it* with thine hand, as *it is* this day.

God is not a man to lie like we many times do. What He says, He fulfills.

- **1 Kings 8:56**
  Blessed *be* the LORD, that hath given rest unto his people Israel, **according to all that he promised**: there hath not failed one word of **all his good promise, which he promised** by the hand of Moses his servant.

God never fails to keep His promise. He promised Abraham a Seed, the Lord Jesus Christ, and He kept His promise (Galatians 3:16).

- **Romans 9:8-9**
  That is, They which are the children of the flesh, these *are* not the children of God: but **the children of the promise** are counted for the seed. For **this *is* the word of promise**, At this time will I come, and Sara shall have a son.

This was part of the promise.

- **Galatians 3:18**
  For if the inheritance *be* of the law, *it is* no more of promise: but **God gave *it* to Abraham by promise**.

The law of Moses required work and good deeds to fulfil. The *"Promise"* was given by faith. It did not require Abraham to do any work or good deed. God just said, in effect, *"I am going to do this all for you."* That is the difference between the promises of God and doing things by the law of Moses. God cannot lie. He keeps His promises.

- **Hebrews 10:23**
  Let us hold fast the profession of *our* faith without wavering; **(for he *is* faithful that promised**;)

If we do not believe that God is faithful in all of His promises, how can we believe that John 3:16 is going to come to pass. *"For God so loved the world, that he gave his only begotten Son, that whosoever believeth in him should not perish, but have everlasting life."* He keeps that promise, too. The promise of His coming in John 14:2-3, *"In my Father's house are many mansions: if it were not so, I would have told you. I go to prepare a place for you. And if I go and prepare a place for you, I will come again, and receive you unto myself; that where I am, there ye may be also."*

The promises of God are true and perfect. He never breaks them. God's promise that he should be heir of the world was not by the law of Moses. It came by the righteousness of faith.

Romans 4:14

"For if they which are of the law *be* **heirs, faith is made void, and the promise made of none effect"** The law of Moses demanded that people had to perform many deeds in order to fulfill its requirements. Those under the law had certain ordinances and sacrifices that they had to follow.

The Yearly Sacrifices of Israel

The Minimum Number of Blood Offerings

Required Yearly by the Nation of Israel

(Numbers 28:3--29:40; Leviticus 23:15-22)

Daily, Weekly, and Monthly Offerings

DAILY OFFERINGS: 730
WEEKLY OFFERINGS: 104
MONTHLY OFFERINGS: 132

The Seven Feasts of the Lord

FEAST OF THE PASSOVER: 1
FEAST OF UNLEAVENED BREAD: 77
FEAST OF FIRSTFRUITS: 11
FEAST OF PENTECOST: 13
FEAST OF TRUMPETS: 10
FEAST OF ATONEMENT: 10
FEAST OF TABERNACLES: . . . . <u>199</u>

<u>TOTAL YEARLY OFFERINGS</u>: . . **1,287**

Plus freewill offerings and sin and trespass offerings

<u>by individual Israelites</u> as needed and desired.

<u>The law of Moses involved works and many sacrifices. The promise was by faith</u>. Abraham was given a promise by God. He was told that he was going to have a child and, through that son, all the nations of the earth would be blessed by the Lord Jesus Christ.

- Galatians 3:17-18
  And this I say, *that* the covenant, that was confirmed before of God in Christ, the law, which was four hundred and thirty years after, cannot disannul, that it should make the promise of none effect. For if the inheritance *be* of the law, *it is* no more of promise: **but God gave *it* to Abraham by promise.**

This is a reference to Abraham in Genesis Chapters 12 and 15 when God promised him that he would have a seed in number as the stars in the heavens. The law of Moses came 430 years later. The promise was therefore 430 years before the law of Moses. It is very important for us to see that. If we are "*heirs*" by the law, then "*faith is made void.*" We would not need faith. We would not need to trust in the Lord by personal faith.

Romans 4:15

"Because the law worketh wrath: for where no law is, *there is* no transgression" Without the law there is "*no transgression.*" The word, "*transgression,*" means "*to step across.*" There must be something in the way in order to "*step across*" it. If we have a law that limits our speed to 35 mph, and we go 55 mph, we break the law. We "*step over*" the law. We "*transgress*" the law. Without the law there is no "*transgression.*" If there is no speed limit, you can go as fast as you want without breaking any law.

We have laws against adultery. It does not seem to stop some people from breaking these laws, but there are such laws. There are laws against fornication, against murder, and against many other things. That does not stop some people from transgressing these laws.

"The law worketh wrath" There are elements of "*wrath*" connected with the "*law*" of Moses. The law of Moses was given in Exodus 19.

- Exodus 19:8
  And all the people answered together, and said, **All that the LORD hath spoken we will do**. And Moses returned the words of the people unto the LORD.

This is what the people of Israel said. They wanted to "*do*" something. God promised Abraham a seed by faith. They were not satisfied with faith. They wanted to work their way to God's acceptance.

The Lord Jesus Christ Paid It All

As we have said before there are two kinds of religions in the world. One that says you have to do something in order to be saved. The other, the Christian faith, says it is done. Salvation has been finished by the Lord Jesus Christ. He paid it all.

- **John 19:30**
  When Jesus therefore had received the vinegar, he said, **It is finished**: and he bowed his head, and gave up the ghost.

"*It is finished*" is just one word in the Greek. It is TETELESTAI. This verb is in the Greek perfect tense. It refers to something that has been finished in the past with the results continuing into the present and on into the future as well. There is nothing that we can add to the finished work of our Saviour. The Lord Jesus Christ finished the work of redemption. The Jews wanted to do something to earn their salvation.

- **Exodus 20:11-18**
  For *in* six days the LORD made Heaven and earth, the sea, and all that in them *is*, and rested the seventh day: wherefore the LORD blessed the Sabbath day, and hallowed it. Honour thy father and thy mother: that thy days may be long upon the land which the LORD thy God giveth thee. Thou shalt not kill. Thou shalt not commit adultery. Thou shalt not steal. Thou shalt not bear false witness against thy neighbour. Thou shalt not covet thy neighbour's house, thou shalt not covet thy neighbour's wife, nor his manservant, nor his maidservant, nor his ox, nor his ass, nor any thing that *is* thy neighbour's. **And all the people saw the thunderings, and the lightnings, and the noise of the trumpet, and the mountain smoking: and when the people saw *it*, they removed, and stood afar off**.

Here is "*wrath*" right here at the giving of the ten commandments section of the law of Moses.

- **Exodus 19:13**
  There shall not an hand touch it, but he shall surely be stoned, or shot through; whether *it be* beast or man, it shall not live: when the trumpet soundeth long, they shall come up to the mount.

The "*law worketh wrath*." The law is connected with death. Here is the Lord Himself up on Mount Sinai giving the law of Moses. The people could not touch that mount or they would die.

- **Exodus 19:16**
  And it came to pass on the third day in the morning, **that there were thunders and lightnings, and a thick cloud upon the mount, and the voice of the trumpet exceeding loud; so that all the people that** *was* **in the camp trembled.**

They were afraid of God because He could not be approached. He is a holy God, and they were an unholy people.

- **Exodus 19:18**
  And **mount Sinai was altogether on a smoke, because the LORD descended upon it in fire: and the smoke thereof ascended as the smoke of a furnace, and the whole mount quaked greatly.**

The "*law worketh wrath.*" That certainly is true.

Romans 4:16

"Therefore *it is* **of faith, that** *it might be* **by grace; to the end the promise might be sure to all the seed; not to that only which is of the law, but to that also which is of the faith of Abraham; who is the father of us all"** This salvation must be "*by grace.*" God is giving us something we do not deserve. He is giving us unmerited favor. We don't deserve anything. If our eternal salvation came through the "*law*" of Moses, it would be by works. The children of Israel had to do something. They said: "*All that the LORD hath spoken, we will do*" (Exodus 19:8).

This verse teaches that those who are "*of the law*" of Moses, the Jews, can come to Christ by faith. The Gentiles also who are "*of the faith of Abraham,*" can also come to Christ by faith.

Thousands of Jews Were Saved

In the book of Acts, thousands of Jews believed on the Lord Jesus Christ.

We in this dispensation of grace can also have faith in Christ. In that way, Abraham can be the "*father of us all,*" both saved Jews and saved Gentiles. The basis of genuine salvation, either Old or New Testament, is faith.

- **Genesis 28:14**
  And thy seed shall be as the dust of the earth, and thou shalt spread abroad to the west, and to the east, and to the north, and to the south: and **in thee and in thy Seed shall all the families of the earth be blessed.**

Christ, the Promised Seed

God promised Abraham a Seed. Abraham believed God concerning this Seed which was the Lord Jesus Christ.

- **Galatians 3:16**
  Now to Abraham and his Seed were the promises made. He saith not, And to seeds, as of many; but **as of one, And to thy Seed, which is Christ.**

The Lord interprets Abraham's faith in the book of Genesis.

- **Genesis 26:4**
  And I will make thy seed to multiply as the stars of Heaven, and will give unto thy seed all these countries; and **in thy Seed shall all the nations of the earth be blessed;**

Blessing in the Lord Jesus Christ

They can all "*be blessed*" in Abraham's "*Seed*" and only that "*Seed*" Who is the Lord Jesus Christ. He is the promised "*Seed of Abraham.*" God can bless all the families of the earth only in the Lord Jesus Christ.

Romans 4:17

"(As it is written, I have made thee a father of many nations,) before him whom he believed, *even* God, who quickeneth the dead, and calleth those things which be not as though they were."

Verbal Bible Preservation

This quotation is from Genesis 17:5. Notice those words, *"as it is written."* The Greek word for this is GEGRAPTAI. It is a perfect tense, which speaks of something which has been written down with letters, but also continues to the present and on into the future. This teaches Bible preservation of the Words of Hebrew, Aramaic, and Greek. His Words are still preserved to this day based on the meaning of the Greek perfect tense.

Genesis 17:4-5 was written in the past. It still stands written today. I believe in the preservation of the Old Testament Hebrew and Aramaic Words that underlie our King James Bible, and in the New Testament Greek Words that underlie our King James Bible. Though it has been written in the past, God has promised to preserve it for the present, and He has kept that promise.

Perfect Tense Bible Preservation

That perfect tense is a help in proving both the inspiration and the preservation of God's Words.

The *"father of many nations"* is found in Genesis.

- **Genesis 17:4**
  As for me, behold, my covenant *is* with thee, and **thou shalt be a father of many nations**.

That is an actual quotation.

- **Genesis 17:5**
  Neither shall thy name any more be called Abram, but thy name shall be Abraham; **for a father of many nations have I made thee**.

"Abram" was his first name. God changed his name. *"Abram"* means father of

people. "*Ab*" means father, and "*ram*" refers to "*people*." ABRAHAM means "*father of multitudes*."

The "*multitudes*" referred to in this new name are not just the physical Jews. They are everyone of us who have genuinely accepted Jesus Christ as our Saviour. He is our "*father*" in the faith, not in the race, not in the flesh. He is the father of the faithful. That does not mean that the promises of the Jews are now fulfilled in the church.

Jews and the Church--Two Bodies

The Jews are one body of people and the church is another body of people.

God's earthly people are the Jews. One day, God is going to restore them to faith in Christ, the Messiah, when they see Him and behold Him. The saved ones in the church are God's Heavenly people. These two groups are distinct and separate.

The verse speaks of "*God who quickeneth the dead*." That word, quickeneth, means "*to make alive*."

- **John 5:21**

  For as **the Father raiseth up the dead**, and quickeneth *them*; even **so the Son quickeneth whom he will**.

God is able to raise the dead. We must believe this.

- **Ephesians 2:1**

  And **you *hath he quickened***, who were dead in trespasses and sins;

Everyone is spiritually dead before they come to Christ in a genuine faith in Christ.

- **Ephesians 2:5**

  Even when we were dead in sins, **hath quickened us together with Christ**, (by grace ye are saved;)

God the Father is able to "*quicken us*" and make us alive in Christ. That means that He can give us new life, eternal life in Christ.

- **Colossians 2:13**

  And you, being dead in your sins and the uncircumcision of your flesh, **hath he quickened together with him**, having forgiven you all trespasses;

God Sees the End In the Present

Another part of God's power is that He *"calleth those things which be not as though they were."* Those things that *"be not"* are things that have never yet transpired. God sees them as already fulfilled and *"as though they were"* already present. Just think of some of the things that He calls that *"were not,"* but as yet *"as though they were."*

- **Ephesians 1:4**
  According as **he hath chosen us in him before the foundation of the world,** that we should be holy and without blame before him in love:
  I believe in the corporate election or choice of the church as a body. There are all different explanations of election and so on.

Corporate Election

I believe in corporate election of the church as a body. Just as God elected as a corporate body the Jews. They are His chosen people. Not that every one of the Jews are genuine believers in God, but they are His chosen people. The same with the church, He has chosen the church as a body before the foundation of the world. As we believe in Christ as our Saviour, we become members of that chosen body that He chose *"before the foundation of the world."*

That is an illustration of something that was as good as completed, even before it came to pass.

- **1 Peter 1:19-20**
  But with the precious blood of Christ, as of a lamb without blemish and without spot: **Who verily was foreordained before the foundation of the world,** but was manifest in these last times for you,
  We are redeemed by the *"precious blood of Christ"* Who, though He was *"foreordained before the foundation of the world,"* the redemption price was just as good as paid in advance.

The Cross in God's Mind

When Abraham was living, in God's mind, the Lord Jesus Christ, His Son, had already come and paid for Abraham's sins by the shedding of His blood in His death on Calvary, even though it had never yet happened.

• **Revelation 13:8**
And all that dwell upon the earth shall worship him, whose names are not written in **the book of life of the Lamb slain from the foundation of the world**.

Here again is God's Lamb, the Lord Jesus Christ, Who was *"slain from the foundation of the world"* in the mind of God, long before it happened.

When Was The Lamb Slain?

The Lord Jesus was already slain at Calvary even before *"God was manifest in the flesh"* (1 Timothy 3:16). But God saw this thing as an accomplished fact, the *"Lamb slain from the foundation of the world."*

That is why every one of the Old Testament believers, if they had the faith of Abraham, looking forward to that Seed, Christ, could be saved by that personal faith. If they were saved, it was not by keeping the law, but by faith in the Seed of Abraham. Even as we who are saved are saved by faith looking back on the Lord Jesus Christ's sacrifice Who, in the mind of God, was *"slain from the foundation of the world"* for our sins.

• **Revelation 17:8**
The beast that thou sawest was, and is not; and shall ascend out of the bottomless pit, and go into perdition: and they that dwell on the earth shall wonder, whose names were not written in the **book of life from the foundation of the world**, when they behold the beast that was, and is not, and yet is.

Here's the *"book of life"* made *"from before the foundation of the world."* The ones who have rejected the Lord Jesus Christ were not written in that *"book of life."* God knew who was going to believe, and who was not going to believe. So, their names were not there. That is most interesting.

Romans 4:18

"Who against hope believed in hope, that he might become the father of many nations, according to that which was spoken, So shall thy seed be."

Abraham had no logical or reasonable "*hope*" that he was going to become "*the father of many nations.*" Yet he "*believed*" in that "*hope*" and promise which God spoke, "*So shall thy seed be.*" He was totally unable to have any children. There was no hope, yet Abraham believed God's promise that he would have many children.

We were invited to a wedding recently of a couple that was in their 80's. I am sure that we would have never assumed that they were going to have a child. The bride had never been married before. The husband was a widower. As I mentioned before, they were both in their 80's. Why is there any difference in Abraham's case? Abraham was in his 100's. Sarah was in her 90's. "*Against hope*" he believed what God promised him. In the natural, we would never believe they were going to have a child at that age. You can see how much faith Abraham really had. It is "*against*" all "*hope*" to think that he was going to be a father at 100 years of age with his wife Sarah being in her 90's. This is against all hope.

The promise to Abraham was "*spoken.*" Who spoke it? It was "*spoken*" by the Lord Himself.

God's Words Preserved Today

We must believe the Words that the Lord speaks today, too. We must believe we have God's Hebrew, Aramaic, and Greek Words preserved for us even today. That is why in our King James Bible, I believe those preserved Words were accurately translated for us in the English language. So we can say that in the King James Bible we have God's Words kept intact in English.

Originally, the Scriptures come from Hebrew, Aramaic, and Greek, but this translation must be accurate so that we can believe God's Words in our mother tongue also. Abraham believed that which was "*spoken*" by God. That settled it.

- **Genesis 15:5-6**
  And he brought him forth abroad, and said, **Look now toward Heaven, and tell the stars, if thou be able to number them**: and he said unto him, **So shall thy seed be. And he believed in the LORD; and he counted it to him for righteousness.**
  There are billions of stars. In fact there are billions of galaxies. Abraham believed the Words that God spoke to him.

Romans 4:19

"And being not weak in faith, he considered not his own body now dead, when he was about an hundred years old, neither yet the deadness of Sara's womb:"

"And being not weak in faith" Abraham is now about a *"hundred years old."* Despite his age and the *"deadness of Sara's womb,"* he was still *"not weak in faith."* We, as Abraham, must be strong *"in faith."* If some people come along to you and ask, *"Why are you believing the Bible?"* do not be *"weak in faith."* Be strong in faith and say, *"I believe the Bible because it is God's Book."* It is not a matter of reason, but a matter of *"faith."*

Need Salvation Be "Reasonable"?

We are not saved by reason. It is not reasonable for us to believe that by faith in the Lord Jesus Christ we can have forgiveness of sins, be righteous in God's eyes, and be taken to Heaven when we die. It is not reasonable that the Lord Jesus Christ could die in our place for our sins, and the sins of the whole world, and that those that believe on Him could be saved for all eternity. That is not reasonable, but it is by faith that we accept it.

"He considered not his own body now dead, when he was about an hundred years old" Abraham just trusted the Lord. The Lord said He was going to do this, and Abraham believed the Lord was able. Do you believe the Lord could create this universe? Well, He did it. You have to believe it. He did it. If you were talking to the Lord before He created the universe, the billions of stars, the moon, and the planets, would you believe He could do it? That is the issue. *"In the beginning God created the Heaven and the earth"* (Genesis 1:1). If you take those first few words, *"In the beginning God,"* you have the whole thing. If you trust in the Powerful, Omnipotent God, all the rest is easy.

"neither yet the deadness of Sara's womb"

- Genesis 17:17

Then Abraham fell upon his face, and laughed, and said in his heart, **Shall** *a child* **be born unto him that is an hundred years old? and shall Sarah, that is ninety years old, bear?**

- Genesis 18:11

Now **Abraham and Sarah** *were* **old** *and* **well stricken in age;** *and* it ceased to be with Sarah after the manner of women.

Both Abraham and Sarah *"laughed."* *"Sarah laughed within herself"* (Genesis 18:12), but the Lord knew that she laughed. He reminded her that she laughed (Genesis 18:14). In other words she did not believe.

You know what happened to John the Baptist's father, Zacharias, when he did not believe? God told him his name would be John. Zacharias objected to the angel's announcement saying he was an *"old man"* and his wife was *"well stricken in years"* (Luke 1:18). Because he did not believe God's *"Words"* (Luke 1:20), Zacharias was made *"dumb"* and *"not able to speak"* until the baby was born. When Zacharias agreed to name his son John, *"his mouth was opened,"* and he could speak again (Luke 1:63-64). He finally had faith in the Words of the Lord.

- Genesis 18:13

And the LORD said unto Abraham, **Wherefore did Sarah laugh, saying,** Shall I of a surety bear a child, which am old?

- Genesis 18:14

Is any thing too hard for the LORD? At the time appointed I will return unto thee, according to the time of life, and **Sarah shall have a son.**

Sarah was the one who would have this promised son, not Hagar. She was going to have a son. *"Is anything too hard for the LORD?"*

When you finally have genuine faith in the Lord God of Heaven and earth, and in His Son, the Lord Jesus Christ, there's not a single thing *"too hard"* for Him. The only thing that is *"too hard"* for Him is to do something against His will. The only thing *"too hard"* for Him is to sin. It is against His holy character. Other than that, nothing is *"too hard for the Lord"*!

Romans 4:20

"He staggered not at the promise of God through unbelief; but was strong in faith, giving glory to God"

Abraham *"staggered not."* That is a good word, is it not? He did not have a lack of faith. He believed the promises of God. He did not deny any of them. Even though it was almost impossible, against all hope, he did not *"stagger"* through unbelief.

"But was strong in faith, giving glory to God" We must be *"strong."* What God promises, He is going to fulfill.

- **Titus 1:2**
  In hope of eternal life, which **God, that cannot lie, promised** before the world began;
- **1 Corinthians 16:13**
  Watch ye, stand fast in the faith, quit you like men, **be strong**.

Abraham was *"strong in faith."* Our faith cannot be weak. It must be strong.

- **Ephesians 6:10**
  Finally, my brethren, **be strong in the Lord**, and in the power of his might.
- **2 Timothy 2:1**
  Thou therefore, my son, **be strong in the grace that is in Christ Jesus**.

What is it that strengthens our bodies? Good food, good vitamins, good minerals, good water and all the things we need to nourish our bodies.

The Words of God Strengthen Us

What is it that strengthens our soul and makes it strong? It is the Words of God. It is faith. It is prayer. It is fellowship. It is gathering together. It is hearing and listening and believing the Words of God.

Many people *"stagger."* Many people do not believe the Lord. Remember the sons of Noah? Noah said it was going to rain. He preached that for 120 years. Noah was an old man when he died. He lived to be 930. He preached for 120 years that God had promised it was going to rain on this earth. There was going to be a flood that would cover the entire earth. He preached that God told him to build an ark, a huge ship. This ark was going to be able to carry a male and female of every animal on earth. These animals could be young. Noah did not have to carry an adult hippopotamus. You could have a baby hippopotamus. You do not have to have full grown giraffes. You can have baby giraffes. God said two of every animal will go into the ark. Noah was to provide the food (Genesis 6:21). Then God was going to send rain. The people probably began to laugh at Noah. He was a preacher of righteousness (2 Peter 2:5), and they did not believe him. The people did not come into the ark. The only ones who believed him were his wife, his three sons, and their three wives.

Sometimes wives do not believe husbands, and husbands do not believe wives. That is a sad thing when you have a split home. Sometimes our sons or daughters-in-law do not believe, but Noah's sons and daughters-in-law believed this preacher and came into the ark.

Strong Faith Needed

We must have faith in what the Lord has promised. Abraham was *"strong in faith."*

Romans 4:21

"And being fully persuaded that, what he had promised, he was able also to perform"

Four Powerful Words

There are four powerful words in this verse: (1) *"persuaded,"* (2) *"promised,"* (3) *"able,"* and (4) *"perform."*

- **Romans 8:38**
  For I am **persuaded**, that neither death, nor life, nor angels, nor principalities, nor powers, nor things present, nor things to come,

The Greek word for *"persuaded"* means:

*"to bear or bring full, to make full; to cause a thing to be shown to the full; to fulfil the ministry in every part; to carry through to the end, accomplish; things that have been accomplished; to fill one with any thought, conviction, or inclination; to make one certain, to persuade, convince one; to be persuaded, **persuaded, fully convinced or assured**; to render inclined or bent on."*

We Must Be Persuaded

Paul was *"persuaded"* and that is why he was such a good apostle. That is why he could take such beatings and endure starvation as he preached throughout the world. He was stoned, put in prison, and beaten, but he was persuaded that nobody was going to keep him from the love of God. I hope that you and I are persuaded that same way.

- **2 Timothy 1:12**
  For the which cause I also suffer these things: nevertheless I am not ashamed: for I know whom I have believed, and am **persuaded** that he is able to keep that which I have committed unto him against that day.

This was a promise from God.

- **2 Chronicles 6:15**
  Thou which hast kept with thy servant David my father that which thou hast promised him; **and spakest with thy mouth, and hast fulfilled *it* with thine hand**, as *it is* this day.

God spoke with His *"mouth,"* and fulfilled it with His *"hand."*

God Keeps His Promises

Sometimes we speak with our mouths and do not fulfill it with our hands and actions. We do not always do what we promise. God always keeps His *"promises."*

- **Titus 1:2**
  In hope of eternal life, which God, that cannot lie, **promised before the world began;**

Look at that word *"able."* You may promise your spouse or your child a million dollars, but are you able to fulfill that promise? You can promise anything, but being able to fulfill the promise is two different things.

God is able. *"Is anything too hard for the Lord?"* He is able.

- **Ephesians 3:20**
  Now unto **him that is able** to do exceeding abundantly above all that we ask or think, according to the power that worketh in us,
- **Philippians 3:21**
  Who shall change our vile body, that it may be fashioned like unto his glorious body, according to the working whereby **he is able** even to subdue all things unto himself.

God is able to change these bodies into resurrected bodies.

- **2 Timothy 1:12**
  For the which cause I also suffer these things: nevertheless I am not ashamed: for I know whom I have believed, and am persuaded that **he is able** to keep that which I have committed unto him against that day.

God is able to keep us, so we are not lost, once we come to our Saviour by personal, saving faith in Him.

- **Hebrews 7:25**
  Wherefore **he is able also to save** them to the uttermost that come unto God by him, seeing he ever liveth to make intercession for them.

God is "*able to save.*" As they say "*from the uttermost to the guttermost.*" He can save all kinds, all shapes, all varieties of people. The ones that are the hardest for the Lord, He is able to save "*to the uttermost.*"

- **Jude 24**
  Now unto **him that is able to keep you from falling**, and to present *you* faultless before the presence of his glory with exceeding joy,

God is able. How He is able to present sinners, such as we are, faultless in His sight before the presence of His Glory, is amazing. It must be a matter of faith. God promised it, and it is in His Word.

Then notice the fourth word, "*also to perform.*"

- **Deuteronomy 9:5**
  Not for thy righteousness, or for the uprightness of thine heart, dost thou go to possess their land: but for the wickedness of these nations the LORD thy God doth drive them out from before thee, and **that he may perform the word which the LORD sware unto thy fathers, Abraham, Isaac, and Jacob.**

God is a performing God.

- **Jeremiah 1:12**
  Then said the LORD unto me, Thou hast well seen: for **I will hasten my word to perform it.**

He performs that which has been promised.

- **Philippians 1:6**
  Being confident of this very thing, that he which hath begun a
  good work in you **will perform** *it* **until the day of Jesus
  Christ:**
  If we're saved, we have the Holy Spirit within us. The Lord is going to
  fulfill His promise and save us to the uttermost until we see Him in Glory in
  Heaven.

Romans 4:22

**"And therefore it was imputed to him for righteous-
ness."** Notice the word, *"therefore."* It means *"because of something."* The
teaching of this verse was made possible because of verse 21, *"And being fully
persuaded that, what He had promised, He was able also to perform."* This
faith, this persuasion, that is the basis of this *"imputation to him for
righteousness."*

What Is Imputation?

The Greek word for "impute" is LOGIZOMAI. It means:

*"to reckon, count, compute, calculate, count over; to take into
account, to make an account of; metaph. to pass to one's account,
to impute; a thing is reckoned as or to be something, i.e. as
availing for or equivalent to something, as having the like force
and weight; to number among, reckon with; to reckon or account;
to reckon inward, count up or weigh the reasons, to deliberate; by
reckoning up all the reasons, to gather or infer; to consider, take
into account, weigh, meditate on; to suppose, deem, judge; to
determine, purpose, decide."*

As I mentioned earlier, another way to understand this is as follows:
*"This word deals with reality. If I "logizomai" or reckon that my
bank book has $25 in it, it has $25 in it. Otherwise I am deceiving
myself. This word refers to facts not suppositions."*
This word appears in this chapter eight different times in the first twelve verses,
three more times at the end of this chapter, making eleven times altogether.
This word LOGIZOMAI is sometimes translated in our King James Bible
"imputed," sometimes *"reckoned"* and sometimes *"counted."* This is an
accountant's term. It is something that is *"counted"* as yours. It is put on your
account as a deposit that you now own.

God's Reckoning

By Abraham's *"faith"* God *"reckoned," "imputed,"* and *"put on his account"* absolute and perfect *"righteousness."* This is what God does to us today when we put our faith and trust in the Lord Jesus Christ. He *"reckons"* us as being absolutely righteous in His eyes. He *"counts"* us as righteous because of what the Lord Jesus Christ has done for us.

Romans 4:23

"Now it was not written for his sake alone, that it was imputed to him" God did not put this account into the Old Testament just so Abraham *"alone"* would know about it. Today, we are saved by the promise concerning Abraham's *"Seed"* Who is the Lord Jesus Christ. Even today we are saved by the promise of Abraham's promised Seed. In other words, the Lord Jesus Christ was the Seed. He was promised to Abraham. By faith in that Seed, the Lord Jesus Christ, we can be saved.

* John 3:16
  For God so loved the world, that he gave his only begotten Son, that **whosoever believeth in him** should not perish, but have everlasting life.

So, it wasn't written only for Abraham's sake, but it was for us too.

Romans 4:24

"But for us also, to whom it shall be imputed, if we believe on him that raised up Jesus our Lord from the dead" It was not just written for Abraham's sake, but also for those of us who are living today. This perfect "righteousness" from God Himself can be *"reckoned to our account."* When we genuinely *"believe on the Lord Jesus Christ,"* (Acts 16:31) God saves us. He also *"imputes"* to us His absolute *"righteousness."* That is what saves us.

Perfectly Righteous For Heaven

We cannot go to Heaven unless we are perfectly righteous in God's sight. He cannot take us there because He cannot permit sin in Heaven. So, how can we get there?

We must have absolute righteousness. How are we going to get it? By our own works? We cannot work for it because that is not enough. We cannot make ourselves righteous. The Lord Jesus Christ was perfectly righteous. When we trust in Him He "*reckons*," or "*imputes*," or "*counts*" His righteousness as our own, and we are saved.

- **Romans 4:11**
And he received the sign of circumcision, a seal of the righteousness of the faith which *he had yet* being uncircumcised: that he might be the father of all them that believe, though they be not circumcised; **that righteousness might be imputed unto them also**:

- **James 2:23**
And the scripture was fulfilled which saith, Abraham believed God, and **it was imputed unto him for righteousness**: and he was called the Friend of God.

The following verses state that God the Father "*raised up Jesus our Lord from the dead.*" Our Lord Jesus Christ's resurrection is a fact that must be believed.

- **Matthew 16:21**
From that time forth began Jesus to shew unto his disciples, how that he must go unto Jerusalem, and suffer many things of the elders and chief priests and scribes, and be killed, **and be raised again the third day**.

- **Acts 2:24**
Whom God hath raised up, **having loosed the pains of death**: because it was not possible that he should be holden of it.

- **Acts 2:32**
This Jesus hath God raised up, whereof we all are witnesses.

All throughout the New Testament we find the doctrine of the resurrection of the Lord Jesus Christ. It is a vitally important fact of history.

- **Acts 3:15**
And killed the Prince of life, **whom God hath raised from the dead**; whereof we are witnesses.

- **Acts 13:37**
But he, whom God raised again, saw no corruption.

- **Romans 8:11**
But if the Spirit of him that raised up Jesus from the dead dwell in you, **he that raised up Christ from the dead shall also quicken your mortal bodies by his Spirit that dwelleth in you**.

- Romans 10:9
  That if thou shalt confess with thy mouth the Lord Jesus, and shalt believe in thine heart that **God hath raised him from the dead**, thou shalt be saved.

Romans 4:25

"Who was delivered for our offences, and was raised again for our justification" It is the Lord Jesus Christ Who was *"delivered for our offences."* And it is He Who was *"raised again for our justification."* I believe that the first *"our"* in this verse refers to everyone in the entire world. The Lord Jesus Christ died for the sins of the whole world. The second *"our"* refers to those of us who are born-again by genuine faith in the Saviour.

What Does "Delivered" Mean?

The Greek word for "delivered" is PARADIDOMI. It means:

"to give into the hands (of another); to give over into (one's) power or use; to deliver to one something to keep, use, take care of, manage; to deliver up one to custody, to be judged, condemned, punished, scourged, tormented, put to death; to deliver up treacherously; by betrayal to cause one to be taken; to deliver one to be taught, moulded; to commit, to commend; to deliver verbally; commands, rites; to deliver by narrating, to report; to permit allow; when the fruit will allow that is when its ripeness permits; gives itself up, presents itself."

The Lord Jesus Christ was indeed *"delivered"* and *"betrayed"* by Judas Iscariot into the hands of evil men. Have you and I betrayed the Lord Jesus Christ? Have we denied Him before people? Have we said, as Peter, *"I know Him not"* (Luke 22:57)? I hope not. He was *"delivered"* up and betrayed into the hands of sinners. Why? *"For our offences,"* and because of our sins. That is why the Lord Jesus Christ was turned over to be crucified for the sins of the world. There are many verses that teach this unlimited atonement of our Saviour.

- Romans 5:5-6
  And hope maketh not ashamed; because the love of God is shed abroad in our hearts by the Holy Ghost which is given unto **us. For when we were yet without strength, in due time Christ died for the ungodly**.

- **Isaiah 53:5-6**
  But **he *was* wounded for our transgressions, *he was* bruised for our iniquities**: the chastisement of our peace *was* upon him; and with his stripes we are healed. All we like sheep have gone astray; we have turned every one to his own way; and the LORD hath laid on him the iniquity of us all.
- **1 Peter 2:24**
  Who his own self bare our sins in his own body on the tree, that we, being dead to sins, should live unto righteousness: by whose stripes ye were healed.

Notice that word, *"for"* in the phrase, *"for the ungodly"* in Romans 5:6 quoted above. There are two Greek words translated by the English word, *"for."* One is ANTI and the other is HUPER. The word ANTI means *"instead of or in the place of."* HUPER, which is used in Romans 5:6, means both *"in the place of"* and also *"for the benefit of."*

The Lord Jesus Christ was *"raised again for our justification."* The Greek word translated *"for"* in this phrase is DIA. It means variously:

"through, 1a) of place, with, in; 1b) of time; throughout; during; 1c) of means; by; by the means of; 2) through; 2a) the ground or reason by which something is or is not done; by reason of; on account of; because of for this reason; therefore; on this account."

The Lord Jesus Christ's resurrection was *"the ground or reason"* by which born-again Christians could be *"justified."*

God's Justification

The Greek word for *"justification"* is DIKAIOSIS. It means: *"**the act of** God declaring men free from guilt and acceptable to him."* In this act, God declares believing sinners to be absolutely righteous in His eyes.

- **Romans 3:24**
  Being justified freely by his grace through the redemption that is in Christ Jesus:
- **Romans 3:26**
  To declare, *I say*, at this time his righteousness: that he might be just, **and the justifier of him which believeth in Jesus**.

The Lord Jesus Christ had to be crucified for our sins, dying for us, in order that we might be declared righteous in the sight of God.

What Happened at Calvary?

Without the Lord Jesus Christ's being delivered for our offences, delivered for our sins, and crucified for the sins of the world, no one could ever be justified in God's sight. The death of the Lord Jesus Christ for the sins of the world had to take place. This is what happened at Calvary as He shed His blood for us sinners. We should be fully persuaded, as Abraham, that what God has promised He is able to perform it, and He will perform it.

Romans
Chapter Five

Romans 5:1

"Therefore being justified by faith, we have peace with God through our Lord Jesus Christ" Notice that first word, *"therefore."* Preachers have always said when you find the word *"therefore"* in the Bible, you should always look and see what it is *"there for."* It is a good little phrase. It is because of personal *"faith"* in the Lord Jesus Christ that we can be and are *"justified."* In Romans Chapter 5, there are at least seven results of justification by genuine faith in our *"Lord Jesus Christ."* In 5:1, we have *"peace with God."* In 5:2, we have *"access by faith"* and *"we rejoice in hope."* In 5:3, *"we glory in tribulation."* In 5:9, *"we are saved from wrath."* In 5:10, we are *"reconciled."* In 5:11, we have *"atonement."* All of these seven results are true of those who have been *"justified by faith"* in the Lord Jesus Christ. That is a wonderful gift to have.

But in addition to having this gift of being *"justified by faith,"* the Lord Jesus Christ also can give the genuine believer His true *"peace."* There are many verses on God's peace, but here are just a few of them.

- **Mark 4:39**
  And he arose, and rebuked the wind, and said unto the sea, **Peace, be still.** And the wind ceased, and there was a great calm.
- **Luke 2:14**
  Glory to God in the highest, and **on earth peace, good will toward men.**

"Peace" by faith in the Lord Jesus Christ can be received by all who trust in Him.

- **John 14:27**
  Peace I leave with you, my peace I give unto you: not as the world giveth, give I unto you. Let not your heart be troubled, neither let it be afraid.

- **John 16:33**
  These things I have spoken unto **you, that in me ye might have peace**. In the world ye shall have tribulation: but be of good cheer; I have overcome the world.

As far as the heathen are concerned, "*the way of peace have they not known*" (Romans 3:17). They have no peace at all. As it says in the book of Isaiah,

- **Isaiah 57:20-21**
  But the wicked *are* like the troubled sea, when it cannot rest, whose waters cast up mire and dirt. **There is no peace, saith my God, to the wicked.**

But we can have God's "*peace*" if we have been justified by faith in the Lord Jesus Christ.

"*Peace*: is a part of the "*fruit of the Spirit.*"

- **Galatians 5:22**
  But the fruit of the Spirit is love, joy, **peace**, longsuffering, gentleness, goodness, faith,

"*Peace*" is one of the manifestations of the fulness of God the Holy Spirit in the life of the yielded Christian.

- **Ephesians 2:14**
  For he is our peace, who hath made both one, and hath broken down the middle wall of partition *between us*;

Christ is "*our peace.*" The only reason anyone can have "peace with God" is because they have been justified by faith in the Lord Jesus Christ.

- **Ephesians 6:15**
  And **your feet shod with the preparation of the gospel of peace**;

The gospel brings "*peace*" to those who trust in Christ. It is a wonderful gospel that we have to proclaim.

- **Philippians 4:7**
  And **the peace of God**, which passeth all understanding, shall keep your hearts and minds through Christ Jesus.

God's "*peace*" can be manifested even in the midst of a troubled world.

I remember an illustration of peace I gave when I was preaching in Newton, Massachusetts. It was at the Immanuel Baptist Church, October 29, 1961. I preached on "*The Gift of Peace.*" After I preached on peace there was the biggest upset in that church that I had ever seen. There was almost a riot that took place. The deacons wanted to upset the preacher. They were stationed on the front row with their arms folded. They wanted me to make an announcement that there was a business meeting the following Wednesday or Thursday whenever it was, but we had already had a church business meeting announced for the same time, so it was impossible to make that particular announcement. They wanted me to make their announcement in the first part of the service. I saw them lined up, my son, D. A., Jr., had heard that they were all planned and ready to work their plan. They had already had a preliminary riot the Sunday night before. So I knew what was up. I planned to preach the sermon first and then make their announcement last. They were upset about that. At the end of the sermon I simply said something to this effect:

> *"Although I do not believe it is constitutional, and is at the same time as a properly called business meeting, and it was not announced properly in advance, yet, at the request of the clerk, I will read the announcement of the meeting."*

I read the announcement of their meeting, but that still did not stop them in their plan. They had already planned to come up onto the platform, storm the pulpit, and read this announcement themselves, thinking that I was not going to read it. As I said, the name of the sermon was *"The Gift of Peace,"* yet there was a complete absence of peace on that occasion. What a riot!

Little Birds Under Niagara Falls

One of the illustrations of peace I used in this sermon was that of a little bird in a nest under Niagara Falls just as quiet and peaceful. Though the water thundered down all around the little birds, they were still peaceful in their nest. The Lord Jesus Christ can give us *"peace"* by being justified by faith. It is a great promise that we have in Him.

Romans 5:2

"By whom also we have access by faith into this grace wherein we stand, and rejoice in hope of the glory of God"

"By whom also we have access by faith" This *"by whom"* goes back and refers to the Lord Jesus Christ. He is the One Who has *"justified"* those who have trusted in Him, thereby giving them His *"peace."* When the verse states that *"we have access,"* it refers only to those who are justified by genuine faith in the Lord Jesus Christ and have been born-again. It does not mean the world of lost people. They do not have any *"access"* to the Lord. They do not have *"peace."*

The Greek word for "access" is PROSAGOGE. It means: *"the act of bringing to, a moving to; access, approach; to God, i.e. that relationship with God whereby we are acceptable to him and have assurance that he is favourably disposed towards him."*

We must have *"access"* to different things. You can have a wireless phone, but without the proper hook-up you cannot to talk to anybody. You will not have "*access*" to anybody. You can have a computer, but if you do not have "*access*" to the World Wide Web, you cannot communicate with that Web. You may have a cell phone, but if you don't have a contract with a wireless network, it hooked up to the proper place, you cannot have "*access*" to anyone by using that phone.

How to Get Access to the Father

So we who are saved have "*access*" to the God of Heaven. The Lord has an open-door policy for believers who are saved. We who have been justified by faith have "*access*" to God by faith "*into this grace wherein we stand.*" It is a wonderful truth to have "*access*" to God the Father through genuine faith in the Lord Jesus Christ at any time, at any moment. Most of us do not have "*access*" to very important people in this world, whether it is the president of a company, the president of a college, the president of a bank, or the President of the United States. The Heavenly Father is not that way. We can have "*access*" to Him at any time. Our Father, though He is busy, He is never too busy for us who love Him and are saved.

This word, "*access*," is used only two other times in the New Testament:

* **Ephesians 2:18**
  For through him we both have **access by one Spirit** unto the Father.

* **Ephesians 3:11-12**
  According to the eternal purpose which he purposed in Christ Jesus our Lord: In whom we have boldness and **access with confidence** by the faith of him.

" into this grace wherein we stand" The Greek word for "*stand*" is HISTEMI. It means many things, such as:

"*to cause or make to stand, to place, put, set; to bid to stand by, [set up]; in the presence of others, in the midst, before judges, before members of the Sanhedrin; to place ; to make firm, fix establish; to cause a person or a thing to keep his or its place; to stand, be kept intact (of family, a kingdom), to escape in safety; to establish a thing, cause it to stand; to uphold or sustain the authority or force of anything; to set or place in a balance; to weigh: money to one (because in very early times before the introduction of coinage, the metals used to be weighed); to stand; to stand by or near; to stop, stand still, to stand immovable, stand firm; of the foundation of a building; to stand; continue safe and sound, stand unharmed, to stand ready or prepared; to be of a steadfast mind; of quality, one who does not hesitate, does not waiver."*

Eternal Security for the Saved

Talk about eternal security, the Bible teaches it right here. We *"stand."* We do not lose our salvation. Once we are saved, once we have regeneration, once the Holy Spirit comes into us and occupies and lives in us, and we are redeemed by the Blood of Christ, we stand firm, and nobody's going to move us from that.

"and rejoice in hope of the glory of God" We who are saved, *"rejoice."* That verb is in the Greek present tense which means a continuous action. We continue to *"rejoice in the hope of the glory of God."* One day He's going to glorify these bodies. It may not be too many more years for some of us. It may be a long time for others. If you are saved, the Lord Jesus Christ one day is going to glorify your body. We should continue to *"rejoice"* in that hope of the Glory of God when we shall behold the Lord Jesus Christ in all of His *"glory."* That is one of the requests He made in His high priestly prayer in the Gospel of John:

- John 17:24
  Father, I will that they also, whom thou hast given me, be with me where I am; **that they may behold my glory, which thou hast given me**: for thou lovedst me before the foundation of the world.

That prayer will be answered. We who are saved should continuously *"rejoice"* in the *"hope"* of that *"glory"* that He's given to us.

Hopelessness in the World

There is a lot of hopelessness around this world because of different problems that exist. But we who are saved have hope in the Lord Jesus Christ.

- **Ephesians 2:12**
  That at that time ye were without Christ, being aliens from the commonwealth of Israel, and strangers from the covenants of promise, **having no hope**, and without God in the world:
- **Colossians 1:5**
  For **the hope which is laid up for you in Heaven**, whereof ye heard before in the word of the truth of the gospel;

This "*hope*" for believers is a firm and real "*hope*" that will come to pass in the future. It is not just a maybe.

- **Colossians 1:27**
  To whom God would make known what *is* the riches of the glory of this mystery among the Gentiles; which is **Christ in you, the hope of glory**:

The born-again Christians not only have the Holy Spirit indwelling them (1 Corinthians 6:19-20), but also the Lord Jesus Christ and God the Father (John 14:23). The Lord Jesus Christ in them is the believer's "*hope of glory.*"

- **1 Thessalonians 4:13**
  But I would not have you to be ignorant, brethren, concerning them which are asleep, **that ye sorrow not, even as others which have no hope.**

Not a Hopeless Sorrow for Saints

We "*sorrow not as others which have no hope.*" There is "*no hope*" for glorified bodies for unsaved people, but for us who are saved, there is. We may cry. We may feel sorry, but not as others who have "*no hope.*" It is a different kind of sorrow. It is a different kind of grief.

- **Titus 2:13**
  Looking for that blessed hope, and the glorious appearing of the great God and our Saviour Jesus Christ;

The Lord Jesus Christ is our "*blessed hope,*" who one day will come at the rapture to take the believers Home, and then return to set up His millennial reign on earth.

Romans 5:3

"And not only _so_, but we glory in tribulations also: knowing that tribulation worketh patience" This is usually very contrary to experience, at least for most of us. Do even most born-again Christians really "_glory in tribulations?_" I believe if we have been "_justified by faith_" in the Lord Jesus Christ, God can help us to "_glory_" even in "_tribulation,_" but it does not come easily.

The Greek word for "_tribulation_" is THLIPSIS. It means: "_a pressing, pressing together, pressure; metaph. oppression, affliction, tribulation, distress, straits._" This could be sickness, financial reverses, and a host of other pressures. Whatever it might be, Paul says he "_glories_" in it.

Glorying in Tribulations

The only way that we can "_glory in tribulations_" and trouble is if we believe that God has brought them to us. We must realize that the Lord Jesus Christ is the Master of our lives. What He sends us we must "_glory_" in it, praise Him for it, and be thankful, knowing that all these troubles and problems lead us who are saved to "_patience._" God wants us to have "_patience._"

In a recent Thanksgiving season, Mrs. Waite and I visited our daughter-in-law. We thought we should not visit her on that occasion because she broke her leg just a week before the holiday. She was in pain. They were going to perform surgery soon. She is saved and loves the Lord Jesus Christ. I said to her, "You are in "tribulation," do you have "_patience_"? This verse says that "_tribulation worketh patience._" She said to me, "_I must have patience. There is nothing I can do. I am just sitting down there flat on the davenport, with my leg in a brace. I cannot move._"

Dear reader, if we do not have enough "_patience,_" the Lord might give us some more "_tribulation._"

- **John 16:33**
  These things I have spoken unto you, that in me ye might have peace. In the world **ye shall have tribulation**: but be of good cheer; I have overcome the world.

- **Romans 8:35**
  Who shall separate us from the love of Christ? _**shall tribulation**_, or distress, or persecution, or famine, or nakedness, or peril, or sword?

"Tribulation" will not separate us from the love of God.

- **Romans 12:12**
  Rejoicing in hope; **patient in tribulation**; continuing instant in prayer;
- **2 Corinthians 1:4**
  Who comforteth us in all our tribulation, that we may be able to comfort them which are in any trouble, by the comfort wherewith we ourselves are comforted of God.

We who are believers in our Saviour have been promised the *"comfort of God,"* even in tight places.

- **2 Corinthians 7:4**
  Great *is* my boldness of speech toward you, great *is* my glorying of you: I am filled with comfort, **I am exceeding joyful in all our tribulation.**

What a man Paul was to be able to be filled with the Spirit of God and rejoice even in trouble! He had plenty of trouble. If you think that you and I have trouble, just look at what Paul went through. He was near death by stoning, by shipwreck, spending *"a night and a day"* being *"in the deep"* (2 Corinthians 11:25).

- **1 Thessalonians 3:4**
  For verily, when we were with you, we told you before that **we should suffer tribulation**; even as it came to pass, and ye know.

What is the connection between *"tribulation"* and *"patience"*? There are many verses on *"patience:"*

- **2 Corinthians 6:4**
  But in all *things* approving ourselves as the ministers of God, **in much patience,** in afflictions, in necessities, in distresses,
- **Colossians 1:11**
  Strengthened with all might, according to his glorious power, **unto all patience** and longsuffering with joyfulness;
- **2 Thessalonians 1:4**
  So that we ourselves glory in you in the churches of God **for your patience** and faith in all your persecutions and tribulations that ye endure:
- **1 Timothy 6:11**
  But thou, O man of God, flee these things; and follow after righteousness, godliness, faith, love, **patience,** meekness.
- **Titus 2:2**
  That the aged men be sober, grave, temperate, sound in faith, in charity, **in patience.**

The Impatience of Age

Why do you suppose Paul names the "*aged men*"? Maybe they need it because they are very impatient. They have lived all their lives. They have had their way when they were younger. They knew how to do this and that, but they cannot do as much as they used to do. The result is that they get a little bit impatient. God tells these older men that they must have "*patience*."

- Hebrews 10:36
  For ye have need of patience, that, after ye have done the will of God, ye might receive the promise.
- Hebrews 12:1
  Wherefore seeing we also are compassed about with so great a cloud of witnesses, let us lay aside every weight, and the sin which doth so easily beset *us*, and **let us run with patience the race that is set before us,**
- James 1:3
  Knowing *this*, that **the trying of your faith worketh patience.**

Romans 5:4

"And patience, experience; and experience, hope:" The Greek word for "*experience*" is DOKIME. It means: "*proving, trial; approved, tried character; a proof, a specimen of tried worth, that which has been tried, approved after the test.*" If we have "*tribulation*," we feel like we are in a vice that is pressing in us on all sides. If we have "*patience*" after that "*tribulation*," we are going to gain "*experience*." We have lived through very difficult times. We do not have to fear what might be coming next. If our life gets a little worse than before, we will be able to put up with it victoriously because God has given us the "*patience*" to put up with it. We now have "*experience*."

I remember all the various difficulties throughout my ministry and life up to this point in time. I tried to be faithful to Christ in everything I did and in every place I preached. This was true when I was with the Navy or the Marines as a Navy Chaplain for five years of active duty, or wherever I was. I tried to be faithful to the Lord and His Words, regardless of what the fitness reports were, or whatever the other people said about me. They wrote up some pretty bad things sometimes because I believed the Bible and my superior officers did not.

Experience Brings Hope

God will permit you to go through what is coming next because of the "*experience*" you have already undergone. After "*experience*" you gain "*hope,*" because you know that the end is near. You know that these uncomfortable trials cannot last forever because you have had the "*experience*" of it before. You have had trouble, but then there is an easement of the pain. God has provided a way out of it.

- **1 Corinthians 10:13**
  There hath no temptation taken you but such as is common to man: but God *is* faithful, who will not suffer you to be tempted above that ye are able; but **will with the temptation also make a way to escape, that ye may be able to bear *it***.

When you go to the dentist and he or she begins to drill, you wonder when that is going to stop; but you have "*hope*" because you know from "*experience*" that it ends after awhile. Your dentist will finish. And so it is, you ladies, with the pain of childbirth. We men have never experienced it, but you know from "*experience*" that the pain will cease and that child will be born. There is hope.

- **2 Peter 3:9**
  The Lord is not slack concerning his promise, as some men count slackness; but is longsuffering to us-ward, not willing that any should perish, but that all should come to repentance.

God knows that in all of our "*tribulation*" we need both "*patience*" and "*hope.*" What are you going through today? What is your "*experience*" and problem today? What is your "*tribulation,*" the thing that is pressing down you today? May this trouble lead you to "*patience.*" May it lead to "*experience,*" because you are going through it and you will pass the test. May it also lead to "*hope*" that it will go away soon. When another "*tribulation*" hits you, you have "*hope*" that the Lord will take you through it just as faithfully, and just as successfully, as He has done in the last one.

Romans 5:5

"And hope maketh not ashamed; because the love of God is shed abroad in our hearts by the Holy Ghost which is given unto us." After we have received this *"hope,"* it *"maketh not ashamed."* The Spirit of God, Who indwells the born-again believer, *"sheds abroad"* God's *"love."* If God has given us *"hope"* for eternal life, for Glory, and for our going to Heaven, why should we be *"ashamed"*?

- Luke 9:26
  For whosoever shall be ashamed of me and of my words, of him shall the Son of man be ashamed, when he shall come in his own glory, and *in his* Father's, and of the holy angels.

Christians must not *"be ashamed"* either of the Lord Jesus Christ, or of His *"Words."*

That is why I believe we must honor the King James Bible and the Greek, Hebrew, and Aramaic *"Words"* which underlie it. I believe that those Greek, Hebrew, and Aramaic *"Words"* are *"Words"* which were authored by the Lord Jesus Christ, given to God the Holy Spirit, communicated to the writers of the sixty-six books of the Bible, and preserved for us unto this day. I believe that the King James Bible is the only accurate English translation of those *"Words."* We do not want to be ashamed of the *"Words"* of Christ.

8,000 Differences Greek Texts

Compared to the Greek Words underlying our King James Bible, there are over 8,000 differences in the New Testament Greek text underlying the new versions, such as the NASV, NIV, RSV, NRSV, ESV, and many others.

- Romans 1:16
  For I am not ashamed of the gospel of Christ: for it is the power of God unto salvation to every one that believeth; to the Jew first, and also to the Greek.
- Romans 9:33
  As it is written, Behold, I lay in Sion a stumblingstone and rock of offence: **and whosoever believeth on him shall not be ashamed**.

Why should we be *"ashamed,"* if we believe in the Lord Jesus Christ?

- **Romans 10:11**
  For the scripture saith, **Whosoever believeth on him shall not be ashamed**.
- **Philippians 1:20**
  According to my earnest expectation and *my* hope, **that in nothing I shall be ashamed**, but *that* with all boldness, as always, *so* now also Christ shall be magnified in my body, whether *it be* by life, or by death.

Why be like Peter, *"ashamed"*of Jesus, when asked three times if he knew Jesus? Peter said, *"No!"* Peter was *"ashamed."*

- **2 Timothy 1:8**
  Be not thou therefore ashamed of the testimony of our Lord, nor of me his prisoner: but be thou partaker of the afflictions of the gospel according to the power of God;
- **2 Timothy 1:12**
  For the which cause I also suffer these things: **nevertheless I am not ashamed**: for I know whom I have believed, and am persuaded that he is able to keep that which I have committed unto him against that day.
- **2 Timothy 2:15**
  Study to shew thyself approved unto God, **a workman that needeth not to be ashamed**, rightly dividing the word of truth.
- **1 1 Peter 4:16**
  Yet if *any man suffer* as a Christian, **let him not be ashamed**; but let him glorify God on this behalf.

Suffering As a Christian

To suffer for our own inconsistencies and our own foolishness is one thing. To suffer because we are a *"Christian,"* we should *"not be ashamed."* Stand right up and be counted!

"because the love of God is shed abroad in our hearts by the Holy Ghost which is given unto us." The *"love of God"* is part of the *"fruit of the Spirit"* (Galatians 5:22-23). *"Love"* is the very first part of the *"fruit of the Spirit."*

- **Galatians 5:22-23**
  "But **the fruit of the Spirit is love**, joy, peace, longsuffering, gentleness, goodness, faith, Meekness, temperance: against such there is no law."

The Holy Spirit for All the Saved

The Holy Spirit of God is given to all saved people in this dispensation of Grace.

During a recent semester, I taught a course on Doctrine III in Philadelphia at the *Bible Baptist Institute* sponsored by the *Christ Independent Baptist Church*. The course took up three Bible doctrines, the doctrine of the Bible, the doctrine of the Holy Spirit, and the doctrine of angels.

In the doctrine of the Holy Spirit, one of the things that must be made clear is the fact that He is given only to born-again Christians. Unsaved people do not have the Holy Spirit living within them.

* **Ephesians 2:2**

   Wherein in time past ye walked according to the course of this world, according to the prince of the power of the air, **the spirit that now worketh in the children of disobedience**:

I believe that every one of the lost "*children of disobedience*" has the false evil "*spirit*" which is from Satan (the "*prince of the power of the air*") not the Holy Spirit.

Romans 5:6

"For when we were yet without strength, in due time Christ died for the ungodly." The Lord Jesus Christ did not come into this world to die for our sins at just any time in history. It was "*in due time.*" It was at the proper time.

* **Galatians 4:4**

   But **when the fulness of the time was come**, God sent forth his Son, made of a woman, made under the law,

This "*fulness of the time*" was exactly at the right time. At that time, "*God sent forth His Son*" into this wicked world to die for the sins of the world. When did He do it? It was "*when we were yet without strength.*"

* **2 Corinthians 12:9**

   And he said unto me, My grace is sufficient for thee: for **my strength is made perfect in weakness**. Most gladly therefore will I rather glory in my infirmities, that the power of Christ may rest upon me.

On this occasion, Paul was "*without strength.*" He had a "*thorn in the flesh*" (2 Corinthians 12:7).

This verse says to the Christians at Rome, "*Christ died for the ungodly.*" I wrote a book entitled "*Calvinism's Error of Limited Atonement.*"

Hyper-Calvinism's Serious Error

The error is in their belief that Christ did not die for all the *"ungodly"* people in the world, but only for the <u>elect</u> *"ungodly."* These Calvinists wrongly teach that the Lord Jesus Christ died only for a certain small group of people. They deny that He died for the sins of the entire world. The Bible teaches that Christ died for the sins of the whole world.

There are many verses that teach this truth.

- **Isaiah 53:5-6**
  But **he *was* wounded for our transgressions**, *he was* bruised for our iniquities: the chastisement of our peace *was* upon him; and with his stripes we are healed. **All we like sheep have gone astray**; we have turned every one to his own way; and **the LORD hath laid on him the iniquity of us all.**

Christ bore the sins of the whole world. The people who are hyper-Calvinists, as we call them, teach that if you believe that Christ died for the sins of the entire world, you must believe in Universalism, that the entire world must be saved. This is not true. Just because the Lord Jesus Christ died for all people, it does not mean that all of us are saved. We can only be saved if we receive Christ as our Saviour thus accepting that He died in our place. The Lord Jesus Christ said:

- **Matthew 11:28**
  Come unto me, <u>**all**</u> **ye that labour and are heavy laden**, and I will give you rest.

He did not just say *"come unto me"* if you are elect. He bids **ALL** of the people in the world to come to Him, believe in Him, and be saved. The invitation is universal. It is not limited to the elect only. Everyone who ever lived is given the gift of credence. As the gospel of Christ is proclaimed and the Holy Spirit works in the heart, the sinner is given a choice of trusting Christ as Saviour, or rejecting Him. Rejection leads to Hell, reception leads to Heaven.

- **John 1:29**
  The next day John seeth Jesus coming unto him, and saith, Behold the Lamb of God, which taketh away **the sin of the world**.

The way that the hyper-Calvinists read this verse is that John just meant the *"world"* of the elect, not the *"world"* generally. It is not a question of sin anymore. The *"sin of the world"* has been *"taken away"* by the Lord Jesus

Christ. The sinner must now receive this provision and genuinely believe in the Saviour, thus appropriating this salvation that Christ has offered.

Why People Go To Hell

If people go to Hell, it is because they have refused the Lord Jesus Christ as the remedy for their sins. He died for their sins, and in their place, but if they refuse Him, they are going to bear their sins for all eternity in Hell in the *"second death"* (Revelation 20:6).

- **John 3:14**
  And as Moses lifted up the serpent in the wilderness, **even so must the Son of man be lifted up**:

If an Israelite looked at that brazen serpent on the pole in the wilderness, he or she would live physically and be healed from the poisonous serpent's bite (Numbers 21:8). As Moses *"lifted up"* the *"serpent in the wilderness,"* so Christ was *"lifted up"* on the cross. Everyone that has been bitten by the sin nature, and all of us are sinners, can look in genuine faith to the Lamb of God and live. That is a picture of the Lord Jesus Christ dying for the sins of the whole world.

- **John 3:18**
  He that believeth on him is not condemned: but he that believeth not is **condemned already, because he hath not believed** in the name of the only begotten Son of God.

The hyper-Calvinist would say a person is condemned because he is not one of the elect. The Bible does not teach that. The Bible teaches that he is *"condemned"* because he has not believed. It would be unjust of God to *"condemn"* someone to Hell when it was not the person's fault. God does *"condemn"* people to Hell because they have not *"believed"* in His Son. It is not that Christ has not died for this person's sins, but though He has died for his sins, he refuses to accept this sacrifice.

- **Romans 5:6**
  For when we were yet without strength, in due time **Christ died for the ungodly**.

Does that mean only the *"ungodly"* elect? No. It means all of the *"ungodly"* of the world. It includes all of us.

- **2 Corinthians 5:19**
  To wit, that God was in Christ, **reconciling the world unto himself, not imputing their trespasses unto them**; and hath committed unto us the word of reconciliation.

- 1 Timothy 2:5-6

  For *there is* one God, and one mediator between God and men, the man Christ Jesus; **Who gave himself a ransom for all**, to be testified in due time.

The "*ransom*" was "*for all*," not just for the elect. In my judgment, all these verses are clear.

- **Hebrews 2:9**

  But we see Jesus, who was made a little lower than the angels for the suffering of death, crowned with glory and honour; **that he by the grace of God should taste death for every man**.

- **2 Peter 2:1**

  But there were false prophets also among the people, even as there shall be false teachers among you, who privily shall bring in damnable heresies, even **denying the Lord that bought them,** and bring upon themselves swift destruction.

The Lord Jesus Christ has even "*bought*" these "*false prophets*." He has paid for their sins, but they have rejected Him. They deny Him. This does not mean they are saved, but it means Christ has made provision for them if they would only receive that provision.

- **1 John 2:2**

  And he is the propitiation for our sins: and not for ours only, **but also for *the sins of* the whole world**.

The Bible teaches Christ is the "propitiation" for the "*sins of the whole world.*" The only thing that sends a man or woman to Hell is rejecting the Lord Jesus Christ as their Saviour.

I remember years ago what Pastor Carl Elgena at Bethel Baptist Church in Cherry Hill, New Jersey, used to say. "*It turns out that those who go out calling and knocking on doors just happen to find more of the elect than those that don't.*" He did not believe that Christ died only for the elect.

Christ Died For Everyone

There was a man who used to teach with me at Shelton College, Cape May, New Jersey. His name was Dr. Nigel Lee from South Africa. Dr. Lee said that when he preaches the Bible he does not say *"Christ died for your sins."* I asked, *"Dr. Lee, you cannot preach that?"* He said, *"No, because Christ may not have died for these people, they might not be the elect."* I said, *"If I believed that, I could not preach the gospel to anybody. I must preach Christ died for every one's sins."* This includes everyone reading this, and everyone in the world. Every person in the world is able to believe in the Lord Jesus Christ and be saved. This invitation is not just for the elect.

Romans 5:7

"For scarcely for a righteous man will one die: yet peradventure for a good man some would even dare to die." Why did the Lord Jesus Christ die for an *"ungodly"* world? It says in verse 6 that Christ died for the *"ungodly."* The word *"for"* is used in the sense of *"on our behalf"* and *"as our substitute."*

Paul said a strange thing. He said *"for a righteous man"* one will *"scarcely"* die. Normally people do not die in the place of people who are *"righteous."* If a person is *"good,"* some *"dare to die."* But God does not consider us as either *"righteous"* or *"good,"* but *"ungodly."* Yet the Lord Jesus Christ died for us who were *"ungodly."* Mothers have died for their children, snatching them from a burning building, because they loved their little child. They probably did not realize that they were going to die, but some of them did die. People have died while rescuing people from rivers, fires and storms. They thought they could live. They rescued the victim, and then they themselves died.

Would you die for anybody? Just figure it out now. Here you have a person who is both *"righteous"* and *"good."* If a bullet were coming toward that person standing near you, would you step in front of the bullet and die in this person's place? Would you or would you not? We may die for our loved ones. We may try to prevent harm from our spouses or our children.

Romans 5:8

"But God commendeth his love toward us, in that, while we were yet sinners, Christ died for us." When the Lord Jesus Christ *"died for us,"* we were neither *"righteous"* nor *"good."* We were *"yet sinners."* Yet, even in that state, *"God commendeth his love toward us."*

In the Civil War, I understand you could go into the service for a friend or for a relative so they would not have to serve in the military. Perhaps that person might have had a family to care for. If he had enough money, he could hire a substitute to fight in his place. Some of these substitute men who went into the Civil War died. They died for the men they represented.

Take the worst *"sinner"* you can think of. The Lord Jesus Christ died for those kinds of *"sinners."* The motive for this was God's *"love toward us."* It was the kind of *"love"* that made His Son come from Heaven's Glory. The sinless Son of God came to take the place of the most wretched *"sinner"* on the face of the earth. All of us are included in this term.

Take the most wretched *"sinner"* you can think of. Take for example, the mass-murderer who ate the flesh of the ones he slew. He put them in the refrigerator, and he ate some of them. He had skulls that he froze. He was so wicked, so bad, that he did not even survive to face death row. Other prisoners hated him so much that they murdered him in prison. The inmates took the law into their own hands. Yet this is the kind of person that the Lord Jesus Christ came to die for. He came to take their place. In fact, somebody asked us if we would send a gospel tract or a Bible to that very mass-murderer. We did this. He was on our Bible For Today mailing list. When he was killed in prison we wondered how did he get on our mailing list? Well, someone wanted to send him the Gospel.

The Width and Depth of God's Love

God the Father sent His Son into the world for sinners, to take their place. That is real love. There is no question about that. To die for a *"good man,"* or for a *"righteous"* man is one thing, but it is truly miraculous for the Lord Jesus Christ to die for the *"ungodly"* or for *"sinners."* God's *"love"* here is AGAPE *"love."* It is the strongest kind of *"love."* The evil nature and deeds of the objects of that *"love"* have no effect on its strength and sincerity. It is wide and it is deep.

Romans 5:9

"Much more then, being now justified by his blood, we shall be saved from wrath through him." This verse teaches clearly that born-again Christians have been *"justified"* by the Lord Jesus Christ's *"blood."* I wrote a tract entitled *"Fourteen Biblical Effects of the Literal Blood of Christ."* It is in the back of my book on *JOHN MAC-ARTHUR'S HERESY ON THE BLOOD OF CHRIST* (**BFT #2185**).

The Lord Jesus Christ shed His *"blood,"* and we who are saved have been *"justified by His blood."* *"Without shedding of blood is no remission"* of sins (Hebrews 9:22). When the Lord Jesus Christ died for our sins, He shed His *"blood."* The clear teaching on the Blood of Christ is a very important doctrine of the Christian faith. It has also become a controversial subject due to the false teaching on this subject by Dr. John MacArthur. Here are some of the important verses on *"blood"* in the Bible.

- **Leviticus 17:11**
   For the life of the flesh *is* in **the blood**: and I have given it to you upon the altar to make an atonement for your souls: **for it** *is* **the blood** *that* **maketh an atonement for the soul**.

Notice that this verse sets forth a Biblical principle which is true both in the Old and New Testaments. It makes it clear that it is not the *"death"* of the slain animal that makes *"atonement for the soul."* It is the *"blood"* that is put upon the altar that does this.

So in the case of the Lord Jesus Christ's atonement, the New Testament speaks about both the *"death"* of the Lord Jesus Christ, as well as His *"blood."*

Christ's Blood and Christ's Death

While it is true that the Lord Jesus Christ shed His *"blood"* at His *"death"* on the cross, God speaks specifically about Christ's *"blood"* in many ways that He does not say about His *"death."*

The Bible speaks clearly about the fact that it is the Lord Jesus Christ's *"blood"* that redeems, justifies, and does many other marvelous things for the saved ones. That is why I believe that the *"blood"* of the Lord Jesus Christ is on the mercy seat of Heaven to this day. I believe it is incorruptible *"blood"* (1 Peter 1:18-19). I believe that the Scriptures teach this.

I do not believe, as John MacArthur believes, that the blood of the Lord Jesus Christ is just like your blood and my blood. He teaches that it is just *"human blood"* that is no different from yours and mine. If that were the case how could that *"blood"* cleanse us from sin? There are many things about MacArthur's teaching that are false. That false teaching is growing by leaps and bounds. That is the teaching that is being taught in many schools, even Fundamentalist schools.

"We shall be saved from wrath through him" There are many verses on *"wrath."* Such as *". . . Flee from the wrath to come"* (Matthew 3:7) and *". . . The wrath of God abideth on him"* (John 3:36).

- **Ephesians 2:3**
  Among whom also we all had our conversation in times past in the lusts of our flesh, fulfilling the desires of the flesh and of the mind; **and were by nature the children of wrath,** even as others.

- **1 Thessalonians 1:10**
  And to wait for his Son from Heaven, whom he raised from the dead, *even* Jesus, **which delivered us from the wrath to come.**

God's *"wrath"* will not be poured out upon those of us who are saved and who have been *"justified"* by the *"blood"* of the Lord Jesus Christ. He has delivered us.

- **1 Thessalonians 5:9**
  For God hath not appointed us to wrath, but to obtain salvation by our Lord Jesus Christ,

- **Revelation 6:16**
  And said to the mountains and rocks, Fall on us, and hide us from the face of him that sitteth on the throne, **and from the wrath of the Lamb:**

The Lord Jesus Christ, during the seven-year tribulation period, will exercise His justice and in His judgment, He will exercise holy Divine *"wrath"* as He judges the wicked, lost rebels. They will *"flee"* from the *"wrath of the Lamb."*

- **Revelation 19:15**
  And out of his mouth goeth a sharp sword, that with it he should smite the nations: and he shall rule them with a rod of iron: **and he treadeth the winepress of the fierceness and wrath of Almighty God.**

God in His grace has saved us from His *"wrath."* There is no more *"wrath"* if we have His Salvation. We do not need to fear the *"wrath"* of God any longer.

Romans 5:10

"For if, when we were enemies, we were reconciled to God by the death of his Son, much more, being reconciled, we shall be saved by his life." Here is a contrast with the *"death"* of the Lord Jesus Christ at Calvary where He shed His blood to *"justify"* us, and His *"life"* that He now lives for us in Heaven. When we were His *"enemies,"* those of us who are saved *"were reconciled to God by the death of His Son."* This was His *"death"* on Calvary's cross where He shed His blood for our sins.

The Greek word for *"reconciled"* is KATALLASSO. It means: *"to change, exchange, as coins for others of equivalent value; to reconcile (those who are at variance); return to favour with, be reconciled to one; to receive one into favour."* God does not have to be *"reconciled"* to us. Some theologians are teaching this. On the contrary, sinners must be *"reconciled"* to God. If we have been *"reconciled,"* we shall be *"saved by His life."*

Three Tenses of God's Salvation

God's *"salvation"* is in three tenses: past tense, present tense, and future tense. If we have been born-again, (1) God has saved us from the penalty of sin. (2) He is saving us from the practice of sin. (3) One day He will save us from the presence of sin.

When it says, *"we shall be saved by his life,"* what does it mean? The Lord Jesus Christ right now is alive. He is at the right hand of God the Father.

- **Romans 8:34**
  Who *is* he that condemneth? *It is* Christ that died, yea rather, that is risen again, who is even at the right hand of God, **who also maketh intercession for us**.

The Lord Jesus Christ is our great High Priest *"making intercession for us."* He is helping us who are saved so we do not stumble and disgrace Him.

Everyone of us who are saved, I am sure, has gone through or will go through, in some way or other, a point that if we crossed that line we would be a disgrace to God. May God help us not to go over that line. May He keep us and guard us by His *"life."* If we have gone over that line at one time, may we not go over another line. He is making *"intercession"* for us that we may do what he wants us to do.

- **Hebrews 7:25**
  Wherefore he is able also to save them to the uttermost that come unto God by him, **seeing he ever liveth to make intercession for them**.

  In the Old Testament, the high priests died. Every time one high priest died, another one of Aaron's sons had to become high priest to take his place. Not so with the Lord Jesus Christ. He is our great High Priest, after the order of Melchizedek. He *"ever liveth to make intercession"* for His own children. He never dies. He lives. He is now saving us *"by His life."* He is at God the Father's right hand.

- **1 John 2:1**
  My little children, these things write I unto you, that ye sin not. And if any man sin, **we have an advocate with the Father**, Jesus Christ the righteous:

  An *"advocate"* is like a lawyer who represents us who are saved. An *"advocate"* is one that represents us. The Greek word for *"advocate"* is PARAKLETOS. It means many things: '

  > *"summoned, called to one's side, esp. called to one's aid; one who pleads another's cause before a judge, a pleader, counsel for defense, legal assistant, an advocate; one who pleads another's cause with one, an intercessor;* <u>*of Christ in his exaltation at God's right hand, pleading with God the Father for the pardon of our sins;*</u> *in the widest sense, a helper, succourer, aider, assistant; of the Holy Spirit destined to take the place of Christ with the apostles (after his ascension to the Father), to lead them to a deeper knowledge of the gospel truth, and give them divine strength needed to enable them to undergo trials and persecutions on behalf of the divine kingdom."*

Christ As Our Advocate

When Satan points Christians out to the Lord and says, *"Look at those vicious persons down there, don't you see how disgusting they are?"* God the Father points to the blood of Calvary on the Mercy Seat in Heaven. He tells the Devil, when challenged by him, *"My Son died for the sins of that one down there who is disgracing me. Devil go away."* We have an *"Advocate"* with the Father who pleads our cause.

- **Revelation 12:10**
  And I heard a loud voice saying in Heaven, Now is come
  salvation, and strength, and the kingdom of our God, and the
  power of his Christ: for **the accuser of our brethren is cast
  down, which accused them before our God day and night.**
  That is the Devil's position right now. The Lord Jesus Christ will save us "*by
  His life*" because "*He ever liveth to make intercession for us*" as our "*High
  Priest*" and as our "*Advocate.*"

Romans 5:11

**"And not only *so*, but we also joy in God through our
Lord Jesus Christ, by whom we have now received the
atonement."** This verse gives us the seventh out of seven results of the
believer's being justified by faith. God's Word tells us that because our sins
have been taken away, we can have "*joy in God.*"

By the Lord Jesus Christ we who are saved have "*received the atonement.*"
That word, "*atonement,*" occurs 69 times in the King James Bible's Old
Testament, but only in this one place in the entire New Testament. The Greek
word for "*atonement*" is KATALLAGE. It means:

> "*exchange; of the business of money changers, exchanging
> equivalent values; adjustment of a difference, reconciliation,
> restoration to favour; in the NT of the restoration of the favour of
> God to sinners that repent and put their trust in the expiatory death
> of Christ.*"

The word's basic meaning is "*an exchange*" of something for something. In the
"*atonement*" spoken of here, God exchanged the Christian's sin for His absolute
"*righteousness.*"

- **2 Corinthians 5:21**
  For he hath made him *to be* sin for us, who knew no sin; **that
  we might be made the righteousness of God in him.**

Exchange of Sin For Righteousness

This verse makes it clear that Christ took our "*sin*," and we took
His "*righteousness.*" That is the exchange. That is the
"*atonement.*"

- **Leviticus 17:11**
  For the life of the flesh *is* in the blood: and I have given it to
  you upon the altar to make an atonement for your souls: for **it**

is the blood *that* maketh an atonement for the soul.

The word in Hebrew for *"atonement"* comes from the verb KAPHAR. It means several things:

> *"to cover, purge, make an atonement, make reconciliation, cover over with pitch; to coat or cover with pitch; (Piel) to cover over, pacify, propitiate; to cover over, atone for sin, make atonement for; to cover over, atone for sin and persons by legal rites; (Pual) to be covered over; to make atonement for; (Hithpael) to be covered."*

We are saved by Christ's *"life."* What a wonderful state of affairs! We who are sinners lost and bound for Hell, when we trust Christ and receive Him as our Saviour, we are redeemed. We are set free from sin. We are on our way to Heaven. We have escaped the Lake of Fire.

Seven Results of Justification

There are seven things that happen because we are justified by faith in Christ. Romans Chapter 5 tells us what these seven things are:

1. Verse 1, we have peace with God.
2. Verse 2, we have access to God.
3. Verse 2, we rejoice in hope of God's glory.
4. Verse 3, we glory in tribulation.
5. Verse 9, we're saved from wrath.
6. Verse 10, we're reconciled to God.
7. Verse 11, we received an atonement.

This should cause us great joy.

Romans 5:12

"Wherefore, as by one man sin entered into the world, and death by sin; and so death passed upon all men, for that all have sinned" Notice how it says, *"by one man."* A woman by the name of Eve started *"sin"* entering into the world (Genesis 3:6). Yet it is the *"man"* whom God holds responsible for the *"sin"* entering into the world and *"death by sin."* Because of that *"one man,"* Adam, *"death passed upon all men."* Because of this, God considers that *"all have sinned."* We who are the husbands, are the heads of our families. We cannot take our wives and make them the scapegoats for anything that happens in our home. We must bear the responsibility, and this is what God did in the Garden of Eden.

Why All The Cemeteries?

Because *"death passed upon all men,"* there are millions of graveyards all over the world. The cause of these cemeteries is what happened in Genesis Chapter 3. It was because of what Adam did. God holds Adam responsible. Because of Adam's sin, *"death passed upon all men,"* and God considers that *"all have sinned."* He holds every man, woman, and child in the world as sinners.

The background of this is in the book of Genesis.

- **Genesis 3:1-6**
  Now the serpent was more subtil than any beast of the field which the LORD God had made. And he said unto the woman, Yea, hath God said, Ye shall not eat of every tree of the garden? And the woman said unto the serpent, We may eat of the fruit of the trees of the garden: But of the fruit of the tree which *is* in the midst of the garden, God hath said, Ye shall not eat of it, neither shall ye touch it, lest ye die. And the serpent said unto the woman, Ye shall not surely die: For God doth know that in the day ye eat thereof, then your eyes shall be opened, and ye shall be as gods, knowing good and evil. And **when the woman saw that the tree *was* good for food, and that it *was* pleasant to the eyes, and a tree to be desired to make *one* wise, she took of the fruit thereof, and did eat, and gave also unto her husband with her; and he did eat**.

Satan quoted only part of a verse. He knows the Bible. He is a created angel. He rebelled against God and fell from his position. At the suggestion of his wife, Eve, Adam ate what God said not to eat. He ate of that forbidden fruit from the Tree of the Knowledge of Good and Evil.

- **Genesis 2:15-17**
  And the LORD God took the man, and put him into the garden of Eden to dress it and to keep it. And the LORD God commanded the man, saying, **Of every tree of the garden thou mayest freely eat**: **But of the tree of the knowledge of good and evil, thou shalt not eat of it**: for in the day that thou eatest thereof thou shalt surely die.

Sin entered the whole human race because of this act. Some people might say: *"What is wrong with eating fruit?"* We eat fruit all the time. We eat bananas, and oranges, and apples, and cherries, and peaches, and plums. I enjoy fruit, but that is not the issue. The issue was disobedience to what God had commanded. When we disobey what God says, that is the serious part of it. That is why sin entered into this world. Then physical and spiritual *"death"* began to reign.

Death--Spiritual and Physical

Spiritually, Adam and Eve died immediately. Physically, Adam and Eve began to die slowly. God said, *"In the day that thou eatest thou shall surely die."* His body became decrepit.

Today, we waste away faster than Adam did. He lived 930 years in all. A recent Vice President's father died at the age of 90. That's a good old age these days. Now, some live to be 100 or more, but no one lives over 900 years any more, or even close to that age. After the universal flood in Noah's days, physical conditions on the earth have made it impossible to live that long.

- **Isaiah 14:11-12**
  Thy pomp is brought down to the grave, *and* the noise of thy viols: the worm is spread under thee, and the worms cover thee. **How art thou fallen from Heaven, O Lucifer, son of the morning!** *how* art thou cut down to the ground, which didst weaken the nations!

"Lucifer" or *"light-bearer"* is a name for Satan. He is a counterfeiter. He counterfeits darkness for light. This verse speaks of Satan's *"fall from heaven."*

- **Isaiah 14:15**
  Yet thou shalt be brought down to Hell, to the sides of the pit.

- **Isaiah 14:17**
  That made the world as a wilderness, and destroyed the cities thereof; **that opened not the house of his prisoners?**

Satan *"opened not the house of his prisoners."* Only the Lord Jesus Christ can open the prison gates and free them by His redemption when they trust Him by genuine faith in His finished work on Calvary.

- **1 Timothy 2:12-14**
  But I suffer not a woman to teach, nor to usurp authority over the man, but to be in silence. For Adam was first formed, then Eve. **And Adam was not deceived, but the woman being deceived was in the transgression**.

Adam knew full well that he was forbidden to take of the forbidden fruit, yet he followed Eve's suggestion and took it. Eve was *"deceived"* and *"was in the transgression."* Though Adam *"was not deceived,"* he also sinned.

Adam's Sin Caused Three Things

Because of Adam's sin three things are true:

1. **Sin entered into the world of men and women.** Before Adam sinned there was no sin among human beings. The wicked angel, Lucifer, had sinned and took a number of the evil angels with him. The evil angels today are on Satan's side. There was no sin on the earth until Adam sinned.

2. **Physical death began to set in.** God promised, *"In the day that thou eatest thereof* [of the tree], *thou shalt surely die."*

3. **God concluded all have sinned.** God concluded the entire universe of mankind, from the time that Adam was born until the time that there are no more human beings in the world, that every one of them are born sinners. This result was all because of what that one man, Adam, had done.

Regardless of our own personal sin, we are all concluded under sin. Adam was the representative of the whole human race. The Lord Jesus Christ is the representative of all of those who are redeemed among the human race.

Bishop B. F. Westcott, who together with Professor F. J. A. Hort, got a false Greek New Testament together in 1881, said to the Arch Bishop of Canterbury in 1890,

> *"No one I suppose holds that the first three chapters of Genesis, for example, gives a literal history. I could never understand that anyone reading them with open eyes could think that they did."*

Genesis does give us a literal history, including the fall of man in the Garden of Eden. In saying this, Westcott denies the creation of the world, the fall of man, and many other things.

Professor Hort, Westcott's partner in their false Greek text, had similar ideas about Genesis. In 1886, he wrote:

> *"The authors of the article doubtless assume the strictly historical character of the account of the fall in Genesis. This assumption is now in my belief no longer reasonable."*

Well, who said it had to be reasonable. God said it, and it's true.

Again, Hort wrote:

"But the early chapters of Genesis remain a divinely appointed parable or apologue, setting forth important practical truths on subjects which, as matter of history, are outside our present ken."
In fact, Hort later said in 1848 in his *Life and Letters of Hort*,

"I am inclined to think that no such state as Eden, I mean the popular notion, ever existed, and that Adam's fall in no way differs from the fall of each of his descendants as Coleridge justly argues."

There are ministers and others in our own day who deny the historicity of Genesis and the fall of men. I totally disagree with both Westcott and Hort on this and many other issues. It was surprising to me to find out that Samuel Schnaiter, a leading Department Head at *Bob Jones University* in Greenville, South Carolina, uses one of Westcott's books as a textbook in his classes. In a tape-recorded message at Heritage Bible Church in Greenville, SC, Schnaiter made this statement concerning Westcott who denies the historicity of Genesis:

"Westcott in particular still has, as far as I'm concerned, the best commentary on the book of Hebrews."

I have a problem with this.

Do Not Use Westcott or Hort

In my studied opinion, no Fundamentalist college, university, or seminary should use any textbooks by either Westcott or Hort who are deniers of God's Words in Genesis and in many other places.

Romans 5:13

"For until the law sin was in the world: but sin is not imputed when there is no law" The law of Moses was not in effect until Exodus 19. This verse is referring to Genesis 3. Until the law of Moses, though *"sin was in the world,"* without such a law, *"sin is not imputed."* When there is no rule on the books, sin cannot be prosecuted.

When there is a speed-limit sign, you can be arrested for going so many miles per hour beyond that speed. If there is no sign, sometimes you can get away with it. From Adam to Moses *"sin"* was *"in the world,"* but it was *"not imputed."* When Cain slew Abel, God did not slay him. It was in the dispensation of age of conscience, before the law of Moses.

- Numbers 35:31
  Moreover ye shall take no satisfaction for the life of a murderer, which *is* guilty of death: but **he shall be surely put to death**.

God had mercy on Cain because there was no law. Sin was "*not imputed*" until the law.

- Genesis 9:6
  Whoso sheddeth man's blood, by man shall his blood be shed: for in the image of God made he man.

The Death Penalty

The death penalty was given by God. A law has to be on the books before there is a penalty against it, but not so with the judgment of sin in the Garden of Eden as far as physical death is concerned.

There did not have to be any law at all. God said this is going to take place without any law. God said He was going to keep His promise. Adam sinned on the day that he ate the fruit from the forbidden tree. Though he died spiritually instantly, it took Adam 930 years to die physically. He was headed for death. If he had not sinned, he would have been able to live in that perfect body that God made for many more years. But "*sin*" entered in and "*death*" by sin. The oldest man, Methuselah, died at the age of 969 years.

- Genesis 25:7
  And these *are* the days of the years of Abraham's life which he lived, **an hundred threescore and fifteen years**.

Abraham died at age 175. As time passed, people's lives became shorter and shorter. Sin brought physical death. God's penalty was there even though there was no law of Moses at that time.

Romans 5:14

"Nevertheless death reigned from Adam to Moses, even over them that had not sinned after the similitude of Adam's transgression, who is the figure of him that was to come." "*Death reigned from Adam to Moses.*" Moses was the instigator of the law. Though the law was not imputed normally, that did not matter as far as "*death*" is concerned. The sentence of death was carried out. Even those who "*had not sinned*" after Adam had the penalty of death. Adam was a "*figure*" or a picture of Him that was to come, the Lord Jesus Christ, Who "*was to come.*"

As Adam was the head of the human race and got us into sin, so the Lord Jesus Christ is the head of the new group of people called "*believers*" who trust in Christ, bringing them salvation and redemption.

Many deaths are recorded in Genesis 5. In Genesis 3, Adam sinned. God had said, "*In the day that thou eatest thereof thou shalt surely die*" (Genesis 2:17). In Genesis 5, those named lived so many years, begat so many children, and they died. In fact, from Genesis 5:9 to 5:31, no less than nine times we read, "*and he died.*" "*So death passed upon all men.*" God kept His promise. God always keeps His promises. "*The wages of sin is death, but the gift of God is eternal life through Jesus Christ our Lord.*"

That "*death*" is not only physical "*death,*" but it also is spiritual "*death*" until we come to Christ. Men, women, boys, and girls are under the threat of "*death*" physically; yes, but they are also under the threat of eternal "*death*" in Hell, unless they flee from the wrath to come, genuinely trust the Lord Jesus Christ, and receive Him as their Saviour.

- **1 Corinthians 15:45**
  And so it is written, The first man Adam was made a living soul; **the last Adam *was made* a quickening spirit**.

The question may be asked, "*Is it fair?*" Often we, as human beings, ask about the fairness of God.

God Is Always Fair

Was it fair for God to judge all of us, make all of us die physically because of Adam's sin? Was it fair for the Lord Jesus Christ to die for the sins of the whole world so that they by genuine personal faith in Him might be justified? It is the same thing. It is just as fair for Adam to get us into sin as it is for Christ to get us out of the sin trouble by believing in and trusting in Him.

The "*last Adam,*" the Lord Jesus Christ, was the One Who can redeem those who exercise saving faith in Him.

Romans 5:15

"But not as the offence, so also *is* the free gift. For if through the offence of one many be dead, much more the grace of God, and the gift by grace, *which is* by one man, Jesus Christ, hath abounded unto many." Adam's consequences are different from those of the *"last Adam."* The *"last Adam"* is another term for the Lord Jesus Christ. The first Adam had an *"offence,"* and the *"last Adam"* brought the *"gift of grace"* (giving us something we do not deserve). It is the difference of being *"dead"* because of Adam's sin, and having the possibility of the *"gift of grace"* and salvation through the Lord Jesus Christ.

There are similarities between the first Adam and the *"last Adam."* In the first place, they have both influenced many. The first Adam influenced many to die physically and spiritually. The *"last Adam"* influenced many, because there are multitudes through the centuries who have looked to *"the Lamb of God"* and have been saved by faith in His death and the shedding of His blood. The first Adam made a bad decision in the Garden of Eden, the *"last Adam"* made a good decision to follow the will of His Father in the Garden of Gethsemane and on Mount Calvary.

Romans 5:16

"And not as *it was* by one that sinned, *so is* the gift: for the judgment *was* by one to condemnation, but the free gift *is* of many offences unto justification." In Adam's case, there was one *"offence"* and only *"one that sinned."* In the case of the Lord Jesus Christ, He provided a "free gift" for *"many offences unto justification."*

Remember, in John Chapter 1, when John the Baptist saw the Lord Jesus Christ coming to him, he said, *"Behold the Lamb of God which taketh away the sin of the world"* (John 1:29b). That is what the Lord Jesus Christ did. He took away many, many sins.

The first Adam ended in condemnation and judgment because of disobedience. What the *"last Adam"* accomplished was the *"free gift"* of *"justification"* by genuine faith in His finished work on the cross. The condemnation was not only unto physical death, but also unto eternal death. Death by definition is a separation.

The Three Kinds of Death

There are three kinds of death: (1) Physical death is a separation of the spirit and soul from the body. (2) Spiritual death is a separation of the spirit and soul from God during this life. (3) Eternal death is the eternal separation of the spirit, soul, and body from God in the Lake of Fire.

Condemnation is mentioned many times.

- **Matthew 20:18**
  Behold, we go up to Jerusalem; and the Son of man shall be betrayed unto the chief priests and unto the scribes, **and they shall condemn him to death,**

- **Luke 23:40**
  But the other answering rebuked him, saying, Dost not thou fear God, **seeing thou art in the same condemnation?**

Before he was saved, this repentant thief was still a sinner. He was still lost. He was a murderer. He was a thief. Though he was on that cross, he looked in obedient faith to the Lamb of God, the Lord Jesus Christ. That look of faith snapped sin's fetters and set him free. The Lord Jesus took him to the Paradise of Heaven that very day. He was no longer in any condemnation or judgment.

- **John 5:24**
  Verily, verily, I say unto you, He that heareth my word, and believeth on him that sent me, hath everlasting life, **and shall not come into condemnation**; but is passed from death unto life.

- **Romans 8:1**
  There is therefore now no condemnation to them which are in Christ Jesus, who walk not after the flesh, but after the Spirit.

Adam got us into condemnation, but Christ opens the door to *"justification."*

What Is God's Justification?

"Justification" is God's judicial declaration that, though we are sinners, through Christ's death on the cross for our sins when we genuinely trust Him, believe in Him, and receive Him as our Saviour, He declares us absolutely righteous on the books of Heaven.

The books are wiped clean. Our sins are gone. As far as **our standing** with God is concerned, we are absolutely righteous. If we are not declared righteous by God, we can never go to Heaven.

What about **our state** as redeemed ones here below? It should be the goal of every born-again Christian to have their **state** on earth approach their **standing** in Heaven.

- **Romans 4:5**
  But to him that worketh not, but believeth on him that justifieth the ungodly, **his faith is counted for righteousness.**

- **Romans 8:33**
  Who shall lay any thing to the charge of God's elect? *It is* **God that justifieth.**

God is the One who declares us righteous when we are regenerated through faith in Christ.

- **Galatians 3:8**
  And the scripture, foreseeing that **God would justify the heathen through faith**, preached before the gospel unto Abraham, *saying*, In thee shall all nations be blessed.

God's justification through Christ is what we get if we are saved, rather than condemnation through Adam.

Romans 5:17

"For if by one man's offence death reigned by one; much more they which receive abundance of grace and of the gift of righteousness shall reign in life by one, Jesus Christ.)" These are more contrasts between Adam and the *"last Adam."* The first contrast is Adam's *"offence"* versus the Lord Jesus Christ's *"gift of righteousness."*

The second contrast is that Adam caused physical *"death"* to reign, whereas the Lord Jesus Christ made it possible to *"reign in life."*

When Does New Life Begin?

When does this *"reign"* **take place? I believe it begins the minute a sinner is born-again by the power of God through the Holy Spirit, as he has genuine faith in the Lord Jesus Christ. I believe it continues on into Heaven where the saved will live and** *"reign in life"* **forever.**

Look at a few verses on *"life."*

- **John 1:4**
  In Him was life; and the life was the light of men.
- **John 3:16**
  For God so loved the world, that he gave his only begotten Son, that whosoever believeth in him should not perish, but have **everlasting life**.

Right now we who are saved have *"everlasting life."* When we *"reign in life,"* that means we *"reign"* right now. The redeemed can *"reign in life"* because they possess everlasting life.

- **John 5:24**
  Verily, verily, I say unto you, He that heareth my word, and believeth on him that sent me, **hath everlasting life**, and shall not come into condemnation; but is passed from death unto life.

Many saved people think they have *"everlasting life"* only when they die. This is incorrect. This verse says that the minute a person believes, he *"has everlasting life."* They do not have to wait until they die. If a person does not have eternal life while he is living, he will not have it when he dies. It is just as simple as that. You must trust the Lord Jesus Christ now while you are living or you will never have eternal life afterwards. The chorus that we sing sometimes, is true: *"Life begins when Jesus comes in."*

- **John 10:10**
  The thief cometh not, but for to steal, and to kill, and to destroy: **I am come that they might have life**, and that they might have *it* more abundantly.
- **John 10:28**
  And I give unto them eternal life; and they shall never perish, neither shall any *man* pluck them out of my hand.
- **Acts 3:15**
  And killed **the Prince of life**, whom God hath raised from the dead; whereof we are witnesses.

- Colossians 3:4
  When Christ, *who is* our life, shall appear, then shall ye also appear with him in glory. (KJV)

If we are saved, the Lord Jesus Christ is *"our life,"* and we can *"reign in life"* because of what He has done for us.

Romans 5:18

"Therefore as by the offence of one *judgment came* upon all men to condemnation; even so by the righteousness of one *the free gift came* upon all men unto justification of life." Though the words *"the free gift"* are in italics and therefore are not found in the Greek Words underlying this verse, they are added by the King James translators to illustrate further the sense of *"the gift"* referred to in verse 17. This *"gift of righteousness"* (v. 17) of the Lord Jesus Christ resulted in *"justification of life."* This indeed was a *"gift"* rather than the result of our own good deeds. A *"gift"* is something you do not deserve. It is something you do not merit. Maybe you do not even want this gift.

Many people receive *"gifts"* during the so-called *"Christmas season."* If they do not like the *"gifts,"* they return them to the store for exchange. It is the same with the Lord Jesus Christ. He gave us the *"gift"* of His own Life. He died for the sins of the world, shedding His blood for them, He was buried, and He rose again bodily from the grave.

Millions Reject God's Gift

There are millions and millions of men, women, boys, and girls all over this world who do not want that *"gift."* They reject it. The *"gift"* must be accepted, and received. It must be taken before it can be ours.

Here are a few verses on God's *"gift."*

- John 4:10
  Jesus answered and said unto her, **If thou knewest the gift of God**, and who it is that saith to thee, Give me to drink; thou wouldest have asked of him, and he would have given thee living water.

And the Lord Jesus Christ did give this woman that *"living water."* She went away from that well saved.

- Romans 6:23
  For the wages of sin *is* death; **but the gift of God *is* eternal life through Jesus Christ our Lord.**
- 2 Corinthians 9:15
  Thanks *be* unto God for **his unspeakable gift.**
- Ephesians 2:8
  For by grace are ye saved through faith; and that not of yourselves: ***it is* the gift of God:**

Salvation is the "*gift of God.*" It is not by the works we do, but it is by genuine saving faith in the Lord Jesus Christ.

Romans 5:19

"For as by one man's disobedience many were made sinners, so by the obedience of one shall many be made righteous." Here is the contrast again.   This time it is a question of "*disobedience*" versus "*obedience.*"

The Result of Adam's Disobedience

Adam disobeyed God. God had told him not to eat of the fruit of the tree in the middle of the garden. He ate of that fruit because his wife Eve ate of it. Because of Adam's disobedience in listening to his wife rather than the Lord God, every man, woman, and child have been made sinners and subject to both physical and eternal death unless they trust the Lord Jesus Christ as their Saviour.

On the contrary, because of the "*obedience*" of the Lord Jesus Christ, many can be "*made righteous.*" This does not mean that everybody living is going to be made righteous. Only those who genuinely trust in the Lord Jesus Christ and receive His "*gift*" of eternal life are made righteous.

Because of Adam's "*disobedience,*" all of us were made sinners. Here are a few important verses about "*sinners.*"

- Matthew 11:19
  The Son of man came eating and drinking, and they say, Behold a man gluttonous, and a winebibber, **a friend of publicans and sinners.** But wisdom is justified of her children.

Are you not glad that the Lord Jesus Christ is a friend of publicans and sinners? We are all sinners. If the Lord Jesus Christ were not our friend, we could never be saved.

- **Matthew 26:45**

    Then cometh he to his disciples, and saith unto them, Sleep
    on now, and take *your* rest: behold, the hour is at hand, and
    the Son of man is betrayed into the hands of sinners.

While the Lord Jesus prayed all night in the Garden of Gethsemane, Peter,
James, and John fell asleep. The Lord Jesus was facing Calvary. He was facing
death as a payment for the sins of the whole world. *"Sinners"* who came to that
garden that night wanted to take the life of the Saviour. There is nothing more
evil or wicked than to desire to take the life of the Lord Jesus Christ Who came
"to seek and to save that which was lost" (Luke 19:10).

- **Mark 2:17**

    When Jesus heard *it*, he saith unto them, They that are whole
    have no need of the physician, but they that are sick: I came
    not to call the righteous, **but sinners to repentance**.

That is why the Lord Jesus Christ came. He has many candidates for His
assistance. Everyone of us that is living on this planet is a candidate for the
Lord's salvation since all of us are *"sinners"* because of what Adam did. What
Adam did made us all *"sinners."* What Christ did makes those who trust Him
confidently able to have His eternal life and a Home in Heaven.

- **Romans 5:8**

    But God commendeth his love toward us, in that, **while we
    were yet sinners**, Christ died for us.

- **1 Timothy 1:15**

    This *is* a faithful saying, and worthy of all acceptation, that
    Christ Jesus came into the world to save sinners; of whom
    I am chief.

This is the purpose of Christ's coming into the world. Whatever Adam did, the
Lord Jesus Christ undid.

Romans 5:20

"Moreover the law entered, that the offence might abound. But where sin abounded, grace did much more abound:" The law of Moses entered to make the *"offence"* very clear and *"abound."*

The Three Parts of Moses' Law

There were three parts to the law of Moses: (1) the Ten Commandments, (2) the ceremonial law, and (3) the civil law.

But where *"sin abounded, grace did much more abound."* In other words, God's *"grace"* was in greater abundance than the *"offences."*

Let us look at a few verses that talk about God's *"grace."* Grace is getting something we do not deserve.

- **John 1:14**
  And the Word was made flesh, and dwelt among us, (and we beheld his glory, the glory as of the only begotten of the Father,) **full of grace and truth**.

If the Lord Jesus Christ, the *"Word"* that was *"made flesh,"* was not *"full of grace,"* every person ever born would be in serious trouble with the Lord.

- **John 1:17**
  For the law was given by Moses, **but** grace and truth came **by Jesus Christ**.

- **Acts 20:32**
  And now, brethren, I commend you to God, **and to the word of his grace**, which is able to build you up, and to give you an inheritance among all them which are sanctified.

Studying God's Words

The Words of God, as we read, study, and learn of them, give us grace. It is a wonderful gift.

- **Romans 3:24**
  Being justified freely **by his grace** through the redemption that is in Christ Jesus:

- **Romans 5:2**
  By whom also we have access **by faith into this grace** wherein we stand, and rejoice in hope of the glory of God.
- **Romans 5:15**
  But not as the offence, so also *is* the free gift. For if through the offence of one many be dead, **much more the grace of God, and the gift by grace,** *which is* by one man, Jesus Christ, hath abounded unto many.
- **Romans 5:17**
  For if by one man's offence death reigned by one; much more they which receive **abundance of grace** and of the gift of righteousness shall reign in life by one, Jesus Christ.)
- **Romans 6:1**
  What shall we say then? Shall we continue in sin, that **grace may abound**?
- **2 Corinthians 8:9**
  For **ye know the grace of our Lord Jesus Christ**, that, though he was rich, yet for your sakes he became poor, that ye through his poverty might be rich.

  This morning Mrs. Waite and I read 2 Corinthians 8:9. What was the *"grace of our Lord Jesus Christ"*? *"Though He was rich"* and has all the glories of Heaven, yet *"He became poor."* He came to this wicked world. He was crucified, smitten, laughed at, and scorned.

Poverty to Riches through Christ

"He became poor that ye through His poverty might be rich." That is what the substitutionary work of our Lord Jesus Christ brought us who are saved. He took our *"poverty"* and we took His *"riches."* That is grace.

Paul had a *"thorn in the flesh."* God did not take it away from him. No one knows what the *"thorn"* was. Maybe it was bad eyesight or something else. He prayed three times for the Lord to take away this thorn in the flesh. The Lord did not take it away. He gave him His grace.

- **2 Corinthians 12:9**
  And he said unto me, **My grace is sufficient for thee**: for my strength is made perfect in weakness. Most gladly therefore will I rather glory in my infirmities, that the power of Christ may rest upon me.

- **Ephesians 1:7**
  In whom we have redemption through his blood, the forgiveness of sins, **according to the riches of his grace;**
- **Ephesians 2:5**
  Even when we were dead in sins, hath quickened us together with Christ, **(by grace ye are saved;)**
- **Ephesians 2:7**
  That in the ages to come he might shew **the exceeding riches of his grace** in *his* kindness toward us through Christ Jesus.
- **Titus 2:11**
  For **the grace of God that bringeth salvation** hath appeared to all men,
- **Titus 3:7**
  That **being justified by his grace,** we should be made heirs according to the hope of eternal life.
- **Hebrews 4:16**
  Let us therefore come boldly unto **the throne of grace,** that we may obtain mercy, and find grace to help in time of need.

The destination of a believer's prayer toward Heaven is called "*the throne of grace.*"

When a Christian Prays

When a Christian prays, he can enter into the very presence of the Lord Jesus Christ who is at God the Father's right hand.

Romans 5:21

"That as sin hath reigned unto death, even so might grace reign through righteousness unto eternal life by Jesus Christ our Lord." Here is the situation in a nut shell. Adam, because of his sin, wickedness, and disobeying God, brought physical and eternal death on the whole body of men, women, boys, and girls. On the other hand, the Lord Jesus Christ brought "*righteousness*" and "*eternal life.*"

Let's look at a few verses on "*eternal life.*"

- **John 3:15**
  That whosoever believeth in him should not perish, but have **eternal life.**

The Lord Jesus Christ was lifted up on Calvary's cross for us.

- **John 6:66-68**
  From that *time* many of his disciples went back, and walked no more with him. Then said Jesus unto the twelve, Will ye also go away? Then Simon Peter answered him, Lord, to whom shall we go? **thou hast the words of eternal life.**

The Lord Jesus had talked about the feeding of the 5,000. He talked about appropriating what His body and His blood accomplished under the figure of "*eating*" and "*drinking*" something. Because these difficult things were not understood, "*many of his disciples*" went away and "*walked no more with him.*" The Lord spoke some very deep things to them, and because of that many people went back and walked no more with Him. When the twelve were asked if they were leaving Him also, Peter said: "*To whom shall we go?*" The Lord Jesus alone had "*the words of eternal life.*"

Eternal Life--Nowhere Else to Go

Where are you going to go for "*eternal life*"? Where are you going to go for your sin, darkness, wickedness, unrighteousness, and condemnation? There is nowhere to turn except to the Lord Jesus Christ.

- **John 10:28**
  And I give unto them eternal life; and they shall never perish, neither shall any *man* pluck them out of my hand.

When we trust Christ and are saved, nobody is able to take away that eternal life.

- **Romans 6:23**
  For the wages of sin *is* death; **but the gift of God *is* eternal life** through Jesus Christ our Lord.

The Lord Jesus Christ makes the difference.

- **1 John 5:11**
  And this is the record, **that God hath given to us eternal life**, and this life is in his Son.

I am so thankful that the Lord Jesus Christ, the "*last Adam,*" made it possible for us to have eternal life, and that life is in His Son.

Romans Chapter Six

Romans 6:1

"What shall we say then? Shall we continue in sin, that grace may abound?" If you hit your finger with a hammer, it would hurt. When you stop hitting it, it feels much better. Should you keep hitting your finger with a hammer so you will feel good when you stop? That is the question. Suppose a thief steals a diamond ring from a woman's house, and later repents. The newspapers write him up and tell the readers what a wonderful man he is because he is giving this wonderful diamond ring back to this lady. *"Shall we continue in sin so that grace may abound?"* The graciousness is that the woman forgave the man. The man does not have to pay any penalty. He does not have to go to jail. Should he steal another diamond ring from somebody else so that he can have all this publicity again? That is foolishness!

We should not *"continue in sin"* at all. There are Scripture verses to tell us who are saved how we can stay out of sin. Have you sinned with your body in the last hour? Think of it. I'm not asking for a confession. Have you sinned with your words in the last ten minutes? Have you sinned with your thoughts in any way, shape, or form in the last ten` minutes? Think about it. If the Lord is able to keep us from sinning with our body, our words, and our thoughts, why can we not have continual victory over sin? Not that we are sinlessly perfect, but why cannot God give us victory over the practice of sin in our lives, if we are saved? That's the whole issue in these eleven verses.

- 1 John 2:1
  My little children, these things write I unto you, **that ye sin not**.
  And if any man sin, we have an advocate with the Father,
  Jesus Christ the righteous:

God does not want us to sin if we are saved. We are sinners, but He does not want us to sin.

- **1 Peter 4:3**
  For the time past of *our* life may suffice us to have wrought the will of the Gentiles, when we walked in lasciviousness, lusts, excess of wine, revellings, banquetings, and abominable idolatries:

We who have been redeemed do not have to "*continue in sin.*" That is our past life before we were saved. We do not have to practice sin.

- **1 John 1:9**
  If we confess our sins, he is faithful and just to forgive us *our* sins, and to cleanse us from all unrighteousness.

God has a remedy for us. We do not have to "*continue in sin.*" He will help us.

Romans 6:2

"God forbid. How shall we, that are dead to sin, live any longer therein?" The phrase "*God forbid*" has drawn criticism from some people who do not like the King James Bible. They say the translators used dynamic equivalence here because the word "*God*" is not in the Greek text. That is correct. The Greek phrase is "ME GENOITO." It means "*may it not be, may it never come to pass, or may it never happen.*" In 1611, or even today, "*God forbid*" conveys this picture clearly, does it not? "*May God forbid this thing. May it never happen. May it never, never, never come to pass.*" This phrase is used only twenty-four times in the entire King James Bible, nine in the Old Testament and fifteen times in the New Testament.

Versions' Dynamic Equivalence

If this is really an example of dynamic equivalence, what about the over 2,000 examples of dynamic equivalence in the New King James Version where they have either taken away, added, or changed the Words of God in other ways? What about the over 4,000 examples in the New American Standard Version where they have done this to the Words of God? What about the over 6,653 examples of dynamic equivalence in the New International Version where they have done this to the Words of God?

Though other versions make a practice of using dynamic equivalence, the King James Bible does not.

"How shall we, that are dead to sin, live any longer therein?" How can "*dead*" people live? If we are "*dead to sin*" how can we "*live any longer therein*"? The Bible teaches in Romans 5 that through Adam's sin, "*physical death*" came upon the whole world. This verse is talking about spiritual death, a different kind of death. If we are saved, God reckons us to be "*dead*" as far as sin is concerned.

- **Romans 6:8**
  Now **if we be dead with Christ**, we believe that we shall also live with him:
- **Colossians 2:20**
  Wherefore **if ye be dead with Christ** from the rudiments of the world, why, as though living in the world, are ye subject to ordinances,
- **2 Timothy 2:11**
  It is a faithful saying: **For if we be dead with *him***, we shall also live with *him*:
- **Romans 6:6**
  Knowing this, that **our old man is crucified with *him***, that the body of sin might be destroyed, that henceforth we should not serve sin.
- **Galatians 2:20**
  I am crucified with Christ: nevertheless I live; yet not I, but Christ liveth in me: and the life which I now live in the flesh I live by the faith of the Son of God, who loved me, and gave himself for me.

All of these verses teach that, as to his position before God, the believer was "*crucified with Christ.*" When Christ died, if we're saved, we died with Him.

Romans 6:3

"Know ye not, that so many of us as were baptized into Jesus Christ were baptized into his death?" Normally, when you think of being "*baptized*," you think of water baptism. That is generally what it is in Scripture. In the book of Acts, after different people believed on the Lord Jesus Christ, they were "*baptized*" or immersed in water. The baptism spoken of in this verse is of a different sort. It is a "*baptism*" performed by God the Holy Spirit.

The Picture of Baptism

We are an independent Baptist church. We believe that the best picture of what the Holy Spirit has done for us is the picture of water baptism by immersion where the saved ones are put under the water. It is a picture of our death, burial, and resurrection with the Lord Jesus Christ.

Sprinkling is not a picture of death, burial, or resurrection of Christ. It is not pouring. The best picture of what the Holy Spirit did to us was to be immersed in water. We are "*baptized*" into His death. The following verse is the best verse that shows us what the Holy Spirit has done for us in the baptism of the Holy Spirit. We are not talking about speaking in tongues as Charismatic and Pentecostal people often say.

- **1 Corinthians 12:13**
  For by one Spirit are we all baptized into one body, whether we be Jews or Gentiles, whether we be bond or free; and have been all made to drink into one Spirit.

The baptism of the Holy Spirit is one of the five ministries of the Holy Spirit to the Christian.

Two Ministries to the Unsaved

The Holy Spirit has two ministries to the unsaved: (1) His reproving of sin, righteousness, and judgment; and (2) His restraining of sin.

Five Ministries to Christians

1. The baptism of the Holy Spirit when we believe in Christ.
2. The indwelling of the Holy Spirit when we believe in Christ.
3. The sealing by the Holy Spirit when we believe in Christ.
4. The regeneration by the Holy Spirit when we believe in Christ.
5. The filling by the Holy Spirit when we meet the Scriptural conditions.

These first four take place immediately upon being saved by faith and are not necessarily experienced by any feeling on our part. The filling can occur at anytime and is experienced in our hearts and souls as the Holy Spirit fills us for service. We can continue to be filled and controlled by the Holy Spirit. When we are baptized by the Holy Spirit into the death of Christ, He joins us to the Lord Jesus Christ. We are also joined to every other believer in Christ. *"For by one Spirit are we all baptized into one body, whether we be Jews or Gentiles, whether we be bond or free; and have been all made to drink into one Spirit"* (1 Corinthians 12:13).

I do not agree with having Jews who have been redeemed by genuine faith in the Lord Jesus Christ holding separate church services. Once a Jew is saved, he is a Christian. Though he is a Jew by birth, he is now a Christian by choice. I would like to have any Jews who become saved come here to our church. We do not have to have a separate service for them. We are now one body in Christ.

As far as God sees it, when we are saved, we died with the Lord Jesus Christ. Scripture tells us that we were also buried with Christ when He was buried in the tomb. We were also raised with Christ when He was raised. We also ascended with Christ when He ascended to the Father's right hand. We are also seated with Christ in Heaven where He is today.

- **Ephesians 2:6**
  And hath **raised *us* up together, and made *us* sit together in Heavenly *places*** in Christ Jesus:

We died with Him. We were buried with Him. We arose with Him. We ascended with Him. We are seated with Him. We are down here on this earth, but as far as our position and standing goes, we are with the Lord Jesus Christ, in Heaven.

Everything that the Lord Jesus Christ did for us, we did with Him. That is how God sees it. That is hard for us to grasp and understand. We who are redeemed, are *"in Christ."* That phrase, *"in Christ,"* is used seventy-six times in our King James New Testament.

- **Romans 8:1**
  There is therefore now no condemnation to them which are **in Christ Jesus**, who walk not after the flesh, but after the Spirit.

- **Romans 12:5**
  So we, *being* many, are one body **in Christ**, and every one members one of another.

- **1 Corinthians 15:22**
  For as in Adam all die, even so **in Christ** shall all be made alive.

- **2 Corinthians 5:17**
  Therefore if any man *be* **in Christ**, *he is* a new creature: old things are passed away; behold, all things are become new.
- **Galatians 3:28**
  There is neither Jew nor Greek, there is neither bond nor free, there is neither male nor female: for ye are all one **in Christ Jesus**.
- **Ephesians 1:3**
  Blessed *be* the God and Father of our Lord Jesus Christ, who hath blessed us with all spiritual blessings in Heavenly *places* **in Christ**:

God sees us as completed. The body of Christ consists of all the genuinely saved believing Christians.

- **Ephesians 2:10**
  For we are his workmanship, created **in Christ Jesus** unto good works, which God hath before ordained that we should walk in them.
- **Ephesians 2:13**
  But now **in Christ Jesus** ye who sometimes were far off are made nigh by the blood of Christ.

This is a truth that is taught in Scripture which must be believed, even though we might not understand it fully.

Romans 6:4

"Therefore we are buried with him by baptism into death: that like as Christ was raised up from the dead by the glory of the Father, even so we also should walk in newness of life." We who are saved died with the Lord Jesus Christ, but that was not enough. We were *"buried with Him by baptism."* The Holy Spirit did this for us, on our behalf. We died with Him, we were buried with Him, we have been raised with Him, and we are seated with Him. All because we are *"in Christ."* What about walking *"in newness of life"*?

- **2 Corinthians 5:17**
  Therefore if any man *be* **in Christ**, *he is* a new creature: old things are passed away; behold, all things are become new.

What Is New When Saved?

We have many new things. What is new when we are saved?

1. We have a new Father.
2. We have a new Heavenly relationship with the Lord Jesus Christ.
3. We have a new relationship with our brothers and sisters in Christ.
4. We have a new forgiveness.
5. We have a new Home in Heaven.
6. We have a new sanctification, a new justification.

- **Galatians 6:15**
  For in Christ Jesus neither circumcision availeth any thing, nor uncircumcision, but **a new creature**.

God calls us who are redeemed "*a new creature*." You have heard of the "*creature*" from the Black Lagoon, well, we are a "*new creature*." Not like the Black Lagoon "*creature*." In this verse, it is not a "*creature*" in a bad sense, but a "*creature*" is simply that which God has created.

- **Ephesians 4:24**
  And that ye put on **the new man**, which after God is created in righteousness and true holiness.

Once we are saved we are a "*new man*" or a new woman.

- **Colossians 3:10**
  And have put on the **new *man***, which is renewed in knowledge after the image of him that created him:

- **Hebrews 10:19-20**
  Having therefore, brethren, boldness to enter into the holiest by the blood of Jesus, By **a new and living way**, which he hath consecrated for us, through the veil, that is to say, his flesh;

- **Revelation 5:9**
  And they sung **a new song**, saying, Thou art worthy to take the book, and to open the seals thereof: for **thou wast slain, and hast redeemed us to God by thy blood** out of every kindred, and tongue, and people, and nation;

We have many new things. We should walk in newness of life. We are new people if we are saved.

John MacArthur teaches that the word "*blood*" is only a metonym or a figure of speech for death, that it is not literal "*blood*." He says that "*blood*" does not mean "*blood*." In this verse, Revelation 5:9, there are two things spoken of as distinct, not mixed: (1) the death of the Lord Jesus Christ ("*thou wast slain*") and (2) the blood of the Lord Jesus Christ ("*and hast redeemed us to God by thy blood*") is entirely separate from His being "*slain*." There are two parts to our Lord's redemption. They concern His substitutionary "*death*" and His redeeming shed "*blood*."

"**we also should walk in newness of life.**" That word "*walk*" is a very descriptive expression which is used in the New Testament repeatedly.

● **Romans 13:13**
   Let us walk honestly, as in the day; not in rioting and drunkenness, not in chambering and wantonness, not in strife and envying.

Dr. Lewis Sperry Chafer, the founder of *Dallas Theological Seminary* and my teacher for 4 years, was a godly man. Dr. Chafer wrote a book called *He That is Spiritual.* I taught that book to the Bible Institute students there in Dallas at the Southern Bible Training School for Negroes.

One of Dr. Chafer's emphases in this book is the "*walk in the Spirit.*"

Three Conditions for Being Filled

There are three conditions for the filling of the Holy Spirit in the believer. Two are negative, and one is positive: (1) Grieve not the Spirit, (2) quench not the Spirit, and (3) walk in the Spirit.

Dr. Chafer reminded his readers that when we walk, each step is an incipient (or first stage) fall. If you do not put the other foot down in front of you, you will fall down flat on your face. God wants to remind us that none of us is going to stay on a plateau. We will have serious problems unless we realize this danger.

● **1 Corinthians 10:12**
   Wherefore **let him that thinketh he standeth take heed lest he fall.**

As we walk each step, we must make sure that the other foot comes down. That is a warning. We are to walk honestly.

● **2 Corinthians 4:2**
   But have renounced the hidden things of dishonesty, **not walking** in craftiness, nor handling the word of God deceitfully; but by manifestation of the truth commending ourselves to every man's conscience in the sight of God.

- 2 Corinthians 5:7
  (For we **walk** by faith, not by sight:)

Living Is Not Walking

Do you know what these new versions such as the New International Version do with that word, *"walk"*? The Greek word is PERIPATEO. It means literally *"to walk around."* Many new English versions, in various places, incorrectly translate the word "walk," by the word *"live."* There is a great deal of difference between *"living"* and *"walking."* I am sure everyone here is *"living,"* but you are not *"walking."* The word for *"walk"* is a very good image and word picture for what it is.

"Walking" with the Lord Jesus Christ is a step-by-step process. We *"walk"* by faith.

- Galatians 5:16
  This I say then, **Walk in the Spirit**, and ye shall not fulfil the lust of the flesh.
- Ephesians 2:2
  Wherein in time past ye **walked according to the course of this world**, according to the prince of the power of the air, the spirit that now worketh in the children of disobedience:

May God deliver us from our former *"course"* we *"walked"* in when unsaved. It was a terrible *"course."*

- Ephesians 4:1
  I therefore, the prisoner of the Lord, beseech you that ye **walk worthy** of the vocation wherewith ye are called,
- Ephesians 4:17
  This I say therefore, and testify in the Lord, that ye henceforth **walk not as other Gentiles walk**, in the vanity of their mind,
- Ephesians 5:8
  For ye were sometimes darkness, but now *are ye* light in the Lord: **walk as children of light**:
- Ephesians 5:15
  See then that ye **walk circumspectly**, not as fools, but as wise,

"Circumspectly" means that redeemed ones are to *"walk"* looking around in all directions, being careful lest they fall.

- **Colossians 1:10**
  That ye might **walk worthy of the Lord** unto all pleasing, being fruitful in every good work, and increasing in the knowledge of God;
- **Colossians 4:5**
  Walk in wisdom toward them that are without, redeeming the time.
- **1 Thessalonians 2:12**
  That ye would **walk worthy of God**, who hath called you unto his kingdom and glory.
- **1 Thessalonians 4:1**
  Furthermore then we beseech you, brethren, and exhort *you* by the Lord Jesus, that as ye have received of us **how ye ought to walk** and to please God, *so* ye would abound more and more.
- **1 Peter 4:3-4**
  For the time past of *our* life may suffice us to have wrought the will of the Gentiles, **when we walked in lasciviousness**, lusts, excess of wine, revellings, banquetings, and abominable idolatries: Wherein they think it strange that ye run not with *them* to the same excess of riot, speaking evil of *you*:

My wife and I went back to our 50th High School graduation anniversary at *Berea High School*, Berea, Ohio. Our fellow classmates were amazed that I was still a dedicated Christian and living to please the Lord Jesus Christ. They just could not understand it. One of our friends was almost saved Dick Golwitzer was a friend from our class of 1945 who almost was saved, but he did not accept the Lord Jesus Christ as his Saviour. He not only rejected Christ himself, but he thought for sure I would not last too long either. Fifty years later the man could not believe that I was still the same, and still believed in the Lord Jesus Christ.

The unsaved world thinks it is strange that Christians do not walk in the same riotous way as the world walks. These lost people love to live for self, for Satan, and for this world, and not for Christ.

- **1 John 1:7**
  But **if we walk in the light**, as he is in the light, we have fellowship one with another, and the blood of Jesus Christ his Son cleanseth us from all sin.

Romans 6:5

"For if we have been planted together in the likeness of his death, we shall be also *in the likeness* **of** *his* **resurrection:"** The baptism of the Holy Spirit has made the believers *"planted together"* in *"the likeness of His death."* How was the Lord Jesus Christ after He was raised? What was *"the likeness of His resurrection?"*

● Luke 24:6

He is not here, but is risen: remember how he spake unto you when he was yet in Galilee,

When the two Marys came to the tomb the angel said, *"He is not here, but He is risen."* We who are saved are going to have bodies that are resurrected bodies like the Lord Jesus Christ's resurrected body.

● John 20:19

Then the same day at evening, being the first *day* of the week, **when the doors were shut** where the disciples were assembled for fear of the Jews, came Jesus and stood in the midst, and saith unto them, Peace *be* unto you.

Though the doors were shut, the Lord Jesus Christ was able to go through the doors. I cannot walk through a door as long as it is shut, but the Lord Jesus' resurrected body could go between the protons, neutrons, and electrons in the atoms of that door.

● Luke 24:42

And **they gave him a piece of a broiled fish**, and of an honeycomb.

The Lord Jesus Christ could eat with His resurrected body. He did not have to, but he could.

● Romans 8:34

Who *is* he that condemneth? *It is* **Christ that died, yea rather, that is risen again**, who is even at the right hand of God, who also maketh intercession for us.

● Philippians 3:21

Who shall change our vile body, that it may be fashioned like unto his glorious body, according to the working whereby he is able even to subdue all things unto himself.

Our resurrected body will be exactly like that of the Lord Jesus Christ.

● 1 John 3:2

Beloved, now are we the sons of God, and it doth not yet appear what we shall be: but we know that, **when he shall appear, we shall be like him**; for we shall see him as he is.

We who have been *"planted together in the likeness of His death"* will be also *"in the likeness of His resurrection."* That is a wonderful prospect.

Our friend has said several times that she will be glad when she gets a new body without all her arthritis and pains. From time to time, we all have had some pain in our body, however slight, but one day all that pain will all be over. We who are saved will have a body like unto the Lord Jesus Christ's perfect body.

Romans 6:6

"Knowing this, that our old man is crucified with *him*, that the body of sin might be destroyed, that henceforth we should not serve sin." Our *"old man"* refers to the old sin nature that every human being inherited from Adam. He passed this sin nature on to the whole human race. We got it from our fathers and mothers.

Sin's Root and Sin's Fruit

There are two things about sin. (1) There is sin which is the root. (2) There are sins which are the fruit of that root nature.

The *"old man"* is that sin nature that we all have. We who are saved are not going to lose that sin nature until we get our resurrected bodies. We will continue to have the potential to sin. The *"old man"* loves to sin. The only thing that can restrain it is God the Holy Spirit Who indwells every born-again Christian.

As God sees it, *"our old man is crucified with him, that the body of sin might be destroyed."* The Christian's co-crucifixion with the Lord Jesus Christ is to disannul the *"body of sin."*

The Christians at Colossi were apparently lying one to another.

The word for *"destroyed"* is KATARGEO. The word means:

"to render idle, unemployed, inactivate, inoperative; to cause a person or thing to have no further efficiency; to deprive of force, influence, power; to cause to cease, put an end to, do away with, annul, abolish; to cease, to pass away, be done away; to be severed from, separated from, discharged from, loosed from any one; to terminate all intercourse with one."

- **Ephesians 4:22**
  That ye **put off concerning the former conversation the old man,** which is corrupt according to the deceitful lusts;
- **Colossians 3:9**
  Lie not one to another, seeing that **ye have put off the old man with his deeds;**

- **1 Corinthians 6:13**
  Meats for the belly, and the belly for meats: **but God shall destroy both it and them**. Now the body *is* not for fornication, but for the Lord; and the Lord for the body.
- **1 Corinthians 15:26**
  The last enemy *that* **shall be destroyed** *is* death.
- **2 Thessalonians 2:8**
  And then shall that Wicked be revealed, whom the Lord shall consume with the spirit of his mouth, and **shall destroy with the brightness of his coming**:

God will render that "*Wicked*" man of sin inoperative. He will not annihilate him. Jehovah's Witnesses believe in the annihilation of the soul. This is false. The devil and all those who reject the Lord Jesus Christ as Saviour will be in the Lake of Fire for all eternity.

- **Hebrews 2:14**
  Forasmuch then as the children are partakers of flesh and blood, he also himself likewise took part of the same; that **through death he might destroy him** that had the power of death, that is, the devil;

The Lord Jesus Christ is going to make the Devil inoperative.

Suffering For All Eternity to Come

I believe that there is not a sinner in all this world who will be destroyed in the sense of wiped out of existence. God is going to make them exist in suffering for all eternity to come. They will have everlasting existence in the Lake of Fire (Revelation 20:15).

I hate the thought of it, but if you and I do not persuade our loved ones and our friends to be saved by genuine faith in the Lord Jesus Christ, they will spend all eternity in the "*Lake of Fire and brimstone*" (Revelation 20:10, 14-15). I believe that the Lord is going to provide for those sinners bodies which will not be able to burn up. They will have asbestos-type of bodies. That is the only word that I can use to describe the bodies. Governments are trying to get rid of all the asbestos because it kills people. Whatever is the present day counterpart of asbestos, the Lord will make it so the unbelievers will have to feel the pain and fire of Hell.

It is terrible, but this is what it says in the book of Luke in the Lord Jesus Christ's account of the rich man and Lazarus. The rich man died and was sent to Hell. He lifted up his eyes "*being in torment*" (Luke 16:23). God is not going to completely annihilate Satan, He is going to render him inoperative and then He is going to cast him into the Lake of Fire "*where the beast and the false prophet are*" (Revelation 20:10). It is like a big tank. When an anti-tank weapon hits that tank, it renders that tank inoperative. It does not wipe it out. It just makes it a pile of steel and leaves those inside the tank dead.

That is what God wants believers to do with their "*old man.*" We should not serve sin. Because of this, "*henceforth we should not serve sin.*" We do not have to be a slave to the sin nature anymore. We are free.

- **Luke 16:13**
  No servant can serve two masters: for either he will hate the one, and love the other; or else he will hold to the one, and despise the other. Ye cannot serve God and mammon.
- **Romans 7:6**
  But now we are delivered from the law, that being dead wherein we were held; that **we should serve in newness of spirit**, and not *in* the oldness of the letter.
- **1 Thessalonians 1:9**
  For they themselves shew of us what manner of entering in we had unto you, and how **ye turned to God from idols to serve the living and true God**;

God wants us to serve the Lord Jesus Christ rather than be bound with the old sin nature.

Romans 6:7

"For he that is dead is freed from sin." When you are "*dead*," you do not have to pay taxes. You do not have to get up in the morning. You do not have to get dressed. You do not have to eat. You do not have to mow the lawn. You do not have to comb your hair. You do not have to take a shower. You are free from everything you have to do.

We Owe the Devil Nothing

If we who are saved are considered by God as being really "*dead*," we must realize that we have died with Christ. We are not obligated anymore to serve Satan. The world that is lost is obligated to be the Devil's servants. They have to do what their father wants them to do (John 8:44). They can do nothing but follow him in separation from the Lord Jesus Christ.

If we are saved, God has made provisions for us in everything that we need. He has equipped us for victory over the world, the flesh, and the devil.

Romans 6:8

"Now if we be dead with Christ, we believe that we shall also live with him:" This is one of the wonderful things about how God figures things. If we *"be dead with Christ,"* we *"shall also live with Him."* As we see from other New Testament verses, we are also ascended with Him, seated with Him, and, one day, we are going to live with Him for all eternity. The Scriptures are filled with these precious truths. Jesus said:

- **John 14:3**
  And if I go and prepare a place for you, I will come again, and receive you unto myself; that **where I am, *there* ye may be also**.

One day we will live with Him.

- **John 17:24**
  Father, I will that they also, whom thou hast given me, be with me where I am; that they may behold my glory, which thou hast given me: for thou lovedst me before the foundation of the world.

That is the promise of the Lord Jesus Christ for His believers. He wishes that we will be with Him, and we are going to be with Him. We shall live with Him for all eternity.

- **Philippians 1:23**
  For I am in a strait betwixt two, **having a desire to depart, and to be with Christ;** which is far better:

There is no *limbo* like the Catholics talk about. There is no purgatory or half-way house. If we are saved, we will depart and *"be with Christ"* immediately.

I could not get that through one Catholic lady's head who was one of the ladies in our Bible study. We have had over twenty-five years of Bible studies here in our home. I do not know if I ever got through to her on this. I hope I did. I hope she accepted Christ as her personal Saviour.

- **2 Corinthians 5:8**
  We are confident, *I say*, and willing rather to be **absent from the body, and to be present with the Lord**.

When and if this lady is saved, she will go Home to be with the Lord. Her spirit will be absent from her body and she will be with Christ. When some of the rest of us in our church go Home to be with the Lord, we will go immediately into His presence. The younger ones who are saved will take a little longer to go Home to be with the Lord. We do not know when that will be for any of us. The younger ones could be in an airplane crash or an automobile crash. If we are saved, we will depart and be with Christ immediately. There are no "if's, and's, or but's." There is no middle ground. We are instantaneously with

Christ.

One person was asking me about cremation. He did not want to be cremated. The wife wanted to save a little money on the burial cost, so she had him cremated. One of the friends of this man was concerned that this Christian man was cremated. She wondered what had happened to him. He is "*with Christ.*"

I Am Against Cremation

I am against cremation. I think a person should be buried. But even if your body is burned up with 10,000 degrees of heat, if you are genuinely redeemed, you will still depart and be with Christ when you die.

The fire is one of the ingredients of what Hell will be like. It is a terrible thing. Mrs. Waite and I asked one of the undertakers one time in Bridgeport, Connecticut about cremation. He showed us the ovens in the crematory. I asked the man what he did to cremate the bodies. He explained how he puts the body in the cremation oven, turns up the heat very high and burns it up. He told us he had to grind up the bones because they would not burn up. Then I asked him the $64,000 question. "*Sir, when you get ready to die, what are you going to do? Are you going to be cremated?*" He very quickly said, "*No!*"

* **Colossians 3:1**
  If ye then be risen with Christ, seek those things which are above, where Christ sitteth on the right hand of God.

We who are saved are "*risen with Christ*" as far as God is concerned.

Romans 6:9

"Knowing that Christ being raised from the dead dieth no more; death hath no more dominion over him." Once the Lord Jesus Christ had been "*raised from the dead*," then "*death hath no more dominion over Him.*" Christ did not die for His own sins. He died for the sins of the world. Death could not hold Him. He rose and gained victory over death forever.

Romans 6:10

"For in that he died, he died unto sin once: but in that he liveth, he liveth unto God." John the Baptist talked about this.

- John 1:29
  The next day John seeth Jesus coming unto him, and saith, **Behold the Lamb of God, which taketh away the sin of the world.**

The Old Testament word KAPHAR could only cover sin, but the Lord Jesus took it away. *"He died unto sin once."* He was not a sinner, but He took our sins in His own body.

- 2 Corinthians 5:21
  For **he hath made him** *to be* **sin for us, who knew no sin**; that we might be made the righteousness of God in him.

The Lord Jesus Christ lives continuously, and because He lives in a continuous sense, *"He ever liveth to make intercession"* for those who are saved. (Hebrews 7:25). He will never die any more.

The Mass Is Unscriptural

The Roman Catholics cannot kill Him, even though they try in every single Mass that they have. As far as they are concerned, the body and blood of Christ are literal. The elements of the Eucharist are not literal as far as the Bible is concerned. When the Roman Catholic priest says certain Latin words, Roman Catholic false theology teaches that the bread and the wine become the body of Christ and the blood of Christ. The Lord Jesus Christ is being crucified again. The Roman Catholic churches are doing this all over the world at every Mass that is held. The book of Hebrews tells us that the Lord Jesus died once for sin, never to die again (Hebrews 7:27; 9:26, 28).

Romans 6:11

"Likewise reckon ye also yourselves to be dead indeed unto sin, but alive unto God through Jesus Christ our Lord." Here is the victory over the sin nature. The first point in victory for those who are saved is to *"reckon"* themselves *"to be dead indeed unto sin."* If we are born-again, we died with Christ. God says we are to *"reckon"* it to be so.

The Greek word for "*reckon*" is LOGIZOMAI. It is variously translated as "*counted, imputed, or reckoned.*" We have to count on it. The word means:

> "*to reckon, count, compute, calculate, count over; to take into account, to make an account of; metaph. to pass to one's account, to impute; a thing is reckoned as or to be something, i.e. as availing for or equivalent to something, as having the like force and weight; to number among, reckon with; to reckon or account; to reckon inward, count up or weigh the reasons, to deliberate; by reckoning up all the reasons, to gather or infer; to consider, take into account, weigh, meditate on; to suppose, deem, judge; to determine, purpose, decide.*"

The definition continues:

> "*This word deals with reality. If I "logizomai" or reckon that my bank book has $25 in it, it has $25 in it. Otherwise I am deceiving myself. This word refers to facts, not suppositions.*"

My dad was a senior navigator. He had a boat in Vermilion, Ohio, and in Naples, Florida. He was a boater. He studied navigation. He was in the Navy in World War I. He liked the ships and he liked the sea. I do not know anything about navigation, but he did. He is with the Lord now. There is an expression in navigation called "*dead reckoning.*" I looked that up because I knew partially what it meant. It means:

> "*the finding of a ship's position by an estimate based on data recorded in the log, as speed and the time spent on a certain course, rather than by more precise means, as astronomical observations or Loran.*"

"*Dead reckoning*" is used when a ship's captain wonders about his position. He goes to his navigation log and finds out what course he has been on, how long he has been on it, and what his speed is. In this way, he can find his approximate position. By using the stars or LORAN or some other modern electronic means of navigation, he could find a more accurate position. Suppose there is no sun or stars, then you have to do some "*dead reckoning.*" You have to depend on what is written in your navigation log. So with born-again Christians today, we must "*reckon*" as true what God has written in His Word.

Reckoning Ourselves Dead

We must *"reckon"* ourselves *"to be* [continually] *dead indeed unto sin, but alive unto God through Jesus Christ our Lord."* All three of the verbs (*"reckon,"* *"to be,"* and *"alive"*) are in the present tense. In the Greek language, the present tense means continuous action. We must continuously *"reckon"* that we died with Christ. We must count on it, and hold it to be true.

Then we who are saved must believe that we are continually *"alive unto God."* This is the answer to the problem of the sin nature. We no longer have to yield to these temptations from that sin nature. We no longer have to say whatever the sin nature wants me to say. My body does not have to sin. I have a sin nature, but I can say "No" to that sin nature. I no longer have to obey my mouth when it wants to utter sinful words. I do not have to sin. If I choose to sin, that is up to me, but I do not have to. I am freed from that. I do not have to think thoughts of evil. If I do sin with my body, my words, or my thoughts, I must confess this and get God's forgiveness.

● 1 John 1:9

If we confess our sins, he is faithful and just to forgive us *our* sins, and to cleanse us from all unrighteousness.

Answer to the Sin Nature

This continual *"reckoning"* ourselves to be *"dead indeed unto sin"* is the answer to the power of the sin nature over our lives.

We do not have to go along with it. We do not have to obey it. We do not have to say "Yes" to it. But we do have to remember we are *"alive unto God"* because the Lord Jesus Christ has given us new life.

Someone has said when sin knocks on the door of your heart, your mouth, your life, your body, and that knock is heard by you, send the Lord Jesus Christ to answer the door. That's a good statement, is it not?

Romans 6:12

"Let not sin therefore reign in your mortal body, that ye should obey it in the lusts thereof." This expression is a negative prohibition in the Greek present tense. In the present tense prohibition, it means to stop an act already in process. The negative prohibition in the aorist tense means not even to begin to do something. This is in the present tense which means to stop doing something already in progress. These Christians to whom Paul was writing there at Rome, Italy, were letting sin *"reign"* in their *"mortal bodies."* Paul said: *"Stop it! That is enough!"* We do not have to let that old sin nature continue to *"reign"* if we have been freed from the power of that sin nature and the Lord has given us the Person of the Holy Spirit within us. We do not have to continue to let sin *"reign"* in our mortal bodies. There are various Scriptures on *"reigning."*

- **Romans 5:14**
  Nevertheless **death reigned from Adam to Moses**, even over them that had not sinned after the similitude of Adam's transgression, who is the figure of him that was to come.

Death continued to take over the whole landscape and everyone died because of Adam's sin.

- **Romans 5:21**
  That as **sin hath reigned unto death**, even so might **grace reign through righteousness** unto eternal life by Jesus Christ our Lord.

The Greek word for *"reigned"* is BASILEUO. It means:

  "to be king, to exercise kingly power, to reign; of the governor of a province; of the rule of the Messiah; of the reign of Christians in the millennium; metaph. to exercise the highest influence, to control."

Paul was telling the Christians at Rome to stop letting the old sin nature be king over them or to reign in their mortal body.

The Choice is Ours

The sin nature does not have to *"reign."* We do not have to obey it or answer to it. The choice resides with us.

We can stop letting that sin nature reign in our life, or we can go ahead and let it reign.

- **Luke 8:25**
  And he said unto them, Where is your faith? And they being afraid wondered, saying one to another, What manner of man is this! for **he commandeth even the winds and water, and they obey him.**

Born-again Christians who profess the name of the Lord Jesus Christ do not seem to want to obey Him. The elements obey Him. The winds obey Him. The water obeys Him. All nature obeys Him. Some of us seem to say, "*I don't want to obey Him.*" He must be the Lord of our lives. We must obey Him. We should not obey the "*lusts*" thereof. There are many verses against "lust."

- **Matthew 5:28**
  But I say unto you, That whosoever looketh on a woman to **lust** after her hath committed adultery with her already in his heart.

We do not have to obey. Our sin nature has all kinds of "*lusts.*" We may be saved by grace with God the Holy Spirit in our bodies, but we still have to deal with these lusts that the sin nature has.

We have seen various things in the news have we not? We have seen the lust of our former President, the lust of the former Speaker of the House, the lust of the Speaker to be, and of various others who have had to resign. The one that has the most "*lust*" is not going to resign. He or she will stay right there in office.

- **Mark 4:19**
  And the cares of this world, and the deceitfulness of riches, and **the lusts of other things** entering in, choke the word, and it becometh unfruitful.
- **Romans 1:24**
  Wherefore God also gave them up to uncleanness through **the lusts of their own hearts,** to dishonour their own bodies between themselves:
- **Romans 13:14**
  But put ye on the Lord Jesus Christ, and make not provision for the flesh, **to *fulfil* the lusts *thereof*.**
- **Galatians 5:16**
  This I say then, Walk in the Spirit, and **ye shall not fulfil the lust of the flesh.**

Walk--A Step at a Time

God the Holy Spirit inside the saved, born-again Christian is able to stop the Christian from fulfilling the *"lust of the flesh."* We need to walk in the Spirit. *"To walk"* means to take a step at a time. It is not something that you have already arrived at. You must take one step at a time. Dr. Chafer used to say, *"Every step is an incipient fall."*

- 1 Corinthians 10:12
  Wherefore let him that thinketh he standeth **take heed lest he fall.**

Moment-By-Moment Dependence

Walking in the Spirit is a moment-by-moment dependence upon God the Holy Spirit.

- Ephesians 4:22
  That ye put off concerning the former conversation the old man, **which is corrupt according to the deceitful lusts**;
- Titus 2:12
  Teaching us that, **denying ungodliness and worldly lusts**, we should live soberly, righteously, and godly, in this present world;
- James 1:15
  Then when **lust hath conceived**, it bringeth forth sin: and sin, when it is finished, bringeth forth death.

Death lies at the end of lust, sin and wickedness.

- 1 Peter 2:11
  Dearly beloved, I beseech *you* as strangers and pilgrims, **abstain from fleshly lusts**, which war against the soul;

The bodily lusts war against the soul. The spirit and the soul is what God wants to keep clean as well as our bodies.

- 1 John 2:15-16
  Love not the world, neither the things *that are* in the world. If any man love the world, the love of the Father is not in him. For all that *is* in the world, **the lust of the flesh**, and **the lust of the eyes**, and the pride of life, is not of the Father, but is of the world.

We do not have to let sin reign and rule in our bodies. Paul tells the Roman believers to stop it and to quit it. He would say the same to every one of us who are saved in our own world today.

Romans 6:13

"Neither yield ye your members *as* instruments of unrighteousness unto sin: but yield yourselves unto God, as those that are alive from the dead, and your members *as* instruments of righteousness unto God."

This verse begins with a *"neither"* which is a negative. The verb *"yield"* is in the Greek present tense. Like the preceding verse, 12, here is a negative prohibition in the present tense which means to stop an action already in progress. This means that these Christians in Rome, to whom Paul was writing, were in the continued process of *"yielding"* their members *"as instruments of unrighteousness unto sin."* That included their hands, their feet, their eyes, their legs, their fingers, their mind, and all the other *"members"* of their body. Paul told them to stop it!

Threefold Genuine Victory

Here, then, is the threefold remedy for fulfillment for genuine victory in the Christian life.

1. Continue to reckon yourself indeed dead unto sin, and alive unto Christ.

2. Stop letting sin reign in your mortal bodies.

3. Stop yielding your members as instruments of unrighteousness unto sin.

- Matthew 5:30
  And if thy right hand offend thee, cut it off, and cast *it* from thee: for it is profitable for thee that one of thy **members** should perish, and not *that* thy whole body should be cast into Hell.

- **James 3:5**
  Even so the tongue is a little **member**, and boasteth great things. Behold, how great a matter a little fire kindleth!

That word "*member*" means part of our body.

- **Psalm 33:2**
  Praise the LORD with harp: **sing unto him with the psaltery *and* an instrument of ten strings.**

There is a book that my mother-in-law gave me when I was first saved called *An Instrument of Ten Strings*. This book was written by William Pettingil. He was one of the editors of the Old Scofield Reference Bible. Dr. Pettingil made the analogy that

---

Our Instrument of Ten-Strings

The body is like a ten-string instrument. We have two eyes, two ears, two feet, two hands, one mouth, and one heart. That is our instrument of ten-strings.

Once we are saved, we should want to praise our Lord on all of our "*strings*" that the Lord has given us.

- **Psalm 144:9**
  I will sing a new song unto thee, O God: upon a psaltery *and* **an instrument of ten strings** will I sing praises unto thee.

May all of our "*members*" praise the Lord. We have an instrument that we must continue to yield unto the Lord to be used of Him.

"but yield yourselves unto God, as those that are alive from the dead, and your members *as* instruments of righteousness unto God." The Greek word for "*yield*" is PARISTEMI. Depending on the context, it means:

> "*to place beside or near; to set at hand; to present; to proffer; to provide; to place a person or thing at one's disposal; to present a person for another to see and question; to present or show; to bring to, bring near; metaph. i.e to bring into one's fellowship or intimacy; to present (show) by argument, to prove; to stand beside, stand by or near, to be at hand, be present; to stand by; to stand beside one, a bystander; to appear; to be at hand, stand ready; to stand by to help, to succour; to be present; to have come; of time.*"

PARA means "*beside or near*" and TITHEMI means "*to put or place*." The resultant meaning of this term is to place our "*members*" or bodies along side, or near the Lord for His use. That is what it means literally. That is what we need to do. We should not be like Peter who stood near the enemy. He put the members of his body close to the enemy's fire. Because he was there to watch the end of what would happen to the Lord Jesus, he denied the Lord three times.

We are to continue to yield our members, all ten strings, unto the Lord. We are to put them at His disposal at all times. Does He want our mouth? Let Him have it. Does He want our eyes? Give them to Him. Does He want our ears to listen to His praises? Let Him have them. Does He want our feet to go where He wants us to go? Let Him have them. Does He want our hands to do His work? Give them to Him. Does He want our heart which is the most important member? Of course He does. Let Him have it! Proverbs tells us this.

- **Proverbs 23:26**
  My son, give me thine heart, and let thine eyes observe my ways.

The Heart Is the Key to All

If the Lord has our heart, He will have the use of all of the other members of our body.

Romans 6:14

"For sin shall not have dominion over you: for ye are not under the law, but under grace." As I mentioned before, sin, the nature is the root and sins are the fruit of that nature. Sin is the nature that we have from Adam right straight down the line. We are Adamic and we have inherited a sin nature and that will never change.

I know there are some churches and groups who say that we can somehow get entirely sanctified. They say that we can obliterate that whole sin nature. Well, that is not possible. The Scriptures do not teach that.

In Romans 7 we will see this clearly. The sin nature will never be eradicated, but, if we are saved, it can be controlled by the Holy Spirit of God. If we are born-again, the Holy Spirit indwells us. It is the Holy Spirit Who must do battle with that old sin nature. The root is the sin nature. The fruit is the sins that come from that sin nature.

When Paul wrote that *"sin shall not have dominion over you,"* he is speaking of the sin nature. That Greek word for "dominion" is KURIEUO. It means:

"to be lord of, to rule, have dominion over; of things and forces; to exercise influence upon, to have power over."

The noun that is related to this verb is KURIOS. It is the word, *"Lord,"* which is used for our Lord Jesus Christ. What Paul is saying is that the *"sin"* nature does not need to have lordship over you who are saved. Each believer has the Holy Spirit of God given to him or her by the Lord Jesus Christ. They can moment-by-moment, as they *"walk in the Spirit"* (Galatians 5:5:16), be kept from sin. Not that we are sinlessly perfect or ever will be sinlessly perfect, but God can control our sin nature if we allow Him to do so with the result that *"sin shall not have dominion"* over us. There are many verses on *"dominion."*

- **Zechariah 9:10**
  And I will cut off the chariot from Ephraim, and the horse from Jerusalem, and the battle bow shall be cut off: and he shall speak peace unto the heathen: and **his dominion** *shall be* from sea *even* to sea, and from the river *even* to the ends of the earth.

- **Romans 6:9**
  Knowing that Christ being raised from the dead dieth no more; **death hath no more dominion over him**.

- **Romans 7:1**
  Know ye not, brethren, (for I speak to them that know the law,) how that **the law hath dominion over a man** as long as he liveth?

- **1 Peter 5:10-11**
  But the God of all grace, who hath called us unto his eternal glory by Christ Jesus, after that ye have suffered a while, make you perfect, stablish, strengthen, settle *you*. **To him** *be* **glory and dominion** for ever and ever. Amen.

- **Revelation 1:5-6**
  And from Jesus Christ, *who is* the faithful witness, *and* the first begotten of the dead, and the prince of the kings of the earth. Unto him that loved us, and washed us from our sins in his own blood, And hath made us kings and priests unto God and his Father; **to him** *be* **glory and dominion** for ever and ever. Amen.

The Lord Jesus Christ is the One Who should have *"dominion."* He will have *"dominion"* in the future, and He does have *"dominion"* over all of the things which are His. He is the Creator. He is the Saviour. He is the Lord. He wants *"dominion"* over our lives.

Sin, the nature, and sins, the fruit of that nature, *"shall not have dominion over"* the believers because they are *"not under the law, but under grace."* Under the law of Moses, the Israelites did not have God the Holy Spirit indwelling them. The Holy Spirit came and went and left them here and there, but not so in the New Testament under grace. The age of the church is different from the age of the Law. When we are saved by faith in Christ and we trust in

Him as our Saviour and Redeemer, we are told by the Words of God that the Holy Spirit enters into our bodies. Our bodies become His "*temple*" (1 Corinthians 6:19-20). He will never leave that "*temple*." That is why we can never perish.

The Holy Spirit Never Leaves Us

Once we are saved and the Holy Spirit enters our bodies, He will never leave us.

I do not agree with those who say that a Christian can be demon-possessed. I do not believe that the Devil can come in and possess what the Holy Spirit has already claimed for His own. I realize that Satan and demons can **influence** the believers as he influenced Peter. The Lord told His disciples that He was going to be crucified at Jerusalem by the elders and chief priests and then to rise again on the third day (Matthew 26:21-23). Then the apostle Peter opened his big mouth. Part of me is glad he did so, because he represents all of us who are saved. That is what some of us may have done. Peter rebuked Him and said, "*Be it far form Thee, Lord: this shall not be unto Thee*" (Matthew 26:22). Peter was expecting the Lord Jesus Christ to be the King of Kings and Lord of Lords right then. Peter wanted the Lord to reign and to deliver the Jews from the Romans. What did the Lord tell him? He said: "*Get thee behind me, Satan*" (Matthew 26:23). Here Satan was influencing, though not indwelling, Peter.

Satan can influence the Christian, but cannot possess the Christian. Grace has given us a new picture. It has given us a Saviour and the Holy Spirit to reign inside of us with the power of God. We who are saved have a new nature that the law of Moses never could give those who are under the law until the Lord Jesus came to die for our sins.

Romans 6:15

"What then? shall we sin, because we are not under the law, but under grace? God forbid." Just because we are "*under grace*," we should not "*sin*." Yes, God can forgive believers' sins (1 John 1:9), but this does give them a license to sin.

God Forbid

This expression, *"God forbid,"* let me just touch on it once again. This term appears in our King James Bible twenty-four times, nine in the Old Testament and fifteen in the New Testament. Those who are critical of the King James Bible remind their audiences that the word *"God"* is not in the Greek text. They say this is *"dynamic equivalency."* Because of this, these critics say I should be quiet about the over 6,653 dynamic equivalencies of the New International Version, the over 4,000 dynamic equivalencies of New American Standard Version, and the over 2,000 dynamic equivalencies in the New King James Version. These same critics will never be able to even come close to finding this amount of what they term, *"dynamic equivalencies"* in our King James Bible.

I have been reading Dean John W. Burgon's book, *Inspiration and Interpretation.* We have reprinted it for the Dean Burgon Society. Dean Burgon, in 1861, used the term, *"God forbid."* That was in the 1800's. In other words, from 1611 to 1861 the term *"God forbid"* was still being used. Even today, some people wonder if we should use *"God forbid."* The Greek words behind this are ME GENOITO. It means literally, *"may it not be, or come to pass, or may it never even once happen."* Does not this meaning come across clearly by the term *"God forbid"*?

Romans 6:16

"Know ye not, that to whom ye yield yourselves servants to obey, his servants ye are to whom ye obey; whether of sin unto death, or of obedience unto righteousness?" Obedience determines a Christian's servitude. If we yield to our sin nature as our "lord," we become a *"servant"* to that sin nature. The Greek word for *"servant"* is DOULOS. It means:

"a slave, bondman, man of servile condition; a slave; metaph., one who gives himself up to another's will; those whose service is used by Christ in extending and advancing His cause among men; devoted to another to the disregard of one's own interests; a servant, attendant."

To Whom Do We Yield?

If we yield our members as servants to unrighteousness as unto sin, we are servants or slaves to sin. But if we yield our members unto the Lord, as He wants us to, we will be servants or slaves to Him, leading to *"righteousness."*

- Galatians 1:10
  For do I now persuade men, or God? or do I seek to please men? for if I yet pleased men, I should not be **the servant of Christ**.

We often try to please other people. It is all right to please others, if we can, but if it is a question between pleasing people and pleasing the Lord, we must please the Lord.

- Galatians 1:10
  For do I now persuade men, or God? or do I seek to please men? **for if I yet pleased men, I should not be the servant of Christ**.

We must not yield ourselves unto sin to obey, but unto the Lord as servant-slaves. The successful Christian life that is pleasing to the Lord is a form of *"slavery."* Why do I say this at the risk of being misunderstood? Because of the meaning of the word *"servant"* in the Greek language. Though there are many other words translated "servant" in our King James Bible, this word is DOULOS. It means:

> *"a slave, bondman, man of servile condition; a slave; metaph.,* ***one who gives himself up to another's will;*** *those whose service is used by Christ in extending and advancing His cause among men;* ***devoted to another to the disregard of one's own interests;*** *a servant, attendant."*

This is a very serious word. I am not talking about physical slavery such as we had during Civil War days. I am talking about *"spiritual slavery."* Those of us who have been saved by genuine faith in the Lord Jesus Christ should be completely obedient to and controlled by the Lord Jesus Christ. As the relation of a *"servant-slave"* to his *"master,"* so we should do everything that our *"Lord"* would want us to do. Is there anything wrong with that?

The Lord Jesus Christ died in our place. He gave His life for us. He shed His blood for us. He redeemed us at the cross of Calvary. He bought us with His blood. Should we not give Him our best and obediently yield unto Him? In fact, I believe that any saved person who does not obey the Lord Jesus Christ is living in sin! I also believe that there are countless professing (and even possessing) believers who are living in the sin of disobedience to their Lord and Master! This is a shame, and it must hurt the heart of our God.

In the United States Navy, the only response to a direct order is, "*Aye, aye sir.*" I was a Navy Chaplain five years on active duty. I served with the Marines two of those years. That is the response with a salute, "*Aye, aye sir.*" When our Saviour, in His Bible, in His Word, gives us directions, commands, and direct orders, "*Aye, aye sir,*" or "*Yes, Sir,*" or "*Speak, LORD; for thy servant heareth*" (1 Samuel 3:9) should be our response.

Spiritual Slavery to Christ

There is nothing wrong with spiritual slavery to the Lord Jesus Christ. He will never lead us astray. He will never take advantage of us if we yield ourselves to Him as His servant or His slave. He will do us good and not evil. We must realize that we are to obey the Lord and serve Him. We are not to be servants or slaves to sin.

Romans 6:17

"But God be thanked, that ye were the servants of sin, but ye have obeyed from the heart that form of doctrine which was delivered you." We were "*slaves of sin*" before we were saved. Some of you reading this book may not be saved, may not be born-again, may not be regenerated. So, you are a slave, a "*servant of sin.*" You are a servant of Satan. You are in Satan's army. You are Satan's child (John 8:44), and the Lord Jesus wants to snap those fetters away from Satan and deliver you into the precious kingdom of His dear Son (Colossians 1:3).

● **Isaiah 14:17**
That made the world as a wilderness, and destroyed the cities thereof; *that* **opened not the house of his prisoners**?

This is speaking about Satan. This is talking about Lucifer. Satan does not want to set His prisoners free. He wants to keep them enslaved.

We Are Born Children of Satan

Before we were saved, if we are presently saved, we were in the power of Satan (Ephesians 2:2). We were born into this world as a child of Satan. Many people do not believe that. The modernists and the liberals say we are all the children of God. No, we are not.

There are two fatherhoods. The Lord Jesus told the Pharisees in the Gospel of John:

- **John 8:44**
  Ye are of *your* father the devil, and the lusts of your father ye will do. He was a murderer from the beginning, and abode not in the truth, because there is no truth in him. When he speaketh a lie, he speaketh of his own: for he is a liar, and the father of it.

Do you suppose they liked hearing that? Nobody wants to hear that. There are two fatherhoods. The Devil is one father. When we are born we become members of his family. We are the children of the Devil. When we are born-again we are in God's family. God wants every single human being on the face of the earth in His family. Satan does not want to open "*the house of his prisoners*".

- **Luke 4:18**
  The Spirit of the Lord *is* upon me, because he hath anointed me to preach the gospel to the poor; he hath sent me to heal the brokenhearted, **to preach deliverance to the captives**, and recovering of sight to the blind, to set at liberty them that are bruised,

One of the things that the Lord Jesus Christ was to do, while here on earth in His first coming, was "*to preach deliverance to the captives.*" This is what the Lord Jesus Christ wants to do right now. He wants to break Satan's prisoners out of their prison house and make them saved by personal and genuine faith in His finished work on the cross.

- **2 Timothy 2:26**
  And *that* they may **recover themselves out of the snare of the devil**, who are taken captive by him at his will.

Every last person before he is saved is in the "*snare of the devil.*" If you are not saved, you are still in the "*snare of the devil.*"

- **Galatians 5:1**
  Stand fast therefore in the liberty **wherewith Christ hath made us free**, and be not entangled again with the yoke of bondage.
- **Hebrews 2:14-15**
  Forasmuch then as the children are partakers of flesh and blood, he also himself likewise took part of the same; **that through death he might destroy him that had the power of death, that is, the devil**; And deliver them who through fear of death were all their lifetime subject to bondage.

Satan "*had the power of death.*" He wants to keep the people in his bondage. The Lord Jesus wants to free us.

- **Mark 7:6**
  He answered and said unto them, Well hath Esaias prophesied of you hypocrites, as it is written, This people honoureth me with *their* lips, **but their heart is far from me.**

It is not enough to obey the doctrine with our "*lips,*" but we must obey with our "*heart.*"

- **Acts 8:36-37**
  And as they went on *their* way, they came unto a certain water: and the eunuch said, See, *here is* water; what doth hinder me to be baptized? And Philip said, **If thou believest with all thine heart**, thou mayest. And he answered and said, I believe that Jesus Christ is the Son of God.
- **Acts 11:23**
  Who, when he came, and had seen the grace of God, was glad, and exhorted them all, **that with purpose of heart they would cleave unto the Lord**.

We must have "*purpose of heart*" and also "*cleave unto the Lord.*"

- **Romans 10:9-10**
  That if thou shalt confess with thy mouth the Lord Jesus, and shalt **believe in thine heart** that God hath raised him from the dead, thou shalt be saved. **For with the heart man believeth unto righteousness**; and with the mouth confession is made unto salvation.

We have a verse on our offering gift box that gives a similar sentiment.

- **2 Corinthians 9:7**
  Every man **according as he purposeth in his heart**, so let him give; not grudgingly, or of necessity: for God loveth a cheerful giver.

As it says in Proverbs, "*My son, give me thine heart*" (Proverbs 23:26.) There are many, I am sure, reading this book who used to be servants or slaves to sin.

You who have been saved, have obeyed from the heart the teaching of the Lord Jesus Christ when he said,

- Matthew 11:28
  Come unto me, all ye that labour and are heavy laden, and I will give you rest.

Delivered From Satan's Grasp

If you are saved, you came unto the Lord Jesus Christ, and you genuinely believed in Him as your Saviour. He has given you eternal life. If you are reading this and have not yet done that, I pray that right now you will do that. God wants you to be delivered from Satan's grasp, from Satan's power, Satan's hold, and Satan's family by personal and genuine faith in His Son, the Lord Jesus Christ.

Romans 6:18

"Being then made free from sin, ye became the servants of righteousness." That was a wonderful, wonderful day. If you are reading this and you have trusted the Lord Jesus Christ as your Saviour, you remember the time, the place, and even the hour, perhaps, when this took place and you became *"free"* from that old Devil, *"free"* from his clutches, *"free"* from his hold on you, *"free"* from the sin nature.

There is a gospel chorus that says, *"This one thing I know. God in His mercy pardoned me. Snapped sin's fetters and set me free. This one thing I know."* This is a good gospel song. When the Lord Jesus Christ comes into our lives and we are saved through faith in Him, we are no longer servants or slaves in bondage to sin and the Devil. We become the servants and the slaves of *"righteousness."* Therefore we should live a life of righteousness and please the Lord Jesus Christ who saved us and called us with a Holy calling.

- 1 Peter 4:4
  Wherein they think it strange that ye run not with *them* to the same excess of riot, speaking evil of *you*:
  If you live a righteous life, sinners around you are going to wonder why you are living a righteous life. They will wonder why you are not sinning like they are. They will wonder why you do not go to the same places, drink the same substances, and do the same things as they do. They will wonder and *"speak evil of you."* The world might think it is strange, but once we have been freed from the bondage of sin and slavery to the Devil, we can live to please the

Lord Jesus Christ Who has given us life eternal.

Romans 6:19

"I speak after the manner of men because of the infirmity of your flesh: for as ye have yielded your members servants to uncleanness and to iniquity unto iniquity; even so now yield your members servants to righteousness unto holiness." In the old life, if we are saved, we used to yield our *"members servants to uncleanness."* We yielded our eyes to the Devil, our hands to the Devil, our ears to the Devil, our feet to the Devil, our mouths to the Devil, and our hearts to the Devil. We were the Devil's children.

Once we are saved, we are to *"yield"* our *"members servants to righteousness unto holiness."* As I have said before, the idea of *"servants"* is from a Greek word that means *"slaves."* What does it mean to *"yield"*? The Greek word is PARISTEMI . PARA means *"along side of"* and HISTEMI which means *"to place."* The resultant meaning is:

"to place beside or near; to set at hand; to present; to proffer; to provide; to place a person or thing at one's disposal; to present a person for another to see and question; to present or show; to bring to, bring near; metaph. i.e to bring into one's fellowship or intimacy; to present (show) by argument, to prove; to stand beside, stand by or near, to be at hand, be present; to stand by; to stand beside one, a bystander; to appear; to be at hand, stand ready; to stand by to help, to succour; to be present; to have come; of time."

Are You At His Disposal?

For you as a born-again Christian to *"yield"* to the Lord Jesus Christ means that you place yourself along side of the Lord and therefore *"at His disposal,"* so that He can use you whenever He desires.

For example, if you have a cup from which you drink your juice, that cup should be at your disposal so when you get thirsty you can use it to drink. It should be *"yielded"* to you if it is your cup. That cup must be *"at your disposal."* That cup must *"yield"* to you. That is what this word means, among many other things, *"to place at the disposal of someone."*

We must *"yield"* our members--our bodies--unto righteousness and unto the Lord Jesus Christ. What if the cup you wanted to fill with water was filled with motor oil? What would you have to do? You would have to pour that oil out so it can *"yield"* to your wishes and use. That cup must be at your disposal all the time. You should be able to fill it with whatever you might want, whether it be juice, water, or milk. That is the way the Lord Jesus Christ wants every member of our body, at His disposal at all times. That is a difficult thing for everyone of us because we want to be the lord and master of our own lives. Like the *Burger King* motto, we want to have it *"our way."*

What did the Lord Jesus Christ say to His Father at the most crucial time in His whole ministry? In the Garden of Gethsemane He prayed to His Father to remove *"this cup"* (whatever that may have been). Some believe He was praying that He not die in the Garden but on the cross. Others believe the *"cup"* was Calvary and His bearing the sins of the world.

● **Luke 22:42**
Saying, Father, if thou be willing, remove this cup from me: nevertheless **not my will, but thine, be done**.

His attitude was clear. That is the attitude that all of us who are saved should have. We should want to *"yield"* our members as instruments for the Lord to be used when, where, and how He wants.

Some of the words of a popular gospel song are: *"I'll go where you want me to go dear Lord, I'll say what you want me to say, and I'll be what you want me to be."* Many of those who sing these words do not mean it. If the Lord should call our children to the foreign field as missionaries away from us, many might say, *"No, I want to keep them here. I want to grab on to them."* Yielding our members to the Lord means they are at His disposal to do whatever He would have us to do.

Mrs. Waite went to *Moody Bible Institute*--the *"Old"* Moody. It has all changed now. It is sliding and drifting like all the other schools. She told me that these young people, at a real strong preaching service, would come down and yield themselves to the Lord. They would yield to the Lord's will whatever He would have them to do. But that did not last for most of them. Some of them did go and do what the Lord wanted them to do. Others just turned right around and went their own way. The Lord Jesus Christ wants us to yield to Him sincerely and in perpetuity.

Romans 6:20

"For when ye were the servants of sin, ye were free from righteousness." When we were lost, we were *"servants of sin"* and slaves to the old nature and the old Devil. We were absolutely *"free from righteousness."* We could not do anything righteous. It says in the book of Isaiah that all our righteousnesses are like *"filthy rags."*

- **2 Corinthians 5:21**
  For he hath made him *to be* sin for us, who knew no sin; that **we might be made the righteousness of God in him.**

Our Standing--Absolutely Righteous

We were "*free from righteousness*" before we were saved, but "*in Christ*" we were "*made*" righteous. In our standing before the Lord we are absolutely righteous. Even when we were lost we may have seemed righteous, but God said we were "*free,*" that is, without any form of God's righteousness.

- **Matthew 5:20**
  For I say unto you, That **except your righteousness shall exceed *the righteousness* of the scribes and Pharisees,** ye shall in no case enter into the kingdom of Heaven.

  If we compare ourselves with somebody else, we might think we are righteous, but if we're not saved, no matter how righteous we seem to be from the standards of mankind, in God's eyes we are not righteous.

Romans 6:21

"What fruit had ye then in those things whereof ye are now ashamed? for the end of those things *is* death." Before we were saved, all we knew how to do was "*to eat, and to drink, and to be merry*" (Ecclesiastes 8:15). That is one of the important cries of the world. This is the theme of those in the old life of sin. After a recent Sunday morning service, one of the folks came up to me and said: "*Just the thought of that old life makes me sick.*"

I Have No Desire to Go Back

I can look back on my old life before I was saved. Though I used to enjoy it, now I have no desire to go back to that old life under the domination of sin and of Satan.

I was not as bad a boy as I might have been. I used to dance, but when I was saved, I stopped dancing because I knew that this was not proper for me as a young Christian boy at the age of sixteen. I also had a fifteen-piece dance band. I played the saxophone and clarinet in my band. I thought, "*I do not have to dance now. I will just stay in my dance band and that will be all right. Nobody would have to know that Waite is no longer dancing. They would not have to know that I had a conviction against dancing. I will just hide that conviction behind my dance band.*"

Then, the man that led me to Christ got ahold of me. His name was Uncle Charlie Allen, a former drunk whom the Lord Jesus Christ saved. He was the head janitor in our Berea High School, Berea, Ohio. We call them "*custodians*" now. He said to me: "*All those people dancing around are dancing because of your music. That is not Christian.*" Well, I understood that. I quit my band. I could see that those band members were arguing and swearing during practices. I did not want any part of that mess, so I left the band. The new leader was right there, ready to take over. He bought all the music stands and the music, and took over.

I still had my "*W*" on the music stands, standing for "*Waite.*" There was another boy who was a Christian and became a preacher. His name was Lynn. He was a carnal believer and he went to dances in those early days before he got straightened around. He was at a dance at his school. He went to a different high school than ours. Lynn asked somebody where Waite was. He knew I used to own that band. He saw Waite's music stands with the "W"on them, but did not see Waite. Only about twenty or thirty-years later did he tell me this story. He knew that a change had taken place in Waite and that he was now a Christian. This was a testimony of a young man who straightened out his life thereafter, and later became a Baptist Pastor. He and I have been dear friends ever since.

The Lord Jesus Christ saved me in 1944 when I was a high school senior. I was the first student in that school that dear Uncle Charlie Allen led to Christ. He was as happy as he could be. Through the influence of a few of us who were saved, we led several others in our class to the Lord. When our class of 1945 graduated, Uncle Charlie told me that he had graduated with our class, with all these who were born-again. It is amazing! Uncle Charlie only had a 6th grade education, but there was one thing he knew. He knew the Lord Jesus Christ as his Saviour, and he served Him faithfully. The Lord saved me through that man's faithful witness.

Paul asked the question, "*What fruit had ye then in those things whereof ye are now ashamed*" There is no good "*fruit*" in the past life. Fruits are important.

- **Matthew 7:16**
  Ye shall know them by their fruits. Do men gather grapes of thorns, or figs of thistles?

We should be ashamed of the evil works of the flesh

- **Galatians 5:19**
  Now the works of the flesh are manifest, which are *these*; Adultery, fornication, uncleanness, lasciviousness, Idolatry, witchcraft, hatred, variance, emulations, wrath, strife, seditions, heresies, envyings, murders, drunkenness, revellings, and such like: of the which I tell you before, as I have also told *you* in time past, that they which do such things shall not inherit the kingdom of God.

Everyone Has the Old Flesh

Every person living has the old flesh, even those who are saved. As such, even the saved are capable of every one of these sins. By the power of God the Holy Spirit, Who indwells those who are born-again, we do not have to yield to these things.

We have been enabled to manifest the fruit of the Holy Spirit instead of the works of the old flesh.   The *"fruit of the Spirit"* is *"love, joy, peace, longsuffering, gentleness, goodness, faith, meekness, temperance"* (Galatians 5:22-23).   That is the *"fruit of the Spirit."*

We should not be *"ashamed"* of anything in our Christian life.

- **Mark 8:38**
  Whosoever therefore shall be ashamed of me and of my words in this adulterous and sinful generation; of him also shall the Son of man be ashamed, when he cometh in the glory of his Father with the holy angels.
- **Romans 1:16**
  For I am not ashamed of the gospel of Christ: for it is the power of God unto salvation to every one that believeth; to the Jew first, and also to the Greek.

We ought not be *"ashamed"* of the *"gospel of Christ."*

- **Romans 9:33**
  As it is written, Behold, I lay in Sion a stumblingstone and rock of offence: and **whosoever believeth on him shall not be ashamed**.

Why should we be *"ashamed"* of our faith?

- **Philippians 1:20**
  According to my earnest expectation and *my* hope, **that in nothing I shall be ashamed**, but *that* with all boldness, as always, *so* now also Christ shall be magnified in my body, whether *it be* by life, or by death.

- **2 Timothy 1:8**
  Be not thou therefore ashamed of the testimony of our Lord, nor of me his prisoner: but be thou partaker of the afflictions of the gospel according to the power of God;

- **2 Timothy 1:12**
  For the which cause I also suffer these things: nevertheless **I am not ashamed**: for I know whom I have believed, and am persuaded that he is able to keep that which I have committed unto him against that day.

- **2 Timothy 2:15**
  Study to shew thyself approved unto God, **a workman that needeth not to be ashamed**, rightly dividing the word of truth.

- **1 Peter 4:16**
  Yet if *any man suffer* as a Christian, **let him not be ashamed**; but let him glorify God on this behalf.

If you suffer as a sinner you must be ashamed, but if you *"suffer as a Christian"* you should not be ashamed.

- **1 John 2:28**
  And now, little children, abide in him; that, when he shall appear, we may have confidence, **and not be ashamed before him at his coming**.

Are you going to be *"ashamed before Him at His coming"*? I trust not.

Romans 6:22

"But now being made free from sin, and become servants to God, ye have your fruit unto holiness, and the end everlasting life." *"Being made free from sin"*--what a wonderful reality! We who are born-again do not have to sin. We do not have to be evil. We do not have to do that which is wrong and unrighteous. God has enabled us, by the superhuman Power of God the Holy Spirit Who indwells us, to be free from that.

The Sin Nature Is Not Removed

God has not taken the sin nature out of us, but He has given us the Holy Spirit to conquer and control that sin nature. That is why God wants us to "*be filled with the Spirit*" (Ephesians 5:18), that is, completely controlled by the Holy Spirit of God. God delivered us and made us "*free.*"

- **John 8:32**
  And ye shall know the truth, **and the truth shall make you free.**

We have been "*freed*" by the "*truth*" of God's Word.

- **John 8:36**
  If the Son therefore shall make you free, ye shall be free indeed.

The Lord Jesus Christ has made "*free*" those of us whom He has saved.

- **Galatians 5:1**
  Stand fast therefore in the liberty wherewith **Christ hath made us free,** and be not entangled again with the yoke of bondage.

Christ delivered us from sin and "*made us free.*"

- **2 Corinthians 1:9**
  But we had the sentence of death in ourselves, **that we should not trust in ourselves,** but in God which raiseth the dead:

- **Galatians 1:4**
  Who gave himself for our sins, **that he might deliver us from this present evil world,** according to the will of God and our Father:

- **Colossians 1:13**
  Who hath delivered us from the power of darkness, and hath translated *us* into the kingdom of his dear Son:

This "*deliverance*" from the "*power of darkness*" is what the Lord Jesus Christ did when he saved us. He delivered us from the power of Satan.

- **1 Thessalonians 1:10**
  And to wait for his Son from Heaven, whom he raised from the dead, *even* Jesus, **which delivered us from the wrath to come.**

He is a great Deliverer!

- **Hebrews 2:14**
  Forasmuch then as the children are partakers of flesh and blood, he also himself likewise took part of the same; that **through death he might destroy him that had the power of death, that is, the devil;**

"ye have your fruit unto holiness, and the end everlasting life." The *"fruit"* of the Spirit that every born-again Christian is to manifest is: *"love, joy, peace, longsuffering, gentleness, goodness, faith, meekness, temperance"* (Galatians 5:22-23). That is the fruit that God wants us to have. There is a gospel song entitled, *"Nothing But Leaves."* The chorus ends with the words, *"Instead of the fruit He is wanting, we give him nothing but leaves."* This must make our God very sad when He sees His born-again children living, not *"unto holiness,"* but after the *"works of the flesh."*

Romans 6:23

"For the wages of sin *is* death; but the gift of God *is* eternal life through Jesus Christ our Lord." Sin pays *"wages."*

Sin Pays Terrible Wages

Sin pays people their *"wages"* on time. It pays time-and-a-half for *"over-time"* also. It pays double-time on holidays. Yes indeed, sin pays *"wages."*

Adam's heritage was death. God promised him that *"in the day that thou eatest thereof* [of the tree] *thou shalt surely die"* (Genesis 2:17). Because Adam and Eve disobeyed God and sinned, both physical and spiritual death passed upon all of the world. All of us are now dead spiritually when we are born, and all will die physically unless the Lord Jesus Christ returns in the rapture to allow the saved ones to escape that physical death by being changed to His likeness (1 Corinthians 15:51-54; 1 Thessalonians 4:16-17).

The *"gift of God,"* as told us in this verse, is *"eternal life through Jesus Christ our Lord."* In contrast to Adam, the Lord Jesus Christ's heritage is *"eternal life."* There are many verses in our Bible about God's *"gift."*

- **John 4:10**
  Jesus answered and said unto her, **If thou knewest the gift of God**, and who it is that saith to thee, Give me to drink; thou wouldest have asked of him, and he would have given thee living water.

Christ--The Greatest Gift

The Lord Jesus Christ is *"the gift of God."* If we do not have Him, we do not possess the greatest "gift" in all of time and eternity.

- **2 Corinthians 9:15**
  Thanks *be* unto God for **his unspeakable gift**.

This is speaking about the Lord Jesus Christ. This *"gift"* cannot even be put into words; it is an *"unspeakable gift."*

- **Ephesians 2:8**
  For by grace are ye saved through faith; and that not of yourselves: *it is* **the gift of God**:

Salvation is *"the gift of God."*

- **John 3:16**
  For God so loved the world, that **he gave his only begotten Son**, that whosoever believeth in him should not perish, but have everlasting life.

The phrase, *"He gave,"* represents the act of His giving. The gift Itself was *"His only begotten Son."* The motive of the *"gift"* was God the Father's love. The result of this loving *"gift"* was that those who believed in Him and received Him would *"not perish"* but *"have everlasting life."*

- **John 10:28**
  And **I give unto them eternal life**; and they shall never perish, neither shall any *man* pluck them out of my hand.

God gave His own Son as a *"gift."* Now, the Gift Who has been given, gives us who believe, a *"gift."* *"And I give unto them eternal life; and they shall never perish."*

Christ Offers You Eternal Life

If you are reading this book, and have never yet received that eternal life by genuine faith in the Lord Jesus Christ, He offers it to you also.

- **John 17:3**
  And **this is life eternal**, that they might know thee the only true God, and Jesus Christ, whom thou hast sent.

In this verse, the Lord Jesus Christ was praying to His Father.

- **1 John 5:11**
  And this is the record, that **God hath given to us eternal life, and this life is in his Son**.

Romans
Chapter Seven

Romans 7:1

"Know ye not, brethren, (for I speak to them that know the law,) how that the law hath dominion over a man as long as he liveth?" This is a simple open and shut statement. The Mosaic law had *"dominion"* as the Lord or the master as long as a man was living. This is true of any law, whether it is the speed law, or whether it is the income tax law, or the law of Moses. No law can touch us if we are dead. That is the end of its control over us. People have died who have owed thousands of dollars. After they die, no one can collect money from them. Sometimes they can collect from their estate. Basically, death breaks the law's *"dominion"* over us. With some laws we do not agree. Some laws we are opposed to, but we are still under the law. If we are living as a citizen of a certain country, we have to obey the proper laws of that country.

Romans 7:2

"For the woman which hath an husband is bound by the law to *her* husband so long as he liveth; but if the husband be dead, she is loosed from the law of *her* husband."

Before I comment on this second verse of the chapter, let us turn this into a *"let's pretend"* session. Some of you who are younger do not know what that is. There used to be a radio program called, *"Let's Pretend."* The reason I am going to *"pretend"* is that we are getting into some deep and heavy water and some difficult sailing. There is some difficult and controversial doctrine here in verses 2 and 3. In order for us to see clearly God's teachings in these verses, we must not bring our own present status into the equation. Because of this, let's pretend!

There are people who are involved in this situation. They cannot do anything about it now. They are already in the storm. They have a divorce and a remarriage on their hands. But, for the sake of our children and the unmarried, let's pretend that none of us are married. Let us pretend that we are trying to see clearly what God has to teach us about marriage, divorce, remarriage, and the permanence of the marriage institution. In order to do this effectively, dispassionately, and clearly, let us just pretend.

There is so much confusion about divorce and remarriage both in this country and around the world. Let us pretend that no one is married. There are some of our young people who are not married. They are sitting here. How are we going to teach the younger generation what God's standards are? You may have failed in marriage. You may have gotten into trouble, but let us just forget that. God is able to forgive you, even if you have gotten into trouble, whether it was before you were saved or after you were saved and didn't know any better. Let's pretend that none of us are married. What does God teach in regard to the permanency of marriage? Though many others disagree, I believe the Scriptures are clear on this matter.

Here we have, in this verse 2, God's picture of the permanency of marriage. The only dissolution of that marriage is when the husband or the wife dies. Death is the only thing that breaks the marriage bonds. Let us pretend that we are not married, and let us see what God's Words are teaching. To me, I look at the Bible and say that it is as simple as pie. There is not a single person in this world that should be confused by what God teaches. Our young people who are going to be married one day must have a clear idea of the Bible's teachings on the permanence of marriage.

Mrs. Waite and I have been married since 1948. Along with the many blessings we have enjoyed, there have also been a few rocky roads during these decades. When we entered our marriage, both my wife and I had a firm stand that we are together for life, and that has carried us through successfully. Just like a ship at sea that is going down, we have a life boat. We are both in the life boat and are going to stay there until we get to Shore safely. And that Shore is Heaven!

When you go into marriage as young people, and I counsel this with those whom I marry, do not go into this flippantly. The divorce rates are sky-rocketing almost off the charts. The divorce rates used to be one in four, then one in three, then one in two, and lately, over 60% of all marriages end in divorce. Sadly, this is happening even in many of our Bible-believing Christian churches.

Five Ways For Permanent Marriage

(1) Be sure that first of all you are saved. Be certain that the Lord Jesus Christ is your personal Saviour and that you have been washed by His blood, and are born-again by the Holy Spirit.

(2) Be sure that, when you go into your marriage, that you have dedicated yourself completely to the Lord Jesus Christ. Dedication is important.

(3) Be sure that your future mate is also saved, born- again, washed in the blood of Christ, and also dedicated completely to the Lord Jesus Christ. Both of you must be agreeing that you are going to follow whatever the Bible teaches.

(4) Be certain that you both agree that marriage is for life and neither of you will divorce the other.

(5) Then, even after you agree that you both are saved, you both have dedicated yourselves completely to obey the Lord Jesus Christ, and you both are going to follow what the Bible teaches against divorce, there still will be a rocky road ahead of you. Though there still will be fights and battles, and all kinds of things that will come your way, at least you will be starting out right.

Let us get into what God does teach on divorce, remarriage, and the permanence of marriage.

The Marriage Bond Until Death

God teaches us that we are bound to our mates until death breaks that bond.

There are some Scripture verses that I want us to look at. By the way there are a couple of, so called, exception verses such as:

- **Matthew 5:32**
  But I say unto you, That whosoever shall put away his wife, **saving for the cause of fornication**, causeth her to commit adultery: and whosoever shall marry her that is divorced committeth adultery.

- **Matthew 19:9**
  And I say unto you, Whosoever shall put away his wife, **except it be for fornication**, and shall marry another, committeth adultery: and whoso marrieth her which is put away doth commit adultery.

These two verses in Matthew are usually cited as giving some exception against the clear teachings of the Bible in other places that make no provision for divorce and remarriage.

When Clear Contradict Unclear

There is a law of hermeneutics (which is Biblical interpretation) which goes like this: *"Never contradict clear passages of Scripture by some unclear passage that seems to teach something different."* We must always interpret the unclear or questionable passages by the other clear and unquestionable teachings of other passages in the Words of God.

Let us take a look at some of these clear verses before looking at the so-called *"exception"* verses of Matthew. In this way, we can explain satisfactorily the *"exception"* verses in the light of the clear and unmistakable passages. Before taking up the specific verses, let me make this observation. Though the verses often mention the husband taking some action, it is my assumption that it is equally applicable, by extension, to the wife who takes the same action. In other words, it works both ways.

- **Matthew 19:6**
  Wherefore they are no more twain, but one flesh. What therefore God hath joined together, **let not man put asunder**.

God does not want man through divorce or anything else to *"put asunder"* his wife, and vice versa. This is a very clear verse prohibiting divorce.

- **Mark 10:9**
  What therefore God hath joined together, **let not man put asunder**.

- **Mark 10:11**
  And he saith unto them, **Whosoever shall put away his wife**, and marry another, committeth adultery against her.

A Clear Verse on Adultery

This is a verse that teaches very clearly that, if a man divorces his wife and marries another, he *"committeth adultery against her."* Once a person enters marriage, he or she must remain there lest when the partner re-marries, he or she becomes guilty before God of *"adultery"* against his wife, or she against her husband.

- Luke 16:18

   Whosoever putteth away his wife, and marrieth another, **committeth adultery:** and **whosoever marrieth her** that is put away from *her* husband **committeth adultery.**

   In this verse from Luke, the Lord Jesus Christ adds another very clear element surrounding divorce and remarriage. The one who marries a woman who has been married and divorced also *"committeth adultery,"* and vice versa.

- 1 Corinthians 7:10-11

   And unto the married I command, *yet* not I, but the Lord, **Let not the wife depart from** *her* **husband:** But and if she depart, **let her remain unmarried, or be reconciled to** *her* **husband:** and **let not the husband put away** *his* **wife.**

   There are some other clear teachings on marriage. The wife is not to *"depart from her husband"* and vice versa. If she departs, there are only two things for her to do: (1) *"remain unmarried"* or (2) *"be reconciled to her husband."* The husband is not to *"put away"* or divorce his wife and vice versa. Nothing could be stated clearer than in these two verses.

- 1 Corinthians 7:39

   The wife is bound by the law as long as her husband liveth; **but if her husband be dead,** she is at liberty to be married to whom she will; only in the Lord.

Only Death Breaks the Marriage

Here again is a very clear teaching to the effect that only death can break the marriage bond. The wife is *"bound by the law"* as long as her husband *"liveth"* and vice versa. Only *"if her husband be dead"* can she have God's liberty and freedom to marry another, and vice versa.

We must teach our young people that are not yet married what the Scriptures teach concerning marriage. We must also teach them to obey those Scriptures. What if you are already in this situation? Well, you must face up to what Scripture teaches so far as the teaching to your children. You must teach your children faithfully exactly what God's Words teach on this subject. They might say, *"Well, Mom and Dad you did not do it this way."* Well, you tell them that is right, but God has forgiven me, I have confessed it unto Him. I know that I have done wrong but the Scriptures are clear. It is difficult sometimes to get the proper Biblical attitude when we are involved in something. It is hard to get an objective look at the matter.

That is one of the beautiful things about Bible exposition verse-by-verse. You must deal with every verse as you come to it. You cannot back out of it. You cannot get into your shell and say, *"Well, let us not even touch that, let us pick something else and preach on it."* As you know, I did not select this portion of Scripture to pick on anybody, but God picked it. It is in this book that we are studying. It is in the book of Romans, and we are going to teach it. As I say, that is the beautiful part of being a Bible preacher. You can teach what you believe to be true.

Dallas Theological Seminary, where I was trained (1948-1953), taught us that you did not have to stay married all your life. You could use various excuses, including adultery, if you want. They used all kinds of very scholarly-sounding approaches. But I think the Scriptures are against that view and very clear about it.

I married people as a Naval Chaplain five years on active duty. I used to marry quite a few. If they are both unsaved I would marry them, but I would not marry a Christian with a non-Christian. After one or two of those unsaved marriages, where they were getting divorced after one or two months, I said to myself: *"No more . That is the end of it. As long as I am in the military I will not marry them anymore. I will send them to some other Chaplain. I will send them to a modernistic Chaplain to marry them. I am not going to do it any more."*

Marriage Is for Keeps

Marriage is for keeps. It is important that we marry properly. This is something that people are not clear about and they fall into the trap. They are also not teaching their children the teachings of the Scriptures in regard to this subject. When I do marry two believers that are saved, they have stuck together pretty well.

When I do officiate in a marriage, I use the old-fashioned way and wording, "*Until death us do part.*" Many ceremonies have changed the wording of the service completely. The couples often make up their own words, their own laws, their own little sayings. They sometimes say they will stay married "as long as we both agree" or "as long as we love one another." They do not say, "*Until death us do part,*" anymore. That is often taken out of the marriage ceremony. This is done, not just by the modernistic, liberals, and unbelievers, nor the Neo-Evangelicals, but even among some Fundamentalists, separatists, real strong Bible-believing people. Some are watering down the marriage ceremony. Now that we have gone to meddling, let us pretend, remember we must analyze this problem. We must get ourselves in an objective mode.

Romans 7:3

"So then if, while *her* husband liveth, she be married to another man, she shall be called an adulteress: but if her husband be dead, she is free from that law; so that she is no adulteress, though she be married to another man."

I do not know how much clearer words can be concerning the will of God regarding the permanence of marriage than in this verse. Clearly, in the New Testament teachings, death is the only thing that breaks the marriage bond.

Marriage Ended Only by Death

So far as God's Words are concerned, marriage can only be ended by the death of one of the mates. Only after the death of the mate does God give permission to the other mate to remarry.

The woman would not be called an "*adulteress*" if she marries after her husband dies, but if she marries while her husband is still alive, she shall be "*called an adulteress*" and vice versa.

I believe there should be a respectable length of time to elapse before the remarriage of the mate in this situation, out of respect for the deceased mate. Throughout our marriages, we must be certain to act as the Bible commands us to act as husbands and wives. We must really love our mates as God tells us. A husband is to love his wife. A wife should be obedient to her own husband in love. We praise God for the Scriptural answer to various problems of marriage. There are certainly many problems. If both of you come into marriage knowing that the only way out of that marriage is after one of you dies, you will enter that estate with an entirely different mind-set than if you do not believe this.

Romans 7:4

"Wherefore, my brethren, ye also are become dead to the law by the body of Christ; that ye should be married to another, *even* to him who is raised from the dead, that we should bring forth fruit unto God." Here in Verse 4, we have the permanency of marriage used as a picture of the Law of Moses and the grace of the Lord Jesus Christ. Paul stated that the Jews were married to the Law of Moses, but they have "*become dead to the law by the body of Christ.*" Just as death breaks the marriage bond, so "*death*" to the law broke the Jews' bond to the law.

God wanted the Jews, and the Christians of today as well, to be "*married to another.*" We do not have to go through all the blood sacrifices of the Old Testament. We are finished with the law because we are "*married to another,*" even to the Lord Jesus Christ by faith. He was "*raised from the dead.*" The purpose of this union was that the saved should "*bring forth fruit unto God.*" "*Fruit*" is very important in the Scripture.

- **Matthew 7:17-20**
  Even so every good tree bringeth forth good **fruit**; but a corrupt tree bringeth forth evil **fruit**. A good tree cannot bring forth evil **fruit**, neither *can* a corrupt tree bring forth good **fruit**. Every tree that bringeth not forth good **fruit** is hewn down, and cast into the fire. **Wherefore by their fruits ye shall know them**.

God wants us who are saved to bring forth "*good fruit*" to the Lord. After we are "*married*" to the Lord by being born-again and saved by genuine faith in Him, we are obligated to bring forth "*good fruit.*" The Lord Jesus Christ talked more about this.

- **John 15:4**
  Abide in me, and I in you. As the branch cannot bear **fruit** of itself, except it abide in the vine; no more can ye, **except ye abide in me**.

We must stay close to the Lord Jesus Christ in order to bring forth lasting and genuine "*fruit*" unto Him.

- **John 15:5**
  I am the vine, ye *are* the branches: He that abideth in me, and I in him, **the same bringeth forth much fruit**: for without me ye can do nothing.

- **John 15:8**
  Herein is my Father glorified, **that ye bear much fruit**; so shall ye be my disciples.

- **John 15:16**
  Ye have not chosen me, but I have chosen you, and ordained you, **that ye should go and bring forth fruit, and** *that* **your fruit should remain**: that whatsoever ye shall ask of the Father in my name, he may give it you.
- **Galatians 5:22-23**
  But the fruit of the Spirit is love, joy, peace, longsuffering, gentleness, goodness, faith, Meekness, temperance: against such there is no law.

The Holy Spirit's Ninefold Fruit

If we are saved, the Holy Spirit indwells our body, and God wants us to bring forth the Holy Spirit's ninefold *"fruit."*

- **Colossians 1:10**
  That ye might walk worthy of the Lord unto all pleasing, **being fruitful in every good work**, and increasing in the knowledge of God;

  God has told us who are saved that we are now *"married"* to the Lord Jesus Christ and He wants to be producing *"good fruit"* in our lives. The Holy Spirit is the only One who can bring forth *"good fruit"* in our lives. The old flesh is not able to do this.

  There is a gospel song that I have referred to various times, *"Nothing but leaves."* Let me quote you a verse of it,

  "The Master is seeking a harvest in lives He's redeemed by His blood. He seeks for the fruit of the Spirit and works that will glorify God. Nothing but leaves for the Master. Oh how His loving heart grieves. When instead of the fruit He is seeking, we offer Him nothing but leaves."

Only Leaves Instead of Fruit

It is a sad thing to claim to be saved by the blood of Christ, but all we give to Him are leaves instead of fruit. God wants spiritual fruit in our lives.

Romans 7:5

"For when we were in the flesh, the motions of sins, which were by the law, did work in our members to bring forth fruit unto death."

- **Romans 8:8-9**
  So then they that are **in the flesh** cannot please God. But ye are not **in the flesh**, but in the Spirit, if so be that the Spirit of God dwell in you. Now if any man have not the Spirit of Christ, he is none of his.

"In the flesh" is an expression in Scripture which, if used for a person, means that this person is lost.

- **2 Corinthians 10:3**
  For though we walk **in the flesh**, we do not war **after the flesh**:

We who are saved are still in this body, but we should not use carnal weapons.

- **Philippians 3:3**
  For we are the circumcision, which worship God in the spirit, and rejoice in Christ Jesus, and **have no confidence in the flesh**.

Sin Brings Forth Evil Fruit

The *"motions of sins"* are the afflictions and the passions of sin. It brings forth evil *"fruit"* that leads to *"death."*

- **Galatians 5:19**
  Now the works of the flesh are manifest, which are *these*; Adultery, fornication, uncleanness, lasciviousness, . . .

These works are produced by many of those who are lost. Sadly, they are produced too often by those who are saved, but not sanctified by the Lord's power.

When we were *"in the flesh"* and lost, we were not married to Christ. We were in sin. We had the old sin nature (and still do), but the Holy Spirit had not yet entered our bodies because we had never been born-again. This is what happened. We did not have *"fruit"* unto the Lord, but *"unto death."*

There is a verse of Scripture which talks about the young widows who do not re-marry, but live in sin. While the sinning widow lives, she is *"dead while she liveth"* (1 Timothy 5:6). They are not physically *"dead,"* but their quality of life is as *"death."* They are living for self and this is what it means that they are "*dead.*"

● **1 Corinthians 7:39-40**
The wife is bound by the law as long as her husband liveth; but if her husband be dead, she is at liberty to be married to whom she will; only in the Lord. But she is happier if she so abide, after my judgment: and I think also that I have the Spirit of God.

Romans 7:6

"But now we are delivered from the law, that being dead wherein we were held; that we should serve in newness of spirit, and not *in* the oldness of the letter."

Paul, speaking for the Jews who are now saved (as well as for saved Gentiles), said "*we are delivered from the law.*" In other words, the law had no more force or power over them. For the believer, the law is dead. Just like when a husband dies, the wife is free. So Paul was freed because the law died, and now he is married to Christ. Paul and all the Jews who are now saved were formerly held in bondage, but now God wants them to "*serve in newness of spirit, and not in the oldness of the letter.*" The "*letter*" is a word that refers to the "*law of Moses.*" The law could only kill because no one could fulfill it.

There are thousands of different regulations in the Old Testament law of Moses. The Pharisees, the scribes, and all the other Jewish leaders interpreted this law and added many other rules of their own. That is why the Lord Jesus said to the Pharisees that they had made "*the Word of God of none affect by your tradition.*" They made their own additions to that law.

We should not serve "*in the oldness of the letter,*" but "*in the newness of the Spirit.*"

Read the Entire Bible Each Year

We should be reading daily the Words of God in our King James Bible so as to read the entire Bible in one year. This can be done with the *Yearly Bible Reading Schedule,* published by the Bible For Today, at a pace of 85 verses per day.

● **2 Corinthians 5:17**
Therefore **if any man *be* in Christ, *he is* a new creature**: old things are passed away; behold, all things are become new.

We should serve the Lord in the "*newness*" of the Holy Spirit of God. If we are saved, the Holy Spirit of God indwells our bodies, and He wants us to serve and be a slave and do the will of the Lord Jesus Christ from now on until death parts us.

Romans 7:7

"What shall we say then? *Is* the law sin? God forbid. Nay, I had not known sin, but by the law: for I had not known lust, except the law had said, Thou shalt not covet." In this verse 7 we see this expression "*God forbid*," again. It is in the Greek optative mood (ME GENOITO) meaning "*may it not be.*"

The Four Moods in Greek Grammar

There are four moods in Greek grammar.
1. The imperative mood is used to issue a command.
2. The indicative mood is used in making a positive statement.
3. The subjunctive mood, is used in doubtful or uncertain sentences.
4. The optative mood is used in sentences that express wishes.

Hence the term, "*God forbid*," being in the optative mood, was a strong wish that the action in question would not come to pass.

In answer to the question, "*Is the law sin?*" the King James Bible made very clear the answer by its rendition of "*God forbid.*" Just because we cannot keep the law of Moses does not mean it is "*sin.*" Is it sin to have a law about speed limits? No, it is not sinful. There is a law in New Jersey that says you can only travel 25 miles per-hour when the houses are so many feet apart. Just because we might violate the law does not make the law wicked or sinful. We are the ones who violate it and are sinful and wicked. Is the law of Moses sin? No! Paul said, "*I had not known sin, but by the law.*" In other words, when there came a law which said you cannot do this or that, then you knew what sin was because that law told me I could not do it.

If my neighbor has a grove of oranges or apples, and there was no written law against it, I could just go and grab all the oranges or apples I could. That would not be stealing because there was no law against it. Once the law comes in that says, "*Thou shalt not steal,*" then I know stealing is sin and I am convicted of sin if I steal. When there is no law, you don't know what the sin is. Paul said, "*I had not known lust, except the law had said, Thou shalt not covet.*" That Geek word "*covet*" is EPITHUMEO. It means:

"*to turn upon a thing; to have a desire for, long for, to desire; to lust*

after, covet; of those who seek things forbidden."
There are various verses about this.

- **Exodus 18:21**
  Moreover thou shalt provide out of all the people able men, such as fear God, men of truth, **hating covetousness**; and place *such* over them, *to be* rulers of thousands, *and* rulers of hundreds, rulers of fifties, and rulers of tens:

When you *"covet"* something, you want more of it. You have to watch out. *"Covetous"* people will want everything you have. They may want your car, your wife, or many other things that belong to you. There are many things that *"covetous"* people want to steal. It is in the old sin nature to *"covet."*

- **Exodus 20:17**
  Thou shalt not covet thy neighbour's house, **thou shalt not covet** thy neighbour's wife, nor his manservant, nor his maidservant, nor his ox, nor his ass, nor any thing that *is* thy neighbour's.

- **Deuteronomy 5:21**
  Neither shalt thou desire thy neighbour's wife, **neither shalt thou covet thy neighbour's house**, his field, or his manservant, or his maidservant, his ox, or his ass, or any *thing* that *is* thy neighbour's.

- **Joshua 7:21**
  When I saw among the spoils a goodly Babylonish garment, and two hundred shekels of silver, and a wedge of gold of fifty shekels weight, **then I coveted them**, and took them; and, behold, they *are* hid in the earth in the midst of my tent, and the silver under it.

The Lord did not act favorably on Achan's sin. In fact, all Israel was under judgment and death because Achan, just one person in that whole tribe, sinned. Do you know what God said about Achan's sin?

They were praying because they went off to Ai to fight a battle. They won a battle in Jericho, and then they went over to Ai to fight with just a few people. The people of Ai just mowed them down. Joshua could not understand it. Here the Lord gave them victory in Jericho, and he could not understand why they could not conquer the people of Ai. Do you know what God said about the sin of Achan who had taken of the cursed stuff of Jericho? He said *"Israel hath sinned"* (Joshua 7:11). Though only one man had sinned, God considered the entire nation of Israel as having sinned. When Joshua was on his face praying for God's help to win the battle of Ai, God said, *"Get thee up; wherefore liest thou thus upon thy face?"* (Joshua 7:10) First things must come first.

Judge Sin Personally

There are certain sins that should not request God's help as the very first priority. The first priority is to judge personally the sin in question and put it out of the way completely. After this has been done, then it is proper to request the Lord to help you.

The Lord did deal with Achan. He slew Achan and all of his family that was apparently in on the sin with him. Was it right of the Lord to kill Achan's family also? Yes indeed. The family apparently wanted the stolen merchandise and gold just as much as their father Achan did. The mother and the children were all in on this with Achan.

- **Luke 12:15**
  And he said unto them, Take heed, and **beware of covetousness**: for a man's life consisteth not in the abundance of the things which he possesseth.

- **Ephesians 5:3**
  But fornication, and all uncleanness, **or covetousness**, let it not be once named among you, as becometh saints;

In this verse, the Lord puts "*covetousness*" in the same general classification as the sins of "*fornication, and all uncleanness.*"

- **Colossians 3:5**
  Mortify therefore your members which are upon the earth; fornication, uncleanness, inordinate affection, evil concupiscence, and **covetousness**, which is idolatry:

In this verse, look at the company that the sin of "*covetousness*" keeps. Notice, this verse identifies "*covetousness*" as "*idolatry*." When you "*covet*" something, you treat that object as an idol and revere it.

- **1 Timothy 3:3**
  Not given to wine, no striker, not greedy of filthy lucre; but patient, not a brawler, **not covetous**;

This verse gives some of the requirements for the office of a pastor-bishop-elder.

No Covetous Pastors

A pastor who is *"covetous"* is Scripturally disqualified. He can not be a pastor. Someone has aptly defined *"covetousness"* as *"the itch for more."* How much *"more"* is not the question. A person who *"covets"* is never satisfied.

The Lord wants us to be satisfied with what the Lord has given us.

• **Hebrews 13:5**
Let your conversation be **without covetousness**; and be content with such things as ye have: for he hath said, I will never leave thee, nor forsake thee.

These are great verses. The law reveals the sin of *"covetousness."*

Romans 7:8

"But sin, taking occasion by the commandment, wrought in me all manner of concupiscence. For without the law sin *was* dead." Here is sin, *"taking occasion."* The Greek word "occasion" is APHORME. It means:

"a place from which a movement or attack is made, a base of operations;(metaphor) that by which endeavour is excited and from which it goes forth; that which gives occasion and supplies matter for an undertaking, the incentive; the resources we avail ourselves of in attempting or performing anything."

Sin's Command Post

When *"sin"* takes *"occasion,"* it has a command post for further evil operations.

"Sin," the nature, *"wrought"* in Paul *"all manner of concupiscence."* The reason for this is that he finally knew that sin was sin. For without the law to tell him what sin was, *"sin was dead."* When the *"commandment"* of the law came along, it made Paul all the more sinful, because he realized he could not keep it.

Romans 7:9

"For I was alive without the law once: but when the commandment came, sin revived, and I died." In the Garden of Eden, there was not a law of Moses. It was the dispensation of innocence, followed by conscience, human government, and promise. In the days of Abraham there was no law of Moses. When the law came in, sin was made plain. Everyone knew what it was. This is what you do, and this is what you do not do! Paul said he was *"alive without the law,"* but when the *"commandment came,"* then *"sin revived"* and he *"died."* Paul was convicted of what he was doing, and he was wrong.

Romans 7:10

"And the commandment, which *was ordained* to life, I found *to be* unto death." The *"commandment"* was hoped to bring *"life,"* but Paul found it to be unto *"death."* The *"commandment,"* to use a modern expression, *"rained on Paul's parade."* It also *"rains on our parade."* Any time God says something for us to do and we do not do it, that is a bad day for us. We use another modern expression, *"it is like a wet blanket that has been thrown over our fire."* And another modern expression is, *"it cramps our style."* Whenever God tells us to do something and we do not want to, we feel ill at ease. That is what Paul means here.

Romans 7:11

"For sin, taking occasion by the commandment, deceived me, and by it slew *me*." Once again, as in verse 8, the expression, *"taking occasion"* is used. The Greek word, OPHORME means:
> *"a place from which a movement or attack is made, a base of operations; metaph. that by which endeavour is excited and from which it goes forth; that which gives occasion and supplies matter for an undertaking, the incentive; the resources we avail ourselves of in attempting or performing anything."*

Paul stated that *"sin"* had *"deceived"* him by means of the *"commandment"* of the law of Moses. Sin was just like a leader of the whole operation in Paul's life. Sin *"deceived"* Paul, and through the *"commandment,"* that same sin nature *"slew"* him. There are many verses on the *"deceitfulness"* of sin.

- **Proverbs 27:6**
  Faithful *are* the wounds of a friend; but the kisses of an enemy *are* deceitful.

Beware of Kissing Enemies

Be careful of the "*enemy*" who kisses you.

Judas was a kisser was he not? He kissed the Lord Jesus Christ in the garden (Matthew 26:49). Judas said: "*Whomsoever I shall kiss, that same is he: hold him fast*" (Matthew 26:48) After Judas "*kissed*" the Lord Jesus Christ, "*then came they, and laid hands on Jesus, and took him*" (Matthew 26:50). The kisses of an enemy certainly are "*deceitful.*"

- **Jeremiah 17:9**
  The heart *is* **deceitful** above all *things*, and desperately wicked: who can know it?
- **Jeremiah 48:10**
  Cursed *be* he that **doeth the work of the LORD deceitfully**, and cursed *be* he that keepeth back his sword from blood.

There are many deceitful workers doing the "*work of the Lord,*" believe me. There are thieves, bandits, and adulterers allegedly doing the "*work of the Lord.*" Whether they are on television, or whether they are in pastoral ministries in local churches, it is a crying shame. God puts a curse on anyone doing the "*work of the Lord deceitfully.*"

- **Matthew 13:22**
  He also that received seed among the thorns is he that heareth the word; and the care of this world, and **the deceitfulness of riches**, choke the word, and he becometh unfruitful.

Many people who lost money in the stock market crash of 1929 committed suicide by jumping out of tall buildings. The "*deceitfulness of riches*" is certainly a fact. "*Riches*" are often here today, and gone tomorrow. When the stock market went down quite a few points, if you had any investments in it, you wondered where your riches had gone. When the market goes up, you have "*riches*" again. "*Riches*" come and go.

- **Mark 7:22**
  Thefts, covetousness, wickedness, **deceit**, lasciviousness, an evil eye, blasphemy, pride, foolishness:

Deceit Defiles

"*Deceit*" comes from within the heart and defiles a man.

- **2 Corinthians 4:2**
  But have renounced the hidden things of dishonesty, not walking in craftiness, nor **handling the word of God deceitfully**; but by manifestation of the truth commending ourselves to every man's conscience in the sight of God.

Some people handle the Bible "*deceitfully.*" This includes modernists, liberals, and, sad to say, even some fundamentalists.

- **2 Corinthians 11:13**
  For such *are* false apostles, **deceitful workers**, transforming themselves into the apostles of Christ.

- **Hebrews 3:13**
  But exhort one another daily, while it is called To day; lest any of you be hardened through the **deceitfulness of sin**.

Paul mentions that "*sin, taking occasion by the commandment, deceived*" him. There are all kinds of deception of sin. It looks so good.

Sin Is Like Cotton Candy

Sin is like cotton candy. I do not know if you remember cotton candy. You look at that thing heaped up large, but by the time you bite into that, it is gone. It is deceitful.

That is the way sin is. It looks so good. It looks so beautiful. Eve thought she had it made when she ate whatever the fruit was in the middle of the garden, but she was trapped by the "*deceitfulness of sin.*"

May none of us want to nibble on what God says not to nibble on. Do not even touch it, do not even look at it. Remember Achan as the example. He saw, he coveted, he took, he hid, he was judged, the Lord slew him. There are many Achans around.

Romans 7:12

"Wherefore the law *is* holy, and the commandment holy, and just, and good." There was nothing wrong with the law of Moses, just like there is nothing wrong with a twenty-five miles per-hour speed limit posted on Park Avenue in Collingswood, New Jersey. There is nothing wrong with a crossbar or the upright holders that holds the crossbar up in the high jump or pole vault events in track.

In high school I was a high-jumper and a pole-vaulter. The upright standards held the crossbar. The object was to get your body over the bar without knocking the bar over. There was nothing wrong with the bar, but every time I missed it, the bar went down. There was nothing wrong with the uprights that supported the bar or with the bar itself. If the bar was knocked down, it was the fault of the jumper who failed to clear it. The same is true with the pole vault. You set the height up to 9 feet, 11 feet, or whatever you might want to jump over. You would try to get over with that pole without breaking your arm or knocking your back out of shape when you miss. Before I was saved I used to curse that bar. That was foolish and idiotic. Many of my fellow high-jumpers and pole-vaulters would curse and swear as well. After I was saved, I never said a word. It was not that bar's fault. That bar is all right. It is neutral. It does not care whether it stays up or is knocked down by the athlete. Like the bar, the law of Moses was good. I was the one who was not good because I failed to get over the bar without knocking it down. So the law of Moses was good, but those who failed to keep it were not good. Paul here says that this law of Moses was "*holy, and the commandment holy, and just, and good.*" I am glad that the Lord Jesus Christ, when He came into this world, took upon Himself all of our sins. By His death on Calvary, He also put away the law of Moses once and for all. We who are saved do not have any responsibility to obey that law. We could not do it anyway, even if we tried. Through the Lord Jesus Christ, we who are saved have been given the righteousness of Christ. That is a wonderful thing that the law could not do.

• **Romans 8:3-4**

For **what the law could not do, in that it was weak through the flesh,** God sending his own Son in the likeness of sinful flesh, and for sin, condemned sin in the flesh: **That the righteousness of the law might be fulfilled in us,** who walk not after the flesh, but after the Spirit.

Weak Through the Flesh

I remember what was said about this verse by Dr. Lewis Sperry Chafer, founder of Dallas Theological Seminary and my teacher for four years. He likened the law of Moses like a fork used to pick up a roast of meat. If the meat were overcooked, when the fork would try to lift up the roast, it would fall down. It was "*weak through the flesh.*" Nothing was wrong with the fork, but the meat was weak and could not stick together to enable it to be picked up by the fork. The Lord Jesus Christ fulfilled the law in our behalf so that we do not have to be under any part of it.

Romans 7:13

"Was then that which is good made death unto me? God forbid. But sin, that it might appear sin, working death in me by that which is good; that sin by the commandment might become exceeding sinful." This is a section of God's Words in the book of Romans that describes a battle inside Paul. I believe it also describes a battle inside a born-again believer's body.

There are different opinions that are offered concerning Romans Chapter 7. Some say this is Paul's conflict within, before he was saved. Some say it is a conflict between the believer's two natures. Others, like John MacArthur, say that the Christian just has one nature. He believes that we who are saved do not have two natures. He believes once we are saved, we only have one nature.

Since the lost have only one nature, if it is an internal battle of the lost, they really do not have much of a battle. They are Satan's children. They do not have God's Holy Spirit living within them. They can do what they want to do. I believe that this Chapter 7 illustrates an internal battle that saved people have. We who are saved cannot win this battle without God's provision.

There are some who teach that Christians can be entirely sanctified once they are saved and they do not sin anymore. If you are married, ask your spouse about that. If you are not married, ask your mother and father about that, or ask your sister and brother if they agree with that theology.

Saved People Have Two Natures

I believe the Scriptures teach clearly that we who are saved have two natures. We have the old nature that we had from Adam through our mothers and fathers. We have a new nature when the Holy Spirit of God comes into our bodies. This gives us a new nature inside, in addition to the old nature that we were born with. Yes, we have the two natures.

In this verse, Paul is talking about the law of Moses which is "*good.*" Yet it is "*made death*" unto him because he could not keep it. When the law says do not do this, and we do it, that makes you sinful. That makes you a transgressor of what is "*good.*"

For instance, if I were to give you something on assignment and if you did not do it, you would have failed in doing what you should have done. Suppose I gave you the assignment of copying out Romans 7:13-25, that we are going to talk about today, in just three minutes without skipping a word. What if you had to do it word perfect with no spelling errors. Could you do it? I do not think any of us could do it perfectly in just three minutes. I do not know if we could do it in ten, or fifteen, or even twenty minutes, exactly word perfect, with all the proper punctuation. That would be an example of giving someone a requirement to do that we could not do. Once we cannot do something that we are supposed to do, we get frustrated. We get to feeling that there is something wrong with us because we fall short of what is expected of us. If it is God's law, certainly we cannot keep that. Neither could the Jews keep their own law of Moses.

The Three Parts of the Mosaic Law

God's law in the Old Testament, the Mosaic Law, was in three parts.

1.   There was the moral law (the Ten Commandments).
2.   There was the civil law (the ordinances).
3.   There was the ceremonial law (the animal sacrifices).

Israel could not keep perfectly all three parts of that law. They could not even keep the first part of it, nor can we today. Because of Israel's failure to keep *"the commandment,"* that *"sin"* might *"become exceeding sinful."* When you have the law and you see you cannot keep it, you are just like the dead. That is what he is saying here. When God says do not do something and we do it, we are in trouble.

We must realize that we are all sinners, *"For all have sinned and come short of the glory of God"* (Romans 3:23).

● **Ecclesiastics 7:20**
For **there is not a just man upon earth**, that doeth good, and sinneth not.

We have a problem if we are trying to keep the law of Moses. We cannot do it. We cannot keep any of God's laws without God's help.

Romans 7:14

"For we know that the law is spiritual: but I am carnal, sold under sin." Here is Paul's admission that *"the law is spiritual."* There is nothing wrong with God's Word. There is nothing wrong with God's requirements. God would not proclaim things that were wicked. He would not tell us to do something that was wrong. Paul admits that he is *"carnal."* He is fleshly. He has the old sin nature. Paul was an apostle. Why did he admit that he is *"carnal"* and subject to the flesh? It is because he is honest. I think all of us must be honest. We have the old wicked sinful nature that is still within us even after we are saved and born-again.

Notice Paul also said, *"I am carnal, sold under sin."* The Greek word for *"sold"* is PIPRASKO. It means:

"to sell; of price, one into slavery; of the master to whom one is sold as a slave;(metaphor) sold under sin, entirely under the control of the love of sinning; of one bribed to give himself up wholly to another's will."

By using this word, Paul said he was *"entirely under the control of the love of sinning."* He was like a *"slave"* of sin. Paul said he did not know what to do. He was in a quandary. He does not come out of his problem until verse 25.

In Romans 7:13-25, the word, *"I,"* is used thirty-six times. You might say Paul had *"I"* trouble. Glasses will not cure that kind of *"eye"* trouble. In just thirteen verses, *"I"* is mentioned thirty-six times. This is an average of three times per verse. We are going to see these different conflicting *"I's."* Ten times Paul used the words, *"my"* or *"me,"* which is also a reference to himself. He realized that he was *"carnal"* and had the Adamic nature like all the rest of us. He realized that he could not escape it.

All of us who are saved should realize this same thing. We have God's Holy Spirit living in our bodies if we are saved. But there is also the old man or the old woman that is also there. It is our old sinful nature that we have inherited from our parents. We have a battle on our hands. The old sin nature does not want to do what the new nature wants us to do. That is our problem.

Romans 7:15

"For that which I do I allow not: for what I would, that do I not; but what I hate, that do I." Notice all of the *"I's"* in the following verses. We will see Paul, as well as saved people today, have what might be called split personalities. The Greek-based term for this is *"schizophrenia."* SCHIZO means *"split"* or *"divided."* PHREN means *"mind."* The resultant meaning of that word is *"split minds."* Not that saved people are insane. I do not want to imply that. But, according to the proper understanding of this chapter, we who are born-again do have a split personality. We have the two *"I's"* within each of us.

There are six times that *"I"* occurs in Verse 15. *"I"* does not mean the same in each instance. Notice when Paul said *"that which I do,"* I believe he refers to the old *"I."* When he said *"I allow not,"* his new nature really did not want to do the action. That is the new *"I"* that saved people have. Notice the next phrase *"for what I would."* That is what Paul really wanted to do with his new nature *"I."* But *"that do I not"* is the old nature *"I."* Notice the third coupling. When Paul said *"but what I hate,"* he is talking about the new *"I."* The response to this is *"that do I,"* which refers to the old sin nature's *"I."* Here is a clear depiction of the struggle that all saved people have between their old *"I"* and their new *"I."* It is indeed a battle within us.

All these verbs, by the way, are in the present tense in the Greek language. As such, these are continuous actions. What Paul *"continues to hate,"* he *"continues to do."* What he *"continues to do,"* he *"continues not to allow."* That which he *"continues not to desire,"* that he *"continues to do."* All these verbs indicate continuous activity and action.

Romans 7:16

"If then I do that which I would not, I consent unto the law that *it is* good." Paul's new nature *"consents"* to the law of Moses that *"it is good."* Here again you have the two *"I"*'s' of Paul. His old *"I"* says, *"If then I do."* The words *"that which I would not,"* apply to the new *"I."* The old *"I"* does it, the new *"I"* says I do not want to do that. There I did it again. The new *"I"* knows it is wrong to sin, whatever the sin may be.

Three Categories of Sins

There are at least three categories of sins:

(1) the sins of the body,

(2) the sins with words, and

(3) the sins with the heart or mind.

The old *"I"* and the new *"I"* are in constant battle and conflict in one or the other, or all of these three areas.

Romans 7:17

"Now then it is no more I that do it, but sin that dwelleth in me." When Paul wrote that *"it is no more I that do it,"* he was saying that his new nature *"I"* was not doing it. On the contrary, it is *"sin that dwelleth in me"* that is doing this evil. This is the old *"I."* We realize that there is a battle. We must also realize that the new nature is not the part of us that is going to lead us into sin, whether it is by our body, our words, or our thoughts. It is rather, the sin nature that dwells within us. This means that the sin nature is still alive and well on planet earth in every one of our bodies even if we are saved. That is a very important fact to remember.

Romans 7:18

"For I know that in me (that is, in my flesh,) dwelleth no good thing: for to will is present with me; but *how* to perform that which is good I find not." This is a very important theological verse. Paul is not questioning the fact that *"in me (that is, in my flesh,) dwelleth no good thing."* The liberals and the modernists do not agree with that. Many of them say that there is a *"spark of the Divine"* in every fallen man, woman, and child. This is totally false. They say that man is basically good. That is their theology. They say all you have to do is fan that little *"spark of the Divine"* and it will burst into greatness. That is the opposite of what this verse is clearly teaching.

There are some people I know right here in Collingswood that are not saved, as far as I know. They are not Christians, but, seemingly, they have many good works. They can give to the band in Collingswood High School. They can contribute to different organizations. They can even give money to plant trees. Is this not good? As far as God is concerned, *"no good thing"* dwells in our old nature. That is hard to understand and to agree to, but we must agree with it. If we do not agree that inside of us (the old nature) is wicked, corrupt, evil, and *"no good thing,"* we are going to be in trouble. We are going to think we can do what we want to do because we are *"good"* inside of us. No, I am not *"good,"* I am bad. You are bad. Does that warp some people's ego? Well, if it warps them, then let it warp them.

Many psychologists say that no one should ever tell anybody they are bad. Instead, just say that they are wonderful and build them up. Paul did not have that philosophy. Paul said that his new nature wanted to live for the Lord, wanted to pray, wanted to read his Bible, wanted to witness, and wanted to do everything that is right. But, on the other hand, because of his old nature, he wrote: *"how to perform that which is good I find not."* The old nature is not able to do this. The Lord Jesus Christ talked about this old nature to Nicodemus.

- **John 3:6**
  That which is born of the flesh is flesh; and that which is born of the Spirit is spirit.

An undertaker can take a dead body and try to make that person look alive. Sometimes they look better dead than alive the way they fix them up. Dead people do not speak. They cannot move. They are dead. *"That which is born of the flesh is flesh."* it will never change. That is the old nature, *"and that which is born of the Spirit is spirit,"* and that will never change.

Two Natures Dwelling Inside Us

So, we have two people, so to speak, living inside of our bodies if we are saved. Now, the unsaved have nothing but the flesh. The Holy Spirit is not in them. They have no conflict! The unsaved does not have to do anything for the Lord. All the unsaved person has to do is live for the flesh and live for the Devil. I am not advocating that, but that is what the lost person has in his heart. There is no battle. God considers man a sinner.

- Jeremiah 17:9
  The heart *is* deceitful above all *things*, and **desperately wicked**: who can know it?
- Psalm 58:3
  The **wicked** are estranged from the womb: they go astray as soon **as they be born, speaking lies**.

If you want to see sin in action just remember your children. Our children were born in 1949, 1951, 1954, 1956, and 1965, so it is a long time since they were little children. It is hard to remember that far back, but I have observed little children as I visit in homes. Whenever they say "No" to mom and dad, that is a rebellion. That is sinful wickedness. If a child takes a cookie that they should not take, and their mother asks if they took it and they say "No," they illustrate this verse. They "*go astray as soon as they are born, speaking lies.*" Even the little ones know how to lie their way out of a lot of things. That is what God says.

- Psalm 51:5
  Behold, **I was shapen in iniquity**; and in sin did my mother conceive me.

This does not mean that conception is sin. It means that the sin nature is passed on to every baby right from conception. Babies, though nice and cuddly, are considered by our God to be sinners, after their birth and even before their birth.

- Isaiah 64:6
  But **we are all as an unclean *thing*, and all our righteousnesses *are* as filthy rags**; and we all do fade as a leaf; and our iniquities, like the wind, have taken us away.

God is very clear on the fact that in every one of us there "*dwelleth no good thing.*" We do not like to be told that from people, but that is what the God of the Bible says about all mankind.

Preaching the Words of God

I am glad that I can preach the Words of God without having to apologize for it. I did not write the Bible. God wrote it. He tells us that we are sinners, and that, in our flesh *"dwelleth no good thing."* There is not a single thing that is *"good"* in God's eyes. It may seem *"good"* in the eyes of people, but not in God's eyes.

Romans 7:19

"For the good that I would I do not: but the evil which I would not, that I do." Here again we have an illustration of the old "I," and the new *"I."* When Paul wrote *"the good that I would,"* he referred to his new *"I"* which really wanted to do *"good."* However, Paul's old *"I"* admitted that *"I do not."* The old flesh does not perform that which the new man wants to do. This same truth is taught in the opposite sense. *"The evil which I would not"* (that is the new *"I"* talking), *"that I do"* (that is the old *"I"* talking). The old nature wins out once again.

None of us believers can win the victory in this battle against the old nature when left to our own human devices. The only way to gain that victory is by using God's provided weapons. Paul repeated this situation over and over in order to emphasize it. Repetition is good for us. The old Latin proverb that we have said many times is so true: *Repetitio mater estudiorum est.* [*"Repetition is the mother of learning."*] That is important.

Romans 7:20

"Now if I do that I would not, it is no more I that do it, but sin that dwelleth in me." Here is another illustration of the two contrasting *"I's."* Follow the reasoning: *"Now if I do"* [the old nature] *"that I would not"* [the new nature], *"it is no more I"* [the new nature], *"but sin that dwelleth in me"* [the old sin nature]. The old sin nature. At least he's got it categorized. Every saved Christian has two *"I's"* that are in conflict continuously. There are no exceptions.

Some Christians who are more or less of the strong Calvinistic bent believe that Christians can not sin. For example, Calvinist John MacArthur does not believe Christians have two natures, but only one. If they sin, they must be lost, according to his reasoning. I do not believe that the Bible teaches us that. I believe the Bible teaches clearly that we have two natures. The old nature can sin, and loves to sin. The new nature cannot sin, it is God's Holy Spirit dwelling within us. The old nature is called our *"flesh"* whose *"works"* are manifested.

- **Galatians 5:19**

  Now **the works of the flesh** are manifest, which are *these*;
  Adultery, fornication, uncleanness, lasciviousness,

You might ask me if I believe born-again Christians can commit these sins of the flesh after they are saved? Yes, that is right, I believe it. Their *"flesh"* is wicked, and unless restrained by the Holy Spirit, is capable of these things. I do not approve of them, but it is possible. Many people disagree with me. They say that once you are saved, you are perfect and it is impossible for you to sin. No, you are not perfect until you get your new body at the resurrection. These works of the flesh are in the believers, and, until we die, the flesh is able to manifest them.

Romans 7:21

"I find then a law, that, when I would do good, evil is present with me." The new *"I"* really wants to *"do good."* There is also the old nature, and Paul wrote that this *"evil is present with me."* Paul speaks this of himself, but if it is true for an apostle, how much more is it true of every other born-again Christian who ever lived.

If Paul the apostle says *"evil is present"* with him, who are you? Who am I? Who is anybody to say that we do not also have *"evil"* within us? We can be sweet and kind, but basically we have within us what God calls *"evil."*

Romans 7:22

"For I delight in the law of God after the inward man:"
That is wonderful is it not? Paul *"delights"* in the *"inward man,"* and in the *"law of God."*

- **Psalm 37:5**

  Commit thy way unto the LORD; **trust also in him**; and he shall bring *it* to pass.

We should have a *"delight"* in the things of the Lord. The *"inward man"* is the one who does this *"delight"* rather than the old sin nature.

Lazarus' sister Mary, like Paul, *"delighted"* in the Lord. While Martha her sister was *"cumbered about much serving"* (Luke 10:40), Mary *"sat at Jesus' feet and heard His Word"* (Luke 10:39). The Lord Jesus told Martha that *"one thing is needful: and Mary hath chosen that good part, which shall not be taken away from her"* (Luke 10:42)

I think of the two disciples on the road to Emmaus after the resurrection of the Lord Jesus Christ. Jesus drew near to them and told them many things concerning Himself.

- Luke 24:27
  And beginning at Moses and all the prophets, **he expounded unto them in all the scriptures the things concerning himself.**

After this Biblical lesson by the Saviour,

- Luke 24:32
  And they said one to another, **Did not our heart burn within us, while he talked with us by the way, and while he opened to us the scriptures?**

They had their *"hearts burn within them."* We must have a warmness and a *"delight"* in the *"law of God."*

Delighting in the Things of God

I am glad that there is something in us, if we are saved, that is able to *"delight"* in God's Word. The old man may be there, but the new man *"delights."* That is one of the evidences that we are saved, when we have a *"delight"* in the things of Scripture, and the things of God. That is a sign that we are saved and have new life.

Romans 7:23

"But I see another law in my members, warring against the law of my mind, and bringing me into captivity to the law of sin which is in my members." Paul has *"another law in his members"* that is opposite of the new nature. That is the old *"I."* Notice what that old *"I"* is doing. It is not just sitting there idle. It is *"warring against the law of his mind."* That Greek word for "warring" is ANTISTRATEUOMAI. It means:

> *"to make a military expedition, or take the field, against anyone; to oppose, war against."*

It is in the Greek present tense which makes this a continuous and unceasing action. That is continuously warring, battling, and fighting. The flesh will not give up. You cannot win in your own strength in this battle against the old *"I,"* and the new *"I."* The old flesh will not give up. That flesh cries out for more, more sin, more self, more destruction.

Notice what the effect of that war is. Paul says that this war results in *"bringing him into captivity to the law of sin which is in his members."*

Breaking Sin's Bondage

No one but the Lord Jesus Christ can break the captive's bondage. You certainly cannot do it in your own strength and in your own self.

- Galatians 5:16-17
  This I say then, **Walk in the Spirit**, and ye shall not fulfil the lust of the flesh. For the flesh lusteth against the Spirit, and the Spirit against the flesh: and these are contrary the one to the other: so that ye cannot do the things that ye would.

That is God's remedy. The Holy Spirit of God is greater and stronger than the flesh that is within us after we are saved (1 John 4:4b).

Paul said, "*I see another law in my members, warring against the law.*" Paul's "*members*" would mean his entire body, including his eyes, his ears, his mouth, his hands, his feet, his tongue, and even his heart. The war of all the members. Because of this "*warring,*" Paul is brought into "*captivity.*"

- 2 Corinthians 10:3-5
  For though we walk in the flesh, we do not war after the flesh: (For **the weapons of our warfare are not carnal, but mighty through God** to the pulling down of strong holds;)Casting down imaginations, and every high thing that exalteth itself against the knowledge of God, and **bringing into captivity every thought to the obedience of Christ;**

Here is a different "*captivity.*" The old nature has us "*captive,*" but Paul says through the victory that is in Christ, we can "*bring into captivity every thought to the obedience of Christ.*"

Thoughts, Words, and Actions

If you can bring into "*captivity,*" through the Lord, your thought-life, you will not have a problem with your words. You will not have a problem with your actions.

That is the "*obedience*" spoken of here.

- **Luke 4:18**
  The **Spirit of the Lord** *is* **upon me**, because he hath anointed me to preach the gospel to the poor; he hath sent me to heal the brokenhearted, **to preach deliverance to the captives**, and recovering of sight to the blind, to set at liberty them that are bruised,

  One of the reasons for the Lord Jesus Christ's coming into the world was to bring "*deliverance to the captives.*"

- **2 Timothy 2:26**
  And *that* **they may recover themselves out of the snare of the devil, who are taken captive by him** at his will.

All the lost world has been made "*captive*" by Satan. The born-again Christian, though free from Satan's captivity, can be made captive by the old nature, the flesh.

Christ--The Answer to All Captivity

We have all kinds of captivity. The Lord Jesus Christ is the answer to all. Paul mentions the "*warring against the law of his mind.*" One of the kinds of captivity concerns the "*mind.*" There are many battles that go on in the mind. There is filthy, smut literature. This pornographic literature feeds the minds of wicked people. May it not be named among us who name the name of the Lord Jesus Christ to look at it, to indulge in it, and to do the things which are portrayed therein. We all have "*minds.*" There is a saved mind, and there is a mind of the lost people.

- **Romans 1:28**
  And even as they did not like to retain God in *their* knowledge, **God gave them over to a reprobate mind**, to do those things which are not convenient;

The lost "*mind*" leads these heathen people to indulge in all kinds of wickedness.

- **2 Corinthians 4:3-4**
  But if our gospel be hid, it is hid to them that are lost: In whom **the god of this world hath blinded the minds of them which believe not**, lest the light of the glorious gospel of Christ, who is the image of God, should shine unto them.

Unsaved people's minds have been "*blinded*" by Satan.

- 1 Timothy 6:5
  Perverse disputings of **men of corrupt minds**, and destitute of the truth, supposing that gain is godliness: from such withdraw thyself.

We who are saved should not have *"corrupt minds."*

- 1 Corinthians 2:16
  For who hath known the mind of the Lord, that he may instruct him? **But we have the mind of Christ.**

God has given to those who are saved the *"mind of Christ."*

- 2 Corinthians 11:3
  But I fear, lest by any means, as the serpent beguiled Eve through his subtilty, **so your minds should be corrupted from the simplicity that is in Christ.**

The devil wants to *"corrupt"* our minds. He wants them corrupted, wicked, and made filthy.

- Philippians 2:5
  Let this mind be in you, which was also in Christ Jesus:

- Philippians 4:7
  And the peace of God, which passeth all understanding, shall keep your hearts and **minds through Christ Jesus.**

God can guard our *"minds."* The battle for the mind can be won if we are saved.

- 1 Timothy 1:18
  This charge I commit unto thee, son Timothy, according to the prophecies which went before on thee, that thou by them **mightest war a good warfare;**

Paul is telling preacher Timothy, the pastor at Ephesus, to *"war a good warfare."* Part of this spiritual warfare is against our minds. It is also against the world, the flesh, and the devil. That is what Paul is talking about in Romans Chapter 7.

- James 4:1
  From whence *come* wars and fightings among you? *come they* not hence, **even of your lusts that war in your members?**

The *"war"* is the lust in our members. It is the old *"I"* again. This is the old sin nature that we inherited from Adam.

- 1 Peter 2:11
  Dearly beloved, I beseech *you* as strangers and pilgrims, **abstain from fleshly lusts, which war against the soul;**

We have a war going on *"against the soul."* I think John Bunyan wrote about *The War Against Man's Soul.* There was a conflict. He had it right. John Bunyan was a Baptist preacher who was put in prison for his beliefs because he would not join the state church of his day.

Romans 7:24

"O wretched man that I am! who shall deliver me from the body of this death?" Paul calls himself *"O wretched man that I am."* If you called somebody *"wretched"* today, they would probably be very offended. Paul was being very honest.

You and I must be honest before the Lord and before one another. We should not and cannot put on a garb of hypocrisy. The masks of Greece in the plays were of two kinds. In the tragedies they would wear a mask on their face that would have the corners of the mouth turned down. If the play was one of victory and happiness, the actors would put on a mask with a smile on their face. Sometimes the actors would wear a neutral-looking mask. We who are saved should not have a mask either of sadness or joy unless it is real. We should be real. The heart should overflow.

Paul realized that his old *"I"* was a *"wretched"* man. Realism is needed. That is the first thing. Secondly, he asked a good question, *"who shall deliver me from the body of this death?"* That is a another good question. It demands a good answer. Paul had discussed this problem in many of the preceding verses in this chapter. He wanted to know who was going to deliver him from this serious problem. I am sure that the sinners in Rome were just as bad in their day as are the sinners in Collingswood, Cherry Hill, Camden, Philadelphia, New York, Boston, Los Angeles, or anywhere else in the world.

- **Isaiah 6:5**
  Then said I, Woe *is* me! for **I am undone**; because **I *am* a man of unclean lips**, and **I dwell in the midst of a people of unclean lips**: for mine eyes have seen the King, the LORD of hosts.

When Isaiah saw the Lord, he realized that he was unclean.

- **John 10:10**
  The thief cometh not, but for to steal, and to kill, and to destroy: **I am come that they might have life**, and that they might have *it* more abundantly.

If you do not have this *"more abundant"* life, you are a little bit dead. Spiritual rigor mortis has not completely set in yet, but spiritually you are slowly getting dead little by little. That's what Paul means.

Paul was looking for a deliverer. He asked *"who shall deliver me?"* Let us look at some of the deliverance of God. The Lord Jesus is a deliverer.

That Word *"Jesus"* means Saviour. Saviour also means "deliverer." Someone that pulls us out of the pit is a savior. Paul said, *"who shall deliver me?"* He did not say *"what shall deliver me?"* He did not say it was money, it was position, it was possessions, it was power, it was our job, it was our rank. Paul asked, *"who shall deliver me?"*

- **Matthew 6:13**
  And lead us not into temptation, but **deliver us from evil**: For thine is the kingdom, and the power, and the glory, for ever. Amen.

That is the disciples prayer to the God of Heaven. He is the only One Who can *"deliver"* us from this body of death, this old nature, and get the victory over it. The simple prayer is *"deliver us from evil."*

- **Luke 4:18**
  The Spirit of the Lord *is* upon me, because he hath anointed me to preach the gospel to the poor; he hath sent me to heal the brokenhearted, **to preach deliverance to the captives**, and recovering of sight to the blind, to set at liberty them that are bruised,

- **Acts 7:9-10**
  And the patriarchs, moved with envy, sold Joseph into Egypt: but God was with him, And **delivered him out of all his afflictions**, and gave him favour and wisdom in the sight of Pharaoh king of Egypt; and he made him governor over Egypt and all his house.

God is a delivering God.

- **Acts 7:34**
  I have seen, I have seen the affliction of my people which is in Egypt, and I have heard their groaning, **and am come down to deliver them**. And now come, I will send thee into Egypt.

God came down to that terrible bondage of Egypt and *"delivered"* His people.

- **2 Corinthians 1:10**
  Who **delivered us** from so great a death, **and doth deliver**: in whom we trust that **he will yet deliver *us***;

- **Galatians 1:4**
  Who gave himself for our sins, **that he might deliver us from this present evil world,** according to the will of God and our Father:

Our God is in the delivering business.

- **Colossians 1:13**
  Who hath delivered us from the power of darkness, and hath translated *us* into the kingdom of his dear Son:

The Lord Jesus Christ did this for all who are saved.

- **1 Thessalonians 1:10**
  And to wait for his Son from Heaven, whom he raised from the dead, *even* Jesus, **which delivered us from the wrath to come.**

Three Tenses of God's Deliverance

.There are three tenses of deliverences that Paul mentions in 2 Corinthians 1:10.

1. *"Delivered* us from so great a *death"* is deliverance and salvation past.
2. *"And doth deliver"* is deliverance and salvation present.
3. *"He will yet deliver us"* is deliverance and salvation future. God is in the delivering business! Paul asked a question that all of us who are saved should ask

---

He saved us from the wrath to come.

- **2 Timothy 4:16-18**
  At my first answer no man stood with me, but all *men* forsook me: *I pray God* that it may not be laid to their charge. Notwithstanding the Lord stood with me, and strengthened me; that by me the preaching might be fully known, and *that* all the Gentiles might hear: and **I was delivered out of the mouth of the lion. And the Lord shall deliver me from every evil work**, and will preserve *me* unto his Heavenly kingdom: to whom *be* glory for ever and ever. Amen.

Paul was in jail and was going to be beheaded. This was his second Roman imprisonment. Everybody left him. They did not want to be around a prisoner.

Talk about the lions. Daniel was delivered from literal lions. It was not a *"lion's den."* It was a *"den of lions."* The lions were present there in that den. When Daniel invaded their space by being thrown in their den, normally they would have snatched him and killed him immediately. The Lord delivered him. He closed the lions' mouths so that they did him no harm. The men that accused Daniel were thrown into this den of lions and were eaten by the lions even before they hit the bottom of the den.

Deliverance Comes From God

Deliverance is in God's hands.

God also delivered the three Hebrew children, Shadrach, Meshach, and Abednego, from the fiery furnace. He did not deliver them **from** the furnace, He delivered them **in** the furnace. No harm came to them, not even the smell of smoke on their garments (Daniel 3:27). The king looked in and asked if they had cast three men in the fiery furnace, because he saw four, and the fourth was *"like the Son of God"* (Daniel 3:24-25). The Lord Jesus Christ was there to help and deliver them. He is a delivering Saviour.

- **Hebrews 2:14-15**
  Forasmuch then as the children are partakers of flesh and blood, he also himself likewise took part of the same; that through death he might destroy him that had the power of death, that is, the devil; **And deliver them who through fear of death were all their lifetime subject to bondage**.

The Lord Jesus Christ is a Deliverer.

Romans 7:25

"I thank God through Jesus Christ our Lord. So then with the mind I myself serve the law of God; but with the flesh the law of sin." Paul's question in Romans 7:24, *"who shall deliver me from the body of this death?,"* is answered in this verse. The only answer to this question is *"Jesus Christ our Lord."* He is the One that has made provision for us to gain the victory over the old nature, the old flesh.

- **Galatians 5:16-17**
  This I say then, **Walk in the Spirit**, and ye shall not fulfil the lust of the flesh. For the flesh lusteth against the Spirit, and the Spirit against the flesh: and these are contrary the one to the other: so that ye cannot do the things that ye would.

Three Needs For the Spirit's Filling

There are at least three things required of believers to be filled with the Holy Spirit of God in our lives. Two requirements are negative, and one is positive.

(1) The first requirement is: *"Grieve not the Holy Spirit"* (Ephesians 4:30). The thing that grieves the Holy Spirit is the presence of known, unconfessed sin.

(2) The second requirement is: *"quench not the Spirit"* (1 Thessalonians 5:19). The thing that quenches the Holy Spirit is saying no to the will of God.

(3) The third requirement is: *"walk in the Spirit"* (Galatians 5:16).

"*Walking*" is a step-by-step procedure. You cannot all of a sudden take an escalator, and you are there without taking a step. That is not what the Christian life is all about. It is a "*walk.*" In a "*walk,*" every step is an incipient fall. If the other foot does not come down, you will lose your balance and fall down. You and I know that on slippery pavement, in slippery weather, you can lose your footing fast. Am I right? This is how Dr. Atkins, the founder of the famous Atkins diet, died. He slipped on the ice, hit his head, and, after a few days, died.

- **1 Corinthians 10:12**
  Wherefore let him that thinketh he standeth take heed lest he fall.

We must be careful not to fall, even if we think we are "*standing.*" We can have many bruised bones if we fall. I remember two or three winters ago. Out there on my front steps there was ice on the edge of each step. I did not see that ice, so I slipped. I really hurt my back badly. We must remember, when we "*walk,*" we are only one step away from falling.

If we "*walk*" by means of the Holy Spirit of God, He can get a hold of our lives. As we study His Word and pray, we can fellowship with the Lord Jesus Christ and God the Father. That is the power that will break the power of the old sin nature over us and give us victory. **"*Walk in the Spirit*,** *and ye shall not fulfil the lust of the flesh.*" That does not mean that the "*lust of the flesh*" goes away. It is always there potentially. It means when we walk in the power of the Spirit of God, we will not "*fulfil the lust of the flesh.*" God the Holy Spirit is greater in power than the flesh.

- **1 John 4:4**
  Ye are of God, little children, and have overcome them: because **greater is he that is in you, than he that is in the world**.

The Holy Spirit of God is a great power in our lives.

The Scripture says "*the flesh lusteth against the Spirit, and the Spirit against the flesh: and these are contrary the one to the other so that you cannot do the things that ye would*" (Galatians 5:17). The walk in the Spirit is a moment-by-moment continuous process.

Different hymns have been written about victory in Christ. Some talk about staying close to the Lord year by year. Other hymns talk about staying close week by week. Still others talk about staying close to the Lord day by day. But the real truth is found in the hymns that tell us we must stay close to the Lord moment-by-moment. That is the secret of success in this battle against the flesh, against the world, and against the devil. It is a moment-by-moment walk by means of the power of the Lord Jesus Christ. Only in this way can we not fulfill the lust of the old nature and the desires of the flesh. There is victory in the Lord Jesus Christ.

- **1 Corinthians 15:57**
  But thanks *be* to God, which giveth us the **victory through our Lord Jesus Christ**.

He is the One Who was victorious over death, victorious over Hell, victorious over all the demons, and victorious over all the other things that came upon Him. And now we who are saved can have the victory through our Lord Jesus Christ, provided we fulfil the requirements God has set forth in His Word. Paul found out where the victory was in the battle he experienced in Romans 7.

With the deliverance of the Lord Jesus Christ, Paul could say, "*with the mind I myself serve the law of God; but with the flesh the law of sin.*"

- **Philippians 4:13**
  I can do all things through **Christ which strengtheneth me**.

If you take Christ out of that equation, you cannot "*do all things.*" You cannot do anything.

- **John 15:5**
  I am the vine, ye *are* the branches: He that abideth in me, and I in him, the same bringeth forth much fruit: **for without me ye can do nothing**.

Christ Alone Can Bring Us Victory

This is the answer to the battle within. The Lord Jesus Christ that giveth us the victory day-by-day and moment-by-moment.

𝕽omans
𝕮hapter 𝕰ight

Romans 8:1

"There is **therefore now no condemnation to them which are in Christ Jesus, who walk not after the flesh, but after the Spirit."** The question is, "Are you *in Christ Jesus*"? If you are saved, born-again, and regenerated by God's Holy Spirit, God's Words say you are "*in Christ.*" If you are not "*in Christ,*" you ought to trust Him and accept Him as your Saviour. If you are "*in Christ*" there is "*no condemnation,*" no judgment, no more Hell, no more Lake of Fire. It is a tremendous victory that the Lord Jesus Christ has wrought, to be in Him and to be saved by His blood. For the believers, there is no judgment that will send them to Hell at the Great White Throne Judgment seat (Revelation 20:11-15). There certainly will be the Judgment Seat of Christ for the believers (1 Corinthians 3:10-15).

Paul says that saved people should "*walk not after the flesh, but after the Spirit.*" This will avoid a negative judgment at the Judgment Seat of Christ provided they continue to walk "*after the Spirit*" rather than "*after the flesh.*" Judgment in Hell is assured for every non-believer that is not "*in Christ.*"

Romans 8:2

"For the law of the Spirit of life in Christ Jesus hath made me free from the law of sin and death." Again, I ask you who are reading this, "Are you *in Christ Jesus*"? If we have been born-again by genuine faith in the Lord Jesus Christ, if we have been regenerated, if we have trusted and accepted Christ who has washed our sins away, God's Words tell us that we are considered to be "*in Christ.*" If that is the case, we have been made "*free from the law of sin and death.*"

- **John 8:32**
  And ye shall know the truth, and **the truth shall make you free**.

The Lord Jesus is that Truth. To know Him is to be *"free from the law of sin and death."*

- **John 8:36**
  If the Son therefore shall make you free, **ye shall be free indeed.**

- **Galatians 5:1**
  Stand fast therefore in the liberty wherewith **Christ hath made us free**, and be not entangled again with the yoke of bondage.

The freedom mentioned here is the result of our being saved and hence *"in Christ."* If indeed we are *"free"* in Christ, we no longer have to worry about being shackled to sin, to the sin nature, to the devil, or to the world. On the contrary, we have been made free by the Lord Jesus Christ. If we're saved, we are free at last, and free indeed!

Romans 8:3

"For what the law could not do, in that it was weak through the flesh, God sending his own Son in the likeness of sinful flesh, and for sin, condemned sin in the flesh:" The law of Moses could not do anything, because it was *"weak through the flesh."* The law was good, but it could not do anything about saving people's souls.

Remember the illustration I gave earlier. Dr. Lewis Sperry Chafer was the Founder of *Dallas Theological Seminary*, and my teacher for the last four years of his life. He gave our class an excellent illustration of the phrase, *"weak through the flesh."* He gave a picture of two things: (1) very well-cooked meat, and (2) a fork that was trying to lift up that meat. Perhaps you have had a Thanksgiving turkey that was very well-done. When you put your fork in the turkey to lift it from the pan to the serving platter, the turkey fell back on to the pan. It fell down because of the *"weakness"* of the flesh. The fork, which represents the law of Moses, is all right. But the weakness of the flesh makes it so the turkey cannot do anything. It just drops to the bottom of the pan. You cannot pick it up with the fork because of the *"weak"* flesh. This is a very good illustration of this point.

God Sent His Own Son

Paul jumped over this weakness of the law and mentioned the solution to the dilemma. It involved *"God sending His own Son,"* the Lord Jesus Christ. God sent His Son from Heaven to earth, and then he sent Him to the cross of Calvary to suffer and die for the sins of the world. In this event, truly *"God was manifest in the flesh"* (1 Timothy 3:16). Perfect God became perfect man. He was the *theanthropos*, the God-Man. In theology, this is called the *"hypostatic union."*

Notice that God the Father sent His Son *"in the **likeness** of sinful flesh."* He did not say *"in the **sameness** of sinful flesh."* There are two similar Greek words which are different. One is **HOMOIOMA** which is this word *"likeness."* The other is **HOMOOMA**. HOMOI is like, but not the same. HOMO is *"sameness."* The Lord Jesus did not come in the *"sameness"* of sinful flesh, just in the *"likeness."* The Lord Jesus Christ was perfect Man and perfect God. That is the great difference. We have that root word for *"same"* [HOMO] in the word "**homo**genized."

The Lord Jesus Christ *"condemned sin in the flesh,"* that is, both the sin nature and sins, which are the fruit of that nature. Because He condemned and judged the sin nature and sins that are the result of that nature, we who are saved can be free.

Romans 8:4

"That the righteousness of the law might be fulfilled in us, who walk not after the flesh, but after the Spirit." Here is the result of God the Father's *"sending His own Son."* It was in order that the *"righteousness of the law might be fulfilled **in** us"* rather than **by** us. The law could not bring righteousness by doing it and keeping it because no one could keep it, but the Lord Jesus fulfilled it. Not a single one in the world can have the righteousness of God fulfilled in them. But, to those saved ones who *"walk not after the flesh, but after the Spirit,"* the *"righteousness of the law"* can be *"fulfilled **in** us"* by God's Divine power rather than **by** us in our own strength.

- **Genesis 15:6**
  And he believed in the LORD; and **he counted it to him for righteousness**.

Faith is *"counted"* or reckoned by God *"for righteousness."*

- **Romans 4:3**
  For what saith the scripture? Abraham believed God, and **it was counted unto him for righteousness**.
- **Galatians 3:6**
  Even as Abraham believed God, and **it was accounted to him for righteousness**.

Genuine faith in the Lord Jesus Christ today, just as in Abraham's day, leads to the reception of God's *"righteousness."*

- **Romans 3:22**
  Even **the righteousness of God** *which is* **by faith of Jesus Christ** unto all and upon all them that believe: for there is no difference:
- **Romans 4:5**
  But to him that worketh not, but believeth on him that justifieth the ungodly, **his faith is counted for righteousness**.
- **Romans 10:10**
  For **with the heart man believeth unto righteousness**; and with the mouth confession is made unto salvation.

The order is genuine belief followed by righteousness. That is a Scriptural truth taught all over the Words of God.

- **1 Corinthians 1:30**
  But of him are ye in Christ Jesus, who of God is made unto us wisdom, and **righteousness**, and sanctification, and redemption:
- **2 Corinthians 5:21**
  For he hath made him *to be* sin for us, who knew no sin; that **we might be made the righteousness of God in him**.

The Father has made the Son to be as a sin offering for us.

Romans 8:5

"For they that are after the flesh do mind the things of the flesh; but they that are after the Spirit the things of the Spirit."

Earmarks of a Lost Person

The *"minding the things of the flesh"* is one of the earmarks of a lost person.

Since the verb for *"minding"* is in the Greek present tense, it means that the ones who are "*after the flesh*" or who are lost, continuously mind the things of the flesh. The Greek word for "*minding*" is PHRONEO. It means variously: "*to have understanding, be wise; to feel, to think; to have an opinion of one's self, think of one's self, to be modest, not let one's opinion (though just) of himself exceed the bounds of modesty; to think or judge what one's opinion is; to be of the same mind i.e. agreed together, cherish the same views, be harmonious; to direct one's mind to a thing, to seek, to strive for; to seek one's interest or advantage; to be of one's party, side with him (in public affairs).*"

These lost people are like the hogs that are constantly "*minding*" their food by looking down all the time eating, eating, and eating. They do not have an upward look. You can just look at the hogs and the pigs and see their eyes are just built to the ground. The hog-type of life, which is the carnal life after the flesh, is a picture of the lost person who continuously minds the things of this old wicked flesh. You cannot tell me that a person who feasts upon hog meat, the garbage, and the filth of this world, is saved. You cannot eat the filth of this world and love it, and mind continuously the things of the flesh, and be saved, in my judgment.

Just as the lost person minds the things of the flesh, so the ones who are saved and walk "*after the Spirit*" continuously mind "*the things of the Spirit.*" There is a distinction made here between the lost and the saved. Those who have been redeemed by the Lord Jesus Christ have a desire to mind and to have an interest in the things of the Holy Spirit of God that He has given to us in His Word.

Romans 8:6

"For to be carnally minded *is* death; but to be spiritually minded *is* life and peace." Are you "*carnally minded*"? Do you mind only the flesh and all that you think of and all that you want? Remember the battle that Paul had with the enemy within, the old nature and the new nature discussed in detail in Romans 7. If the "*carnal mind*" is all that you have in your life, God says it is "*death.*" This is spiritual "*death*" now, and the "*second death*" (Revelation 20:14) in Hell for all eternity. On the other hand, for the saved who are living to please the Lord, they are called "*spiritually minded.*" The result of this is "*life and peace.*"

- **1 Timothy 5:6**
  But **she that liveth in pleasure is dead while she liveth**.

The Scripture uses the terms "*dead*" and "*death*" sometimes literally and physically, and sometimes in a metaphorical and spiritual sense, as presented in the verse listed above. That is death and dead works because it is fleshly. There is no life when living in pleasure and sin, wickedness, and corruption. The unbelievers do not have God's "*peace.*"

- Romans 3:17
  And **the way of peace have they not known:**
- Romans 5:1
  Therefore being justified by faith, **we have peace with God** through our Lord Jesus Christ:
- Galatians 5:22
  But the fruit of the Spirit is love, joy, **peace**, longsuffering, gentleness, goodness, faith,
- Philippians 4:17
  Not because I desire a gift: but I desire **fruit that may abound to your account.**

To be spiritually minded is life and peace. Carnally minded is death. We must be careful about our mind set, that is, what we are looking for, and who we are looking at. There is a battle between the *"carnal mind"* and the *"spiritual mind."*

Romans 8:7

"Because the carnal mind *is* enmity against God: for it is not subject to the law of God, neither indeed can be."

What Is The Carnal Mind?

The *"carnal mind"* is the mind motivated by the flesh. It is all that the unsaved person possesses. If the saved person is not controlled by God the Holy Spirit, he or she might also be operating on the basis of the *"carnal mind."* Such a mind is *"enmity against God."*

That *"mind"* hates God, and God hates that *"mind."* Such a *"mind"* is not *"subject to the law of God,"* nor can it be. It is not controlled by God, but by the person's own flesh. That word *"enmity"* is used only eight times in the King James Bible.

- Genesis 3:15
  And I will put **enmity** between thee and the woman, and between thy Seed and her seed; it shall bruise thy head, and thou shalt bruise his heel.

The Lord is speaking to the serpent which, I believe, was an incarnate form of Satan. He's called the serpent, the Devil, Satan, and the deceiver (Revelation 12:9). This verse describes the hatred between Satan, the seed of the serpent, and the Lord Jesus Christ, the Seed of the woman.

- **James 4:4**
  Ye adulterers and adulteresses, know ye not that the **friendship of the world is enmity with God**? whosoever therefore will be a friend of the world is the enemy of God.

This verse says that the "carnal mind" cannot be "subject" to God's law. The Greek word for "subject" is HUPOTASSO. It means:

> "*to arrange under, to subordinate; to subject, put in subjection; to subject one's self, obey; to submit to one's control; to yield to one's admonition or advice; to obey, be subject; [A Greek military term meaning 'to arrange (troop divisions) in a military fashion under the command of a leader.' In non-military use, it was 'a voluntary attitude of giving in, cooperating, assuming responsibility, and carrying a burden.]'"*

The "*carnal mind*" wants its own way, not the way of the Lord Jesus Christ.

Romans 8:8

"So then they that are in the flesh cannot please God."

The term "*in the flesh*" is the term that the Scripture uses to describe those who are unsaved and not born-again. Those who are "*in the flesh*" do not have God the Holy Spirit dwelling within them. All they have is the "*flesh.*" They do not have the new nature. Because of this, they "*cannot please God.*"

The word "*pleasing*" is used many places in the Scripture.

- **Matthew 3:17**
  And lo a voice from Heaven, saying, This is my beloved Son, in whom **I am well pleased**.

- **Matthew 17:5**
  While he yet spake, behold, a bright cloud overshadowed them: and behold a voice out of the cloud, which said, This is my beloved Son, in whom **I am well pleased**; hear ye him.

- **John 8:29**
  And he that sent me is with me: the Father hath not left me alone; for I do always **those things that please him**.

We must, as the Lord Jesus Christ did, "*please*" the Lord.

- **Galatians 1:10**
  For do I now persuade men, or God? or do **I seek to please men? for if I yet pleased men**, I should not be the servant of Christ.

  The Greek word for "*please,*" is ARESKO. It means:

  > "*to please; to strive to please; to accommodate one's self to the opinions desires and interests of others.*"

I hope you who are reading this seek to "*please*" the Lord Jesus Christ rather than the flesh, the world, or the devil. It is very true that those who are "*in the flesh cannot please God,*" but those of us who have been redeemed by the blood of our Lord Jesus Christ can "*please*" Him, and indeed, we must "*please*" Him.

Romans 8:9

"But ye are not in the flesh, but in the Spirit, if so be that the Spirit of God dwell in you. Now if any man have not the Spirit of Christ, he is none of his." Paul tells the believers in Rome that they are "*not in the flesh.*" They have the "*flesh,*" but God does not consider them to be "*in the flesh.*" As Paul said earlier, it is the lost people who are "*in the flesh*" and those "*in the flesh cannot please God.*" God says: "*That which is born of the flesh is flesh; and that which is born of the Spirit is spirit.*" You cannot mix the two.

Those who have the "*Spirit of God*" dwelling in them are "*in the Spirit.*" Everyone who has been regenerated by saving faith in the Lord Jesus Christ has the Holy Spirit of God indwelling them. Paul wrote: "*What? Know ye not that your body is the temple of the Holy Ghost which is in you, which ye have of God, and ye are not your own? For ye are bought with a price: therefore glorify God in your body, and in your spirit, which are God's*" (1 Corinthians 6:19-20). Paul makes clear that "*if any man have not the Spirit of Christ, he is none of his.*" If you point out a person in this world who does not have the Holy Spirit of God dwelling inside of their bodies, it is a fact that they are lost. They do not belong to the Lord.

I was reading a book recently. In it there is documentation of many godly pastors and Bible teachers in the past who have said that the problem of the world is the churches. The problem with the churches are the people in the churches. The problem with the people in the churches are that most of them are not saved, that is, genuinely converted. They may have made some decision, but the Spirit of God is not in them. The estimate of some is that there is possibly as high as 75 percent of the people in Bible-believing churches who are not saved.

When revival comes, it comes to these unregenerate church people who are in churches. Church members who thought they were saved before are regenerated. It is an interesting thing, but if anyone "*has not the Spirit of Christ he is none of his.*"

I remember that Dr. David Otis Fuller shocked me, and so did Dr. Robert Ketcham, one of the early leaders of the General Association of Regular Baptist Churches (GARBC). Both of these men believed that 90 to 95 percent of the church members, even in fundamental churches, are lost and not saved. Paul tells the church at Corinth: "*Examine yourselves, whether ye be in the faith*" (2 Corinthians 13:5). This should apply to us today as well.

Just because you go to a church, just because you sit there and you claim to believe what the doctrines are, are you sure you are "*in the faith*"? . Be sure the Holy Spirit of God dwells in you and that you are regenerated by genuine faith in Lord Jesus Christ. Remember, "*if any man have not the Spirit of Christ, he is none of his.*" God means what He says.

Romans 8:10

"And if Christ *be* in you, the body *is* dead because of sin; but the Spirit *is* life because of righteousness." In the Gospel of John, he stated that "*we* [both the Father and the Son] *will come unto him, and make our abode with him*" (John 14:23). Though it is true that both the Father and the Son "make their abode" in the believers, it is God the Holy Spirit Who is the primary person in the Godhead Who indwells those who are saved.

• **1 Corinthians 6:19**
     What? know ye not that **your body is the temple of the Holy Ghost *which is* in you**, which ye have of God, and ye are not your own?

The whole Trinity in the Scripture dwells in the ones who are saved and redeemed by the Blood of Christ. The Father, the Son, and the Holy Spirit all dwell in you. The words "*if Christ be in you*" tell us that Christ indwells the believers. One of the themes of the book of Colossians is "*Christ in you the hope of glory*" (Colossians 1:27).

Christ Indwells the Saved Ones

The omniscient, omnipresent, omnipotent Lord Jesus Christ dwells inside of the body of all born-again Christians.

In the words "*the body is dead because of sin,*" the reference is to the "*body*" being spiritually "*dead*" or fitted for death. It is going to die. That "*body*" is made for death because of Adam's sin as mentioned in Romans 5. Because Adam got us into it, we have physical death passed upon the whole human race, but the Holy Spirit of God is life because of righteousness. It is the body versus the Spirit again.

Romans 8:11

"But if the Spirit of him that raised up Jesus from the dead dwell in you, he that raised up Christ from the dead shall also quicken your mortal bodies by his Spirit that dwelleth in you." In this verse, the *"Spirit of Him that raised up Jesus from the dead"* is none other than God the Holy Spirit. And the One Who raised the Lord Jesus Christ up was God the Father. This was a bodily resurrection, regardless of how the modernists, liberals, and unbelievers try to deny this. If you are saved and the Holy Spirit *"dwelleth in you,"* the promise here is that God will also *"quicken your mortal bodies"* by this *"Spirit."* That Greek word for *"quicken"* is ZOOPOIEO. It means:

> *"to produce alive, begat or bear living young; to cause to live, make alive, give life; by spiritual power to arouse and invigorate; to restore to life; to give increase of life: thus of physical life; of the spirit, quickening as respects the spirit, endued with new and greater powers of life; metaph., of seeds quickened into life, i.e. germinating, springing up, growing."*

- **1 Corinthians 15:53-54**
  For this **corruptible** must put on incorruption, and this **mortal** *must* put on immortality. So when this **corruptible** shall have put on incorruption, and this **mortal** shall have put on immortality, then shall be brought to pass the saying that is written, Death is swallowed up in victory.

Who Are *"Mortal"* and *"Corruptible?"*

At the resurrection of believers' bodies, there are two terms that must be understood:

1. *"mortal"* which refers to believers who are still living but subject to death and

2. *"corruptible"* which refers to believers who have died and are in their graves. The word *"mortal"* means *"subject to death."* Those are people who are still living when the Lord Jesus Christ returns in the rapture of the believers

---

Insurance companies publish what they term *"mortality tables."* They estimate the average life span of men and women. The word *"corruption"* means *"decay."* Thus *"corruptible"* speaks of people who are already dead.

Their bodies begin to corrupt as soon as they die.

If we who are saved are alive when the Lord Jesus returns in the rapture, our *"mortal"* bodies, subject to death, will be transformed into glorious and *"immortal"* bodies, never more subject to death. If we who are saved have died, our corruptible bodies in the grave will be changed instantly into incorruptible bodies never more subject to death. Both these transformations will be accomplished by the power of God the Holy Spirit who indwells us.

Romans 8:12

"Therefore, brethren, we are debtors, not to the flesh, to live after the flesh." We who are born-again do not have any debt to our *"flesh."* It does not owe us anything, and we do not owe it anything. We do not have to placate it, because the Lord Jesus has died for that old sin nature, that old flesh. We do not have *"to live after the flesh."*

Romans 8:13

"For if ye live after the flesh, ye shall die: but if ye through the Spirit do mortify the deeds of the body, ye shall live." Living *"after the flesh"* will lead to death. The *"flesh"* will be put into the grave at our physical death. That is its destiny. It will not live forever. The quality of the *"flesh's"* product is also *"death,"* whether in a spiritual sense or physical sense. The *"flesh"* does not lead to spiritual life in any way.

The alternative has to do with the power of God the Holy Spirit. *"Through the Spirit,"* the believers are able to *"mortify the deeds of the body."* The Greek word for *"mortify"* is THANATOO. It means:

"to put to death; metaph. to make to die i.e. destroy, render extinct by death, to be liberated from the bond of anything, literally to be made dead in relation to (something)"

In other words, all the things that you live for, if they are *"fleshly,"* are going to perish. The saying is true: *"Only one life 'twill soon be past. Only what's done for Christ will last."* That is what Paul is talking about here. The new nature will live on into eternity. It will not die like the old *"flesh."* This Greek verb for *"mortify"* is in the Greek present tense. As such, it is a continued action.

• **Colossians 3:5**

Mortify therefore your members which are upon the earth; fornication, uncleanness, inordinate affection, evil concupiscence, and covetousness, which is idolatry.

God wants saved ones to *"mortify"* or *"put to death "* your *"members."* In other words, *"mortify"* your eyes, if you are looking at wicked things; your ears, if you are hearing wicked things; your mouth, if you are saying wicked things; your hands, if you are doing wicked things; your feet, if you are going to wicked places; your heart, if you have wickedness in your heart. This command is to put to death all the members of our bodies.

Three Ways to Manifest Ourselves

I have said it before and I'll say it again. There are at least three ways we can manifest the deeds of the body. (1) One is by actions that we do. (2) A second area is our words. (3) A third area is our thought-life.

---

(1) One is by actions that we do. We do not have to sin. In the next two minutes, if you are saved, you do not have to sin with your body. Or the next five minutes or ten minutes or twenty minutes or thirty minutes, you do not have to sin with your body. Not that we are sinlessly perfect. We do not have to sin with our body. We do not have to punch somebody in the nose or anything like that with our body.

(2) A second area is our words. We do not have to sin with our words. Most of you are not saying a word in this service, so you can last another 5 or 10 minutes without sinning with your words. We do not have to do it. If you do not sin with your words for five or ten minutes, you do not have to sin with your words for 30 or 40 minutes, or one day. God wants us Holy and living for Him.

(3) A third area is our thought-life. If you can put away sin from your thoughts and your hearts for five minutes or twenty minutes you do not have to sin in your thoughts. God wants us pure and holy so that we can be used for Him. God wants us to *"mortify the deeds of the body"* so that we might live pleasing to the Lord Jesus Christ.

Romans 8:14

"For as many as are led by the Spirit of God, they are the sons of God." God wants to lead those of us who are saved. He wants to lead us by the *"Spirit of God."* There is a beautiful gospel song entitled "God Leads His Dear Children Along." Some, God leads through the water, some through the flood, some through the fire, but all through the blood. God leads His dear children along. That was my father-in-law's favorite hymn.

Paul says that as many as are *"led by the Spirit of God"* they *"are the sons of God."* God wants to lead us. This verse makes it clear that if you are led by God's Spirit, you are one of the *"sons of God."* God expects His children to be led and guided by the Spirit of God. God does not want the believers to meander around with the flesh and the world and the old devil. He wants to lead us. The Holy Spirit of God gave us the Scriptures. God wants to lead us through the Words of God. He wants to lead us into green pastures.

Romans 8:15

"For ye have not received the spirit of bondage again to fear; but ye have received the Spirit of adoption, whereby we cry, Abba, Father." The Spirit of God is not a *"Spirit of bondage."* The spirit of the world, the spirit of the devil, the spirit that we were born with is a spirit of *"bondage"* and *"fear."*

● **Ephesians 2:2**
   Wherein in time past ye walked according to the course of this world, according to the prince of the power of the air, **the spirit that now worketh in the children of disobedience**:

According to this verse, every person has that *"spirit"* when he was born. We were born in sin, born as the devil's child, not God's child. The old devil's spirit gives us *"bondage."* Once we are born-again we are snatched from *"bondage."* The Lord Jesus Christ can snap that *"bondage"* and make the believers free.

On the contrary, those who are saved have *"received the Spirit of adoption, whereby we cry, Abba, Father."* The Greek word for *"adoption"* is HUIOTHESIA. It comes from two words, HUIOS (*"son"*) and TITHEMI (*"to put or place."*) It means, variously:

> *"adoption, adoption as sons; that relationship which God was pleased to establish between himself and the Israelites in preference to all other nations; the nature and condition of the true disciples in Christ, who by receiving the Spirit of God into their souls become sons of God; the blessed state looked for in the future life after the visible return of Christ from Heaven."*

This word for *"adoption"* was used in the Greek culture to indicate that the child had now reached the age where he became a mature son, and was ready to assume adult duties. When I was one or two years old, I was a son of my father, but I wasn't able to inherit his wealth because I was a minor. This verse speaks of an *"adoption"* which made the son a grown-up, so that he could inherit all the wealth of his father even if he were only ten or twelve. That is what *"adoption"* is in the Christian faith. It makes the saved ones full grown, grown-up, and mature sons. That is what God has done for us by means of the regeneration by God the Holy Spirit.

Because saved people have become full grown sons, they can cry *"Abba, Father."* ABBA is an Aramaic term. It means:

> *"father, customary title used of God in prayer. Whenever it occurs in the New Testament it has the Greek interpretation joined to it,*

that is apparently to be explained by the fact that the Chaldee "ABBA" through frequent use in prayer, gradually acquired the nature of a most sacred proper name, to which the Greek speaking Jews added the name from their own tongue."

The Hebrews use this word all the time. It is an endearing term like the English word *"daddy."* My mother sent Mrs. Waite and me on a tour of Israel in 1980. While we were on a lift, going up to the Masada, we stood next to a Hebrew father who had a little boy in his arms. The baby was crying, *"Abba, Abba, Abba."* I told Mrs. Waite to listen. The baby was frightened and cried for his *"father."* That is the Aramaic equivalent. Our little American babies say, *"Ma, Ma, Ma"* or *"Da, Da, Da."* The little children can easily pronounce *"Abba."*

Full-Grown Children of God

When we are regenerated by the Holy Spirit of God, God makes us full grown sons and daughters. We have reached our maturity and are able to receive the complete inheritance of our Heavenly Father. We can then continuously cry out, *"Abba, Father."* We can have a close relationship with the Heavenly Father that we did not have before we were saved, and before the Holy Spirit of God came to us.

This Greek word for "cry" is KRAZO. It means:

"to croak; of the cry of a raven; hence, to cry out, cry aloud, vociferate; to cry or pray for vengeance; to cry; cry out aloud, speak with a loud voice."

It seems strange to compare us with the *"ravens"* when we cry out, but that is the word used. The ravens' sound is loud. It can be heard. So our *"cries"* can also be heard by the Lord. We can speak out with a loud voice and call our Heavenly Father saying *"Abba, Father."*

Romans 8:16

"The Spirit itself beareth witness with our spirit, that we are the children of God:" Does the Holy Spirit *"bear witness"* with your Spirit that you are a child of God? This is a very important question. This is the assurance that you can have in your heart and life, if you are genuinely saved. Notice the phrase in our King James Bible, *"the Spirit itself."* Some have asked about this. They think the word*"itself"* is an error. It is true that God the Holy Spirit is a Divine Person, but in the Greek language, the word for *"itself"* (AUTO) is neuter. This is true because the word it modifies, "Spirit,"

(TO PNEUMA) is also neuter. So the King James Bible translators translated it as a neuter. This is grammatically correct. They did this also in Romans 8:26. It is not that the Holy Spirit is not a Person, but they translated it grammatically. In John 14:17, the King James translators refer to the Holy Spirit by the personal pronouns, "*him*" and "*He*." They did not deny His Personality. So in John 15:26 ("*He*"), John 16:13 ("*He*"), and even in Romans 8:27 ("*He*").

There are three genders in Greek: masculine, feminine, and neuter. The word "*itself*" (AUTO) happens to be neuter in gender. In fact the word "*Spirit*" is neuter (PNEUMA). "*The Spirit itself*" is literally correct for all of the above reasons, so do not get upset about this. People criticize the King James Bible for this and point it out as an error. It is not an error. "*Itself*" is exactly how it should be translated. "*Spirit*" is neuter so "*itself*," which is neuter, is correct. It does not mean that He is not a Person. He is a Person. In the phrase "*we are the children of God,*" the Greek word for "*are*" is in the present tense. It signifies continuous action. It means that the saved people "*are continuously the children of God.*" There is no doubt about it. There's no question about it.

Assurance for Saved People

Saved people have an assurance. This is very necessary. If you do not have assurance of your salvation, I wish today, right now, that you would genuinely trust the Lord Jesus Christ for His eternal salvation and have that assurance.

If you do not have assurance that you are saved, then you might as well be lost. Let me say that again. If you do not have the assurance of your salvation, you might as well be lost. If you are hanging in the balance, if you are asking, "Am I or am I not saved?" if you do not know for certain, you had better know right now. Trust the Lord Jesus Christ as your Saviour, receive Him, be regenerated by the Spirit of God, and have the assurance of eternal life. The Spirit of God bears witness with our human spirit that "*we are continuously children of God.*"

Romans 8:17

"And if children, then heirs; heirs of God, and joint-heirs with Christ; if so be that we suffer with *him*, that we may be also glorified together." If we are God's "*children*," we have been placed in "*adoption*" as full-grown sons. Because of this, we are "*heirs of God and joint-heirs with Christ*." We are not little babies. Everyone who has come to Christ by faith and is regenerated by the Spirit of God is a full- grown, mature son, and therefore we are His heirs, "*heirs of God*."

Not only that, but we are "*joint-heirs with Christ*." Everything that the Lord Jesus Christ has is ours also. Everything that God the Father owns and has is ours. If we are saved, we are full-grown, grown-up children of God and heirs. We are going to enjoy that glory. That is going to be a tremendous day. We are joint-heirs with Christ.

Paul then adds: "*if so be that we suffer with him, that we may be also glorified together*." Suffering is brought into verse 17 because that is a part of our life. It is a part of every Christian's life who is living for the Lord. If you do not have a bit of suffering, I wonder if you are a Christian. There must be suffering.

- **2 Timothy 3:12**
  Yea, and **all that will live godly in Christ Jesus shall suffer persecution.**

Joined With Christ in Three Ways

There are three joint-words in this text that have the Greek word SUN ("*with*.")

1.   The first is "*joint-heirs with Christ*," joint-heirs.
2.   The second is "*we suffer with Him*," joint- suffering.
3.   The third is "*glorified together*," joint-glory.

We glory together, suffer together, and are heirs together. Just like all the things we said earlier in the book of Romans, if we are saved, we died with Christ, we were buried with Christ, we are raised with Christ, we are seated with Christ, we are going to be coming back with Christ, and we will reign with Christ for one thousand years during the Millennium. We are "*in Christ*."

- **Galatians 4:1**
  Now I say, *That* the **heir**, as long as he is a child, differeth nothing from a servant, though he be lord of all;

In the Old and New Testament, children did not inherit anything. They had to wait until they were older before they inherited. But God, Himself, has made Christians adopted, full-grown children of God. We can inherit. We are no longer servants. We are no longer babies. The very youngest of anyone who is saved, even if just for one day, he is regenerated by the Holy Spirit of God. Then God has made him an heir and joint-heir with Christ. It is a wonderful truth.

Romans 8:18

"For I reckon that the sufferings of this present time are not worthy to be compared with the glory which shall be revealed in us." Why is Paul bringing up this suffering? Why is he being negative? Some people criticize those who bring up negative things. That is what life is all about. There are sufferings.

The Greek word for *"reckon"* is LOGIZOMAI. It means:

"to reckon, count, compute, calculate, count over; to take into account, to make an account of; metaph. to pass to one's account, to impute; a thing is reckoned as or to be something, i.e. as availing for or equivalent to something, as having the like force and weight; to number among, reckon with; to reckon or account; to reckon inward, count up or weigh the reasons, to deliberate; by reckoning up all the reasons, to gather or infer; to consider, take into account, weigh, meditate on; to suppose, deem, judge; to determine, purpose, decide. [This word deals with reality. If I "logizomai" or reckon that my bank book has $25 in it, it has $25 in it. Otherwise I am deceiving myself. This word refers to facts not suppositions.]"

Since it is in the present tense in the Greek language, Paul continues to "reckon" this matter. Paul talks about the *"sufferings of this present time."* He had many of these. But he *"reckons"* that they are *"not worthy to be compared with the glory which shall be revealed in us."*

- **1 Peter 2:19**

  For this *is* thankworthy, if a man for conscience toward God endure grief, **suffering wrongfully.**

It is all right to *"suffer,"* so long as it is *"wrongfully."* Here is a catalogue of Paul's suffering from his own testimony.

- **2 Corinthians 11:23-28**
  Are they ministers of Christ? (I speak as a fool) I *am* more; in **labours** more abundant, in **stripes** above measure, in **prisons** more frequent, in deaths oft. Of the Jews five times received I **forty *stripes* save one.** Thrice was I **beaten with rods,** once was I **stoned,** thrice I suffered **shipwreck,** a night and a day I have been in the deep; In **journeyings** often, *in* **perils of waters,** *in* **perils of robbers,** *in* **perils by *mine own* countrymen,** *in* **perils by the heathen,** *in* **perils in the city,** *in* **perils in the wilderness,** *in* **perils in the sea,** *in* **perils among false brethren;** In **weariness** and **painfulness,** in **watchings** often, in **hunger** and **thirst,** in **fastings** often, in **cold** and **nakedness.** Beside those things that are without, that which cometh upon me daily, **the care of all the churches.**

I believe that when Paul was stoned at Lystra, he died (Acts 14:19). His spirit and soul went to Glory, the *"third Heaven"* (2 Corinthians 12:2). If you look in the book of Acts in chapter 14, you will see that it was about 14 years before Paul wrote 2 Corinthians 12. In Acts 14:19, we read that *"there came thither certain Jews from Antioch and Iconium, who persuaded the people, and, having stoned Paul, drew him out of the city,* **supposing he had been dead.**" In the next verse, we read that: *"Howbeit, as the disciples stood round about him,* **he rose up,** *and came into the city: and the next day he departed with Barnabas to Derbe."* (Acts 14:20). I believe Paul died, but God raised him up and took him up to the *"third Heaven."* He knew what Heaven was. He wrote about it. That's why he could say, *"the sufferings of this present time are not worthy to be compared with the glory which shall be revealed in us."*

- **Matthew 25:31**
  When **the Son of man shall come in his glory,** and all the holy angels with him, then shall he sit upon **the throne of his glory:**

There is going to be *"Glory"* up in Heaven.

- **John 1:14**
  And the Word was made flesh, and dwelt among us, **(and we beheld his glory, the glory as of the only begotten of the Father,)** full of grace and truth.

John said that he *"beheld His glory."* Peter, James, and John, the big three, were on the Mount of Transfiguration when the Lord Jesus Christ was transfigured with tremendous glory (Matthew 17:1-8; and Mark 9:2-8).

- **John 17:5**
  And now, O Father, glorify thou me with thine own self with **the glory which I had with thee before the world was.**

- **John 17:24**
  Father, I will that they also, whom thou hast given me, be with me where I am; **that they may behold my glory**, which thou hast given me: for thou lovedst me before the foundation of the world.
- **Acts 7:55**
  But he, being full of the Holy Ghost, looked up stedfastly into Heaven, **and saw the glory of God**, and Jesus standing on the right hand of God,
- **2 Peter 1:17**
  For he received from God the Father **honour and glory**, when there came such a voice to him from **the excellent glory**, This is my beloved Son, in whom I am well pleased.

His garments became *"exceeding white as snow"* (Mark 9:3). Peter was there and said, *"let us make three tabernacles, one for Thee, and one for Moses, and one for Elias"* (Mark 9:5). There were three altogether. Peter was, in effect, bringing down the Lord Jesus Christ to the level of Moses and Elijah. He is not on an even level. He is God the Father's only *"beloved Son"* (Mark 9:7), in Whom He is well pleased.

Romans 8:19

"For the earnest expectation of the creature waiteth for the manifestation of the sons of God." Even the *"creatures,"* including the sheep, the goats, the wolves, the cattle, and all the other animals on earth, are waiting for the redemption and *"manifestation of the sons of God."* We are going to get into that later. They were made subject to bondage. They had not sinned. It was Adam that sinned. That was a wicked thing. These creatures are now eating each other and are wild. Before the fall they were not eating each other nor were they wild. They were tame and serving the Lord. They did not even eat meat. They were herbivorous (Genesis 1:29-30). During the millennial reign of the Lord Jesus Christ, many conditions will change, including the status of various *"creatures."*

Animals Delivered From Bondage

Paul then said: *"the creature waiteth for the manifestation of the sons of God."* We who are saved will get our resurrected bodies one day. When the Lord Jesus Christ returns to set up the Millennial age of glory for His 1,000-year reign on this earth, the animals will be delivered from their *"bondage"* too.

The following conditions will prevail:

* **Isaiah 11:6-9**

"The wolf also shall dwell with the lamb, and the leopard shall lie down with the kid; and the calf and the young lion and the fatling together; and a little child shall lead them. And the cow and the bear shall feed; their young ones shall lie down together: and the lion shall eat straw like the ox. And the sucking child shall play on the hole of the asp, and the weaned child shall put his hand on the cockatrice' den. They shall not hurt nor destroy in all my holy mountain: for the earth shall be full of the knowledge of the LORD, as the waters cover the sea."

One of our people asked me the other day how we get a "*millennium*" from the Bible. The word "*millennium*" comes from Latin. It means "*thousand years.*" In Revelation 20:2-7, this phrase is used no less than six times. There is no reason not to take it literally. During this time, many of the unfulfilled prophecies of the Old Testament prophets will be fulfilled. One of the things to be fulfilled is that these creatures that are poisonous and killers are going to be tamed by the Lord Jesus Christ Who is the King of Kings and Lord of Lords.

Romans 8:20-21

"For the creature was made subject to vanity, not willingly, but by reason of him who hath subjected *the same* in hope, Because the creature itself also shall be delivered from the bondage of corruption into the glorious liberty of the children of God." That does not mean that cats and dogs are going to go to Heaven. We had a lady right over here near us who died about twenty years ago. She must have had 100 cats. Her house had a horrible odor when she died because of all those cats. They had to completely re-do all the walls and floor. She believed that cats went to Heaven. That is not what this is teaching here. Dogs and cats do not go to Heaven, but they will be delivered from the bondage they are now in. The time of their deliverance will be in the millennium. Let us look at the context of what I quoted earlier from Isaiah 11. It shows the timing of the "*deliverance*" from "*bondage of corruption*" will be when the Lord Jesus Christ returns to earth to set up His millennial reign.

- Isaiah 11:1-9

And there shall come forth a rod out of the stem of Jesse, and a Branch shall grow out of his roots: And the spirit of the LORD shall rest upon him, the spirit of wisdom and understanding, the spirit of counsel and might, the spirit of knowledge and of the fear of the LORD; And shall make him of quick understanding in the fear of the LORD: and he shall not judge after the sight of his eyes, neither reprove after the hearing of his ears: But with righteousness shall he judge the poor, and reprove with equity for the meek of the earth: and he shall smite the earth with the rod of his mouth, and with the breath of his lips shall he slay the wicked. And righteousness shall be the girdle of his loins, and faithfulness the girdle of his reins.

The **wolf also shall dwell with the lamb**, and the leopard shall lie down with the kid; and the calf and the young lion and the fatling together; and a little child shall lead them. And the cow and the bear shall feed; their young ones shall lie down together: and the lion shall eat straw like the ox. And the sucking child shall play on the hole of the asp, and the weaned child shall put his hand on the cockatrice' den. They shall not hurt nor destroy in all my holy mountain: for the earth shall be full of the knowledge of the LORD, as the waters cover the sea.

You know that "*wolves*" and "*lambs*" do not "*dwell*" together peacefully today. There is no question about it. There must be a literal fulfillment of this prophecy.

The Golden Rule of Interpretation

There is what has been called "*The Golden Rule of Bible Interpretation.*" It says:

"*When the PLAIN SENSE of Scripture makes COMMON SENSE, SEEK NO OTHER SENSE. Therefore, take EVERY WORD at its primary, ordinary, usual, literal meaning, UNLESS the facts of the immediate context, studied in the light of related passages, and axiomatic and fundamental truths, indicate CLEARLY otherwise. God in revealing His Word, neither intends nor permits the reader to be confused. He wants His children to understand.*"

That is what we have in these verses. One day, when the Lord Jesus comes back to rule on this earth, there is going to be a complete change. The *"creature"* is going to be delivered from its *"bondage."* Can you imagine a little child leading a lion, or a tiger, or any other ferocious animal? In the millennium that will be the case. *"And the cow and the bear shall feed; their young ones shall lie down together: and the lion shall eat straw like the ox"* (Isaiah 11:7). Can you imagine what a *"bear"* would do with a *"cow"* today? These will take place when the Lord Jesus Christ is reigning.

Many other prophecies will be fulfilled as well at that time. Consider these animals. Just think of those poor animals eating one another. That is just the way it is. That was not the case in the original creation. If you notice, for instance:

- **Genesis 1:29-30**
  And God said, Behold, I have given you every herb bearing seed, which *is* upon the face of all the earth, and every tree, in the which *is* the fruit of a tree yielding seed; to you it shall be for meat. And to every beast of the earth, and to every fowl of the air, and to every thing that creepeth upon the earth, wherein *there is* life, *I have given* every green herb for meat: and it was so.

The herbs, the vegetables, the fruits and the nuts were the food of man and of the animals. Animals did not eat each other. People did not eat the animals until after the flood (Genesis 9:3). They did not eat chicken and steak, and various things along that line. They ate herbs, vegetables, fruits, and nuts.

Sin entered and the whole thing was changed around. In Genesis chapter 6, when God told Noah to build an ark for the saving of the souls of men, eight souls were saved: Noah and his wife, Shem, Ham, and Japheth, and their wives. He also said to take a male and a female, two of every single kind of animal which you have, and of the clean animals he was to take seven pairs of each so they could sacrifice those animals to the Lord (Genesis 7:2-3).

You can imagine, if you have hungry lions, tigers, and bears mixed in with dogs, cats, monkeys, and other such animals, they would eat them. They would not be able to stay alive. They did not have that problem at that time of Noah. He did not have to have animal flesh for food for some of these animals. He had fruits, vegetables, herbs, and nuts for them all to last the entire year. What about after the flood?

- **Genesis 9:3**
  Every moving thing that liveth shall be meat for you; even as the green herb have I given you all things.

There is now a difference. This is when the beasts began to eat each other, and man began to eat animal flesh. If you watch those nature shows on television you see the lions and tigers that go in packs and kill those wildebeests. They just jump up on them, tear their necks open, kill them and begin to eat them. That is just the way it is. It is a dog-eat-dog activity, you might say. That is the way the animals are living now, but one day it will be peaceful. They will not be killing each other. They will be eating herbs in the millennial reign of Christ.

Man's life will be prolonged. We will not live for only eighty or ninety years. I heard just the other day a lady lived to be 105 years-old. My wife's aunt lived to be a few months short of 103 years-old. During the millennium, people will live to be 1,000 years-old just like before the flood. Just like Methuselah who lived to be 969 years-old. In the Millennium Age of Christ, longevity will be restored. Not only will the animals be freed, but also mankind will be freed as well. The curse of death will be prolonged.

As it says in Isaiah 65:20, "*The child will die an hundred years old.*" In today's terms, a child could be ten years old and still be considered a child. If he lives to be a hundred, that is ten times ten. But, if the child starts at age 100, 100 times ten would be 1,000. This passage is teaching that a child might live to be 1,000 years of age.

God also likens man's days to that of a tree. He said: "*As the days of a tree are the days of my people*" (Isaiah 65:22). If you look at those old Sequoia and Redwood trees, many of them are over 1,000 years-old. This is a picture of the possible length of human life during the millennial reign of the Lord Jesus Christ on this earth.

Romans 8:22

"For we know that the whole creation groaneth and travaileth in pain together until now." Creation continues to groan and moan and make loud noises as it were. Some scientists have told us that nature is in the minor key. You who are musical know that there is a major key and a minor key on the piano and on other instruments. In nature when you hear the sounds of all of the animals, and the movement of the trees, and various other things, some of these scientists tell us it is in a minor key. That is probably because of the fall of Adam. I cannot verify this. I am not a scientist, and I do not know all about this, but that is what they say. This "*moaning*" in pain is because of the curse.

- **Genesis 3:17**
  And unto Adam he said, Because thou hast hearkened unto the voice of thy wife, and hast eaten of the tree, of which I commanded thee, saying, Thou shalt not eat of it: **cursed *is* the ground for thy sake**; in sorrow shalt thou eat *of* it all the days of thy life;

There was a curse and that is why the whole creation "*groaneth and travaileth in pain*" until the Lord Jesus Christ returns and redeems it. He is the King of Kings and Lord of Lords and will reign for 1,000 years.

Romans 8:23

"And not only *they*, but ourselves also, which have the firstfruits of the Spirit, even we ourselves groan within ourselves, waiting for the adoption, *to wit*, the redemption of our body." We who are old or young, as the case may be, God says that, if we are saved, we have the *"firstfruits of the Spirit."*

The Holy Spirit indwells the believers' bodies. He is the *"firstfruits"* or down-payment toward the believers' *"redemption of our body."* This is called in this verse an *"adoption."*

In our present state, Paul says we *"groan within ourselves."* Being a present tense in the Greek language, it means a continuous *"groaning."* There are many *"groans"* that people have while they are in this world. Whether it is a toothache, arthritis, back pain, or whatever it may be, groaning prevails. There are some of us who are not in pain very often and maybe some of us have never been in pain, like some of you younger people. I do not know. The whole creation is *"groaning"* and *"waiting"* for the *"redemption of our bodies."*

When we get new bodies they will be bodies like unto the body of our Lord Jesus Christ. We will have no aches and pains. Our eyes will not need glasses. We will not need to have a lot of liniments and rubbing compounds in order to alleviate the pains in our backs.

All of us are groaning in pain for some reason or another. Some people reading these words have arthritis. One day we will have new bodies and have no more pain, for the *"former things are passed away"* (Revelation 21:4). That is what we are waiting for, *"the redemption of our bodies."*

Romans 8:24

"For we are saved by hope: but hope that is seen is not hope: for what a man seeth, why doth he yet hope for?" The *"hope"* of our salvation is in the future, when we get resurrected bodies, or when we go Home to be with Christ. Our salvation is not a hope-so salvation. It is not an indefinite thing. It is definite, but it is yet future. That is what our *"hope"* is in a Scriptural sense. The Scriptural *"hope"* is true. It is verifiable. It will be fulfilled in the future.

The redemption of our bodies is going to be a *"hope"* for the future, but *"hope that is seen is not hope."* If you can see *"hope,"* you are not saying you *"hope"* it comes to pass. It is already here.

Paul said, *"for what a man seeth, why doth he yet hope for?"* The Lord has given us some things in the future. He has not given us the ability to have everything in our salvation right here and now.

The Three Tenses of Salvation

1. salvation past--from the penalty of sin,
2. salvation present--from the power of sin, and
3. salvation future--from the presence of sin.

Salvation is in three tenses. We have part of that salvation. The completion, the redemption of our body, is yet future, when our bodies (if we are saved) will be made just like that of our Lord Jesus Christ.

Romans 8:25

"But if we hope for that we see not, *then* do we with patience wait for *it.*" *"If we hope"* in the future for a resurrected body, we are hoping for a body that is perfect, a body that will not rot, a body that will not waste away, and a body that will not have pain or sorrow. If we have *"hope,"* then we wait for it with patience. If we have no *"hope,"* all the patience in the world will not help.

If you are not sure you are saved, for instance, you need assurance. If you are not trusting the Lord Jesus Christ as your personal Saviour and Redeemer, you should trust Him and have true assurance. You need to have that future *"hope"* that one day you will be made like unto Christ. One day you will be in Heaven, rejoicing with Him as He said in John 14.

*   **John 14:3**
    And if **I go and prepare a place for you,** I will come again, and receive you unto myself; that where I am, *there* ye may be also.

The Lord Jesus is preparing for the believers a *"place."* This *"place"* is a future *"hope."* We should *"with patience wait for it."* The word *"patience"* occurs thirty-three times in the New Testament.

*   **Titus 2:13**
    Looking for that blessed hope, and the glorious appearing of the great God and our Saviour Jesus Christ;

*   **Romans 5:3**
    And not only *so,* but we glory in tribulations also: **knowing that tribulation worketh patience;**

When we have *"tribulation"* and trials, it gives us more *"patience."* We know we cannot do anything about it. We have to wait for it and be *"patient."*

- **Romans 15:4**
  For whatsoever things were written aforetime were written for our learning, **that we through patience and comfort of the scriptures might have hope**.

The Scriptures give us *"patience"* and *"comfort."*

- **1 Thessalonians 1:3**
  Remembering without ceasing your work of faith, and labour of love, and **patience of hope in our Lord Jesus Christ**, in the sight of God and our Father;

- **Hebrews 10:36**
  For **ye have need of patience**, that, after ye have done the will of God, ye might receive the promise.

He does not answer His promises immediately.

- **Hebrews 12:1**
  Wherefore seeing we also are compassed about with so great a cloud of witnesses, let us lay aside every weight, and the sin which doth so easily beset *us*, and **let us run with patience the race that is set before us**,

- **James 5:11**
  Behold, we count them happy which endure. **Ye have heard of the patience of Job**, and have seen the end of the Lord; that the Lord is very pitiful, and of tender mercy.

Job certainly had to be *"patient."* He had much pain and suffering.

Some people cannot wait until they open presents for different occasions, but they have to be *"patient."* Some cannot wait to eat, they are so hungry, but they have to be *"patient."* Some people have *"patience,"* and some people do not.

Romans 8:26

"Likewise the Spirit also helpeth our infirmities: for we know not what we should pray for as we ought: but the Spirit itself maketh intercession for us with groanings which cannot be uttered." The Spirit of God, if we are saved, indwells us. He helps our weaknesses and *"infirmities"* continuously. He knows that we know not what to pray for specifically as we ought to know. The Greek word for *"itself"* is AUTO. It is a neuter pronoun because it modifies the word for *"Spirit"* (PNEUMA) which is also neuter. As I explained before, God the Holy Spirit is a Person, not just an influence or a force. This is a grammatical agreement and does not deny His Personhood.

Paul also talked about how the Holy Spirit *"maketh intercession for us with groanings which cannot be uttered."* The Holy Spirit of God Who lives in the bodies of born-again Christians intercedes for us. He makes *"intercession"* before God the Father for the things that we need according to the will of God. The kind of *"intercession"* that the Holy Spirit makes is *"with groanings which cannot be uttered."* This is not some kind of Pentecostal experience. This is not some speaking in tongues experience. It is *"groanings"* that cannot be uttered or spoken. We have to believe it. It is in the Words of God.

The Holy Spirit makes intercession for us by telling God the Father of what we have need. Have you ever been so sick that you cannot even talk? Have you been in so much pain that you just sit there? You cannot pray. The Holy Spirit of God can make intercession for us and help us by talking to the Lord in our behalf so that He might help us.

Romans 8:27

"And he that searcheth the hearts knoweth what *is* the mind of the Spirit, because he maketh intercession for the saints according to *the will of* God." Notice that God the Father is the One Who *"searcheth the hearts"* of the saints. God the Father *"knoweth what is the mind of the Spirit, because he maketh intercession for the saints according to the will of God."* The Holy Spirit makes intercession and pleads on behalf of the saved ones.

Sometimes we talk and ask the Lord for things that are not according to the will of God. We ask the Lord for things that we ought not ask Him for, and for things that we ought not have. Sometimes He gives them to us and we get in trouble. Sometimes He withholds from us those things and we stay out of trouble. By way of contrast, the Holy Spirit of God never makes a mistake in His intercession. He always makes *"intercession"* for us to the Father according to *"the will of God."* That is a great truth to cling to and to know.

The Father knows what is the mind of the Holy Spirit. We also have another Person of the Trinity Who makes *"intercession"* for us as well. He is the Lord Jesus Christ Himself.

- **Romans 8:34**
  Who *is* he that condemneth? *It is* Christ that died, yea rather, that is risen again, who is even at the right hand of God, **who also maketh intercession for us**.

Here is the Lord Jesus Christ, as well as the Holy Spirit, Who *"makes intercession for us."*

- **Hebrews 7:25**
  Wherefore he is able also to save them to the uttermost that come unto God by him, **seeing he ever liveth to make intercession for them**.

The Lord Jesus Christ is our High Priest at the Father's right hand. *"He ever liveth to make intercession for us."*

Romans 8:28

"And we know that all things work together for good to them that love God, to them who are the called according to *his* purpose." This verse does not mean that every single item in our life is going to be good, but for those who continuously love God, things work together for good in the long run, as we say. The hard things, and the easy things are all mixed in together. When you bake a cake, I am told, you put salt and sugar in it, as well as many other ingredients. You take those ingredients which, in and of themselves are not very tasty, yet mixed together, they make a good cake. All things are *"working together."* The good things, the bad things, the knocks, the hits, the disappointments, the Lord is working all of them together for our good. He wants to make us better Christian people who are more dedicated and in love with Him and with His will.

This *"working together"* is for only those *"who are the called according to his purpose."* Those that are saved, genuine believers in the Lord Jesus Christ are those who are *"called according to his purpose."*

Romans 8:29

"For whom he did foreknow, he also did predestinate *to be* conformed to the image of his Son, that he might be the firstborn among many brethren." Here we have in one verse the concepts of both *"foreknowledge"* and *"predestination."* Many people get confused about these particular doctrines. Those who the Lord Jesus Christ *"foreknew"* in advance He did *"predestinate."* But what was it that God did *"predestinate"* the saved people to be? It tells us the answer right here in this verse.

The object and purpose of Biblical *"predestination"* is limited in function. God's goal for every saved person is that they will one day *"be conformed to the image of his Son, that he might be the firstborn among many brethren."* The Lord Jesus Christ is our elder Brother. He is the One that God wants us to *"conform"* to. When we who are saved get new resurrected bodies, they will be like the Lord Jesus Christ's body. That is what this verse teaches us concerning God's *"predestination."* This does not negate the *"whosoever will"* of the gospel message.

● **Revelation 22:17**
   And the Spirit and the bride say, Come. And let him that
   heareth say, Come. And let him that is athirst come. And
   whosoever will, let him take the water of life freely.
It is not a question of *"predestination"* in the sense that only those who are of

the elect can believe on the Lord Jesus Christ and be saved. The Words of God are clear that **whosoever will** can come unto the Lord Jesus Christ and trust in Him.

● **John 3:16**

For God so loved the world, that he gave his only begotten Son, that **whosoever believeth in him** should not perish, but have everlasting life.

The "*predestination*" here is to be "*conformed to the image of His Son.*" Every saved person who is born-again will one day be "*conformed*" to the very "*image*" of the Lord Jesus Christ. That is God's goal for every saved person. "*We shall be like Him because we shall see Him as He is*" (1 John 3:2).

Romans 8:30

"Moreover whom he did predestinate, them he also called: and whom he called, them he also justified: and whom he justified, them he also glorified." In this verse there is a picture of God's redemptive work. There is no time with God. He is in eternity past, present and future. We, on the other hand, are creatures of "*time.*" We have watches on our wrists. We have clocks on our walls. We are late or early to wherever we are supposed to go. We are creatures of time, but God is not.

Notice the order of events in this verse: "*whom he did predestinate*" [that is, to be conformed to the image of His Son], "*them he also called.*" If we are saved, we have been "*called.*"

Next, "*he also justified.*" Those who are "*called*" by the gospel presentation, and who believe that gospel by personal faith in the Lord Jesus Christ, are made absolutely "*just*" in the eyes of God. If we are saved and born-again, we have been declared righteous. Then these predestinated, called, and justified ones God "*also glorified.*" That is in the past tense. We who are saved are not glorified yet, but as far as God is concerned it is just as good as done. It has already been accomplished. When He saves us we are already looked upon as being "*glorified*" and in the presence of the Lord Jesus Christ. Since we are "*in Christ,*" we who are saved are right now in the very presence of God in Heaven with new bodies, and glorified at the Father's right hand with Christ beholding His glory. This is all possible because God is not a Person beholden and limited to "*time.*"

● **1 Corinthians 15:49**

And as we have borne the image of the earthy, **we shall also bear the image of the Heavenly.**

That is our glorification.

- **1 John 3:2**
  Beloved, now are we the sons of God, and it doth not yet appear what we shall be: but we know that, when he shall appear, **we shall be like him**; for we shall see him as he is.

Our glorified bodies will be like that of the Lord Jesus Christ with the exception of the scars in His hands that he bore in the cross of Calvary for the sins of the world. We will be made like unto Him. As far as God is concerned, we are already *"predestinated," "called," "justified,"* and *"glorified"* in Heaven even though we are not there yet.

Romans 8:31

"What shall we then say to these things? If God *be* for us, who *can be* against us?"   One with God is said to be a majority. That is true. Paul said of the saved ones, *"If God be for us, who can be against us?"* Abraham Lincoln once reportedly said, "We should not ask God to be on our side, rather, we must ask that we might be on God's side." That is the difference. We must want to be on God's side, and not ask God to be on our side. *"If God be for us who can be* [successfully] *against us?"* If God is for us that does not mean He is never going to chasten us and scold us and get us into shape. As a Father, He wants His daughters and sons to be good daughters and good sons. Sometimes the Father has to chasten or discipline His children.

- **Proverbs 3:11**
  My son, **despise not the chastening of the LORD**; neither be weary of his correction:
- **1 Corinthians 11:32**
  But when we are judged, **we are chastened of the Lord**, that we should not be condemned with the world.

The Lord wants us to be His good children for Christ.

- **Hebrews 12:5-8**
  And ye have forgotten the exhortation which speaketh unto you as unto children, My son, **despise not thou the chastening of the Lord,** nor faint when thou art rebuked of him. For **whom the Lord loveth he chasteneth**, and scourgeth every son whom he receiveth. **If ye endure chastening**, God dealeth with you as with sons; for what son is he whom the father **chasteneth** not? But if ye be without **chastisement**, whereof all are partakers, then are ye bastards, and not sons.

I am not in the habit of chastising some other person's son or daughter. When our children were growing up, four sons and a daughter, when they needed it, I had to discipline them. If they did not need it, I hope that I did not discipline them. Two rules I always tried to follow in the discipline of our children. (1) Only when they needed it, (2) but, always when they needed it.

My wife and I did not see eye-to-eye on certain things, but I, as the father, was responsible under God for my children so we disciplined my way. The Father, the Lord God of Heaven and earth, is responsible for us if we are saved. He is *"for us,"* but He wants to shape us up to be made like unto His glorious Son.

Romans 8:32

"He that spared not his own Son, but delivered him up for us all, how shall he not with him also freely give us all things?" How wonderful it was that God the Father *"spared not His own Son."* First of all, He *"spared not"* His Son by sending Him from Heaven. Secondly, He *"spared not"* His Son by having Him to go to the cross of Calvary to die in the place of all the sinners of all time. This was filled with pain and suffering. He, the perfect sinless Saviour, Who had no sin of any kind, bore in His body the sins of the world (1 Peter 2:24; John 1:29b).

"For Us All"--Unlimited Atonement

Notice the words, *"but delivered him up for us all."* That is unlimited atonement. God the Father delivered up God the Son, the Lord Jesus Christ *"for us all."* The word *"us"* includes all the people who ever lived in the world. It is not limited to the *"elect"* only, though they are included. God the Father delivered up the Son of God to the cross of Calvary for all of us, so that all of us might be able to be saved by faith, by genuinely trusting in the Lord Jesus Christ.

The last part of this verse speaks of an additional truth: *"how shall he not with him also freely give us all things?"* Now the Son of God has gone back to the Father. He is at the Father's right hand in Heaven. If the believers are in the will of God, He will give us all things. He has promised to *"freely give us all things."*

Dr. Lewis Sperry Chafer, the founder of Dallas Theological Seminary, who was my teacher for the last four years before he went Home to be with the Lord, used to illustrate this verse in his classes this way. He said,

"Men, if I go into a jewelry store and I buy an expensive diamond, do you think that the seller of that diamond will not give me a little piece of brown paper to wrap it in?"

"If God spared not His own Son, but delivered Him up for us all, how

shall he not with him also freely give us all things?" The *"little piece of brown paper"*--the simple things and the tiny things--He can certainly take care of. He will do that for us who are saved, too.

Romans 8:33

"Who shall lay any thing to the charge of God's elect? *It is* God that justifieth." This is a question addressed to *"God's elect."* It refers to those who are saved by genuine faith in God's Son as their Saviour. Who is going to lay anything to the born-again person's *"charge"*? That is what the Devil has been doing against the believers for centuries. The book of Job illustrates this.

- Job 1:11

    But put forth thine hand now, and touch all that he hath, and **he will curse thee to thy face**.

Job was being accused by Satan before God of having bad motives and various other things.

- Revelation 12:10

    And I heard a loud voice saying in Heaven, Now is come salvation, and strength, and the kingdom of our God, and the power of his Christ: **for the accuser of our brethren is cast down**, which accused them before our God day and night.

Satan wants to accuse the Bible-believing, born-again Christians of things and sins that they commit every day.

The answer to any *"charges"* against God's children is found in the phrase, *"It is God that justifieth."* Justification is the way that God declares the sinners who genuinely trust in the Lord Jesus Christ to be absolutely righteous in His sight. Not that we are absolutely righteous in our own selves. As to our **state**, we are still sinners. As to our **standing**, we are absolutely and perfectly declared righteous in the sight of God because of what the Lord Jesus Christ has done for us on Calvary's cross.

Romans 8:34

"Who *is* he that condemneth? *It is* Christ that died, yea rather, that is risen again, who is even at the right hand of God, who also maketh intercession for us." The question is asked by Paul, *"Who is he that condemneth?"* This implies that believers might be sent to Hell for all eternity. This can never happen because *"it is Christ that died"* for our sins so we might be saved by genuine faith in Him. He not only died for us, but He *"is risen again"* bodily from the dead. Not only that, but also, the Lord Jesus Christ is *"at the right hand of God the Father."* The right hand is the hand of power, blessing, and authority.

The next truth in this verse is that the Lord Jesus Christ "*maketh intercession for us*." The Lord Jesus Christ intercedes for saved people. What is an intercessor? It is someone who argues on your behalf. It is a lawyer or an attorney. It is someone who stands between the believer and God in order to assist and to help them.

We who are saved have the Holy Spirit of God within us, as we saw earlier in this chapter. He makes intercession for us. In this verse we have the Lord Jesus Christ, who is at the Father's right hand, making intercession for us.

- **Hebrews 7:25**
  Wherefore he is able also to save them to the uttermost that come unto God by him, **seeing he ever liveth to make intercession for them**.

All the priests of the Old Testament died. When the high priest died, his oldest son became the high priest in his place. When this priest died, his oldest son would be the high priest. And so on, all the way down the line.

We have a High Priest in Heaven, the Lord Jesus Christ, Who "*ever liveth*." He has no time off or rest. He does not need rest. He is on duty twenty-four hours a day. What is He doing? He is making intercession for those of us who are saved. He is not interceding for the lost or for those who have not trusted Christ, but only for the saved. He is interceding and making it so that we believers can be in fellowship one with another and with God the Father and God the Son.

Romans 8:35

"Who shall separate us from the love of Christ? *shall* **tribulation, or distress, or persecution, or famine, or nakedness, or peril, or sword?"** The question is who is going to "*separate us from the love of Christ*." There are two types of genitives in the Greek and English languages. There is the objective genitive and the subjective genitive. You could read this Scripture and understand who could "*separate us from the love of Christ*," in the sense of the "*our love for Christ*." Or you could take it as "*Christ's love for us*." That is the way I believe it should be understood here. The meaning is "*Who can separate us from Christ's love for us*."

- **John 3:16**
  For God so loved the world, that he gave his only begotten Son, that whosoever believeth in him should not perish, but have everlasting life.

God so loved us, He will never take away that love. I believe once you are born-again you will never be lost. That does not mean you are always perfect, but once you are saved, you are safe and not lost. You will never be separated ever from the "*love of Christ*."

Nothing Can Separate From Christ

"Tribulation" cannot separate us. That is the trouble that pushes in upon us.

*"Distress"*cannot separate us. *"Persecution"* will not do it. Paul was persecuted severely.

*"Famine"*cannot separate us. Hunger will not separate us from Christ's love for us.

"Nakedness," without good clothing in the cold weather cannot separate us from the love of Christ.

*"Peril"*cannot separate us.

*"Sword"*cannot separate us from Christ's love; death by the *"sword"* will take us to Glory to be with Christ forever.

Paul received the *"sword."* Paul was martyred for Christ. Paul was beheaded, according to tradition, with a short sword, called a MACHAIRA. This *"sword"* was used for capital punishment. His head was cut off. Did that separate him from the love of Christ? No, it took him to Glory. That was his entrance to Glory. Nothing will separate us from the love of Christ. There is a Friend that we have Who said:

- **Hebrews 13:5**
  Let your conversation be without covetousness; and be content with such things as ye have: for he hath said, **I will never leave thee, nor forsake thee**.

- **Proverbs 18:24**
  A man that hath friends must shew himself friendly: and **there is a friend that sticketh closer than a brother**.

That Friend is none other than our Lord Jesus Christ.

- **Hebrews 13:6**
  So that we may boldly say, **The Lord is my helper**, and I will not fear what man shall do unto me.

Romans 8:36

"As it is written, For thy sake we are killed all the day long; we are accounted as sheep for the slaughter." The phrase, *"as it is written"* is an important expression. The Greek word for that phrase is GEGRAPTAI. It is a perfect tense. That perfect tense in Greek indicates an action which has taken place in the past, it exists in the present, and will continue to exist on into the future.

Verbal Plenary Bible Preservation

When God says, *"it is written,"* this means His Words that He has given us in Hebrew, Aramaic, and Greek. This is a firm promise that God's original Hebrew, Aramaic, and Greek Words, although written in the past, stood complete in the Lord Jesus Christ's present time, and they will stand preserved and complete down to all future time.

Paul quoted from the Old Testament when he wrote: *"we are killed all the day long; we are accounted as sheep for the slaughter."*

- **Psalm 44:22**
  Yea, for thy sake are we killed all the day long; **we are counted as sheep for the slaughter.**

Born-again believers are not much accounted for in the eyes of the world. The ones who are worldly do not think much of the believers who are saved. They think: *"These people believe in Heaven which is strange. They want to live for the Lord Jesus Christ. They are foolish. They spend time in the Word of God by reading their Bibles."*

When the Scripture says *"we are accounted as sheep for the slaughter,"* it says something about the value the world puts on Christians. What good are sheep, except for the slaughter? What good are Christians except to be killed? That is what Paul found out very definitely in his day. We may find out that even more in our day, even in this country. It has come to that in other countries. There is persecution of Christians around the world. They are counted as being of no value. They are expendable. *"For thy sake though we are killed."* Let it not be for our own wickedness, but for His sake *"we are accounted as sheep for the slaughter."* We are of no account in the eyes of the world, but of great account for the Lord Jesus Christ. We who know Him are of much value to Him.

Fanny Crosby, the blind hymn writer, wrote a song entitled, *"Take the World But Give Me Jesus."* That is a good phrase. Would that all of us would agree with it. George Beverly Shay used to sing another song written many years ago entitled, *"I'd Rather Have Jesus Than Anything."* I would rather have Jesus than all that this world can give.

Romans 8:37

"Nay, in all these things we are more than conquerors through him that loved us." We who are saved are "*more than conquerors.*" In what things? In the things mentioned in verse 35: In "*tribulation,*" in "*distress,*" in "*persecution,*" in "*famine,*" in "*nakedness,*" in "*peril,*" and in "*sword.*" In all of these things, Paul says, "*we are more than conquerors.*" We are not just "*conquerors*" or victors, but above "*conquerors,*" better than "*conquerors,*" "*more than conquerors.*" How is this possible? It is certainly not through ourselves, but it is "*through him that loved us,*" the Lord Jesus Christ, who saves those who trust Him. He has given us a victory over the old Devil himself. Satan is a defeated foe. We no longer have to be in his clutches. We no longer have to be in his power, in his grip. We no longer are his child, if we have trusted the Lord Jesus Christ as our Saviour. We are no longer in bondage. We no longer have to follow this wicked world. We do not have to, because "*we are more than conquerors through him that loved us.*" We do not have to follow the old wicked flesh that dwells in everyone of us who are saved. If we are saved, we can be "*more than conquerors*" because Christ has loved us, gave Himself for us, and made our victory possible.

Romans 8:38-39

"For I am persuaded, that neither death, nor life, nor angels, nor principalities, nor powers, nor things present, nor things to come,"

"Nor height, nor depth, nor any other creature, shall be able to separate us from the love of God, which is in Christ Jesus our Lord." Paul said "*I am persuaded.*" Are you persuaded? I hope that you are persuaded. The Greek word for "*persuaded*" is PEITHO. It means:

"*be persuaded; to be persuaded, to suffer one's self to be persuaded; to be induced to believe: to have faith in a thing; to believe; to be persuaded of a thing concerning a person; to listen to, obey, yield to, comply with; to trust, have confidence, be confident.*"

If you are "*persuaded*" about something, you are sure of it. If you are saved and trusting the Lord Jesus Christ, you will one day depart from this life. Your spirit and soul will depart from your body and be "*with Christ; which is far better.*" Are you "*persuaded*" that this is the case? Will "*death*" separate you from the "*love of God*"? No, it will not. Or, if you are lost, "*death*" is going to separate you from the Lord Jesus Christ for all eternity in the Lake of Fire. Will "*life*" separate you from the "*love of God*"? If you are unsaved, you are right now in this life "*separated*" from the Lord Jesus Christ (John 3:36).

If you are born-again, will *"angels"* or *"principalities"* or these powers of darkness separate you from the *"love of God"*? Paul knew what death was, and that did not separate him from the *"love of God."* He was dragged out of the city in Acts chapter 14, in the city of Lystra. He was stoned and dragged out of the city because the disciples thought he was dead. Then he said he knew a man fourteen years ago in 2 Corinthians.

- **2 Corinthians 12:2**
  I knew a man in Christ above fourteen years ago, (whether in the body, I cannot tell; or whether out of the body, I cannot tell: God knoweth;) **such an one caught up to the third Heaven**.

Paul knew that *"death,"* or *"life,"* or *"angels,"* or *"principalities,"* or *"powers,"* or *"things present,"* or *"things to come"* could not *"separate"* him from the *"love of God."*

Again you have the question of whether the phrase *"love of God"* is an objective genitive or a subjective genitive in English and in Greek. Should this phrase, *"the love of God"* be understood to be *"our love for God"* (objective) or *"God's love for us"* (subjective)? I believe it is the subjective genitive which would mean, *"God's love for us."* I do not believe that we should separate our love for Him either. Nothing is able to separate us from God's love for us. Notice that this "love" is all *"in Christ Jesus our Lord."* There is no other Way to get into this "love" except through the Lord Jesus Christ. Think of some of these verses about God's love for us.

- **John 3:16**
  For **God so loved the world**, that he gave his only begotten Son, that whosoever believeth in him should not perish, but have everlasting life.

That is God's *"love."* The saved ones are not going to be separated from that *"love."*

- **Romans 5:8**
  But **God commendeth his love toward us**, in that, while we were yet sinners, Christ died for us.

- **Ephesians 2:4**
  But God, who is rich in mercy, **for his great love wherewith he loved us**,

- **Ephesians 5:2**
  And walk in love, **as Christ also hath loved us**, and hath given himself for us an offering and a sacrifice to God for a sweetsmelling savour.

- **Ephesians 5:25**
  Husbands, love your wives, even **as Christ also loved the church**, and gave himself for it;

That's a command to husbands! Husbands are to love their wives as the Lord

Jesus Christ loved the church.

- **1 John 4:9-10**

  In this was manifested **the love of God toward us**, because that God sent his only begotten Son into the world, that we might live through him. **Herein is love**, not that we loved God, but that **he loved us**, and sent his Son *to be* the propitiation for our sins.

- **1 John 4:19**

  We love him, because **he first loved us**.

We could not love Christ without His first loving us.

- **Revelation 1:5**

  And from Jesus Christ, *who is* the faithful witness, *and* the first begotten of the dead, and the prince of the kings of the earth. **Unto him that loved us**, and washed us from our sins in his own blood,

The Lord Jesus Christ is the author of the book of Revelation as well as the other sixty-five books of our Bible. The Lord Jesus Christ's "*love*" is permanent. His love is not fickle. It is not an Indian-giver sort of "*love*" when He gives us eternal life.

- **John 10:27-29**

  My sheep hear my voice, and I know them, and they follow me: And I give unto them eternal life; and they shall never perish, **neither shall any *man* pluck them out of my hand. My Father, which gave *them* me, is greater than all; and no *man* is able to pluck *them* out of my Father's hand.**

If you are saved, you are in the "*hand*" of the Lord Jesus Christ. You are also in the Father's "*hand.*" You have double protection. Nobody is going to separate you from that "*love.*" That is a wonderful grace that God has given to us in His Son, the Lord Jesus Christ!

𝕽𝖔𝖒𝖆𝖓𝖘 𝕮𝖍𝖆𝖕𝖙𝖊𝖗 𝕹𝖎𝖓𝖊

Romans 9:1

"I say the truth in Christ, I lie not, my conscience also bearing me witness in the Holy Ghost" Paul begins this chapter by telling the believers in Rome that he does not lie. It is a good thing for us never to lie. The Lord Jesus said that He is *"the Way, the Truth, and the Life"* (John 14:6). Paul had to make this clear, especially when he is going to talk about the terrible curse that he said he would be willing to take (Romans 9:3). He must preface this by saying, *"I lie not, my conscience also bearing me witness in the Holy Ghost."* Paul was seriously grieved and affected by the unbelieving Jews all around him. The Lord Jesus Christ was a Jew, and Paul was also a Jew, but he found his countrymen all about were rejecting the Saviour, the Lord Jesus Christ.

Romans 9:2

"That I have great heaviness and continual sorrow in my heart." *"Heaviness and continual sorrow"* were in Paul's *"heart"* because these unsaved people around him, his fellow kinsmen, were lost. A consuming grief was his. Ask yourself this question, *"When is the last time, if at all, that you and I had sorrow and grief for anyone who is lost?"* Just think about that. Those who are lost are apart from Christ. Their destiny is Hell, the Lake of Fire. I believe that we should, as Paul, have sorrow and grief because of those who are on their way to a Christless eternity, damnation, and judgment in Hell. Paul was not a hypocrite; he had genuine and *"continual sorrow."*

Romans 9:3

"For I could wish that myself were accursed from Christ for my brethren, my kinsmen according to the flesh:" This is the most serious and bold statement by Paul on this subject of his lost brethren after the flesh. Paul could *"wish"* that he were *"accursed from*

Christ" for his *"brethren"* the Jews.   The Greek word for *"accursed"* is
ANATHEMA. It means:

> *"a thing set up or laid by in order to be kept; specifically, an*
> *offering resulting from a vow, which after being consecrated to a*
> *god was hung upon the walls or columns of the temple, or put in*
> *some other conspicuous place; a thing devoted to God without hope*
> *of being redeemed, and if an animal, to be slain; therefore a person*
> *or thing* **doomed to destruction***; a curse; a man accursed, devoted*
> *to the direst of woes."*

Paul is saying here that he *"could wish"* that he were *"doomed to destruction"*
if only his fellow Israelites around him could be saved. I do not believe that any
of us today would want to doom ourselves to Hell. To save some lost people
Paul wrote this wish to his friends in Rome. It would not be possible to be
"doomed to destruction" once a person is born-again, but the desire was voiced
by Paul. It is a noble sentiment.

Romans 9:4

**"Who are Israelites; to whom *pertaineth* the adoption,
and the glory, and the covenants, and the giving of the
law, and the service *of God*, and the promises;"** Paul lists the
past benefits of his kinsmen called *"Israelites."* Those followers of Abraham
had a past. They had an *"adoption"* by God. God picked them. God chose
them. The nation of Israel was a special line of God's choice. God has freedom
of choice. He had a choice of Abraham first, and then a special son, Isaac, and
then Isaac's special son Jacob, and then on down the line to the Lord Jesus
Christ.

These Israelites had the *"adoption,"* a close filial relationship to the Lord.
Not like the Gentiles and the heathen who were the ancestors of most of us.
Israel had a special *"covenant"* relationship to the Lord. They partook of the
SHEKINAH *"glory"* when they went through the wilderness. SHAKAN is one
of the Hebrew words meaning *"to dwell."* The SHEKINAH *"glory"* was the
dwelling *"glory"* of God. Everywhere they went in the wilderness wanderings,
the cloud of God's *"glory"*was above the tabernacle. When the glorious cloud
by day and the pillar of fire by night moved, the Israelites moved. That is how
God manifested Himself. That *"glory"* was a visible thing for all the Israelites
to see. We today do not have that.

Israel also had the *"covenants."* The word *"covenant,"* (or one of its
forms) is used two hundred eighty times in the King James Bible; two hundred
fifty-six times in the Old Testament and the rest in the New Testament. Though
there were some covenants before this, the Abrahamic covenant begins the
covenants made to Israel. The other three are the Mosaic covenant, the

Palestinian Covenant, and the New Covenant. Israel had "*covenants*" or agreements with God. God gave these "*covenants*" to Israel, who were a special people.

The giving of the Law of Moses was a frightening event. The power of God was shown. The smoke and fire from Mount Sinai made the people afraid. The law of Moses dealt with the ten commandments, and various civil and ceremonial laws.

Law Was to Israel, Not the Church

This law was given to Israel, not to the church. These promises made to Israel will be fulfilled literally in the future of Israel. They must not be spiritualized and applied to the church.

This is what Harold Camping of Family Radio and other Amillennialists and covenant theologians have been teaching. There is a special entity called the nation of Israel. God has given Israel a past, a present, and a future. Covenant theologians believe that the promises of Israel (the Jews) are fulfilled in us the believers, or the church. That is not true. God said what He meant, and He meant what He said.

God is going to fulfill all the promises of the Old Testament that He made to Israel. Many of those promises will be fulfilled in the Millennium, the thousand-year reign of the Lord Jesus Christ on this earth. You do not have to spiritualize God's promises of the Old Testament. The Bible clearly states that

"The wolf also shall dwell with the lamb, and the leopard shall lie down with the kid; and the calf and the young lion and the fatling together; and a little child shall lead them. And the cow and the bear shall feed; their young ones shall lie down together: and the lion shall eat straw like the ox. And the sucking child shall play on the hole of the asp, and the weaned child shall put his hand on the cockatrice' den." (Isaiah 11:6-8)

No one has to spiritualize these things as the Amillennialists do. No, these things will take place. There will be peace. *"They shall not hurt nor destroy in all my holy mountain"* (Isaiah 11:9a). The millennium of the Lord Jesus Christ will bring peace. *"Millennium"* is a good word. It comes from the Latin MILLE (thousand) and ANNUS (year). It means *"a thousand years."*

The millennium of the Lord Jesus Christ is when He is reigning and ruling here upon this earth and many things will change. The promises of God to His people Israel will be fulfilled. Those living at the time will have longevity during the millennium. No longer will a child die at the age of ten and be called a child. If he die at one hundred years of age, he will still be called a mere "*child*" (Isaiah 65:26). If a child will die at one hundred that means that people might live ten times that child's age, or at the age of one thousand years. In other words, there will be people walking around during the millennium who will be as old as Methuselah. He died at 969 years of age.

There will be many topographical changes that will take place also. There will be changes in the desert near Jerusalem. The Bible says that "*the desert will rejoice, and blossom as the rose*" (Isaiah 35:1). That is not just a figure of speech. It indeed will be literally fulfilled. There will be waters from the city of Jerusalem that will go forth and heal the Dead Sea, and the whole desert area will blossom and prosper. All of these Israelites have these "*promises*" which God has promised to them.

Romans 9:5

"Whose *are* the fathers, and of whom as concerning the flesh Christ *came*, who is over all, God blessed for ever. Amen." When you see the word "*fathers*" in the New Testament, it is speaking of the Old Testament "*fathers*," not the church fathers, but the "*fathers*" of the Israelite nation--Abraham, Isaac, and Jacob. Those are the lead "*fathers*." Jacob, who is also named "*Israel*," had twelve sons. These are called the twelve tribes of Israel. As to His perfect Humanity, the Lord Jesus Christ came from the tribe of Judah. He is the eternal God Who became incarnated by means of the Virgin birth. It is true that, "*concerning the flesh, Christ came*" from the "*fathers*." He was a Jew, and that was very important.

The Lord Jesus Christ Is God

Notice there is a comma after the phrase, "*over all*." The word, "*God*," is in apposition to the word, "*Christ*." This is a clear teaching of the Deity of the Lord Jesus Christ. Our King James Bible has an excellent translation of the Greek text here as elsewhere. It says that the Lord Jesus Christ "*is over all*," also that He is "*God*," and as such, He is "*blessed forever*." I want you to notice that there are some versions and perversions of the Words of God that change the Deity of Christ right here at this verse. Westcott and Hort and their text changed this.

Let me quote to you from the Revised Standard Version (RSV) sponsored by the *National Council of Churches* (NCC) which is an apostate group of churches.

"to them belong the patriarchs, and of their race, according to the flesh, **is the Christ. God who is over all be blessed for ever. Amen."** (Romans 9:5) (Revised Standard Version)

This is an erroneous version in many places and especially in this verse. Notice that after the word *"Christ,"* this false translation puts a period. Then they change the subject and say that *"God* [meaning God the Father, NOT God the Son] *who is over all be blessed for ever."* They start a new sentence. They deny completely here that the Lord Jesus *"Christ"* is identified as being *"God."* On the contrary, here is a tremendously powerful verse that shows clearly that the Lord Jesus Christ is true Deity and is *"God"* blessed forever.

Romans 9:6

"Not as though the word of God hath taken none effect. For they *are* not all Israel, which are of Israel:" The *"Word of God"* should take *"effect"* in the lives of believers. It was not always the case with *"Israel,"* however. This is a very important point. Just because a person is a member of the line of Abraham, Isaac, and Jacob, God does not consider them to be the true *"Israel."* The true *"Israel"* were those who had been looking by faith forward to the cross of Calvary and the Lamb of God Who died for the sins of the world. Those are the real Israelites. In the same way, not all members of some churches are genuine Christians. They can call themselves Baptists, or Presbyterians, or Lutherans, but that does not make them born-again Christians just because they name the name. They must each have genuine personal faith in the Lord Jesus Christ as their Saviour and Redeemer. That gives them eternal life and regeneration. While it is true that many genuine cars are kept in garages, it is also true that just because you are in a garage does not make you a car. To be a true Israelite, there must have been a genuine faith in a coming Saviour like Abraham had. It is not simply by birth. You and I cannot be born Christians either. We must have genuine personal faith in the Lord Jesus Christ ourselves to make us Christians.

Romans 9:7

"Neither, because they are the seed of Abraham, *are they* all children: but, In Isaac shall thy seed be called." There is always a battle in the Middle East and the Palestine area between Abraham's two sons. Abraham had Isaac (representing Israel), but he also had Ishmael (representing the Arabs.) They are battling. There is a battle in Jerusalem over the West Bank and in many other places. The late Jassar Araphat, the former Palestinian leader, was a hard core Communist-terrorist. He was a butcher who countenanced slaughter, murder, and torture. Some in our country were trying to make deals between this murderer and the leaders of

Israel. It will never last. Those who follow Araphat's ways will continuously break every agreement that is made. Remember Lenin? He was one of the early Communist leaders. He said, *"Promises are like pie crusts--made to be broken."* They will break their promises whenever it is to their advantage to do so.

The Jewish *"seed of Abraham"* is having trouble. It is only in *"Isaac"* that God's true *"seed"* shall be *"called."* It is not through Ishmael's Arab seed. In God's sovereignty, He chose to bless Isaac and his greater *"Seed,"* the Lord Jesus Christ.

Romans 9:8

"That is, They which are the children of the flesh, these *are* not the children of God: but the children of the promise are counted for the seed." The *"children of the flesh"* refers to the Ishmaelites. Ishmael was a son of Abraham, but he was a son of the *"flesh,"* because Hagar was his mother rather than Sarah. He was not a son of the promise. The *"children of the promise"* are the children of Isaac whose mother was Sarah. They are the ones *"counted for the seed."* God promised Abraham a son and a seed as the stars of the sky and as the sand of the seashore. He would have children. But he could not wait for God to fulfill the promise. He made a deal with Sarah and her handmade Hagar, who produced Ishmael. The Lord Jesus Christ came through Isaac, not through Ishmael.

Romans 9:9

"For this *is* the word of promise, At this time will I come, and Sara shall have a son." The background for this *"word of promise"* is in Genesis 15. This was God's *"promise"* to Abraham and Sara. That *"promise"* could not be fulfilled in anything but Abraham's wife. It could not be fulfilled by some handmaid off the street brought in to have conception of children and to have Ishmael born. Abraham could not wait. He was wrong in this.

Sometimes we cannot wait to have God's Words fulfilled. We rush things. We go off "half-cocked," as they say. We go off with the flesh. We want to do things our way, rather than waiting to do things God's way.

● **Genesis 18:14**
Is any thing too hard for the LORD? At the time appointed I will return unto thee, according to the time of life, and **Sarah shall have a son.**

Sarah was barren. She could not have children!

Abraham loved Ishmael. Ishmael was his firstborn even though it was through Hagar the handmaid. It was not his real wife. Ishmael was a man of the field. He was strong. He was probably handsome and rugged.

● **Genesis 17:19**
And God said, **Sarah thy wife shall bear thee a son indeed**; and thou shalt call his name Isaac: and I will establish my covenant with him for an everlasting covenant, *and* with his seed after him.

God had freedom of choice. He set aside the firstborn in favor of the second born. Isaac was the son of *"promise."* That is up to God. He can do this. It is His freedom of choice. He can pick and choose just like you and I can pick and choose. We should remember that and not fault the Lord for it.

Romans 9:10-11

"And not only *this***; but when Rebecca also had conceived by one,** *even* **by our father Isaac; (For** *the children* **being not yet born, neither having done any good or evil, that the purpose of God according to election might stand, not of works, but of him that calleth;)"** Rebekah was Isaac's wife. She was the one through whom Isaac was to have the chosen seed. This is the line that was going to run through Jacob, and not through Esau. The two sons of Abraham were Ishmael and Isaac. The two sons of Isaac were Jacob and Esau. God chose one and not the other.

Notice that God did not want *"works"* to determine His purposes. He wanted His purposes to be determined by Himself who *"calleth."* Here is God's freedom of choice. Notice in this verse 11 the word *"election."* The Greek word for *"election"* is EKLOGE. It means: *"the act of picking out, choosing."*

The Calvinists and the Hyper-Calvinists like to fasten upon this word, *"election,"* and make it always refer to salvation. That is not the case. In fact, there are very few instances in Scripture where the word *"election"* or *"choice"* refers to salvation. This *"election"* or *"choice,"* in this verse, refers to picking or choosing one of the two children from whom the Lord Jesus Christ would be born. That is God's Sovereign choice. That is **His** freedom of choice.

Let it be understood that there are moderate Calvinists. Though there are some of their beliefs I disagree with, I want to turn my attention here to what is known as hyper-Calvinists.

Five Errors of the Hyper-Calvinists

Let me go over some of the unscriptural things on the subject of
"*election*" that are taught by the hyper-Calvinists.

1. They teach that none of us can be saved unless we have been
   previously "*elected*" by God, Who has "*elected*" a small number
   of people in the world.

2. They teach that if you have not been previously "*elected*," you
   cannot accept Christ and receive Him as Saviour.

3. They teach that the Lord Jesus Christ did not die for the sins of
   the entire world, but only for the sins of the "*elect.*"

4. They teach that God did not love the entire world, but only the
   "*world*" of the "*elect.*"

5. To do this, they twist and grossly mis-interpret John 3:16 as to
   the meaning of "*world*," "*whosoever*," and "*perish*" in this verse.
   They add three of their own words after each of these terms ["*of
   the elect*"] in order to interpret the verse the way they think it
   means, even though by so doing it is a gross distortion of the
   verse.

The hyper-Calvinists interpret John 3:16 like this:

- **John 3:16**
  For God so loved the world **[of the elect]**, that he gave his
  only begotten Son, that whosoever **[of the elect]** believeth in
  him should not perish **[of the elect]**, but have everlasting life.

I believe this is a travesty of Biblical interpretation. I believe it is a
travesty of God's love of the world. I believe it is bending and twisting of the
Scriptures. It has done great harm to the cause of Christ. If a person really
believes that only the "*elect*" can be saved and only the "*elect*" are loved by
God, and God does not love anybody who is not "*elect,*" that means I cannot tell
an audience that God loves them unless I know everyone for sure is saved. I
cannot tell you that God loves you if I believed like they do. I cannot tell you
also that Christ died for your sins, if Christ did not die for your sins, because
you may not be of the "*elect.*" I would not be able to preach the gospel clearly
taught in the Bible if I believed that. I firmly believe that these views are
heretical and apostate. This position is a false and "*another gospel*" (2
Corinthians 11:4; Galatians 1:6).

There was a man who believed this hyper-Calvinism very strongly. He
was one of my fellow-teachers when I was teaching at *Shelton College* in Cape

May, New Jersey. He was from South Africa. On one occasion I said unto him, *"How can you preach the gospel?"* He said, *"I do not tell that Christ died for their sins."* He was tongue-tied. I asked him, *"If you have an audience, either a radio audience, or a live audience, how do you preach?"* He could not give an answer.

This word *"election"* in this verse is God's choice as to which of these two sons He was going to pick and choose to be the inheritor of the blessings of God from whom the Lord Jesus Christ, the Saviour of the world, was going to be born. God's choice had nothing to do with works, whether good or evil. He did not wait for Esau to be born to find out if Esau was better than Jacob or vice versa. They were both a little bit questionable in many things. He didn't ask anything about works. Before these sons were born God just said, *"All right, the line of my Son, the Lord Jesus Christ, is going to come through Jacob the second born rather than Ishmael the firstborn."* That is it. That was God's sovereign choice.

We must acknowledge God's power, right, and authority to choose. He is the great God of the universe. He chose to create the stars and the galaxies, every one of them. He chose to create man, and from man to make woman. He does all things right. He created all the animals of the earth.

Romans 9:12

"It was said unto her, The elder shall serve the younger." That is an interesting phenomenon in Scripture. *"The elder shall serve the younger."* The *"elder"* usually has the greatest place at the table and the greatest inheritance. It was the law of the firstborn.

In the Old Testament economy the elder son, the firstborn, would get twice as much as any of the other children, a *"double portion."* (Deuteronomy 21:17). That was the law of the firstborn. They would have double the inheritance. That was a great thing.

Do you realize that God in the Old Testament quite often changed this law about the firstborn? He often switched the blessing from the firstborn to the second born. Notice the comparison with the *"first man Adam"* and the *"last Adam"* (1 Corinthians 15:49). The Lord Jesus Christ, even though He was *"last,"* is preferred to the *"first man."* It was the first Adam that God takes away and puts in his place the last Adam. The Lord Jesus Christ is the God of all, and He's the one Who is first. God rejected the first Adam. Christ is the One who is to be exalted.

Consider Abraham. His firstborn was Ishmael. God set him aside and chose Isaac his second born. Consider Isaac's children, Jacob and Esau. God laid aside the firstborn, Esau, and He said He was going to take Jacob instead. Consider Joseph. Manasseh was the firstborn and Ephraim was the second born. When Jacob was going to bless the sons of Joseph, his eyes were dim.

Joseph, who was in Egypt, brought his two children to his father to be blessed. Joseph brought Jacob's hands up so that the right hand would go upon the firstborn, Manasseh, and the left hand would go upon the second born, Ephraim. But Jacob crossed his hands and blessed the second born rather than the firstborn.

God's Sovereignty in His Choice

God's sovereignty has operated to discount the firstborn and go to the second in cases of His choosing. That is what it was in the case of Joseph. The crossing of Jacob's hands is a picture of the cross of Christ. By that cross, the Lord took away the sin of Adam by the sacrifice of the "*last Adam*" Who was predominant. Throughout the Old Testament, it seems to be God's plan that "*the elder shall serve the younger.*"

Romans 9:13

"As it is written, Jacob have I loved, but Esau have I hated." Love and hate are two difficult things to understand. The phrase, "*As it is written*," was a reference to the book of Malachi.

- Malachi 1:2-3
  I have loved you, saith the LORD. Yet ye say, Wherein hast thou loved us? *Was* not Esau Jacob's brother? saith the LORD: **yet I loved Jacob, And I hated Esau**, and laid his mountains and his heritage waste for the dragons of the wilderness.
- Matthew 10:37
  He that loveth father or mother more than me is not worthy of me: and he that loveth son or daughter more than me is not worthy of me.

If you love your children more than the Lord Jesus Christ you are "*not worthy*" of Him. It is a comparative love.

- Luke 14:26
  If any *man* come to me, and **hate not his father, and mother, and wife, and children, and brethren, and sisters, yea, and his own life also**, he cannot be my disciple.

"*Hate*" in this case could be defined as "*loving less*" than someone else. You have to love the Lord Jesus Christ first, and anyone else comes under the meaning of "*loving less*" which is akin to "*hate.*"

This is, I believe, a picture of God's love and His hatred. I do not think that God hates anything but sin in a real absolute sense, but some things He loves less, and therefore he hates. Who was Esau? He was a man of the field. He was a hairy man.

Remember Rebekah's scheme to get the blessing on Jacob instead of Esau? Jacob was told by his mother that Esau was out in the field getting some venison for his father. She explained, *"When Esau comes back with the venison your father is going to bless Esau and not you."* She had a plan. Rebekah told Jacob to put goat's skin on Jacob's hands because Esau's hands were hairy and Jacob's hands were smooth. Also the smell of the field would be there. Because his father could not see well, so he would think Isaac was Esau. Rebekah said she would dress the goat so that Isaac would think it was venison. *"I will serve it and you can take it in there and get the blessing"* she said.

"And Rebekah heard when Isaac spake to Esau his son. And Esau went to the field to hunt for venison, and to bring it. And Rebekah spake unto Jacob her son, saying, Behold, I heard thy father speak unto Esau thy brother, saying, Bring me venison, and make me savoury meat, that I may eat, and bless thee before the LORD before my death. Now therefore, my son, obey my voice according to that which I command thee. Go now to the flock, and fetch me from thence two good kids of the goats; and I will make them savoury meat for thy father, such as he loveth: And thou shalt bring it to thy father, that he may eat, and that he may bless thee before his death." (Genesis 27:5-10)

Jacob was a conniver. Do we have mothers who are connivers? Sometimes we do. The father asked who Jacob was. Jacob said that he was Esau. The father said that *"the voice was Jacob's voice, but the hands are the hands of Esau"* (Genesis 27:22). Isaac blessed Jacob. Esau came later and told his father that he blessed the wrong son. Isaac said, I have *"blessed him, yea, and he shall be blessed"* (Genesis 27:33). Esau wept. Esau was a man of the flesh. Esau was a man of the world. Esau sold his birthright for some red pottage, some soup (Genesis 25:29-34). Jacob was a great deceiver himself. Jacob's name means *"deceiver."* It also means *"heel holder"* or *"someone who grabs onto the heal."* Jacob was not perfect, but God loved him.

I want you to remember another thing about Verse 13. It is the phrase, *"As it is written."* That is a perfect tense in the Greek language which means something that takes place in the past, continues to the present, and will continue into the future. This is God's stamp every time you see GEGRAPTAI which is the Greek word whose root is GRAPHO, which is *"to write."*

Every time you see *"it is written"* in Scripture, remember that God is saying that He has preserved entirely and perfectly His Words--His Hebrew, Aramaic, and Greek Words. It is something that has been written down in the past. It has been preserved right down to the present. It will continue to be preserved, word perfect, right into the future. That is why we dare say that God has preserved the Hebrew, Aramaic, and Greek Words which underlie our *King James Bible*. God promised to preserve it. These words right here, "*it is written,*" are another evidence that God preserves His Words.

Romans 9:14

"What shall we say then? *Is there* unrighteousness with God? God forbid." This accusation that there is "*unrighteousness with God*" is behind those who criticize Him for choosing Jacob rather than Esau. People might rise up and say, "*Why did God do this?*" These same people might accuse God of taking a child, a son, or a daughter in death. When that happens, there are various reactions. The world looks at God, shakes a finger at the Lord, and yells out and screams out in criticism and condemnation. The world removes themselves farther from the Lord.

What might the saved believer do? First, the believer might ask the question why does God do this? Is God unrighteous? Why did He do this to me? Why is it that I am picked out? Secondly, I would trust that this calamity would draw the believer closer to the Lord. These things came about for a purpose. If the Lord was behind it, He did it for a reason. He has permitted it.

All God's Purposes Are Righteous

The Lord has His purposes in all of these things. He sometimes takes His born-again ones to the woodshed for one reason or another. In any kind of pain or whatever it is that lays us low, we must ask the Lord, what is there for me in this? What trial and temptation is there for me to escape? What can I learn from this? How can I draw closer to Thee? These are some of the questions that we should ask the Lord. "*Is there unrighteousness with God? God forbid.*"

- **Genesis 18:25**
  That be far from thee to do after this manner, to slay the righteous with the wicked: and that the righteous should be as the wicked, that be far from thee: **Shall not the Judge of all the earth do right?**

This was said by Abraham when God was ready to judge Sodom and Gomorrah for their sin. The sins of Sodom are prevalent today as well.

Former President Clinton pushed the sodomites, the lesbians, and all the gay rights people with the result that they supported him. Others in government are pushing this as well. When God was about to judge Sodom, Abraham pled with the Lord. For God to have *"unrighteousness"* is ridiculous. God and *"unrighteousness"* are poles apart. They are not even in the same plane. It is impossible even to think of it. **"Shall not the Judge of all the earth do right?"**

- **Psalm 92:15**
  To shew that the LORD *is* upright: *he is* my rock, and *there is* **no unrighteousness in him**.

Is God unrighteous? No, He is not.

- **Isaiah 55:6-9**
  Seek ye the LORD while he may be found, call ye upon him while he is near: Let the wicked forsake his way, and the unrighteous man his thoughts: and let him return unto the LORD, and he will have mercy upon him; and to our God, for he will abundantly pardon. For my thoughts *are* not your thoughts, neither *are* your ways my ways, saith the LORD. For *as* **the heavens are higher than the earth, so are my ways higher than your ways, and my thoughts than your thoughts**.

There's a definition of unrighteousness in 1 John.

- **1 John 5:17**
  All unrighteousness is sin: and there is a sin not unto death.

According to this definition, if God is unrighteous, He is a sinner. That is so outlandishly false. Is God unrighteous? Certainly not.

- **1 John 1:9**
  If we confess our sins, he is faithful and just to forgive us *our* sins, **and to cleanse us from all unrighteousness**.

If God cleanses us from all unrighteousness obviously, He, Himself, could not be unrighteous.

In Him is no sin. We are not to criticize our God for His freedom of choice. He chose what line from which the Lord Jesus Christ would be born.

Romans 9:15

"For he saith to Moses, I will have mercy on whom I will have mercy, and I will have compassion on whom I will have compassion." Here is an illustration of God's sovereignty once again in Exodus chapter 33.

- Exodus 33:19
  And he said, I will make all my goodness pass before thee, and I will proclaim the name of the LORD before thee; **and will be gracious to whom I will be gracious, and will shew mercy on whom I will shew mercy**.

Here Pharaoh was ready to hold back His people from their freedom.

- Isaiah 55:7
  Let the wicked forsake his way, and the unrighteous man his thoughts: and let him return unto the LORD, and he will have mercy upon him; and to our God, for **he will abundantly pardon**.

Does the Lord have mercy on those today who are living? I believe that He does. Does He have compassion on those of us who are living today? Yes, I believe that He does. He has freedom of choice. Why do I say that?

- Romans 5:8
  But **God commendeth his love toward us**, in that, while we were yet sinners, Christ died for us.

- John 3:16
  For **God so loved the world**, that he gave his only begotten Son, that whosoever believeth in him should not perish, but have everlasting life.

That is the compassion of God. That is the mercy of God on all of us. As far as the compassion of the Lord Jesus Christ:

- Matthew 9:36
  But when he saw the multitudes, **he was moved with compassion on them**, because they fainted, and were scattered abroad, as sheep having no shepherd.

- Matthew 14:14
  And Jesus went forth, and saw a great multitude, **and was moved with compassion toward them**, and he healed their sick.

- Matthew 15:32
  Then Jesus called his disciples *unto him*, and said, **I have compassion on the multitude**, because they continue with me now three days, and have nothing to eat: and I will not send them away fasting, lest they faint in the way.

He fed the 5,000 men plus women and children because He had "*compassion*." God said "*I will have mercy on whom I will have mercy, and I will have compassion on whom I will have compassion.*"

- **1 Peter 3:8**
  Finally, *be ye* all of one mind, **having compassion one of another**, love as brethren, *be* pitiful, *be* courteous:

God wants the believers to have compassion on one another. God wants us to be merciful, pitiful, and to have sincerity. God is a God of compassion.

We are going to see next week that God not only had compassion on some, but He hardened Pharaoh's heart. I have spoken about this previously. Some people asked the question about whether God hardened Pharaoh's heart, or if Pharaoh hardened his own heart. At that time I looked this up. Both of these things were true. It says in Scripture that God hardened his heart, and that Pharaoh hardened his own heart. About six times each, these two statements are mentioned. God had mercy on the Israelites, but He certainly judged the Egyptians at the time of Israel's exodus from Egypt.

Romans 9:16

"So then *it is* not of him that willeth, nor of him that runneth, but of God that sheweth mercy." The line of Christ was God's freedom of choice by taking Abraham's second born son, Isaac. By taking Isaac's second born, Jacob, he was in the line from which the Lord Jesus Christ would be born. This choice was "*not of him that willeth, nor of him that runneth, but of God that sheweth mercy.*" It is not the human beings in this equation who made this decision. The Lord is in charge. He is a "*merciful*" God.

- **Luke 18:13**
  And the publican, standing afar off, would not lift up so much as *his* eyes unto Heaven, but smote upon his breast, saying, **God be merciful to me a sinner**.
- **Hebrews 2:17**
  Wherefore in all things it behoved him to be made like unto *his* brethren, **that he might be a merciful** and faithful high priest in things *pertaining* to God, to make reconciliation for the sins of the people.

Our Saviour is "*merciful.*"

- **Hebrews 8:12**
  For I will be merciful to their unrighteousness, and their sins and their iniquities will I remember no more.

God's Infinite Freedom of Choice

In the first part of this chapter, we see God's freedom of choice as He sees that His Son is going to be born of Israel. It was going to be a special birth, and down a special line. God is not unrighteous to select Isaac instead of Ishmael, to select Jacob instead of Esau, and to select all the necessary things down the line until the birth of our Saviour. God is the One Who has purposed these things, and they are in His plan.

We ought to be thankful that God has a plan for us. Are you not glad, if you are saved, that the plan of salvation by faith in the Lord Jesus Christ was brought to you? If you are saved, are you not happy and glad that you have accepted and received Him as your personal Saviour and Lord? That was in God's Sovereign plan.

Romans 9:17

"For the scripture saith unto Pharaoh, Even for this same purpose have I raised thee up, that I might shew my power in thee, and that my name might be declared throughout all the earth." There was a special purpose for that Pharaoh, the king of Egypt at the time of Moses. Egypt is a big country. We still have problems with Egypt today. Pharaoh was *"raised up"* especially of God. People might question why God *"raised up"* a man like that. He hardened his heart and he was judged, because this was God's purpose. Again, this is God's freedom of choice, which is a part of His Divine sovereignty. I mentioned that God has a freedom of choice.

God's Purpose With Pharaoh

The purpose of *"raising up"* Pharaoh was that God could then show His *"power"* unto him. The *"power"* of God could not be evidenced to Pharaoh unless he resisted the Lord. Pharaoh was evil, but God planned it that way. Pharaoh was so evil that he would not let the children of Israel go. Israel wanted to go out into the wilderness and serve God, but Pharaoh refused to permit this. Pharaoh hardened his heart. He was a wicked, evil man. Every time Pharaoh hardened his heart, God judged.

God sent ten plagues or judgments against Egypt. How would you like it if our rivers turned into blood? All the fish died. Then the frogs came up. How would you like frogs everywhere? Then lice, the third judgment, all over man and beast. The fourth judgment was fleas. Lice and frogs are bad enough, but fleas! The fifth judgment was a very grievous murrain, a terrible plague on the cattle that would kill them. The sixth judgment was boils on man and on beast. The seventh plague was large, heavy hail that could be felt. Crops would be destroyed. The eighth plague was locusts. The ninth plague was thick darkness, you could not see anything. The tenth plague was the death of the firstborn.

God raised up Pharaoh and hardened his heart that the "*power*" of God might be shown in Egypt and that God's "*Name might be declared throughout all the earth*." God's judgments were "*against all the gods of Egypt*" (Exodus 12:12). The Egyptians worshiped the lice. They worshiped the frogs. They worshiped the Nile River god.

Romans 9:18

"Therefore hath he mercy on whom he will *have* mercy, and whom he will he hardeneth." The Lord hardened Pharaoh's heart. I talked about this earlier. There are eleven places where the Bible says God hardened Pharaoh's heart and three places where it says that Pharaoh hardened his own heart.

- **Exodus 4:21**
  And the LORD said unto Moses, When thou goest to return into Egypt, see that thou do all those wonders before Pharaoh, which I have put in thine hand: but **I will harden his heart,** that he shall not let the people go.

Pharaoh was a special person raised up by God.

- **Exodus 7:3**
  And **I will harden Pharaoh's heart**, and multiply my signs and my wonders in the land of Egypt.

- **Exodus 7:13**
  And **he hardened Pharaoh's heart**, that he hearkened not unto them; as the LORD had said.

- **Exodus 9:12**
  And **the LORD hardened the heart of Pharaoh**, and he hearkened not unto them; as the LORD had spoken unto Moses.

- **Exodus 10:1**
  And the LORD said unto Moses, Go in unto Pharaoh: for **I have hardened his heart,** and the heart of his servants, that I might shew these my signs before him:

- **Exodus 10:20**
  But **the LORD hardened Pharaoh's heart**, so that he would
  not let the children of Israel go.
- **Exodus 10:27**
  But **the LORD hardened Pharaoh's heart**, and he would not
  let them go.
- **Exodus 11:10**
  And Moses and Aaron did all these wonders before Pharaoh:
  and **the LORD hardened Pharaoh's heart**, so that he would
  not let the children of Israel go out of his land.
- **Exodus 14:4**
  And **I will harden Pharaoh's heart**, that he shall follow after
  them; and I will be honoured upon Pharaoh, and upon all his
  host; that the Egyptians may know that I *am* the LORD. And
  they did so.
- **Exodus 14:8**
  And **the LORD hardened the heart of Pharaoh king of
  Egypt**, and he pursued after the children of Israel: and the
  children of Israel went out with an high hand.
- **Exodus 14:17**
  And I, behold, **I will harden the hearts of the Egyptians**, and
  they shall follow them: and I will get me honour upon Pharaoh,
  and upon all his host, upon his chariots, and upon his
  horsemen.

On the other hand it says:

- **Exodus 8:15**
  But when Pharaoh saw that there was respite, **he hardened
  his heart**, and hearkened not unto them; as the LORD had
  said.

Here is Pharaoh cooperating with the Lord. You cannot blame the Lord all the
time because it is Pharaoh who hardened his own heart.

- **Exodus 8:32**
  And **Pharaoh hardened his heart** at this time also, neither
  would he let the people go.
- **Exodus 9:34**
  And when Pharaoh saw that the rain and the hail and the
  thunders were ceased, he sinned yet more, and **hardened his
  heart**, he and his servants.

There are five references which just say his heart was hardened. It doesn't
say if God hardened his heart or if he hardened his own heart. There are three
places where Pharaoh hardened his own heart. There are eleven places where
God hardened Pharaoh's heart. Pharaoh was a special person used for a special

purpose.

Romans 9:19-20

"Thou wilt say then unto me, Why doth he yet find fault? For who hath resisted his will?" "Nay but, O man, who art thou that repliest against God? Shall the thing formed say to him that formed *it,* Why hast thou made me thus?" In these verses is God's reply to people finding fault with Him. The question is asked, *"For who hath resisted his will?"* Satan certainly is one who resists God's will.

- Zechariah 3:1
  And he shewed me Joshua the high priest standing before the angle of the LORD, and **Satan standing at his right hand to resist him.**
- Acts 7:51
  Ye stiffnecked and uncircumcised in heart and ears, **ye do always resist the Holy Ghost**: as your fathers *did*, so *do* ye.

They find fault with God.

Why Pharaoh's Hardened Heart?

People ask why God hardened Pharaoh's heart. This was in God's will, God's purpose, and God's plan. The only way that Israel could have gotten out of the land of Egypt was by means of the hardness of the heart of Pharaoh. Finally, Pharaoh told them to get out. Afterwards, he changed his mind. Half way through the Red Sea, as the Lord opened up the Red Sea for the Israelites to cross over, Pharaoh and his army tried to cross over. God shut that sea up and drowned Pharaoh's army.

It was because of the hardness of Pharaoh's heart that God's people left Egypt. God had promised to Israel a past, a present, and a future. His blessing was to be found in the land of promise. The Israelites were down in Egypt for over 430 years in bondage and slavery (Exodus 12:40). The way God used to get the children of Israel out of Egypt was to make a wicked, evil Pharaoh that hardened his heart. God was not responsible for it. Pharaoh played right into God's hands by hardening his heart. Because Pharaoh hardened his heart, God brought judgment number one, number two, number three, and all ten judgments, until Pharaoh finally yielded to the will of God and let the people go.

One of the important questions in these verses is: *"Shall the thing formed say to him that formed it, Why hast thou made me thus?"*

- **Deuteronomy 32:18**
  Of the Rock *that* begat thee thou art unmindful, and **hast forgotten God that formed thee.**

- **Isaiah 43:21**
  This people have I formed for myself; they shall shew forth my praise.

  I am not an artificer in clay. I am sure I used clay when I was a young boy, as many of us did. After I had made a dog or a cat, or a house, or whatever it was that I made, what if that clay started talking and asked me why I made them in the way that I did? It would be foolish and ridiculous. God is the God of all creation. He has the power to make any creature that He wishes. He is able to perform His will upon that creature.

Romans 9:21

"Hath not the potter power over the clay, of the same lump to make one vessel unto honour, and another unto dishonour?" The potter can make from the clay anything he wants. We do not have as many potters today as in former years. We do have some pottery stores where the wives like to shop and see what they can buy. My mother used to bake things in a kiln. She had that kiln in Naples, Florida. She made all kinds of dishes and plates in it. I thought they were a little bit silly, but she liked them.

The potter is a picture that is used in the Words of God for God himself as the Master Potter.

- **Isaiah 29:16**
  Surely your turning of things upside down shall be **esteemed as the potter's clay**: for shall the work say of him that made it, He made me not? or shall the thing framed say of him that framed it, He had no understanding?

It is really illogical for the heathen who make their own gods, and after making them, believe that these gods made their makers. That seems a little silly, but that is what they have.

- **Isaiah 64:8**
  But now, O LORD, thou *art* our father; **we *are* the clay, and thou our potter**; and we all *are* the work of thy hand.

- **Jeremiah 18:3-6**
  Then I went down to the **potter's house**, and, behold, he wrought a work on the wheels. And the vessel that he made of clay was marred in the **hand of the potter**: so he made it again another vessel, as seemed **good to the potter to make it.** Then the word of the LORD came to me, saying, O house of Israel, cannot I do with you **as this potter?** saith the LORD. Behold, **as the clay is in the potter's hand**, so are ye in mine hand, O house of Israel.

Here is a picture of a visit to a potter's house.

God Is The Potter

The Lord is the Potter and we are the clay.

There is no way in the world, unless we are haughty, proud, and arrogant, that we can dictate to the God of Heaven and earth. Yet, we have people who are dictating to Him all the time. They are usually unsaved people shaking their fist in the face of our God saying that He is not worthy. They ask why God did this, why did He do that, or why did he cause this calamity or that calamity. He is the One Who is the Potter, and we are the clay. If we are born-again, we should want Him to use us in any way He sees fit. We should want Him to mold us. Our bodies are houses of clay.

In the book of 2 Corinthians, the Bible says that we are made of clay and the "*earthen vessels*" which are our bodies are vessels of clay (2 Corinthians 4:7). This is so the "*power may be of God and not of us.*" If we were so splendid, so impervious to pain, so superhuman, that people could see how wonderful we are, then God would not have any glory. He has made us just pots, just "*earthen vessels,*" vessels of clay. If there is any power at all it must come from within us as the Lord Jesus Christ, if we are saved, indwells us and gives us this power (Philippians 4:13). He must shine forth from us, not because of who we are, but because of Who He is. God is a wonderful Potter.

Romans 9:22

"What **if God, willing to shew** *his* **wrath, and to make his power known, endured with much longsuffering the vessels of wrath fitted to destruction:"** In this verse, we see that God had both *"wrath"* as well as *"longsuffering."* God is a *"longsuffering"* God.

God's Longsuffering And Pharaoh

He was *"longsuffering"* with Pharaoh who was obstreperous, who was obstinate, who was set in his ways, who had hardened his heart against the Lord.

God poured out His wrath upon him and judged him until that rascal came to his senses and let God's people go.

God's Longsuffering And the Flood

God was *"longsuffering"* in the days of Noah. He did not allow the waters to kill and inundate all that lived. He spared eight people.

He waited. Noah probably invited many people to come into the ark. They probably laughed at Noah because it had never rained up to that time. It is just like when we invite people to come to Christ today, and many times they laugh us to scorn. They want to know why they must come to the Lord Jesus Christ and be saved. It is because they are lost. The lost world needs to come to Christ the Saviour.

Though the other people probably laughed at Noah, his wife and children did not laugh at him. They knew him long enough to know that God put into his heart to build that ark. It was a huge ship. It was large enough to be able to take care of two of every kind of animal and seven of the clean animal pairs. There was no rain on the earth as yet. There was only a mist to water the ground (Genesis 2:6). People had never seen rain.

Here was a man who was told by God to build an ark for the saving of himself and his family, and two of every kind of animal, in addition to the seven pairs of clean animals. Noah believed God. God was *"longsuffering."* He waited. In fact, it says in Genesis 6:3 that man's *"days shall be one hundred and twenty years."* If man's days would be that many years before the flood came, it means that it would have been possible for Noah to have been a *"preacher of righteousness"* (2 Peter 2:5) for these *"one hundred and twenty years."* This was very possible since they lived many years in those days. Noah was 950 years old when he died (Genesis 9:29). It was entirely possible for 120 years, as Noah was building that ark, that he invited people to join him. I am sure that some of the people laughed at him because of his prediction of a flood of waters that would destroy them all.

God's Longsuffering And Lot

God was *"longsuffering"* also in the days of Lot when Lot was dragged out of the city of Sodom and Gomorrah. When the wicked city of the Sodomites was going to be judged with fire and brimstone, Lot came out.

His wife reluctantly came out. She looked back, and was turned into a pillar of salt (Genesis 19:26). The fire killed her just like it killed those in Sodom and Gomorrah. Their two daughters came out. They were no good. They committed incest with their father, but God was merciful and *longsuffering."*

Abraham plead with the Lord. He asked the Lord if there were 50 righteous people in that city would He spare the city (Genesis 18:24)? Yes, the Lord said He would spare the city for fifty righteous people. Abraham changed the number from fifty to forty-five to forty to thirty to twenty, and finally to ten (Genesis 18:24-32). The Lord said He would spare the city if there were only ten righteous people. The *"longsuffering"* of God. God is *"longsuffering"* today in this wicked world.

God Is Still Longsuffering

God is still *"longsuffering"* today.

- **2 Peter 3:9**
  The Lord is not slack concerning his promise, as some men count slackness; but **is longsuffering to us-ward, not willing that any should perish,** but that all should come to repentance.

One day God is going to judge this world. He is *"longsuffering."*

Is everyone reading this saved? I trust that you are born-again receiving Christ as your Saviour. It is not only the elect who can be saved. That is what the hyper-Calvinists would teach us. No, God is *"not willing that any should perish."* That is why we send out missionaries.

One Day Judgment Will Come

One day the judgment will come, and it will be too late. There came a time in the days of Noah before the flood when God shut the door (Genesis 7:16). No longer was the invitation open. God shut the door of the ark. It began to rain. When this happened, I am sure that everyone said they wanted to enter that ark. But it was too late. For everyone of us, there is an invitation to those who need to trust Christ as Saviour.

When the time comes, and you have rejected the call, someday it is going to be too late. The door will be shut. It is not too late today, so trust the Lord Jesus today.

Romans 9:23

"And that he might make known the riches of his glory on the vessels of mercy, which he had afore prepared unto glory," This verse speaks of the *"vessels of mercy."* It is in contrast to the *"vessels of wrath"* in verse 22, who were *"fitted to destruction."* Those who do not trust Christ will head to the *"destruction"* of Hell. In this verse, God makes known the *"riches of His glory."* Do you have these *"riches"*? *"Riches"* in material things do not last for eternity. Can you take any of that with you? If you go to Hell you cannot take gold or silver. If you go to Heaven you cannot take gold or silver. You take only what you have done for the Lord Jesus Christ here on this earth. You can take with you the *"riches"* of God, spiritual *"riches."* Let me read a few verses about God's *"riches."*

- **Romans 2:4**
  Or despisest thou **the riches of his goodness** and forbearance and longsuffering; not knowing that the goodness of God leadeth thee to repentance?
  If we are saved we have the "*riches*" of God.
- **Romans 11:33**
  O **the depth of the riches** both of the wisdom and knowledge of God! how unsearchable *are* his judgments, and his ways past finding out!
- **Ephesians 1:7**
  In whom we have redemption through his blood, the forgiveness of sins, **according to the riches of his grace**;
  God is a rich God. He has given "*riches of grace*" to those who believe.
- **Ephesians 1:18**
  The eyes of your understanding being enlightened; that ye may know what is the hope of his calling, and what **the riches of the glory** of his inheritance in the saints,
- **Ephesians 2:7**
  That in the ages to come he might shew **the exceeding riches of his grace** in *his* kindness toward us through Christ Jesus.
  God is a rich God, and He wants to give us "*riches*" as well.
- **Ephesians 3:8**
  Unto me, who am less than the least of all saints, is this grace given, that I should preach among the Gentiles **the unsearchable riches of Christ**;
- **Ephesians 3:16**
  That he would grant you, **according to the riches of his glory,** to be strengthened with might by his Spirit in the inner man;
- **Philippians 4:19**
  But my God shall supply all your need **according to his riches in glory** by Christ Jesus.
- **Hebrews 11:26**
  Esteeming the reproach of Christ **greater riches than the treasures in Egypt**: for he had respect unto the recompence of the reward.
  Paul is talking about Moses now.

That Greek word translated "*riches*" is PLUTOS. You have heard of Pluto, the dog. PLUTOS refers to someone who is rich. A plutocrat is a rich ruler. Plutocracy is the rule of the rich, by the rich, and for the rich.

I do not know what we have in Washington, DC. In the Lord Jesus Christ, we have many riches. He wants to make them available to us who are born-again. You may have all the riches in the world, but if you do not write yourself a check, or go to the bank and withdraw those riches, the riches are not available to you.

The Riches of God

If you are saved, and have the Lord Jesus Christ as your Saviour, you have the availability of all the riches of God in Heaven to be ministered unto you. You only have to believe it and ask the Lord to help you out. Tell the Lord you are poor in spirit, poor in heart, and you want the Lord Jesus Christ's riches.

Jesus knew about that.
- **2 Corinthians 8:9**
  For ye know the grace of our Lord Jesus Christ, that, though he was rich, yet for your sakes he became poor, **that ye through his poverty might be rich**.

This refers to God's rich mercy and salvation by genuine faith in His Son, the Lord Jesus Christ.

Romans 9:24

"Even us, whom he hath called, not of the Jews only, but also of the Gentiles?" The *"call"* of Christ in salvation is to everyone in the world. Again, I repeat, the hyper-Calvinists teach that the *"call"* of God is limited only to the elect whom He had chosen aforetime. They teach that this is not a universal call. They are wrong. The Lord Jesus Christ *"called"* everyone.
- **Matthew 11:28**
  Come unto me, **all *ye*** that labour and are heavy laden, and I will give you rest.

That is a universal invitation or *"call."*
- **John 3:16**
  For God so loved the world, that he gave his only begotten Son, that **whosoever believeth in him** should not perish, but have everlasting life.

This is also a universal invitation or *"call."*

It is true that in the Old Testament God called the Jews to Himself. We who are Gentiles had nothing in Him. Is it not wonderful that in the New

Testament, God invites Gentiles to come to His Son also? In the Old
Testament, we who are Gentiles had nothing. We were not Jews. The high
priest went into the presence of God once a year with his robes and all. He had
the 12 stones in his mitre. Those stones represented the twelve tribes of Israel,
including Levi, Joseph, and all the others. You and I who are Gentiles were not
there. When he went in to represent the people, it was the children of Israel for
whom he asked the Lord for forgiveness for that year. It was not us, the
Gentiles. We were heathen. We were without Christ.

Now, in the New Testament when Christ has come, and Israel has rejected
the Lord, He has opened up the door for us heathen people with a heathen
background. Our background was with the idle worshipers and corruptness and
wickedness that went with it. In addition to the Jews, God has opened the doors
for us who are Gentiles to receive His redemptive forgiveness by genuinely
accepting the Lord Jesus Christ as Saviour.

Romans 9:25

"As he saith also in Osee, I will call them my people,
which were not my people; and her beloved, which was
not beloved." Calling His "*people*" and "*beloved*" who were not His
"*people*" nor "*beloved*," required God's grace.

- **Hosea 2:23**
  And I will sow her unto me in the earth; and I will have mercy
  upon her that had not obtained mercy; and **I will say to *them***
  ***which were* not my people, Thou *art* my people**; and they
  shall say, *Thou art* my God.

God's Gracious Salvation Fountain

This is God's grace, opening up the wellspring, the fountain of
salvation for those of us who are Gentiles, lost and undone, and
not simply the Jews. We were not "*beloved*" before, but now,
through genuine faith in the Lord Jesus Christ, we can be called
"*beloved*." We were not God's "*people*" before, but if we are
saved, we are now His "*people.*"

- **Romans 1:7**
  To all that be in Rome, beloved of God, **called *to be* saints**:
  Grace to you and peace from God our Father, and the Lord
  Jesus Christ.

These Romans were saved Christians. Probably most of them were Gentiles.

God wants all of us to trust the Lord Jesus Christ. When this happens, we will be *"accepted in the beloved,"* the Lord Jesus Christ Himself (Ephesians 1:6).

Romans 9:26

"And it shall come to pass, *that* in the place where it was said unto them, Ye *are* not my people; there shall they be called the children of the living God." Here again we see an illustration of God's grace. Salvation is by genuine faith in the Lord Jesus Christ. This salvation is open to the Gentiles as well as to the Jews. Paul was saved and he was a Jew. The Lord met him on the road to Damascus. He was ready to kill, crucify, imprison, and murder Christians. God called him and saved him. Once saved, both Jews and Gentiles can be called *"children of the living God."*

* **John 1:12**

   But as many as received him, **to them gave he power to become the sons of God**, *even* to them that believe on his name:

John is talking about the Lord Jesus Christ. Those of us who were not children of God before, by trusting in Him genuinely, we can be saved.

Romans 9:27

"Esaias also crieth concerning Israel, Though the number of the children of Israel be as the sand of the sea, a remnant shall be saved:" No matter how many Jews reject the Lord Jesus Christ as their Messiah, *"a remnant shall be saved."* Paul was part of that believing *"remnant."* There are Christians today that were formally Jews, but now have been saved and are therefore part of this remnant even today. When the ten northern tribes of Israel went into the Assyrian captivity, a *"remnant"* came back under Ezra and Nehemiah. When the two Southern tribes went into Babylonian captivity, only a *"remnant"* came back under Ezra and Nehemiah.

Among professing "Christian" churches today, there is only a *"remnant"* who are thoroughgoing, sound Bible-believing churches. The greater number of these churches have gone into liberalism or neo-evangelicalism. Look at all the modernistic churches of our day. Look at the theological apostasy of the Roman Catholic Church and the Greek Orthodox Church. Look at the strong liberalist leadership in the Methodist churches, Lutheran churches, Episcopal churches, Unitarian churches, and even many of the Baptist churches. They have forsaken the doctrines of the Christian faith as taught clearly in the Bible. We have just a *"remnant,"* a small group of people who are *"earnestly contending for the faith which was once delivered unto the saints"* (Jude 1:3).

I do not buy into this thing that so many millions and millions of people over in Africa or India and different places are getting genuinely saved. I wish it were true, but I do not believe it. The preachers can wave their hands over them, the people can raise their hand and profess with their mouth faith in Christ, but are they genuinely saved? That is what some people say. There is a great church growth movement in these days. They look mainly for large numbers of followers, and in so doing, curtail and diminish their message. I believe that the Lord grows the churches little by little, just like He grows children and families, little-by-little, one at a time. It is just not this mass situation. A remnant shall be saved.

- **2 Kings 19:30**
  And **the remnant** that is escaped of the house of Judah shall yet again take root downward, and bear fruit upward.
- **Isaiah 10:20**
  And it shall come to pass in that day, *that* **the remnant of Israel**, and such as are escaped of the house of Jacob, shall no more again stay upon him that smote them; but shall stay upon the LORD, the Holy One of Israel, in truth.

That is going to be true in the Millennial reign of Christ.

Jewish Tribulation Evangelists

After the rapture of the Church when all born-again people have been caught up to be with the Lord (1 Thessalonians 4:16-18), there is going to be a seven-year period called the tribulation. At that time, a remnant of Israel is going to be saved. God will save 144,000 Jews during that time. This will be 12,000 out of each of the twelve tribes. They will then preach the gospel throughout the world and will lead many others to a saving faith in the Lord Jesus Christ.

God is going to miraculously redeem many people. Isaiah 66:8 asks, *"shall a nation be born at once?"* The answer is *"Yes."* As soon as they are led to Christ, the Antichrist will slay them (Revelation 13:15) if they do not have the mark of the beast on their right hand or in their foreheads (Revelation 13:16); but, still, a *"remnant"* will be saved.

Romans 9:28

"For he will finish the work, and cut *it* short in righteousness: because a short work will the Lord make upon the earth."

One Day, Judgment Will Come

There is going to be a day when the Lord will stop all of His grace and longsuffering. Then He will pronounce judgment upon this wicked world. I believe that is what is being referred to here in this verse. We do not know when that day will take place, but we must be prepared for eternity. Eternity is long. Eternity is where everyone who ever lived will one day be. Time will be no more.

The important question is, *"Will our spirits and souls and bodies be in the Lake of Fire or will they be in Heaven where the Lord Jesus Christ is?"* I trust it we will be in Heaven. If we genuinely trust the Lord Jesus Christ as our Redeemer, we are going to be in Heaven rather than Hell.

Romans 9:29

"And as Esaias said before, Except the Lord of Sabaoth had left us a seed, we had been as Sodoma, and been made like unto Gomorrha." Here again is the picture of Sodom and Gomorrah. In addition to references in the Old Testament, these two evil cities are referred to in Matthew 10:19; Mark 6:11; 2 Peter 2:6; and Jude 1:7. The phrase, *"Lord of Sabaoth,"* is an interesting expression. It means *"the Lord of Hosts, the Lord of the armies of Heaven."*

Did you know that *"the Lord is a Man of war"* (Exodus 15:3) and has armies? Millions upon millions of powerful and holy angels are a part of God's army. God's grace is the only thing that can make it possible for us to be saved and to have this *"seed"* of believing Christians. As I said before, only four people left Sodom and Gomorrah. One of them, Lot's wife, looked back and was destroyed (Genesis 19:26). The three that came out were not too much better than she was. The Lord spared them and delivered them from this overthrow.

Have You Been Born-Again?

I hope everyone reading this has been delivered from Satan and sin, and has been born-again by genuine faith in the Lord Jesus Christ and saved.

Romans 9:30-31

"What shall we say then? That the Gentiles, which followed not after righteousness, have attained to righteousness, even the righteousness which is of faith."

"But Israel, which followed after the law of righteousness, hath not attained to the law of righteousness." Here are the Gentiles who had not followed after righteousness. They had no law of Moses. Those heathen just worshiped sticks and stones and idols as well as the moon, the stars, and the sun. Israel, on the other hand, was zealous to fulfill the law of Moses, but they did not fulfill it. They could not fulfill it. There was no way to fulfill it because the law of Moses could not be fulfilled by anyone except the Lord Jesus Christ Himself. They did not attain to righteousness because they went about it the wrong way, but the Gentiles *"have attained to righteousness, even the righteousness which is of faith."* That is the only way you can get righteousness. God is the only one that prepares it and we receive it by genuine faith in the Lord Jesus Christ and His finished work for sinners.

There was a chaplain in the service when I was a Navy Chaplain for five years on active duty. His name was Chaplain Maddox. He was a Southern Baptist Chaplain. Our church has no relationship to the Southern Baptist Convention for a number of reasons. We are Independent Baptists. Chaplain Maddox used to give an illustration about salvation. He said God's salvation was like a train pulling up to a station. Where you board that train at the station, there is a platform. You step onto that platform to get on that train. That illustrates what a person's personal faith is. It is like the platform you step on to get on that train. The platform does not take you to your destination, it is the train. The train is like God's perfect salvation that takes you all the way to Heaven. The righteousness of God is what is perfect. You do not have to run out in front of the train and pull it to its destination. That train has an engine, but you must step on that train by means of the platform of faith.

There are at least eleven verses that talk about God's righteousness. Perfect righteousness before God is only accepted and received by our faith and our trust. It is not what we do. Israel wanted to do it. In fact ,before the Lord gave them the Law of Moses, they said "*all that the Lord hath spoken we will do* (Exodus 19:8). They did not mean it, but they said it. The Lord Jesus has done the complete work for our salvation. As our Saviour exclaimed as He hung on the cross of Calvary, "*It is finished*" (John 19:30).

- **Genesis 15:6**
  And **he believed in the LORD**; and he counted it to him for **righteousness**.

Faith equals "*righteousness*" before God.

- **Romans 1:17**
  For therein is **the righteousness of God** revealed from faith to faith: as it is written, **The just shall live by faith**.

- **Romans 3:22**
  Even **the righteousness of God *which is* by faith of Jesus Christ** unto all and upon all them that believe: for there is no difference:

- **Romans 3:26**
  To declare, *I say*, at this time **his righteousness**: that he might be just, and the justifier of him which believeth in Jesus.

- **Romans 4:3**
  For what saith the scripture? **Abraham believed God**, and it was counted unto him for **righteousness**.

- **Romans 4:5**
  But to him that worketh not, but believeth on him that justifieth the ungodly, **his faith is counted for righteousness**.

- **Romans 4:13**
  For the promise, that he should be the heir of the world, *was* not to Abraham, or to his seed, through the law, but through **the righteousness of faith**.

- **Romans 10:10**
  For **with the heart man believeth unto righteousness**; and with the mouth confession is made unto salvation.

- **Galatians 3:6**
  Even as **Abraham believed God**, and it was accounted to him for **righteousness**.

- **Galatians 5:5**
  For we through the Spirit wait for the **hope of righteousness by faith**.

- **James 2:23**
  And the scripture was fulfilled which saith, **Abraham believed God**, and it was imputed unto him for **righteousness**: and he was called the Friend of God.

The only people God takes to Heaven are absolutely perfectly righteous. If you want to get into Heaven by your own *"righteousness,"* forget it. If I am going to get to Heaven by my own *"righteousness,"* forget it. The only type of people our God takes to Heaven are those who are absolutely 100% perfect in His sight.

How To Get 100% Perfection

The only way anyone can receive this 100% perfection in God's eyes is by genuine faith in the Lord Jesus Christ, Who provided for the Christian His own absolute *"righteousness."* The Lord Jesus Christ died in order that those who are born-again might have His *"righteousness"* reckoned or imputed unto them.

We cannot do this by ourselves. That is why the Gentiles received God's *"righteousness"* and Israel missed out. Israel missed out because they sought to receive God's *"righteousness"* by their own works and deeds. All Israel wanted to do was to work. The Gentiles found this by faith in the Saviour, the Lord Jesus Christ.

Romans 9:32

"Wherefore? Because *they sought it* not by faith, but as it were by the works of the law. For they stumbled at that stumblingstone;" The Jews *"stumbled"* at the *"stumbling stone"* of simple, yet genuine faith in the Lord Jesus Christ. They just could not understand it.

I do not think that many people understand this today. If you were to tell people generally that there is a righteousness that God wants to give them, and it is going to be a righteousness which is only received by truly trusting the Lord Jesus Christ by faith. They do not understand it. They cannot understand it. They do not believe that is the way it can be. It is difficult to understand. Israel lost out because they thought God's *"righteousness"* could be obtained by *"the works of the law"* of Moses. Faith was too simple for them.

Need Heart-Faith, Not Head-Faith

There is a type of faith that is shallow. There is a type that is with the head without the heart. If a person says that he has faith in the Lord Jesus Christ with the head only, rather than with the heart, they are lost.

I was lost for the first sixteen years of my life, and yet, every single Sunday morning when I went to the Methodist Church, we repeated the Apostles Creed, "*I believe in God the Father creator of Heaven and Earth . . .*" The Roman Catholics say this also, do they not? With my head, I said every word of that Creed, but I was lost. I was unsaved and bound for Hell until I genuinely trusted the Lord Jesus Christ with my heart.

- **Romans 10:10**
  For with the heart man believeth unto righteousness; and with the mouth confession is made unto salvation.

The Jews missed God's salvation because they attempted to obtain it by works rather than by faith.

- **Romans 10:4**
  For **Christ *is* the end of the law for righteousness to every one that believeth**.

- **John 1:17**
  For the law was given by Moses, *but* grace and truth came by Jesus Christ.

Romans 9:33

"As it is written, Behold, I lay in Sion a stumblingstone and rock of offence: and whosoever believeth on him shall not be ashamed." The Jews stumbled at the "*stumblingstone*" that God's righteousness could be received by faith. They said it has to be made by works, by what we do.

Here is the final verse in the chapter. Notice the words in this verse, "*it is written.*" As I have said many times before, these words point to the preservation of the Hebrew, Aramaic (and, extension, Greek) Words of the Bible. The Greek word is GEGRAPTAI. It is the perfect tense of the verb GRAPHO. The perfect tense in Greek deals with three points of time: (1) the past; (2) the present, and (3) the future. In this case, it teaches that the Old Testament Hebrew Words alluded to in Isaiah 28:16 were written in the past, preserved right down to the time Paul quoted from them, and will be preserved on into the future.

A Bible Preservation Phrase

Wherever it is found in the New Testament, the phrase, "*it is written*" always means that God has preserved His written Hebrew, Aramaic, and Greek Words of the Old and New Testaments.

"*Sion*" is a hill in Jerusalem, the city of David. Because the Jews rejected the Lord Jesus Christ as their Saviour, He was made to them "*a stumblingstone and rock of offence.*" Paul also says that "*whosoever believeth on him shall not be ashamed.*" We who have been saved should never be ashamed of the Lord Jesus Christ, our Saviour.

"Ashamed of Jesus"
By Joseph Griggs

"Jesus, and shall it ever be
A mortal man ashamed of Thee?
Ashamed of Thee, Whom angels praise,
Whose glories shine thro' endless days.

Ashamed of Jesus! Sooner far
Let evening blush to own a star;
He sheds the beams of light divine
O'er this benighted soul of mine.

Ashamed of Jesus! That dear Friend,
On Whom my hopes of heav'n depend!
No! When I blush, be this my shame,
That I no more revere His Name.

Ashamed of Jesus! Yes, I may,
When I've no guilt to wash away;
No tear to wipe, no good to crave,
No fears to quell, no soul to save."

- **1 Corinthians 1:23**
  But we preach Christ crucified, **unto the Jews a stumblingblock**, and unto the Greeks foolishness;
  The Jews stumble at faith in Christ. They cried out for Him to be crucified.
- **1 Peter 2:8**
  And a stone of stumbling, and a rock of offence, *even to them* which stumble at the word, being disobedient: whereunto also they were appointed.
- **Isaiah 28:16**
  Therefore thus saith the Lord GOD, Behold, I lay in Zion for a foundation **a stone, a tried stone, a precious corner** *stone,* **a sure foundation**: he that believeth shall not make haste.
- **Isaiah 8:14**
  And he shall be for a sanctuary; but for **a stone of stumbling and for a rock of offence** to both the houses of Israel, for a gin and for a snare to the inhabitants of Jerusalem.

The Lord Jesus Christ should not be a *"stone of stumbling"* to those who are born-again. We should take the Words of God at its face value, and agree with God Who says we must genuinely believe on the Lord Jesus Christ to get His righteousness. We must not make Christ a *"stone of stumbling."* If you have trusted Him as your Saviour, He is a stepping stone instead of a stumbling stone. For those who are lost and have rejected Christ, He has become a *"stumbling stone and rock of offense."*

Romans
Chapter Ten

Romans 10:1

"Brethren, my heart's desire and prayer to God for Israel is, that they might be saved." Notice, Paul calls these Christians "*brethren.*" They are "*brethren.*" They are born-again believers in Christ. They are related to the Lord Jesus Christ as sons and daughters of His. Most of these believers were Gentiles. Paul was the minister to the Gentiles. When the Lord saved him, this is what He said to him:

- **Acts 9:15**
  But the Lord said unto him, Go thy way: for **he is a chosen vessel unto me, to bear my name before the Gentiles**, and kings, and the children of Israel:

The apostle Peter was a minister unto the Jews (Galatians 2:7). In this verse, addressing the Gentile brethren, Paul expressed one of his deepest desires. He goes apart from these Gentiles back to his own Jewish race.

He said, "*my heart's desire and prayer to God for Israel is, that they might be saved.*" I hope we have some "*heart's desires.*" I hope we have some genuine feelings in our hearts that are Christian, and that are Biblical. May we communicate these feelings to others that they might be saved. Not only having desires, but also a "*prayer.*" We can have all kinds of desires for good things, but God also wants us to pray about these things and ask the Lord for that which is right and that which is good. The Israelites were lost in trespasses and sins.

Before the Lord stopped him, Paul was in the same spiritual condition. He was lost. Paul was out to slaughter Christian believers. He was on the road to Damascus, Syria. As an unconverted Pharisee, Paul would travel a long distance in order to imprison or to kill Christians. The Lord Jesus stopped him. Paul was an Israelite of the tribe of Benjamin. He was a zealous man, but the Lord stopped him. As a Christian his prayer was that all the Israelites would be saved. Notice the prayer and the content. The prayer was not that his kinsmen might be popular. He did not pray that they might continue in existence. He did not pray that they might be financially well off. He did not pray that they might be healthy. He prayed that they might be saved. That is a valid prayer for anybody in the world.

We can pray for our friends, and even our enemies, that they might be saved, rightly related to the Lord Jesus Christ by faith, and with a Home in Heaven guaranteed. They need the righteousness of the Lord Jesus Christ put upon them by faith, with redemption which is theirs, that gives them a righteous standing before God. This is a tremendously important prayer.

Some people these days, the neo-evangelicals, the liberals, and the modernists, do not like that last word of the verse, "*saved.*" They say you cannot say that word. Well, the Bible uses it repeatedly. The King James Bible uses "*saved*" fifty-seven times in the New Testament. The word "*save*" is used fifty-nine times. It is a Biblical word, and I am going to continue to use it. It is an important word. Some people say you have to use some other word because people do not understand that word. Why would they not? It is in the Bible. If people do not understand it, teach them its meaning. To be "*saved*" means to be delivered. Every single person in this world has a sin problem. They must be "*saved*" and delivered from that problem. The Lord Jesus Christ is the only answer to that serious problem. He is able to save sinners from their sins if they repent of their sins and genuinely trust in His finished work at Calvary.

People who are apart from Christ need salvation. Paul prayed that these Israelites would be saved, and we can pray that our friends, neighbors, loved ones, and relatives can be "*saved*" as well. That is a good prayer. "*Saved*" is a good term! No problem with that term. Another term some people do not like us to use is "*born-again.*" That is also a Bible term. In fact these critics are changing the meaning of "*born-again*" into something foreign to the Bible's intention (see John 3:3, 7; 1 Peter 1:23). Paul's prayer was for the Israelites that "*they might be saved.*" That was an important prayer.

An Illustration of Being Saved

It is just like a person drowning in the water. For years and years I was a Red Cross Water Safety Instructor. I instructed many Junior and Senior Life Saving swimming classes. It has been a long while since I have been teaching these classes. For those who are in the water and drowning, there are four things on our Red Cross Water Safety Chart that Life Saving personnel need to do. In this order:

(1) The first word is *"row."* If someone is out in the water, and there is a boat nearby, you should get in a boat and row out to them. That is the first line of defense.

(2) The second word is *"throw."* If you do not have a boat, but you do have a ring buoy with a rope on the end, you can throw it to them and pull them in.

(3) The third word is *"tow."* You can take a towel, a board, a belt, or something that can be extended to the drowning person and tow them in. Because of the danger involved, you do not touch them. You stay away from them.

(4) The fourth word is *"go."* As a water safety instructor or a life guard, the last line of defense is to go where the drowning person is, get a proper hold on the victim, and bring him or her into safety. The reason for this being the last resort is that the Life Guard might drown unless they really know what they are doing. A person who is drowning needs to be saved physically, delivered from that water, or face a certain death.

Romans 10:2

"For I bear them record that they have a zeal of God, but not according to knowledge." Paul is a witness to the effect that the Israelites had a *"zeal of God, but not according to knowledge."* The Greek word for *"zeal"* is ZELOS. It means:

> *"excitement of mind, ardour, fervour of spirit; zeal, ardour in embracing, pursuing, defending anything; zeal in behalf of, for a person or thing; the fierceness of indignation, punitive zeal an envious and contentious rivalry, jealousy."*

It is based on feelings and emotions.

Balanced Zeal Is Good

There is nothing wrong with *"zeal"* as such, provided it is aimed at the right object. There is nothing wrong with *"knowledge,"* provided that it does not reason contrary to God's Words. These two things should be in proper balance.

These Jews had a real *"zeal."* The wild wing of Islam has *"zeal."* They want to kill both Jews and Christians. I am talking about the mean, hard-hearted Muslims, who are out to slaughter the believers in Christ. That is part of their religion. Before he was saved, Paul had a lot of *"zeal."* He wanted to kill the Christians. We who are saved need to have *"zeal,"* but we must have *"knowledge"* as well. There needs to be a balance.

God's Will Is In God's Words

A full knowledge of God's Words gives us a full knowledge of God's will. If you just have a hard-hearted intellectual personality without any feelings toward anyone else, you will not care whether they are lost or saved. You will not care if they are in sickness or in trouble. You will have no empathy, no sympathy, no feeling at all.

The charismatics have gone to terrible extremes in emotionalism and *"zeal."* The Toronto Blessing Movement is one example of this. My wife and I went up there a couple of years ago when we were in Toronto at meetings. We took our video camera into this Toronto Blessing. The people were whooping, yelling, barking like dogs, falling down and being, what they term, *"slain in the spirit."* It was absolutely ridiculous. Where is that found in the Bible? It is not found there. It is very far-out. It was Satanic as far as we could see. We have that on video, about an hour of it. After the preaching, many people lined up in about four in lines. It must have stretched out fifty in each line. Each person in the lines had what they call a *"catcher"* to stand behind them. They had someone in front of them to *"slay them in the spirit."* Then they would fall back and be caught by the *"catcher."* What does that prove? Where is that in Scripture? They have great *"zeal."* We wanted to take pictures of that *"slaying in the Spirit"* activity, but we were forbidden to do it. They had enough of the slaying of the spirit in the audience that we could video, but we could not take the after-meeting events. It was amazing *"zeal,"* but not according to *"knowledge."*

That is what Israel was doing. They tried to establish their own righteousness, but they did not have enough knowledge in the things of the Lord. What does excessive knowledge do?

Dr. M. R. DeHaan was the founder of the Radio Bible Class ministry. When I was a student at the University of Michigan, I used to go to his Detroit Bible class every Friday night. He taught the book of Hebrews. Some of us Christian students were taken to that class by Mr. David McRoberts who was a Chef at the University of Michigan hospital. Here was a layman who loved the Lord, and who loved young people, and wanted them to get sound teaching in the Words of God. I will ever be grateful to that dedicated layman, because it was through Dr. DeHaan's ministry that I gave my heart and life to be a servant of the Lord. Up until this time I had intended to be a medical missionary and was taking pre-medical courses. I changed to pre-theology in order to be prepared to serve my Saviour in the ministry that He might open up for me.

At that time, Dr. DeHaan was working with the Grand Rapids Dutch Reformed Church. He told us that, in his opinion, the trouble with these Dutchmen and the Christian Reformed people in his church was this: Their theology was **"CLEAR AND SOLID AS A CAKE OF ICE--AND JUST AS COLD."** That was an excellent example of having cold knowledge and intellectualism with very little heart, feelings for the lost, or feelings for the things of the Lord. May the Lord deliver us from this imbalance! We must have a balance--knowledge and heart.

Paul contrasts *"zeal"* with *"knowledge."* I could have *"zeal"* about tuning our church piano instead of having a piano technician like Dick Carroll tune it for us. That would be foolish. I do not have the *"knowledge"* of how to tune a piano. There are all kinds of things that we can get off-base on. As I said before, you could have a zeal to save someone's life who is drowning out in the Atlantic Ocean, but if you have no training in life saving, and you do not know what you are doing, you could really be in trouble.

Both Zeal and Knowledge Needed

"Zeal" without *"knowledge"* or *"knowledge"* without *"zeal"* is certainly something we should avoid. There must be a balance.

Romans 10:3

"For they being ignorant of God's righteousness, and going about to establish their own righteousness, have not submitted themselves unto the righteousness of God." Paul says that the Israelites were *"ignorant of God's righteousness."* In verse 2, he says they lack proper *"knowledge."* How can any of us *"establish their own righteousness"*? What a silly thing. It says very clearly in Scripture, *"There is none righteous, no, not one"* (Romans 3:10). *"For all have sinned, and come short of the glory of God"* (Romans 3:23). There is no way we can get our own *"righteousness."*

Righteousness In The Wrong Way

Israel was ignorant of the way to obtain *"righteousness."* They went about it the wrong way. They tried to *"pull themselves up by their own boot straps"* as we say. This cannot be done.

Where are you looking for *"righteousness"*? Only in the Lord Jesus Christ and what He accomplished at the cross of Calvary can any one in the world have perfect *"righteousness"* in the sight of a righteous God.

I would rather have perfect *"righteousness"* to start with, rather than make it myself. I know nothing about building a house or building an automobile. Rather than building an automobile from scratch, I would rather have a brand new perfect automobile given to me as a gift. Would not that be easier? It is already completed and finished. That is what the Lord Jesus Christ did in providing for the believing sinner His own perfect *"righteousness."* By faith we can accept something that is already completed, already finished. We cannot work for it.

God's Way Or Their Own Way

The Israelites tried to work for and establish *"their own righteousness,"* which they did not have and could not establish in any way. Not only that, but they did not *"submit themselves to the righteousness of God."* It was impossible to achieve *"their own righteousness."* They did not realize that, so they did it in the wrong way.

Romans 10:4

"For Christ *is* the end of the law for righteousness to every one that believeth." The Lord Jesus Christ finished and completed *"the law for righteousness."* He finished this when He died for the sins of everyone in the world at the cross of Calvary. There is nothing anyone can do to add to it.

I had a call from one of our friends. She told me that she has been going on a Website by a Messianic Jew. She said,

> *"He has me confused because he is saying different things from what you are preaching. He wants us to have Kosher foods. He wants us to obey the Jewish customs and feasts. He wants us to obey the Jewish laws and the Mosaic law."*

I told this lady that this is absolutely unnecessary.

Christ Fulfilled the Law

"Christ is the end," the finish, the completion, of all the righteousness *"of the law to everyone that believeth."* We who are saved have the *"righteousness"* of Christ. He has fulfilled all of the law of Moses. We do not have to go back into the law of Moses in any way.

Three Parts of Moses' Law

There are three parts to the law of Moses.

1. The first part is the ten commandments or moral law.
2. The second part is the judgments or civil laws.
3. The third part is the ordinances or the ceremonial laws.

We who are Christians are not under any part of that law of Moses.

All the ten commandments but one are repeated in the New Testament, and that is why we follow these nine commandments. The only commandment which is not repeated in our New Testament is *"Remember the Sabbath Day, to keep it holy"* (Exodus 20:8; Deuteronomy 5:12) It is not in the New Testament. We worship on the Lord's Day, the first day of the week rather than on

Saturday, the seventh day of the week. We are not under any part of the law.

- **Genesis 15:6**
  And **he believed** in the LORD; and **he counted it to him for righteousness**.

The prescription and formula that God gives is *"faith=righteousness."* The Jews want to say that *"works"* can bring this about. Their formula is *"works= righteousness."* This really equals unrighteousness.

- **Romans 1:17**
  For therein is **the righteousness of God revealed from faith to faith**: as it is written, The just shall live by faith.

- **Romans 3:22**
  Even **the righteousness of God** *which is* **by faith of Jesus Christ** unto all and upon all them that believe: for there is no difference:

God's perfect *"righteousness"* is received by faith and faith alone.

- **Romans 3:26**
  To declare, *I say*, at this time **his righteousness**: that he might be just, and the justifier of him which believeth in Jesus.

- **Romans 4:3**
  For what saith the scripture? Abraham believed God, and **it was counted unto him for righteousness**.

- **Romans 4:5**
  But to him that worketh not, but believeth on him that justifieth the ungodly, **his faith is counted for righteousness**.

- **Romans 4:13**
  For the promise, that he should be the heir of the world, *was* not to Abraham, or to his seed, through the law, but through **the righteousness of faith**.

- **Romans 10:10**
  For **with the heart man believeth unto righteousness**; and with the mouth confession is made unto salvation.

- **Galatians 3:6**
  Even as Abraham believed God, and **it was accounted to him for righteousness**.

- **Galatians 3:5**
  He therefore that ministereth to you the Spirit, and worketh miracles among you, *doeth he it* by the works of the law, or **by the hearing of faith**?

- **James 2:23**
  And the scripture was fulfilled which saith, Abraham believed God, and **it was imputed unto him for righteousness**: and he was called the Friend of God.

All the way through Scripture, we see that the only way to obtain perfect absolute holiness, righteousness, and justification in God's eyes, is by genuine faith in the Lord Jesus Christ.

Our Standing And Our State

We are righteous in the eyes of God once we are saved. Once we are born-again, we are absolutely righteous in the sight of God. That does not make us perfectly righteous here upon this earth. That is our state. Our standing before God is perfect righteousness.

Our state, living upon this earth, is imperfect. Let us try to make our state equal to our standing. God said, *"Because it is written, Be ye holy; for I am holy"* (1 Peter 1:16). God does not want to make us unholy. He wants Christian believers to have His perfect righteousness by faith.

Romans 10:5

"For Moses describeth the righteousness which is of the law, That the man which doeth those things shall live by them." The law of Moses required *"doing"* many things. The righteousness by faith in Christ has to do with belief and trust in the Saviour. God imputes His righteousness to those who genuinely trust in the Lord Jesus Christ. That does not mean that the redeemed should not live for the Lord. That does not mean we should not try to please Him after we are justified by faith and made righteous. The law had nothing to do with faith as far as receiving righteousness. The Jews tried to *"establish their own righteousness,"* which was wrong to do. They did it by works instead of by grace through faith. There are many verses on the contrast between works versus faith.

- John 6:28-29

   Then said they unto him, What shall we do, **that we might work the works of God?** Jesus answered and said unto them, This is **the work of God, that ye believe on him whom he hath sent.**

The only way to *"work the works of God"* as the Lord Jesus Christ stated is to *"believe on Him Whom He hath sent,"* that is, to genuinely believe on and trust in the Lord Jesus Christ as Saviour.

- Romans 4:5

   But to him that **worketh not**, but believeth on him that justifieth the ungodly, **his faith is counted for righteousness.**

- **Galatians 2:16**

  Knowing that a man is not justified by the **works of the law, but by the faith of Jesus Christ**, even we have believed in Jesus Christ, that we might be **justified by the faith of Christ**, and not by the **works of the law**: for by the works of the law shall no flesh be justified.

Some Israelites were trying to work the works of the law to do what they could do. Others looked, by faith, to the cross. These were the redeemed and justified Israelites. Those are the saved who looked, by faith, to the cross of Calvary. Everyone of those Jewish offerings pointed to Calvary and the shed blood of the Lord Jesus Christ. Some of those Jews were saved. However, Paul said that most of them were not doing it right.

- **Galatians 3:2**

  This only would I learn of you, Received ye the Spirit by the **works of the law**, or by **the hearing of faith**?

How did we, if we are saved, receive the Holy Spirit of God into our lives, into our bodies? Was it by doing some "*works*"? Or was it by faith in Christ? It was by faith in Christ.

Romans 10:6-7

"But the righteousness which is of faith speaketh on this wise, Say not in thine heart, Who shall ascend into Heaven? (that is, to bring Christ down *from above*:) Or, Who shall descend into the deep? (that is, to bring up Christ again from the dead.)" The question is "*Where do you go to get the righteousness that is by faith?*" Do you have to climb to Heaven? That is a long way off. That is the picture here. Do you have to go down to Sheol or Hades which is the place of the dead? No, we do not have to go very far. It is not a long distance call. The Person Who can give us righteousness is not far away, but He is near at hand. Righteousness is received by genuine faith in the Lord Jesus Christ. We can exercise that faith right where we are. We do not have to "*ascend into Heaven*" in order "*to bring Christ down*" again, nor could we.

Three Important Future Events

One day the Lord Jesus Christ is going to come down from Heaven.

1.   First, there will be the rapture of the Church, the snatching away into the air of the born-again believers;

2.   Second, there will be seven years of the Tribulation Period on this earth;

3.   Third, Christ will come back with the believers to set up His one-thousand-year reign (the millennium) upon this earth.

He will come back, but we don't have to wait until He comes back to get faith and righteousness. We can do that where we are.

There is no long-distance race that has to be run to get this righteousness. The question was asked in one of our Bible Studies, *"Can you tell me where in the scripture it says Christ descended into Hell?"* The basis of this comes from Ephesians 4:9 *"(Now that he ascended, what is it but that he also **descended first into the lower parts of the earth?**"* The reason for this view is found from this verse and in a phrase of the Apostle's Creed.

"I believe in God, the Father Almighty,
the Maker of Heaven and earth,
and in Jesus Christ, His only Son, our Lord:
Who was conceived of the Holy Spirit,
born of the Virgin Mary,
suffered under Pontius Pilate,
was crucified, dead and buried.
He descended into Hell. . . ."

The word *"Hell"* is interpreted by many to be the equivalent of HADES. This word, HADES, comes from two Greek words, "A" ("not") and "EIDO" (to see). It means *"the unseen world."*

The Two Sections of Sheol

I believe the Lord Jesus Christ went to the Paradise section of Sheol or Hades and released those saved Old Testament saints from that place and took them to Heaven after His resurrection.

Luke 16:19-31 speaks about the rich man and Lazarus. In this true story, the Lord Jesus Christ teaches that, up until His ascension to Heaven, there were two separate compartments for the departed spirits in the Old Testament. This place was called Sheol in Hebrew and Hades in Greek. There was a blessed section for the righteous, and there was a tormented section for the lost. The rich man went into the place of torment (Luke 16:23). He was in "*torments.*" Lazarus, a beggar, was carried into "*Abraham's bosom*" (Luke 16:22) which was a place of blessing. I believe that the Lord Jesus Christ, after His resurrection, emptied the Paradise section of Sheol and took these souls to Heaven.

Remember what the Lord Jesus Christ told the repentant thief on the cross? He defended the Lord Who had "*done nothing amiss*" (Luke 23:41). Then he "*said unto Jesus, Lord, remember me when thou comest into thy kingdom*" (Luke 23:42). After this step of faith on the part of that thief, the Lord Jesus Christ told him, "*Verily I say unto thee, To day shalt thou be with me in paradise*" (Luke 23:43). The Lord went to the "*lower parts of the earth*" (Ephesians 4:9). I believe He went to the "*paradise*" section of Sheol. This thief was "*with Him in paradise.*"

Paradise Now the Third Heaven

According to 2 Corinthians 12:4, "*paradise*" was removed from the "*lower parts of the earth*" to the "*third Heaven.*"

I believe Paul was writing about himself in this verse. He was "*caught up to the third Heaven*" (2 Corinthians 12:1) which was also called "*into paradise*" (verse 4). The thief on the cross said, "*Lord, remember me when thou comest into thy kingdom*" (Luke 23:42). The Lord Jesus replied, "*Verily I say unto thee, To day shalt thou be with me in paradise*" (verse 43). At that time, "*paradise*" was in the "*lower parts of the earth.*"

To be saved, people do not have to "*descend into the deep*" and "*bring up Christ again from the dead.*" He has already been raised from the dead. There is no necessity for a long-distance journey to get righteousness. The Israelites were trying to achieve this in the wrong way. They were working, working, working, and puffing and huffing, and trying to find God's righteousness.

Romans 10:8

"But what saith it? The word is nigh thee, *even* in thy mouth, and in thy heart: that is, the word of faith, which we preach;" The *"word"* about obtaining God's righteousness is near. It is *"in thy mouth, and in thy heart."* In other words, it is just as close as your heart is. It is just as close as your mouth is. In the next verses, we will see the coordination between the mouth and the heart. Paul is talking about the *"word of faith"* which he preaches. Paul preached salvation by genuine personal faith in the Lord Jesus Christ. It is not that we should not have works after we have the faith and are saved, but salvation must precede works, and works must follow salvation.

There is a figure of speech made up of two Greek terms. The figure is called a *"hysteron proteron."* *"Hysteron"* means *"last"* and *"proteron"* means *"first."* It is putting the last first rather than putting the first first. No, you must put the first, first and the last, last. It is the same as putting *"the cart before the horse."* The horse must be in front of the cart. The horse pulls the cart, it does not push it. Faith and works are like the horse and the cart. Many modernists, liberals, and unbelievers want to put works first. They say we are saved by works or by what we do. The Bible says we are saved by *"faith."* After we are saved by *"faith"* God expects and requires that we have works that will glorify Him.

- **Ephesians 2:8-10**

   For **by grace are ye saved through faith**; and that not of yourselves: *it is* the gift of God: **Not of works**, lest any man should boast. For we are his workmanship, **created in Christ Jesus unto good works, which God hath before ordained that we should walk in them.**

We are not saved by *"works,"* but believe me, once we are saved we better have some *"works"* for the Lord, to show what we are doing to honor the Lord Jesus Christ. We must not have a *hysteron proteron* (the cart before the horse). We want to have the *"faith"* first that saves us, then we must work for the Lord.

Modernists and liberals love to see works. I am afraid to say there are some modernists and liberals who are theological apostates that have better works than some fundamental Christians. At least, it seems that way to me. Those who profess belief in the Lord Jesus Christ too often have worse works, worse deeds, worse lives. It is a terrible situation. Even members of the Christian Science religion, who are complete apostates and heretics, do not do many immoral things. They are seemingly perfect. God wants us first to be saved by His grace through faith in the Lord Jesus Christ, and then live for Him, and have some evidence of that faith.

Romans 10:9

"That if thou shalt confess with thy mouth the Lord Jesus, and shalt believe in thine heart that God hath raised him from the dead, thou shalt be saved." This is the *"word of faith"* that Paul preaches to the Christians at Rome, Italy as He is writing to them. He told them that to be *"saved,"* they must *"confess with their mouth the Lord Jesus"* and *"believe in their heart that God hath raised Him from the dead."*

The Greek Meaning of Confession

The Greek word for *"confess"* is HOMOLOGEO. It means:

"to say the same thing as another, i.e. to agree with, assent; to concede; not to refuse, to promise; not to deny; to confess; declare to confess, i.e. to admit or declare one's self guilty of what one is accused of; to profess; to declare openly, speak out freely; to profess one's self the worshiper of one; to praise, celebrate."

It comes from two Greek words. HOMO means *"the same."* LOGEO means *"to say or speak."* *"Confess,"* therefore, means to speak the same thing that God says about His Son. It means to agree with God that the Lord Jesus Christ is your Saviour and perfect Deity. It means that He is perfect God and perfect Man.

The Lord is not only a perfect Human Being. He is also perfect deity, God the Son and the Son of God. The liberals and the modernists talk about Jesus as being only a human being. The members of the Christian Science church talk about Jesus as only a human being. Even Muslims talk about Jesus, the human being. They believe there was a Jesus, but He is not *"Lord Jesus"* to them. When Paul speaks of *"Lord Jesus,"* he is referring to His absolute Deity coupled with his perfect Humanity. He was the Incarnated God. He was for all eternity past, God the Son and the Son of God. In His incarnation, He became perfect Man, the Son of Man. This confessing and agreeing with your mouth the *"Lord Jesus"* is needed.

But Paul mentions another vital truth which includes the heart. He adds, *"and shalt believe in thine heart, that God hath raised him from the dead."*

Genuine Heart-Belief Needed

Heart-belief is necessary in addition to speech from the mouth. So many times we have mouth-speech, but no heart-belief. We can have heart-belief, but no mouth-speech also. God wants us to use our mouth as a witness for our Saviour, but we are not to be mouthy. We must not only talk the talk, but must also walk the walk, as people say. God wants us to believe in our hearts. Genuine heart-belief is what saves our souls. Heart-belief is what gives us eternal life. Heart-belief is what makes us righteous before God.

This heart-belief includes faith in the bodily resurrection of the Lord Jesus Christ. Only then can the person be *"saved."*

Christ's Bodily Resurrection

The bodily resurrection of our Saviour is the most wonderful and stupendous miracle in all the Scriptures. This miracle transformed the body in which He was crucified into a glorified body. He was never to die again.

In the Old Testament, temporarily there were a few who were raised from the dead, but they died again. In the New Testament the Lord Jesus Christ resuscitated three people. Those people, no doubt, died again. These were wonderful miracles, but the bodily resurrection of our Saviour was more wonderful than any of those.

- **Matthew 27:53**
  And came out of the graves after his resurrection, and went into the holy city, and appeared unto many.

We believe these people, without doubt, all died again. The Lord Jesus Christ, on the other hand, broke the bonds and bands of death and was resurrected bodily from that grave. He was transformed. You did not see a dead corpse in that tomb after three days and three nights. Mary and those who came to the tomb did not see a dead body. The tomb was empty.

That same body in which He was crucified was transformed and resurrected. It was made immortal and incorruptible. It did not see corruption. The body which they saw on the road to Emmaus was the Lord Jesus Christ's transformed, resurrected body. It was the body the disciples saw when the doors in the upper room were closed. He entered into that room, by going right straight through the doors. His glorified body could do this. The Lord had a body, but He had the elements that could pierce even through doors.

Genuine Heart-Belief Saves

By our *"belief in our heart"* that God performed the miracle of raising Christ from the dead we will be saved by faith in that Saviour.

Romans 10:10

"For with the heart man believeth unto righteousness; and with the mouth confession is made unto salvation." It is very clear that it is *"with the heart"* that people *"believe unto righteousness."* I have said many times, there is a battle between the head and the heart. There is a great deal of difference between the head and the heart. As it says in Romans 10:2, there is a contrast between *"zeal,"* which is a matter of the *"heart,"* and *"knowledge,"* which is a matter of the head. We need both.

We could not get very far in our activity whether it is teaching, or business, or homemakers, without a head to think through things. On the other hand, we also need a healthy attitude of the *"heart."* I realize that there are some scientists that apparently are heartless. There are some criminals who are heartless. There are some liars who seem to be heartless. Many people seem to me to be heartless. God wants us to have both in a proper balance. Faith in the Lord Jesus Christ gives us a righteousness before God that no man can gainsay or contradict.

Paul adds another dimension to this. He wrote that *"with the mouth confession is made unto salvation."* Notice that word *"unto."* I do not believe that *"confession"* is the CAUSE of salvation. Our *"confession"* is made *"unto"* our *"salvation"* that we already have by genuine *"heart-faith"* in the Lord Jesus Christ. Because we have been saved, we are confessing Him before men. We are agreeing with God that He is our Saviour. We are bearing witness to Him *"unto"* the *"salvation"* that He has given *"unto"* us.

- **Psalm 107:2**

    Let the redeemed of the LORD say *so*, whom he hath redeemed from the hand of the enemy;

    If we have a know-so salvation and we are assured of it, we ought also to have a *"say so"* salvation. That varies with each individual. Some of us prefer to be fairly quiet. Maybe we can just leave one of our gospel calendars which has some verses of Scripture on the back as we eat in different restaurants. That is fine. Some of us may want to pass out a sound gospel tract. These are important days. The day of death is unknown. I know not the day of my death. The wages of sin is death. The day of salvation is now. *"Behold, now is the accepted time; Behold, now is the day of salvation"* (2 Corinthians 6:2). The day of judgment is coming. God has *"appointed a day, in the which He will judge the world"* (Acts 17:31). The Lord Jesus Christ invites people to His salvation.

- **John 5:24**
  Verily, verily, I say unto you, **He that heareth my word, and believeth on him that sent me, hath everlasting life**, and shall not come into condemnation; but is passed from death unto life.

  Some, as I said, will just pass out tracts or leave a verse of Scripture. Some will write letters. Some will witness in other ways. Some will go visiting, knocking on doors, and encouraging people to trust Christ. We are all different, but our mouth should be ready to talk about our salvation.

- **1 Peter 3:15**
  But sanctify the Lord God in your hearts: and *be* **ready always to** *give* **an answer to every man that asketh you a reason of the hope that is in you** with meekness and fear:

"Let the redeemed of the Lord say so" (Psalm 107:2a)

- **Matthew 10:32**
  Whosoever therefore shall confess me before men, him will I confess also before my Father which is in Heaven.

Willing to Confess Christ

We ought to be willing. We ought to be privileged to confess that we are saved before a lost and dying world. He will confess us before the Father which is in Heaven.

- **Mark 16:15**
  And he said unto them, **Go** ye into all the world, and **preach the gospel to every creature**.

We are to go. We are to tell about our Saviour. Men of God are to *"preach."* That is why we have missionaries.

- Acts 1:8
  But ye shall receive power, after that the Holy Ghost is come upon you: and **ye shall be witnesses unto me** both in Jerusalem, and in all Judaea, and in Samaria, and unto the uttermost part of the earth.
- Acts 4:33
  And with great power gave the apostles **witness of the resurrection of the Lord Jesus**: and great grace was upon them all.

They did "*witness*" after they were saved.

- Acts 22:15
  For **thou shalt be his witness** unto all men of what thou hast seen and heard.

Because we possess God's "*salvation*," we should want to tell others about it.

Uncle Charlie Witnessed to Me

What was the first thing I did when I was saved as a high school senior? It was in the month of October, 1944. I was only 16 years-of-age. Our high school janitor was "*Uncle Charlie*" Allen. He was used of the Lord to bring me to salvation by personal faith in the Lord Jesus Christ. He led me to Christ in the boiler room of Berea High School, in Berea, Ohio, a suburb of Cleveland. It was very hot down there, so when he told me about Hell I got the picture. He told me about the Lord Jesus Christ as our Passover Lamb, which was prefigured by the blood of the lamb, which was put on the top and the side posts of the doors in Egypt. He told me I had to trust in the Lord Jesus Christ or I would suffer in Hell for all eternity. I did trust in my Saviour and was saved at that early age.

After I accepted the Lord Jesus Christ, the first thing I did was to go to my friend, Tommy Seaton, who was the son of our dentist. I said,

"*Tom you have to accept Christ. You have to believe on Him and trust Him. Hell is real. A burning fiery Hell is real.*"

I believed it very strongly at that time when I was first saved in 1944, and I still believe it just as strongly today. Do you know what Tom did? He sort of smiled and laughed. That was a rebuff to me as a new Christian. I didn't know what to say. I thought for certain he would trust the Lord Jesus Christ as his Saviour like I had done. But he did not. I learned many times since then that this is a popular reaction. That does not bother me at all. My Lord said, *"Confess me before men"* (Matthew 10:32; Luke 12:8)

Tell the story of salvation whenever you feel the Lord is leading you to do it. Do not push yourself outside of your own sphere of influence, but if the Lord leads you, speak to this one or that one about your Saviour, regardless of what they do. The reaction is not up to you. You cannot save a soul. I cannot save a soul. The person's heart must *"believe unto righteousness."* That person must believe in and receive the Lord Jesus Christ personally. Just like the sower that went forth to sow.

Four Kinds of Soil

There are four kinds of soil. Only the good soil brought forth fruit.

1. **The rocky soil did not do much.**
2. **The thorny soil did not do much.**
3. **The soil by the wayside did not do much.**
4. **The good soil was the only one that produced fruit.**

Our job is to be sowers of the Words of God, and sowers of the Lord Jesus Christ.

Paul stated: *"For with the heart man believeth unto righteousness."* That is what the Jews did not get in their minds. They wanted to attain *"righteousness"* by their own *"works."* They could not achieve it in this way. God said that He has already finished salvation's work. He has done it all. If you are saved, God's Son has given you His perfect *"righteousness."* He has made it all possible. All you have to do is to have genuine trust in God's Son, believe in Him, and be saved. The Jews did not want any part of God's Son. They crucified Him. Pilate asked: *"Shall I crucify your king?"* (John 19:15). The Jews said, *"We have no king but Caesar"* (John 19:15).

Do not worry about what people say or think about you. On the other hand, be concerned about what the Lord Jesus Christ thinks about you. That is the very important difference. Not that you want to be ugly, mean, or hateful so that everybody will hate you. No! Try to be as pleasant as you can be. Try to be as winsome as you can, but when your Saviour meets the opposition of the Satanic crowd that you may be with, *"Count it all joy"* (James 1:2). Do not be surprised at the *"fiery trial which is to try you"* (1 Peter 4:12). Be faithful to the Lord.

Romans 10:11

"For the scripture saith, Whosoever believeth on him shall not be ashamed." Here is another *"whosoever"* in Scripture. There are many such references.

- **John 3:16**
  For God so loved the world, that he gave his only begotten Son, that **whosoever believeth** in him should not perish, but have everlasting life.

This is not limited to the *"elect."*

- **Revelation 22:17**
  And the Spirit and the bride say, Come. And let him that heareth say, Come. And let him that is athirst come. **And whosoever will, let him take the water of life freely.**

Again, this *"whosoever"* invitation is not just limited to a few. It was for all.

In this eleventh verse, Paul urges the believers not to *"be ashamed."* We who are born-again should never be ashamed of the Lord Jesus Christ our Saviour.

- **Mark 8:37-38**
  Or what shall a man give in exchange for his soul? **Whosoever therefore shall be ashamed of me** and of my words in this adulterous and sinful generation; **of him also shall the Son of man be ashamed,** when he cometh in the glory of his Father with the holy angels.

Defend God's Words

I use that verse many times when I am defending the Words of Hebrew, Aramaic, and Greek that underlie our King James Bible. *"Whosoever therefore shall be ashamed of me and of my Words."* There is a serious and a ferocious battle, even among Fundamentalists of our day, over the Hebrew, Aramaic, and Greek Words of Scripture underlying our King James Bible. In this verse, the Lord Jesus Christ justifies and honors our battle for His very Words!

- **Romans 1:16**
  For **I am not ashamed of the gospel of Christ**: for it is the power of God unto salvation to every one that believeth; to the Jew first, and also to the Greek.

- **Romans 9:33**
  As it is written, Behold, I lay in Sion a stumblingstone and rock of offence: and **whosoever believeth on him shall not be ashamed.**

- **Philippians 1:20**
  According to my earnest expectation and *my* hope, **that in nothing I shall be ashamed**, but *that* with all boldness, as always, *so* now also Christ shall be magnified in my body, whether *it be* by life, or by death.

When he wrote this, Paul was about to die for his faith. He was in prison ready to be beheaded by the short sword of Roman judgment. He did not want to be ashamed as he was facing death.

I hope when you and I are facing death (and none of us know the day of our death), we will not be "*ashamed*" of our Lord Jesus Christ. We should not be ashamed to witness. We should not be ashamed to tell people that He has redeemed and saved us. Our spirits and souls will go directly into His presence upon our death. As we are dying, it may be painful, but there is no pain or suffering in death itself. As David wrote, death is only a "*shadow*" for the saved people (Psalm 23:4). The process of dying is one thing, the final result of death is quite another. I hope we will not be ashamed, as Paul prayed that he was not ashamed.

- **2 Timothy 1:8**
  Be not thou therefore ashamed of the testimony of our Lord, nor of me his prisoner: but be thou partaker of the afflictions of the gospel according to the power of God;

Paul was a prisoner in 2 Timothy. He told pastor Timothy he should not be ashamed of him.

- **2 Timothy 1:12**
  If we suffer, we shall also reign with *him*: **if we deny *him*, he also will deny us:**

- **2 Timothy 2:15**
  Study to shew thyself approved unto God, **a workman that needeth not to be ashamed**, rightly dividing the word of truth.

- **1 Peter 4:16**
  Yet if *any man suffer* as a Christian, **let him not be ashamed**; but let him glorify God on this behalf.

- **1 John 2:28**
  And now, little children, abide in him; that, when he shall appear, we may have confidence, **and not be ashamed before him at his coming.**

Not Be Ashamed At His Coming

When the Lord Jesus returns, if He should come today, this instant, this day, this hour, would any of us be ashamed when we see the Lord Jesus Christ face to face? John does not want any of us to be ashamed of Him *"at His coming."* Or, when we go Home to be with the Lord at death, if He should not return before we die, I hope that we would not be ashamed, but will be able to say, *"Lord I have done what I could. I wasn't perfect. No man, woman, or child is perfect, but I did what I could."* I hope that He will say to us, *"Well done, thou good and faithful servant"* (Matthew 25:21). Faithfulness is important.

Romans 10:12

"For there is no difference between the Jew and the Greek: for the same Lord over all is rich unto all that call upon him." Paul is speaking here about the new natures of the saved, born-again people. There is no difference as to their salvation and their standing before God. In their flesh, however, there are differences in sex, in size, in color of skin, in income, and in many other things. In Scripture, sometimes God makes a difference in various groups, and sometimes He makes no difference.

- Exodus 11:7
  But against any of the children of Israel shall not a dog move his tongue, against man or beast: that ye may know how that **the LORD doth put a difference between the Egyptians and Israel**.

When the plagues of Egypt came and they were judged by the plagues, all the judgments of God were on that terrible city. God *"put a difference between the Egyptians and Israel."* God put a difference for Israel in all these plagues. They did not get any locusts. They did not get any flies. They did not get any darkness. In all of these things God made a difference.

- Leviticus 10:10
  And that ye may put **difference between holy and unholy**, and between unclean and clean;

- Acts 15:9
  And **put no difference between us and them**, purifying their hearts by faith.

- **Romans 3:22-23**
  Even the righteousness of God *which is* by faith of Jesus Christ unto all and upon all them that believe: **for there is no difference**: For all have sinned, and come short of the glory of God;

  So it is, in this verse 12, there is no difference. Paul says that *"the same Lord over all is rich unto all that call upon him."* The Jews are from Abraham right down the line in a linear descent. The Greeks are non-Jews. We could call them Gentiles. If you are not a Jew, you are a Gentile. We have the same Lord no matter who we are. If you are saved, you are no longer either a Jew or a Gentile, but a Christian, a member of the *"church of God"* (1 Corinthians 10:32).

  Now, in the case of today, the availability of the Lord is open to both the saved and the lost. The lost do not avail themselves of Him. But He is available to them if they would only accept Him and receive Him. They can accept Him as Lord and Saviour. That is what the unsaved need to do, to call upon the Lord. He is rich.

The Lord Is Rich

The Lord is full of riches. He shows Himself to be rich upon all them that call upon Him. Somebody who is rich can give what is requested. The Lord is rich and He can give what is requested for those who call upon Him.

If we are saved, we need to call upon the Lord, pray, and ask Him to help us. If a person is lost, he also needs to call upon the Lord for personal salvation from sin. He is just as rich for the lost, as well as for the saved.

There are all sorts of riches that the Lord has there for us (Romans 11:33; Ephesians 1:7; 2:7; 3:8; 3:16;). He is the same Lord, and we can call upon Him whether lost or saved. That is the need of those who are lost, to repent of their sins, call upon and genuinely trust the Lord Jesus Christ and be saved. There is no greater need that the lost have. Some think they need a different car or a different house. The Lord said we must call upon the name of the Lord and be saved (Acts 2:21). He is the same Lord and *"rich unto all."* He is not obligated to one group or another. He is interested in everyone.

Romans 10:13

"For whosoever shall call upon the name of the Lord shall be saved." Here is one of God's universals. It is found in the word "*whosoever.*"

God's "Whosever" Provision & Offer

God's provision and offer for His eternal salvation is for
"*whosoever.*" It is for everyone in the world, not only for the
elect that God had chosen beforehand.

But it is effective only for those who genuinely believe in the Lord Jesus Christ
as their Saviour. God's salvation is for "*whosoever*" who "*calls upon the name
of the Lord.*" There are many "*whosoevers*" in Scripture.

- **John 3:15**
  That **whosoever believeth in him** should not perish, but have
  eternal life.

- **John 3:16**
  For God so loved the world, that he gave his only begotten
  Son, that **whosoever believeth in him** should not perish, but
  have everlasting life.

- **John 4:14**
  But **whosoever drinketh of the water** that I shall give him
  shall never thirst; but the water that I shall give him shall be in
  him a well of water springing up into everlasting life.

- **Acts 2:21**
  And it shall come to pass, *that* **whosoever shall call on the
  name of the Lord** shall be saved.

- **Acts 10:43**
  To him give all the prophets witness, that through his name
  whosoever believeth in him shall receive remission of sins.

It is not "whosoever" of the elect, or of the chosen ones, or of the predestinated
ones. The Bible's terms are for "*whosoever believeth in Him.*"

- **Revelation 22:17**
  And the Spirit and the bride say, Come. And let him that
  heareth say, Come. And let him that is athirst come. And
  whosoever will, let him take the water of life freely.

Does that mean that if I call upon the name of the Lord I can believe on the
Lord Jesus Christ? Yes!

The Ability of Credence

The late Pastor Carl Drexler of Runnemede, New Jersey, used to say, "*Every person in the world has been given the ability of credence* [belief]. *It is available to all.*"

That is a good way of putting it. God has not prohibited any of us from believing on the Lord Jesus Christ. That is a person's own decision. That is up to a person's own will. Each person must decide either to believe in the Lord Jesus Christ, or not to believe.

The people who are the hyper-Calvinists say, "*No, not everyone is able to believe. Only the 'elect' can believe in Christ. The non-elect are not able to believe in Christ no matter what they do or even if they really want to.*" This is a false and unbiblical "*gospel.*"

I remember our former pastor of Bethel Baptist Church in Cherry Hill, New Jersey, Dr. Carl Elgena. He solved the problem of the "*elect*" being saved this way. He said: "Those who knock on doors and give the gospel to people in their community just happen to find more of the '*elect*'" than those who don't."

The Great Open Door of Salvation

God's salvation is a great open door. It is not universal salvation, because that would mean that everybody would be saved. It is a whosoever invitation to be saved, to call on, and believe on the Lord Jesus Christ and be saved.

Romans 10:14

"**How then shall they call on him in whom they have not believed? and how shall they believe in him of whom they have not heard? and how shall they hear without a preacher?**" It is important for people to "*believe*" on the Lord Jesus Christ, but they first must hear about Him.

- **Hebrews 11:6**
  But without faith *it is* impossible to please *him*: **for he that cometh to God must believe that he is,** and *that* he is a rewarder of them that diligently seek him.

Sinners must "*call*" on the Lord after they have heard of His plan of salvation. You have to believe that there is somebody there in order to "*call.*" Why would anyone call on someone if they did not believe that there is someone there to respond to that call? If this room were empty and I began to call on someone who was not here, that would be a little stupid. If there were a person here, then I could call on them. You begin by believing that somebody is there, then you can call on them.

God Calls Atheists Fools

There are many atheists in the world today who do not believe that there is a God. The Communists have this as a plank in their religion doctrines. It is part of their theory of atheism. God has an answer to that from Scripture, "*The fool hath said in his heart, There is no God*" (Psalm 14:1). God calls men and woman, and boys and girls fools if they do not believe there is such a person such as God.

But after a person wants to "*call*" on the Lord, how can this be done if they have never "*heard*" about Him? That is why we need missions today. People of the world must "*hear*" about the gospel of our Saviour. They have to hear, and Paul then asks, "*and how shall they hear without a preacher?*"

I believe that is one reason I began this church we have here, **The Bible For Today Baptist Church**. I wanted more people to understand the gospel, believe in the Lord Jesus Christ, and be saved. The question is often asked, "*Are the heathen lost if they have never heard the gospel?*" Yes, I believe they are lost. The heathen are "*without excuse*" (Romans 1:20). That is why we need missions today. Those who have not heard about the Lord Jesus Christ need to be told.

That is why a fourth of our offerings which come to our ministry here go to missions. We now have one missionary family that our church has sent out, and six other missionaries. At present, though we are a small church, we send out over $1,000.00 each month to support them. The Bible speaks of the need for missions. Every person who attends our church has a responsibility to give to missions.

- **John 20:21**

  Then said Jesus to them again, Peace *be* unto you: as *my* Father hath sent me, **even so send I you**.

God the Father sent God the Son, the Lord Jesus Christ, as a foreign missionary to this wicked world. Aren't you glad He came?

- **Matthew 28:19**

  Go ye therefore, and teach all nations, baptizing them in the name of the Father, and of the Son, and of the Holy Ghost:

- **Mark 16:15**

  And he said unto them, **Go ye into all the world**, and preach the gospel to every creature.

That is our goal. That is why we are preaching so that they will hear.

- **Acts 1:8**

  But ye shall receive power, after that the Holy Ghost is come upon you: and **ye shall be witnesses unto me** both in Jerusalem, and in all Judaea, and in Samaria, and unto the uttermost part of the earth.

Preaching the gospel is vital.

- **Mark 16:15**

  And he said unto them, Go ye into all the world, and **preach the gospel** to every creature.

- **Acts 4:2**

  Being grieved that they taught the people, and **preached through Jesus the resurrection from the dead**.

These Jews were angry at the disciples because they preached the resurrection of the dead.

- **Acts 5:42**

  And daily in the temple, and in every house, **they ceased not to teach and preach Jesus Christ**.

That is evangelism and that is preaching.

- **Acts 8:4-5**

  Therefore they that were scattered abroad **went every where preaching the word**. Then Philip went down to the city of Samaria, and **preached Christ unto them**.

Preaching is part of hearing, and it is part of God's plan for this world.

- **Acts 8:25**

  And they, when they had testified and **preached the word of the Lord**, returned to Jerusalem, and **preached the gospel** in many villages of the Samaritans.

- **Acts 8:35**

  Then Philip opened his mouth, and began at the same scripture, and **preached unto him Jesus**.

- **1 Corinthians 1:18**

  For the **preaching of the cross** is to them that perish foolishness; but unto us which are saved it is the power of God.

- **1 Corinthians 15:14**

  And if Christ be not risen, **then *is* our preaching vain**, and your faith *is* also vain.

- **Ephesians 3:8**

  Unto me, who am less than the least of all saints, is this grace given, that **I should preach among the Gentiles** the unsearchable riches of Christ;

- **2 Timothy 4:2**

  Preach the word; be instant in season, out of season; reprove, rebuke, exhort with all longsuffering and doctrine.

That is proper Biblical preaching. As Paul asked, *"how shall they hear without a preacher?"*

Romans 10:15

"And how shall they preach, except they be sent? as it is written, How beautiful are the feet of them that preach the gospel of peace, and bring glad tidings of good things!" Sorry to say, we have many preachers who are pastors in churches all over this country and all over this world who have never been "*sent*." I do not believe that modernists and liberal preachers have ever been "*sent*" by the Lord. They were never called. How would the Lord Jesus Christ call an unsaved preacher to preach hypocrisy, iniquity, unbelief, and apostasy? God never called those preachers, yet they are there.

The Roman Catholic priests, and various other preachers who are not saved, have never been sent by God. God sends those who are saved and called. Whenever Bible-believing churches call an ordination council, they usually ask the candidate about three things: (1) His salvation, (2) His doctrines, and (3)

His call to the ministry.

"*How beautiful upon the mountains are the feet of him that bringeth good tidings, that publisheth peace; that bringeth good tidings of good, that publisheth salvation; that saith unto Zion, Thy God reigneth!*" That is a quotation from Isaiah 52:7. It is wonderful to be able to bring the good news of the gospel of the Lord Jesus Christ. It is a great thing to preach the gospel. God says their feet are "*beautiful*" because they are walking with the gospel of God's grace and salvation.

Key to Verbal Bible Preservation

Remember that the expression, "*as it is written*," always refers to what happened in the past, has remained unto the present and on into the future. In this case, it means Isaiah wrote down those words in his day, the words were still preserved in the Hebrew text in Paul's day, and will still be preserved down to our day and on into the future. This shows the preservation of the Words of Hebrew, Aramaic, and Greek underlying our King James Bible. It is shown right there by the use of the Perfect Greek tense.

Romans 10:16

"But they have not all obeyed the gospel. For Esaias saith, Lord, who hath believed our report?" It is very true that people "*have not all obeyed the gospel.*" This is true, even of those who have heard about the Lord Jesus Christ's death, burial, and resurrection. Many of these have still not believed and obeyed the gospel. It is not our job to force people to obey and to believe. We cannot do that, even if we tried. That is not humanly possible. Our job is like the sower who "*went forth to sow*" (Matthew 13:3). The seed is the Words of God. As the Words of God are sown, and as the gospel is preached, the soil of the heart must be good soil to bring forth fruit and to become a born-again Christian. You will not get any genuine faith on the hard "*way side*" (Matthew 13:19) ground; or on the "*stony*" (Matthew 13:20) ground; or on the ground of "*thorns*" (Matthew 13:22). You might get a little growth at first, but then the plant just falls away. Only upon the "*good ground*" (Matthew 13:23) does the seed bring forth real and lasting fruit. Paul then quotes Isaiah.

- Isaiah 53:1
  Who hath believed our report? and to whom is the arm of the LORD revealed?
- Isaiah 53:4-5
  Surely he hath borne our griefs, and carried our sorrows: yet we did esteem him stricken, smitten of God, and afflicted. But **he *was* wounded for our transgressions, *he was* bruised for our iniquities:** the chastisement of our peace *was* upon him; and with his stripes we are healed.

It is sad when people do not want to believe and be saved. It is sad to us. We do not like to hear about it, but that is the way it is. We must be steeled to that fact. We must understand that this is the way it is. You do not sow seeds out in the yard with the result that every one of those seeds will come up. Just some come up. Regardless of the results (which we must leave in the hands of our God) we must be faithful sowers of the seed.

Romans 10:17

"So then faith *cometh* by hearing, and hearing by the word of God." True saving *"faith"* comes by *"hearing the Word of God."* Faith in the Lord Jesus Christ, Whom we have never seen, is possible as we learn about Him in the Words of God.

We Must Hear God's Words

Saved people must also hear the Words of God if they are to be strengthened in their faith. These things do not come by reading comic books or other kinds of literature of the world. It is the Words of God.

That is why it is so important that we are reading and studying the right Bible. That is why it is important that we use and defend the King James Bible in the English language. It is the only accurate translation of the preserved Hebrew, Aramaic, and Greek words that underlie it. The new versions and perversions have many dangerous pitfalls both in their texts, their translators, their technique of translation, and their theology. Here is an example.

- John 6:47

Verily, verily, I say unto you, He that believeth **on me** hath everlasting life.

Perverted Versions Omit "On Me"

This is a very simple gospel verse. The Greek text which underlies the modern versions leaves out two words, "*on me.*" This includes the Westcott and Hort text, the Nestle/Aland text, and the United Bible Societies text. They all leave out the important words, "*on me.*" The New American Standard leaves out, "*on me.*" So does the New International Version, just to name a few versions. The verse goes something like this in those versions.

"*Whoever believes has everlasting life.*" They do not say anything about believing "*on me.*" These words refer to the Lord Jesus Christ. Without genuine faith in Him, there can be no "*everlasting life.*" That is a false gospel. If you leave out the words, "*on me,*" you do not have the Words of God. Dr. Jack Moorman has enumerated a total of 356 doctrinal passages where the false New Testament Greek Words of the Westcott and Hort type of texts such as Nestle/Aland and United Bible Societies are in doctrinal error. This 100- large page book is **BFT #2956** for a gift of **$10.00 plus shipping and handling.** Dr. Moorman also has a book of over 500-large pages which details over 8,000 differences between the Nestle/Aland Greek text compared to the New Testament Words underlying the King James Bible. It is **BFT #3084** for a gift of **$64.00 plus shipping and handling**.

It is very important that we have the proper Scripture so that we can get the proper hearing and the proper faith. I think it is true, not only for the unsaved to have genuine faith in Christ, but also for the believers who are saved, so they can have the proper Bible and continue to have their faith growing soundly. That is why I preach the Words of God, "*in season and out of season*" (2 Timothy 4:2) in our Bible For Today Baptist Church and ministries. It is in the Words of God where our faith is strengthened. There is a hymn which goes, "*My faith has found a resting place, not in device nor creed.*" That "*resting place*" is to be found in the Lord Jesus Christ and in the accurately translated Words of God.

Romans 10:18

"But I say, Have they not heard? Yes verily, their sound went into all the earth, and their words unto the ends of the world." Many people have heard the gospel in whole, and others only in part. The "*words*" in this verse refer back to Psalm 19:4 "*their words to the end of the world.*" There is a sense in which God's general revelation through the created universe has been heard "*unto the ends of the world*" even though they have not heard in a special revelation of the Words of God.

- Psalm 19:1
  The heavens declare the glory of God; and the firmament sheweth his handiwork.

- Romans 1:20
  For **the invisible things of him from the creation of the world are clearly seen**, being understood by the things that are made, *even* his eternal power and Godhead; so that they are without excuse:

A general revelation of God's creation should lead people to abandon all forms of idolatry. God's special revelation is His Hebrew, Aramaic, and Greek Words given to us in the Bible. That is why we have to get out to the people what the Bible teaches about sin, our Saviour, and salvation by God's grace through personal faith. It is not enough to have the sound go out into all the earth. Israel knew about the Lord because the prophets told them. Their sound in that sense went out, but there is a difference between special revelation and really going into the hearts of the people as the Bible is preached, versus just the sounds of nature.

God Condemns Idolatry

God condemns the heathen who worship idols which they have made when the heathen can see what God has made. The heathen did not make the trees. They did not make the stars. They did not make the moon. They did not make the earth. They did not make the sun.

If they would open up their hearts, they could see that they were wrong in worshiping an idol which they themselves had made. They need special revelation of the Words of God in the gospel of the Lord Jesus Christ.

Romans 10:19

"But I say, Did not Israel know? First Moses saith, I will provoke you to jealousy by *them that are* no people, *and* by a foolish nation I will anger you." Paul says clearly that the nation of Israel knew the Words of God. They knew the Scriptures. The prophets had told them. The Words of God were written down. Eventually Israel had the Pentateuch, the first five books of Genesis, Exodus, Leviticus, Numbers, and Deuteronomy.

Moses is quoted here from Deuteronomy 32:21. Israel is going to be provoked "*to jealousy*" by the Gentiles. God has spent much time and effort to try to redeem Israel. In effect, Israel said to Him, "*no, we are not interested.*" God just lays His hand on the Gentiles (those that are non-Jews). In effect, he says to these Gentiles: "*Now, you can come to Christ. I have opened up salvation to you. You can have everlasting life by genuinely believing in the Lord Jesus Christ.*" Because of God's opening up salvation opportunity to the Gentiles as well as the Jews, the Jews got angry and jealous because God had laid them aside temporarily. We are going to see that more in the next chapter. We will see that God has laid Israel aside and blinded the Jewish people for the most part. There are only a few, a remnant, who are saved and born-again in this dispensation.

The Heathen Were Shut Out

Think of all the feasts God gave to Israel. Think of all the commandments that God gave to them. Think of the law of Moses. Think of the day of atonement in Leviticus 16. Once a year the high priest went into the holy of holies and confessed the sins of His people, Israel, in order that they might be delivered and be forgiven. The Gentiles were not a part of this forgiveness. This had nothing to do with us. In the high priest's garments, he had twelve stones. Each stone represented one of the twelve tribes of Israel. The Gentiles were completely shut out. They were heathen and lost.

Since Israel has turned its back on the Lord Jesus Christ, He said, "*All right, now whosoever will may come to me for salvation.*" The Lord is rich for the Jew and the Gentile, and whosoever will call upon the name of the Lord shall be saved.

God used "*foolish nations*" when His people were sent into captivity because of their sins. In around 700 B.C., God sent His northern ten tribes of Israel into Assyria. In around 600 B.C., He sent His two southern tribes of Judah and Benjamin into Babylon. These were "*foolish nations.*" They were judged because of their sins. God took them out of the land because they had sinned against Him. God used the heathen nations to judge the sins of His people, Israel. Sometimes He does that even today.

Romans 10:20

"But Esaias is very bold, and saith, I was found of them that sought me not; I was made manifest unto them that asked not after me." Originally the Gentiles did not ask anything about the Lord. In this verse, Paul quoted from Isaiah 65:1. The Gentiles did not know the Lord. In fact, they did not want to know Him. They were heathen idolaters. Occasionally, in the Old Testament, God made an exception. I think of Ruth, the heathen Moabitess. She had a no-account background. She was of the Moabite clan. Naomi, who was a Jew, went to sojourn in Moab. Her two sons married two wives who were Moabitish women. One of these Moabitish women was Ruth. When Naomi's two sons died, Ruth and Orpah, the two daughters-in-law, were left without their husbands. Naomi was going back to Palestine where she belonged. The famine was over. She told her daughters-in-law that she had no more sons for them to marry. She suggested that they remain in Moab and marry one of the heathen men. Ruth did not follow this suggestion.

God put His hand upon Ruth and she said, "*Intreat me not to leave thee, or to return from following after thee: for whither thou goest, I will go; and where thou lodgest, I will lodge: thy people shall be my people, and thy God my God:*" (Ruth 1:16) God, in His grace, opened the heart of Ruth, who was a lost heathen girl in the Old Testament time. She became a proselyte Jew. She married Boaz and became in the line of King David.

A Few O.T. Gentiles Were Saved

So there were exceptions in the Old Testament, where God opened the hearts and lives to be saved for some Gentiles, but this was not true in general. I am glad that God has made it possible for us who never asked about Him to find Him and be saved by faith in the Lord Jesus Christ. Our heathen ancestors never asked about the Lord. They were interested in tree gods, sun gods, moon gods, and the idols that were made of silver, and wood, and stone.

The Eskimos have their gods. The American Indians have their totem pole gods. That was our parentage and history. If Paul had not gone over to Macedonia in Asia Minor which is a part of Europe, our ancestors probably would have never heard the gospel either. If that gospel would have stayed in Asia Minor and had not gone over across the sea and reached our continent, perhaps we would never have heard either. If Paul had stayed over in the Holy Land and not gone to Europe, we may have not heard about the gospel. God made it clear that the Gentiles were opened up.

- **John 1:10-11**
  He was in the world, and the world was made by him, and the world knew him not. He came unto his **own**, and his **own** received him not.

That first "*own*" is a neuter. It refers to His own things, like the things which He created. The second "*own*" is masculine. That refers to His own people, the Jews. He came unto His own (His own creation), and His own (His own people the Jews) received Him not.

- **John 1:12**
  But **as many as received him**, to them gave he power to become the sons of God, even to them that believe on his name:

The Lord Jesus Christ was rejected by His own people, so God passed over the Jews, and opened up the gospel to those of us who are Gentiles. That is a great blessing to all of the Gentiles.

Romans 10:21

"But to Israel he saith, All day long I have stretched forth my hands unto a disobedient and gainsaying people."
The Lord was disappointed with His people Israel so many times. He was angry with them often in the wilderness. He said of Israel in the wilderness, they *"have tempted me now these ten times, and have not hearkened to my voice"* (Numbers 14:22). The Lord was ready to kill them all and make of Moses a *"greater nation and mightier than they"* (Numbers 14:12). Moses plead with the Lord not to do this. The Lord accepted His intercession. Moses and Aaron also provoked the Lord. Instead of speaking to the rock to bring forth water, they *"smote the rock twice"* (Numbers 20:11) in disobedience of the Lord's Word. Because of that they did not enter into the Promised Land themselves. Moses saw it from afar, but Aaron did not. Immediately Aaron went up onto mount Hor where God slew him. Eleazar took Aaron's high priestly garments and became the high priest. Moses saw the land from mount Pisgah where he died (Deuteronomy 3:27). When Moses asked the Lord if he could go over Jordan, the Lord said, *"Speak no more unto me of this matter"* (Deuteronomy 3:26). When the Lord makes a decision, that is final.

God's Stretched-Out Hands

Why was the Lord *"stretching forth"* His hands? There are two meanings when God stretches forth His hands. He can stretch forth His hands in judgment, or He can stretch forth His hands in pleading.

That is what the Lord seems to be doing in this instance. I think of the Lord Jesus Christ in Matthew 23 when He wept over Jerusalem. He wanted Israel to repent and receive Him as their Saviour.

God cannot make anybody come to Him who does not want to. God cannot make anyone believe on Him and be saved who does not want to. He had stretched forth His merciful hands toward Israel. He sent His Son from Heaven to redeem Israel, the Gentiles, and the whole world if they would trust Him.

Israel Was Disobedient to God

God calls Israel a *"disobedient and gainsaying people."* They were disobedient to the clear commands of the Lord. They did not do what God told them to do.

That Greek word for *"gainsaying"* is ANTILEGO. It means:

"to speak against, gainsay, contradict; to oppose one's self to one, decline to obey him, declare one's self against him, refuse to have anything to do with him."

Those were obstructionists who did not want to do anything the Lord wanted them to do. They talked against, spoke against, and contradicted the Lord and the Lord's Words. The Lord is gracious, but He tells the truth about what Israel has done. Not that He has by-passed Israel completely, but He has now opened the door to the Gentiles for which we are glad.

Romans
Chapter Eleven

Romans 11:1

"I say then, Hath God cast away his people? God forbid. For I also am an Israelite, of the seed of Abraham, of the tribe of Benjamin." God most certainly has not "*cast away His people*" of Israel. There are some that teach that God has "*cast away*" national Israel. For instance, Mr. Harold Camping, the President of Family Radio Stations, teaches clearly and wrongly that there is no longer any national Israel either now, or in the prophetic future. What is the nation of Israel doing over there now in Palestine? That is a national state of Israel. Mr. Camping says that Israel now has become the church. He believes that all the promises of Israel in the past have now been fulfilled in the church. This is absolutely false. God has a future for national Israel. The church and Israel are not the same at all.

In this verse, Paul said he himself was "*an Israelite, of the seed of Abraham, of the tribe of Benjamin.*" If God indeed has "*cast away His people,*" then Paul would have been "*cast away.*" He was one of the remnant that were believers of his day. You might think that the Lord would "*cast away His people*" because it was the people of Israel who crucified the Lord Jesus Christ. The leaders of Israel rose up against their Messiah. They tortured and killed Christians. They took them into prisons. The Christians were persecuted for many years. So, some have raised the question, "Has God "*cast away*" Israel?" No not at all.

Romans 11:2

"God hath not cast away his people which he foreknew. Wot ye not what the scripture saith of Elias? how he maketh intercession to God against Israel, saying"

Here is a picture which definitely states that *"God has not cast away His people which He foreknew."* God knew ahead of time all about Israel's past, present, and future. God had what we might call a *"corporate election"* or choice of the nation of Israel. Not that all the Israelites individually were good or bad, but our omniscient God looked down through the corridors of time and picked Abraham, the father of the Israelitish people, the father of the Jews. He chose that nation, that people, that group. It was a corporate or group election.

Corporate Election of the Church

I believe He has done the same with the *"Church which is His body"* (Ephesians 1:22-23). I believe it is a *"corporate election."* God chose the entire corporate body. As *"whosoever will"* (Revelation 22:17) believes in the Lord Jesus Christ and is saved, he or she becomes a member of that body, which body He had chosen from eternity past.

"Elias" is the Greek spelling of the Hebrew word *"Elijah."* Elijah thought he was all alone. He thought he was the only one left who stood for the Lord. He thought all the other prophets and all other Israelites had been cast away. This was not correct, but he was lonely.

Romans 11:3

"Lord, they have killed thy prophets, and digged down thine altars; and I am left alone, and they seek my life."

Elijah thought he was *"left alone."* Have you ever felt alone? Some of you live alone. Some of you live with people around you and you still feel alone. Elijah felt alone because he was God's prophet who was forthright and honest in his preaching. In 1 Kings 17:1 Elijah told King Ahab that it was not going to rain until he said it would. King Ahab was angry. Everything dried up. There was no grass. Elijah the prophet had withheld the rain. This was a miracle that God had given to that prophet.

Then, in 1 Kings 18:5, Ahab sent Obadiah to search for grass to feed his horses and mules. Obadiah was a compromised prophet. He was in the household of Ahab, eating wicked Ahab's food. He was also comfortable being around wicked Queen Jezebel. She had killed and slaughtered many of God's prophets (1 Kings 18:4).

When Elijah had his contest with the 450 prophets of Baal and 400 prophets of the groves (1 Kings 18:19), where was Obadiah? Elijah was alone in this contest. Elijah said that the God who answered by fire would be the Lord God of Israel. The prophets of Baal tried to call down fire. They cut themselves and did everything possible, but they could not get any fire. First of all, Elijah made an altar, put the sacrifice on the altar, then poured barrels of water on that sacrifice. That would be humanly impossible to have fire burn that up. The prophets of Baal could not do it. God's prophet Elijah called down God's fire from Heaven. Fire burned up that offering and everything else (1 Kings 18:38). Then God told Elijah to slay all the prophets of Baal (1 Kings 18:40).

Then he fled because Queen Jezebel got after him (1 Kings 19:2). In chapter 18 there was God's victory on Mount Carmel; yet in chapter 19 the victory seemed to be forgotten. Jezebel heard about how her favorite prophets of Baal were slain. She was not only a worshiper of Baal, she was also a vicious, filthy, immoral queen. As Elijah was fleeing, as he was alone out there in the desert somewhere, he requested to die (1 Kings 18:4.) It is too bad that he could not face up to this wicked woman. Some women can be very frightening.

Elijah said, *"I am left alone, and they seek my life"* (1 Kings 18:3). We feel sometimes that we are alone. Was Paul left alone? He was one of the few Israelites who was saved. Is Israel left alone? Just a few people are saved from Israel. God raised up Elijah for this very purpose. Are we left alone?

Sometimes it seems like a lonely path, but remember, if the Lord Jesus Christ is our Saviour, if the Holy Spirit of God indwells us, if we are born-again and regenerated by the Spirit of God, He is with us, even if we feel like we are alone.

- **Hebrews 13:5-6**
  Let your conversation be without covetousness; and be content with such things as ye have: for he hath said, **I will never leave thee, nor forsake thee**. So that we may boldly say, The Lord is my helper, and I will not fear what man shall do unto me.

The Lord Jesus Christ will never leave us alone.

The Field of God's Harvest

The field of God's Harvest is vast and wide;
Yet each must serve in his place.
The Lord of the Harvest has planned it well,
And provides a supply of His grace.

All over the world brave servants proclaim
And show forth the true message of love;
Knowing full well when the telling is o'er,
They must give a report up above.

Sometimes it may seem they serve quite alone
And the enemy's weapons too strong;
But God's in His Heaven surveying it all,
So press on, for it won't be long.

So keep to the task, to the work, to the fray,
Not counting the heartache and loss.
For He was not willing that any should perish;
And for this He went to the cross.

By Gertrude Grace Sanborn

Romans 11:4

"But what saith the answer of God unto him? I have reserved to myself seven thousand men, who have not bowed the knee to *the image of* Baal." Just think, the Omniscient, all-knowing God could look at the landscape of Israel at that time and could pick out 7,000 men (maybe in addition to this there were woman and children) who had not bowed to the image of Baal. So, in reality, Elijah was not alone.

How many others are like our church? There are still others who stand firm for the Scriptures, preach out of and defend the King James Bible, are separatist, fundamental Baptists all over this world. We are not alone. We are not the only ones. I know there are many who are compromising. There are many Baptists who use other versions and do not preach straight and true from the preserved Words of God. God found 7,000 in Elijah's day who were standing true.

Keep Standing For God's Words

So when we get that lonely feeling, God sometimes has to remind us that there are 7,000 others who are standing with us, even though we don't know exactly where they are. Some wonder if they are the "*only pebble on the beach.*" No, there are many more pebbles who stand where they need to stand. It is unfortunate there are many more people who do not stand right. There are many churches and believers who are wishy-washy and compromising on many of the things they say and preach from the Words of God. They do not believe as we believe.

Romans 11:5

"Even so then at this present time also there is a remnant according to the election of grace." Even when Paul was writing to the church at Rome, he said there was a "*remnant*" of believers. There were a few that were saved even of Israel. Even though most of the Israelites were lost, Paul said there was a "*remnant according to the election of grace.*" God chose Israel corporately, that is, as a whole group. There were some saved Jews then, even as there are some Jews who are saved today. This is the "*election*" of God's grace which led them to know Christ.

In Timothy's family there were some Jews and some Gentiles, but Timothy was saved. Others were saved also. So a "*remnant,*" a small number, were saved. One day God will raise up Israel as a nation. They will look on the Lord Jesus Christ Whom "*they have pierced*" (Zechariah 12:10), trust Him, and be saved. But this revival among the Jews did not happen when Paul was writing. Only a "*remnant*" was saved in his day.

Romans 11:6

"And if by grace, then *is it* **no more of works: otherwise grace is no more grace. But if** *it be* **of works, then is it no more grace: otherwise work is no more work."**

"Grace" and *"works"* are separate. Many people teach that faith in Christ is a work. Harold Camping of Family Radio, for example, teaches this false doctrine. He says that a person cannot believe in and receive the Lord Jesus Christ as Saviour because that is a work. *"Faith"* is not a *"work."* It says this right here in this verse. *"Grace"* and *"works"* are opposites. Mr. Camping and other hyper- Calvinists say that a person cannot have faith. They teach that God must give you faith. These people believe that only the elect can be saved. They believe that the Lord Jesus Christ died only for the sins of the elect rather than, as Scripture clearly teaches, for the sins of every person who ever lived in the world. These people teach that a person is totally unable to believe in the Lord Jesus Christ. They teach that God must give a person *"special faith"* so that he can believe in Christ, and He only gives this to the elect. If God does not give this to you, you cannot believe and are condemned to Hell for all eternity.

I do not hold to this. I believe it to be false doctrine and even could be considered heresy. It is a disgraceful teaching. I believe that everyone of us in the world has the ability to trust the Lord Jesus Christ as our Saviour. God has given human beings this ability by His creation of them with freedom of the will. Many people do not trust Christ. Many people do not believe in the Lord Jesus Christ and are not saved, but at least they have the ability to be saved and it is their own fault (not God's fault) if they refuse to trust the Saviour. If they were not able to do so, how could God justly condemn them to Hell for not doing so? That would not be right for a just and righteous God.

The Error of the Hyper-Calvinists

The hyper-Calvinists say that God must give you the faith. No. *"Faith cometh by hearing, and hearing by the Word of God"* (Romans 10:17). Faith is something that you and I place in the Lord Jesus Christ in order to be saved for all eternity. We genuinely believe in Him after the Gospel is preached. Surely the Holy Spirit of God is in the Gospel and is moving on our hearts, but we must by our own free will open the door of our heart and life. It is by faith we trust Christ. These people say faith is a work. *"Grace"* is not *"work,"* *"work"* is not *"grace."*

- Ephesians 2:8-9

   For **by grace are ye saved through faith;** and that not of yourselves: *it is* the gift of God: Not of works, lest any man should boast.

That is the way God works. That is the way He saves people, whether it concerns Israel or the Gentiles.

Romans 11:7

"What then? Israel hath not obtained that which he seeketh for; but the election hath obtained it, and the rest were blinded" Israel, as a nation, wanted big things. They wanted to be the head and not the tail, but when they sinned, God packed them off into captivity. He took into Assyrian captivity the ten Northern tribes of Israel in about 700 B.C. They were there for many years. Because of their sins, God sent into Babylonian captivity the two Southern tribes of Judea in about 600 B.C. They were there for seventy years.

God said that every seven years they were to let the land rest. They were not to plant anything. Instead of obeying this, Israel planted crops. They did not let their land rest. In order to give the land rest, God sent the two southern tribes into seventy years of captivity in Babylon. In that way, the land got rest.

Israel was a very proud people. They wanted to be the chief nation. God works His will in His own ways. God put them down. *"But the election hath obtained"* God's blessing. This refers to the *"remnant"* who were saved by trusting in the Lord Jesus Christ. The remnant hath obtained what they were looking for through salvation, through faith in Christ, but the rest of the nation of Israel *"were blinded."* The one who puts the blinders on people today is Satan.

- 2 Corinthians 4:3-4

   But if our Gospel be hid, it is hid to them that are lost: **In whom the god of this world hath blinded the minds of them which believe not,** lest the light of the glorious Gospel of Christ, who is the image of God, should shine unto them.

It is a sad thing to be blind. My wife just got a letter from a friend of ours in Washington state. She is a wife of a pastor. He is a fundamental, Bible-believing preacher who uses and defends the King James Bible. He has been a friend of ours for many years. His wife is going blind. It is a sad thing. She has to use a magnifying glass to read. She still goes to the church to help, but it is hard for her to see and read. Her condition has to do with her **hyper**-thyroidism. My wife has **hypo**-thyroidism which is less thyroid secretion than she should have. This other woman has too much thyroid secretion. This has affected her eyes. We have known a blind friend in Collingswood who is now with the Lord. We know of a fellow pastor who is going blind. Hymn writer Fanny Jane Crosby was blind, but wrote thousands of hymns despite this blindness. Israel as a whole was spiritually "*blinded,*" but some were able to see.

Romans 11:8

"(According as it is written, God hath given them the spirit of slumber, eyes that they should not see, and ears that they should not hear;) unto this day."

Verbal Preservation Attacked

Notice those words again, "*it is written.*" Every time we see this phrase, it is a proof of Bible preservation of God's Hebrew, Aramaic and Greek Words. That very important doctrine is now being attacked by even fundamentalist schools.

The fundamentalists in *Central Baptist Seminary* in the Minneapolis, Minnesota area have written a book called: *The Bible Version Debate*. In that book, their professors say that the Hebrew and Aramaic Old Testament Words are not preserved. They teach that there are holes and errors in those Words. The same professors say that the Greek New Testament Words are not preserved either. They teach that there are errors and holes in them as well. This is from a fundamentalist school.

I may have already told you this that there is a coalition of seven schools that take this same position as Central Baptist Seminary which is one of the seven. The seven schools are listed on the next page. They dislike the Textus Receptus upon which our King James Bible was based. They are Westcott and Hort people. They want the false versions. In a recent book, they say that all versions are the "*__Word__ of God*" in the sense of only the message, ideas, concepts, or thoughts. They have banded themselves together as a "*Coalition for the Preservation of Scripture.*" That is a nice high sounding name is it not? The question is "*What Scripture?*" They certainly do not mean our *Textus Receptus* Scripture, because they are opposed to those Words. They certainly do not mean our King James Bible's Masoretic Hebrew and Aramaic Words, because they are opposed to those Words. Also, "What do they mean by '*Scripture*'"? They do not mean the "Words" of Scripture, but only the "*message, thoughts, ideas, concepts, and truth*" of the Scriptures. This is serious error!

If they go along with what is written in Central Baptist Seminary they do not have any Old Testament Hebrew and Aramaic Words preserved for sure. Where will their so-called "*scribal errors*" end? With this weakness of Hebrew and Aramaic Words, how can they have Old Testament English translations that are accurate? They do not have any Greek New Testament Words preserved for sure. How can they have any New Testament English translations that are accurate? One of my friends in Canada sent me an article where Northwestern Baptist Seminary has favorably reviewed this book, *The Bible Version Debate*, by Central Baptist Seminary.

Northwestern Baptist Seminary was formerly approved by the General Association of Regular Baptist Churches (GARBC). Before they changed the system, this seminary was one of their approved agencies and seminaries. It is located on our West Coast. The seminary's Dean has recommended that everybody read this book. I have an answer to some of these distortions. I call it *Fundamentalist Distortions on Bible Versions*. It is eighty pages in length and is **BFT #2928-P @ $7.00 + $3.00 S&H.** I think many of their doctrines are blasphemous against the Words of God.

The Seven "Coalition" Schools

Here are the seven "Fundamentalist" schools in this "*Coalition.*"

1. *Bob Jones University* in Greenville, SC

2. *Detroit Baptist Seminary* in Detroit, MI

3. *Central Baptist Seminary* in the Minneapolis, MN area

4. *Calvary Baptist Seminary* in Lansdale, PA

5. *Northland Baptist College* in Wisconsin

6. *Maranatha Baptist Bible College* in Watertown, WI

7. *Clearwater Christian College* in Clearwater, FL

Dr. E. Robert Jordan started out as a fundamentalist who loved and defended the King James Bible. He began Calvary Baptist Seminary on that basis, but now it is way off base on the King James Bible and other things. I saw the video put out by these nine men from seven Fundamentalist schools.

Verbal Preservation of the Bible

When Paul says, *"it is written,"* he is asserting verbal preservation of the Bible. It means the Words have been written down in the past in Hebrew, Aramaic, or Greek; they have been preserved right to when Paul wrote it in this verse; and they will be preserved on into the future.

God has promised to preserve His Hebrew , Aramaic, and Greek Words right unto the present day. God had given Israel *"the Spirit of slumber."* They had *"eyes that they should not see, and ears that they should not hear; unto this day."* There are some Old Testament Scriptures which talk about this.

- Isaiah 44:18

    They have not known nor understood: for he hath shut their eyes, that they cannot see; *and* their hearts, that they cannot understand.

That is the way with lost people today that are not saved.

- Isaiah 29:10

    For the LORD hath poured out upon you the spirit of deep sleep, **and hath closed your eyes**: the prophets and your rulers, the seers hath he covered.

- Isaiah 6:9

    And he said, Go, and tell this people, Hear ye indeed, **but understand not**; and see ye indeed, **but perceive not**.

In other words, Israel cannot see. They cannot hear. They are blind and deaf. They are slumbering and sleeping. Nobody who is sleeping can hear or see physically, unless they have a dream of some kind. This is Israel's condition. Paul laments it. He is sad about it. Nevertheless, they are in the Spirit of slumber. It is an *"insensibility or torpor of mind."* It is a *"spirit of stupor."* People who dope themselves these days are in a "slumber" as well. Drugs will put people into a stupor and "slumber" faster than anything. These Israelites were slumbering. According to this verse, it was God Who gave them this *"spirit of slumber."*

Romans 11:9

"And David saith, Let their table be made a snare, and a trap, and a stumblingblock, and a recompence unto them:" In this verse, Paul quoted from the Psalms.

* **Psalm 69:22**
  Let their table become a snare before them: and *that which should have been* for *their* welfare, *let it become* a trap.

These unsaved Jews have rejected both God's Words and the Lord Jesus Christ. There are three words used here that we should understand carefully. The word, *"snare,"* is PAGIS which means:

> *"snare, trap, noose; of snares in which birds are entangled and caught implies unexpectedly, suddenly, because birds and beasts are caught unawares; a snare, i.e. whatever brings peril, loss, destruction; of a sudden and unexpected deadly peril; of the allurements and seductions of sin; the allurements to sin by which the devil holds one bound; the snares of love."*

The word for *"trap"* is THERA. It means:

> *"a hunting of wild beasts to destroy them; metaph. of preparing destruction for men."*

Satan's Snares and Traps

Like birds or beasts caught unawares, so Satan wants to get Christians in a *"snare"* or a *"trap."*

The word for *"stumbling block"* is SKANDALON. It means:

> *"the movable stick or trigger of a trap, a trap stick; a trap, snare; any impediment placed in the way and causing one to stumble or fall, (a stumbling block, occasion of stumbling) i.e. a rock which is a cause of stumbling; fig. applied to Jesus Christ, whose person and career were so contrary to the expectations of the Jews concerning the Messiah, that they rejected him and by their obstinacy made shipwreck of their salvation; any person or thing by which one is (entrapped) drawn into error or sin."*

Satan wants everyone of us to stumble. He wants us to be entrapped by him, snared by him, and stumbled by him.

* **Jude 24**

   Now unto him that is **able to keep you from falling**, and to present *you* faultless before the presence of his glory with exceeding joy

The Lord Himself is able to keep *"from falling"* those of us who are saved. We do not have to stumble. We do not have to fall into any *"snare," "trap,"* or *"stumbling block."* The Lord Jesus Christ and the Holy Spirit of God are with us if we are saved. If people are not saved, they have no means of warding off the attacks of Satan who wants every one to stumble.

I have seen stumbling in a church where I was a member. In that church the senior Pastor and the assistant Pastor both committed adultery and left the ministry. This *"stumbling"* is serious among even professing Christians. Can you imagine what happens when the preacher falls? All the people have looked up to him because he has preached the Words of God to them. When the preacher falls, the confidence in the preacher falls as well. It is very important that men and women of God do not fall or stumble. Sometimes Christians stumble. It hurts their families, their influence in the community, as well as their church testimony. It is extremely hurtful.

Romans 11:10

"Let their eyes be darkened, that they may not see, and bow down their back alway." Again, Paul quotes the next verse of Psalm 69 (v. 23). He applies it to the Israelites who are lost and have not found the faith in the Lord Jesus Christ as their Saviour. Not only are their eyes *"darkened,"* but they also *"bow down their back alway."* The Greek Word for *"bowing down"* is SUGKAMPTO. It means:

   "to bend together, to bend completely; metaph. to subject one to error and hardness of heart, a figure taken from bowing the back by captives compelled to pass under the yoke."

I suppose this *"yoke"* is some low thing where the Israelites were shackled while in captivity. In other words, Paul was saying of Israel, *"Let them be in misery. Let them be in trouble. Let them be enslaved."* That is David's prophecy of those who reject the Lord. This wish is what is called an imprecatory prayer, that is, a prayer that invokes a curse or bad luck on someone. It occurs often in the Psalms. We who are believers should not cast a curse upon somebody, but if it is in the Scripture we should read it and believe it.

Romans 11:11

"I say then, Have they stumbled that they should fall? God forbid: but *rather* through their fall salvation *is come* unto the Gentiles, for to provoke them to jealousy." Here is both bad news and good news in this verse.

Bad News and Good News

The bad news is that Israel had stumbled and fallen. They wanted to reject the Lord Jesus Christ rather than to receive and accept Him. The good news is that, because of their fall, the gates of Glory and grace were opened up to us Gentiles who had a heritage of being heathen idol worshipers who were lost and bound for Hell.

Now the way is opened for former unbelievers in the Gentile world to be saved by God's grace and go to Heaven for all eternity. What is meant by bringing in the subject of *"jealousy"*? I believe it means that when the Jews see all these people who are Gentiles being saved and turning to Christ, Paul is hopeful that these Jews will be jealous of the Gentiles. Whereas the Jews used to have the Lord all to themselves, now they must share Him with the heathen Gentiles who were former idol worshipers. Now, all of a sudden, Israel sees that their God's salvation is opened up to us who had been previously heathen. We can now genuinely believe in, trust the Lord Jesus Christ, and be saved. Paul says that Israel is one day going to be jealous.

They might think, *"How dare can God open up His eternal life to these cursed Gentiles."* Many Orthodox Jews spit even at the mention of the Name of the Lord Jesus Christ. There is a hatred there. There is jealousy there. It is good news that, through the Jews' rejection of the Lord Jesus Christ, salvation has come to the Gentiles. This does not mean that all Gentiles are saved. It means that salvation is available to all of us who are Gentiles as well as to the Jews.

Christ's Rebuke of Hyper-Calvinism

The Lord Jesus Christ said, "*Come unto me all ye that labor and are heavy laden and I will give you rest* . . . " (Matthew 11:28a). This verse puts the lie to Hyper-Calvinism's error.

The Lord Jesus had spoken to the Jews primarily up to this point in Matthew, but at the end of Chapter 11, He turns to everyone of us in the world, Jew and Gentile alike. This is what He meant by the words, "*Come unto me **ALL** ye that labor*." The word, "*all*," means "*all*." None are excepted, all are included, whether Jews or Gentiles. Praise God for this universal invitation.

Romans 11:12

"Now if the fall of them *be* the riches of the world, and the diminishing of them the riches of the Gentiles; how much more their fulness?" It is a sad thing that the Lord's own people, the Jews, did not receive Him. Because they did not receive Him, His salvation has been opened up to us Gentiles. Praise God for that. One day the Jews will have a full blessing from the Lord as they turn unto Him. That is what Paul is teaching here in Romans Chapter 11. There is going to be a future for Israel. One day they will be the head and not the tail of the nations. One day they will accept and turn unto their Messiah whom they rejected and crucified. He said to them: "*Ye shall not see me henceforth, 'till ye shall say, Blessed is He that cometh in the name of the Lord*" (Matthew 23:39).

In the meantime, Israel has been blinded. One day they are going to be unblinded. They are going to have their slumber stopped. They are going to be awakened. They are going to trust Christ as their Saviour. There are some Bible teachers (like Harold Camping of Family Radio Stations) who say there is no future for national Israel. They are wrong. The Bible clearly teaches, in both the Old and the New Testaments, that there will be a future fullness of blessings for Israel.

Romans 11:13

"For I speak to you Gentiles, inasmuch as I am the apostle of the Gentiles, I magnify mine office:" Paul is writing here to the church at Rome. In Rome, Italy, there were many who were Gentile Christians. There were not too many Jews in Rome at that time. Basically, that church at Rome was a Gentile church.

Our church here in Collingswood is basically a Gentile church. Paul was the apostle to the Gentiles. Peter was the apostle to the Jews.

- **Acts 9:15**

  But the Lord said unto him, Go thy way: for **he is a chosen vessel unto me, to bear my name before the Gentiles**, and kings, and the children of Israel:

Paul did preach some to the children of Israel, but basically it was to the Gentiles.

- **Acts 22:21**

  And he said unto me, Depart: **for I will send thee far hence unto the Gentiles**.

- **Acts 26:17**

  Delivering thee from the people, and *from* **the Gentiles, unto whom now I send thee,**

- **Galatians 2:7-8**

  But contrariwise, when they saw that *the Gospel* of the uncircumcision *was* committed unto me, as the Gospel of the circumcision was unto Peter; (For **he that wrought effectually in Peter to the apostleship of the circumcision, the same was mighty in me toward the Gentiles:**)

Paul continued to glorify and honor his office as a preacher to the Gentiles. I guess that is my ministry as well, I am a preacher and minister to the Gentiles. There are various Jewish ministries all over the country that minister to the Jews, but the Lord has not called me to that ministry. If I meet a Jew I can tell him the Gospel and I do. But that is not my particular ministry. Paul magnified his office.

There are many Gentiles in the world who are lost. There are many Gentiles in your city, in every city, in Africa, and all over the world. We must throw out the net and sow the Gospel seed, so that they may be saved. We need to do this with the Jews as well.

This is the Dispensation of Grace

Right now, in this particular dispensation of grace, it is the Gentiles who are the key recipients of Christ. The believing Jews make up only a remnant at this present time.

The Vice President spoke at an American Jewish Congress meeting in Philadelphia recently. He honored one of the Jewish leaders for being a builder and having a home for many of the Jewish elderly. He praised Israel, but they are not saved Israel. They are lost Israel. That is what is over there in Palestine and in Jerusalem.

People might ask whether this prophecy that the Lord is going to raise up Israel is being fulfilled right now in Israel. The fact that they are a nation is fine. That is a point in their favor, but that is not the fulfillment of God's prophecy. God promised that He would send for the Jews from all over the world and bring them back to the land (Isaiah 11:12). That is when God is going to bring them back to their land fully as saved Israel. The ones over in Palestine now are lost. Most of them are not even orthodox Jews. A lot of them are only reformed Jews. There are very few true Jews. Most of them are Jews by birth, but not orthodox Jews by their faith. One day the Lord will save many of them, but now, the Gentiles are on the main highway of God's plan. Not that God cannot save the Jews, but the Gentiles are the main ones trusting Christ today.

We must keep our eyes fixed on the goal to go into all the world, not just the Jews, and preach the Gospel unto every creature.

- **Romans 1:16**
  For I am not ashamed of the Gospel of Christ: for **it is the power of God unto salvation to every one that believeth; to the Jew first, and also to the Greek.**
  The Gospel is open for all, but the main track these days are the Gentiles.

Romans 11:14

"If by any means I may provoke to emulation *them which are* my flesh, and might save some of them." Paul wanted to be a soul winner to his own people if he could. He was a minister to the Gentiles. He was writing to the church at Rome, Italy who were mostly Gentiles, but he still wanted to lead to the Lord as many of his Jewish brothers as he could. He wanted to *"provoke to emulation,"* in other words, he wished to make his own people angry in order that he might *"save some of them."*

Romans 11:15

"For if the casting away of them *be* the reconciling of the world, what *shall* the receiving *of them be*, but life from the dead?"

If The Jews Had Accepted Christ

Can you imagine what would have happened if the Jews had been the sole recipients of the Lord Jesus Christ's Words in the Old Testament? The Old Testament had all the promises of Israel. If they were the sole recipients, it would mean that the entire rest of the world, except for that little spot in Palestine and Jerusalem, would still be heathen. They would still be worshiping and bowing down to idols if Paul, the minister to the Gentiles, had not taken the Gospel of the grace of God across over to Asia Minor and Europe to evangelize and cause many of the people to be saved and to become Christians.

I realize that Christianity is just a sham all over the world. Many are just in name only, but at least they have something that is there, and they are not worshiping idols. Some Gentiles are still worshiping various idols: perhaps it was money, or fame, or drugs, or sex, or sin, and many other things. It is the Gospel of Christ that can remove such idols from people.

Paul then mentions a contrasting thought. Just think about it, if when God cast off Israel and it lead to the *"reconciling of the world"* of the Gentiles, what is going to happen when *"the receiving of them"* takes place? It will be like bringing *"life from the dead."* Israel will then be the head and not just the foot among the nations.

- Isaiah 66:8

  Who hath heard such a thing? who hath seen such things? Shall the earth be made to bring forth in one day? *or* **shall a nation be born at once?** for as soon as Zion travailed, she brought forth her children.

This is referring to the time when the nation of Israel will be saved as a nation or *"born at once."* This will happen when the 144,000 Jewish evangelists preach the Gospel and millions of Jews will be converted to Christ.

National Israel will be saved, born-again, regenerated and then what is going to happen? There will be even a greater blessing. If the casting away is a blessing, how much more the receiving of it? That is what is going to happen.

Romans 11:16

"For if the firstfruit *be* holy, the lump *is* also *holy*: and if the root *be* holy, so *are* the branches." The *"Firstfruit"* could refer to the Lord Jesus Christ. He was *"holy."* The *"lump"* is also *"holy"* because it is made up of the dough from the *"firstfruit"* which is then mixed with water. So with the *"root."* If the *"root"* is *"holy"* then the *"branches"* are also *"holy."* The *"root"* is a reference to the Lord Jesus Christ. He is called a *"root out of a dry ground"* (Isaiah 53:2).

Christ the Only Source of Salvation

What he is saying here is that the Lord Jesus Christ is the very *"root"* and source of salvation.

He is absolutely *"holy"* and sinless in His Person. He wants those who have trusted in Him also to be *"holy."*

Romans 11:17

"And if some of the branches be broken off, and thou, being a wild olive tree, wert graffed in among them, and with them partakest of the root and fatness of the olive tree;" The *"branches"* which have been "broken off" refer to Israel who has rejected the Lord Jesus Christ as their Saviour from sin.

The *"wild olive tree"* refers to the Gentiles at Rome who have been *"graffed in among them"* who are Jews. These Gentiles were a *"wild olive tree"* without any connection with the Lord. Look at the wildness of people today. The word *"wild"* is a descriptive word for many. These who are saved partook of the *"root and fatness of the olive tree."*

Saved Ones Grafted Into Christ

We who are saved have been grafted into Christ.

- **John 15:5**

  I am the vine, **ye *are* the branches**: He that abideth in me, and I in him, the same bringeth forth much fruit: for without me ye can do nothing.

- **John 10:10**

  The thief cometh not, but for to steal, and to kill, and to destroy: **I am come that they might have life**, and that they might have *it* more abundantly.

The Lord Jesus Christ is the "*Root out of a dry ground*" (Isaiah 53:2). The branches have been broken off and those who are saved partake of that Saviour, the Lord Jesus Christ. We ought to be thankful to the Lord. I am sad that Israel has been "*broken off*" by the Lord, but that is His business and plan. It would be nice if we could all be saved, Jews and Gentiles as well, but that does not happen. Israel was broken off and we who are Gentiles were taken from wildness and put into the "*olive tree.*" This is the center of the Lord's blessings for today.

Romans 11:18

"Boast not against the branches. But if thou boast, thou bearest not the root, but the root thee." Paul cautions the Gentiles at Rome not to "*boast*" against these poor branches which have been "*broken off.*" In other words, do not hate them. Do not look down on them. Many people today hate the Jews for one reason or another. Many also hate other races. They seem to hate many people. God does not want us to do that. He does not want us to be against these "*branches*" which have been broken off. We should pray for them. The Bible urges us to "*Pray for the peace of Jerusalem*" (Psalm 122:6). We ought to be concerned for them that as many as possible might be saved. We ought to send the Gospel forth wherever possible to the Jews.

Paul then gives the reason why the Gentiles should not boast against Israel, the branches. "*But if thou boast, thou bearest not the root, but the root thee.*" Remember, those who are Gentiles are joined to the Root Who came out of Israel. They were broken off, and you are the ones that are come from this Root now. The Root holds you up. The Root is the Lord Jesus Christ. We are just grafted in temporarily. They are broken off, and one day they will be coming back into the tree again. Israel's blindness has made it possible for the Gentiles to come in and have salvation given them. Praise God for that. The next half of this Chapter 11 will show how God is going to restore to Himself the nation of Israel.

Romans 11:19

"Thou wilt say then, The branches were broken off, that I might be graffed in." Here is a continuation of the grafting in of us, the Gentiles. Paul is talking to these Gentile Christians of Rome, Italy. He speaks to them directly. He wants them to remember clearly that *"The branches were broken off, that [they] might be graffed in."*

The Jews--God's Chosen People

The natural branches are the Jews, God's chosen people. Many times we do not like to think of the Jews as God's chosen people because they do many things that do not honor the Lord and His Words. This is because they are in unbelief. They have not turned to the Lord Jesus Christ.

As we know, unbelievers do unbelieving things. They have been broken off. The branches are no longer in place, but they are still God's chosen people. God is going to return and bless them.

The Church--Also A Chosen People

But in the breaking off of the Jews, the Lord now has another chosen people, the church, the believers in the Lord Jesus Christ. These people have agreed with Christ and have accepted His call when He said, *"Come unto me, all ye that labor and are heavy laden, and I will give you rest"* (Matthew 11:28).

This new body is the church. It consists of genuine saved, born-again Christians in this age of grace.

It is a wonderful privilege to be saved as a former Gentile, but it is also a sad thing that the Lord Jesus Christ was rejected by His own people when he came into this world (John 1:10-12). It is bad news and good news as I have said before. Israel was broken off and nobody likes to see a broken people and those who are in unbelief. I do not like to see it. I would rather have them all as a group come unto Christ and be saved. Some Jews are saved and have become a part of the church. There is still a remnant who are saved in these days. It is like a father or mother who take one of their kidneys out of their body in order to save their child who is dying from a kidney disease. One kidney is taken off and it is grafted in so that the child might live. This is the blessing of God. Though we cannot fully comprehend it, we must believe that it is in God's love and mercy that this has happened.

Romans 11:20

"Well; because of unbelief they were broken off, and thou standest by faith. Be not highminded, but fear:" Notice the reason that God broke off His people Israel. It was because of their *"unbelief"* in His Son, the Saviour.

- **John 1:10-12**
  He was in the world, and the world was made by him, and the world knew him not. **He came unto his own, and his own received him not.** But as many as received him, to them gave he power to become the sons of God, *even* to them that believe on his name:

  Unbelief was the cause for God's breaking off His people, Israel. Paul reminded these Gentiles that they *"stand by faith."* They were not to be *"highminded, but fear."* Both these Christians at Rome, and those of us who are saved, stand by faith.

- **John 3:16**
  For God so loved the world, that he gave his only begotten Son, **that whosoever believeth in him should not perish, but have everlasting life.**

  It is by our faith and not by our works that we stand complete in our Saviour. He is our Foundation. *"Other foundation can no man lay than that is laid, which is Jesus Christ* (1 Corinthians 3:11). Paul adds: *"But let every man take heed how he buildeth thereupon"* (1 Corinthians 3:10b). So we stand by faith but we must be careful how we build on the Lord Jesus Christ, our Foundation.

  Paul issues a warning to these Christians at Rome, and to us as well. He wrote: *"Be not highminded, but fear."* That expression, *"be not highminded,"* is a negative command, or what we call a prohibition. In the Greek language, there are two kinds of prohibitions. One uses the present tense and the other uses the aorist tense. If it is a prohibition in the aorist tense, it would mean, *"Do not even begin to be highminded."* The prohibition in this verse is in the present tense. The present prohibition says to stop an action already begun. The meaning would be *"Stop being highminded."* Apparently the Roman Christians were being very *"highminded"* due to a number of things. Paul says *"Stop it!"* We who are believers today should take this same warning to heart. We should also continue to have a *"fear"* of the Lord, knowing that He means business and does not want us to stray from Him.

What Is Being Highminded?

What is being *"highminded"*? The Greek word for this is **HUPSELOPHRONEO**. The simplest meaning for it is *"to be proud."* It is thinking of ourselves that we are something great. We are somebody. We have status. Perhaps we have wealth. We have nice clothes, nice cars, nice houses, and everything is going well. God warns everyone of us who are saved today that we are not to be *"highminded."* We should be humble minded, the opposite of *"highminded."*

The Jews were highminded and God cut them off. Then, Paul says, *"but fear."* They are to continue to fear the Lord and trust the Lord. Paul wants them to be careful. Paul writes, *"Wherefore let him that thinketh he standeth take heed lest he fall"* (1 Corinthians 10:12). In all of our lives as saved people, we must remember that we *"stand by faith."* We must not only *"stand by faith,"* but we must also *"live by faith."* One of God's principles is *"The just shall live by faith."* He holds this very dear to His heart and has repeated it no less than four times in the Bible (Habakkuk 2:4; Romans 1:17; Galatians 3:11; Hebrews 10:38).

Romans 11:21

"For if God spared not the natural branches, *take heed lest he also spare not thee."* Here is another warning to the Christians of Rome and to us today. We must beware. God did not spare the natural branches of the Jews. In other words, when God called His people out of the Ur of the Chaldees, he picked Abraham, his son Isaac, and his son Jacob.

These were the fathers. These were the ones He blessed. These were the natural branches. From Abraham's lineage came the Lord Jesus Christ.

I do not think Paul is thinking about losing your salvation once you have been saved by faith in Christ. You cannot lose what is eternally yours. You cannot be unborn if you are born of God by faith in Christ.

Beware of Disobedience

If you are one of His children, however, you must beware of being disobedient to the will of God. That is why we must be careful. Paul was very clear when he wrote to those believers at Rome: "*Take heed lest he also spare not thee.*"

The Lord may bring trials into your life. He may bring difficulties, troubles, or persecutions in our way. When this happens, we must be very careful that we still walk by faith and stay close to the Lord and His Words.

- **Ephesians 2:8-9**

  For **by grace are ye saved through faith; and that not of yourselves:** *it is* **the gift of God**: Not of works, lest any man should boast.

Since our salvation is by God's grace through our genuine faith in our Saviour, we must be careful to walk and live by faith.

Romans 11:22

"Behold therefore the goodness and severity of God: on them which fell, severity; but toward thee, goodness, if thou continue in *his* goodness: otherwise thou also shalt be cut off." Here is another of Paul's warnings. These Christians were at Rome. You remember what happened to Rome. It turned out to be the seat of the Roman Catholic Church. This local church of Rome did not heed the Words of God found in the New Testament. They did not walk by faith, but they walked by works. They were not able to last for very long because of it.

Today in the city of Rome there is a small district called Vatican City. It is a place that is opulent and wealthy, yet pagan and idolatrous. That church advocates the worship of idols, worship of Mary, and the worship of the saints. They even say that Mary was "*assumed*" bodily into Heaven. The Roman

Catholic Church believes in the immaculate conception of Mary which means they think she was absolutely sinless. These heresies have grown up in that little place in Rome, Italy, since Paul wrote to the Christians at Rome in his day.

We can take heed as well. Paul told his readers to "*Behold therefore the goodness and severity of God.*" The "*severity of God*" fell on the Jews who rejected the Saviour. The "*goodness*" came to the Gentiles who were now able to trust the Saviour and be saved for all eternity.

We Must Grow in God's Grace

God wants those of us who are saved to "*grow in grace, and in the knowledge of our Lord and Saviour Jesus Christ*" (2 Peter 3:18). He wants us to continue in our faith and our trust. He wants us to read our Bibles. He wants us to trust the Lord Jesus Christ on a day-by-day basis. He wants us to walk by faith, not by sight. He wants us to continue. What good is it if we just start in a race and stop after the first couple of yards? He wants us to continue in this race until we come to the finish.

- Hebrews 12:1-2

  Wherefore seeing we also are compassed about with so great a cloud of witnesses, **let us lay aside every weight, and the sin which doth so easily beset** *us*, **and let us run with patience the race that is set before us,** Looking unto Jesus the author and finisher of *our* faith; who for the joy that was set before him endured the cross, despising the shame, and is set down at the right hand of the throne of God.

We must continue in God's "*goodness.*" Then another warning is sounded, "*thou also shalt be cut off.*" The words, "*cut off,*" do not refer to our loss of salvation. I do not believe, as some teach, that once you are saved, if you sin, you lose your salvation. I do not believe that. If you are genuinely saved, born-again and God the Holy Spirit has regenerated you and given you new life, you are saved for eternity. If you sin after being saved, what then?

- 1 John 1:9

  If we confess our sins, he is faithful and just to forgive us *our* **sins,** and to cleanse us from all unrighteousness.

God wants His saints to be "*cleansed from all unrighteousness.*" If we sin, that does not make us lost. Rather, it makes us disobedient Christians, disobedient sons, or disobedient daughters. God wants us straight.

The warning is that we will be *"cut off"* from His blessings, from His favor, from His smile of approval, and from His saying, *"Well done, thou good and faithful servant,"* (Matthew 25:21), when we enter into Heaven.

Romans 11:23

"And they also, if they abide not still in unbelief, shall be graffed in: for God is able to graff them in again."

Israel Will Receive Christ One Day

One day Israel will *"look on Him whom they have pierced"* (Zechariah 12:10). One day Israel will be restored as a nation and as a people. They will believe on the Lord Jesus Christ and be saved.

The promise is that *"if they abide not still in unbelief, shall be graffed in,"* that is, back into the fullness of the olive tree with Christ as the Root. God is able to graft them in again, and to make them the head and not the tail.

We have been reading, in the book of Deuteronomy, through the Bible. My wife and I read this morning that some of the priests on Mount Gerizim (Deuteronomy 17:12) will stand to call forth various blessings. Also, on Mount Ebal (Deuteronomy 17:13), some of the priests will call forth various curses. The curses are listed in Deuteronomy 27 and the blessings in Deuteronomy 28. One day these blessings will overtake Israel.

I am glad that there is a remnant of Jews who have trusted in the Lord Jesus Christ as their Saviour. Paul was part of that remnant. He was a Christian. He was saved. He genuinely trusted the Lord Jesus Christ, even though he was born a Jew. Some of the Jews, even today, trust Christ and are saved, but they are only a tiny remnant in number.

Romans 11:24

"For if thou wert cut out of the olive tree which is wild by nature, and wert graffed contrary to nature into a good olive tree: how much more shall these, which be the natural *branches*, be graffed into their own olive tree?" We who are Gentiles, were *"wild by nature."* The Gentiles have shown their "wildness" by their worship of idols and the worship of gold and silver. The same is true in countries all over the world. In China they have Buddhism, and Shintoism, Taoism, and other Eastern Religions. They have forsaken God. They are wild Gentiles. Look at the Gentiles in this country. Look at the Gentiles in Collingswood, in Cherry Hill, in Haddonfield, in Camden, and you will see they are wild and getting wilder. In fact, as this is written, the city of Camden, New Jersey, (which borders Collingswood) has been named *"the most dangerous city in the United States of America."* It leads the country in murder, rape, thefts, and in other crimes.

Lately on the television news they were talking about intermural wrestling. They told about girls wrestling boys and boys wrestling girls. They were talking about certain sexual holds and various other things. What are we coming to? We are in a wild situation here in this country.

We have all kinds of dope, narcotics, adultery, fornication, and divorces. Many are mean and going wild. We have road rage. Brother David Gammelgard, who was visiting us from Washington State, told me he does not think much of the traffic situation over in Philadelphia. He was going fifty-five miles per hour when some man stopped right in front of him. This is wild. I am glad our friend's doors were locked and that this driver did not have a gun and did not kill him. Just because our friend was driving the speed limit this man was angry. He told me other stories, too. He drives big rigs. He pulls big trailers. He told me about a man somewhere in Colorado who was angry for some reason, and this man got right in front of him and stopped. People are wild today for no reason.

We who are *"wild"* by nature, we Gentiles, God grafted us into the olive tree of the Lord Jesus Christ. Now it is opened to us. We are no longer just Gentiles and people who are not a part of the Lord's work.

The Jews Will Be Grafted Back

When it is God's time, He will graft the Jews back into the olive tree. They will then be faithful and trust the Lord Jesus Christ as their Saviour.

Romans 11:25

"For I would not, brethren, that ye should be ignorant of this mystery, lest ye should be wise in your own conceits; that blindness in part is happened to Israel, until the fulness of the Gentiles be come in." Paul wants these brethren in Rome, Italy, not to be "*wise in their own conceits.*" This is another caution that Paul lays down. If we are "*wise*" in this manner, we think we know everything. We are simply looking down our nose at other people. That is not the way we ought to do it. Paul does not want the believers to be ignorant of God's mystery. A mystery is God's sacred and holy secret.

The secret is, "*blindness in part is happened to Israel.*" There are two parts to this. First, it is a "*blindness in part*" only. It does not mean the whole are blinded. Secondly, this "*blindness*" is only temporary. It was only "*until the fulness of the Gentiles be come in.*"

What is this "*fullness of the Gentiles*"? The Gentiles are ruling over the other nations today. Israel is not running the nations at this time.

● Luke 21:24

And they shall fall by the edge of the sword, and shall be led away captive into all nations: and **Jerusalem shall be trodden down of the Gentiles, until the times of the Gentiles be fulfilled**.

The "*fullness of the Gentiles*" will stop when God stops dealing with the Gentiles and begins again to deal with His people, Israel. We do not know when that time will be.

The Rapture Is Imminent

Someone asked me the other day if I believed that the coming of the Lord Jesus Christ in the rapture is imminent. That is, it may occur at anytime. I told them *"Yes, I believe it is imminent."* There is no prophecy that must be fulfilled before the rapture by the Lord Jesus Christ of all born-again believers. They will be caught up in the air to be with the Lord Jesus Christ for ever (1 Thessalonians 4:16-18).

After this event, there will be Daniel's seventieth week (Daniel 9:24) of seven years known as the tribulation. The person then asked me if I believed the rapture would be soon. I told him that I did not know about that. It depends on what you mean by "soon." It is certainly "sooner" than in Paul's day almost two thousand years ago. Though there are no prophecies to be fulfilled prior to the rapture, there are general signs for the second phase of the Lord Jesus Christ's coming to the earth to set up His millennial reign. This begins seven years after the rapture of the church. I cannot say necessarily that the Lord Jesus Christ will come back in my lifetime. We cannot know this for certain. He may come today. He may come while we are having this service. It is imminent. It may occur at anytime.

We cannot be dogmatic. I have seen people who have made dogmatic statements about the return of the Lord. They are absolutely positive that the Lord will return in their lifetime. Many of these people are dead and the Lord has not come back yet. I have heard Harold Camping the president of Family Radio say that the Lord was coming back in 1994. The Lord did not come back visibly in 1994, but I heard him say He returned in an invisible way and will return visibly in 2011. Harold Camping is a false prophet.

Christ's Return-Time Is Unknown

The Lord Jesus Christ said that *"in such an hour as ye think not the Son of Man cometh."* There is no prediction as to exact time when He will return.

We must look up. The Lord Jesus said, "*And when these things begin to come to pass, then look up, for your redemption draweth nigh*" (Luke 21:28). This is not referring to the rapture, but to His return to set up the Millennial reign.

It May Be Today

One day, and it may be today,
We shall hear His great commanding shout,
And while we are busy at our tasks,
He will come to take us out.

"Come up, come up hither!"
And, in a moment--"a twinkling"--It will be
We shall be with Him
Whom we so long have yearned to see.

With wondrous joy, we shall hear His voice
Which bids the dead to rise and leave earth's shroud
Our dear, dear dead that we have missed so long
They rise in beauty to meet us in the cloud.

Fulfilled His promise, we'll rise
And leave behind earth's tears and fears
The things we could not understand or comprehend
To be together with Him, eternal years.

To be with Him, wherever that may be,
Our glorious Lord, in His blest company.
So let us wait and sing hope's sweetest song;
One day! Hold fast! It won't be long.

By Gertrude Grace Sanborn

Romans 11:26

"And so all Israel shall be saved: as it is written, There shall come out of Sion the Deliverer, and shall turn away ungodliness from Jacob:" One day *"all Israel shall be saved."* This is a promise of God. It will happen. Harold Camping does not believe this. He believes that there is no future at all for national Israel. Years ago I called him and read this verse to him. I do not bother calling him anymore because he over-talks you and you cannot get a word in edgewise. He will not be changed. He believes there is no future for national Israel and that is all there is to it. He believes that the church is Israel. That is his erroneous belief which I do not believe at all.

God says clearly, *"And so all Israel shall be saved: as it is written, There shall come out of Sion the Deliverer, and shall turn away ungodliness from Jacob:"* This gives the time when *"all Israel shall be saved."* It is the time when the Lord Jesus Christ will come down and His feet will touch the Mount of Olives (Zechariah 14:4; Acts 1:11).

The Battle of Armageddon

The Lord Jesus Christ is coming back before the battle of Armageddon (Revelation 16:16). In Revelation 19:11-21, this battle is clearly depicted. He will return with His saints. He will catch up all who are born-again into the air at the rapture and then return with us to earth to reign with him for one thousand years.

He is coming back with us in order to put down this terrible rebellion that will take place at Armageddon. The word means literally *"the hill of Megiddo."* It is outside of Jerusalem. At this battle of Armageddon, the Lord Jesus Christ will put down the many thousands of His enemies who will make war on Jerusalem and the saints. Blood will flow to the horses bridles (Revelation 14:20). There will be mass killing. The enemies from the north countries will come down as well as from the South, the East, and the West. All nations will come down against Israel. The Lord Jesus will come out of Mount Sion and *"all Israel shall be saved"* physically and spiritually they will turn to their Messiah as well. At that time, the Lord Jesus Christ *"shall turn away ungodliness from Jacob.*" "*They shall look on Him whom they pierced, and they shall mourn for him, as one mourneth for his only son*" (Zechariah 12:10).

Notice at the beginning of this verse the three little words that we always stop on, "*it is written.*" That is the perfect tense, and, as I have said before, in the Greek language the perfect tense refers to something that occurred in the past, was preserved to the present and on into the future. Paul was quoting from Joel.

● **Joel 3:16**

   The LORD also shall roar out of Zion, and utter his voice from Jerusalem; and the heavens and the earth shall shake: but **the LORD** *will be* **the hope of his people**, and the strength of the children of Israel.

This whole concept of the preservation of the Hebrew, Aramaic, and Greek Words of the originals, which I believe has been accomplished, has been now denied by some leading Fundamentalist schools. This Bible Preservation doctrine concerns the very Words of those original languages, not merely the thoughts, concepts, or message only.

There has been formed now a coalition of seven Fundamentalist colleges, universities, and seminaries. Each of these seven schools denies that God even **PROMISED** to preserve the original Hebrew, Aramaic, and Greek Words of the Bible. **(1)** Bob Jones University heads the list of these seven schools. **(2)** Detroit Baptist Seminary, **(3)** Central Baptist Seminary, and **(4)** Calvary Baptist Seminary are three of the other leaders who have been highly influenced by the Bob Jones University training. These schools and their teachers are smashing the Bible's verbal preservation. They do not believe that the Hebrew, Aramaic, and Greek Words of the original Bible have been preserved for us to this day. They believe only the message and the ideas have been preserved. <u>I believe this belief and doctrine is a heresy</u>. It is paganism. These four schools are fundamental in other doctrines, but not in this area. <u>This is an apostate belief. It is not Scriptural</u>. The three other schools to be added to the four mentioned above are **(5)** Maranatha Baptist Bible College in Watertown, Wisconsin; **(6)** Northland Baptist College in Wisconsin; and **(7)** Clearwater Christian College in Clearwater, Florida.

Schools Deny Verbal Preservation

All seven of these schools got together and formed a "*Coalition for the Preservation of the Scripture.*" This is a very deceptive title, because nowhere did they define the words, "preservation" or "Scripture." Nine teachers from these seven schools have a video out called *Fundamentalism and the Word of God*. In this video, nine men are around the table telling about the text and translation of the Bible. They are all saying basically that the Words of God in the Hebrew, Aramaic, and Greek texts are not preserved to this day. It is just simply the "Word" that has been "preserved." By "Word" they mean only the "thoughts, ideas, concepts, or message" in general, but NOT the very "Words." This is gross and very clever deception. Many of them say they love the King James Bible, but the Greek text that they use in these schools undermines the King James Bible in 5,604 places, including more than 8,000 Words in the Greek texts they use in class.

How can they love what is the English translation when they are demolishing the Greek Words on which that translation is based? That is what these schools are doing. And I oppose this teaching strongly.

Romans 11:27

"For this *is* my covenant unto them, when I shall take away their sins." This promise to have the "*Deliverer*" Who will "*come out of Sion*" so that "*all Israel shall be saved*" is called here God's own "*covenant.*"

What Is A Covenant?

The Greek word for *"covenant"* is DIATHEKE. It means:

"a disposition, arrangement, of any sort, which one wishes to be valid, the last disposition which one makes of his earthly possessions after his death, a testament or will; a compact, a covenant, a testament."

There are various other Biblical covenants that God made with man at different times. This is a special and an important covenant whose fulfillment must depend on God's supernatural, miraculous, and omnipotent power.

The Northern ten tribes of Israel were taken into Assyrian captivity in roughly 700 B.C. The Southern two tribes of Judah and Benjamin were taken into Babylonian Captivity about 100 years later or roughly in 600 B.C.

Here is another *"covenant."* The terms are clear: *"this is my covenant unto them, when I shall take away their sins."*

- **Jeremiah 50:20**

  In those days, and in that time, saith the LORD, the iniquity of Israel shall be sought for, and *there shall be* none; and the sins of Judah, and they shall not be found: **for I will pardon them** whom I reserve.

It is a wonderful thing that one day God is going to take away the sins of Israel. Has He taken away your sins? You have to answer that question for yourself. You can have your sins forgiven by genuinely receiving the Lord Jesus Christ as your Saviour.

- **John 1:29**

  The next day John seeth Jesus coming unto him, and saith, **Behold the Lamb of God, which taketh away the sin of the world**.

The Old Testament could not take away sins. Sin was only said to be *"covered,"* but the Lord Jesus Christ can *"take away"* sins. How can he do that? By trusting in Him as our Saviour and genuinely believing that you are a condemned sinner and the Lord Jesus Christ died in your place for your sins. That's how your sin and mine can be taken away. One day God is going to take away the sin of Israel. Right now He can take away your sin. If you genuinely trust in the Lord Jesus Christ as your Saviour, He will take away your sin, never to be remembered again. *"As far as the east is from the west, so far hath He removed our transgressions from us"* (Psalm 103:12).

If you keep going East do you ever meet West? No, you do not. But if you go North, eventually you will meet South. God did not say this in this verse. He said *"as far as the East is from the West."* It just keeps going and going. We who are saved should recognize our sins. We should love the Lord Jesus Christ even more than those who claim they have no sin. The Lord Jesus Christ said about the woman that wiped His feet with tears from her eyes and dried them with the hair of her head, *"Wherefore I say unto thee, Her sins, which are many, are forgiven; for she loved much: but to whom little is forgiven, the same loveth little"* (Luke 7:47). Only the Lord Jesus Christ is able to take away our sins. He is the only One. It is not the church, not the Mass, not the communion service, not anything, but the Lord Jesus Christ alone. He is one day going to take away the sin of Israel as well, when they turn to Him in humble belief.

Romans 11:28

"As concerning the Gospel, *they are* enemies for your sakes: but as touching the election, *they are* beloved for the fathers' sakes." The *"Gospel"* of the Lord Jesus Christ is not received by the Jews. It is considered their *"enemy."* Paul was an enemy of the *"Gospel"* before he was saved. He killed Christians. He imprisoned Christians. He went to Damascus, the capital of Syria, to find every Christian he could, to put them in prison, and to slay them. Then the Lord Jesus Christ got a hold of his life and turned him around.

Jews Are "Enemies" of the Gospel

The Jews are *"enemies"* of the Gospel. Those who are orthodox Jews spit at the Gospel of the Lord Jesus Christ. They spit at the mention of His Name. An Orthodox Jew does not want anything to do with the Lord Jesus Christ. When an Orthodox Jew is saved today, he loses his family. He loses his friends. They kick him right out. It is just like the Muslims who come to Christ. Their family will not have anything to do with them either.

But there is another side of that coin. "*As touching the election*" refers to God's choice of the Jews. His chosen people are His beloved. How can God call them beloved when they have rejected His Son? Their leaders told the crowds to say "*crucify Him, crucify Him*" (John 19:6; Mark 15:11). It was because God's love even overcomes their wickedness and their sin. "*they are beloved for the fathers' sakes.*" The "*fathers*" would refer to Abraham, Isaac, and Jacob. God made some promises to these "*fathers.*" He said to Abraham, "*in thee shall all families of the earth be blessed*" (Genesis 12:3). This meant that Christ was going to come to fulfill that promise of blessing to every family who received Him. God keeps His promises.

One day He is going to make things right. The Jews are beloved for the fathers' sake. His chosen people are laid on the shelf for now. Blindness in part has come unto them, but one day many of them are going to turn unto the Lord Jesus Christ and be saved.

Romans 11:29

"**For the gifts and calling of God *are* without repentance.**" God's "*gifts and calling*" are "*without repentance.*" That is, He does not change His mind about them. When God made these promises to Abraham to bless all families of the earth in him, he did not have any children. Sarah could not have any children. She was childless. God promised Abraham, even before he had any children, that through him "*shall all families of the earth be blessed*" (Genesis 12:3). Then Isaac was born. Then Jacob was born. Then the twelve sons of Jacob were born. Through Jacob's son, Judah, came David, and through David came the Lord Jesus Christ. God thus fulfilled His promise and "*calling.*"

God is not going to change His mind. Dr. Jack Hyles wrongly taught that this verse made it possible for an adulterous preacher to come back into the pulpit and continue to preach. He wrongly believed that this verse proves that the sinning pastor can keep on preaching even though he has committed adultery. That is not what this verse is teaching. Such an adulterous pastor has given up the qualifications required by a pastor listed in Titus 1:6-9 and in 1 Timothy Chapter 3:1-7. These are specific qualifications for the pastoral ministry.

God Will Restore Israel

What this verse does teach is that one day God is going to restore the children of Israel back to their place of blessing. It will happen when they trust the Lord Jesus Christ when He comes *"out of Sion"* as the *"Deliverer."*

Romans 11:30

"For as ye in times past have not believed God, yet have now obtained mercy through their unbelief:" Paul now talks about the Gentiles in Rome who, *"in times past have not believed God."* They were idol worshipers of stone, wood, silver, and gold, who had not *"believed God."* Now, because of Israel's rejection of their Messiah, the Lord Jesus Christ, these Gentiles *"have now obtained mercy through their unbelief."* That is the way it is.

Mercy For the Gentiles

A *"mercy"* has been obtained because the Jews have rejected the Lord Jesus Christ and opened up a way for us who are Gentiles to trust Christ and to be saved. It is very sad that Israel has rejected Christ, but, in spite of this, it is fortunate for the Gentiles who can now receive the Lord Jesus Christ and be saved for all eternity.

Romans 11:31

"Even so have these also now not believed, that through your mercy they also may obtain mercy." We should be merciful to the Jews. We ought to try to win them to Christ. We ought not hate them or be unkind to them, even if they are the enemies as far as the Gospel is concerned. Because of the *"mercy"* God gave to the Gentile Christians in Rome, God might also extend His *"mercy"* to them so that they can be saved as we preach the Gospel to them.

There is a whole group of Christians that have various ministries to the Jews. They have translated the New Testament from Greek into Hebrew for the Jews. This particular mission is located in Greenville, South Carolina. They hand out New Testaments in Hebrew so the Jews can read the Gospel of the Lord Jesus Christ. That's a good thing to have. I have received some of these Hebrew New Testaments also. It is based on the Textus Receptus Greek Text rather than the false Westcott and Hort critical type of text.

We must be merciful to them so that they can come to Christ. Although they are blinded in part, a remnant can still be saved if we pray for them and work with them.

Romans 11:32

"For God hath concluded them all in unbelief, that he might have mercy upon all." Every single person in the whole world has been "concluded" (*"shut up and enclosed"*) in unbelief that *"He might have mercy upon all"* of us. All of us, whether Jew or Gentile, before we came to Christ, were unbelievers. We did not believe on the Lord Jesus Christ. God is always just.

- **Romans 3:22-23**

  Even **the righteousness of God** *which is* **by faith of Jesus Christ unto all and upon all them that believe**: for there is no difference: For all have sinned, and come short of the glory of God;

All Are In Unbelief

God has concluded every single person, whether Jew or Gentile, *"in unbelief."*

You talk about an even playing-field, that is a good expression. I suppose it would be very seriously wrong to have one team's side on a hill and the other team's side in a valley. You have to have the playing-field the same for both teams so that everybody can run under the same conditions. That is what God has done. He wants to be fair. He says: *"Jews, if you are unbelieving, you are lost. Gentiles, if you are unbelieving you are lost. Both of you come to Christ and be saved equally."* It is the same Gospel that saves both the Jew and/or the

Gentile.

Romans 11:33

"O the depth of the riches both of the wisdom and knowledge of God! how unsearchable *are* his judgments, and his ways past finding out!" Here is God's deep *"riches."* He has boundless, bottomless riches. We can never find the depth of God's riches. What are some of the riches that God can give to us? In Ephesians, we find riches of *"spiritual blessings."* *"Blessed be the God and Father of our Lord Jesus Christ, who hath blessed us with all spiritual blessings in Heavenly places in Christ:"* That is our God if we are born-again.

For saved people, there are the riches of God's forgiveness. There are the riches of eternal life. These are only part of the depth of His riches. There are the riches of a Heavenly Home where no sorrow or tears can dwell, for the former things have passed away. Those are God's riches if you genuinely trust in the Lord Jesus Christ as your Saviour. The redeemed ones have riches of blessings here as they live to please the Lord and blessings in Heaven when they leave this life.

The Depth of God's Riches

God's riches are said to have *"depth."* The Greek word for this is BATHOS. It is the same word that is part of the word *"bathosphere."* This is a spherical vehicle used when men go down to the deepest parts of the oceans. These deep riches apply to God's *"wisdom and knowledge."* No mortal can come even close to God's *"wisdom and knowledge."* He is omniscient. God's *"judgments"* and *"ways"* are *"past finding out."*

- Isaiah 55:7-9
  Let the wicked forsake his way, and the unrighteous man his thoughts: and let him return unto the LORD, and he will have mercy upon him; and to our God, for he will abundantly pardon. For my thoughts *are* not your thoughts, neither *are* your ways my ways, saith the LORD. For **as the heavens are higher than the earth, so are my ways higher than your ways, and my thoughts than your thoughts**.

God is infinite. We are finite. He is timeless. We are creatures of time. One day the clock will run out on our life, and our bodies will be buried. If we are saved, our spirits and souls will go to Heaven. If we are lost, our spirits and souls will go to Hell. We are creatures of time, but God is the Creator of eternity. He is the One Who created us all.

- **1 Corinthians 1:30**
  But of him are ye in Christ Jesus, who of God is made unto us wisdom, and righteousness, and sanctification, and redemption:

He is a great God. He is wise. His ways we do not know except through the Scriptures.

Do you have a rich friend? What do you do if you have a rich friend? Do you ask them for favors? If you have a real close friend who has a million dollars and you have a need for a car, what might you do? Would you ask them for a loan or perhaps a gift? He has a million dollars so he can afford a car even if it is a second hand car. What would you ask him for?

If you are connected by genuine faith in the Lord Jesus Christ to the Heavenly Father, you have all the riches of time and eternity at your disposal. They are not the physical type that we often think are the best type. They are the things that are underneath the physical. They are spiritual things which are far greater. We have but to ask our Heavenly father to help us, and to give us of His riches. We can ask Him to bless our lives and to encourage us in the way which is so difficult many times. He will help us. He is rich, and we are connected to Him by faith in Christ.

Romans 11:34

"For who hath known the mind of the Lord? or who hath been his counsellor?" The *"mind of the Lord"* would include what He is thinking about. Like Isaiah wrote: *"My thoughts are not your thoughts"* (Isaiah 55:8). His thoughts are completely different from those of humans.

God's Mind Only in His Words

We can know the *"mind of the Lord"* only through His Words, the Scriptures, the Words of God. That is the only place we can find His *"mind"* and how He thinks. God has revealed His *"mind"* from Genesis through Revelation. He has revealed at least part of His *"mind,"* not all of it. God is infinite. He is omniscient, or all-knowing.

The next question in this verse is *"who hath been His counsellor?"* This whole idea of counseling is a strange phenomena indeed. In the pastoral counseling chambers of many churches, sin develops more than in any other place in a minister's life. Because of the subject matter, the intimacy, the one on one nature of it, counseling is indeed morally dangerous. Many preachers who have gone into full-time counseling have stopped preaching. This is what happened in some of the situations in churches that I know about. Adultery developed from the counseling situation. I believe how Pastor Carl Elgena believes in regard to counseling. He was our pastor at *Bethel Baptist Church* in Cherry Hill, New Jersey, for many years. He said, "I do my counseling three times a week. In the Sunday morning service, the Sunday evening service, and the mid-week Prayer Meeting. His faithful preaching of the Words of God was his counseling. *"Counsellor"* is one of the names of the Lord Jesus Christ in Isaiah.

- **Isaiah 9:6**

  For unto us a child is born, unto us a son is given: and the government shall be upon his shoulder: **and his name shall be called** Wonderful, **Counsellor**, The mighty God, The everlasting Father, The Prince of Peace.

Most of the new versions do not have this name as a separate name. They combine two nouns, making *"Wonderful"* into an adjective and make only one name of it, *"Wonderful Counselor."* In so doing, these new versions wrongly take away the comma between *"Wonderful"* and *"Counsellor."* The King James Bible has it right and is strict to the Hebrew following all the accent marks.

The Lord Jesus is the One that can help us in our problems and difficulties. We are not going to counsel the Lord. That is what the world is trying to do all the time. They are telling the Lord what to do, how to do it, how to run His world, how to run His affairs. People seem to like to dictate to the Lord. I do not believe that is what we ought to do. I believe some of the televangelists on television are doing this. They are saying, *"Lord you must heal this person."* They are telling the Lord how to run His affairs. The Lord does not need any advice from us.

Romans 11:35

"Or who hath first given to him, and it shall be recompensed unto him again?" Have any of us human beings *"first given to Him"*? No. The Lord is always the First Mover. John 3:16 tells us that. *"God so loved the world"* that He gave the Gift of His only begotten Son. That was His gift. He was the Initiator of that gift. We cannot give to Him first. Before we were saved, we did not know the Lord. We were unsaved. We never knew Him. We did not want to know Him. We were lost. We had gone our own way. We were headed for destruction. All of a sudden the Lord picked us up and let us hear the call of the Gospel of the Lord Jesus Christ.

After Salvation, Christ Must Be Lord

If we have been born-again, we came unto the Saviour and we were saved. After we have been saved, we can give to the Lord our life, our money, our time, our talent, and whatever He wants to have from us. We cannot give to Him anything that pleases Him before we are saved.

This is the great error of so-called *"Lordship Salvation"* such as taught by John MacArthur and others. He gave first in order to save us. When we were *"dead in trespasses and sins"* (Ephesians 2:1), we could not make the Lord Jesus Christ our *"Lord"* and Master which is what *"Lordship Salvation"* teaches. Only after we are born-again can we make the Lord Jesus Christ the absolute *"Lord"* of our life.

- 1 John 4:19

   We love him, because he first loved us.

Romans 11:36

"For of him, and through him, and to him, *are* all things: to whom *be* glory for ever. Amen." The words, *"of Him,"* indicate that the God of the Bible in three Persons--the Lord Jesus Christ, God the Father, and God the Holy Spirit--is the Source of all things. He is the Creator of the world. There is nothing made that He did not make.

The words *"through him"* indicate that by His means God produces everything. By means of Him are all things. The words *"to him"* indicate that God is the Owner of all things. To Him all things belong. Of Him, through Him, and to Him encompasses everything imaginable in our human brains.

You Belong to the Saviour

If you are genuinely saved, your heart and life belongs to the Lord Jesus Christ. We must praise the Lord. We must thank the Lord. We must be genuinely and completely in love with the Lord. We must be humbled by the Lord. We must serve the Lord with gladness so that He would be pleased to call us brethren and one day would say, *"Well done, thou good and faithful servant: thou hast been faithful over a few things, I will make thee ruler over many things: enter thou into the joy of thy lord"* (Matthew 25:21).

Romans
Chapter Twelve

Romans 12:1

"I beseech you therefore, brethren, by the mercies of God, that ye present your bodies a living sacrifice, holy, acceptable unto God, *which is* your reasonable service."
In this first verse of the Chapter, Paul makes a demand on all born-again *"brethren."* It is a practical demand. He starts out where most believers do not want to be. By the use of the word, *"I beseech,"* it is a soft request. The Greek word for it is PARAKALEO which means:

> *"to call to one's side, call for, summon; to address, speak to, (call to, call upon), which may be done in the way of exhortation, entreaty, comfort, instruction, etc.; to admonish, exhort; to beg, entreat, beseech; to strive to appease by entreaty; to console, to encourage and strengthen by consolation, to comfort; to receive consolation, be comforted; to encourage, strengthen; exhorting and comforting and encouraging; to instruct, teach."*

God's Continuous Request

Being in the present tense in Greek, it is a continuous request to all the Christians at Rome. By the use of this term *"beseech,"* this is not an order, but a strong entreaty and request. This is what God wants to request of every born-again Christian.

What is the basis of this request? It is based upon the *"mercies of God."* That is a good basis. When you have a request that has a good basis, it is more easily accepted, adopted, and obeyed. God showed us mercy in saving us. God showed the Christians at Rome mercy in redeeming their souls from sin and the Gentile wickedness all around them. The plea is addressed only to brethren, that is, saved men and women, as well as boys and girls. God does not address this request to lost people, because they cannot perform it. They do not have the *"mercies of God"* behind them. God has not saved their soul. To us who have been redeemed, this is a continuous request that the Lord would make to us.

Notice the substance of the request. It is *"that ye present your bodies."* You might say, *"I have a body. I can eat what I want to eat. I can wear what I want to wear. I can go where I want to go."* Why does the Lord want me as a saved person to present my body unto Him? Well, that is the only thing that the Lord has to work with among human beings here on this earth. He has the Holy Spirit of God Who indwells each believer. He wants the saved ones to *"present"* their bodies. The Greek word for *"present"* is PARISTEMI. This means:

> *"to place beside or near; to set at hand; to present; to proffer; to provide; to place a person or thing at one's disposal; to present a person for another to see and question; to present or show; to bring to, bring near; metaph. i.e to bring into one's fellowship or intimacy; to present (show) by argument, to prove; to stand beside, stand by or near, to be at hand, be present; to stand by; to stand beside one, a bystander; to appear; to be at hand, stand ready; to stand by to help, to succour; to be present; to have come; of time."*

It comes from two Greek words, PARA (*"along side of"*), and HISTEMI (*"to stand"*). The liberal meaning of the word then would be *"to stand along side of."* Someone who is *"standing along side of"* the Lord would be close to Him. He would be at the Lord's use and disposal, so that He could use him. If I would want to drink a drink of water right now, I would have nothing to drink with. I have no cup in my hand. I have no water available. I would have no way to drink. When God wants to use us, if we are like that cup and water way off in the kitchen somewhere, He is not going to be able to use us. He wants us to have our bodies close to Him so they are at His disposal and use when He wants to use them.

Living, Yet A Sacrifice

Notice what is involved in this presentation. It involves the use of the "*body*" as "*a living sacrifice.*" The two words, "*living*" and "*sacrifice*" are usually thought to be opposites. Usually "*sacrifices*" are slain, rather than "*living.*" Obviously, this is a special kind of a "*sacrifice.*"

- **Acts 7:42**

   Then God turned, and gave them up to worship the host of Heaven; as it is written in the book of the prophets, O ye house of Israel, have ye offered to me slain beasts and **sacrifices** *by the space of* forty years in the wilderness?

   There are multitudes of "*dead sacrifices*" in the Old Testament. In fact, if you look at the book of Leviticus, Chapter 23, and Numbers, Chapters 28 and 29 you will find over 1,200 obligatory offerings every single year during Israel's seven annual feasts. In addition to this, the Israelites offered many freewill offerings also. Here is a list of these offerings as I mentioned earlier in the book.

The Yearly Sacrifices of Israel

The Minimum Number of Blood Offerings

Required Yearly by the Nation of Israel

(Numbers 28:3--29:40; Leviticus 23:15-22)

Daily, Weekly, and Monthly Offerings

DAILY OFFERINGS: 730

WEEKLY OFFERINGS: 104

MONTHLY OFFERINGS: 132

The Seven Feasts of the Lord

FEAST OF THE PASSOVER: 1

FEAST OF UNLEAVENED BREAD: 77

FEAST OF FIRSTFRUITS: 11

FEAST OF PENTECOST: 13

FEAST OF TRUMPETS: 10

FEAST OF ATONEMENT: 10

FEAST OF TABERNACLES: 199

TOTAL YEARLY OFFERINGS: . . 1,287

Plus freewill offerings and sin and trespass offerings

by individual Israelites as needed and desired.

These totals do not count the five special offerings mentioned in Leviticus Chapters 1, 2, 3, 4, and 5. All of these Old Testament offerings were "*dead offerings.*"

God does not want us dead. God wants us "*living,*" and yet He wants us to be "*sacrifices.*"

Our Lives Daily on God's Altar

God wants us continuously *"living"* for Him, and yet living a sacrificial life. Our lives should be placed on His altar to be used by the Lord anytime He wants to use them. That is what His plea means.

This *"living sacrifice"* must be *"holy, acceptable unto God"* so that God can use us, not only continually, but successfully for His glory. He can use us continuously. Such use the Lord might make of us is called a *"reasonable service."* It is agreeable to our reasoning capacity because God has redeemed us by genuine faith in the Lord Jesus Christ. He has placed in our body God the Holy Spirit, which we have from God. We are indeed *"not our own"* because we have been *"bought with a price"* of the shedding of the blood of the Lord Jesus Christ for us on Calvary's cross (1 Corinthians 6:19-20).

Romans 12:2

"And be not conformed to this world: but be ye transformed by the renewing of your mind, that ye may prove what *is* that good, and acceptable, and perfect, will of God." After the positive presentation plea, Paul gives an important negative command. He says, *"be not conformed to this world."* If God wants our bodies to be holy and acceptable unto Him, He does not want us to be *"conformed to this world."*

This negative command is in the Greek present tense. As I have said before, the Greek language has two different ways to say a prohibition or negative command. If it is a negative in the aorist tense, it means do not even begin to do a certain action. You have not done it. If this were in the aorist tense, it would mean, *"Do not even begin to be conformed to this world."* But this command is not in the aorist tense. It is a Greek present tense prohibition or negative command. It means to stop an action already in progress. It would mean here, *"Stop being conformed to this world."*

Apparently the Christians in Rome, like many of the Christians living today in various parts of the world, were conforming themselves to this world. Paul tells them to stop it. This includes the conformation of the mind and character to the pattern of this world. It includes what the world thinks, what the world says, what the world does, where the world goes, and what the world eats.

The Meaning of "Conformed"

The Greek word for "*conformed*" is SUSCHEMATIZO. It means: "*to conform one's self (i.e. one's mind and character) to another's pattern, (fashion one's self according to).*"

The Old Testament spoke of such dedication as well.

* **Deuteronomy 10:12-13**

  And now, Israel, **what doth the LORD thy God require of thee, but to fear the LORD thy God, to walk in all his ways, and to love him, and to serve the LORD thy God with all thy heart and with all thy soul,** To keep the commandments of the LORD, and his statutes, which I command thee this day for thy good?

  Next, Paul gives an opposite command to "*stop being conformed to this world.*" This is a positive rather than a negative command. It is "*be ye transformed.*" As a Greek present tense, this indicates a continuous action. It is also in the passive voice. That means that we cannot actively transform ourselves, but we must be passive in this process. This transforming power must be done by means of another's power. This is the force of the passive voice. Paul is literally saying to the Christians at Rome, "*Continue to be being transformed into a different form.*"

The Meaning of "Transformed"

The Greek word for "*transformed*" is METAMORPHOO. It means: "*to change into another form, to transform, to transfigure; Christ's appearance was changed and was resplendent with divine brightness on the mount of transfiguration.*"

God wants every born-again Christian to be transformed. How is this to be done? This is to be done "*by the renewing of your mind.*"

Renewed by the Words of God

Our minds must be *"renewed"* by the Holy Spirit of God, and by the Words of God as the Holy Spirit of God can teach us.

By this means, every born-again Christian is able to *"be transformed."* All of us need to be more *"transformed"* than we are presently. There is always room for improvement. Think of what type of life you were living when you were lost. Think of your actions. Think of your words. Think of your activities. After you have been saved, you can be transformed and completely metamorphosed, transfigured, and changed into another form by the Words of God, the Scriptures, as the Holy Spirit of God is able to *"renew your mind."*

The result of this transformed mind is in order *"that ye may prove"* something. The Greek word for *"prove"* is DOKIMAZO. It means:

"to test, examine, prove, scrutinize (to see whether a thing is genuine or not), as metals; to recognize as genuine after examination, to approve, deem worthy."

Examining the Will of God

What are we to *"prove"* or examine? We are to *"prove"* three things about the *"will of God."* You will find that the will of God is *"good, acceptable, and perfect."*

1.   First of all, *"the will of God"* is *"good"* for us. This is true even though we may not want to do it. The Greek word for *"good"* is AGATHOS. It means:

"of good constitution or nature; useful, salutary; good, pleasant, agreeable, joyful, happy; excellent, distinguished; upright, hono rable"

God's *"will"* is always for our betterment. It is always for our benefit and our profit. God never commands anything in His Words that is not for our benefit and help to us.

2.   Second, *"the will of God"* is also *"acceptable"* for us. Even though it may seem difficult. It may move us to a different location, a different place,

or to a different job. It might take away our money. It might take away our health. We still must find that it is the "*acceptable will of God.*"

3.   Third, "*the will of God*" is "*perfect*" and complete. The Greek word for "*perfect*" is TELEIOS. It means:

"*brought to its end, finished; wanting nothing necessary to completeness; perfect; that which is perfect; consummate human integrity and virtue; of men; full grown, adult, of full age, mature.*"

God's will is not immature. It is mature. God's will for our lives is what we ought to do and what we ought to be. It is necessary for completeness.

The Need for Renewed Minds

If we are not renewed in our "*minds,*" we will be greatly hindered. If our "*minds*" are still carnal, and fleshly, and willful, rather than guided by the Holy Spirit and by God's Words, we are not going to test out, "*prove,*" and see that God's will is "*good, acceptable, and perfect*" for us. When we are into the Scriptures and when God has a hold of our bodies, He will be able to show us all about His "*will.*"

The Lord Jesus Christ knew about His Father's "*will*" in the Garden of Gethsemane. He said "*Not my will, but thine, be done*" (Luke 22:42). Even though that was a very heavy burden, including the cross of Calvary and bearing the sins of the entire world, He was willing to do His Father's will. He, the sinless One, took upon Himself the awful wicked sins of the world. It was a terrible thing, but it was God's will for the Lord Jesus Christ and He accepted it willingly. It was "*good,*" it was "*acceptable,*" and it was "*perfect,*"

Romans 12:3

"For I say, through the grace given unto me, to every man that is among you, not to think *of himself* more highly than he ought to think; but to think soberly, according as God hath dealt to every man the measure of faith." Paul speaks of God's "*grace given unto me.*" He was now an apostle, but before he was a man who chased Christians in order to imprison and slay them (Acts 26:10). He was called by the Lord. God gave him "*grace.*" The grace of God was very important to Paul. He wrote of this in 2 Corinthians 12. He had a *"thorn in the flesh"* (2 Corinthians 12:7). Though Paul prayed to be delivered from this *"thorn,"* the Lord refused to remove it. We do not know for sure what that *"thorn"* was. Maybe it was something about his eyes, but we do not know. Perhaps it was not specified so that we can put our *"thorn"* in this blank, whatever it may be. Maybe for you or me it is shingles, or arthritis, or a broken foot, or a car accident, or something else. He prayed about this *"thorn."* But the Lord said He was not going to take it away from him. Instead of this, the Lord told Paul, *"My grace is sufficient for thee: for my strength is made perfect in weakness"* (2 Corinthians 12:9). Paul's response to the Lord's *"grace"* was: *"Most gladly therefore will I rather glory in my infirmities, that the power of Christ may rest on me"* (2 Corinthians 12:9). Certainly God's *"grace"* was *"sufficient"* unto him.

"to every man that is among you, not to think *of* himself more highly than he ought to think; but to think soberly, according as God hath dealt to every man the measure of faith." Paul is pleading with his readers for them not to be proud, arrogant, or boastful.

- **Proverbs 13:10**

    Only by pride cometh contention: but with the well advised *is* wisdom.

If you have many contentions, the cause for them is *"pride."*

Now, who has *"pride"*? When spouses have disagreements and contentions with each other, which one has the *"pride"*? They often blame one another. But we can be sure that *"pride"* is the source of such *"contention."*

- **Proverbs 16:18**

    Pride *goeth* before destruction, and an haughty spirit before a fall.

- **Mark 7:21-22**

    For **from within, out of the heart of men, proceed** evil thoughts, adulteries, fornications, murders, Thefts, covetousness, wickedness, deceit, lasciviousness, an evil eye, blasphemy, **pride**, foolishness:

It is the old and carnal nature that gives us that *"pride."* Paul says we ought not to think *"more highly"* than we ought to think about ourselves.

- **1 Timothy 3:6**

    Not a novice, lest being **lifted up with pride** he fall into the condemnation of the devil.

This refers to the qualifications of a pastor/bishop/elder. He must not be a *"novice"* lest he would be *"lifted up with pride."* That was the Devil's sin was it not? The Devil addressed five "*I wills*" to God. The fifth one was: "*I will be like the most high*" (Isaiah 14:14). In other words, he wanted to exalt himself in pride.

We can think a little bit, but we should not think "*more highly than we ought to think*" of ourselves. I do not believe the way those people do, who abase themselves down to the level of nothingness. That is not what God wants us to do. On the other hand, I do not agree with those who push themselves up to this self-esteem mode like the preacher in California's "crystal cathedral." No, I do not believe we ought to be that way either.

Be What the Lord Wants Us to Be

We need to be exactly like the Lord tells us to be, not to think more highly of ourselves than we ought to.

On the other hand, we should "*think soberly.*" That is to think with a sound mind, sanitarily, and helpfully. This should be "*according as God hath dealt to every man the measure of faith.*" We all have different measures of faith that God has dealt to us, and we are not to think more highly then we ought to think, but think in a sober and self-controlled manner of ourselves.
Some people say that no one thinks very much of them. Many times people do not even know we are around. Sometimes they think we are no good. They are against us, but we still ought not to think "*more highly than we ought to think.*"

Romans 12:4

"For as we have many members in one body, and all members have not the same office:" Paul now uses a comparison concerning our bodies. The comparison begins by saying "*as we have many members in one body.*" He is speaking of the human body. He would include our hands, feet, lungs, eyes, nose, and every other part, important and unimportant. We have many parts in our bodies. It is true that "*all members have not the same office.*" They all have different actions and purposes.

In the next verse, Paul is going to talk about the local church as a body. None of us has exactly the same office in a local church. All of us are different. We trust that each of us would have the same basic faith in the Lord Jesus Christ as our Saviour. We trust that all of us have the same Bible and are standing for our King James Bible. As far as we are concerned, we know that the King

James Bible is the only accurate translation of the Words of God in English. We know that the Hebrew/Aramaic and Greek Words that underlie it are the exact preserved Words of the originals. We are all different people with different backgrounds, different education, different looks, different intelligence, different ages, different sizes, different shapes, and so on. Some of us are male, and some of us are female. We have a different status as far as income is concerned. We do not all have the same office, the same duties, the same things to do. We all deal with our problems differently. This is an important thing for us to realize and deal with.

You know that to start with. If you ever attend a Baptist church business meeting, you would see right away various differences in both minor and major things. You would see that people have varied purposes. They are all different. That is good, not bad. If we had only hands, we could not walk. If we had only feet we could not talk. So, it is necessary in a local church such as our 𝔅𝔦𝔟𝔩𝔢 𝔉𝔬𝔯 𝔗𝔬𝔡𝔞𝔶 𝔅𝔞𝔭𝔱𝔦𝔰𝔱 ℭ𝔥𝔲𝔯𝔠𝔥 that we have differences. We all have the ability to do things as a group and as a body in different ways. One person or a few people should not do everything in a local church.

Romans 12:5

"So we, *being* many, are one body in Christ, and every one members one of another." As is the human body, so is the "*one body in Christ.*" He is writing to the local church in Rome. I realize that there are different views on the church and the "*body*" of Christ. There are some that hold that there is a universal church of all saved people which is referred to as the "*body*" of Christ. Others hold that it is the local church that is the "*body*" of Christ. In this view, those who are saved, yet not members of a proper local church, are in the "*family of God.*" At Dallas Theological Seminary I was taught the first view, but I understand that the vast majority of references to the "*church*" in the New Testament are to "*local churches.*"

1 Corinthians 12 talks about the local church at Corinth as a "*body*" with "*members one of another.*" I think that any church that comes together has different members and gifts of things that each can do. I think this is what Paul is talking about in this verse.

Only Saved Church Membership

If a person is not saved, he or she should not be a member of a local church because he or she is not a member of the *"family of God"* by regeneration and new birth.

Romans 12:6

"Having then gifts differing according to the grace that is given to us, whether prophecy, *let us prophesy* according to the proportion of faith;" Paul now begins a list of various *"gifts"* which differ according to the *"grace"* given to the members in the local church. The first gift mentioned is *"prophecy."* I do not believe that this gift of *"prophecy"* as mentioned here is for this age. It was in existence during Paul's time before the completion of the New Testament in around 90 A.D. There were prophets. The Words of God had not been completed when Romans was written.

- 1 Corinthians 13:8

   Charity never faileth: **but whether *there be* prophecies, they shall fail**; whether *there be* tongues, they shall cease; whether *there be* knowledge, it shall vanish away.

No Tongues With Completed Bible

I believe that *"when that which is perfect shall come"* (1 Corinthians 13:10) refers to the Words of God, the Scripture. The Scripture had not yet been completely given at this time. It says *"tongues . . . shall cease."* It says *"prophecies, they shall fail."* I believe they have failed when the Bible was completed. With the completed Bible, we do not need any more prophets. The Lord has given us His Revelation. His Words in the Scripture are all that we need to know. We should not have any *"prophet"* giving us more revealed truth. God has completed that revealed truth.

Some people redefine the word, "*prophet.*" They interpret it as only a "*preacher.*" Many people do this today, even fundamentalists. I do not think that is the way to go. We should not redefine "*prophecy*" or "*prophet.*" The Greek word for prophecy is PROPHETEIA. It means:

> "*prophecy; a discourse emanating from divine inspiration and declaring the purposes of God, whether by reproving and admonishing the wicked, or comforting the afflicted, or revealing things hidden; esp. by foretelling future events; Used in the NT of the utterance of OT prophets; of the prediction of events relating to Christ's kingdom and its speedy triumph, together with the consolations and admonitions pertaining to it, the spirit of prophecy, the divine mind, to which the prophetic faculty is due; of the endowment and speech of the Christian teachers called prophets; the gifts and utterances of these prophets, esp. of the predictions of the works of which, set apart to teach the gospel, will accomplish for the kingdom of Christ.*"

The Meaning of "Prophecy"

From these definitions, "*prophecy*" must involve supernatural, Divine revelation. This gift has ceased after the completion of the Bible. It cannot be transformed into preaching. However, when Paul wrote Romans, this gift of "*prophesy*" was still in the local church and he encouraged them to use this God-given gift for the Lord.

Romans 12:7

"Or ministry, *let us wait* on *our* ministering: or he that teacheth, on teaching;" The gift of "*ministry*" is giving of a service wherever or whatever it might be. It includes helping people. Not only are preachers to be "*ministers*" or servants, but every believer has a ministry to others, a ministry to the Lord, and a service that he or she should perform. Every person in a local church must find what their ministry is and then to try to do it. Paul exhorts the believers, "*let us wait on our ministering.*" Let us not be slack concerning our ministry and service that God has given us.

Paul exhorts the ones who have been given the gift of "*teaching*" to wait "*on teaching.*" There are in every local church some gifted teachers who can both teach the Words of God, whether men or women. Mrs Waite teaches women. It says in Titus 2:3-4 that the older women should teach the "*young women.*" She teaches husband-loving lessons. One of the things that the older women are supposed to teach the "*young women*" is "*to love their husbands.*" She has been used of the Lord in these classes. She started when she was in her 40's now she is in her 70's. There are still some younger women that want her to teach them, so she keeps teaching. After she finished teaching the ladies at Hammonton, they wrote her a letter. They and their husbands were very happy about her ministry. We must teach faithfully. We are not to teach anything contrary to the Words of God. In fact there is a caution in James:

- **James 3:1**

  My brethren, **be not many masters [teachers],** knowing that we shall receive the greater condemnation.

Teachers Have Responsibility

If you are a teacher, you must not teach amiss. You must be prepared and know your subject. You should know the Words of God, otherwise God will give you "*greater condemnation.*" There are many false teachers out in the world, and we who are "*teachers*" must teach clearly, carefully, and Scripturally.

Romans 12:8

"Or he that exhorteth, on exhortation: he that giveth, *let him do it* with simplicity; he that ruleth, with diligence; he that sheweth mercy, with cheerfulness." The next of God's "*gifts*" to the local church is "*exhortation.*" The Greek word for "*exhortation*" is PARAKALEO. It means, variously:

> "*to call to one's side, call for, summon; to address, speak to, (call to, call upon), which may be done in the way of exhortation, entreaty, comfort, instruction, etc.; to admonish, exhort; to beg, entreat, beseech; to strive to appease by entreaty; to console, to encourage and strengthen by consolation, to comfort; to receive consolation, be comforted; to encourage, strengthen; exhorting and comforting and encouraging; to instruct, teach.*"

Being in the present tense, it implies continuous activity in this wide-ranging compass of meanings.

Exhortation Needed

This is a needed gift for every local church. Pastors are to *"exhort"* as they preach God's Words (2 Timothy 4:2). Many people have serious difficulties and problems. God has called born-again believers to be comforters and encouragers to those who are in trouble.

We must strengthen them in the things of the faith. That is a good and helpful gift and I hope that many in our church and other churches have this gift. We should know how to encourage, strengthen, and comfort others. The Scriptures certainly give us exhortation.

Scriptural "Giving"

The next of God's *"gifts"* to the local church regards *"giving."* Paul urges those who are giving to *"do it with simplicity."* The Greek word for *"simplicity"* is HAPLOTES. It means:

"singleness, simplicity, sincerity, mental honesty; the virtue of one who is free from pretence and hypocrisy; not self-seeking, openness of heart manifesting itself by generousity."

Our *"giving"* should be *"free from pretence and hypocrisy."*

There should be no boastfulness or showing off. Remember in Mark 12:41-44 the rich cast in much into the treasury, but the poor widow cast in only two mites. I am sure the rich made a big splash and fanfare when they deposited their money. I am also sure that the poor widow did not show off as she put in her two mites. The Lord Jesus Christ said she put in more than the rich men because they *"did cast in of their abundance, but she of her want did cast in all that she had, even all her living"* (Mark 12:44). There should not have been any fanfare. We should give privately, secretly, and *"with simplicity."* This is why we have an offering box at the back of our church. It gives opportunity for those who give or who do not give to our ministry to do so quietly and privately.

How Much Should You Give?

You might ask how much should we give to the Lord? That is entirely what the Lord would lead us to do. Some give 10% some give more. Some of us have more to give than others. Some give more and some give less. 1 Corinthians 16:2 tells us to give "*as God hath prospered*" us. 2 Corinthians 9:7 tells us: "*Every man according as he purposeth in his heart, so let him give, not grudgingly, or of necessity: for God loveth a cheerful giver.*"

This is the verse that we have on our church's gift box.

The next of God's "*gifts*" to the local church regards those who "*rule.*" The Greek word for "*ruleth*" is PROISTEMI. It means:

"*to set or place before; to set over; to be over, to superintend, preside over; to be a protector or guardian; to give aid; to care for, give attention to; profess honest occupations.*"

Presiding Over Things

There is a need in the local church for someone to "*preside*" over or be in charge of things. This includes such things as witnessing, the treasury, the ministry of music, or taking care of the flowers. This is a gift that God wants us to give. The one that "*ruleth*" or is in charge of things must have "*diligence.*"

The Greek word for "*diligence*" is SPOUDE. It means:

"*haste, with haste; earnestness, diligence; earnestness in accomplishing, promoting, or striving after anything; to give all diligence, interest one's self most earnestly.*"

Pastors Must Be Diligent

A pastor, as well as others who might *"rule"* in a local church, must be diligent. There are many details to care for in any local church, including bulletins, inviting people to services, visitation, witnessing, advertising, care of the building, and many other responsibilities.

We should do all these things *"with diligence"* and earnestness, promoting things so that they should be properly cared for. God wants things to be done decently and in order.

The next of God's *"gifts"* to the local church regards those who *"show mercy."* The one that shows *"mercy"* should do it *"with cheerfulness."* The Greek word for *"showing mercy"* is ELEEO. It means:

"to have mercy on; to help one afflicted or seeking aid; to help the afflicted, to bring help to the wretched; to experience mercy"

Do you know any *"afflicted"* people? If so, you should help them. That is *"showing mercy."* There are people with all sorts of problems and difficulties. Maybe you do not have one in your own life, but maybe you have a relative that is in trouble. If that is the situation, you must *"show mercy"* to them and help them *"seeking aid."* Maybe it is a spouse. Maybe it is someone who is a friend.

Showing Mercy Cheerfully

Some people do not come to you and say they need some help, but they do need help. If you spot them and help them in a kind way, that is what it means to *"show mercy."* This should be done with *"cheerfulness"* rather than an attitude of obligation.

I believe that the family of God should help the family of God. But I do not believe in the social gospel. I do not believe it is taught in Scripture. The apostate modernist churches have a social gospel. They give aid to the whole world. Not that there is anything wrong with giving aid to the whole world, but there are so many people in the whole world that there is not enough money to go around or enough people to help. We should aid our fellow believers who need assistance. That is why many churches have a deacons fund to help those in the congregation who have special problems.

The Social Gospel is Unscriptural

The Lord Jesus Christ did not tell us to go into the whole world and feed the world, or cloth the world, or house the world, or to provide medical care for the world. There is nothing wrong with any of these things, but the Lord Jesus Christ told His apostles: *"go ye into all the world, and preach the gospel to every creature"* (Mark 16:15). The *"gospel"* cannot pass away. It is not physical. It is spiritual. It is something people can take with them , be saved, and go Home to glory. This is true no matter what these people have in the way of worldly goods.

When Paul went on his missionary journeys, he did not have the funds to provide all these things that these big churches are providing in the way of world relief. There is nothing wrong with that, but as the Lord Jesus Christ said to a man when someone died in his family, *"Let the dead bury their dead: but go thou and preach the kingdom of God"* (Luke 9:60). Let the person's family take care of their needs and help them. Perhaps the government agencies or private agencies could take care of these things. If they want to do that, they should do so. However, we as believers who have limited funds and limited people, just cannot perform these social gospel activities without limiting their primary task of bringing the gospel and redemption to a lost world.

When the Lord Jesus Christ sent out his disciples two-by-two, He sent out his twelve apostles (Matthew 10:5- 20) as well as seventy others (Luke 10:1-17). He commanded the twelve *"that they should take nothing for their journey, save a staff only; no scrip, no bread, no money in their purse"* (Mark 6:8). They were not to feed, to clothe, and to house. They were to be fed and to preach the coming of the Lord Jesus Christ. We should *"show mercy"* on fellow believers. As the Lord leads us, certainly, if we can, we would want to help those who are not saved. But the primary purpose of the church is to preach the gospel to the lost and to especially help, as needed, those who are in the household faith.

Paul took collections, for example, for the poor saints in Jerusalem (Romans 15:26; 1 Corinthians 16:1). He took collections for the believers who were in need. If we are *"showing mercy,"* we should help those who need help.

Most people do not tell you that they are in need. I don't know how you can find that out except being close to them. We have people right here in our church who, I am sure, have some needs. We need to *"show mercy"* to them and help them. Now, notice we are to do this *"with cheerfulness."* You should not do it with a grumbling spirit and attitude. Do it with *"cheerfulness"* and readiness of mind that it may be honored by the Lord.

Romans 12:9

"Let love be without dissimulation. Abhor that which is evil; cleave to that which is good."

Sincere Love

Here is godly *"love."* The Greek word for *"dissimulation"* is UNHYPOCRITOS. It means: *"unfeigned, undisguised, sincere."* It is literally *"without hypocrisy,"* or showing off.

What would it be if you had a *"hypocritical love"*? It would be a *"feigned"* love which is *"insincere."* Many people smile with their teeth only. Other people smile with their hearts. Others smile with both their teeth and their hearts. Unfortunately, there is such a thing as false love. This world has a lot of syrupy and gooey kind of love, but you do not know what is in the heart. God says that believers are to have "love" which is sincere and *"without hypocrisy."* We should love one another as Christian believers in our church and for believers in other fundamental churches. We should respect one another with a strong and godly *"love."*

The opposite of *"love"* is *"abhorrence."* Though our *"love"* should not be *"insincere,"* yet we should *"abhor that which is evil."* We are not to *"love"* evil in any way. We are to stand aside from *"evil"* and give it up, because it is wrong. We are to dislike it and have a horror regarding any kind of *"evil,"* beginning with the *"evil"* that is in our own hearts and lives, as well as in our families and in our world. We are to despise it and abhor it.

On the other hand, we are to *"cleave to that which is good."* That word *"cleave"* is used in Genesis also.

- **Genesis 2:24**

  Therefore shall a man leave his father and his mother, and shall **cleave** unto his wife: and they shall be one flesh.

That is also quoted in the New Testament in the Gospel of Mark.

- **Mark 10:7-8**

  For this cause shall a man leave his father and mother, and **cleave** to his wife; And they twain shall be one flesh: so then they are no more twain, but one flesh.

The Greek word for "*cleave*" is KOLLAO. It means:

> "*to glue, to glue together, cement, fasten together; to join or fasten firmly together; to join one's self to, cleave to*"

If you have a good glue, it will stick. That is what we are to do to the "good." It is also what we are to do to our "wives." We are to "*cleave*" to them, and not leave them.

- **Acts 11:23**

  Who, when he came, and had seen the grace of God, was glad, and exhorted them all, that with purpose of heart they would **cleave** unto the Lord.

What are some of the things that are "*good*" that we should "*cleave*" to? The Words of God are "*good*." God the Father, God the Son, and God the Holy Spirit are "*good*." All the things that the Lord has for us in the commands of the Scriptures are "*good*." We are to "*cleave*" or stick to those things as glue.

We are to hate the "*evil*" and to love and "*cleave*" to the "*good*." Many people do not think we should have the emotion of hatred of any kind. God says we are to hate "*evil*" and to love the "*good*." The word "*abhor*" is a synonym for hate, detest, and dislike.

Romans 12:10

"Be kindly affectioned one to another with brotherly love; in honour preferring one another;"

Meaning of "Kindly Affectioned"

The Greek word for "*kindly affectioned*" is PHILOSTORGOS. It means: "*the mutual love of parents and children and wives and husbands; loving affection, prone to do to love, loving tenderly; chiefly of the reciprocal tenderness of parents and children.*"

God wants these believers at Rome to have a "*tender love*" for one another like people in a family. The local church, whether it is in Rome, whether it is in Collingswood, or wherever it is, should have a family kind of love. It is also called a "*brotherly love*." It is a love that sisters and brothers should have. It is true, realistically, that sometimes sisters and brothers do not love each other. They have fights and battles. I have two sisters. While we were growing up in our family home, sometimes there were battles. This "*brotherly love*" is a different kind of thing. This is a "*brotherly love*" that is sincere and genuine because those in the local church should be born-again. As such, we are brothers and sisters in the Lord Jesus Christ.

Genuine Affection=Fewer Fights

Should genuine affection prevail with one another in the local church, there certainly would be fewer fights, less bitterness, less contention, less strife, and more unity. They would bless and honor such love.

The words "*in honour preferring one another*" indicate that Paul wants Christian people to want to fellowship with genuine believers rather than those in the world. If we have as our closest friends those who are lost and in their sins, we will be in serious trouble sooner or later. We may begin to want to be with them, think like they think and do what they do.

God wants us to prefer true believers, saved people. I know some saved people can be very cantankerous, evil, and wicked, walking out of fellowship with the Lord. I trust that our close fellowship would not be with these people either. Not that we are to spurn the unsaved. We are to witness to them. We are to be kind to them and do what we can to love them for the sake of our Saviour, but our closest, most intimate friends should be those that love the Lord Jesus Christ in sincerity. We should indeed "*prefer one another*" in love. If this were practiced, there would be less marital fighting and fewer, if any, divorces.

Romans 12:11

"Not slothful in business; fervent in spirit; serving the Lord;" God does not want us who are saved to be "*slothful.*" I've never seen a sloth, but they are described as very slow-moving and lazy. God does not want us to be "*slothful*" in any business or other activity. God does not want us to be lazy. Here is one definition of a "*sloth*."

> "*a) any of a family (Bradypodidae) of <u>slow-moving</u>, tree-dwelling edentate mammals of tropical Central and South America that hang, back down, from branches and feed on fruits and vegetation, including a three-toed species (genus Bradypus) and a two-toed species (genus Choloepus) b) any of various families of extinct, ground-dwelling edentate mammals*"

On the other hand, we must move through our lives being "*fervent in spirit.*" This is the opposite of "*slothful.*" The Greek word for "*fervent*" is ZEO. It means:

> " *to boil with heat, be hot; used of water; metaph. used of boiling anger, love, zeal, for what is good or bad etc.; fervent in spirit, said of zeal for what is good*"

The Meaning of "Fervent"

From the meaning of the word, this is a "*boiling*" up in zeal for doing that which is right. We are to be "*fervent.*"

May our God give us the fervency, heat, and boiling as we serve the Lord. It is a hot attitude. It is the heat and zeal for that which is good. Something that boils usually gets a reaction. If you put your finger in boiling water, you will have a reaction will you not? Boiling in "*fervency in spirit*" will get a reaction also. God wants us to be hot and heated for the Lord, not for self, not for anger, and not for the devil.

All of this "fervency" is to be used in "*serving the Lord;*" The Greek word for "*serving*" is DOULEUO. It means:

> " *to be a slave, serve, do service; of a nation in subjection to other nations; metaph. to obey, submit to; in a good sense, to yield obedience; in a bad sense, of those who become slaves to some base power, to yield to, give one's self up to.*"

Continuous Service for the Lord

It is in the Greek present tense and therefore signifies a continuous action. We are to be continuously *"serving the Lord."* That is the way that *"fervency"* is; not for self, but for the Lord.

We do not want to be slothful in any of our business even for self, but especially for the Lord. We are to be boiling up just as hot and warm- hearted as we can. It is service for the Lord, saying *"yes"* to Him whatever His orders are. It means serving willingly and continuously all the days of our lives. It is not a case that when you reach twenty, thirty, forty, fifty, sixty, seventy, eighty, ninety or one hundred years of age you can cease *"serving the Lord."* No, God expects us continuously to serve the Lord.

Caleb did not stop serving the Lord. He was eighty years old when he said *"Lord give me this mountain"* (Joshua 14:12). He said he was strong and could go in and out, fight this battle, and defeat those giants. He took the land for the Lord at the age of eighty. There is no let up. We are to continue to serve the Lord.

Give Me This Mountain

Give me this mountain, O Lord I pray

Give me the victory O'er the hard things today.

Give me this mountain, Thy promise I claim.

Give me this high place;

Thus to praise Thy Name.

Give me this mountain, What matter my age.

Give me provision The battle to wage.

Give me this mountain, O Lord I pray,

Though there are giants That stand in the way

Grant me Thy blessing, O Lord I long.

Give me this mountain; I'll climb with a song.

(Joshua 14:12)

By Gertrude Grace Sanborn

Romans 12:12

"Rejoicing in hope; patient in tribulation; continuing instant in prayer;" One of the important parts of the *"fruit of the Spirit"* is joy (Galatians 5:22). We should be *"rejoicing"* if we are born-again. We have something to rejoice about if we are saved. The Lord Jesus Christ has saved us. He died for our sins and rose again and is in Heaven today. In all of our *"rejoicing"* we should have an attitude of *"hope."* The world uses *"hope"* like the fictional door-to-door salesman, Elmer Blurt, who used to say, as he was knocking on a customer's door, *"I hope nobody is home, I hope, I hope, I hope."* We who are old-timers probably remember him. He did not want to face the people at whose doors he was knocking. The *"hope"* in the Bible is a sure thing that will happen sometime in the future. It is future, but not uncertain. It is very certain and it will come to pass.

- Titus 2:13

    Looking for **that blessed hope**, and the glorious appearing of the great God and our Saviour Jesus Christ;

That is a sure thing. It is called a "*blessed hope*" because it is yet future, but it is absolutely certain. This refers to the rapture of the believers. We can rejoice in this "*hope*."

- **Romans 15:4**

  For whatsoever things were written aforetime were written for our learning, that we through patience and comfort of the scriptures **might have hope.**

The Words of God give us "*hope*" as we read our Bibles.

- **Colossians 1:5**

  For the **hope which is laid up for you in Heaven,** whereof ye heard before in the word of the truth of the gospel;

That "*hope*" is just as sure as anything that is present. It is as certain as our being alive, but it is a future possession, therefore it is a called a "*hope*." We have a great "*rejoicing*" because we have many wonderful blessings in store for us up in Glory.

But because we who are born-again have various troubles here on earth, God wants us to be "*patient in tribulation.*" It is difficult to be "*patient.*" The Greek word for "*tribulation*" is THLIPSIS. It means:

"*a pressing, pressing together, pressure; metaph. oppression, affliction, tribulation, distress, straits.*"

Most people want deliverance now from this pressure.

Patient Through All Distress

God may or may not want to deliver us from this tribulation, but one thing He desires of us, He wants us to be "*patient*" through every part of that distress. God wants to teach us "*patience*" but that takes time.

"*Tribulation*" is one way for us to learn "*patience*" (Romans 5:3). It takes a little bit of time. We would like deliverance now would we not? Right now, in our tribulation, whatever it might be, we have to be patient. As this sermon was preached, I had shingles on the left side of my head. It felt like sunburn and was tender. I wondered when this would go away. I did not know. They said it would take about six months. I had to be "*patient*" in that "*tribulation.*" I am sure the Lord wanted me to be empathetic and sympathetic to others who have pain. "*Tribulation*" should find us "*patient.*" We must ask the Lord to help us accomplish this.

Constant Prayer in Tribulation

In all of our *"rejoicing"* and in all of our *"tribulation,"* we should never fail to be *"continuing instant in prayer."*

The *"prayer"* is for many of our spiritual and physical needs, including *"patience."* The Lord gave me *"patience"* to live through my shingles and I certainly did pray to Him asking Him for His help and healing in His own time. We must ask the Lord what He will have us for His cause during our present situation before we get to Glory.

Romans 12:13

"Distributing to the necessity of saints; given to hospitality." God wants the Christians at Rome to be *"distributing to the necessity of saints."* This would include those things that the born-again believers need. In earlier pages, I talked about how I do not believe the Scriptures teach the social gospel. The modernist and liberal churches believe in the social gospel: that is, feed the world, clothe the world, house the world, and get jobs for the world. The New Evangelicals like Billy Graham and others believe in the social gospel. They believe there are two gospels: (1) the gospel of salvation, and (2) the gospel of feeding, clothing, and housing the world. Unfortunately, some fundamentalists are also given over to the social gospel. The Association of Baptists for World Evangelism (ABWE) with its hospitals, fighting HIV and AIDS, building houses, and many other current programs, now believes in the social gospel. I am not against hospitals or food. I eat every day. I am not against having a job. I am not against clothing. I wear clothes. Is that the scriptural mandate for the Christian church? No. That is the issue.

At Calvary Baptist Seminary in Lansdale, Pennsylvania, their annual gathering for fundamentalists discussed the social responsibility for churches and Christians. They wrongly and unscripturally pushed the social gospel.

No Social Gospel!

You cannot ride both "*gospels*," the true and the false. As I mentioned earlier, the Lord Jesus Christ sent His disciples out two-by-two and told them not to take coats, script, food, or money. He told them to eat whatever they were fed. The disciples did not take food to give to people. They took the gospel of salvation by genuine faith in the Lord Jesus Christ. They gave out the good news.

- Romans 15:26

  For it hath pleased them of Macedonia and Achaia to make a certain **contribution for the poor saints** which are at Jerusalem.

If we who are saved had all the money in the world, we could give to the whole world. We do not have enough people to do this. God wants us to take care of our Christian family. These were "*poor saints*" that received the "*contribution*" from the Christian believers in "*Macedonia and Achaia.*"

- 1 Corinthians 16:1-3

  Now **concerning the collection for the saints**, as I have given order to the churches of Galatia, even so do ye. Upon the first *day* of the week let every one of you lay by him in store, as *God* hath prospered him, that there be no gatherings when I come. And when I come, whomsoever ye shall approve by *your* letters, them will I send to bring your liberality unto Jerusalem.

You take the collection on the first day of the week. Then you send it to the "*poor saints*" which are at Jerusalem. This is speaking of believers.

- 2 Corinthians 8:4

  Praying us with much intreaty that we would receive the gift, and *take upon us* the fellowship of **the ministering to the saints**.

- **2 Corinthians 9:1-8**

  For as touching **the ministering   to the saints**, it is superfluous for me to write you: For I know the forwardness of your mind, for which I boast of you to them of Macedonia, that Achaia was ready a year ago; and your zeal hath provoked very many. Yet have I sent the brethren, lest our boasting of you should be in vain in this behalf; that, as I said, ye may be ready: Lest haply if they of Macedonia come with me, and find you unprepared, we (that we say not, ye) should be ashamed in this same confident boasting. Therefore I thought it necessary to exhort the brethren, that they would go before unto you, and make up beforehand your bounty, whereof ye had notice before, that the same might be ready, as *a matter of* bounty, and not as *of* covetousness. But this *I say*, He which soweth sparingly shall reap also sparingly; and he which soweth bountifully shall reap also bountifully. Every man according as he purposeth in his heart, *so let him give*; not grudgingly, or of necessity: for God loveth a cheerful giver. And God *is* able to make all grace abound toward you; that ye, always having all sufficiency in all *things*, may abound to every good work:

  It is for the "*saints*" and believers. It is a clear scriptural injunction.

- **Galatians 6:10**

  As we have therefore opportunity, let us do good unto all *men*, especially unto them who are of the household of faith.

  There is nothing wrong with helping all men, but we are to help "*especially*" the "*household of faith.*"

Social Gospel Is Spreading

If believers have a need, we must help them if we are able. This is what *"distributing to the necessity of saints"* means. Unfortunately, the teaching of the social gospel is penetrating the churches, even those that are called *"fundamental."* I want to be sure that we are clear Scripturally that the primary purpose of the churches is NOT to go ye into all the world and clothe the world, feed the world, or house the world. Rather, it is to *"Go ye into all the world, and preach the gospel to every creature"* (Mark 16:15). That is our primary mission in the Bible-believing churches.

I am not hard-hearted. Everyone needs all these things, but if we do not keep in mind our priorities, our funds, our mission, and our goals, we are going to be in trouble. We will be taken over just like the Salvation Army has been taken over for the pure but false social gospel.

The Salvation Army used to be for the true gospel preaching . Now it is just for the false social gospel of feeding, clothing, and housing the world. There is nothing wrong with it. It is just like the history of the YMCA. It stands for the Young Mens' Christian Association. The YWCA stands for the Young Women' Christian Association. Both the YMCA and the YWCA used to preach the gospel. Now, all they have is athletic programs and swimming pools. I am not against swimming pools, but this is how people pervert things. Very quickly the gospel of salvation is gone. That is wrong. The gospel always must be there, and be primary in all we do.

We Need to Have Hospitality

The next thing the believers in Rome should be doing is that they should be *"given to hospitality."* The literal meaning of the Greek word for *"hospitality,"* PHILONEXIA, is the *"love to strangers."*

There were many Christian people in the early churches, and in Rome, Italy as well. They did not have hotels and motels to stay in as they traveled from place to place. The Christians were to entertain them and give them a place to stay. They were to feed them and give them the use of a bed so they could sleep. In fact, this practice was included in one of the qualifications of a pastor.

- **1 Timothy 3:2**

  A bishop then must be blameless, the husband of one wife, vigilant, sober, of good behaviour, **given to hospitality**, apt to teach;

The very fact that our 𝕭𝖎𝖇𝖑𝖊 𝕱𝖔𝖗 𝕿𝖔𝖉𝖆𝖞 𝕭𝖆𝖕𝖙𝖎𝖘𝖙 𝕮𝖍𝖚𝖗𝖈𝖍 meets in our former living room is an indication that I as the Pastor and my wife both are "*given to hospitality.*" I am glad of that. We have opened our home for the saints of the Lord to worship with us each week. Pastors must be "*given to hospitality.*" They must like people and be willing to care for them. They must be willing to have them in their home.

- **Titus 1:8**

  But **a lover of hospitality**, a lover of good men, sober, just, holy, temperate;

This is also a reference to the qualifications of the pastor/bishop/elder. They must love the strangers and open their home to them, otherwise they are to be disqualified for this office.

Romans 12:14

"Bless them which persecute you: bless, and curse not." These words bring an even more difficult task for the saints of God.

Continue To Bless Persecutors

The Christians are told to "*bless them which persecute you.*" Both the verbs "*bless*" and "*persecute*" are in the Greek present tense. This represents continuous present action. The saved people are to "*continue to bless*" those who "*continually persecute*" them.

This is a very difficult task. The Lord Jesus Christ also talked about this in His Sermon on the Mount.

- Matthew 5:44

  But I say unto you, Love your enemies, **bless them that curse you, do good to them that hate you,** and pray for them which despitefully use you, and persecute you;

That is not easy.

- Luke 6:28

  Bless them that curse you, and pray for them which despitefully use you.

Paul was a person who practiced this. He must have had the power of God on him because it is humanly difficult and impossible. But it is divinely possible.

- 1 Corinthians 4:12

  And labour, working with our own hands: **being reviled, we bless; being persecuted, we suffer it:**

Paul was a man of God.

- James 3:8-10

  But the tongue can no man tame; *it is* an unruly evil, full of deadly poison. Therewith bless we God, even the Father; and therewith curse we men, which are made after the similitude of God. **Out of the same mouth proceedeth blessing and cursing. My brethren, these things ought not so to be**.

That's exactly what it should be.

The Jews were persecuting Paul. When they persecute you, you are to bless them. The Lord Jesus Christ was persecuted by the Romans as well as the Jews. They *"crucified the Lord of Glory"* (1 Corinthians 2:8). Pilate asked: *"What shall I do then with Jesus which is called Christ?"* (Matthew 27:22a). The crowd of *"chief priests and elders"* (Matthew 27:20) yelled out *"Let Him be crucified"* (Matthew 27:22b). That is exactly what they did to our Lord.

In the phrase *"curse not,"* the verb is also in the present tense. It becomes, therefore, a present tense prohibition. As I have said before, there are two types of prohibitions in the Greek language. One uses the aorist tense and would mean *"do not begin an action."* If this were the case, it would mean, *"Don't even begin to curse anybody."* But in this instance, it is a Greek present tense prohibition. The Greek present tense means to stop an action already in progress.

Stop Cursing the Persecutors

Paul is saying to these Roman Christians to *"stop your cursing those that are persecuting you."* Apparently, the Christians at Rome were cursing out and ridiculing those who were persecuting them. They were making a big scene. Paul tells them to *"stop it!"* He says the same thing to us if this is our situation.

Romans 12:15

"Rejoice with them that do rejoice, and weep with them that weep." This is a verse that demands what we call Christian sympathy and even empathy. Believers at Rome and believers today are to *"rejoice with them that do rejoice."* One reaction often found in people who observe others who are *"rejoicing"* is jealousy. They are jealous at the other person's joy because maybe they are sad. Jealousy is not to be our reaction. We are to *"rejoice with them."*

Perhaps the next order is even much more difficult to follow. It is to *"weep with them that weep."* We are not to turn our back on them. Those who have sorrow in their hearts and lives are weeping for various things. Maybe some of those you know are weeping about certain things. We as Christians should sympathize with them and enter into their suffering. This is what the Lord Jesus Christ did at Lazarus' tomb.

The shortest verse in the English Bible is *"Jesus wept"* (John 11:35). Why did the Lord Jesus Christ weep? He knew what He was going to do. He knew He was going to raise Lazarus from the dead. He knew He was going to say, *"Lazarus come forth"* (John 11:43). He knew that Lazarus was going to come forth bound with grave clothes. The Lord Jesus Christ said to those gathered around Lazarus, *"loose him, and let him go"* (John 11:44). The reason the Lord wept was in deep sympathy for Mary and Martha. They were weeping because they had lost their brother. In like manner, we who are saved must have Christian sympathy for those who *"weep."* Some say the Lord Jesus Christ wept because of their unbelief that He could raise Lazarus from the dead.

Romans 12:16

"Be of the same mind one toward another. Mind not high things, but condescend to men of low estate. Be not wise in your own conceits." In this verse also there is an element of Christian sympathy. The English word, *"sympathy,"* is from two Greek words, SYN and PATHOS. SYN is *"with"* and PATHOS is *"feeling."* So the word means a *"feeling with"* someone else, putting yourself in their place. That is what we need. It is not always there, even among saved people.

Be of the Same Mind

We are to *"be of the same mind one toward another."* We are to be sympathetic. Are they rejoicing? Are they weeping? Whatever their temperament or predicament, we need to be of the *"same mind"* with them. We need to be on the same page with them.

The other part of that verse urges born-again people to, *"Mind not high things."* This is a prohibition once again in the Greek present tense. It means to stop an action already in progress. Paul is telling these Roman Christians to *"stop minding high things."* From the structure of the sentence, we can see that they were doing this.

Stop Minding High Things

The Christians at Rome were minding high things. What do we mean minding *"high things?"* I think they were trying to have fellowship with the high society. They were trying to rub shoulders with the high group and let the little people out in the cold.

Paul wanted them to stop that wrong activity. Stop paying attention to those who are high and mighty. Those who are way up in the high echelons might be more handsome, more affluent, better dressed, or more intelligent than the rest of the people.

On the contrary, these believers were to *"condescend to men of low estate."* Those were just the common and normal people. That is what God says. There is nothing wrong with people of *"low estate."* If they love the Lord they are as good as anyone else. Under the Lord we are all equal as far as our relationship with the Lord is concerned. So, stop minding these high things by striving for people of high station and success as your close friends. On the contrary, be sympathetic and have sweet fellowship with those even of lower estate who are a little bit less well-off perhaps. Maybe they are a little bit less intelligent, less beautiful or handsome, or even ugly. Maybe they are deformed. Maybe they only have one leg.

Stop Being Conceited!

Here is another Greek present prohibition. It means to stop an action already in progress. Paul was telling these believers to *"stop being wise in your own conceits."* They were apparently all puffed up and filled with self, and selfish things, rather than what they could do for someone else. Paul says *"Stop doing that and being wise in your own conceit. Think of others."*

Romans 12:17

"Recompense to no man evil for evil. Provide things honest in the sight of all men." The Greek word for *"recompense"* is APODIDOMI. It means:

> *" to deliver, to give away for one's own profit what is one's own, to sell; to pay off, discharge what is due; a debt, wages, tribute, taxes, produce due; things promised under oath; conjugal duty; to render account; to give back, restore; to requite, recompense in a good or a bad sense."*

This verb is in the Greek present tense. It is a present tense prohibition. It means stop doing the thing that you are doing. This is something that the Christians at Rome were guilty of. They were *"recompensing"* and giving back evil for evil. That's a normal and natural thing. That is what people of the world do. That is in the Old Testament law of Moses, *"eye for eye, tooth for tooth*" (Exodus 23:23-25; Matthew 5:38). That was justice in the Old Testament, but in the New Testament God has a higher standard for the born-again Christians.

That is why the Lord Jesus Christ summed up the Old Testament when He stated what we call the golden rule, "*whatsoever ye would that men should do to you, do ye even so to them: for this is the law and the prophets.*" In other words, do not render evil for evil. I remember what a lady in *Bethel Baptist Church* used to say with her red hair flashing, "*I don't get mad I get even.*" That is the natural thing. She was kidding of course. People might say, "*If somebody does me evil I will get back at them.*" That is where road-rage comes in. People get killed and shot on the highway because of this. One of our friends from Washington state was not going fast enough on the highway in Philadelphia for a young man. The boy stopped his car in front of my friend, in anger. He got angry and stopped dead right in front of his car and Brother Gammelgard had to step on his brakes. God says stop it. Don't continue to recompense and give back evil for evil.

No Thievery Among the Saints

The last part of the verse says that believers are to "*provide things honest in the sight of all men.*" There should be no dishonesty or thievery in any way among saved people. This provision must be "*in the sight of all men.*" No one should be able to accuse you of stealing.

Make it clear that you are on the up- and-up and not on the questionable side of life. We are never out of the sight of the Lord. Not only are we to be honest in the sight of the Lord, but also we are to be honest in the sight of other people so that they cannot criticize us in any way. We do not want people to say, "*I do not know about that fellow. I am not sure he is honest.*" Many evangelists are getting into trouble about money. There are people who are taking money which does not belong to them. Sad to say, there is too much fraud in the so-called "Christian community." We must be "*honest in the sight*" of all men, both lost and saved alike. I remember a Baptist Pastor who stole money in one church, and yet is currently serving as a Pastor in another Baptist church. I believe he has disqualified himself because of his thievery.

Romans 12:18

"If it be possible, as much as lieth in you, live peaceably with all men." Notice that there is an *"if"* clause in this sentence. Paul stated, *"If it be possible."* Why do you think this clause is there? I think it takes into consideration about *"men"* who do not want to *"live peaceably"* with you. If this is the case, just try your best, *"as much as lieth in you."* I cannot prevent somebody else from getting angry with me, hating me, and being at war with me. I cannot do anything about this but I will try my best to *"live peaceably"* with these people, even though they do not want to *"live peaceably"* with me.

- Luke 6:26

  Woe unto you, when all men shall speak well of you! for so did their fathers to the false prophets.

  We must have a strong belief in the Scriptures otherwise we will be like the false prophets whom everyone loved. You cannot always have everyone loving you if you are preaching Scripturally and they are living in error. If you preach right and they are living wrong, they are not going to be praising you for standing for truth.

- Matthew 24:9

  Then shall they deliver you up to be afflicted, and shall kill you: and **ye shall be hated of all nations for my name's sake.**

- Proverbs 16:7

  When a man's ways please the LORD, he maketh even his enemies to be at peace with him.

Being At Peace With All

That *"peace"* does not always mean your enemies love you, but they will stay away from you. They know what you have and they are not going to tangle with you. They know you are right, they do not agree, but they will be at peace with you.

Look at that clause, *"as much as lieth in you."* This implies that some have one thing that *"lieth in them"* and others have other things that *"lieth in them.*" Saved people are all different. We should not make excuses such as "*I am Scotch, Dutch, or German, so I cannot help myself.*" That is one excuse that some make. We of the **Bible For Today Baptist Church** should try our very best to "*live peaceably with all men.*" Being in the Greek present tense, this implies that we are to "*continuously live peaceably with all men.*" That is what God would have us so that we would not dishonor the Lord or His gospel.

Romans 12:19

"Dearly beloved, avenge not yourselves, but *rather* give place unto wrath: for it is written, Vengeance *is* mine; I will repay, saith the Lord." In this verse there is a very kindly address that Paul used for the Christians at Rome. He called them "*dearly beloved.*" That is a very intimate phrase. Paul had never met these believers, but because they are "*in Christ*" and He is Beloved, so they are beloved. They are not only beloved, but they are "*dearly beloved.*"

Any of us who are born-again are beloved to each other and to the Lord. Paul addresses these Christians in Rome in this way before he has a word of criticism of them. He says to them, "*avenge not yourselves.*" This is a Greek present tense prohibition and signifies that the people involved are to stop an action already begun. Paul tells them to "*quit avenging yourselves.*" They had been doing that. I am sure that such a command did not ingratiate Paul to these Christians at Rome. He was smacking them on the hand. He is criticizing them. None of us like criticism.

The Meaning of "Avenge"

That Greek word for "*avenge*" is EKDIKEO. It means:

" *to vindicate one's right, do one justice; to protect, defend, one person from another; to avenge a thing; to punish a person for a thing.*"

In the Old Testament there are many things that were wrong and should be "*avenged.*"

- **Exodus 23:4-5**

  If thou meet thine enemy's ox or his ass going astray, thou shalt surely bring it back to him again. If thou see the ass of him that hateth thee lying under his burden, and wouldest forbear to help him, thou shalt surely help with him.

  That is not the person's avenging himself on his enemy. He is obliged to return the animals. God is the One Who gives vengeance. He will set things right.

- **Psalm 94:1**

  O LORD God, to whom vengeance belongeth; O God, to whom vengeance belongeth, shew thyself.

Do Not Avenge Yourself

We cannot satisfactorily *"avenge ourselves."* If we go after someone who hates us by bumping his car, or calling him names, is that going to stop his hatred? No! It will probably get worse.

There is an increase and an acceleration of evil when you start fooling around with the flesh. The flesh just loves to mix-it-up, as they say. Pretty soon you end up in a brawl, and that is not good for anybody. At the Great White Throne Judgment when the Lord Jesus Christ will judge the sinners of all the world from all the ages, then fair judgment will be meted out. He will repay every single thing that anyone has done amiss. The judgment of the eternal fire of Hell awaits them if they have rejected the Lord Jesus Christ as their Saviour.

What is the answer of the Bible to *"avenging"* yourself? The answer is *"give place unto wrath"* (Romans 12:13). In other words, just move over and give *"wrath"* a little space. Do not let *"wrath"* get to you. You need to bite your tongue. Maybe when you were younger that is what you did. You can do that even when you are older. There are some things in our older years that are worse than in our younger years. I know young people often have more anger, wrath, and explosive emotions than the older people. There are some of these old people that are just as angry, mean, and ugly. We must keep ourselves from these people. We who are older as well as those who are younger, must keep sweet. It is hard to do sometimes. The *"fruit of the Spirit is love, joy, peace, longsuffering, gentleness, goodness, faith, meekness, temperance* [self-control]" (Galatians 5:22-23). That is what the Lord has to do with young and old Christians alike. We must *"give place unto wrath"* (Romans 12:13). Just let it go its way. Just let it blow over.

Then Paul quotes the Old Testament. He begins the quotation in this verse with the phrase, "*it is written.*" Psalm 94:1 or Nahum 1:2 could be the verses referred to. Whenever this phrase is used, it is in the Greek perfect tense. The perfect tense indicates an action that happened in the past, continues into the present, and will continue on into the future. When God says, "*it is written,*" that means the words referred to were written in the past and preserved to the present and future. The same Hebrew and Aramaic Words which were written right down letter for letter are preserved to the time when Paul was writing. These Words will continue to be preserved into the future. That is why I believe in Biblical preservation of the Hebrew, Aramaic, and Greek Words of the originals.

That is one thing that those seven schools on a recent video do not believe in. There were nine different people from seven schools which spoke on this video. I have a copy of this video and my answer to it. It is available as **BFT #2928-P**. It is 80 pages for a gift of **$7.00 + $3.00 S&H**. The chairman of this group, David Doran from Detroit Baptist Seminary said "*All of you men believe in Bible preservation don't you?*" All the men nod their heads and agreed that they believed in what they say is "*Bible preservation.*"

Re-Definition of Preservation

However, they cleverly and deceitfully re-define the term "*Bible preservation*" to mean that they have the "<u>*Word*</u> *of God,*" but not the "<u>*Words*</u> *of God.*" To them, there is a difference. Though in the Bible, these terms are equated, these fundamentalist schools have re-defined this term which has resulted in confusion and clever deception. These men and their schools falsely define and limit the "*Word*" of God to mean only the "*message, ideas, thoughts, or concepts,*" but not the "*Words*" of God.

That is why one of these men, Kevin Bauder, at this writing, President of Central Baptist Seminary in the Minneapolis, Minnesota, area could make such a contradictory statement. He said he could hold up the King James Bible and the Textus Receptus and say that this is the "*Word*" of God. Then he said he could also hold up the New American Standard Version and say that is the "*Word*" of God. These two statements cannot possibly be understood unless there has been a drastic re-definition of the term "*Word.*" Why do I say that?

The Serious Deviation of the NASV

The Greek text underlying the New American Standard Version differs from the Greek text underlying the King James Bible in 5,604 places for a total of over 8,000 Greek Words.

This information is found in **BFT #3084.** It is 535 large pages by Dr. Jack Moorman of London, England. It is available for a gift of **$54.00 + $6.00 S&H.**

How can both of those be the "*Word*" of God if you mean the "*Words*" of God and yet have over 8,000 differences in their Greek texts? They believe in semantics and they have the shadings of meanings right down to a fine tuning. Things that differ are not the same. Therefore how can a man hold up the King James Bible and The New American Standard Version and say they are both the "*Word*" of God unless they re-define "*Word*." They mean only the "*message, thoughts, ideas, or concepts*" of God, but not the very Hebrew, Aramaic, and Greek "*Words*" of God.

Romans 12:20

"Therefore if thine enemy hunger, feed him; if he thirst, give him drink: for in so doing thou shalt heap coals of fire on his head." Do you have any "*enemies*"? I am sure that each of us does. Can we count them on one hand or two? Do we need our fingers and our toes also to count them? What is a "*non-friend*"? Is a "*non-friend*" also an "*enemy*"? Someone who is a friend is obviously not an "*enemy.*" When we know a person well, and know everything about them, sometimes it is harder to be a friend to them than before. If you just see people superficially, it is easier to say they are a friend. When we know the ins-and-outs, sometimes it is harder to say they are our friend. I hope people will not say that about us. I hope that our private life is every bit as good and as Christian as our public life.

Friendship

Oh, the comfort--the inexpressible comfort

Of feeling safe with a person,

Having neither to weigh thoughts,

Nor measure words--but pouring them

All right out--just as they are--

Chaff and grain together--

Certain that a faithful hand will

Take and sift them--

Keep what is worth keeping--And with the breath of kindness

Blow the rest away.

By Dinah Craik

But what should born-again Christians do with their *"enemies"*? Paul said: *"Therefore if thine enemy hunger, feed him; if he thirst, give him drink: for in so doing thou shalt heap coals of fire on his head."* In other words, if you take this advice, your enemies will have more judgment on top of them at the judgment of God than before, because you have not done anything against them. You have helped them. That is the most upsetting thing that an enemy can have happen to him. He will not know how to handle that. It is very upsetting to them.

Returning Good For Evil

They cannot understand how anyone can return good for evil. That does not figure for our *"enemies."* That does not compute. They will be dumbfounded. They will not know what to say or how to act. If we return evil to their evil, then they will know how to act. They will expect this to happen. Then they will do more evil to us.

The principle of helping your "*enemy*" is also taught in the Old Testament. If your enemy's ox goes astray, you must "*surely bring it back to him*" (Exodus 23:4). That's God's principle even in the Old Testament.

I could list a number of names of people who have made me their "*enemy*" through the years. You could do the same. People have done us evil all of our lives. If we live soundly for our Lord Jesus Christ, some will without doubt continue to do us evil. What should our reaction be to this? Do not stop living for your Saviour just because others are doing evil to you. Stick with the Lord and He will repay and He will honor your ministry. Do not let your enemies take away your blessing and victory in your Redeemer.

Romans 12:21

"Be not overcome of evil, but overcome evil with good." Once again we meet up with a Greek present tense prohibition. As before, this indicates an action already in progress that must be stopped. Paul is saying here, "*stop being overcome of evil*." These Christians at Rome were being "*overcome*" and conquered by evil. Paul says, "*Stop it.*" The Greek word for "*overcome*" is NIKAO. It means:

> " *to conquer; to carry off the victory, come off victorious; of Christ, victorious over all His foes; of Christians, that hold fast their faith even unto death against the power of their foes, and temptations and persecutions; when one is arraigned or goes to law, to win the case, maintain one's cause.*"

We use this root in English in "*Nike*" missiles or "*Nike*" shoes. They apparently were being completely absorbed by evil. Paul is saying: "*Stop letting the evil overcome you, conquer you, and be a victor over you. On the contrary, overcome evil with good. Conquer that old evil by means of good.*" That is the Christian way and the Biblical way. People used to call Christians "*sissies.*" Maybe they still do. The early Christians would not reject the Lord Jesus Christ when under persecution. They stood for the Lord and were burned at the stake because of it. Their persecutors thought these Christians were "*simple.*" Perhaps they were "*simple.*" But one thing is certain. they "*overcame evil with good.*" They continued to "*carry off the victory.*" Whatever evil comes our way, we are to "*overcome*" it with that which is "*good*" and pleasing to the Lord Jesus Christ. That will "*overcome*" anything that is against us, and God will be pleased with us. Is this not what we who are saved are after? We should want our God to be pleased with us. We should not want simply to go through life with smooth sailing. We should want His blessing, whatever kind of "*sailing*" that might mean.

When we who are redeemed go into the presence of God, I hope that we would want to hear from our Saviour, *"Well done, thou good and faithful servant"* (Matthew 25:21). Forget whatever *"evil"* might come to you. You just keep living faithfully for the Lord Jesus Christ and He will honor you for it.

Romans

Chapter Thirteen

Romans 13:1

"Let every soul be subject unto the higher powers. For there is no power but of God: the powers that be are ordained of God." This chapter discusses a very important and often misunderstood topic, *"What are Bible-Defined Rulers?"* What are rulers? What is government? What are the *"higher powers"*? Who are we to obey? Who are we not to obey? These questions will be discussed by Paul in this chapter.

A few years ago a book came out called *"A Fearful Master."* It takes a documented and critical look at the United Nations. The author took his title from a simile about government used by an earlier patriot in our country who said: *"Government is like fire--a useful servant, but a FEARFUL MASTER."* Fire can cook our food, burn our garbage, keep us warm, but it can also get away from us and burn our houses down. Government can also get away from us and turn to tyranny and despotism. Let us see what the Bible says concerning this.

When Paul wrote *"let every soul be subject,"* he is talking principally to the believers at Rome, though it can be applicable to all people, even though they may be non-Christian. The Greek word for *"subject"* is HYPOTASSO. It means:

"to arrange under, to subordinate; to subject, put in subjection; to subject one's self, obey; to submit to one's control; to yield to one's admonition or advice; to obey, be subject. It is a Greek military term meaning 'to arrange [troop divisions] *in a military fashion under the command of a leader.' In non-military use, it was 'a*

voluntary attitude of giving in, cooperating, assuming responsibility, and carrying a burden.'"

The verb is in the Greek present tense indicating that those addressed should be continuously *"subject"* to these *"higher powers."* There is much controversy about what this means. Paul gives a partial definition of *"powers"* in this verse. He says that *"there is no power but of God."* The Greek word for *"power"* is EXOUSIA. It has a wide range of meanings:

"power of choice, liberty of doing as one pleases; leave or permission; physical and mental power; the ability or strength with which one is endued, which he either possesses or exercises; the power of authority (influence) and of right (privilege); the power of rule or government (the power of him whose will and commands must be submitted to by others and obeyed); universally; authority over mankind; specifically; the power of judicial decisions; of authority to manage domestic affairs'; metonymically; a thing subject to authority or rule; jurisdiction; one who possesses authority; a ruler, a human magistrate; the leading and more powerful among created beings superior to man, spiritual potentates; a sign of the husband's authority over his wife; the veil with which propriety required a woman to cover herself; the sign of regal authority, a crown."

This gives the source of *"power."*

Source of Power and Authority

God Himself is the source of all Biblical *"power"* and authority. He is also the One Who gives that *"power"* and authority to all different elements of society.

We must be careful about the definition of the meaning of *"power"* as used in the Bible or of *"government"* which could be considered as Biblical. Are all governments Biblical? No, I do not believe they are. They do not all meet the Bible's definitions of *"powers."* I will explain how the Bible defines Biblical government *"powers."* Paul wrote that *"the powers that be are ordained of God."* God is the source of all order and authority. Such *"powers"* are *"ordained of God."* The Greek word for *"ordained"* is TASSO. It means:

"to put in order, to station; to place in a certain order, to arrange, to assign a place, to appoint; to assign (appoint) a thing to one; to

appoint, ordain, order; to appoint on one's own responsibility or authority; to appoint mutually, i.e. agree upon."

God wants everything to fall in line with His proper and rightful authority which He has "*ordained.*" The Lord Jesus Christ spoke of His "*power*" given unto Him.

- **Matthew 28:18**

  And Jesus came and spake unto them, saying, **All power is given unto me in Heaven and in earth.**

Governmental authorities can not outstrip the Lord Jesus Christ in "*power.*" He has the highest power. God the Father, God the Son, and God the Holy Spirit have the highest power. There is no power but from God. God is the one Who grants this power. The Lord Jesus Christ said "*all power is given unto me in Heaven and in earth.*" These authorities, these higher superior things, are higher than we are. These things which are more superior than we, are what is being talked about here. This "*power*" or authority is "*ordained*" and set apart, and arranged by the Lord Himself. We do not get the definition of what "*power*" is and what rulers are until we get to Verse 3.

Romans 13:2

"Whosoever therefore resisteth the power, resisteth the ordinance of God: and they that resist shall receive to themselves damnation." When we resist God's "*power,*" we "*resist the ordinance of God.*" When people will not receive the gospel of the Lord Jesus Christ that He died for our sins, that He was buried, and that He rose again and say they do not want it, that is resisting the very "*power*" of God. That is the greatest "*power*" of all, God's ability to save us.

- **Romans 1:16**

  For I am not ashamed of the gospel of Christ: for it is **the power of God unto salvation to every one that believeth;** to the Jew first, and also to the Greek.

All power and authority comes from God.

When Paul wrote of "*resisting the power,*" I realize that he is talking about earthly power here, but there is a higher "*power*" than all earthly power. One day the Lord Jesus Christ will assume that earthly "*power*" to rule and reign upon this earth for 1000 years in the millennium.

Christ's 1,000-Year Reign

I believe in a millennium, a 1,000-year reign by the Lord Jesus Christ, where He will be the "King of Kings and Lord of Lords" (Revelation 17:14; 19:16). All the kings and all the lords will be under Him. He will be the "*power*."

God has placed **proper** authorities in place, not **improper** authorities. Improper authorities are not from God. They are from the Devil. The Devil has some "*powers*" also (Romans 8:38-39; Ephesians 6:12; Colossians 2:15.) When the Lord Jesus Christ came to earth, He "*spoiled principalities and powers*," defeating them, "*nailing it to His cross*" (Colossians 2:14-15).

Notice the words, "*Whosoever therefore resisteth the power, resisteth the ordinance of God: and they that resist shall receive to themselves damnation*." What do these words mean? If the "*power*" is genuinely following the Biblical pattern, people who "*resist the power*" are truly "*resisting the ordinance of God*." As such, they will "*receive to themselves damnation*."

Unbiblical "Powers"

But what if these "*powers*" are unbiblical? This is where valid "*civil disobedience*" is proper. This is what Peter meant when he said, "*we ought to obey God rather than men*" (Acts 5:29b). As born-again Christians, we should obey laws and rules that are not against our Bibles. But if those laws and rules interfere with our worship of the Lord Jesus Christ that is another matter. We must obey God first and foremost. We will look at some examples in Scripture that illustrate this. When the civil law, the "*power*," is interfering with God's "*power*," which is the "*highest power*," this is when "*we ought to obey God rather than men*" (Acts 5:29b).

In the Book of Exodus (Exodus 1:17) the Jewish midwives did not obey Pharaoh's command to kill the male babies. The rule from Pharaoh to the midwives was that when a male child was born to a Hebrew he was to be killed. The midwives did not listen to that "*power*." This was false "*power*." It was against the will of God. If every Jewish boy had been killed, the Lord Jesus Christ would have never been born. God knew about this. The midwives feared God. When they saw the Jewish male babies born, they did not kill them. One of the babies they kept alive was Moses. His mother nursed him for awhile. When she could no longer keep him quiet, she put him in a little ark in the Nile River (Exodus 2:3). When Pharaoh's daughter saw that little Hebrew boy in the river, she took him home and raised him as a prince in the house of Pharaoh. That was justifiable *"civil disobedience"* against an unjust law against God's Word.

Another example is found in the Book of Esther. Queen Vashti was ordered by her husband, who was the King, to come and appear before a group of drunken men. She was ordered to show these men *"her beauty"* (Esther 1:11). Perhaps she had to take off all her clothes. I do not know. This would have been wrong and immoral. So Vashti refused to obey that king because it was a wrong *"power."* She was not going to be like a prostitute or some street walker in front of all these men. She refused to come to this meeting because it was an unjust and ungodly order (Esther 1:12). Because of her stand, Vashti was removed as a queen.

Obeying God Rather than Men

Quite often there is a penalty when we refuse to obey an unscriptural law, choosing instead *"to obey God rather than men"* (Acts 5:29b). There are usually consequences that follow this action. We must be willing to deal with those consequences if we follow the Lord and not men.

Then remember the penalty that had to be paid by Daniel. There were 120 princes and over them were three presidents. Daniel was the first president (Daniel 6:1-3). The king saw in Daniel an excellent spirit (Daniel 6:3). Because of this, the king was going to make Daniel *"over the whole realm"* (Daniel 6:3). The other two presidents did not like Daniel. They developed a plan to do away with him.

- **Daniel 6:5**

  Then said these men, **We shall not find any occasion against this Daniel, except we find** *it* **against him concerning the law of his God.**

What a testimony. Would to God that each of us would have the same kind of testimony.

Their plan was to ask the king to make a law that no one could "*ask a petition of God or man for thirty days*" (Daniel 6:7).

Daniel's Penalty for Bowing Down

The penalty for praying was to be cast into a "*den of lions.*" Daniel refused to obey this unscriptural law. He went to his home, the windows being open, and three times a day he faced Jerusalem and prayed unto his God (Daniel 6:10).

He did not alter his habit of prayer in any way, despite the king's decree and the penalty of death by the lions. These two other presidents observed Daniel as he was praying, went to the king and reported to him what they had seen and heard. Though the king did not want to do it, because of his own decree, he put Daniel into the den of lions. The Lord "*shut the lions' mouths*" (Daniel 6:22). This showed the tremendous power of God because Daniel was righteous. The king did not sleep that night (Daniel 6:18). In the morning the king got right up and went to that den. He asked Daniel if his God was able to "*deliver him from the lions*" (Daniel 6:20). Daniel replied, "*My God hath sent his angel, and hath shut the lions' mouths, that they have not hurt me: forasmuch as before him innocency was found in me; and also before thee, O king, have I done no hurt.*"

The king was glad for Daniel's deliverance. He brought the men who had accused Daniel and threw them into the den of lions. The hungry lions broke their bones even before they came to the "*bottom of the den*" (Daniel 6:24).

Then another example of disobeying an unscriptural law concerned the three Hebrew servants who were friends of Daniel.

- **Daniel 3:6**

  And **whoso falleth not down and worshippeth** shall the same hour be cast into the midst of a burning fiery furnace.

The Penalty for Standing Up

Shadrach, Meshach, and Abednego were told by the king to fall down and worship this huge statue of himself every time the music played. That was the unscriptural law made by Nebuchadnezzar. These three men were Hebrew men. They were worshipers of the Lord. They were not about to bow to any image.

The first commandment says they were not to worship any graven image (Exodus 20:5). They knew this commandment and they stood firm. The king tried to get them to bow down again, but they still would not bow down. The punishment was the fiery furnace. They were thrown into the fiery furnace. They said, *"If it be so, our God whom we serve is able to deliver us from the burning fiery furnace, and he will deliver us out of thine hand, O king"* (Daniel 3:17). They were thrown into the furnace which was heated seven times hotter than ever before (Daniel 3:19).

Later, the king went to the furnace and looked into it. He looked into the furnace and remembered that they had *"cast three men bound into the midst of the fire"* (Daniel 3:24).

Protection From the Son of God

The king saw *"four men"* instead of three. He said that *"the form of the fourth is like the Son of God"* (Daniel 3:25). That is the King James Bible's accurate translation from the Hebrew. The NIV and the NASV and other modern versions wrongly say the fourth was like *"a son of the gods,"* thus removing what we call a *"Christophany"* or an appearance of the Lord Jesus Christ before His incarnation.

The Lord Jesus Christ was there protecting these people from the fires of that furnace. All three of these men came out of the furnace without even the smell of fire on their garments. No part of their clothing was burnt. God spared them from the consequences of disobedience of the king's unscriptural order.

Another example of refusing to obey unscriptural orders concerns the New Testament apostles. The council and the high priest reminded them that they were not to *"teach in this name."* Peter and the other apostles told him *"we ought to obey God rather than men"* (Acts 5:29b).

● **Acts 5:42**

And daily in the temple, and in every house, **they ceased not to teach and preach Jesus Christ.**

Notice that they had teaching and preaching in houses in the New Testament, just like we do here in our 𝕭𝖎𝖇𝖑𝖊 𝕱𝖔𝖗 𝕿𝖔𝖉𝖆𝖞 𝕭𝖆𝖕𝖙𝖎𝖘𝖙 𝕮𝖍𝖚𝖗𝖈𝖍. We are going to continue to *"teach and preach"* the Lord Jesus Christ and His Words. There are rules in God's Word for disobeying unlawful, unjust, ungodly orders and rules. These orders are not Biblical and therefore do not come under the classification of being what the Bible calls *"higher powers."* We should always try to do that which is honoring to our Saviour.

Romans 13:3

"For rulers are not a terror to good works, but to the evil. Wilt thou then not be afraid of the power? do that which is good, and thou shalt have praise of the same:" In this verse and those that follow, we find a clear definition of what the Bible calls genuine *"rulers."* Notice this definition. *"For rulers are not a terror to good works, but to the evil."* According to this Biblical definition of *"rulers,"* does this fit with Adolph Hitler, Joseph Stalin, Fidel Castro, Mao Tse-Tung, Saddam Hussein, and other terrorists? Of course it does not fit. These *"rulers"* are not Biblical *"rulers"* and do not come into the definition of this chapter. Rather than being **not** *"a terror to good works,"* they **are** a *"terror to good works."*

Definition of Biblical Government

We must understand what the definition is. Would to God we would have good and solid Biblical government. In fact, if this is the case, when we *"do that which is good"* will *"have praise"* of that government. If, however, we do not have Biblical rulers, we must always follow God's Words, rather than man's.

• **Acts 5:29b**

Then Peter and the *other* apostles answered and said, **We ought to obey God rather than men.**

That is an important verse. If someone tells us to do evil, whether it is our mate, whether it is our boss where we work, whether it is family, whether it is the government, whether it is the president, whoever tells us to do evil, God commands that *"We ought to obey God rather than men"* (Acts 5:29b). When men and rulers do not contradict God's Words, this is all right. We should follow their wishes. We can then be free here in the United States to obey the *"powers that be."* There is not a problem there. If the *"rulers"* want us to drive on the right side of the street instead of the left that is fine, but you must not do this in England where they drive on the left side of the street. However, if anyone wants us to act contrary to the laws of God, *"we ought to obey God rather than men."*

Consequences of Obeying God

We must always bear in mind, however, that there will always be consequences for obeying God rather than men. Many people will not like us if we obey God rather than men.

I believe in the pretribulation rapture (or snatching away) of the born-again. After the true believers are raptured and taken away, the seven-year tribulation will occur. There is going to be a penalty for not worshiping the false image of the Satanic beast. Those who will not worship that image will be put to death (Revelation 13:15). There are always consequences for doing the right thing.

As Bob Jones, Sr. used to say, *"Do right until the stars fall."* Someday they are going to fall, but they have not fallen yet. Dr. Jones also used to say, *"Never do wrong in order to get a chance to do right."* Many people follow the philosophy called *"casuistry."* That is a philosophical name for the belief that *"the end justifies the means."* Many people have taken this as their method of operation. The end might be a beautiful thing. People following this philosophy will take any means in order to reach that end, even if it means stealing, adultery, compromise, or something else. They believe if it is a good end, they will do it.

That is the problem, among many other things, that I have with Evangelist Billy Graham. He started out all right in 1949. All of a sudden he began holding hands with the modernists, liberals, and Roman Catholics. He justified it by saying he was evangelizing and preaching the gospel so that more will be saved. But we should never do wrong in order to get a chance to do right. The end, beautiful evangelizing and people getting saved, does not justify the bad means to achieve it. The means must be right as well as the end.

Romans 13:4

"For he is the minister of God to thee for good. But if thou do that which is evil, be afraid; for he beareth not the sword in vain: for he is the minister of God, a revenger to execute wrath upon him that doeth evil." If a man is the Biblical type of ruler, he is called *"the minister of God"* for *"good."* If, on the other hand, you have a Biblical ruler and you *"do that which is evil, be afraid; for he beareth not the sword in vain."* That Greek word for *"sword"* is MACHAIRA. It is a short sword of about eighteen inches in length. It was used for capital punishment by Rome as their method of execution before and after the crucifixion. Biblically sound government punishes evil and rewards good. Do that which is good, but be afraid if you do evil, because capital punishment could be used against you. Capital punishment for first degree murder is in the Old Testament and in the New Testament as well. This is one of the verses which shows this teaching.

A Biblically sound *"ruler"* is called *"the minister of God, a revenger to execute wrath upon him that doeth evil."* The following names that have been *"rulers"* have not executed *"wrath upon him that doeth evil."* On the contrary, they were evil themselves. This would include such people as Hitler, Malosovich, Stalin, Castro, Mao Tse-Tung, Sadam Hussein and many others. They are certainly not executing wrath against evil. They are executing wrath against those that do good. The saved Christian is under no obligation to obey their evil wishes.

Let us look at a few rulers in Scripture, even though they might not have been saved, that have done good, and therefore could be called *"ministers of God."*

A Good Ruler

The first one that comes to mind is the Pharaoh who was in charge of Egypt in Joseph's day. He elevated Joseph to the second in command of the whole kingdom (Genesis 41:39-41). He put him in charge when the seven years of famine were predicted. He was a good Pharaoh.

Nebuchadnezzar glorified the Lord for His majesty and goodness (Daniel 4:37). The Lord made his fingernails grow like claws. He looked like some kind of a beast. Finally he realized that he was not in charge of everything, but it was the Lord that ruled in the affairs of men (Daniel 4:32). He was bowed down and repentant (Daniel 4:37). He finally turned out all right.

Darius who appointed Daniel as the first president of three presidents was a good ruler (Daniel 6:2). Cyrus of Persia in the Book of Ezra was used by the Lord to send back the Jews to rebuild the temple and he was a good ruler (2 Chronicles 36:23; Ezra 1:2). Artaxerxes in Nehemiah's day was also used of the Lord to send back the Jews to build the walls and the temple itself (Ezra 6:14). King Agrippa was also a good king.

- **Acts 26:32**

   Then said Agrippa unto Festus, **This man might have been set at liberty, if he had not appealed unto Caesar.**

Agrippa listened to Paul. He listened fully. He listened to the Jews' accusations against him for just preaching the gospel of Christ. He was a fair governor and ruler even in Paul's day.

Christ, The Fairest Ruler of All

The Lord Jesus Christ will be the fairest ruler of all in His Millennial Kingdom when He rules for 1,000 years upon this earth.

He certainly will be a fair and good ruler. The Lord Jesus Christ will rule with a rod of iron, but that will be all right because He will be fair and just. The Lord Jesus Christ will be the ruler. Everything will be fair and in His power.

He will be a monarch ruling, but He will be fair because He is the Son of God, and God the Son. This will be a different situation when He rules and reigns in the Millennium. There will be 1,000 years of peace.

Romans 13:5

"Wherefore ye must needs be subject, not only for wrath, but also for conscience sake." To all good and Biblically defined *"rulers"* we believers should be *"subject."* There are two reasons for being in subjection to good *"rulers."* The first reason is because of the *"wrath"* of the ruler if we do evil. This *"wrath"* might lead to our imprisonment or even death. The second reason is *"for conscience sake."* We should want to have a clear *"conscience"* at all times.

- **Acts 24:16**

  And herein do I exercise myself, **to have always a conscience void of offence toward God, and *toward* men**.

  We should try to obey the laws and the rules whatever they might be so that we would not have a guilty *"conscience."* We break rules sometimes because we are human, like the speed limits here and there. If we have cruise control it is helpful. It is helpful to me because I don't have to wonder or worry about the speed I am going. We must be *"subject"* to proper rules and proper laws. Not only for *"wrath"* because we are going to get penalized, but also because we want to keep a good *"conscience"* before the Lord. That is important indeed.

Romans 13:6

"For for this cause pay ye tribute also: for they are God's ministers, attending continually upon this very thing." Every April 15th we in the United States have a date with the International Revenue Service (IRS). This is when our taxes are due. Because of the need for good and Biblical *"rulers,"* Paul ordered the believers: *"pay ye tribute."* The Greek word for *"tribute"* is PHOROS. It means: *"tribute, esp. the annual tax levied upon houses, lands, and persons."*

The reason for our payment of taxes is because these good and Biblical rulers are to be *"attending continually upon this very thing."* This is one of the problems with our governments, both city, county, state, and federal. They are not waiting continually on this very thing.

Two Duties of Biblical Government

This is broken down in two headings:

1.   praising those who do "*good*" and

2.   condemning and judging those who do "*evil.*"

I think it is unfortunate that our government has gotten out of hand. It is large. It is not only ruling and protecting, which it ought to do, but it has expanded to be a welfare state for not only this country, but for the whole world. I think that there is a serious difficulty here. The United States Constitution grants only limited government, rather than unlimited government. I believe, as many have said, "*that which governs least, governs best.*" We cannot police the whole world. What is going to happen when our own country is attacked and yet all of our military and missiles are somewhere else in the world? What about our own homes, our own mothers, our own fathers, and our own children?

Romans 13:7

"**Render therefore to all their dues: tribute to whom tribute is due; custom to whom custom; fear to whom fear; honour to whom honour.**" We who are saved have a "*duty*" to "*render*" to all parties that which is "*due*" to them. This includes "*tribute to whom tribute is due; custom to whom custom*" is due. This would include sales tax, tolls, various indirect taxes on goods, as well as real estate, state and local income taxes.

In addition to the monetary obligation, there are two other intangible things, "*fear*" and "*honour.*" Some people downplay the word "fear." The Greek for this word is PHOBOS. It means "*fear, dread, terror; that which strikes terror.*" It has real literal meaning and should not be watered down to some innocuous sense. For believers, there are certain people we are to "*fear*" and others whom we should "*honor.*" The Lord wants the believers to be in line with proper respect and proper authority. We who are Christians should respect the office of our country's president. We give honor to that office even though we might disagree with some of the policies of that office. Whether they are Democrats or Republicans, we are to give honor to the office. The same goes for our mayors and governors of our states. The person may be wrong, but the office we should respect. That is the distinction. It is somewhat difficult to make that distinction. Often we focus on the person and not the office. God wants us to be respectful, but He also wants us to have a clear definition of what a real Biblical ruler is.

Many years ago, Billy Graham went over to Communist Russia. They did not at that time claim they were no longer Communist. Today they say they are no longer Communist. Do not believe it. There are many people in Russia today who are still in office. They just call their form of government by a different name in order to get billions of dollars from the USA and other free governments. Russia has received our billions. Just the other day the head man in Russia said he does not like what we are doing in NATO. Before they had the sham of taking away the word Communist to describe their Russian government, Billy Graham went over there. This is what he told the people: *"You have an absolute duty, according to the Bible, to obey all your rulers here in Communist Russia."* That is absolutely false. These rulers were killing and torturing Christians and individual people. They were slaughtering people and taking them to Siberia to slave labor camps. I believe to teach obedience to a corrupt government is a wrong interpretation of the Bible. That is why, here in Chapter 13, we have a Biblical definition of what a ruler is.

A ruler honors that which is right and Biblical, a real Biblical ruler does this. A real Biblical ruler punishes evil which is against the Scripture. Not the reverse, and when that is reversed the believers are under no obligation to obey that which is false. I go back to the book of Acts:

- **Acts 5:29b**

Then Peter and the *other* apostles answered and said, **We ought to obey God rather than men.**

Romans 13:8

"Owe no man any thing, but to love one another: for he that loveth another hath fulfilled the law." Notice that word *"owe."* The Greek word for this is OPHELLO. It means:

"to owe; to owe money, be in debt for; that which is due, the debt."

We are in a debt-ridden society. According to the Internet, as of January 10, 2005, the public debt now stands at $4,414,821,750,455.19. This is so high I do not even know how to name it. It looks like $4 trillion to me. I do not know what your debt is personally, but there is a bumper sticker that says it for many people: *"I owe, I owe, it's off to work I go."*

Here is another kind of debt. Paul tells the believers at Rome: *"Owe no man any thing, but to love one another."* This is a debt that every believer who is saved, born-again, and regenerated by the Spirit of God owes to one another in their local churches and among other Christian people.

That verb *"owe"* is in the present tense. Since it is in the negative, it is a prohibition. As I have said many times before, whenever you have a present tense in the negative it means to stop an action already in progress. If you had the aorist tense in the negative it would mean, *"do not even begin"* an action.

Stop Owing Brotherly Love

Here, being in the present tense, it means to stop an action in progress. Apparently these saved people in the church of Rome, Italy were owing love to the brethren. Paul was saying *"Stop owing fellow believers your love. On the contrary, love one another."*

Paul stated that *"he that loveth another hath fulfilled the law."* Not that all of the law was *"fulfilled,"* but true *"love"* toward God and man fulfills the Ten Commandments which relate both to God and to man. The next verse speaks of some of the commandments. The first four refer to the Lord and the last six refer to human beings. If you have genuine love you are going to fulfill some of the law of Moses.

Romans 13:9

"For this, Thou shalt not commit adultery, Thou shalt not kill, Thou shalt not steal, Thou shalt not bear false witness, Thou shalt not covet; and if there be any other commandment, it is briefly comprehended in this saying, namely, Thou shalt love thy neighbour as thyself." This sounds like salvation by works. It is not. These people Paul was writing to were saved people. They were believers. There is nothing wrong with believers having good works that please the Lord. A saved person should be a pattern of good works after he has been saved. If you take an unbeliever who is lost, he or she can do nothing to save himself. It is all by God's grace through faith in the Lord Jesus Christ. He is the One who has saved us.

These are rules and governing principles for believers. Notice Paul names five of the Ten commandments right here in Verse 9. In Exodus 20:3-17, we have the Ten Commandments listed. He lists commandment 6, 7, 8, 9, and 10. He lists them a little out of order. *"Thou shalt not commit adultery"* is listed in Exodus 20 after *"Thou shalt not kill."* These are the commandments that Paul says love fulfills.

The Serious Sin of Adultery

Take the first one: *"Thou shalt not commit adultery"* **is a very serious sin.** It is committed, not only by the world of unbelievers, but also, sad to say, by those who claim to be Christians.

It is altogether too common of a practice. Adultery is the taking of another man's wife or another woman's husband and having sexual relations with them. If you have genuine and true love, you are not going to hurt another person's spouse by this sin. Genuine love would prevent that. This love is AGAPE love. It is God's love. It is Christian love. If you really love that person you are not going to break up his or her home. That is what adultery does. It breaks up homes. Sometimes it does not. Sometimes the persons just continue to live. I know a person here in New Jersey who had two families. He had a lawfully wedded wife and children, and he had an unlawfully unwedded woman and children. If you love your spouse with Christian love, you are not going to commit adultery with someone else's spouse.

The same can be said about the commandment *"Thou shalt not kill."* If you have true, genuine, Christian love for a person, you are not going to kill him or her. Genuine love is fulfillment of that part of the law. You do not kill or murder people if you love them.

The same holds true with the third commandment listed, *"Thou shalt not steal."* If you genuinely love a person you are not going to take his house, his car, his money, or his clothes. You are not going to hold him up for anything at all. Love is a fulfillment of that particular commandment against stealing.

Then Paul lists *"bearing false witness,"* which is lying to or about people. If you really have genuine Christian love for people, you are not going to use falsehood. You are going to speak the truth. You will not speak with a forked tongue as the Indians say, but your statements will be a true report rather than a false one. We have witnesses in courts many times who bear false witness. That is called perjury.

We have had a former President, Bill Clinton, who committed perjury. This is *"bearing false witness"* while under oath to tell the truth. People apparently did not think much about it. In fact, the polls have reported that many thought that it was all right for the President to lie under oath. Because of his activities, the U. S. House of Representatives impeached President Clinton by a majority vote and sent the case on to the U. S. Senate. The Senate did not convict him of impeachment. We have perjury on every hand in our country. It is sometimes difficult for a judge in a court of law to detect whether a person is lying or telling the truth. If a person has genuine love for another person he is not going to lie against him or her. He is going to tell the truth. Love fulfills the law of not "*bearing false witness.*"

The fifth commandment listed, "*Thou shalt not covet,*" is also obeyed if there is genuine love. If you really love a person, you do not want to "*covet*" what another person owns. "*Covetousness*" is really the precursor of stealing and theft. When a person covets or wants something that belongs to someone else, he or she becomes like Achan in the Old Testament. He saw and then coveted a Babylonian garment (Joshua 7:20-21), as well as some gold and silver items, and hid them in his tent. God judged the whole nation of Israel because of his covetousness (Joshua 7:11). God said "*Israel hath sinned.*"

If you had genuine love for a person, you would not want to "*covet*" that person's car, or home, or suit, or hat, or dress, or whatever it might be. You will let the person have these things and be thankful that the person has enough money to buy a suit, or home, or car, or hat, or whatever it might be that you might "*covet.*" Love is a fulfillment of the law against covetousness.

Christian Love Fulfills The Law

Then Paul comments on how "love" fulfills other commandments. He said, "*if there be any other commandment, it is briefly comprehended in this saying, namely, Thou shalt love thy neighbour as thyself.*" In other words, true Christian love is the answer to many other commands in the Old Testament as well as those listed.

The sin of "*adultery,*" which was mentioned first in this list, is probably one of the most widespread sins in the Old Testament and in our day as well.

- **Leviticus 20:10**

  And the man that committeth adultery with *another* man's wife, *even he* **that committeth adultery with his neighbour's wife, the adulterer and the adulteress shall surely be put to death.**

If a person who committed adultery today were living in the Old Testament time, he or she would be "*put to death.*" I wonder what the population in the United States of America would go down to if this were practiced today.

- **Proverbs 6:32-33**

But **whoso committeth adultery with a woman lacketh understanding: he** *that* **doeth it destroyeth his own soul.** A wound and dishonour shall he get; and his reproach shall not be wiped away.

This person is a bit stupid, and this act is eating into his own soul. This is a real wound because it is a dishonorable thing.

I think of a young man who was an assistant Pastor in our area who committed adultery with the choir leader. What lives he ruined! What a ministry he ruined! I remember when he was ordained to the gospel ministry. I was there at his ordination council meeting. I was there at his ordination ceremony. As we placed our hands upon that young man, a talented young man who was going into the gospel ministry, I had the prayer of dedication for this man. This adulterous affair ruined his home, it broke up the church relationship, and that man is out of the ministry. He finally divorced his first wife. He then took another wife who later died. He now has a third wife. His first wife has now died as well. This adultery is a terrible thing. I think of his children. I think of his daughter who had a baby by illegitimate sexual relations with another man. I think of his son marrying someone who is lost and unsaved and bound for Hell. I think of his family. It is truly a *"wound and dishonour."* It does not stop with the party that commits adultery.

This was also true in David's case. He committed adultery with Bathsheba, the wife of Uriah the Hittite (2 Samuel 11). God said He was going to pass that on to his children (2 Samuel 12:11). God did pass that down to his children. His sons as well as David were dishonored. It was a terrible thing.

Romans 13:10

"Love worketh no ill to his neighbour: therefore love is the fulfilling of the law." Here in brief form Paul states again what he has mentioned in Verses 8 and 9. He says that *"love worketh no ill to his neighbour."* If there is genuine *"love"* in operation, there will be no resultant ill, evil, or bad to any one close to you. It is impossible.

If you have brothers and sisters, do you love them? Do they love you? Do you work evil to them? Do they work evil to you? Do you have fights and spats? If so, is there genuine Christian love in operation? No, there is not. Just put yourself in that position. I have two sisters. I know what it means to have a couple of siblings. I was not saved when we were growing up. I was not saved until I was almost seventeen-years-old as a senior in high school. I did not know what Christian love was. When I was angry with my older sister, I would pound her in the back until my Dad got after me and I stopped that pounding. If I had genuine and true love for my sister I would not have pounded her on the back. I am ashamed of these actions, and now have Christian love for both of my sisters. It shows how my Saviour's love has changed my actions and attitudes. He can do this if we allow God the Holy Spirit to control us. If we have genuine Christian love, we are not going to hurt or do evil to people. "*Love is the fulfilling of the law.*" It is a very simple thing, but sometimes simple things escape us.

Romans 13:11

"And that, knowing the time, that now it is high time to awake out of sleep: for now is our salvation nearer than when we believed." The first Greek word for "*time*" in this passage is KAIROS. It means a special "*time*" or a season. It is the word KAIROS. Paul was living in wicked days. I do not know if it were any more wicked than it is in the days in which we live. We are living in very wicked times too. Paul is saying you know the season or the "*time.*"

The second word translated "*time*" is HORA. It refers to a special "*time*" or hour rather than a general season. It is "*high time to awake out of sleep.*" "*Sleep*" is good, but we must heed the warning of Psalm 127:2, "*It is vain for you to rise up early, to sit up late, to eat the bread of sorrows: for so **he giveth his beloved sleep.**" We all need our sleep. Sometimes when it is difficult to sleep, I quote that verse to the Lord. I say to Him, "*Lord, you have promised to give your beloved sleep.*" Because I am saved, I am one of His "*beloved,*" so I ask Him to keep His promise in Psalm 127:2.

It is difficult to get to sleep when you are bothered. I asked one of our friends when we visited her husband in the hospital if she were getting rest. She said she got rest sometimes, but she indicated to me that she was usually not sleeping. She has a serious problem sleeping. In fact, her husband almost died one time. I asked her if she got some rest? She said she was getting a little bit of rest.

It says in the Book of Proverbs 20:13, "***Love not sleep**, lest thou come to poverty; open thine eyes, and thou shalt be satisfied with bread.*" That is true. This is a picture of the field of the sluggard which is all overgrown with weeds and nettles. He does not want to turn on his bed because he is so lazy.

Wake Out of Spiritual Sleep

It is time spiritually to *"wake out of sleep."* When God saved us, if we are regenerated, He took us out of the sleep of death and the sleep of sin. He awoke us. He gave us life. It is time to *"awake out of sleep."* We should not want to go back into the sleep of the unregenerate world. We don't want to go back into the world of sleep. That world is hypnotic. It is a world that is sleeping in sin.

I do not know why people want to use narcotics to fall into drowsiness. I do not understand it. I want to be awake. I want my mind to be able to think about the things of the Lord and about the things I am trying to do.

I remember when I had chemotherapy for my cancer of the lymph glands back in 1985 and 1986. They put poison drugs into my veins once a month for nine months in order to take care of that cancer. The Lord took care of it. As of this date, I am in remission from cancer. I had a big growth on the right side of my neck. It was Hodgkin's Disease. They dripped those drugs in my veins which made me sleepy. I realize they put you to sleep so you will not throw up. The poison makes you vomit. Then you have to take pills through the mouth for three or four days which is more of that chemotherapy. You have to lie flat on your back. You cannot even turn because you might throw up. You can counteract that by taking some other drugs which make it so you do not throw up. These drugs put you to sleep even more. I never bothered taking this other drug. When I got home, once a month from that ordeal at the hospital, I tried to work in my office at first. I gave up on that. The next months that followed I just rested when I got home. If that is a "high," being sleepy and not being able to think, I do not want any "highs." The nurses would sometimes tell me that I would get a great *"high"* and it will be wonderful. That is not my idea of wonderful. I want my mind awake because I think that is what the Lord would have us to do.

These people who smoke marijuana and take all of these other types of drugs just to get *"high,"* I do not understand it. Instead of getting *"high"* it seems to me that they are getting *"low."* I do not understand these opium dens in China. They are just filled with smoke and all the rest with people just sleeping. God said *"it is time to awake out of sleep,"* the sleep of the world, the sleep of death, and the sleep of sin.

When Paul wrote *"for now is our salvation nearer than when we believed,"* what did he mean? In the New Testament there are three tenses or time-frames when referring to God's salvation. If we are born-again, **in the past tense (1) God saved us from the penalty of sin**. We no longer have to pay in Hell fire for all eternity for our sins. The penalty has been paid by Christ. That is salvation past.

If we who are saved follow the Lord, read His Word, and are walking moment by moment in the power of the Holy Spirit of God, **in the present tense (2) God wants to save us from the power of sin in our lives**. We do not have to serve sin. The Lord Jesus died for our sin nature as well as for our sins which are the fruit of that nature. With the Holy Spirit's help, we can live for Christ. We don't have to be under the power of sin. That is salvation present.

In the future tense (3) God will save us from the presence of sin. We will be in the presence of God in Heaven. We will be absolutely perfect, absolutely righteous, and absolutely sinless. *"Our salvation is nearer than when we believed"* in the future sense. We are closer to the day when we receive our new, transformed bodies. If you were saved ten years ago, the time when the Lord Jesus takes you Home to Glory is nearer than when you believed. If you believed in the Lord fifty years ago, the time is still nearer. This is what Paul is saying.

There is nothing you can do for the Lord on earth here after you are dead. If you are saved, you go Home to Glory. It will be all over. As that little saying says, *"Only one life 'twill soon be passed, only what's done for Christ will last."* That is so true. The world says, *"You only go around once, so live, live, live till you die."* The Christian should say *"live for Christ while you are alive, not for self, sin, the world, or Satan."* *"It is high time to awake out of sleep."*

Do not sleep with the world. Be alert, be ready to go, because your salvation, when you go Home to be with Christ, is *"nearer than when you believed."* We do not know when that day will come. If you are not saved, woe unto you when death comes, because your spirit and soul will not go Home to be with Christ. They go to a very serious penalty of Hell fire, damnation, and suffering. Those of us who know Christ will go into His presence. Then we will have to give an account.

Romans 13:12

"The night is far spent, the day is at hand: let us therefore cast off the works of darkness, and let us put on the armour of light."

Yes, *"the night is far spent,"* in the sense that each day the believer lives in this night of sin brings us closer to the day of God's eternal Home in Heaven.

This is a spiritual figure here.

Our Past Life Was Darkness

Paul refers to the night of darkness, the night of sin, the night of living in this wicked and sin-cursed world as past. In Verse 9, for instance, Paul lists some of this past wickedness that is gone. This includes such sins as adultery, killing, stealing, bearing false witness, and covetousness. That is past. That is in the old life.

We should not continue in this night of sin. The *"day"* of salvation future and God's eternity is *"at hand"* for us. Because of this, we should negatively *"cast off the works of darkness"* from our lives and positively, we should *"put on the armour of light"* in that which pleases our Lord Jesus Christ Who has saved us.

The works of darkness are the works of the flesh (Galatians 5:19-21). We no longer have to fulfill these seventeen sins that are listed there. We should let the Lord produce in us the fruit of the Holy Spirit.

● **Galatians 5:22-23**
   But the fruit of the Spirit is love, joy, peace, longsuffering, gentleness, goodness, faith, meekness, temperance . . ."

This is the *"fruit of the Spirit."*

We who are redeemed by personal and serious faith in the Lord Jesus Christ do not have to follow the works of darkness. We are to *"cast them off."* If you are on a ship that is about to leave port, the last thing that you do is to *"cast off"* the lines that bind you to the shore. If you are on a sailboat or a larger vessel, you always have these lines, whether large or small. To get free of the land, you must *"cast off"* the lines that bind you to it. When you do *"cast off"* the lines, make sure you are either completely on the dock or on the boat, but not in between. That can be very hazardous. Some people have fallen into the river because they have not decided what they are going to do, whether to go or to stay behind.

Cast Off the Darkness of Sin

When God says to "*cast off the works of darkness*," do not get in between, living half-dark and half-light. You will fall into the worse darkness than ever. Cast it off and then you will be free of its evils. You do not have to be worried about it anymore. You do not have to be worried about serving the "*works of darkness*" or the works of sin. Cast them off.

Then, after you cast off the "*works of darkness*," you have to put something on. You "*put on the armour of light*." The Lord Jesus Christ is the "*Light of the world*" (John 8:12b). He said "*he that followeth me shall not walk in darkness, but shall have the light of life*" (John 8:12b). The Word of God is light. It is a "*lamp unto my feet, and a light unto my path*" (Psalm 119:105). The Word of God is light and can lead us into light. He wants us to "*put on*" the light as armor. Armor protects. Armor is usually heavy.

David resisted the armor of Saul (1 Samuel 17:38-39). It was like a work of "*darkness*" and it had to be "*cast off*." David could not use it. Remember when David went out to fight Goliath the giant, Saul said he would help David. He gave him his own armor to go out and meet this giant. This man was 9' 9" tall (1 Samuel 17:4). He was huge. He was threatening Israel. David had just come from the sheep to bring a little food to his brothers (1 Samuel 17:17-18). His brothers were angry at him. They wanted to know why David had left his few sheep in the wilderness (1 Samuel 17:28). That giant had been challenging the armies of Israel for forty days, each morning and each evening (1 Samuel 17:16). Then David asked this question, "*Is there not a cause?*" (1 Samuel 17:29) This man had "*defied the armies of the living God*" (1 Samuel 17:28, 36).

David already knew the shepherd's life. One time a bear came out after him and the Lord gave him the power to slay the bear. Another time a lion came out to get the sheep, and the Lord gave him the power to slay the lion. He said that Goliath was no different from the lion or the bear. He said the Lord that gave him the power to slay the lion and the bear will give me the power to slay this Goliath (1 Samuel 17:37). Saul said that David could not go up against Goliath without armor. So little David put on Saul's armor. "*From his shoulders and upward,*" Saul was "*higher than any of the people*" (1 Samuel 10:23). You can imagine David wearing Saul's armor. David tried it on and said no, "*I cannot go with these*" (1 Samuel 17:39). David resisted Saul's armor. It was like the armor of "*darkness*." That was not the way that the Lord was going to defeat Goliath.

David put on the "*armour of light*" as it were. He had strong faith in the Lord Who had delivered him in the past with simple things. He took his sling which he was accustomed to using. Then he went to the brook and picked up five smooth stones (1 Samuel 17:40). He put them in his pouch. David put one of those stones in his sling and then went out to meet the giant. David swung that sling and hit Goliath in the forehead (1 Samuel 17:49). Goliath came tumbling down. The Lord gave Israel the victory by David's special armor which was as an "*armour of light.*"

God says we who are saved must put on "*armour.*" Armor is heavy. That is why some policemen get shot and killed, because they refuse to put on their protective armor. They do not want to wear it because it is heavy. They do not move well. They do not look as nice. They do not look as macho and suave. So they leave their armor home. As they go in to confront the people that are shooting at them, many of them are killed because they have left their body-armor home. Other officers are saved and spared because they have their armor on. God tells the saved ones to "*put on the armour of light.*"

Light Is Found in God's Words

How are we to get light? It is found in God's Words. In English, the King James Bible is the only accurate translation of God's Words from the preserved Hebrew, Aramaic, and Greek Words. We must shun other versions in English because of their unfaithfulness in texts, translators, translation technique, and theology. We must read God's Words and put them into practice. That is where the light is. That is how we find out about the Lord Jesus Christ. He is the "*Light of the world*" (John 8:12b). Put on this armor. It will protect us from evil. It will protect us from sin. It will protect us from every work of darkness. It will protect us from all these things that will come upon us. The armor is given to us in Ephesians.

- Ephesians 6:13
  Wherefore take unto you the **whole armour of God**, that ye may be able to withstand in the evil day, and having done all, to stand.

The Devil is after every born-again believer day-in and day-out. He wants us to fall. To prevent this, God commands us to *"put on the armour of light."* That *"armour of light"* will protect us in the day of calamity.

Romans 13:13

"Let us walk honestly, as in the day; not in rioting and drunkenness, not in chambering and wantonness, not in strife and envying." The armor is going to protect us from the *"rioting and drunkenness . . . chambering and wantonness . . . strife and envying."* God says to the Christian believers at Rome, *"Let us walk honestly."* We should want to walk *"honestly"* and appropriately. God does not want us to be dishonest. He does not want us to be inappropriate in our walk with Him. He wants us to wear an *"armour of light"* that will help us in our Christian walk.

The Greek word for walk is PERIPATEO. It comes from two Greek words, PERI (*"around"*) and PATEO (*"to walk"*). It means, literally, *"to walk around in a circle."*

Walk Does Not Mean Live

Many new versions refuse to use the word *"walk."* Instead they put the word *"live."* This is an error. There is a whole lot of difference between *"living"* and *"walking."* *"Walking"* is in the Greek text and it is in the King James Bible. It is a good translation.

It is a good figure of speech. If you are reading this, you are certainly *"living,"* but you might not be *"walking."* These two things are totally different. *"Walking"* is something that, if we do not put the next step down, we fall.

Walking Is Step-By-Step

"Walking" is a step-by-step process. That is the figure that God wants us to have. To be so cautious in our day-by-day activity for the Lord that we "*walk*" before Him step-by-step so we do not fall. We are only one step from falling. In 1 Corinthians 10:12 Paul says, "*Wherefore let him that thinketh he standeth take heed lest he fall.*" In other words, we should "*walk*" step-by-step "*honestly, as in the day.*"

I heard on the T.V. one time that our government was going to spend billions of dollars for the soldiers in Kosovo to be able to see at night. They will know even as in the daytime whether or not people are friends or foes. We who are saved must "*walk . . . as in the day.*" We should b e able to see what is going on, whether good or evil. If this is true, we should be able to know exactly what we should do and what we should not do.

Notice, this "*walk*" must be "*not in rioting.*" The Greek word for "*rioting*" is KOMOS. It means:

"*a revel, carousal; a nocturnal and riotous procession of half drunken and frolicsome fellows who after supper parade through the streets with torches and music in honour of Bacchus or some other deity, and sing and play before houses of male and female friends; hence used generally of feasts and drinking parties that are protracted till late at night and indulge in revelry.*"

This is the definition of that word and how it has been used in the Greek language historically.

Paul adds that there should also be an absence of "*drunkenness.*" Many people say they do not know whether they are going to get drunk if they drink one drink or two drinks. My suggestion is not to touch any of it. Some people are one drink away from intoxication and a life long habit of alcoholism. The statement in Proverbs 20:1 is, "*Wine is a mocker, strong drink is raging: and whosoever is deceived thereby is not wise.*"

Abstain From Alcoholic Beverages

The Scriptures in the New Testament teach that saved people are to abstain from alcoholic beverages. The Greek word used to teach this is NEPHO or NEPHALEOS. It means:

"sober, temperate; abstaining from wine, either entirely or at least from its immoderate use; of things free from all wine, as vessels, offerings."

I take the meaning *"abstaining from wine"* and *"things free from all wine"* as the primary meaning of this. It is a word that is used not just for pastors or deacons, but also for all Christians. Some Baptist church covenants state that their members should *"abstain from intoxicating drink as a beverage."* The General Association of Regular Baptist Churches (GARBC) used to have that pasted in their churches' hymn books. They have changed that now. It no longer says this. They leave that out. When I was a Navy Chaplain on active duty for five years, I was endorsed by the GARBC. At that time they had this in their constitutions and covenants that church members (not just pastors and deacons) would *"abstain from intoxicating drink as a beverage."*

My regimental Chaplain, Chaplain Vanderpool, said to me one day: *"Chaplain Waite, you go to all of these parties and you are the only Chaplain in the regiment who doesn't drink."* He was trying to get me to drink. I told him that I represented a group of churches whose entire membership had pledged themselves not to drink. Why would I as a Chaplain drink? I do not want to be tempted with alcohol. Before I was saved, my Mom had some beer in the refrigerator and I used to go in there and drink some of that beer. I did not know anything different. I did not know anything about it. I never got intoxicated or drunk, but some people are beer people and get drunk on beer. Some people are wine people and get drunk on wine. They are called winos.

I remember a man that I knew when I was attending the University of Michigan. I was there working at the Michigan Union cafeteria. He was skin and bones. He was a wino. He did not eat much. All he did was drink wine. It was a sad situation. Paul says that all things were lawful unto him but he would not be brought under the power of any (1 Corinthians 6:12b). I do not go to the flame of a match or a candle to see how near I can get before I get burned. My stand and teaching is to stay away and abstain from any and all alcoholic beverages. In that way, it is guaranteed that you will never get drunk. I am never going to get drunk if I never start drinking, whether it is beer, wine, or whisky. Many people think they can drink in moderation. What is moderation?

- **Luke 21:34**

  And take heed to yourselves, **lest at any time your hearts be overcharged with surfeiting, and drunkenness,** and cares of this life, and *so* that day come upon you unawares.

- **Galatians 5:21**

  Envyings, murders, **drunkenness, revellings, and such like:** of the which I tell you before, as I have also told *you* in time past, that they which do such things shall not inherit the kingdom of God.

Another thing Paul forbade to the Christians was "chambering." The Greek word for this is KOITE. It means:

> "*a place for laying down, resting, sleeping in; a bed, couch; the marriage bed; of adultery; cohabitation, whether lawful or unlawful; sexual intercourse.*"

In this context, this represents unlawful sexual relations, whether it is adultery, fornication or homosexuality. Certainly this often is a result of "*drunkenness.*"

Drunkenness Leads to Chambering

In other words, "*drunkenness*" leads to "*chambering*" in many cases. Rioting also might lead to "*chambering.*" Born-again people are to abstain from this sin and walk away from it.

Another prohibited action is "*wantonness.*" The Greek word for this is ASELGEIA. It means:

> "*unbridled lust, excess, licentiousness, lasciviousness, wantonness, outrageousness, shamelessness, insolence.*"

"*Wantonness*" is a work of the flesh and should never be present among believing Christians. Paul says believers are to walk in the day, not in the night. Let us put off the works of darkness. These are works of darkness in this verse.

There was also to be an absence of both "*strife and envying.*" There was "*strife*" between Abraham's cattle and Lot's cattle (Genesis 13:7). They did not have enough land for the two of them. Because of this "*strife,*" they separated one from another. As a result Lot went into Sodom, that filthy city. "*Strife*" is a "*work of the flesh*" (Galatians 5:20). We can differ in opinions, but we do not have to have strife between us. He says to put on the amour of light and walk honestly.

Another "*work of the flesh*" is "*envying*" (Galatians 5:21). You can envy someone's talent. You can envy someone's looks. You can envy someone's clothes or possessions. God says to "*put off*" all of that (Colossians 3:9-9). You do not have to "*envy*" anything. "*Envy*" means I wish that I were like that person. That is what envy is. I really want to be like that person. I would like to have that talent like Tim has to be able to play that violin, or Dick Carroll and his ability to play the piano. We ought to praise God that they have the talent. We ought not to "*envy*" them. "*Envy*" almost makes us hate the person who has the talent. Am I right? People who have skills should not be envied by us. "*Envy*" leads to hatred, and it is a very serious thing.

Romans 13:14

"But put ye on the Lord Jesus Christ, and make not provision for the flesh, to fulfil the lusts thereof." The answer to the avoidance of all the works of darkness is a putting on of "*the Lord Jesus Christ.*" That is just like putting on a garment such as a dress, a shirt, a coat, a tie, shoes, or whatever it might be. We are to "*put on the Lord Jesus Christ.*" How is that different from being saved? If we have genuinely trusted the Lord Jesus Christ as our Saviour and are regenerated by the Holy Spirit of God we have "*Christ in us, the hope of glory*" (Colossians1:27b). We who are saved have God the Holy Spirit dwelling in us (1 Corinthians 6:19-20). In John 14:23, the Lord Jesus Christ made a promise to the ones who "*love Him and keep His Words.*" He told His disciples that both He and the Father will "*come unto them and make Their abode with them.*" From 1 Corinthians 6:19-20 it is clear that God the Holy Spirit indwells all saved people. Therefore, we who are redeemed have the entire Triune God dwelling within us. We speak of the Holy Spirit dwelling in our bodies particularly (which is true), but Christ is also "*in us, the Hope of Glory*" (Colossians 1:27b). The Lord Jesus Christ is omnipresent. He is at the Father's right hand as to His resurrected and glorified Body, but as to His Deity, He is in every genuine believer. That is why we say, "*For where two or three are gathered together in my name, there am I in the midst of them*" (Matthew 18:20). The Lord Jesus Christ is in our midst as we gather in His Name, but He is also in each saved person (John 14:23).

Are You Putting On Christ?

**The difference between the Lord Jesus Christ saving us and
"*putting on*" the Lord Jesus Christ is the difference between
having a suit of clothes in your closet and putting them on. That
is the difference. You have the clothes. You might have the
Lord Jesus Christ as your Saviour, but do you "*put Him on*"?
Are you walking with Him in His power? That is "*putting on the
Lord Jesus Christ.*" It is having Him go with you where your feet
go, and take part in what your hands are doing. It is putting
Him first.**

That is what Paul meant when he said, *"For me to live is Christ, and to die
is gain"* (Philippians 1:21). He put the Lord Jesus Christ first in his life. He
was in a tight place between two things. He did not know which to do. Should
he *"depart to be with Christ"* which would be *"far better,"* or should he *"abide
in the flesh"* which was needful to the Philippians.

So, to *"put on Christ"* means to have His power. He is the *"armour of
light."* He is the One we need to protect us from sin. He will protect us from
guilt, and from all these things which are the works of darkness. The works of
darkness would try to get in and pull us away from the Lord.

After believers *"put on the Lord Jesus Christ,"* we must *"make not
provision for the flesh, to fufil the lusts thereof."* This is a prohibition in the
present tense in the Greek language. It is not a prohibition in the aorist tense
which would mean *"do not even begin to make provision."* Being a present
prohibition, it means to *"stop making provision for the flesh."* These Christians
at Rome were making *"provision for their flesh to fulfill the lusts thereof."* Paul
tells them to *"stop it."* If anyone is making provision to fulfill the lusts of the
flesh, God will tell us the same thing. He would say, *"Stop it."*

What does it mean to make *"provision"*? Different people make various
kinds of *"provisions."* When your lights go out, you provide candles. You can
make *"provisions"* for when the heat goes out. You can get a kerosene burner
of some kind. When you know the food will be gone at the store, you can get
some food in advance. When the money is not there in the bank, you can have
a little cash at home just to make sure. They've made provision. When you go
on a trip, you must make provision. You gas-up your car. You make sure you
have enough oil. You check your tires to see that they are inflated properly. All
these provisions are good, necessary, and prudent.

No Provision for the Flesh

But Paul said that the Christians at Rome and all Christians everywhere and at all times must *"stop making provision for the flesh, to fulfil the lusts thereof."* The word provision breaks down into PRO+VISION. **"PRO"** in Latin means *"before."* *"Vision"* as to do with *"seeing."* It means *"seeing beforehand."*

That is a good thing usually. We ought to be providers. Husbands ought to provide for their families. That is provision, but we should not make provision or foresight for the flesh. The Greek word for *"provision"* is PRONOIA. It means: *"forethought, providential care; to make provision for a thing."* It comes from PRO (*"before"*) and NOIA or NOUS (*"mind, or thought"*).

One of the names for God is JEHOVAH-YIREH or JEHOVAH-JIREH, as some people pronounce it. It means *"Jehovah will see to it"* or *"the Lord will provide."* He is a Provider. He sees to it before we have a need and He provides for us in all the proper ways. But we are to stop *"making provision for the flesh to fulfill the lusts therein."*

I am told that drunkards who want to quit often hide liquor bottles in various places, just in case they need it. They *"make provision for the flesh to fulfil the lusts thereof."* When a smoker say they are going to quit, I understand that some of them hide packs of cigarettes in various places just in case they need a smoke. They are *"making provision for the flesh to fulfil the lusts thereof."*

Provision in a good sense is good. We make provision for our children. We provide them food, nourishment, all the things that we have. We provide bulletins for church services. We make provision to preach the Word. It is good to make provisions for good things.

We should not make provisions for the flesh.

Too Many Fleshly Provisions

Those Christians at Rome, Italy, were making too many provisions for the flesh. I am sure they were guilty of *"rioting."* They were guilty of *"wantonness."* They were guilty of *"drunkenness."* They were guilty of *"chambering."* They were guilty of *"strife."* They were guilty of *"envy."* All of these things are of the flesh. Paul says they were making *"provision for the flesh."* He was not surprised that they were doing these things because they were providing for them. They were getting ready to do these things.

If a doctor says you should not eat certain food, perhaps he said you should not eat ham because of some sickness you might have, your mouth waters every time you see ham. You go to a place where ham is served. You get up close to it and smell it. That is *"making provision."* You want to eat it. It is just like children who have been told not to go near the cookie jar. The child might go to the cookie jar, open the lid and look at those cookies. That is making provision to fulfil the lusts thereof. God says stop it.

Only the Holy Spirit of God can help us who are saved to *"stop making provision for the flesh, to fulfil the lusts thereof."* We are people of flesh. When we are saved and regenerated, God the Holy Spirit comes to live inside of us. That is true, but we still have the old nature of sin fighting with the Holy Spirit of God (Galatians 5:17). You have the new nature and the old nature fighting and warring with each other. Only God's power and *"armour of light"* by putting on the Lord Jesus Christ, having Him walk with us, will prevent us from getting into this wickedness and darkness. May God help us to do this in the day and age in which we live. People are willfully filthy. The world is filthy. I am afraid many Christians are getting filthier and filthier. They are rubbing shoulders with the world. All the sins of the world are rubbing off on them. May it not be true of us.

I'll Build a Fence Around Today

I'll build a fence around today;
Within its limits, I will stay.
Therein I walk my path alone
With none to share or little own.

Within these walls is wondrous peace;
and, tho confined, I find release.
For God's own Son doth walk with me
To comfort and give liberty.

I'll look not thru its sheltering bar,
Nor let tomorrow's problems mar
The peace I have within this wall
Because my Lord arranged it all.

Enough for me to live today
And be content herein to stay
Till God's dear Son doth op' the door
To leave today forevermore."

By Gertrude Grace Sanborn

Romans
Chapter Fourteen

Romans 14:1

"Him that is weak in the faith receive ye, *but* not to doubtful disputations." Paul is talking about those who are *"weak in the faith."* These are probably those who do not know much about the Bible or about the Lord Jesus Christ. Perhaps they were saved only recently. Paul told the born-again people in Rome that they must *"receive"* these weak ones. The usual word for *"receive"* is LAMBANO. The word used here adds a PROS to it and is PROSLAMBANO. It means:

> *"to take to, take in addition, to take to one's self; **to take as one's companion**; to take by the hand in order to lead aside; to take or receive into one's home, with the collateral idea of kindness; to receive, i.e. **grant one access to one's heart**; to take into friendship and intercourse; to take to one's self, to take: i.e. food."*

It is in the Greek present tense and indicates that the believers are to continue to *"receive"* these people without any letup. The prefix PROS means *"near or right next to"* something. You must do that to the ones who are just recently saved and are *"weak in the faith."* In other words, take them "under your wings" as it were. That is what God wants us to do.

Everyone ought to know one another and ought to be friendly one to another. We ought to be concerned with our joys, our fears, our problems, and our difficulties.

Help Build Up Our Brethren

We ought to take each others problems to heart, *"but not to doubtful disputations,"* that is, not to arguments. We are to cause those who are weak to grow in grace and to build them up, not to tear them apart. We should take them close into our hearts and love them. If they love the Lord Jesus Christ, we can love them too.

Romans 14:2

"For one believeth that he may eat all things: another, who is weak, eateth herbs." Paul brings up the question of eating. Later he will bring up the question of the observance of days. There were some Christians who were *"weak in the faith"* and did not want to eat things that were offered to idols. That is in the book of 1 Corinthians (8:10), but I think the background is still here in the church at Rome.

In the pagan temples they would sacrifice lambs, goats, and various animals just like the Jews. The pagans would take that meat after it was sacrificed to the idols and they would sell it on the open market. Some of the weaker Christians said they were not going to eat that meat because it was offered to idols. That was all right. Some people could eat that meat and it did not bother them. So, some ate and others did not eat. That is what Paul is getting at here. The ones who were weak in the faith said they were not going to eat that meat which was offered to idols. They said they were just going to eat *"herbs"* or vegetables. They were going to be vegetarians. There is nothing wrong with that.

I like vegetables myself. In fact, ever since I had cancer in 1985 and 1986 I have been more and more involved with vegetables. I eat some meat too. I was told that red meat makes the body less able to fight cancer which they say is an *"invasive protein substance."* I may be wrong, but they say that is true. I have accepted this. If I am in a home and all they have to eat is red meat, I eat a small portion of it. So I do eat red meat on very rare occasions. I do not want my cancer to return. My wife eats red meat, but I have just chicken, turkey, or fish. I like vegetables, but I am not a vegetarian. You can eat all the red meat you want, this is up to you.

Avoid Stumbling Other Christians

In the situation here in this verse, these meats were offered to idols and some that were *"weak in the faith"* said they were not going to eat this meat because it would cause them to stumble (1 Corinthians 8:9-10). They said that people would see them walking into the place where idol offerings were sold and would not understand. There might have been a large sign saying, *"This meat has been offered to idols. You can come in and buy this meat cheap!"*If people saw them walking into that meat shop, it might cause a weaker Christian to stumble.

Paul realized that there are different kinds of Christians with different levels of growth and understanding of the Lord and His Words. All of us are not the same in our understanding in the things of faith. We must be caring for one another, regardless of our Christian level of growth in Christ. Sometimes you can win an argument and lose a friend. Am I right? I can win an argument and I can lose a lot of friends, because I am a preacher. As I preach the Words of God I must be careful that what I preach and what I say is according to the Words of God. I may lose many friends. Preachers do lose friends. Some preachers are so afraid to preach the truth. They do not want to lose anybody. Many of these preachers have errors in their preaching and they preach little or nothing, just a bunch of fluff. That is not right either. We need the meat of the Words of God, but it must be Scriptural. If I lose friends because I preach the truth, so be it.

Dr. David Otis Fuller, who was a great preacher and defender of the Words of God, wrote three books: *Which Bible, True or False,* and *Counterfeit or Genuine.* In his early years, he was a Westcott and Hort man and loved all the new versions and perversions. All of a sudden he came to the truth that the King James Bible was the proper Bible to use because of its proper and preserved Hebrew, Aramaic, and Greek Words that underlie it. So, he wrote these books. He was on the board of Wheaton College which was and is a Neo-Evangelical school. When Wheaton failed to take a stand on the King James Bible, he got off that board. He said many times, *"I have lost a lot of friends because of my stand on the Word* [meaning Words] *of God, but the friends that I gained are many more and much more valuable then the ones I lost."*

Losing Or Gaining Friends

When we stand for truth, we may lose a lot of friends, but I hope the friends we have gained are much more valuable than the ones we lost. So there are different kinds of born-again Christians. Some are weak, and some are strong. Let us not offend them in *"doubtful things."* Let us draw them to us and to the Lord and His Words.

Romans 14:3

"Let not him that eateth despise him that eateth not; and let not him which eateth not judge him that eateth: for God hath received him." In the local church at Rome, some are despising those that do not eat of this food offered to idols. In the expression, *"Let not him that eateth despise him that eateth not,"* the Greek word for *"despise"* is in the present tense. It is another example of a present tense prohibition.

Present Tense Prohibitions

The rule in Greek grammar indicates that there must be a stopping of an action already in progress. The meaning is *"stop despising him that eateth not."* Those that were eating the meat offered to idols were despising and hating their fellow Christians.

Can you imagine the friction there must have been? I am sure you could just feel it there in that church. There is no peace or unity in this. Paul tells these believers to stop it immediately. This did not make him many friends at Rome, I am sure, when he took to task these Christians who were despising others.

Stop Judging in Doubtful Things

On the other hand, Paul says that the ones who are not eating should not *"judge him that eateth."* This is a Greek present tense prohibition once again. This means to stop an action already in progress. These Christians were judging those who were eating food offered to idols. Those that did not eat were told by Paul to *"stop judging"* the ones who do eat. Here are both factions despising one another, judging one another, and being critical of one another.

You cannot make Christians who have hated each other in the local church for a long period of time stop hating one another. Preachers have tried to do this. I know of a huge church with many factions in it. There are people who sit on one side of the church who do not speak to the people who sit on the other side of the church. When you walk into that church you can feel it. There are all kinds of vibrations of anger. The Spirit of God cannot work successfully under these conditions. No wonder that preachers come and go in churches like this and cannot stay very long. No wonder the Holy Spirit cannot work. No wonder souls are not saved because of the friction of the people.

Paul said, just stop this and try to be at peace one with another. That is a great thing to do is it not? You do not know everything that is in the minds of the people you know and you should be glad you do not know this. If you knew everything that went on in people's minds, you might have a bone or two to pick with them. You would certainly differ with them on some of things they believe and do. Paul says let the weak get stronger and do not enlarge the animosity between the two groups by judging, condemning, or despising.

The reason for Paul's plea for peace between these two groups is found in the last part of the verse where he reminds them that *"God hath received"* them. This is a very important part of this verse.

Take Them As Your Companion

As I said before, that Greek word for "*received*" is not simply LAMBANO which is the regular Greek word to "*receive*" someone, but it is PROSLAMBANO. PROS indicates something that is "*near or close at hand.*" God has taken them as His companion. This applies even to the lowest-of-the-low and even the ones who have been saved by God's grace that lived a life of sin before then. They have been redeemed by the blood of Christ.

God has taken the saved sinner as His companion and made him one of His children. He has made him born-again. He has granted him access to His heart. This is what this word PROSLAMBANO implies. He has taken him into friendship to Himself. Because God has received him, who are we to fight him tooth and nail? If God has received him so should we. God in His grace and mercy receives sinners. How can God receive sinners? That is a good question. How can God take one who has lied, who has stolen, who has committed adultery, who has been a blasphemer, who has sworn, and used God's name in vain, and everything else and receive Him? Well, He can do it because of what the Lord Jesus Christ has done for all the sinners of the world at Calvary's cross. He died for the sins of the whole world. When Paul accepted Christ, and received Him by genuine faith, God received Paul and took him in. It is a wonderful thing in God's grace that he can receive sinners.

* Ephesians 2:8-9

    For **by grace are ye saved** through faith; and that not of yourselves: *it is* the gift of God: Not of works, lest any man should boast.

Romans 14:4

"Who art thou that judgest another man's servant? to his own master he standeth or falleth. Yea, he shall be holden up: for God is able to make him stand." In the local church at Rome, people were judging each other. These Christians were "*another man's servant.*" The Greek word for "*servant*" here is OIKETES. It means:

"*one who lives in the same house as another, spoken of all who are under the authority of one and the same householder; a servant, a domestic."*

This *"servant"* is one who *"lives in the same house as another."* These believers at Rome are all *"in the same house"* as servants. They should not judge each other because they are all fellow-servants. Suppose I had many servants in my house and you had servants in your house. Am I permitted to tell your servants what to do in your house? No. That is none of my business. Furthermore, you ought not tell the servants in my house what to do either.

My wife used to have a certain lady who helped clean our house. Sometimes my wife would ask that lady why she put something in a different place than where it was before. I asked my wife if it bothered her so much, why does she not fire the woman. My wife does not want to do that. She liked the woman and needed her. The lady then can do what she wants and my wife can rearrange things later. Sometimes these servants come in here and seem like the mothers of the house instead of having the mothers be in charge. They come in and arrange and move things around. You wonder what is going to happen next.

The Servant Must Obey His Master

Paul reminds the believers at Rome concerning each person, *"to his own master he standeth or falleth."* It is up to the person's *"master"* who is in charge of that servant to tell him what he is to do.

Then Paul says, *"God is able to make him stand."* That means that for every saved person in the church of Rome, and also every person in local churches today, *"God is able to make them stand."* You will not fall.

If we are born-again, we have a Master, the Lord Jesus Christ. He is the One that we who are saved must appear before at the Judgment Seat of Christ. If people are lost, they will appear before the Lord Jesus Christ at the Great White Throne Judgment and be sent to an eternal Lake of Fire in Hell. If you are saved, *"God is able to make you stand."*

- **Jude 24**

  Now unto **him that is able to keep you from falling,** and to present *you* faultless before the presence of his glory with exceeding joy,

  If we are saved, God is *"able to keep us from falling."* We have a *"standing"* before God the Father in Christ. Because we are in Christ, we are not going to *"fall"* in the sense of losing our salvation. God is able to make us to stand. We should not judge another man's servant. If they are saved, they are the Lord's servants and the Lord will take care of judging them as and when He sees fit.

He is not talking about things that are clearly sinful and wicked which have been spelled out in the Scriptures. This is rather about doubtful things. It is whether you eat this or drink this or not. It is not open sin which is clearly contrary to the Words of God. This is not what Paul is talking about here. These are things that do not make any real difference, such as whether you part your hair on the left side or on the right side. I am saying these are matters of doubtful things that do not make any difference whatsoever. These are small matters that are not spelled out in Scripture either specifically or in principal.

Things Not Clear in Scripture

Paul is telling these Christians not to judge, criticize, or despise one another in these small things which are matters of preference only. These things are not in regard to the Words of God where sin is laid out and specified.

If any believer has been involved in these things which are named in the Bible as clearly wicked and sinful, it is up to us fellow Christians to go along side of that person and try to win them away from that sin. We are to do this very carefully and very gently as the Bible demands.

"Brethren, if a man be overtaken in a fault, ye which are spiritual, restore such an one in the spirit of meekness; considering thyself, lest thou also be tempted" (Galatians 6:1).

Romans 14:5

"One man esteemeth one day above another: another esteemeth every day *alike*. Let every man be fully persuaded in his own mind." Here is a question about certain days of the week, month, or year. Earlier it was a question of eating meat or herbs. I do not know about you, but one day is Sunday, the next day is Monday. Paul is probably referring to some of the Jewish days. Perhaps he is referring to the Sabbath day, or one of the Feasts such as Passover, Unleavened Bread,

Firstfruits, Pentecost, Trumpets, Atonement, or Tabernacles. We could apply it to birthdays, or anniversaries. That becomes a little bit of meddling when talking of these days. When husbands and wives do not remember their anniversaries or birthdays, there often seems to be trouble. Maybe it is another holiday such as: Mother's Day, Father's Day, Children's Day, Valentine's Day, or even Ground Hog's Day. If some people want to celebrate these different days, that is their privilege.

However, I do not believe we should commemorate the signs of the Zodiac. I believe this entire system is Satanic to the core. I think when some people ask you when your birthday is, they want to know what sign of the Zodiac you were born under. Based on your sign they draw conclusions.

Paul's principle is *"Let every man be fully persuaded in his own mind."* Again, these are *"days"* that do not make any difference. Let us not fight among ourselves about these *"days."* I believe there are some *"days"* that have evil connected with their background and history. Take for instance the Christmas season with Rudolf the red-nose reindeer, Santa Claus, and all the other thoughts that go with them. There are so many things that have nothing to do with the birth of the Lord Jesus Christ at all. We have Easter bunnies, Easter parades, and Easter hats that have nothing to do with the resurrection of the Lord Jesus Christ. These are pagan things that have been brought into these days. Many churches revel in these pagan festivals.

Whether it is one *"day"* or another or whatever people think about certain *"days,"* Paul is saying, *"Do not bicker and fight about it and cause a big fury about it."* You can have your own opinions about everything, but let us not make a big fuss in the local church.

Romans 14:6

"He that regardeth the day, regardeth *it* unto the Lord; and he that regardeth not the day, to the Lord he doth not regard *it*. He that eateth, eateth to the Lord, for he giveth God thanks; and he that eateth not, to the Lord he eateth not, and giveth God thanks." If you regard a *"day"* you should regard it unto the Lord. Whatever *"day"* is special to you or not, bring the Lord Jesus Christ into it. Do not leave Him out of any of your days. He wants to be with us in everyone of our joys and our fears and our sorrows. We need to bring the Lord into it.

The same thing is true about eating foods. If a person is eating meat that had been offered to idols and has no conscience against it, he can give God thanks for this. There is thanksgiving and praise to the Lord Jesus Christ. That is the way it ought to be. If we keep the Lord Jesus Christ out of anything that you do or I do, we are wrong. We are to keep Him as a vital part of our daily lives. If we are saved, He is our Friend. There is a sign that is sometimes in people's dining rooms or kitchens and it says, "*The Lord Jesus Christ is the unseen listener to every conversation.*" The Lord Jesus Christ is omnipresent. He is present everywhere in the world. He sees all we do, He hears all we say, and the Lord even knows what is in our hearts. Any "*day*" we keep or not keep, the Lord is right there watching our attitudes. He sees if we are eating or not eating certain foods.

Remember the Lord Every Day

If we have been redeemed, the Lord Jesus Christ must be brought into every part of our lives. He is not simply a one-time per week guest on the Lord's Day, Sunday. We might come to church on Sunday and the next "*day*" forget Him. We might also forget Him on Tuesday, Wednesday, Thursday, Friday, and Saturday. That is not what the Lord wants. He wants us to be remembering Him every day.

There is a verse of Scripture in the Old Testament (Psalm 118:24) which says, "*This is the day which the LORD hath made; we will rejoice and be glad in it.*" When I was a student at the University of Michigan working in the cafeteria, a fellow student said to mek after I quoted this verse to him on a Sunday, that he thought I was applying it only to Sunday. I quoted it on a Sunday, but it is not a verse just for Sunday. Every single "*day*" of the year we can say, "*This is the day which the LORD hath made; we will rejoice and be glad in it.*" My wife told me that when she was a young girl her mother would come into her room in the morning and greet her with that verse. If we really know that the Lord Jesus Christ is our Saviour, He becomes the source of our joy (John 15:11; 17:13). We can rejoice in Him every "*day*" and in every way.

Romans 14:7

"For none of us liveth to himself, and no man dieth to himself." This truth seems very simple and something we ought to know, but Paul puts it in here to remind the believers at Rome. This applies to us as well, wherever we might be. We do not live to ourselves. Others are watching us.

The World Watches Us

We live before a watching-world as some have written. The world is watching and other Christians are watching as well. We do not live to ourselves. This makes us a window to the world.

I realize there is some privacy. All of us have privacy, but when we go out of our homes and we go into this world, people are looking. We do not live to ourself. What we do and how we act is noted by those around us.

What we do not say and what we do not do is also important. Even when it comes our time to die, we must realize that *"no man dieth to himself."*

When Death Comes to the Unsaved

Here is the way you die if you do not know the Lord Jesus Christ as your Saviour. Your spirit and soul go to a conscious place of fiery torment called Hell. One day your body will be resurrected and you will be cast spirit, soul, and body into the Lake of Fire, also called Hell. There will be torment, and it is a terrible, terrible thing. No one who is lost dies to themselves. Their spirit and soul are judged and there is pain in the fires of Hell for eternity.

If you are here and you are saved, if you are born-again and are a Christian, you do not die to yourself either. Not only do people watch you as you die, and how you die, but your spirit and soul go immediately into the presence of the Lord Jesus Christ in Heaven.

There Is No Purgatory

There is no *"purgatory"* like the Roman Catholic Church falsely teaches. There is no limbo where you just go half way. You either go to Heaven or to Hell.

There are only these two destinations, either Heaven or Hell. There is no middle ground. The only place of purgation or cleansing is the cross of Calvary where the Lord Jesus Christ shed His blood to purge and cleanse the believing people from their sins. That is the only *"purgatory"* or place of cleansing, where all the sins of the world were purged or cleansed.

Those of us who are saved go to be with the Lord Jesus Christ the second the spirit and soul leave that body. We attended a memorial service for Mrs. McNalley. I taught her in my Sunday School class at Haddon Heights Baptist Church for many years as well as her husband. Mrs. McNally bought one of our *Defined King James Bibles*. She got that Bible so she could read it. She went Home to be with the Lord. They said she always read her Bible in the morning and spent a couple of hours in prayer. She asked the Lord that she would die peacefully, and according to her son-in-law, that is the way she went. Her *Defined King James Bible* and her glasses were right by her bed and she went Home to be with the Lord happily and peacefully. They put both of these items in her casket during her memorial service for all to see. Will you die as peacefully and go into the very presence of the Lord Jesus Christ in Heaven? Only you can answer this question.

Romans 14:8

"For whether we live, we live unto the Lord; and whether we die, we die unto the Lord: whether we live therefore, or die, we are the Lord's."

- Philippians 1:20-25

  According to my earnest expectation and *my* hope, that in nothing I shall be ashamed, but *that* with all boldness, as always, *so* now also Christ shall be magnified in my body, whether *it be* by life, or by death. **For to me to live *is* Christ, and to die *is* gain.** But if I live in the flesh, this *is* the fruit of my labour: yet what I shall choose I wot not. **For I am in a strait betwixt two, having a desire to depart, and to be with Christ; which is far better:** Nevertheless to abide in the flesh *is* more needful for you. And having this confidence, I know that I shall abide and continue with you all for your furtherance and joy of faith;

If we are saved, Paul's desire for himself should be our desire. At death we *"depart to be with Christ which is far better."*

Paul didn't care whether he lived or died. He was the Lord's. *"To live is Christ, and to die is gain."*

Death Comes to All

Everyone of us is going to die unless the Lord should return and take us away to Heaven in the rapture. Whatever the age may be, whether older ones, or younger ones, we do not know who will die first.

Just like those young students who died in the Columbine school, they died very young. That is what one student was saying on TV concerning that incident. She said to her listeners, *"We think we are young and have our whole lives ahead of us, but look at what happened to our class mates. They were snuffed out just like that and died."* Then she said *"We have to be sure that we are trusting Christ as our Saviour."* She gave a testimony on that TV interview. Those newsmen probably did not know she was going to say that or they would not have used it. I am glad she told it like it was. We all must be ready to die, whether we are young or old.

Romans 14:9

"For to this end Christ both died, and rose, and revived, that he might be Lord both of the dead and living."
This is the reason that the Lord Jesus Christ came into this world. First he came as a Saviour. He came to save the sinners who trust in Him. He came as the incarnate God. That's why 1 Timothy 3:16 is so important,

- 1 Timothy 3:16

  And without controversy great is the mystery of godliness: **God was manifest in the flesh**, justified in the Spirit, seen of angels, preached unto the Gentiles, believed on in the world, received up into glory.

That is a miracle.

"God" Is Absent in New Versions

But the modern versions do not have this in their text. This is because the Westcott and Hort, Critical, Nestle/Aland, United Bible Societies Greek texts leave the word "*God*" out. They do not have "*God was manifest in the flesh.*" In the NASV, the NIV, the RSV, the NRSV, the ESV, and many other modern Bible versions, the truth of the incarnation of the Lord Jesus Christ is gone from 1 Timothy 3:16. It is in our King James Bible because the translators used the proper Greek text.

This incarnation, God becoming flesh, is a great miracle. He was born into this world as perfect God as well as perfect man. He is the *Theanthropos.* This word is made up of the Greek terms THEOS ("*God*") plus ANTHROPOS ("*Man*") combines in what the theologians call a "*hypostatic union*" of One Person in two natures, perfect God and perfect Man. There is no mixing of these natures. In His flesh, as perfect Deity and perfect humanity, the Lord Jesus Christ died for our sins. Then He rose in a bodily resurrection. He ascended up into Heaven and is now seated at God the Father's right hand "*making intercession*" (Romans 8:24; Hebrews 7:25)for the saved ones on earth.

The Lord Jesus Christ had to go through the miracle of becoming truly and perfectly human so that we could realize that He had been through everything that we go through. He feels our every care and burden. He lived three-and-one-half years after His baptism when He began His public ministry. He lived 33 years and knew everything that you and I go through. He had no sin. He resisted any temptation to sin. He had testings. Satan tried to test him, but the Lord Jesus Christ did not sin. He could not sin because He is perfect God and perfect Man. Those who teach that He could have sinned, but did not are in error. He could not have sinned.

Christ Was Not Able to Sin

There are two Latin expressions that put these two viewpoints in contrast. The erroneous position is *posse non peccare* ("able not to sin.") The true position is *non posse peccare* ("not able to sin") But it is still true that the Lord Jesus Christ went through everything that you and I go through yet without sin of any kind (Hebrews 2:17; Hebrews 4:15).

The Lord Jesus Christ "died, *and rose, and revived, that he might be Lord both of the dead and living.*" He is the absolute Sovereign master of two separate kingdoms. He is Lord of the "*dead*" and Lord of the "*living.*" He wants to be the Lord and Master of every saved person. If we are born-again He is the Lord and the Master when we die and go Home to be with Him. He is also Lord of us while we are still living in this world. The Greek word for "*Lord*" is KURIOS. It means:

> "*He to whom a person or thing belongs, about which he has power of deciding; master, lord; the possessor and disposer of a thing; the owner; one who has control of the person, the master; in the state: the sovereign, prince, chief, the Roman emperor; is a title of honour expressive of respect and reverence, with which servants salute their master; this title is given to: God, the Messiah.*"

If you are saved, the Lord Jesus Christ wants to be your Lord and my Lord.

I realize there is such a thing as "*Lordship Salvation.*" This is a serious doctrinal error. "*Lordship Salvation*" taught by John MacArthur and others states that in order for a person to be saved he must first make Christ the Lord of your actions, your words, and even your thoughts. This is impossible. An unsaved person is totally unable to do this before he or she, who is dead in sin, can be saved. The order of the words "*Lordship*" and "*salvation*" are reversed. I believe firmly that after you have "*salvation*" you should then make the Lord Jesus Christ the "*Lord*" and Master of your life. But you cannot reverse these two terms and make Christ your "*Lord*" before you have "*salvation*" or in order for you to achieve "*salvation.*"

When Paul was saved, the first question he asked was "*Lord, what wilt thou have me to do?*" (Acts 9:6b). That is what He wants everyone of us to do. Be saved, and then ask the Lord Jesus Christ to be your Lord in every area of your life. Tell Him that we want to be obedient to Him. That should be our prayer to the Lord Jesus Christ.

Romans 14:10

"But why dost thou judge thy brother? or why dost thou set at nought thy brother? for we shall all stand before the Judgment Seat of Christ." There must have been among the believers at Rome all sorts of bickering and fighting within the various groups. Does this sound familiar? Do we not have such church fights today in most, if not all, of our Fundamental churches?

Asking Two Questions

Paul had a solution to this problem. He merely asked two questions and then made a statement. He asked first of all, *"Why dost thou judge thy brother?"* The second question was *"Why dost thou set at nought thy brother?"* He is referring to small things that would be considered doubtful things. These are things that could go either way. Why are you saying that your brother or sister in Christ is of no account and does not know what they are doing?

Paul's clear statement to these believers is that *"we shall all stand before the Judgment Seat of Christ."* In other words, let us all wait and see what the Lord Jesus Christ will do for us, with us, and to us at the Judgment Seat of Christ for all who have been regenerated. This judgment will take place whether you have been saved for just a few years or for many years. If you are not saved at all, you will not appear before the Judgment Seat of Christ. You will be at the Great White Throne Judgment. This is a different judgment which will end in the Lake of Fire. This present judgment is for born-again Christians only.

- **2 Corinthians 5:10**

  For we must all appear before the **Judgment Seat of Christ**; that every one may receive the things *done* in *his* body, according to that he hath done, whether *it be* good or bad.

Paul is again speaking about saved people. At this judgment, the Lord Jesus Christ will examine what each believer has done after we have been saved. We are going to be judged at this *"Judgment Seat of Christ"* for what we have done for Him in the body, *"whether it be good or bad."* That is what Paul means here. We shall all stand before the Judgment Seat of Christ.

- **1 Corinthians 3:11-15**

    For other foundation can no man lay than that is laid, which is Jesus Christ. Now if any man build upon this foundation **gold, silver, precious stones, wood, hay, stubble; Every man's work shall be made manifest: for the day shall declare it, because it shall be revealed by fire; and the fire shall try every man's work of what sort it is. If any man's work abide which he hath built thereupon, he shall receive a reward. If any man's work shall be burned, he shall suffer loss: but he himself shall be saved; yet so as by fire.**

What Are You Building On Christ?

How are you building your life on this Foundation, the Lord Jesus Christ, the Rock (Matthew 16:18; 1 Corinthians 10:4)? Are you using materials that will not be combustible such as "*gold, silver, and precious stones*"? When the fires of judgment come, they will stand up. Or is it "*wood, hay, and stubble*"? If so, all these things will burn up. What are you building on that foundation?

Our work will be judged on "*what sort it is*" (1 Corinthians 3:13). The deciding factor is not how much it is. Most of us have very few possessions that are "*gold, silver, and precious stones*" because they are very expensive. There is plenty of "*wood, hay, and stubble*" around. Do you have works which will burn up like "*wood, hay, and stubble*"? These works are worthless from the standpoint of eternity. Do you have valuable works which are done solely for the Lord Jesus Christ like "*gold, silver, and precious stones*"?

- **1 Corinthians 3:14**

    If any man's work abide which he hath built thereupon, **he shall receive a reward**.

That is where the rewards are given out, at the Judgment Seat of Christ. All the works built on Christ our Foundation that are considered by the Lord to be "*wood, hay, and stubble*" will be burned up. If you are born-again you will not lose your salvation. You will escape the fire, but will have nothing to give to the Lord Jesus Christ. This saying is true: "*Only one life 'twill soon be past; only what's done for Christ will last.*" Ask yourself the question, "*Am I building on Christ's Foundation with "gold, silver, and precious stones"* that will abide the fires at the Judgment Seat of Christ?" Or, *"Am I building with "wood, hay, and stubble"?*

- **Romans 2:16**

  In the day when **God shall judge the secrets of men** by Jesus Christ according to my gospel.

God is going to judge the *"secrets"* of every saved Christian at the Judgment Seat of Christ. Nothing will be hidden.

- **1 Corinthians 4:5**

  Therefore judge nothing before the time, **until the Lord come, who both will bring to light the hidden things of darkness, and will make manifest the counsels of the hearts:** and then shall every man have praise of God.

Paul is telling these believers to be patient with these little things that do not make any difference. There Christ will *"bring to light the hidden things of darkness."* He will even *"make manifest the counsels of the hearts."* Again, nothing will remain *"hidden."*

- **1 John 2:28**

  And now, little children, abide in him; that, **when he shall appear, we may have confidence, and not be ashamed before him at his coming.**

That is a good verse. If the Lord should appear today would any of us in this room be *"ashamed before Him at His coming"*? I hope not. Our lives must be living for the Lord Jesus Christ so that we would *"not be ashamed."*

Romans 14:11

"For it is written, *As* I live, saith the Lord, every knee shall bow to me, and every tongue shall confess to God."
Paul begins this verse with the expression *"it is written."* It is used sixty-three times in the New Testament of the King James Bible. The Greek term for this is GEGRAPTAI. As I have said many times before, it is a perfect Greek tense. This tense describes an action or an event that took place in the past whose results remain unto the present and will remain on into the future. This speaks of the preservation of every Hebrew, Aramaic, and Greek original Word found in the Bible.

Preservation of the Bible's Words

Romans 14:11 is a quotation from Isaiah 45:23 which has been preserved. Isaiah wrote it down and every letter and every word is also continued to the present and it has been preserved. It will also be preserved on into the future. That is why I believe strongly in Bible preservation of the Hebrew, Aramaic, and Greek Words.

The leading teachers in the seven Fundamentalist schools, colleges, and universities, that I wrote a book about, do not believe in the Bible preservation of the **Words** of God. The leaders in these Fundamentalist schools deny the preservation of the **Words** of God. This includes Bob Jones University, Detroit Baptist Seminary, Central Baptist Seminary, Calvary Baptist Seminary, Maranatha Baptist Bible College, Northland Baptist Bible College, Clearwater Christian College, and I am sure there are many others. Do you know what they say? They say, not the **Words** of God have been preserved, but only the **Word** of God. They are playing antics with semantics as Dr. David Otis Fuller used to say. They say only the **Word** of God has been preserved. They say they believe in the preservation of the "**Word** of God," but not the "**Words** of God." What do they mean?

The phrase "**Word** of God" has been redefined by these Fundamentalist institutions. Their new and false definition of this is one or the other of the following: the message of God, the thoughts of God, the concepts of God, the truth of God, or the ideas of God. **They do not believe the actual Hebrew, Aramaic, and Greek "Words of God" have been preserved.** But they do not come out clearly and plainly and state this. You have to read their words carefully. It is what they do **NOT** say which is as important as what they **DO** say.

The Lord Jesus Christ said, "*Heaven and earth shall pass away, but my Words shall not pass away*" (Matthew 24:35; Mark 13:31; and Luke 21:33) The preservation of the Hebrew, Aramaic, and Greek words is very important. These schools slip by it. If you do not listen carefully you get the wrong impression. These seven schools made a video with nine of their teachers taking part in it. One of these nine men was Dr. Kevin Bauder. He is now the president of Central Baptist Seminary in the Minneapolis, MN area. On this video he said he could hold up his King James Bible and say "*This is the Word of God.*" He said he could also hold up the Textus Receptus and say "*This is the Word of God.*" He said he could also hold up the New American Standard

Version and say "*This is the **Word** of God also.*" If he says that, both of those are the **Word** of God. Notice his semantics here.

According to the *Scrivener's Annotated Greek New Testament* by Dr. Frederick Scrivener (**BFT #1670**), the Greek text underlying the King James Bible and the Greek text underlying the New American Standard Version differs in 5,604 places. In these places, I counted in the footnotes about 9,970 Greek Words that the Westcott and Hort Greek text, similar to that of the NASV, had either added, subtracted, or changed in some other way. Dr. Jack Moorman actually has prepared a study of over 500 large pages showing the Greek text and English translation of over 8,000 differences in the Greek Words of the Nestle/Aland text and the text underlying the King James Bible (**BFT #3084).** This is a notable difference in **Words**.

"Word" Not Same as "Words"

How can Kevin Bauder say that two documents (KJB and NASV), differing in 8,000 underlying Greek Words, can both be called "*the Word of God*"? He says that both of them are the "*Word of God.*" How can this be unless either one of three things are true:

1.   Perhaps he does not know the facts of the 8,000 word differences; or

2.   Perhaps he knows the facts about the 8,000 word differences, and is lying about them, or

3.   He is redefining what he means by "<u>Word</u>."

The third alternative is true.

He uses a different definition of "**Word**" when he equates them as being identical. He means only the message of God, the thoughts of God, the concepts of God, the truth of God, or the ideas of God. Things equal to the same thing are equal to each other. Things that differ are not the same. Am I right?

8,000 Differences in Greek Words

You cannot say that the King James Bible is the "*Word of God*" in the same sense as the New American Standard Version could be called the "*Word of God*" when the Greek Words underlying them have 8,000 differences.

These schools are saying that it is not the Hebrew, Aramaic, and Greek **Words** of God which are preserved, it is only the message, thoughts, concepts, truth, or ideas.

God's judgments will be meted out on the basis of His Words which He has preserved for all mankind. "*Every knee shall bow*" before the Lord Jesus Christ, whether they are saved at the Judgment Seat of Christ, or lost at the Great White Throne Judgment.

- Isaiah 45:23

  I have sworn by myself, the word is gone out of my mouth *in* righteousness, and shall not return, That **unto me every knee shall bow, every tongue shall swear.**

Original Words Preserved For Today

These underlying Hebrew Words stood written in Isaiah's day. These Words were preserved until Paul's day, and these Words continue to be preserved to our day and on into the future.

- Romans 3:19

  Now we know that what things soever the law saith, it saith to them who are under the law: that **every mouth may be stopped, and all the world may become guilty before God.**

Everyone Will Bow Before Christ

Everyone is going to bow before the Lord Jesus Christ. It would be better to bow to the Lord Jesus Christ now as your Saviour than to wait until the Great White Throne Judgment and have to bow to Him as your Judge and then be sent into Hell.

- 1 John 1:9

  If we confess our sins, **he is faithful and just to forgive us _our_ sins, and to cleanse us from all unrighteousness**.

Romans 14:12

"So then every one of us shall give account of himself to God." Paul told the Christians at Rome that everyone shall give an *"account of himself to God."* He would tell the same thing to any person in any church in the world living today. We must realize that every individual will give an account to the Lord God of Heaven and of earth. Every saved person will appear before the Judgment Seat of Christ. Every lost person will appear before the Great White Throne Judgment. Everyone individually will appear before the Lord Jesus Christ Who is the Judge of every person ever born. You may say that you are going to go into Heaven on the strength of your mother's confession of faith. I have sad news for you. You are not. You cannot go into Heaven because of your father's confession of faith either. God has no grandchildren. He has children. You cannot get your faith from either your father or mother. You are the one who must genuinely trust the Lord Jesus Christ as your Saviour on your own.

- **Ezekiel 18:20**

  The soul that sinneth, it shall die. The son shall not bear the iniquity of the father, neither shall the father bear the iniquity of the son: the righteousness of the righteous shall be upon him, and the wickedness of the wicked shall be upon him.

It is the responsibility of each soul to accept the Lord Jesus Christ.

Everyone of us will give an account of himself or herself to God. We are accountable for whatever we do or whatever we say. I pray that the Lord will give us great victory over our wicked flesh. If we are saved, we have the Holy Spirit of God dwelling within us. He wants to help us and encourage us. He wants to give us power and strength. He does not want us to grieve the Holy Spirit of God by having known unconfessed sin (Ephesians 4:30). He wants us to confess any known sin (1 John 1:9). God wants us to walk in the Spirit that we may not fulfill the lusts of the flesh (Galatians 5:16). He wants us to have our life built upon a solid Rock, the Lord Jesus Christ (1 Corinthians 3:11; 10:4). Upon that Rock Foundation, He wants us to build gold, silver, and precious stones which the fire of judgment cannot burn up (1 Corinthians 3:12-15).

Some of us cannot do much for the Lord Jesus Christ. We are just little people. But whatever we do, let us do it for Him, not for self or for others. We should not parade ourselves around for show like the Pharisees. The Lord Jesus Christ said of them, *"Verily I say unto you, They have their reward"* (Matthew 6:2, 5, 16). All they have is their present *"reward"* to be seen of men, but nothing in eternity. May we who are saved ones never be *"ashamed before Him at His coming"* (1 John 2:28) when we face the *"Judgment Seat of Christ"* (2 Corinthians 5:10).

Romans 14:13

"Let us not therefore judge one another any more: but judge this rather, that no man put a stumblingblock or an occasion to fall in *his* brother's way." This is the thing that Paul wanted these Christians at Rome to be aware. I have said before that there are two different types of prohibitions in Greek. To review, if the prohibition is in the aorist tense, it means not even to begin an action. If, as here, it is a prohibition in the present tense, it means to stop doing an action already in progress. This present tense prohibition is a stop sign.

Five Different "Stop Signs"

These Christians at Rome must have been filled with problems because I counted a total of five different stop signs in these verses before us in this section.

There are two of them here in verse 1. These are prohibitions, negative statements, in the present tense. Stop an action already in progress. There are two in Verse 13. There is another stop sign in Verse 15, another one in Verse 16, and another one in Verse 20. There are 5 stop signs.

This first stop sign is to stop "*judging one another.*" The second one is stop putting a "*stumbling block or an occasion to fall in your brother's way.*" They were judging, condemning, and criticizing each other in the church. Remember in the first part of this chapter it was talking about eating certain foods. Some did want to eat, some did not want to eat. It was food that had been sacrificed to idols. It was sold for a cheaper rate. We read about this also in 1 Corinthians 8:10. This meat was no doubt a very tasty meat. Some stronger Christians said they could eat this meat without harm to their conscience. Idols did not mean anything to them. They felt they could eat that meat.

Others said they were not going to eat this meat. So there was a fight among those that ate and those that do not ate. Paul told these warring Christians to stop judging and condemning one another. These are doubtful things. It was not a matter of clear sin against the Words of God. That would be something we all ought to refuse absolutely. Everyone of us should be united on that. But things which are not specifically taught either by direction or implication in the Scripture, we call doubtful things. Some want to worship a day and some thought every day was alike. Some want to eat and some do not want to eat. These are the doubtful things. We need to stop judging one another about these things.

Here is the thing that Paul says very clearly that every saved person should judge. They should not "*put a stumblingblock or an occasion to fall in his brother's way.*" That Greek word for "*put*" is TITHEMI. It is a prohibition in the Greek present tense. As such, it means that these believers should "*stop putting a stumbling block or an occasion to fall in his brother's way.*" These believers were doing this in their local church. There are a number of uses of a "*stumblingblock*" in Leviticus:

- **Leviticus 19:14**

  Thou shalt not curse the deaf, nor put a **stumblingblock** before the blind, but shalt fear thy God: I *am* the LORD.

That is against the will of God. The deaf cannot hear you and come back at you. The blind cannot see the "*stumblingblock*" and therefore could not avoid it. These are things that God does not want us to do.

- Ezekiel 14:3-4

  Son of man, **these men have set up their idols in their heart, and put the stumblingblock of their iniquity before their face**: should I be enquired of at all by them? Therefore speak unto them, and say unto them, Thus saith the Lord GOD; Every man of the house of Israel that setteth up his idols in his heart, and **putteth the stumblingblock of his iniquity before his face**, and cometh to the prophet; I the LORD will answer him that cometh according to the multitude of his idols;

- 1 Corinthians 8:6-9

  But to us *there is but* one God, the Father, of whom *are* all things, and we in him; and one Lord Jesus Christ, by whom *are* all things, and we by him. Howbeit *there* is not in every man that knowledge: for some with conscience of the idol unto this hour eat *it* as a thing offered unto an idol; and their conscience being weak is defiled. But meat commendeth us not to God: for neither, if we eat, are we the better; neither, if we eat not, are we the worse. **But take heed lest by any means this liberty of yours become a stumblingblock to them that are weak.**

Paul did not want the Christians at Rome or us in our church in our day to be a *"stumblingblock"* to those who are weak thus making them fall. The Greek word for *"stumblingblock"* is PROSKOMMA. It means:

> *"a stumbling block; an obstacle in the way which if one strikes his foot against he stumbles or falls; that over which a soul stumbles i.e. by which is caused to sin."*

The Greek word for the phrase *"occasion to fall"* is a different word. It is SCANDALON. It has a variety of meanings:

> *"the movable stick or trigger of a trap, a trap stick; a trap, snare; any impediment placed in the way and causing one to stumble or fall, (a stumbling block, occasion of stumbling) i.e. a rock which is a cause of stumbling; fig. applied to Jesus Christ, whose person and career were so contrary to the expectations of the Jews concerning the Messiah, that they rejected him and by their obstinacy made shipwreck of their salvation; any person or thing by which one is (entrapped) drawn into error or sin"*

Paul says that these Christian believers at Rome are to stop judging one another and stop putting either a stumblingblock or an occasion to sin in their brother's way.

Do Not Stumble One Another

We must watch ourselves that our lives do not trip and stumble others. We do not know all the times the things that stumble others, but we must look into ourselves and ask ourselves if we are doing or saying something that would cause our fellow believers to stumble.

Romans 14:14

"I know, and am persuaded by the Lord Jesus, that *there is* nothing unclean of itself: but to him that esteemeth any thing to be unclean, to him *it is* unclean." Paul was *"persuaded"* that in the matter of various doubtful things as far as days and various eating habits that *"there is nothing unclean of itself: but to him that esteemeth any thing to be unclean, to him it is unclean."* The Greek word for *"esteemeth"* is LOGIZOMAI. It means:

> *"to reckon, count, compute, calculate, count over; to take into account, to make an account of; metaph. to pass to one's account, to impute; a thing is reckoned as or to be something, i.e. as availing for or equivalent to something, as having the like force and weight; to number among, reckon with; to reckon or account; to reckon inward, count up or weigh the reasons, to deliberate; by reckoning up all the reasons, to gather or infer; to consider, take into account, weigh, meditate on; to suppose, deem, judge; to determine, purpose, decide;*
>
> *This word deals with reality. If I "logizomai" or reckon that my bank book has $25 in it, it has $25 in it. Otherwise I am deceiving myself. This word refers to facts not suppositions."*

"Esteeming" something to be *"unclean"* is *"unclean"* to the person who is doing the *"esteeming."*

When someone who is a father and a husband asks his wife if his shirt is clean, the response is, *"if you are doubtful, it is dirty."* That is exactly what Paul is saying here. If there is any question about it, just stay away from it. The very fact that you raise a question about something shows that it is probably wrong and you should stay away from it.

Romans 14:15

"But if thy brother be grieved with *thy* meat, now walkest thou not charitably. Destroy not him with thy meat, for whom Christ died." Here is another stop sign in this chapter. Again, Paul is concerned that if a Christian *"brother"* is *"grieved"* because another Christian is eating meat offered to idols, he is not walking *"charitably."* There is something wrong if this is the case. From the language used here, this was true of some in the church at Rome. Since it is a prohibition in the present tense, Paul was telling them to *"Stop destroying him."* This action leads to the destruction of other believers.

In the phrase, *"if thy brother be grieved with thy meat,"* the Greek word for *"grieved"* is LUPEO. It means:

"to make sorrowful; to affect with sadness, cause grief, to throw into sorrow; to grieve, offend; to make one uneasy, cause him a scruple ['scruple' means: 'a feeling of hesitancy, doubt, or uneasiness arising from difficulty in deciding what is right, proper, or ethical.']"

Some people might wonder why we should care if a Christian does something that offends another brother and sister in Christ, so long as the action is not specifically contrary to the Scripture. They may think they can do or say what they want to, regardless of the effect on fellow believers. They may be able to do or say things, but Paul is recommending that they do not. It is not a question of sin. We do not sin in these things. These are doubtful things which are not clearly mentioned in the Scriptures.

We Are Our Brother's Keeper

What Paul is saying to these believers in Rome is that they should give up a little bit of their personal liberty and freedom so that they do not cause their fellow believers to fall flat on their faces. In that sense, we are our brother's keeper.

That's what was asked by Cain (Genesis 4:9). Yes, we are, if we are saved. We are members of the family of God. We have a Christian family that is similar to our own earthly family. I just have two sisters, so I didn't know anything about brothers. In our family we had two sisters and I was their only brother. We had to live together and work together as a family. What affected me affected them, and what affected them, affected me. It is the same way in the family of the Lord Jesus Christ.

If a fellow Christian was "*grieved*" with what another Christian ate, that first Christian was not walking "*charitably*." We who are saved should walk in love toward other believers. In our case here in the United States, it may not be the kind of food we eat, but perhaps something we wear, or what we say, or where we go, or how we act. A walk that is not considerate of other believers is not a "*charitable*" walk.

As I mentioned earlier, Paul told the believers to "*stop destroying*" this Christian "*for whom Christ died*." This is a Greek present tense prohibition which means to stop an action which is already in progress. The Greek word for "*destroy*" is APOLLUMI which has various meanings:

"*to destroy; to put out of the way entirely, abolish, put an end to ruin;* **render useless**; *to kill; to declare that one must be put to death; metaph. to devote or give over to eternal misery in Hell; to perish, to be lost,* **ruined**, *destroyed; to destroy; to lose.*"

Believers might be "*rendered useless*" as they are hurt and hindered in their Christian life. They might be destroyed and ruined as far as their testimony is concerned.

The Lord Jesus Christ died for that person. Because of this, we need to stop doing what we have liberty to do if it hurts a fellow Christian. What if you do something that you do not know is harming the other person? You cannot be responsible for that.

Offending Needlessly

However, if the person comes up to you and tells you he or she is offended at something you have done or said, then you have to try to do something about it so as not to offend needlessly.

We should not want to be offensive to fellow saints. We must live "charitably." Stop damaging, grieving, and hurting our fellow believers "*for whom Christ died.*"

Romans 14:16

"Let not then your good be evil spoken of:" In this verse is another stop sign in the Greek present tense prohibition. The force of this construction here is *"Stop letting your good be evil spoken of."* Because of their actions, those Christians at Rome were *"letting their good be evil spoken of."* These believers were doing a good thing as far as they were concerned. They were eating meat which had been offered to idols. There was nothing wrong with it Scripturally, but it was being *"evil spoken of"* all over Rome. It was hurting other people. Many good things that we may do may be *"evil spoken of."* You may pray, which is a good thing to do. But it is a bad thing to do if you are going into a person's room who is sleeping and you begin to pray in a loud voice, thus waking him up. Praying is a good thing to do, but you would be *"evil spoken of"* because of the place, time, and conditions of your prayer.

You can think of other things in that same way. They are good of themselves, but may be done in an inopportune time. You may do good in witnessing to people and tell them how to be saved. This is a good thing. We are to *"redeem the time because the days are evil"* (Ephesians 5:16). There are some occasions when it is not wise to try to lead someone to Christ. For instance, supposing a person in the hospital was having an emergency in his heart. It would be wise to wait until the emergency was over and the doctors and nurses had finished with their treatments before we talked to them about eternity. The person might die on the spot with a heart attack if we interfere with the doctors. I am not saying we should not tell people the gospel. I am saying there is an appropriate time and place and we must be wise and pray that the Lord would give us grace and wisdom to know just when to do what. You should not be discouraged from being a good witness, but you have to be a wise witness.

Romans 14:17

"For the kingdom of God is not meat and drink; but righteousness, and peace, and joy in the Holy Ghost." Here is stop sign four in this section. This is a Scripture concerning the *"kingdom of God."* This expression is used sixty-eight times in our King James Bible. *"Kingdom of Heaven"* is used only thirty-one times and is found only in the Gospel of Matthew. These people wanted to partake of *"meat and drink"* that was offered to idols. Others said they were not going to do this. Some said that they want to worship on a certain day, such as on the Passover. Others said that every day was alike. That is not what the kingdom of God is about. That is not what being saved is all about.

Emphasis of the "Kingdom of God"

Paul gives both a negative and a positive definition of the *"kingdom of God."* Negatively, it is *"not meat and drink."* Positively, it is

1. *"righteousness, and*

2. *peace, and*

3. *joy in the Holy Ghost."*

The *"kingdom of God"* has to do with a *"righteousness"* that only the Lord Jesus Christ can provide. He is the only One who can give the genuinely believing sinner His perfect righteousness (2 Corinthians 5:21). Our sin was taken upon Him and His righteousness was placed upon the believing sinners. There was a substitution of His righteousness for man's sins. That is what the *"kingdom of God"* is. It concerns *"righteousness."* Then it concerns *"peace."* Apart from the Lord Jesus Christ, no one in the world can have true *"peace"* with God. Only the Lord Jesus Christ can give sinful people His peace. As the Lord Jesus Christ told His disciples, *"Peace I leave with you, my peace I give unto you: not as the world giveth, give I unto you. Let not your heart be troubled, neither let it be afraid,"* (John 14:27).

*   **Romans 5:1**

    Therefore **being justified by faith, we have peace with God through our Lord Jesus Christ**:

The Greek word for *"peace"* is EIRENE. It has various meanings:

A Definition of "Peace"

"a state of national tranquillity; exemption from the rage and havoc of war; peace between individuals, i.e. harmony, concord; security, safety, prosperity, felicity, (because peace and harmony make and keep things safe and prosperous); of the Messiah's peace; the way that leads to peace (salvation); of Christianity, <u>the tranquil state of a soul assured of its salvation through Christ, and so fearing nothing from God and content with its earthly lot, of whatsoever sort that is;</u> the blessed state of devout and upright men after death."

That is peace. Are you sure you are saved? Paul says that *"peace"* is what the Kingdom of God is concerned about.

A third thing that concerns the *"kingdom of God"* is *"joy in the Holy Ghost."* You cannot manufacture *"joy."* That is God's part. That is part of the fruit of the Holy Spirit: *"The fruit of the Spirit is love, joy, peace, . . ."* (Galatians 5:22). The Holy Spirit of God is the only One Who can give us genuine *"joy."*

God's Joy Even in Pain

Do you think He can give you His *"joy"* even when you are in pain? Yes, He can. The Holy Spirit of God can go through the pain, piercing that pain, and give you true *"joy."* It is true that the *"joy of the Lord is your strength"* (Nehemiah 8:10).

This is not manufacturable by man or the sinful nature that we have. Only the Holy Spirit can give us joy. Did the Lord Jesus Christ have *"joy"* set before Him as He faced Calvary (Hebrews 12:2)? Yes. Mrs. Waite a few years ago spoke on the ministry of tears to some women at a Mother and Daughter Banquet. She had a number of Scriptural references to weeping and tears and the different affects they had on those who wept.

Did the Lord Jesus have joy at Calvary? Again, I say yes. Paul wrote in the book of Hebrews that He wept and cried out in tears of agony as He faced

Calvary (Hebrews 5:7). This was probably referring back to the Garden of Gethsemane (Matthew 26:36-38). Paul also said of the Lord Jesus Christ that *"for the joy that was set before Him endured the cross"* (Hebrews 12:2). What was that joy? The joy of having sons and daughters and born-again people all the way through the ages to be saved and to become His sons and daughters. The Lord Jesus Christ prayed in agony in the garden of Gethsemane, *"O my Father, if it be possible, let this cup pass from me: nevertheless not as I will, but as thou wilt"* (Matthew 26:39).

Even in pain and in suffering there can be *"joy"* if it is by the Holy Spirit of God. There cannot be true godly *"joy"* by human action. The world talks about that emotion as *"happiness."* There is much slap-happiness. Some of the people who are slap-happy are under the influence of booze or other drugs. They are giddy. That is happiness from the happenstances of the world. I do not think that it is genuine. I saw on the television one night many reporters who were with the president. They were giving out awards. They were clapping and clapping at some woman who was singing. I could not understand very many words she was singing, but they kept giving her encore after encore. They seemed to be happy, but there was no real godly *"joy."* My wife wondered if they were drunk. They were very giddy.

The Joy of the Lord

There is a happiness that the world can assemble because of their circumstances, but there is the *"joy of the Lord"* which is an inner joy produced by God the Holy Spirit regardless of circumstances and in spite of the circumstances. It is a part of the fruit of the Spirit. Spiritual joy knows no bounds. Whether you are in pain, about to die, or whatever it might be, the *"joy of the Lord"* can be your strength.

- **Nehemiah 8:10**
  Then he said unto them, Go your way, eat the fat, and drink the sweet, and send portions unto them for whom nothing is prepared: for *this* day *is* holy unto our Lord: neither be ye sorry; for **the joy of the LORD is your strength.**

That is what the *"kingdom of God"* is. It is *"righteousness, and peace, and joy in the Holy Ghost."*

Romans 14:18

"For he that in these things serveth Christ *is* acceptable to God, and approved of men." When Paul said *"he that in these things, serveth Christ,"* he is speaking of not putting a stumblingblock before the brothers and sisters in Christ thus causing them to fall flat in their face. Paul said that if you do this, you are *"serving Christ"* and are both *"acceptable to God, and approved of men."*

Serving God by Helping Believers

Had you ever thought that it was a service to the Lord Jesus Christ by being good, and helpful to our fellow-believers? Yes, God tells us in this verse that it is a service for Him. That is what this verse is saying. Paul was reflecting on the things that were in the preceding verses such as not stumbling the brethren.

The first thing that is true if we do not stumble the brethren in these things is that it we are *"acceptable to God."* It is something that the Lord would have those of us who are saved to do. Many times those who are saved, and born-again, know that they are on their way to Heaven and have escaped Hell, but they just go about their business without caring about anyone else. The Lord wants the saints to serve the Lord Jesus Christ in these little things. We are His bond slaves and must continue to serve Him.

The second thing that is true if we do not stumble the brethren in these things is that we are *"approved of men."* That is what Paul wanted to be true of himself in the book of Acts. *"And herein do I exercise myself, to have always a conscience void of offence toward God, and toward men"* (Acts 24:16.)

It is difficult to please both God and men at all times. If you have to please only one, please the Lord Jesus Christ. You cannot always please people. People can see whether or not you are thoughtful of other people. They might not even be saved, but it is an "approved" thing to do even in their eyes. They will look at you and see that you are doing things right. They will also see that you have God's *"righteousness, and peace, and joy in the Holy Ghost."* That is being *"acceptable to God and approved of men."* These are two very important things.

Romans 14:19

"Let us therefore follow after the things which make for peace, and things wherewith one may edify another."
Paul encourages the believers at Rome to *"follow after the things that make for peace."* He wanted them to have *"peace"* in the local church there in Rome. It is sad that churches are split over tiny differences of opinion. Obviously, if you are arguing about whether you should eat this meat or that meat, or worship on this day or that day, you are going to have war rather than *"peace."* That is not *"peace"* at any price. That is not what is meant here. It is not *"peace"* by sacrificing Bible truths. It is not what is meant. The *"peace"* spoken about here is *"peace"* in the areas of doubtful things which are not Scripturally founded and grounded, but rather are matters of personal preference.

The Meaning of Edification

The last part of this verse shows what kind of things the believers in the church at Rome should *"follow."* They are to be *"things wherewith one may edify another."* The Greek word for "edify" is OIKODOME. It comes from two other Greek words, OIKOS (*"house"*) and DEMO (*"to build"*). It has a variety of resultant meanings:

"(the act of) building, building up; metaph. edifying, edification; the act of one who promotes another's growth in Christian wisdom, piety, happiness, holiness; a building (i.e. the thing built, edifice)."

We should *"edify"* or "build up" one another. That is what God wants us to do in the local church.

There are two English words that have similar endings: (1) "construction," and (2) "destruction." It is far easier to destruct than to construct. Anybody can tear something down. You can wipe off everything from a table with just one sweep. That is destructive. It is easy to destroy, but to construct is more difficult. We can destroy one another by the things we say, by the things we do, by how we live, by what we do not do, by where we go, and by where we do not go. God wants believers to *"edify another."* He tells us: *"If it be possible, as much as lieth in you, live peaceably with all men"* (Romans 12:18). There is an Old Testament verse which says, *"When a man's ways please the LORD, he maketh even his enemies to be at peace with him"* (Proverbs 16:7). I think the *"he"* in this verse can refer to the man or to the Lord. The Lord can put a clamp on those enemies. Not that they will agree with you, but they do not damage you anymore. You are on the battlefield of the Lord. If your ways please the Lord, they will be *"at peace"* with you. This does not mean that they will agree with you, but they will be *"at peace"* with you.

There are a number of verses dealing with edification and edifying.

- **Acts 9:31**

  Then had the churches rest throughout all Judaea and Galilee and Samaria, **and were edified**; and walking in the fear of the Lord, and in the comfort of the Holy Ghost, were multiplied.

- **Romans 15:2**

  Let every one of us please *his* neighbour for *his* good to **edification**.

- **1 Corinthians 8:1**

  Now as touching things offered unto idols, we know that we all have knowledge. Knowledge puffeth up, but charity **edifieth**.

- **1 Corinthians 10:23**

  All things are lawful for me, but all things are not expedient: all things are lawful for me, but all things **edify** not.

- **2 Corinthians 10:8**

  For though I should boast somewhat more of our authority, which the Lord hath given us for **edification**, and not for your destruction, I should not be ashamed:

- **2 Corinthians 13:10**

  Therefore I write these things being absent, lest being present I should use sharpness, according to the power which the Lord hath given me to **edification**, and not to destruction.

- **Ephesians 4:12**

  For the perfecting of the saints, for the work of the ministry, for the **edifying of the body** of Christ:

- **Ephesians 4:29**

  Let no corrupt communication proceed out of your mouth, but that which is good to the use of **edifying**, that it may minister grace unto the hearers.

- 1 Thessalonians 5:11

Wherefore comfort yourselves together, and **edify one another**, even as also ye do.

Are you *"edifying"* and building one another up in your local church? I hope that you are. How can we build people up? The reason we build people up is because they are not up to where they should be. Everyone of us is different. Everyone of us has different ideas, different walks, different aches and pains, and different purposes in life. We must try to encourage, build up, and *"edify"* in the faith everyone of us who are in our local church. This is an important thing.

Romans 14:20

"For meat destroy not the work of God. All things indeed *are* pure; but *it is* evil for that man who eateth with offence." Once again we meet with another stop sign. It is the fifth in this chapter. Because of the Greek present prohibition used here, Paul is ordering these Christians at Rome to *"stop destroying the work of God."* They were *"destroying"* God's work.

Who is Paul referring to when he talks about *"the work of God"*? He is referring to the Christians in the church at Rome. When you make another believer angry at you for something you have said or done which you should not have said or done, to that extent you *"destroy the work of God."* The Lord is trying to build up people in the faith. He is trying to give them more stability. He is trying to teach them more doctrines, Bible passages, and things whereby they can *"walk worthy of the Lord unto all pleasing"* (Colossians 1:10). When we hurt that Christian needlessly who the Lord is causing to grow little by little, we hurt *"the work of God."*

You cannot grow a butterfly bush overnight. Our neighbor has five of those, and she cuts them down every year. I wondered why she did that. She told me they just grow back the next year. This is true. I have seen it two years in a row. These bushes are only about three feet high. Before the summer is out they end up over my head. I cannot even look out and see into her yard. You cannot grow things overnight.

I have been saved since 1944. I am not in the same spiritual state as I was then. I will grant you that. I was a lost Hell-bound sinner who was saved by the grace of God through personal faith in the Lord Jesus Christ. I was a high-school senior.

Read Genesis Through Revelation

After I was saved I began to read the Words of God. God changed my life. He gave me new desires, a new purpose, and a new direction. As I kept reading my Bible, I began to grow in God's grace and understanding of the Christian Faith. When I was first saved I read my Bible two times a year instead of just once a year. Shortly after I was saved I began reading my Bible from Genesis through Revelation each year at the rate of eighty-five verses per day.

I was building my life, and I am still building my life. I have not yet arrived where the Lord wants me to be even from 1944 when I was saved to the present. The Lord wants me to be my very best for Him. I read the King James Bible every day and I ask the Lord what He would have me to understand from His Word.

God wants us to "edify" and build up one another. He wants us to be built up first. You cannot build up someone else if you are not built up yourself. Am I not correct? How are you going to tell someone else how to build a house if you do not know how to build one yourself. This is important. Paul told the believers at Rome to *"stop destroying the work of God"* by the things that they were doing.

It is true that *"all things indeed are pure"* (see also Titus 1:15). This is certainly true when it comes to doubtful things. We are not talking about sin which is spelled out in the Bible. We are talking about things that do not make any real difference. It is like whether you wear a blue or a red tie, or a red or a green dress. Paul makes a conclusion about such doubtful things. He said that *"it is evil for that man who eateth with offence."* If there is a doubt about it in the mind of the one doing it, then it is an evil thing. We are not to destroy God's work by hurting and harming people. That Greek word for *"pure"* is KATHAROS. It has various meanings in the Greek:

"clean, pure; physically; purified by fire; in a similitude, like a vine cleansed by pruning and so fitted to bear fruit; in a Levitical sense; clean, the use of which is not forbidden, imparts no uncleanness; ethically--free from corrupt desire, from sin and guilt; free from every admixture of what is false, sincere genuine; blameless, innocent; unstained with the guilt of anything."

We should have purity in our lives without any "offences" whatsoever.

Romans 14:21

"*It is* good neither to eat flesh, nor to drink wine, nor any *thing* whereby thy brother stumbleth, or is offended, or is made weak." Here is Paul's conclusion in regard to the doubtful things of "*eating flesh,*" or "*drinking wine,*" or doing anything that "*stumbles*" or "*offends,*" or "*makes weak*" a "*brother*" or sister in Christ. "*Wine is a mocker, strong drink is raging; and whosoever is deceived thereby is not wise*" (Proverbs 20:1). These are things we ought not to do. There are a number of verses that I would call your attention to that talk about offending people.

- **Psalm 119:165**

  Great peace have they which love thy law: and **nothing shall offend them.**

Nothing Should Offend Us!

It is wonderful to be in a position where you know the Words of God so thoroughly that nothing is going to "*offend*" us no matter what people say or do. That is a hard place to be, but if you love the Words of God and you know the Words of God nothing is going to "*offend*" you.

A Bitter Lesson

I had a friend I thought was true--
He said he cared for me.
He seemed to be so faithful,
Was with me constantly.
His arm became my resting place;
His strength became mine too.
And then my heart was broken,
For he proved to be untrue.

I wept before my Father's face,
"Oh God, how can this be,
That this my friend for all these years
Has proven false to me?"
It was a bitter lesson;
But I marvel at His grace,
That He showed me human failure
So I would seek His face.

Came awful trial and sickness
Which laid me low in pain.
I cling to Christ, My Saviour,
Who is every day the same.
He told me things in kindness--
His Words, they were so true.
He whispered soft, "I love you,
And will always care for you."

No matter how I faltered

He stayed by me each day;

He filled my heart with gladness

And never walked away.

How thankful that I found Him

And that he let me be

Forsaken and offended

So He could succor me.

By Gertrude Grace Sanborn

- **Proverbs 18:19**

  A brother offended *is harder to be won* than a strong city: and *their* contentions *are* like the bars of a castle.

This is a sad verse. Sometimes if you offend somebody that is the end of your friendship. They want nothing more to do with you, your Saviour, your Bible, or your Christian faith. Am I not right? I hope you are not offended by little tiny things. I hope it takes big things to offend you. And then, if you are a Psalm 119:165 person, you will not be offended. How many people are so close to the Lord Jesus Christ that "*nothing shall offend them*"? You can apologize to someone whom you have offended, but sometimes you cannot get through to them and get back into their fellowship.

I am glad there are some gracious people who, once you apologize to them, they come back and accept your apology. Are you not glad that some people have some grace. We all make mistakes and we all get foolish sometimes. If we make fools of ourselves and the other person gets mad at us, I hope that we are gracious. When that person comes to us and says he is sorry and asks forgiveness, I hope we will forgive him.

- **Matthew 11:6**

  And **blessed is *he*, whosoever shall not be offended in me.**

- **Matthew 13:41**

  The Son of man shall send forth his angels, and **they shall gather out of his kingdom all things that offend**, and them which do iniquity;

People Offended by the Gospel

There are some people who are offended by the gospel and by truth. If that be the case, you just keep preaching the truth and the gospel. Preach it kindly and with love, but preach it. Do not withdraw the truth just because people are offended.

There are some people that you just leave alone and let them be offended. They are not going to be won no matter what. They are not interested in the things of truth.

- Matthew 26:31

  Then saith Jesus unto them, **All ye shall be offended because of me this night:** for it is written, I will smite the shepherd, and the sheep of the flock shall be scattered abroad.

- 1 Corinthians 8:13

  Wherefore, **if meat make my brother to offend, I will eat no flesh** while the world standeth, lest I make my brother to offend.

Paul had the opportunity to eat all the meat he wanted to, but he would eat only vegetables if his eating meat offended his brother.

- James 3:2

  For **in many things we offend all. If any man offend not in word,** the same *is* a perfect man, *and* able also to bridle the whole body.

Paul says we are to stop destroying people. The Greek word for "*stumble*" is PROSKOPTO. It has a number of meanings:

"*to strike against; of those who strike against a stone or other obstacle in the path, to stumble; to strike one's foot against a stone; i.e. to meet with some harm; to rush upon, beat against; to be made to stumble by a thing; i.e. metaph. to be induced to sin.*"

We often are "*stumbled*" when we see in another person what we disapprove of and what hinders us.

Parents Stumble Their Children

That is all too true when parents are not what they ought to be in their homes. Their children see the sham and are "*stumbled*," and "*offended*," and "*made weak*."

We should not cause other believers to be "*made weak*" because of what we do or say. God wants them strong, and He wants us to be "*strong in the Lord*."

- **Ephesians 6:10**

  Finally, my brethren, **be strong in the Lord**, and in the power of his might.

Romans 14:22

"Hast thou faith? have *it* to thyself before God. Happy *is* he that condemneth not himself in that thing which he alloweth." Paul is saying to these believers at Rome, if they have "*faith*," this is all right. You can eat meat which has been offered to idols and it does not bother you. However, do not interfere with your brother and sister's life and cause them to "*stumble*," to be "*offended*," or to be "*made weak*."

We can indeed be "*happy*" when we do not "*condemn*" ourselves in that which we "*allow*." We ought not to have other people look at us and our lives when they are in shambles because of what we do or say. We have liberty. Paul said that he had liberty. "*All things are lawful for me, but all things are not expedient: all things are lawful for me, but all things edify not*" (1 Corinthians 10:23). He also said, "*All things are lawful unto me, but all things are not expedient: all things are lawful for me, but I will not be brought under the power of any*" (1 Corinthians 6:12).

Romans 14:23

"And he that doubteth is damned if he eat, because *he* eateth not of faith: for whatsoever *is* not of faith is sin." This verse teaches us that if we are in doubt about whether you should eat meat which has been offered unto idols (or whatever a similar thing might be in our present day), we are "*damned*." The Greek word for this is KATAKRINO. It has various meanings:

"to give judgment against, to judge worthy of punishment; to <u>*condemn*</u>*; by one's good example to render another's wickedness the more evident and censurable."*

It is not referring to condemnation in Hell in this verse. It probably refers to being condemned because of this bad judgment. In the case of eating with *"doubt,"* it is sin *"because he eateth not of faith."* You have a *"doubt"* and do not think that what you are doing is right, but that it is going against your convictions. Paul says this is not proper, *"for whatsoever is not of faith is sin."* This applies even in these doubtful things.

When Doubting Is Sin

If you have a question of whether you should say or do something, and you do not have faith that it is in accordance with the Words of God, then Paul says it is *"sin."*

This is a difficult thing to understand. God wants us to have absolute certainty about what we do, what we say, and what we believe. He wants us to be a part of the Scriptures and the harmony of the Words of God. If we do not have that faith, God says it is *"sin."* Let us do things that we know are right.

Make sure you are right and then go ahead with what you are thinking, saying, or doing. Some people have no compunctions or hesitations. They just go ahead and think, say, or do whatever they wish. Others hesitate and perhaps want to pray about it. They are not sure it is right at this time. They ask for a little more time to ponder their choices. There is a decision to be made, but it must be a right decision, not a wrong one.

I say again, be sure that what you think, say, or do is right. Make sure your convictions about the Bible and the Bible's standards are right.

You Must Be Convinced of the Lord

The Lord must be the One to convince you that what you believe is right. It must not come from your wife, husband, or friend. You should have a desire to walk with the Lord. Make sure that anything you think, say, or do is proper before Him and in line with His Words.

𝕽𝖔𝖒𝖆𝖓𝖘
𝕮𝖍𝖆𝖕𝖙𝖊𝖗 𝕱𝖎𝖋𝖙𝖊𝖊𝖓

Romans 15:1

"We then that are strong ought to bear the infirmities of the weak, and not to please ourselves." The *"strong"* Christians should carry the *"infirmities"* of the *"weak."*

- **Galatians 6:1**

  Brethren, if a man be overtaken in a fault, **ye which are spiritual, restore such an one** in the spirit of meekness; considering thyself, lest thou also be tempted.

  Those who are strong in the faith, strong in their positions, strong in the Bible, strong in every way, should not simply sit back with their strength and do nothing for others who are *"weak."* They should not let the people who are *"weak"* suffer, struggle, or go underneath the water.

Help those Weak in the Faith

God wants us to help and to bear the infirmities of those who are weaker or not as strong in the faith in the Lord Jesus Christ as we are.

We have some people in our church, as there are in every church, who are not as strong as others. Some are weak and need a little bit of encouragement. If you are strong in the Lord, let us bear the burdens together and help the weak among us.

- **Galatians 6:5**

For **every man shall bear his own burden**.

We have to bear our own burdens, but when we can help the others bear their burdens, we need to do that. In the clause "*and not to please ourselves*" there is a prohibition in the Greek present tense. This structure means to stop doing an action that they were already doing in the church at Rome. Apparently, these Christians at Rome were pleasing themselves and not caring about anybody else. We should not forget about our fellow believers in Christ in our local church and elsewhere.

- **Proverbs 16:7**

When a man's ways **please the LORD**, he maketh even his enemies to be at peace with him.

- **Romans 8:8**

So then they that are in the flesh **cannot please God**.

- **1 Corinthians 10:33**

Even as I **please all *men*** in all *things*, not seeking mine own profit, but the *profit* of many, that they may be saved.

Paul wanted to please the Lord Jesus Christ, but he said here that he pleased "*all men*." Not in a wrong way, not in a sinful way, but in things that do not make any difference and are not in violation of the Words of God. Paul wanted people to get saved.

- **Galatians 1:10**

For do I now persuade men, or God? or **do I seek to please men**? for if I yet **pleased men**, I should not be the servant of Christ.

Please the Lord Jesus Christ First

There is a point beyond which we cannot please people. We must please the Lord Jesus Christ first and foremost. He wants us to maintain a sound position in our doctrine and beliefs.

- 2 Timothy 2:4

  No man that warreth entangleth himself with the affairs of *this* life; that **he may please him** who hath chosen him to be a soldier.

We must please the Lord Jesus Christ and not ourselves in these matters. These are very important things to bear in mind. The Greek word for "please" is ARESKO. It means:

> "*to please; to strive to please; to accommodate one's self to the opinions desires and interests of others.*"

If it is not a doctrinal issue, we can accommodate ourselves to the interests of others so that they might be saved. We cannot accommodate doctrine. We must hold to the teachings of the Bible without compromise.

Romans 15:2

"Let every one of us please *his* neighbour for *his* good to edification." Here again it is an exhortation to continue to "*please*" our "*neighbour*" in order to accommodate ourselves to them when we can. We are not going to change our theology or our doctrine or our belief in salvation by grace through faith in our Saviour. We are not going to change how we believe, but in the little things that do not matter let us see if we can help them.

The purpose is for their "*good to edification*" and not for their evil. We also do this for their "*edification.*" We should want to build them up in the things of the Lord. That is what needs to be done to people. They need to be built up. We can please them for their good so that they may be strong and built up in the things of the Lord Jesus Christ. Many believers are weak and the weak ones need to be built up. That is what our task is, if we are strong.

Romans 15:3

"For even Christ pleased not himself; but, as it is written, The reproaches of them that reproached thee fell on me." Our Lord Jesus Christ is our example in this action. He "*pleased not himself.*" He pleased His Father. It was pleasing to God the Father that the Lord Jesus Christ should suffer, bleed, and die in our place on the Cross of Calvary. He did not please Himself. If He had pleased Himself, He would not have allowed Himself to be delivered to Pilate nor be crucified.

I remind you that the phrase "*it is written*" is in the perfect tense in Greek. As such, it refers to what David wrote down in the past, which writing continued to Paul's day, and continues on into the future to our day and behind. This speaks about Bible preservation of God's Words.

When Paul refers to the "*reproaches,*" he was quoting from Psalm 69.

● **Psalm 69:9**

For the zeal of thine house hath eaten me up; and **the reproaches of them that reproached thee are fallen upon me.**

The Lord Jesus Christ is the One Who bore our reproaches. He bore the many false things that people speak against us. That is what the word "*reproach*" means. It refers to those people who are against us, upbraid us, and revile us. The Lord Jesus Christ bore all of these things for the believers. He bore in His own body the sins of the world, including the "*reproaches.*"

Not Easy Being a Christian

It is not always easy to be a Christian. Many people do not like our Christian faith. They differ with us on it. They will "*reproach*" us and revile us from time to time. They will say things that are against us. They will speak against us. The Lord Jesus Christ took all those reproaches on Himself. We should not feel the sting of them any longer. He took the sting Himself. That is what this verse is telling the believers.

Romans 15:4

"For whatsoever things were written aforetime were written for our learning, that we through patience and comfort of the Scriptures might have hope." This is a beautiful and important verse on the purpose of the Old Testament. God's Old Testament Words "*were written aforetime.*" All of these Hebrew Words and the few Aramaic Words found in the Old Testament were "*written for our learning.*" This was true in Paul's day for the Christians at Rome and it is true for our day as well. These Old Testament Words were written for the purpose of our "*learning.*" We who are saved must read God's Words, Old and New Testaments, in order to learn the things God has for us therein. We must receive the blessings of the Old Testament Scriptures that God has placed there for us who are believers in His Son as our Saviour. They are for our "*learning.*"

God's Way of Bringing Us Hope

There is something more for the believer in the Old Testament. Another purpose of these Words is in order that the born-again believers, *"through patience and comfort of the Scriptures might have hope."* If we read them and believe them, the Scriptures give us *"patience."* There is *"patience"* found in the Old Testament Scriptures because they speak of a future fulfillment of God's promises. That future is what we have to be *"patient"* about. Many of us are anxious and are not *"patient."* God says if you get into the Scriptures and learn from them you will find both the *"comfort"* and the *"patience"* that they are able to give to you. There are many verses in regard to *"comfort."*

- 2 Corinthians 1:3-6

  Blessed *be* God, even the Father of our Lord Jesus Christ, the Father of mercies, and the **God of all comfort**; Who **comforteth us** in all our tribulation, that we may be able to **comfort them** which are in any trouble, by the **comfort** wherewith we ourselves are **comforted of God**. For as the sufferings of Christ abound in us, so our consolation also aboundeth by Christ. And whether we be afflicted, *it is* for your consolation and salvation, which is effectual in the enduring of the same sufferings which we also suffer: or whether we be **comforted**, *it is* for your consolation and salvation.

- 1 Thessalonians 4:18

  Wherefore **comfort one another** with these words.

The Words of God gives us *"comfort"* especially when people have died. The Scriptures in the Psalms are *"comforting."* Even in the books of Genesis, Exodus, and Leviticus and all the other Scriptures are *"comforting"* in their special ways.

Read the Old Testament Also

Many people say that they do not want to bother with the Old Testament. They just want the New Testament. The Old Testament was *"written aforetime"* for our *"learning."*

Those Scriptures give us *"patience and comfort"* as well as *"hope."* The Old Testament saints did not have it too easy. They had many difficulties. Think of David and how God defeated all his enemies. Think of King Asa who had one million Ethiopians from North Africa coming after him. Asa did not know what to do. He simply prayed to the Lord. The Lord has no problem with helping, whether there be many or few. The Lord answered that prayer and defeated the million Ethiopians by His grace. When we read of these events, it gives us hope, patience, and comfort. We trust that God will intercede for us even when we think that things are going bad for us, even as He did for the Old Testament saints.

Romans 15:5

"Now the God of patience and consolation grant you to be likeminded one toward another according to Christ Jesus:" This is a benediction. We have another benediction in Verse 13, *"Now the God of hope fill you with all joy and peace in believing, that ye may abound in hope, through the power of the Holy Ghost."* Here is another evidence of our Lord being *"the God of patience and consolation."*

The Greek word for *"consolation"* is PARAKLESIS. It's various meanings include:

"a calling near, summons, (esp. for help); importation, supplication, entreaty; exhortation, admonition, encouragement; consolation, comfort, solace; that which affords comfort or refreshment; thus of the Messianic salvation (so the Rabbis call the Messiah the consoler, the comforter); persuasive discourse, stirring address; instructive, admonitory, conciliatory, powerful hortatory discourse."

It is the same word translated *"comfort."* The God of the Bible is a consoling God and a God of patience. He wants the believers there at Rome to continue *"to be likeminded one toward another according to Christ Jesus."*

Likemindedness Is Important

This *"likemindedness"* is not according to us and our own feelings. We may have many thoughts and want everybody to agree with us. This *"likemindedness"* must be in accordance to Christ Jesus and according to His Words. That is the thing that we must know, memorize, and go along with in our doctrines.

The Greek word for *"like mindedness"* is PHRONEO. Its various meanings are:

"to have understanding, be wise; to feel, to think; to have an opinion of one's self, think of one's self, to be modest, not let one's opinion (though just) of himself exceed the bounds of modesty; to think or judge what one's opinion is; to be of the same mind i.e. agreed together, <u>cherish the same views, be harmonious</u>; to direct one's mind to a thing, to seek, to strive for; to seek one's interest or advantage; to be of one's party, side with him (in public affairs)."

Churches Should Be Harmonious

It is always good in a church to be harmonious. Sometimes in a church there is not harmony, but disharmony. The word for that is *"cacophony."* That is bad harmony, where everyone is fighting and at one another's throat. God wants us to be *"likeminded"* and *"cherish the same views."*

We hold to the doctrines of the Scriptures here in our church. We believe that the Scriptures are God's Words kept in tact. In English this is our *King James Bible*. We appreciate this Bible, and we stand for the things of Christ. We're Baptist and we believe in these doctrines of the faith.

Romans 15:6

"That ye may with one mind *and* one mouth glorify God, even the Father of our Lord Jesus Christ." God wants every saved person to glorify Himself. That Greek word for *"glorify"* is

DOXAZO.

It has various meanings:

"*to think, suppose, be of opinion; to praise, extol, magnify, celebrate; to honour, do honour to, hold in honour; to make glorious, adorn with lustre, clothe with splendour; to impart glory to something, render it excellent; to make renowned, render illustrious; <u>to cause the dignity and worth of some person or thing to become manifest and acknowledged</u>.*"

God wants us "*to cause His dignity and worth to be manifested and acknowledged.*" He wants the believers at Rome, and us today as well, to do this "*with one mind and one mouth.*"

Minds and Mouths Glorifying God

It is good to be of "*one mind,*" but we must also be of "*one mouth*" as we "*glorify God.*" We should be unified in our "*mind*" and in our "*mouths.*" We who are saved people should be united both in what we say as well as what we believe. Some people have mostly "*mind*" and no "*mouth.*" Some people have "*mouth,*" but not so much "*mind.*" We must have both.

We must be thinking about the things that concern our Lord Jesus Christ. The Scriptures "*were written aforetime*" for our edification and our doctrine. We can praise and glorify the Lord with our "*mouths*" as well as what we do and what we think.

What we think usually comes out in some way, does it not? You cannot keep your "*mind*" to yourself too long. You can often take a look at somebody's face and you can tell many things. You cannot always tell exactly what somebody is thinking.

Words Start in the Mind First

However, soon what is on the mind comes out in words that are said, whether it is anger, whether it is gratitude, whether it is praise, whether it is joy, or whatever it might be.

Our God wants us to be in *"one mind."* We need to glorify our great God *"with one mind and one mouth"* and cause Him to be exalted and manifested in His dignity and in His work.

Romans 15:7

"Wherefore receive ye one another, as Christ also received us to the glory of God." As we noted earlier, the Greek word for *"receive"* is PROSLAMBANO. It has various meanings:

> *"to take to, take in addition, to take to one's self; <u>to take as one's companion</u>; to take by the hand in order to lead aside; <u>to take or receive into one's home, with the collateral idea of kindness; to receive, i.e. grant one access to one's heart</u>; to take into friendship and intercourse; to take to one's self, to take: i.e. food."*

Since *"receive"* is in the Greek present tense, it is a continuous action. It means to continue to *"receive"* one another. In other words, every one of the members of this local church in Rome (and the same in any local church of our day), we are to *"receive one another to ourselves as one's companion."* The Greek verb is not simply LAMBANO which means *"to take,"* but it is PROSLAMBANO. PROS conveys the meaning of *"to, toward, or near."* PROSLAMBANO conveys the meanings cited above. It is indeed a rich and meaningful verb.

These Christians at Rome were to have a real relationship one toward another and so are we at our local churches today. We are to receive one another.

Receiving One Another

Apparently the believers in Rome were not always receiving one another and had to be reminded to do this by Paul. Sometimes it is difficult for some people *"to receive"* someone who is a different color, size, sex, dress, income level, health status, or intelligence, but Paul says *"to receive"* in the Lord even these people. Believers are to take them into their hearts as one of their own.

The Lord Jesus Christ *"received"* us to Himself. He forgave our sins if we are saved and have genuinely believed in and trusted in Him. Just as He "*received*" us, so we should "*receive*" one another. That is a wonderful goal for us to aim at, is it not?

Romans 15:8

"Now I say that Jesus Christ was a minister of the circumcision for the truth of God, to confirm the promises *made* unto the fathers:" The Lord Jesus Christ ministered to the "*circumcision,*" which is another word for the Jews. Later on we will see in this chapter that Paul says He is also a minister to the Gentiles. Most of us in our church are Gentiles. There were many Gentiles in the church at Rome also. Paul is simply saying that the Lord Jesus Christ came unto His own people, the Jews, and they didn't receive Him, or accept Him, they rejected Him and crucified Him. "*But as many as received him, to them gave he power to become the sons of God, even to them that believe on his name:*" (John 1:12).

The Lord Jesus Christ never set aside any of the promises made to Abraham, Isaac, and Jacob. All the Old Testament promises that were made to the Old Testament Israelites will come to pass and be fulfilled to the letter.

Last week when we talked about the Biblical Dispensations, we talked about the Dispensation of Innocence when Adam and Eve were in the garden. The Dispensation of Conscience was after God threw them out of the Garden. When the flood came, it was the Dispensation of Human Government. Then there was the Tower of Babel and the Dispensation of Promise when God took one man, Abraham, and promised to give him a land, a people, and a nation as the sands of the sea. Then he had a son, Isaac. Isaac had a son, Jacob. Those promises to the fathers Abraham, Isaac, and Jacob and all of the Old Testament promises have not been fulfilled in the church. After that came the Dispensation of the Law of Moses. We are now in the Dispensation of Grace or the Church. Then comes the Millennial reign of the Lord Jesus Christ.

Many people today are teaching that the Israelites are the same as the church and that the church is the same as Israel. No! This is called Covenant Theology.

God's Promises Will Be Fulfilled

God is going to fulfill every promise He made to the Old Testament fathers. The Lord Jesus Christ is going to take care of that. Most of these promises will be fulfilled during the Millennium when the Lord Jesus Christ will reign on this earth. That will last 1,000 years. That is the time when the Lord Jesus will confirm and fulfill every promise made to Israel. They will have the land. They will have the land completely.

They have never yet occupied fully all the land that was promised to them, but they will in the Millennial Reign of Christ. They will be the chief nation on this earth. The Lord Jesus Christ will reign out of Jerusalem. Israel will be the "*head, and not the tail*" (Dt. 28:13). People will honor them. Now, they are just a little tiny remnant of things. That is what that verse is teaching. He is going to come back, and He will "*confirm the promises made to the fathers.*"

Romans 15:9

"And that the Gentiles might glorify God for *his* mercy; as it is written, For this cause I will confess to thee among the Gentiles, and sing unto thy name." The Lord not only is going to deal with Israel, but notice in this verse He is going to see that "*the Gentiles . . . glorify God for his mercy.*" The Lord Jesus Christ is not only interested in the Jews, but also in us Gentiles. The church at Rome was a Gentile church. Our Bible for Today Baptist Church is also a Gentile church currently. God is interested in those of us who are not Jews. He wants us to be saved. He wants us to "*glorify God for His mercy.*" That is what this verse says.

It Is Written=Bible Preservation

Paul uses the term "*as it is written*" once again. It is still a strong testimony for the Bible preservation of the Hebrew, Aramaic, and Greek Words of the Bible. As a Greek perfect tense, Paul is talking about God's Words that were written in the past that have been preserved to the present, and into the future.

Paul could quote from these Words. We can quote from them in the future as well. The Words of God are permanent and are preserved. He quotes this Old Testament Psalm.

- **Psalm 18:49**

  Therefore will **I give thanks unto thee, O LORD, among the heathen,** and sing praises unto thy name.

The Gentiles one day were going to be made to glorify God and to sing His praises, even though at the time of this Psalm the Jews were prominent. The Gentiles were of no consequence. Our Gentile ancestors were idol worshipers and Satanically motivated. They did not know Christ. They did not know God. All of a sudden the Gentiles who did not know God have come into the blessings of Christ and the blessings of the Father because the Jews rejected the Saviour and therefore we are able to accept Him and receive Him.

In the clause, "*I will confess to thee among the Gentiles, and sing unto thy name,*" the Greek word for "*sing*" is PSALLO. It means:

> "*to pluck off, pull out; to cause to vibrate by touching, to twang; to touch or strike the chord, to twang the strings of a musical instrument so that they gently vibrate; **to play on a stringed instrument, to play, the harp**, etc.; to sing to the music of the harp; in the NT to sing a hymn, **to celebrate the praises of God in song**.*"

They had musical instruments in David's day though they were not as sophisticated as our instruments today. We should "*sing unto His Name*" as well. Singing of hymns and gospel songs is an important part of our worship of the Lord. We do a lot of singing in our church and seek to glorify the Lord Jesus Christ in this way.

Romans 15:10

"And again he saith, Rejoice, ye Gentiles, with his people." Paul then quotes another Old Testament verse.

- **Deuteronomy 32:43**

  Rejoice, O ye nations, *with* his people: for he will avenge the blood of his servants, and will render vengeance to his adversaries, and will be merciful unto his land, *and* to his people.

Five References the Old Testament

Before Paul quotes from the Old Testament he says either *"it is written"* or he uses the word, *"again."* In the first half of Romans 15:1-17, Paul makes five different references to the Old Testament.

(1) In verse 3, he uses *"it is written;"*

(2) in verse 9, he uses *"it is written;"*

(3) in verse 10, he uses *"again;"*

(4) in verse 11, he uses *"again;"* and,

(5) in verse 12, he uses *"again."*

The Scriptures indeed are a *"comfort"* to those who read and follow them. The Scripture quoted here is about the Gentiles. The Gentiles are those who are just plain heathen. *"Gentiles"* is another word for *"heathen."* Gentiles are those who were unsaved and not Jews. Those who are saved in this age of grace are rejoicing. In the Millennial reign of the Lord Jesus Christ multitudes of the Jews will be saved and glorify the Lord as their Messiah. They will be looking on Him whom they have pierced as it says in the book of Zechariah.

- Zechariah 12:10

  And I will pour upon the house of David, and upon the inhabitants of Jerusalem, the spirit of grace and of supplications: and **they shall look upon me whom they have pierced**, and they shall mourn for him, as one mourneth for *his* only *son*, and shall be in bitterness for him, as one that is in bitterness for *his* firstborn.

Jews & Gentiles Rejoicing Together

The saved Gentiles and the saved Jews will rejoice together. At the present time, Israel has been "blinded." Some of them are saved, but most of them are lost because they have rejected the Lord Jesus Christ as their Saviour.

Romans 15:11

"And again, Praise the Lord, all ye Gentiles; and laud him, all ye people." Paul again quotes the Old Testament from the book of the Psalms.

- Psalm 117:1

  O praise the LORD, all ye nations: praise him, all ye people.

Again the Lord is referring to the fact that Gentiles such as we are and such as the Christians at Rome were, will be able to praise the Lord and thank Him for his salvation by genuine faith in the Lord Jesus Christ. Paul is again reminding them that not only the Jews, but also the Gentiles have a place in God's purposes.

Romans 15:12

"And again, Esaias saith, There shall be a root of Jesse, and he that shall rise to reign over the Gentiles; in him shall the Gentiles trust." Once more Paul quotes from the Old Testament concerning our Saviour.

- Isaiah 11:1

  And there shall come forth a rod out of the stem of Jesse, and a Branch shall grow out of his roots:

This *"Branch"* out of the *"stem of Jesse"* was a reference to the Lord Jesus Christ Who was of the lineage of David. Jesse was David's father.

The Lineage of Mary and Joseph

The Lord Jesus Christ's lineage is given in two places in the New Testament. It is found in Matthew Chapter 1 and again in Luke Chapter 3. In Matthew 1 it is his legal father Joseph's lineage through David's son Solomon and Jechonias (Matthew 1:6 and 1:11). In Chapter 3 of Luke it is Mary's lineage through David's son Nathan (Luke 3:31).

Nathan was a different son of David and he escaped the curse placed upon

Jechonias which is another name for Jehoiakim who tore up God's Words, threw them into the fire, and burned them (Jeremiah 36:28-30). Because he did this Jeconias was cursed and his line was cursed. Mary's line escaped this curse. Her line came through David through Nathan (Luke 3:31). Joseph was our Lord's legal father though he was not the real father. The Lord Jesus Christ had no human father. God the Father was His Father working through God the Holy Spirit (Luke 1:35).

The *"root of Jesse"* shows that it is through David's line that the Lord Jesus Christ should come. The Messiah came through David's line. When the Antichrist appears upon this earth, and deceives the people, he will show that he comes through David, the *"root of Jesse."* because that is the prophecy that the Messiah had to be in the line through David (Luke 1:32). I do not know if he is going to be able to prove that or if he will be able to forge documents or genealogies and try to prove to the people that he is from David's line and out of the *"root of Jesse."* I think it is going to be difficult. Most of the Jews today do not know their lineage. Most of them do not know from what tribe they are. They are all confused, but the Antichrist is going to have to prove his genealogy.

Christ Fulfilled All Requirements

The Lord Jesus Christ is the only genuine One Who can come to fill all the requirements of the Messiah, and that is why He is called *"Christ."* The word CHRISTOS is the Greek for *"anointed one."* Messiah is from the Hebrew word MAWSHIYACH. It means *"anointed one."* Messiah and Christ are terms meaning the same thing, one in Hebrew and the other in Greek.

Since the Lord Jesus Christ is the only One Who can fulfill the requirements of the Messiah, the Jews must accept Him and no other One. Some of the Orthodox Jews are looking for Messiah. That is why they go to the wailing wall in Jerusalem outside the Western wall ,which is the only part of the original temple that is still standing. At that wailing wall, the women are on one side of a partition and the men are on the other side. They move their bodies and sway and say these prayers. They have their little caps on and they have small portions of the Scriptures. They put small pieces of paper with prayers written on them in the cracks in the wall. They are wailing, crying, and looking for the coming of Messiah. He has already come. They are looking for someone in Whom they do not believe. One day the Jews will look unto their Messiah Whom they have pierced (Zechariah 12:10) and mourn for Him as the mourning of an only Son.

When will that take place? When will the Lord Jesus Christ reign? When has He ever reigned over the Gentiles? He is not reigning over these Gentiles now. Look at the heathen people all around us in the United States and other countries. All around us the Lord Jesus Christ is not ruling and reigning, but one day He will. He will be reigning in the Millennial reign of Christ, when He reigns for one thousand years.

"*Thousand Years*" Used Six Times

In verses two through seven of Revelation 20, there are six different references to a "*thousand years.*"

1. Satan will be bound for a "*thousand years*" (verse 2).

2. Satan's deception stops for a "*thousand years*" (verse 3).

3. The saved will reign with Christ a "*thousand years*" (v. 4).

4. The rest of the dead did not live until the "*thousand years*" were finished (verse 5).

5. Believers will reign with Christ a "*thousand years*" (v. 6).

6. After these "*thousand years*" are expired, Satan will be loosed from his prison to deceive the nations (verse 7).

Golden Rule of Bible Interpretation

"*When the PLAIN SENSE of Scripture makes COMMON SENSE, SEEK NO OTHER SENSE. Therefore, take EVERY WORD at its primary, ordinary, usual, literal meaning, UNLESS the facts of the immediate context, studied in the light of related passages, and axiomatic and fundamental truths, indicate CLEARLY otherwise. God, in revealing His Word, neither intends nor permits the reader to be confused. He wants His children to understand.*"

Harold Camping, the president of Family Radio, says that those references of a *"thousand years"* do not mean a true *"thousand years,"* but only a long period of time. The preceding "Golden Rule of Bible Interpretation" demands that the *"thousand years"* be taken literally. Mr. Camping is wrong in his interpretation here and in many other places as well.

When Paul referred to *"he that shall rise to reign over the Gentiles; in him shall the Gentiles trust,"* he was referring to the Lord Jesus Christ in His Millennial reign. The Jews will be uppermost at that time, and He will reign from Jerusalem. Some people will be saved during the Tribulation period and even during the Millennium. The desert shall blossom as the rose (Isaiah 35:1). Fresh water will come into that desert (Ezekiel 47:8-11) and they will plant trees in the desert places where now is only sand (Isaiah 41:19). All the promises of God will be fulfilled. People will live longer. Their days will be *"as the days of a tree"* (Isaiah 65:22). According to Internet sources, some Redwood trees can be up to 367 feet tall and live to 2,000 years. Some Sequoia trees can be up to 311 feet tall and live up to 3,200 years. This might mean that people will live as long as they did before Noah's flood. Methuselah lived 969 years (Genesis 5:27). Isaiah had this to say:

- **Isaiah 65:20**

  There shall be no more thence an infant of days, nor an old man that hath not filled his days: for **the child shall die an hundred years old**; but the sinner *being* an hundred years old shall be accursed.

Think about this a while. Suppose there is a six-year-old *"child."* His life expectancy would be about sixty or ten times six. If the *"child"* is still called a child when he dies at an *"hundred years old,"* one hundred times ten would be 1,000. I believe longevity is going to be increased just like it was in the days before the flood. There is nothing wrong with these bodies that they could not live longer. That is the way God made us. It is sin that causes us to become diseased. During Noah's flood the canopy of water came down flooding the earth. When this happened, that canopy stopped surrounding the earth to filter the harmful rays of the sun. Now those harmful rays age us and make us sick. When the canopy surrounded the earth, it made the whole earth a tropical paradise. That's why you have flora and fauna of tropical types in the North Pole, because they were frozen in there after the flood. Everything was tropical. Dr. Henry Morris and Dr. John Whitcomb have written this book on *The Genesis Flood* (BFT #59) which explains this in great detail.

It is amazing to see all of these different things that will happen during the Millennial reign of our Saviour. During the Millennium we are going to have an atmosphere that will permit these human bodies to live up to even a thousand years just like in the pre-flood days. The Lord Jesus Christ will reign over the

Gentiles. The Jews will be the leading nation on earth at the time. This is more or less what we have been talking about in the discussion on the seventh dispensation of the Millennial reign of Christ. "*In Him shall the Gentiles trust.*" We who were former Gentiles and have genuinely trusted in the Lord Jesus Christ ought to be praising the Lord for all He has done for us.

Romans 15:13

"Now the God of hope fill you with all joy and peace in believing, that ye may abound in hope, through the power of the Holy Ghost." "*The God of hope*" is a great Name for the Lord. Back in verse 5 He is called "*the God of patience and consolation.*" Now, He is called "*the God of hope.*" We are not hopeless.

In Ephesians, Paul described the Gentiles as "*having no hope and without God in the world*" (Ephesians 2:12). We who are saved and were formerly called "*Gentiles*" were "*without God*" in this world. Now that we are born-again and have the Lord Jesus Christ, we have some hope now. We have hope for eternal life. We have a confident hope. Paul wanted the believers at Rome to have "*the God of hope*" to fill them "*with all joy and peace in believing.*"

Continual Faith Brings Joy & Peace

The Greek word for "*believing*" is in the present tense. It implies a continuous faith and trust in this "*God of hope.*" It is that continuous believing that brings "*all joy and peace.*"

The Lord Jesus Christ told his own, "*Peace I leave with you, my peace I give unto you: not as the world giveth, give I unto you. Let not your heart be troubled, neither let it be afraid*" (John 14:27). He can give us a "*joy and a peace*" that the lost world knows nothing about.

The world's happiness is based on happenstances, whether it is a new hat, a new coat, a new dress, a new car, a new boat, a new home, or whatever it might be.

The Source of Abounding Hope

The source of God's abounding *"hope"* is the *"power of the Holy Ghost."* The Holy Spirit of God is the One Who gives us the power to *"abound in hope."* He gives us the power to be filled with *"joy and peace."* These godly qualities are only given by the Spirit of God. In fact these are part of the fruit of the Spirit.

- **Galatians 5:22**

  But the fruit of the Spirit is love, **joy, peace**, longsuffering, gentleness, goodness, faith,

  If we are saved, the *"God of hope"* can fill us with His joy, His peace, and His hope by the power of the Holy Spirit of God. There is a good definition we sometimes quote for that word *"peace."* It is

  "the tranquil state of a soul assured of its salvation through Christ, and so fearing nothing from God and content with its earthly lot, of whatsoever sort that is."

That is what God's peace is. In this country we have so many things, yet many of us are not content. Paul said, *"Not that I speak in respect of want: for I have learned, in whatsoever state I am, therewith to be content"* (Philippians 4:11). That is possible only by the power of the Holy Spirit.

Romans 15:14

"And I myself also am persuaded of you, my brethren, that ye also are full of goodness, filled with all knowledge, able also to admonish one another." Paul is confident that these believers at Rome were *"full of goodness"* and *"filled with all knowledge."* That *"knowledge"* is not knowledge of the world, although that is good to have. We who are saved are able to have a better knowledge than the world. It is the knowledge of God's Words. It is the knowledge of God's will. It is the knowledge of the things of eternity.

We Must Read the Old Testament

These believers at Rome did not have the complete New Testament like we have. They had only the Old Testament, but they were to read it and study it. The purpose and power of the Old Testament is given in this verse: *"For whatsoever things were written aforetime were written for our learning, that we through patience and comfort of the Scriptures might have hope"* (Romans 15:4).

Paul was *"persuaded"* that they were also *"able also to admonish one another."* I believe *"admonition"* is important. Paul believed firmly that they were able and completely empowered to *"admonish one another."* They were capable of it.

Knowledge Precedes Admonition

If we are not filled with the knowledge of the Words of God, we cannot admonish anybody. We cannot teach anybody. We must know the Words of God first. That is the secret of proper admonition.

The Greek word for *"admonish"* is NOUTHETEO. It is a compound word made up of two words, NOUS (*"mind"*) and TITHEMI (*"to put or place"*). It means *"to admonish, warn, or exhort."* We must often place some wisdom into the minds of our fellow believers in order to *"admonish"* them. Sometimes it means *"to exhort"* and sometimes *"to warn"*. What happens when somebody admonishes, exhorts, warns us, or puts something into our minds? Sometimes we are angry with them. Sometimes we do not want to follow them. Paul told these believers they must first have a complete knowledge of the Words of God before they *"admonish"* fellow Christians.

Paul was *"persuaded"* that these Christians at Rome were *"filled with all knowledge"* of God's Words and thus were *"able also to admonish one another."* You do not have to wait for the pastor or some other official of the church to admonish fellow believers. Every born-again Christian should be *"filled with all knowledge"* so that they can admonish one another. When we who are saved see something going amiss in one of our friends' lives, we can step aside and say, "Did you notice this verse in the Bible?" We can admonish and exhort others to stay on the right track according to the Scripture. Such admonition should bring peace and harmony in the church, not discord and division.

Each individual believer should be equipped to admonish and instruct others according to the Bible. There is a former psychologist named Dr. Bobgan and his wife Deidre who have written many books on psychology. They are teaching that believers ought to be able to guide, help, and encourage one another rather than the professional psychologists or even pastors. He believes strongly that knowledgeable individual Christians should be able to *"admonish"* fellow believers and help them. These things, I think, are very clear. This is one of the verses that is used to *"admonish"* one another. Other verses on this subject are Colossians 3:16; 1 Thessalonians 5:12; and 2 Thessalonians 3:15.

This word NOUTHETEO is where we get the English word *"nouthetic."* There is a whole school of counseling called "nouthetic counseling." The psychiatry that follows Freud teaches that the counselor is to just listen to the person without saying a word to direct him or her. The nouthetic counselor says, when you have a good understanding of the situation, you should give the person advice and admonish them.

In the Christian realm the Lord wants us to have an opinion. We just do not sit there and let the people do what they want to do. This is one of the things I was talking about several weeks ago. I was talking to an individual who is going to a psychiatrist who is lost and unsaved. The psychiatrist does not care what this individual does. They might be sinning. They might be perverts. Freud's teachings would say for the counselor to keep silent and be non-directive. As I was talking to this individual I told him that this psychiatrist may help him with his mental health, but not to listen to him when he talks to him about things that are moral or things of Scripture. He does not know what is straight up and straight down regarding the Bible. He is leading this person astray and he should not listen.

Romans 15:15

"Nevertheless, brethren, I have written the more boldly unto you in some sort, as putting you in mind, because of the grace that is given to me of God." Paul was very bold in his writing because God had given him much *"grace."* He is saying very boldly from the previous verse that they ought to *"admonish one another."*

He does not want to admonish them too strongly. He wants to remind them of these things. They should help another. They should bear one another's burdens and so fulfill the law of Christ (Galatians 6:2). When needful, they were to admonish one another with the knowledge of the Words of God that they had.

Romans 15:16

"That I should be the minister of Jesus Christ to the Gentiles, ministering the gospel of God, that the offering up of the Gentiles might be acceptable, being sanctified by the Holy Ghost." Paul was a servant of the Lord Jesus Christ. As he spoke to these Gentile Christians at Rome, he wanted to be a good *"minister,"* as he faithfully was *"ministering the gospel of God."* That was his purpose and mission. The Lord Jesus Christ had sent him to the Gentiles (Acts 9:15). He had one thing in mind; he was an evangelist and preacher of the gospel of the Lord Jesus Christ. That was a very important mission. Paul was concerned *"that the offering up of the Gentiles might be acceptable."* The words *"offering up"* means bringing to the altar the sacrifice that they made. It implies bringing the Gentiles to Christ for service. Whatever service any of us might try to do for the Lord Jesus Christ, we should be concerned that it *"might be acceptable, being sanctified by the Holy Ghost."*

The work that we do for the Lord must be sanctified by the Holy Spirit. If not, the work is in vain. We can do anything we want on our own. We can talk on our own in our own flesh, but if the Lord Jesus Christ our Saviour and the Holy Spirit of God are not behind what we do and say, it all goes up in smoke. It is not permanent. The Lord is permanent. Only this type of ministry is *"acceptable"* to the Lord and it is *"sanctified by the Holy Ghost."*

Romans 15:17

"I have therefore whereof I may glory through Jesus Christ in those things which pertain to God." Paul was happy for the work these believers were doing *"in those things which pertain to God."* He gloried in these things *"through Jesus Christ."* When all else fails, when all the things around us seem to be murky, difficult, and very hard, we can still glory through the Lord Jesus Christ. He can bring us peace and glory through the Spirit of God by believing and taking part in those things that pertain to God and His work. Those things that pertain to God are settled, stable, and do not change. We change and our circumstances change.

We must *"endure hardness as a soldier of Jesus Christ"* (2 Timothy 2:3).

We can always "*glory*" in the things that "*pertain to God*" because He is always up in Heaven where it is peaceful, perfect, righteous, and sinless. If we get into difficulty down here, we just simply "*seek those things which are above.*" Paul tells us in the book of Colossians:

- **Colossians 3:1**

  If ye then be risen with Christ, **seek those things which are above**, where Christ sitteth on the right hand of God.

Everything is peaceful up there above the clouds.

We flew recently on a short flight from Philadelphia to Elmira, New York for a Bible conference. We flew in a little commuter plane. It was a propeller plane with seats for only thirty-seven. We flew at an altitude of about twenty thousand feet in the air where everything was calm and peaceful. When we flew closer to the earth it was choppy and bumpy. It makes you not want to land because when you land it is bumpy. The Lord is above the clouds up in that high altitude with no choppiness, only absolute perfection, peacefulness, and quietness without a single bump or thump.

Setting Our Affections Above

We must "*set our affections on things above*" especially when we are experiencing the difficulties of this life. There are many difficulties. There are all sorts of aches, pains, and problems. We must do as Paul did and "*glory through Jesus Christ in those things which pertain to God.*"

Romans 15:18

"For I will not dare to speak of any of those things which Christ hath not wrought by me, to make the Gentiles obedient, by word and deed." Paul says he is not going to be a boaster and a bragger except to say what the Lord Jesus Christ has done for him and through him. We should not boast. We should not dare to speak of "*things which Christ has not wrought.*" We should not want to be puffed up like toads. Paul is very thankful that the Lord had used him to bring the Gentiles to faith in and obedience to the Lord Jesus Christ. These Gentiles were "*obedient by word and deed.*"

It is one thing to be saved, but it is another thing to be "obedient" not just "*by word*" but also by "*deed.*" Both are necessary. It is possible (though inconsistent) to be saved and yet disobedient to the Lord "*by word*" and disobedient to the Lord by "*deed.*" God wants every born-again saint to be "*obedient*" to Him. In the book of Exodus the people of Israel promised their obedience.

- **Exodus 24:3**

  And Moses came and told the people all the words of the LORD, and all the judgments: and all the people answered with one voice, and said, **All the words which the LORD hath said will we do.**

They pledged that they would do all that the Lord hath said and be obedient, but they were not obedient.

We can have a pledge in our marriage, for example, and promise to live with this man or this woman till death do us part. If we fail in our promise, we are obedient only in "*word*" but not in "*deed.*"

- **Deuteronomy 8:20**

  As the nations which the LORD destroyeth before your face, so shall ye perish; because **ye would not be obedient** unto the voice of the LORD your God.

God took them into captivity because they were disobedient to His Words.

- **Philippians 2:8**

  And being found in fashion as a man, he humbled himself, and **became obedient unto death,** even the death of the cross.

The Lord Jesus Christ was not only "*obedient*" to His Heavenly Father by "*word,*" but also by "*deed.*" He was "*obedient unto death.*"

So, these Gentiles at Rome and other places where Paul ministered were "*obedient.*" We should be "*obedient*" to the Lord Jesus Christ "*by word and deed.*" I appreciate those of you who come faithfully to our services Sunday-in-and-Sunday-out. May you be "*obedient*" to the Lord Jesus Christ in every area of your life. May I also be "*obedient*" to the Lord Jesus Christ in every area of my life by my "*words*" and by my "*deeds.*" May I be doing what my Lord and Saviour wants me to do.

Romans 15:19

"Through mighty signs and wonders, by the power of the Spirit of God; so that from Jerusalem, and round about unto Illyricum, I have fully preached the gospel of Christ."

The reference Paul gives concerning "*mighty signs and wonders*" is a reference to apostolic power. These "*signs and wonders*" are not performed today. Fuller

Theological Seminary had a professor who was writing books on *"signs and wonders."* The Charismatic movement has its *"signs"* and false *"wonders."* It is thought that Paul wrote this letter to the Romans from Corinth in about 60 A.D. He says he has *"fully preached the gospel of Christ"* from Jerusalem all the way to Illyricum. Notice that Paul *"fully preached."* He left nothing out and put nothing in that should not have been in his preaching. Paul would one day come as a prisoner to Rome. He would be preaching in the prison also.

There are a number a verses which talk about various *"signs and wonders."*

- **Exodus 7:3**

  And I will harden Pharaoh's heart, and **multiply my signs and my wonders** in the land of Egypt.

- **Numbers 14:11**

  And the LORD said unto Moses, How long will this people provoke me? and how long will it be ere they believe me, **for all the signs** which I have shewed among them?

- **Deuteronomy 4:24**

  For the LORD thy God *is* **a consuming fire**, *even* a jealous God.

- **Nehemiah 9:10**

  And **shewedst signs and wonders upon Pharaoh,** and on all his servants, and on all the people of his land: for thou knewest that they dealt proudly against them. So didst thou get thee a name, as *it is* this day.

Three Periods of Many Miracles

These were miracles in Moses' time. There are three historical periods in the Bible where there were many miracles:

1. Miracles in the time of Moses;

2. Miracles in the time of Elijah; and,

3. Miracles in the time of the Lord Jesus Christ and His Apostles.

Such miracles are not for this age of Grace.

- **Matthew 24:24**

  For **there shall arise false Christs, and false prophets, and shall shew great signs and wonders**; insomuch that, if it were possible, they shall deceive the very elect.

  The *"false prophets"* of today are showing false *"signs and wonders."* This is Apostolic power only, and yet the Charismatic movement all over the world is growing rapidly. Theses false teachers are using false *"signs and wonders."*

- **John 4:48**

  Then said Jesus unto him, Except ye see **signs and wonders**, ye will not believe.

  The Lord Jesus Christ chastised the Jews who had to see *"signs and wonders."*

- **Acts 2:22**

  Ye men of Israel, hear these words; Jesus of Nazareth, a man approved of God among you by miracles and **wonders and signs**, which God did by him in the midst of you, as ye yourselves also know:

  The Lord Jesus Christ was approved *"by miracles and wonders and signs."*

- **Acts 2:43**

  And fear came upon every soul: and many **wonders and signs** were done by the apostles.

New Testament Signs & Wonders

These were apostolic *"wonders and signs."* When the New Testament was completed in AD 90 to 100, these *"signs and wonders"* ceased. We no longer have to prove anything by *"signs and wonders."* The Words of God have been given to us and we have no more need of these special sign gifts. They have disappeared.

- **2 Corinthians 12:12**

  Truly the signs of an apostle were wrought among you in all patience, **in signs, and wonders**, and mighty deeds.

  There is a serious caution about all of this.

- **2 Thessalonians 2:9**

  Even him, whose coming is after the working of Satan with all power and **signs and lying wonders,**

Satan has a lot of power also. According to this verse, Satan will deceive people by *"signs and lying wonders."* He will cause all kinds of miracles to be performed. You read about such *"signs"* at Fatima. You read about the appearances of Mary and about statues weeping. In my judgment, these are *"lying wonders."* They are not proper or Scriptural. Genuine *"signs and wonders"* from the Lord ceased when the apostles died.

Paul stated that he *"fully preached the gospel of Christ."* I try to do the same. What a wonderful thing to *"fully preach the gospel."* What is the *"gospel"* and what is not the *"gospel"*? Campus Crusade is an organization that does not *"fully preach the gospel."* It says there are four spiritual laws. Those four spiritual laws are not complete. They are not *"fully preaching the gospel"* because they leave out that men, women, boys and girls are all sinners and are lost and bound for Hell. They give out nice wonderful things and tell them to believe this and to believe that and then they are saved. There are thousands, according to their founder, the late Bill Bright, who have been *"led to Christ."* There is nothing in these Four Spiritual laws about people being sinners. This is a serious and dangerous flaw. As Dr. Lewis Sperry Chafer used to tell us, *"Men, you haven't preached the gospel until you've given people something to believe."* There are a number of things that must occur before a person is genuinely saved:

1.   First, a person has to believe, in order to be saved, that they are a sinner before God and lost. Nobody who is already saved is going to want to be saved all over again. They are already saved. They have to believe that they are under the power of sin.

2.   Second, they must repent or change their minds about their sin and hate it rather than love it, and also about the Saviour who can save them.

3.   Third, they must believe that the Lord Jesus Christ died on Calvary's cross in their place and took their sins on His own body (1 Peter 2:24).

4.   They must accept and receive this Saviour by genuine faith.

We must be *"fully preaching the gospel of Christ."*

Romans 15:20

"Yea, so have I strived to preach the gospel, not where Christ was named, lest I should build upon another man's foundation:" Paul very wisely did not want to *"preach the gospel"* where *"Christ was named,"* that is, where the people had already heard the gospel clearly. He did not want to *"build upon another man's foundation."* That is why he went from place to place into new territories.

What *"foundation"* should a Bible-believing, gospel-preaching church be built upon? I can think of at least six things that should go into such a *"foundation."*

Six Foundations for a Church

    1.   The church should use and defend the right Bible. In English, I believe this to be the King James Bible. They need to be encouraging the reading of this Bible by all of their attenders on a daily basis.

    2.   The church should be separated from apostasy (such as is found in the National and World Councils of Churches), from compromise (such as is found in the National Association of Evangelicals and the Billy Graham Evangelistic Association), and from the Charismatic tongues movements.

    3.   The church should be built upon expository, verse by verse preaching and teaching. As Paul commanded Pastor Timothy, *"Preach the word; be instant in season, out of season; reprove, rebuke, exhort with all longsuffering and doctrine"* (2 Timothy 4:2).

    4.   The church should believe and preach the pre-Tribulation rapture of the redeemed Christians followed by the thousand-year millennial-reign of the Lord Jesus Christ. It should believe in and preach the premillennial return of Christ to set up the thousand years of peace upon this earth.

    5.   The church should be dispensational. It should know about the seven dispensations in the Bible and especially that there are major differences between law and grace and Israel and the church.

    6.   The church should be Baptist by doctrine. We have not built our 𝕭𝖎𝖇𝖑𝖊 𝕱𝖔𝖗 𝕿𝖔𝖉𝖆𝖞 𝕭𝖆𝖕𝖙𝖎𝖘𝖙 𝕮𝖍𝖚𝖗𝖈𝖍 on another's foundation.

I believe these are important foundations on which to build a church in our days. I know of no church in the borough of Collingswood that is built upon these above six foundations. If you go to the next town over you will not find a church with these six foundations either. Even the next town over from there.

You can find some of these qualifications in some churches, but not all of these qualifications in any of them. There is a dearth of sound churches in our area. I do not want to build on another's foundation either. Recently there has begun a separated and sound church in the area that is attempting to do what we are doing here. It is a sister church. May we have many more of like faith.

Paul wanted to start it out right. There are real advantages of building a house yourself. I have never built a house myself, but I am told that is the case. My dad built a house himself. My mom was in a house right next to her brother-in-law in Naples, Florida. She talked my Dad into building a house for her on the water just exactly to her specifications, and he did. He did not really want to do it, but he did it for her. They are both Home with the Lord now, but they had that house. She could make everything just exactly like she wanted to. She had her kitchen exactly like she wanted it and all the other rooms as well.

There is something about building a church from scratch. You just start in, and that is what we did in the **Bible For Today Baptist Church**. We started on October 4, 1998. We said if we only have three people in our living room (my wife, and I, and one other person) that would be fine. We had more people than that when we began, and, though we do not have droves of people, we still have more than that today. When you build on another's foundation you do not know what you are building on.

Romans 15:21

"But as it is written, To whom he was not spoken of, they shall see: and they that have not heard shall understand." Paul is talking about the Gentiles. He does not want to build on a Jewish foundation, but he wants to be with the Gentiles to which the Lord Jesus Christ had called him (Acts 9:15).

"It Is Written"=Verbal Preservation

Paul uses again the phrase *"it is written."* The Greek word is GEGRAPTAI. It is found sixty-three times in the New Testament of the King James Bible. It is in the Greek perfect tense of the verb GRAPHO. It speaks of Bible preservation of the Hebrew, Aramaic, and Greek Words of the Old Testament. That tense indicates words spoken or written in the past which continue to the present and on into the future. Paul is quoting from Isaiah.

- **Isaiah 52:15**

  So shall he sprinkle many nations; the kings shall shut their mouths at him: **for *that* which had not been told them shall they see; and *that* which they had not heard shall they consider.**

Isaiah is speaking about the opening of the door of faith to the Gentiles in order that they may be saved. Paul is speaking about this verse which is still true at the time of his writing. It is also true when we are talking about it today. That is the wonderful thing about the phrase "*it is written.*" This is a picture of how the Gentiles will come to know Christ as their Saviour. That was certainly true. Paul was the missionary and the apostle to the Gentiles.

Romans 15:22

"For which cause also I have been much hindered from coming to you." Paul was so busy in leading Gentiles to Christ he was "*hindered*" from coming to them at Rome. The word "*hindered*" is used in other places as well.

- **1 Thessalonians 2:18**

  Therefore we would have come unto you, even I Paul, once and again; but **Satan hindered us.**

In this case it was Satan who "*hindered.*" There are all kinds of hindrances from doing the Will of God. The Greek word for "*hinder*" is EGKOPTO. It means: "*to cut into, to impede one's course by cutting off his way; hinder.*" The "*cutting off his way*" could be accomplished by putting an obstacle right in front of them. If I were to attempt to go out a door and two or three people were right in front of that door, I would not be able to move through the door. These people would be "*hindering*" me by "*cutting off my way.*" That would be cutting off my exit. Paul was hindered from going to visit, though he really wanted to visit them.

Romans 15:23

"But now having no more place in these parts, and having a great desire these many years to come unto you;" When Paul said there was "*no more place in these parts*," he was referring to the place from where he was writing. He was supposedly writing from the city of Corinth which is in the southern part of Greece. He was implying that he had preached all around that area and really wanted to come to Rome. He had a "*great desire*" to come to Rome. He had this desire for "*many years.*" Paul wrote this letter in about A.D. 60.

Do you ever have a "*great desire*" to see somebody? Have you ever been away from some people and after awhile you really want to see them? I know when I was over in Okinawa as a Naval Chaplain serving with the Marines for twelve months without my family, I had a "*great desire*" to see them. Paul had never been to Rome. He had never seen them, but he had written them. He had heard about them. Others had brought word about them. He had a "*great desire*" for these "*many years*" to go there and see these Christians.

Romans 15:24

"**Whensoever I take my journey into Spain, I will come to you: for I trust to see you in my journey, and to be brought on my way thitherward by you, if first I be somewhat filled with your *company.*"** Paul thought he was going to go to Spain. If you look on a map of Spain and of Italy, you can see where he wanted to go. As I mentioned before, Paul was writing this from Corinth. As far as we know, he never got to Spain. He wanted to be there and be "*filled*" with their company and have fellowship with them, just like it is a joy to have fellowship with you here in our church. The singing, the praise, and the prayers are important. Paul wanted to be where other believers were.

We have a missionary that is coming soon. He is a missionary to Papua, New Guinea. He is a man whom we have known for many years. He said I just like to come and fellowship with those of like precious faith. He knows that we believe the King James Bible and that we are separated and Fundamental people who believe the Bible just like he does. He wants to show some slides and tell us about his work. He just wanted to come. He wants to come here and to fellowship with us of like precious faith.

Paul wanted also to be filled with the company of fellow-Christians. Paul thought he was going to take his journey peacefully, but that never happened.

Romans 15:25

"**But now I go unto Jerusalem to minister unto the saints.**" Paul would not go to Rome at this time, but he had to "*go unto Jerusalem.*" He was at Corinth and was going to sail all the way to Jerusalem. He was going "*to minister unto the saints*" by way of bringing them an offering that had been given by the believers in Macedonia and Achaia. He wanted to "*minister*" or "*serve.*" He did not want to go to boss them. He did not want to go and take all their money. He wanted to give them service. That is what a preacher ought to do. That is what a missionary ought to do. That is what an apostle ought to do. They ought to serve and "*minister unto the saints.*"

There is nothing wrong with that word "*saints.*" This is a term that must never be used exclusively by the Roman Catholic Church. They use the term for those whom they have "*canonized*" as "saints," whether or not they had been born-again and are genuinely "*saints*" in the Biblical sense of the word.

What Is a Saint?

Every genuine believer who has been saved and born-again is a "*saint*" of God. The Greek word for "*saint*" is HAGIOS. The plural is HAGIOI. The root meaning is "*separate ones.*" The Greek verb form is HAGIAZO. It means:

"to render or acknowledge, or to be venerable or hallow; to separate from profane things and dedicate to God; consecrate things to God; dedicate people to God; to purify; to cleanse externally; to purify by expiation: free from the guilt of sin; to purify internally by renewing of the soul."

Those who have been separated unto God by genuine faith in the Lord Jesus Christ, and have been regenerated, and have God the Holy Spirit living within their bodies are called holy ones or "*saints.*"

Ninety-eight times the King James Bible has used either the word "*saint*" or "*saints.*" Both the New American Standard Version and the New International Version have it listed only sixty-eight times. They have taken one of these words away thirty times. The New Century Version has the word only one time. Most of these Bibles do not like to use the word "*saints.*" I think they are trying to placate the Roman Catholic Church. I think they are trying to get an ecumenical Bible with ecumenical words and flavor. They do not want to have anybody as "*saints*" except those whom the Roman Catholic Church has canonized.

Romans 15:26

"For it hath pleased them of Macedonia and Achaia to make a certain contribution for the poor saints which are at Jerusalem." Macedonia and Achaia are in Northern and Southern Greece respectively. These believers were Gentiles. The "*saints*" at Jerusalem were basically saved Jews. In this instance you have an illustration of the Gentiles helping the Jews. Later on we shall see the connection there. Paul wanted to go to Jerusalem with a *"contribution for the poor saints."*

No Social Gospel

The New Testament teaches us to help born-again believers who are less fortunate than we are and need our help. I do not believe the New Testament teaches what is called the *"social gospel,"* which means that we should feed, clothe, and house everyone in the world.

We cannot do this even if we wanted to. We do not have enough resources in funds, time, or people. But if the people are saved and born-again, they are of our extended Christian family (1 Timothy 5:8). As such, we are to do everything in our power to help them if they have a genuine need and we are able to do so. Paul and the people in Macedonia and Achaia wanted to help those "poor saints" in Jerusalem.

Romans 15:27

"It hath pleased them verily; and their debtors they are. For if the Gentiles have been made partakers of their spiritual things, their duty is also to minister unto them in carnal things." In this verse we see Paul's reasoning as to why the Gentiles felt the need to help the Jewish *"saints."*

Giving Ungrudgingly

Notice first of all Paul stated *"it hath pleased them"* to make this *"contribution."* This is the beautiful part of Christian giving. That is how our giving should be. It should not be *"grudgingly, or of necessity"* (2 Corinthians 9:7).

That is why our church has placed on our offering box at the door, *"God loveth a cheerful giver"* (2 Corinthians 9:7). This giving by the Gentile Christians was happy and pleasing to the Lord. It was not like pulling teeth.

They were happy to give to the *"poor saints"* at Jerusalem.

Next, Paul said *"and their debtors they are."* What this means is that these Gentiles in Macedonia and Achaia owed a debt to these Jews in Jerusalem because the Jews in Jerusalem were the ones from whom the Lord Jesus Christ came. He was the One who had saved them by His grace and had given them eternal life. They were *"debtors"* to those Jews in Jerusalem because they were the family of the Saviour.

Paul stated that *"the Gentiles have been made partakers of their spiritual things."* This is a reference to the spiritual salvation that people can have through faith in the Saviour Who came through the line of Abraham, Isaac, Jacob, and David. Because of this, *"their duty is also to minister unto them in carnal things."* What Paul is saying is that the *"duty"* of these Gentiles is also to minister unto the saved Jews in Jerusalem in *"carnal things."* This includes money and the other necessities of this life. This is not *"carnal"* in the sense of sinfully *"carnal,"* but merely tangible things. They have the spiritual things by genuine faith in the Lord Jesus Christ. They have redemption, salvation, and forgiveness of sins through the Jewish Messiah, as the Lord Jesus Christ said to the woman at the well (John 4:25).

It is good for Bible-believing Christians to have a *"duty,"* an obligation, or a feeling that we ought to owe something to somebody. For instance, the person who led you to the Lord Jesus Christ, do you not have a *"duty"* or a debt to that person or those people where you found the gospel and God's salvation? You should want to help and support them.

Uncle Charles Allen, our high school janitor (We used to call them janitors; now you say custodians or building engineers). Uncle Charlie led me to genuine faith in the Lord Jesus Christ. He has been with the Lord for many years, but while he was here, I was happy to visit him and to help him. We have an eternal *"debt"* to those who have given us spiritual life through the Lord Jesus Christ. We owe them, we want to thank them, we want to go back to them and say *"thank you"* for introducing us to the spiritual life that they gave us by leading us to our Saviour. That is what these Gentiles in Macedonia and Achaia had--a *"debt"* that they owed and that they wanted to pay back. They took up an offering for the poor and struggling *"saints"* living in Jerusalem.

Romans 15:28

"When therefore I have performed this, and have sealed to them this fruit, I will come by you into Spain." Paul wanted to *"seal"* this *"fruit"* or contribution by performing the delivery of the gift to those in Jerusalem. When he had taken that contribution Paul planned to come to Rome on his way to Spain. He was going to come right by them. Paul's plan went wrong. As far as we know, Paul never made it to Spain. He never made it voluntarily even to Rome. He made it to Rome at Roman government expense. He made it as a prisoner of the Roman government. Paul was warned not to go to Jerusalem (Acts 21:11). Agabus (Acts 21:10) warned him that he was going to be in trouble there. Paul went, however, because he felt obligated to take this offering to the poor saints at Jerusalem even at the risk of his own life.

The writing of Acts was approximately A.D. 60. This letter to the Romans was also written in about A.D. 60, the same year. That is where the historical picture of Acts 21 is found. In Acts 21, Paul became a prisoner of the Jews. In Acts 22, 23, 24, 25, and 26, he was put on trial. Then in Acts 27 he appealed to Caesar, so the Roman government sent him on a ship to Rome. The ship almost sank, as you know, in Chapter 28. The storm came and Paul landed on the island of Melita. He finally made it to Rome. When he arrived at Rome, the Roman government allowed him to speak to his fellow Christians. Fellow believers could come to Paul's "*lodging*" (Acts 28:23) and hear him preaching the Words of God. So the Lord had other plans for the way Paul would one day visit Rome.

Romans 15:29

"And I am sure that, when I come unto you, I shall come in the fulness of the blessing of the gospel of Christ." Paul was "*sure*" that he would eventually come to the believers in Rome. Though his coming to Rome was not at a time and in a manner that he had anticipated, he knew that when he would come to them, it would be "*in the fulness of the blessing of the gospel of Christ.*"

The "*gospel of Christ*" indeed brings many "*blessings.*" Just think of the "*blessings*" that we who are born-again have through the good news about the Lord Jesus Christ. He died for all the sinners of the world, taking on Himself their sins "*in His own body on the tree*" (1 Peter 2:24). Paul planned to come to those Christians at Rome in all the "*fulness*" of these gospel "*blessings.*"

Seven Gospel Blessings

Here are a few blessings that the *"fulness"* of the true and Biblical *"gospel of Christ"* (Romans 1:16) can bring to those who have genuinely accepted it:

1. The gospel can free us from having to follow a sinful life.

2. The gospel can give us forgiveness with God.

3. The gospel can give us the Holy Spirit to indwell us.

4. The gospel can give us redemption.

5. The gospel can give us a pardon.

6. The gospel can give us a Home in Heaven.

7. The gospel can free us from further obedience to the slavery of the sin nature. We don't have to obey that old sin nature. Sometimes we do, but we are free. The power of the Holy Spirit can enable us.

Some people only have the *"gospel"* and not the *"fulness of the blessings"* of that *"gospel."* They will be *"saved yet so as by fire"* (1 Corinthians 3:15) when these Christians stand before *"the Judgment Seat of Christ"* (2 Corinthians 5:10). In the lives of *"carnal"* Christians (1 Corinthians 3:1, 3) there is no joy. There is no peace. There are no blessings. There is no overflow of God's grace to speak out the gospel to others, or even to give out a gospel tract.

The blessings of the gospel are something for which we can thank the Lord. When Paul finally arrived in Rome, he was in chains. When he wrote this letter, he did not know he was going to be in chains, but when he got to Rome he was in chains as a Roman prisoner.

Romans 15:30

"Now I beseech you, brethren, for the Lord Jesus Christ's sake, and for the love of the Spirit, that ye strive together with me in *your* prayers to God for me." Paul was begging these believers *"for the Lord Jesus Christ's sake, and for the love of the Spirit,"* even before he got there, to pray for him. It seems that many people stop this verse with the words *"that ye strive together."* Sad to say, many churches *"strive together"* and that is all that they are doing. They are battling, fighting, and criticizing together.

　　When people ask you to pray for them do you pray for them? I always say *"as the Lord brings you to mind I will pray for you."* Paul asked the believers at Rome to *"strive together with me in your prayers to God for me."* Though Paul was an apostle, he still needed the strength that comes from prayer. He needed the saints to pray on his behalf. I need saints to pray for me. You need saints to pray for you.

Pray For Each Other's Needs

We all need to pray for each other's needs. We all have needs, whether it is various cares, health problems, a death of a loved one, or any other needs that we have.

Romans 15:31

　　"That I may be delivered from them that do not believe in Judaea; and of the saints." Notice the specific prayer that Paul wanted the believers at Rome to make on his behalf. It was *"That I may be delivered from them that do not believe in Judaea; and that my service which I have for Jerusalem may be accepted of the saints."* Notice these two separate and proper requests that were a concern to Paul.

　　1. Paul wanted to be *"delivered from them that do not believe in Judaea."* There were many people who were unbelievers in Judaea. The Jews who hated the Lord Jesus Christ also hated Paul. They wanted to kill Paul (Acts 23:12). They wanted to stone him (Acts 14:19). God did answer that prayer.

　　2. Paul wanted his *"service"* to be *"accepted of the saints."* He wanted them to receive the gifts he had for them in a proper manner. This prayer was answered also.

　　God is said to have *"delivered"* others and has promised *"deliverance"* for His own.

- **Daniel 3:28**

  Then Nebuchadnezzar spake, and said, Blessed *be* the God of Shadrach, Meshach, and Abednego, who hath sent his angel, and **delivered his servants** that trusted in him, and have changed the king's word, and yielded their bodies, that they might not serve nor worship any god, except their own God.

Rather than the three Hebrew children being burned up in the fiery furnace, God delivered them (Daniel 6:27).

- **2 Corinthians 1:10**

  Who delivered us from so great a death, and **doth deliver**: in whom we trust that he will **yet deliver** *us*;

- **Colossians 1:13**

  Who hath **delivered us** from the power of darkness, and hath translated *us* into the kingdom of his dear Son:

- **1 Thessalonians 1:10**

  And to wait for his Son from Heaven, whom he raised from the dead, *even* Jesus, which **delivered us** from the wrath to come.

- **2 Thessalonians 3:2**

  And **that we may be delivered from unreasonable and wicked men**: for all *men* have not faith.

- **2 Timothy 3:11-12**

  Persecutions, afflictions, which came unto me at Antioch, at Iconium, at Lystra; what persecutions I endured: but out of *them* all **the Lord delivered me.** Yea, and all that will live godly in Christ Jesus shall suffer persecution.

- **2 Timothy 4:17**

  Notwithstanding the Lord stood with me, and strengthened me; that by me the preaching might be fully known, and *that* all the Gentiles might hear: and **I was delivered** out of the mouth of the lion.

Sometimes we need physical prayer for deliverance. People who are in the military over in the battlefields need prayer for physical deliverance. Most of them are not saved. They need to be delivered so they can hear the gospel preached to them and be saved for all eternity. I hope that there are faithful chaplains stationed with each unit.

I was a naval chaplain on active duty for five years. One of my years was on the Military Sea Transportation Service (MSTS) duty. I was not on duty constantly, but I was relieving other chaplains who had leave coming to them. I took Army Troops from Brooklyn, New York to Bremerhaven, Germany, and Southampton, England. I was Chaplain on a ship that took army troops from the Brooklyn Army Terminal. I just passed it the other day when I was up there visiting with some preachers. When the troops were going over to England and Germany for combat, they did not know what was going to happen to them. Because of this uncertainty, they flocked to the Bible studies and church services in greater numbers. It is interesting. When the battle was coming, there were decisions made for Christ, and much greater numbers would come to the church services and to the Bible studies.

The Need For Faithful Chaplains

The troops that are going into combat today need faithful chaplains. There are many modernist, unbelieving chaplains in the Service. They have no saving gospel to preach. Pray for the chaplains who are godly chaplains and preach the Words of God, that they may be effective as they preach the gospel to deliver these people from their sins and offer them eternal life.

We have to pray for their physical deliverance and for faithful chaplains who preach the gospel so that people will be saved spiritually.

Romans 15:32

"That I may come unto you with joy by the will of God, and may with you be refreshed." This was a third prayer request made by Paul. He wanted to come to the Christians at Rome *"with joy by the will of God."* He was concerned about the *"will of God"* and we should be concerned about this as well. But he also wanted to have real Christian *"joy"* when he arrived at Rome. A preacher who has no genuine spiritual *"joy"* cannot impart that *"joy"* to the congregation. An apostle who goes all the way over to Rome with no *"joy"* is not going to bring them any *"joy"* either. They needed some *"joy."* All of us need *"joy."* Part of the fruit of God's Holy Spirit is "joy."

Paul's Three Prayer Requests

1. Paul wanted to be "*delivered from them that do not believe in Judaea.*"

2. Paul wanted his "*service*" to be "*accepted of the saints.*"

3. Paul wanted to come to the Christians at Rome "*with joy by the will of God.*"

Paul said the purpose of his coming with "*joy*" was that both Paul and the believers might "*be refreshed.*" He wanted to come "*by the will of God.*" I am sure that at that time he did not realize he would come in chains as a prisoner of Rome to be tried for his life. That is how he came. I am sure he did not know he was going to come to Rome by way of a shipwreck where he almost lost his life. But indeed he came by the will of God.

A Refreshing Fellowship of Saints

The stated purpose of Paul's coming concerned a "*refreshing.*" He wanted it to be a mutual refreshing fellowship when he saw them. Are you "*refreshed*" in the fellowship of our local church? Is it refreshing to hear the songs of Zion, to hear the Words of God, and the prayers of the saints? I hope that it is refreshing. Paul wanted to be refreshed with joy.

- John 15:11

  These things have I spoken unto you, **that my joy might remain in you, and** *that* **your joy might be full**.

- John 16:20

  Verily, verily, I say unto you, That ye shall weep and lament, but the world shall rejoice: and ye shall be sorrowful, but **your sorrow shall be turned into joy**.

- Acts 13:52

  And **the disciples were filled with joy**, and with the Holy Ghost.

- **Acts 20:24**

  But none of these things move me, neither count I my life dear unto myself, **so that I might finish my course with joy**, and the ministry, which I have received of the Lord Jesus, to testify the gospel of the grace of God.

- **Romans 5:11**

  And not only *so*, but **we also joy in God through our Lord Jesus Christ**, by whom we have now received the atonement.

- **1 Peter 1:8**

  Whom having not seen, ye love; in whom, though now ye see *him* not, yet believing, **ye rejoice with joy unspeakable** and full of glory:

The Christian life can be a life of joy if the Holy Spirit of God fills us for service.

- **Jude 24**

  Now unto him that is able to keep you from falling, and to present *you* **faultless before the presence of his glory with exceeding joy,**

Do you think there is going to be sadness in Heaven? Do you think that there is going to be crying in Heaven? No, there is going to be "*exceeding joy.*"

Romans 15:33

"Now the God of peace *be* with you all. Amen." This phrase, "*the God of peace*," occurs five times in the New Testament: Here and in Romans 16:20; Philippians 4:9; 1 Thessalonians 5:23; and Hebrews 13:20. There are many other references to God's "*peace.*"

- **John 14:27**

  Peace I leave with you, my peace I give unto you: not as the world giveth, give I unto you. Let not your heart be troubled, neither let it be afraid.

- **John 16:33**

  These things I have spoken unto you, that **in me ye might have peace**. In the world ye shall have tribulation: but be of good cheer; I have overcome the world.

- **Philippians 4:7**

  And the **peace of God**, which passeth all understanding, shall keep your hearts and minds through Christ Jesus.

- **Romans 5:1**

> Therefore being justified by faith, we have **peace with God** through our Lord Jesus Christ:

Our God certainly is a *"God of peace."*

I have given you the definition of peace before, but let me repeat it here. It has been defined as this:

> *"the tranquil state of a soul assured of its salvation through Christ, and so fearing nothing from God and content with its earthly lot, of whatsoever sort that is."*

That is real *"peace."*

The Only Source of True Peace

The Lord Jesus Christ is the only One Who can give us that *"peace."* God's *"peace"* is something that *"passeth all understanding"* and it alone can *"keep our hearts and minds through Christ Jesus"* (Philippians 4:7).

Romans
Chapter Sixteen

Romans 16:1

"I commend unto you Phebe our sister, which is a servant of the church which is at Cenchrea." Paul commends *"Phebe"* whom he called a *"sister."* That would indicate that she was a saved woman. Many times pastors, preachers, apostles, and missionaries say very little about women. I commend women who love and serve the Lord Jesus Christ as well.

Women Deacons Are Unscriptural

Paul continues his description of her by calling her a *"servant of the church which is at Cenchrea."* The Greek word for *"deacon"* is DIAKONOS. It means:

"one who executes the commands of another, esp. of a master, a servant, attendant, minister; the servant of a king; a deacon, one who, by virtue of the office assigned to him by the church, cares for the poor and has charge of and distributes the money collected for their use; a waiter, one who serves food and drink."

It is in the feminine gender. But just because the word DIAKONOS is used here does not mean that she is a deacon. Some Baptist churches have *"deaconesses."* I believe that office is unscriptural.

"Servant" Versus "Deacon"

This word for *"servant"* is used for many things. It means *"to minister"* and is used for many people in the Bible *"who serve."* It doe not refer to an official *"deacon"* every time it occurs in the Bible. In 1 Timothy 3:10, 13, there is a specific reference to the office of deacon. In this instance, however, Phebe was a *"servant"* or *"helper"* in the church.

Someone who serves the church has many things that they can do. They can pray for the church. They can help clean the church. They can give to the church. There are all kinds of things that a person can do. This servant was at the church at Cenchrea. If you look at a map, Cenchrea is part of Corinth. Remember Paul wrote this letter from Corinth which is the Southern part of Greece. Cenchrea is an Eastern port of Corinth. Phebe was ministering there at Corinth on Cenchrea which is on the East. In the next verse we see that she is going to change her direction and location.

Romans 16:2

"That ye receive her in the Lord, as becometh saints, and that ye assist her in whatsoever business she hath need of you: for she hath been a succourer of many, and of myself also." When Phebe was going to go to Rome, Paul asks those believers in Rome to *"receive her in the Lord, as becometh saints, and that ye assist her in whatsoever business she hath need of you."* The Greek word for *"receive"* is PROSDECHOMAI. It means:

> *"to receive to one's self, to admit, to give access to one's self; to admit one, receive one into intercourse and companionship; to receive one (coming from some place); to accept (not to reject) a thing offered; to expect: the fulfilment of promises."*

The Greek word is the usual DECHOMAI which means *"to receive."* PROSDECHOMAI is a much stronger word.

Being Glad to See People

Paul was telling the believers at Rome not simply to say hello to her, but to be really sincere in receiving her. They were to be glad that she is there as she comes to them. That is the way we should be with people who come to our church here. We must receive them and accept them for what they are. Not one of us is perfect. All of us are imperfect, but we are trying to serve the Lord the best we can and that is all we can do.

Paul wanted the Christians at Rome to "*receive her in the Lord, as becometh saints.*" Some people do not act like "*saints.*" We are "*saints*" if we are saved. This church was to be receiving Phebe "*as becometh saints.*" Their reception of Phebe should be as was fitting and suitable to the "*saints.*"

They were to "*assist her.*" It is one thing to "*receive*" somebody, but it is another thing to "*assist*" them. Paul does not limit their assistance to this lady Phebe. Whatever business she had need of, they were to help her. This would include for her to lodge, her food, and whatever other needs might present themselves.

Phebe had a testimony that "*she hath been a succourer of many, and of myself also.*" The Greek word for "*succourer*" is PROSTATIS. It means:

"*a woman set over others; a female guardian, protectress, patroness, caring for the affairs of others and aiding them with her resources.*"

This was the ministry Phebe had when she was in Cenchrea. Paul indicates that since she had been a helper to others, so they are to be a helper to her when she arrives. In fact, Paul said that Phebe had given him assistance.

Romans 16:3

"Greet Priscilla and Aquila my helpers in Christ Jesus." Priscilla and Aquila were friends and helpers of Paul. In Acts 18:2, 18, 26 we read about Priscilla and Aquila. They were "*tent makers*" along with Paul (Acts 18:3). They did not know the full details concerning the Lord Jesus Christ and His teachings. Paul got them aside and taught them clearly about the things of the Lord (Acts 18:26). He helped them learn more about the things of Christ. According to this verse, Priscilla and Aquila also went over there to Rome. Paul said that they were his "*helpers in Christ.*"

Be a Helper for the Lord

If all that could be said of you was that you are a helper of a pastor, or a missionary, or another Christian, that is a great thing to say. All of us can be helpers one to another. We can give of our time and of our energies.

Priscilla and Aquila were a husband and wife team who helped Paul.

Romans 16:4

"Who have for my life laid down their own necks: unto whom not only I give thanks, but also all the churches of the Gentiles." The Greek word for *"who"* is plural. As such, it could refer back to Phebe, and Priscilla and Aquila, or it could refer only to Priscilla and Aquila alone. Since the closest plural group to the *"who"* is Priscilla and Aquila, I believe the following comments refer to these two alone. Paul said that they *"laid down their own necks."* That is an interesting expression. One meaning that has been offered is: *"to be ready to incur the most imminent peril to life."* There certainly is a risk involved in this. This may have included risking their own literal lives. It might also mean that they supplied from their own resources funds and money that depleted their reserves. That is no doubt what they have done. They have *"laid down their necks"* and they have given of their own lives, their own money, and their own resources at a very great risk, because of their love and respect for Paul.

Because of this, not only Paul *"gave thanks, but also all the churches of the Gentiles."* The churches of the heathen Gentiles that had believers in them all over that area were being helped also by Priscilla and Aquila. These believers also gave thanks for this husband and wife team.

Do you thank the Lord for any husband and wife team that you know of? By the use of the Greek present tense, Paul continuously gave thanks. It is good to be a thankful Christian. To be unthankful and ungrateful is not right and is not pleasing to the Lord. We should not do this just once a year at Thanksgiving time. It should be a daily task. We should thank the Lord with all that is in our being and all that we have. Paul was mindful of these who had helped him. He gave thanks unto them, and we should do the same.

Romans 16:5

"Likewise *greet* the church that is in their house. Salute my wellbeloved Epaenetus, who is the firstfruits of Achaia unto Christ." Paul told the believers in Rome to greet *"the church that is in their house."* Here is an example of a *"church"* or a called-out assembly that met in a *"house."* Priscilla and Aquila had a *"church"* that met in their house in the same way that our 𝕭𝖎𝖇𝖑𝖊 𝕱𝖔𝖗 𝕿𝖔𝖉𝖆𝖞 𝕭𝖆𝖕𝖙𝖎𝖘𝖙 𝕮𝖍𝖚𝖗𝖈𝖍 meets in our house. There is nothing wrong with meeting in a house. The early church did this, and we are doing it as well. To have a church in your house, there were many things that the wife, Priscilla, had to arrange for. She had to arrange for seats and space. Maybe she had to move out some of her own furniture to make room for this church in their house. I do not know what size the church was. We are not told.

There are house-churches all over the world. Some house-churches have to meet in secret for fear of their lives. I have been told that there are many municipalities in our country that are cracking down on home churches. Did you know that? These municipalities are saying that these home churches cannot meet. I do not know what states they are, but I read somewhere that this has been true. If they start cracking down on the church that is in our house here, it would be against the First Amendment of our United States Constitution. This Amendment clearly teaches that there should be freedom of three things: (1) religion, (2) speech, and (3) assembly.

It is interesting that various municipalities are not wanting churches in houses. If conditions worsen in our country and our normal freedoms disappear, there may be many more churches that would have to meet in houses rather than in large buildings. The Communists in China and Russia have driven many of their people out of their churches. The one thing in Russia is that they have state-approved churches which are heretical in their teachings. They are not real Bible-believing and Bible-preaching churches. They are run by ministers who are in league with the Communist government. They have to clear all of their messages in writing before they can preach them. What a horrible thing. Because of this, there are many "unregistered" churches in Russia. They do not register with the state. They do not want any control of their preaching the Bible by the state. As a result, many of those churches are meeting in homes.

Paul also wanted these believers in Rome to *"salute my wellbeloved Epaenetus."* Here is a man whom Paul calls *"wellbeloved."* Paul loved him in the Lord. He was the *"firstfruits of Achaia unto Christ."* Achaia is down in Southern Greece. He was the first one in that entire region whom Paul led to the Lord Jesus Christ. It reminds me of my own experience of coming to know Christ as my Saviour. As I have said before, I was the first one that our high school janitor, Uncle Charlie Allen, led to the Lord after 10 or 15 years of faithful witnessing. This made him very happy.

Romans 16:6

"Greet Mary, who bestowed much labour on us." Paul also wants the church to *"greet Mary."* She was no doubt just a lowly woman, but Paul wanted them to greet her. In this last Chapter of this book, Paul has a balance between the greeting of the men and the greeting of the women. What did Mary do? Paul said that she *"bestowed much labour on us."*

The Greek word for *"labour"* is KOPIAO. It means:

*"to grow weary, tired, exhausted (with toil or burdens or grief); to labour with **wearisome effort**, to toil; of bodily labour."*

Paul was a tent maker by profession in order to give himself food to live. Maybe she helped him in this *"wearisome effort"* of making tents, I do not know.

Who was this Mary?

The Six Different Mary's

There are six different Mary's in the Bible.

1. Mary the Mother of Jesus. We know about that Mary.

2. Mary Magdalene from Magdala out of whom the Lord cast out seven demons.

3. Mary, the sister of Lazarus and Martha.

4. Mary of Cleapus, the mother of James the less.

5. Mary the mother of John Mark, sister of Barnabus.

6. Mary a Christian who lived in Rome who is greeted by Paul in this particular verse.

These are little people who have helped Paul. He is thankful for them. He is praising the Lord for them. They are in the Bible and that is why I talk about them. When I preach the Word, I preach the whole Word and do not leave out any detail.

Romans 16:7

"Salute Andronicus and Junia, my kinsmen, and my fellowprisoners, who are of note among the apostles, who also were in Christ before me." These two people mentioned here were probably a husband and wife team. Andronicus is a male name and Junia is a female name. They were Paul's *"kinsmen."* The Greek word for *"kinsmen"* is SUGGENES. It means:

> *"of the same kin, akin to, related by blood; in a wider sense, of the same race, a fellow countryman."*

So they were either *"fellow countrymen"* or *"of the same race"* and therefore Jews, the same race as Paul. I believe they were part of the Jewish community that were saved.

Notice Paul calls them *"my fellowprisoners."* I wonder if they were put into prison like Paul? Paul had many imprisonments. In Acts 16 he was thrown into prison at Philippi. He was put into prison at Rome two different times. It sounds like this husband and wife team were also cast into prison as Paul was and this is why he has called them his *"fellowprisoners."* As the poet has said, *"Iron bars do not a prison make."*

Free Even if Imprisoned

You can be free in Christ no matter if you are in a prison, or whether you are in your own conditions which seem like a prison at times. God is able to give you freedom and blessing. He can make you a joyful Christian wherever you are.

This couple was also *"of note among the apostles."* They were *"notable and illustrious."* The Greek word for *"apostles"* is APOSTOLOS. It comes from two other Greek words, APO (*"from"* or *"forth"*) and STELLO (*"to send"*). Not that these two people were official *"Apostles"* like the twelve selected by the Lord Jesus Christ. They were merely Christians who were *"sent forth"* with the gospel of salvation. The Bible knows nothing of women apostles, women preachers, women evangelists, or women deacons.

Today we do not have any official Apostles other than the ones the Lord Jesus Christ chose. He chose twelve and one of them, Judas, hanged himself. I believe that he was Satanic and lost. I believe that the Lord chose him because

He knew he would betray Him. It was a warning to us to be careful in our choices of leaders. Then in the Book of Acts the disciples nominated two others and selected Mathias (Acts 1:26). I do not believe that either of those men were destined to replace Judas. I believe Paul was the Apostle chosen by the Lord Jesus Christ from Heaven after his bodily resurrection. I think Paul was the one that took the place of Judas. To sum up, these two who are named in this verse were *"apostles"* with a small *"a."* They were those sent forth like missionaries are today.

Another thing Paul mentioned about this couple was that they *"were in Christ before me."* That means they were older in the Lord than Paul. There are some things that a young Christian, just recently saved, does not know from the Scriptures that one who is a little older in the Lord can know because they have been with Christ a longer time.

When I began my nineteen-year teaching in the School District of Philadelphia, the first couple of years were horrible, as far as I was concerned. The students were boisterous, disobedient, cursing, and blaspheming. I kept order, but I came home tired out every day. I worked from 8:00 a.m. in the morning and I got home at about 4:00 p.m. in the afternoon. The first couple of weeks I lay down in bed when I got home. It was tough. The Lord had to help me. I needed the job to support my wife and five children, so I kept going. I do not know how I lasted nineteen years, but I did. It got easier to put up with as I taught more years, but I had to learn how best to cope with the battle conditions that existed and still exist in the Philadelphia schools. What people used to say about a teacher who had taught nineteen years, for instance, was this: *"Does that teacher have 19 years of teaching experience, or does he or she have only one year of experience 19 times?"*

As with any teaching experience, so it is sometimes with those who have been saved for many years. Just because they have been saved for many years does not necessarily mean that they have profited, as they should have, from this experience. Sad to say, some older Christians seem like *"duds."*

We Must Grow in the Lord

Some people have been saved a long time, but they have not grown an inch in spiritual things. They still fall short of where they should be with the Lord. God says that we ought to *"grow in grace and in the knowledge of our Lord and Saviour Jesus Christ"* (1 Peter 3:18). Born-again believers should not want to stay spiritual babies and stunted in growth.

I would hope that as we read and study God's Words, we would *"grow in grace and in knowledge."* If this happens, we who have been saved before others will be able to lead them and help them to know the things of Christ.

Paul says that these two, Andronicus and Junia, were *"apostles"* and *"in Christ"* before he was. I am sure that Paul looked to them. They could help him and give him some encouragement in the things of the Lord. May we be able to do that same thing also.

Romans 16:8

"Greet Amplias my beloved in the Lord." Paul now asked the believers to *"greet Amplias."* He is a man who is Paul's *"beloved in the Lord."* He loves him *"in the Lord."* Just because he says he is his *"beloved in the Lord"* does not mean he is a boyfriend of his. Some people try to read this into this verse.

Christians can have genuine Christian love one for another. Whether it is a fellow man or a fellow woman. There is Christian love that the world knows nothing of.

Amplias was a friend that *"sticketh closer than a brother,"* (Proverbs 18:24). He was Paul's friend and, as it says, *"A friend loveth at all times and a brother is born for adversity"* (Proverbs 17:17). Amplias was a *"brother"* and probably had a lot of *"adversity."* What do those two verses mean? They mean if you really stick close, like a brother, no matter how much the adversity comes, how much the trouble comes, how much the difficulty comes, that brother will stick right with you, will roll with the punches, will help you, and will not forsake you. Amplias was a man *"beloved in the Lord"* and beloved by Paul.

Romans 16:9

"Salute Urbane, our helper in Christ, and Stachys my beloved." Stachys is another who is called *"beloved."* Urbane is just simply *"our helper in Christ."* The Greek word for *"helper"* is SUNERGOS. It means: *"a companion in work, or a fellow worker."* Notice the number of names Paul lists in the first fourteen verses of this Chapter. There is a total of twenty-four names. It reminds me of the Lord Jesus Christ Who knows the names of those whom He saves.

- **John 10:3**

    . . . He calleth His own sheep by name, and leadeth them out.

Remembering Peoples' Names

Does the Lord Jesus know all the names of His own? Yes, he does. If you are born-again, He knows your name and my name. Paul, though he was a human being, was an Apostle, and he remembered the names of these people.

Some pastors, when they leave a church, they do not even remember the names of people. They forget everybody. They just do their own thing and get some other people involved. Paul was not that way. He remembered people who helped and assisted him. I am sure he remembered the people who did not help him too, but he does not talk about them here. Some people gave him trouble and he mentions some of them in his later epistle (2 Timothy 4:10, 14-15). Urbane was a helper of Paul. I hope we can help other people and ourselves as well.

Romans 16:10

"Salute Apelles approved in Christ. Salute them which are of Aristobulus' *household.*" Here is a man, Apelles, who is called *"approved in Christ."* The Greek word for *"approved"* is DOKIMOS. It comes from the verb DOKIMAZO which means:

"to test, examine, prove, scrutinise (to see whether a thing is genuine or not), as metals; to recognise as genuine after examination, to approve, deem worthy."

This type of "testing" is with a view to passing the test and therefore being *"approved"* after the testing.

There is another kind of testing which attempts to test with the idea of having the person or thing fail the test. This is often translated *"tempt."* The Greek word for this is PEIRAZO. It means:

"to try whether a thing can be done; to attempt, endeavour; to try, make trial of, test: for the purpose of ascertaining his quantity, or what he thinks, or how he will behave himself; in a good sense; in a bad sense, to test one maliciously, craftily to put to the proof his feelings or judgments; to try or test one's faith, virtue, character, by enticement to sin; to solicit to sin, to tempt; of the temptations of the devil; after the OT usage; of God: to inflict evils upon one in order to prove his character and the steadfastness of his faith; men are

said to tempt God by exhibitions of distrust, as though they wished to try whether he is not justly distrusted; by impious or wicked conduct to test God's justice and patience, and to challenge him, as it were to give proof of his perfections."

PEIRAZO is to try and test with the thought and the hope that they will fail the test. Satan tempted the Lord Jesus Christ to test Him and to make Him fall. He did not fall. He is sinless. He is perfect. DOKIMAZO is to test and to try with the hope that you are going to pass the test. That's the difference between these two Greek words.

After trial and testing you pass the test. You pass the trial. You are no longer in trouble. It is just like the person who tests his parachute. He picks up two parachutes. One is the main chute, the other is the emergency chute. He is testing that first chute. He does not hope it will fail and he will fall down to his death. On the contrary, he is hoping that the chute will pass the test and be approved.

Are You "Approved In Christ"?

Apelles is a man *"approved in Christ."* In other words, when the Lord Jesus Christ sits at the Judgment Seat of Christ, the believers who have been judged are going to be *"approved"* at that time. *"Approved"* because they have been tried by the Lord and those things that are bad will be taken away and not judged at all.

Romans 16:11

"Salute Herodion my kinsman. Greet them that be of the *household* of Narcissus, which are in the Lord." Paul greets Herodion and all those in the *"household of Narcissus, which are in the Lord."* The term *"in the Lord"* is used for those who are born-again. Paul called some of these believers *"helpers"* and some *"approved."* He said that some were *"in Christ before him,"* and some were just *"in the Lord,"* but they are all saved people.

Romans 16:12

"Salute Tryphena and Tryphosa, who labour in the Lord. Salute the beloved Persis, which laboured much in the Lord." Here is a team of women. I remember an incident while I was a Naval Chaplain attached to the Marine Corps in Okinawa. In our battalion we had both a commanding officer and an executive officer. There was a master sergeant in the battalion who was a Christian. For various reasons, he would refer to both these officers as Tryphena and Tryphosa. That was not very respectful, but sometimes they more as women than as men.

The Meaning of "Labour"

These two women *"laboured much in the Lord."* They did not just labor for themselves. The Greek word here for *"labour"* is KOPIAO. It means:

"to grow weary, tired, exhausted (with toil or burdens or grief); to labour with wearisome effort, to toil; of bodily labour."

This is a strong word which indicates *"wearisome"* labor. They were tired when they finished working. Paul mentioned another who also *"laboured much in the Lord."* His name was Persis. As before, this word for *"labour"* is also KOPIAO. It indicates hard work. Here are people who were not afraid of strenuous labor. There are people who labor a little and people who labor much. These were laboring to wearisome toil. Paul was also one who labored. I am sure when he got through with his first missionary journey he was exhausted, wearied, and bone-tired. After the second missionary journey, I am sure he was weary also. After the third missionary journey, Paul was even more tired. He went all over the then-known world with the gospel message. Eventually he went to Rome as a prisoner, which was like a fourth missionary journey, because he preached Christ all the way along. I am sure he was extremely tired because he, like these people, had much *"labor"* for the Lord.

Romans 16:13

"Salute Rufus chosen in the Lord, and his mother and mine." Rufus was *"chosen in the Lord."* This term *"chosen"* is used in various ways in the New Testament.

- **John 15:16**

  Ye have not chosen me, but I have chosen you, and ordained you, that ye should go and bring forth fruit, and *that* your fruit should remain: that whatsoever ye shall ask of the Father in my name, he may give it you.

We Choose Each Other

If we are born-again, we choose Him, but He also chose us. He loved us before we ever knew about Him. When we trust the Lord Jesus Christ, we become one of His *"chosen in the Lord."* *"We love Him, because He first loved us"* (1 John 4:19)

The believers at Rome were also to *"salute"* or greet the mother of Rufus as well. She is called *"his mother and mine."* She was probably not Paul's literal mother, but she was like his mother. She took care of him apparently. I am reminded of Jesus' words on the cross concerning His mother. He had a conversation with Mary and John the apostle. *"When Jesus therefore saw his mother, and the disciple standing by, whom he loved, he saith unto his mother, Woman, behold thy son!"* (John 19:26). He said to John about His mother Mary, *"Behold thy mother."* The Lord Jesus Christ was dying, would be buried, would rise again from the dead, and would go back to Heaven. He would not be physically on this earth anymore at that time. He told the Apostle John to take care of Mary. She would be just like his mother. He told Mary to take care of the Apostle John just like he would take care of her. The Apostle John was the *"one whom Jesus loved"* (John 13:23; 20:2; 21:7, 20). He was the one who walked close to the Lord. The Lord Jesus Christ had loved him and he was close to him at the last supper. He leaned on Jesus' breast at the last supper (John 21:20). He was one of two who went in to the final trial of the Lord Jesus Christ (John 18:15). Peter and John were there and then Peter left at the trial. Peter denied the Lord three times. John was the only Apostle of the twelve who was at the cross of Calvary.

Romans 16:14

"Salute Asyncritus, Phlegon, Hermas, Patrobas, Hermes, and the brethren which are with them." Paul names five more of the *"brethren"* that he wants the believers at Rome to greet. Though he names these five men, he does not tell us anything about them. You have seen in these first fourteen verses of this chapter many of Paul's friends that he knew and called by name. He commended them and encouraged the Christians at Rome to love them, to use them, and to have them as their helpers. They were helpers of Paul. Though there is no doctrine involved, I believe that these fourteen verses teach us that the apostle Paul remembered people by name. He was a people-person, as we say. Some people say about the pastoral ministry that it would be a wonderful ministry if you didn't have any people to put up with. Of course, that would be impossible. Some say this about the teaching profession. It would be a wonderful profession if you did not have to deal with any students. They are the ones who give you trouble. Obviously, you have to have students in order to be a teacher, and you have to have people in order to be a pastor of a church.

Paul was a man who did not shirk his duty of praising people for the right things. He did not try to butter them up to get something from them or to take advantage of them. He was a grateful missionary. We ought to be grateful also for those fellow believers in our own church. We can pray for them by name and be thankful for all their help. The Lord Jesus Christ knows everyone of the names of those He has redeemed. *"He calleth His own sheep by name, and leadeth them out"* (John 10:3b).

Romans 16:15

"Salute Philologus, and Julia, Nereus, and his sister, and Olympas, and all the saints which are with them." Here are more greetings for four other people. *"Philologus"* means *"lover of the Word."* Julia is probably the wife of Philologus. Nereus' sister is not named, but Paul wants to greet her also. Paul greeted different people from different times and different places. Paul knows these people well and wants them to understand. He names these people and is grateful for them. Paul also mentions *"the saints which are with them,"* not just these four that are mentioned. These are saints, set apart ones, saved ones, who Paul is also greeting in Rome.

Romans 16:16

"Salute one another with an holy kiss. The churches of Christ salute you." This *"holy kiss"* was the way that Christians greeted one another when they met each other and when they said goodbye. This *"holy kiss"* was usually on the cheek, men with men and women with women. We have some churches today that still practice that custom. It is a little difficult in the day in which we live to have it a really *"holy"* type of *"kiss."* If not *"holy"* it could lead to sin. Many churches have taken this expression in a different way.

That Greek word for *"kiss"* is PHILEMA. It means:

"a kiss; the kiss with which, as a sign of fraternal affection, Christians were accustomed to welcome or dismiss their companions in the faith."

The ending EMA on PHILEMA is a suffix that means *"the result of something."* PHILOS is the word *"love"* and EMA is *"the result of love."* So, we should greet one another *"with the result of love and affection."* A warm handshake and/or a kind and cordial greeting with our words would qualify as a *"result of our love one for another"* so that there is Christian warmth. Some people seem to have greetings to each other which might sound warm, but the heart is cold. That is not the way either. You should have a holy greeting accompanied by warmth and sincerity.

Paul Founded Many Churches

When Paul wrote *"the churches of Christ salute you,"* he was referring to the various churches that had been founded up until that time. He was writing from Corinth, a main city of Southern Greece, and he was saying that all the saints in the churches of that area saluted them. Paul founded most of those churches. He was a missionary.

Romans 16:17

"Now I beseech you, brethren, mark them which cause divisions and offences contrary to the doctrine which ye have learned; and avoid them." Here in the midst of personal greetings, Paul puts in a very important verse that contains some vital doctrine. He uses the phrase "*I beseech you*" the same as he did in Chapter 12.

•Romans 12:1

> **I beseech you therefore, brethren,** by the mercies of God, that ye present your bodies a living sacrifice, holy, acceptable unto God, *which is* your reasonable service.

The Greek word for "*beseech*" is PARAKALEO. It means:

> "*to call to one's side, call for, summon; to address, speak to, (call to, call upon), which may be done in the way of exhortation, entreaty, comfort, instruction, etc.; to admonish, exhort; to beg, entreat, beseech; to strive to appease by entreaty; to console, to encourage and strengthen by consolation, to comfort; to receive consolation, be comforted; to encourage, strengthen; exhorting and comforting and encouraging; to instruct, teach.*"

What is Paul urging them to do? The first thing Paul wanted these born-again believers to do is to "*mark*" certain people. The Greek word for "*mark*" is SKOPEO. It means:

> "*to look at, observe, contemplate; to mark; to fix one's eyes upon, <u>direct one's attention to, any one</u>; to look to, take heed to thyself.*"

Continue To Mark False Teachers

The Greek word for "*mark*" is in the imperative mood. As such it is a command for Christians to obey without question. The verb is also in the present tense. This Greek form shows that this "*marking*" should be a continuous action. They were to continue to "*mark them who cause divisions and offenses contrary to the doctrine which ye have learned.*" This is an important action that must be taken toward the ones included by Paul in this verse. This is a verse on what is called the doctrine of biblical separation.

- **Genesis 13:11**

  Then Lot chose him all the plain of Jordan; and Lot journeyed east: and **they separated themselves the one from the other**.

  The concept of separation began very early in the Bible. Lot and Abraham raised cattle. Since there was not enough room for all the cattle, Abraham gave Lot his choice. Lot pitched his tent toward Sodom. The reason they separated was because there was a division and fighting among their herdsmen (Genesis 13:7). Sometimes separation is necessary.

- **2 Corinthians 6:17**

  Wherefore come out from among them, and **be ye separate**, saith the Lord, and touch not the unclean *thing*; and I will receive you,

  This is what God wants us to do.

- **Hebrews 7:26**

  For such an high priest became us, *who is* holy, harmless, undefiled, **separate from sinners**, and made higher than the heavens;

  The Lord Jesus Christ was separate from sinners. He was not mixed in with the sins of sinners, and we have to be separate from sinners as well. What about separation from disorderly believers?

- **2 Thessalonians 3:6**

  Now we command you, brethren, in the name of our Lord Jesus Christ, that ye **withdraw yourselves** from every brother that walketh disorderly, and not after the tradition which he received of us.

Withdrawing From Fellow-Believers

There are times when we must withdraw from fellow-believers and Christians who are walking in an ungodly fashion. We should separate from them lest we be polluted with what they are doing.

- **1 Corinthians 5:11**

  But now **I have written unto you not to keep company,** if any man that is called a brother be a fornicator, or covetous, or an idolater, or a railer, or a drunkard, or an extortioner; with such an one no not to eat.

Now, if a person is unsaved we would have to go out of the world for us not to encounter one of those people because there are all sorts of fornicators and idolaters and everything else of those who are unsaved. The point of this verse is that if a Christian "*brother*" or sister (by implication) is any of these things, other Christians should separate from them.

- **Ephesians 5:11**

  And **have no fellowship with the unfruitful works of darkness,** but rather reprove *them.*

This is a very clear standard that God has about separating from all "*unfruitful works of darkness.*" Not only is separation required, but also "*reproof*" of such "*works of darkness.*"

Mark and Avoid False Teachers

What are obedient believers to do according to this 17th verse in Romans 16? We are to "*mark,*" that is, "*fix our eyes upon these people and direct our attention to*" any one who "*cause divisions and offences contrary to the doctrine which ye have learned.*" These who cause such "*divisions*" are not by any means limited to Roman Catholics, apostate modernist Protestant liberals, or new evangelical compromisers. Some of them go under the name of Fundamentalist yet they fall under this category, sad to say, in one or more of their activities. When we find such people, the second thing Paul ordered the believers at Rome to do was to "*avoid them.*"

The Greek word for "*avoid*" is EKKLINO. It means:

"*to turn aside, deviate (from the right way and course); to turn (one's self) away,* **to turn away from**, *keep aloof from one's society;* **to shun one**."

This is a clear imperative command that should not be disobeyed.

What are some of such people who "*cause divisions and offences contrary to the doctrine which ye have learned"*? John MacArthur comes to mind right away. He has caused *"divisions and offences contrary to the doctrine."* The Biblical doctrine of *"the blood of Christ"* is that blood is said to perform at least fourteen different things (Cf. **BFT #2185** *John MacArthur's Heresy on the Blood of Christ*). MacArthur, on the other hand, teaches that *"blood"* does not mean literal *"blood"* but is a metonym or figure of speech for *"death."* Though he claims to have changed his position on this (but I am not certain that he really has), he formerly denied the eternal Sonship of Christ. He denied that the Lord Jesus Christ was the eternal Son of God. He believed that Christ just became a Son upon His birth. He also denies the two natures of the believer. He does not think that saved people have two natures, the flesh and the spirit. He believes that they have only one nature.

He believes in what I would call salvation by works. It is a form of what is called *"Lordship Salvation."*

Mark and Avoid John MacArthur

I believe that after salvation the Lord Jesus Christ should be made Lord of our lives. If a person tries to make Jesus Lord of thought, word, and deed before being redeemed and saved, this is first impossible, and second this is an attempt to gain salvation by human works. This is what MacArthur believes and teaches. How can a Hell-bound sinner be perfect? You have to be saved first and then you can make Christ Lord of your life. John MacArthur should be both *"marked"* and *"avoided"* for these *"contrary doctrines."*

Another division and offence which is contrary to doctrine clearly taught in the Bible is that taught by at least four leading Fundamentalist schools: (1) Bob Jones University; (2) Detroit Baptist Seminary; (3) Central Baptist Seminary; and (4) Calvary Baptist Seminary. Though the Bible clearly teaches that God has promised to preserve His Hebrew, Aramaic, and Greek Words, they deny it. The claim that there is only a promise of the *"Word"* of God, but not the *"Words"* of God. By *"Word of God"* they mean only concepts, message, ideas, teachings, or truth, but not *"Words."* Because of this major false doctrine, we ought to *"mark"* and *"avoid"* these schools and others who follow them as well.

The list could go on and on. It would include Billy and Franklin Graham with their ecumenical evangelism. It would include the *Promise Keepers*, and many other people and movements. There are so many that we are to "*mark*."

The preacher who is faithful unto the Lord will obey this verse. Paul says, continue to "*mark*" such people and movements.

Marked and Avoided People

Someone who is doctrinally off is causing division. Anybody who is not lined up with the Word of God as it ought to be is causing division and should be both "*marked*" and "*avoided*."

This verse is speaking of things that are "*contrary to the doctrine which ye have learned*." The "*doctrine*" must be that which is clearly taught in the Bible. If it is not in the Bible we ought not to follow it, but if it is in the Bible we ought to follow it. We ought to follow the Bible's doctrines. We must be aware that there are others leading us astray from the Bible doctrine and causing division. God says of those people, faithful Christians are to mark them, look at them, observe them, fix your eyes upon them, put an "X" on them, and draw people's attention to them.

Whom Should We "Avoid"?

The second imperative and command to believers is to "*avoid*" such people. We must separate from them. In other words, we must not have fellowship with those who are contrary to the Bible's doctrine. We believe there are false teachers that are very false teachers all over this world. There are Jehovah Witnesses, Christian Science people, Roman Catholicism, and all the other cults and false religions of the world. We must "*mark*" them and "*avoid*" them. These are some of the ones that are not in accordance with true Biblical doctrine. We can say hello to them, and be friendly to them, but we must not have close fellowship with them, and we must obey this verse.

Romans 16:18

"For they that are such serve not our Lord Jesus Christ, but their own belly; and by good words and fair speeches deceive the hearts of the simple." These who fail to follow the teachings of the Bible are actually *"causing divisions and offences contrary to the doctrine"* of the Bible. Paul says in this verse that they *"serve not our Lord Jesus Christ."* The Greek word for *"serve"* is DOULEUO. It means:

"to be a slave, serve, do service; of a nation in subjection to other nations; metaph. to obey, submit to; in a good sense, to yield obedience; in a bad sense, of those who become slaves to some base power, to yield to, give one's self up to."

These false teachers do not *"serve"* the Lord Jesus Christ but *"their own belly."* These people that are *"causing divisions contrary to the doctrine"* are not serving as slaves to the Lord Jesus Christ. They are not doing His will and His will alone.

What do they do? They *"serve their own belly."* I suppose they like to eat. I suppose that is part of it. Those who like to eat a lot must have money to eat. Maybe they get the money by having the false doctrine and teachings. They are servants of their own affections and their own desires. Whatever feels good to them is what they are doing. These false teachers are contrary to the doctrine of the Lord Jesus Christ.

Notice what else they do: *"by good words and fair speeches deceive the hearts of the simple."* The deception is a very clever deception.

False Teachers Pollute Believers

False teachers are always seeking after Bible-believing Christians to pollute them with their false doctrines. False teachers very seldom go after the non-believers. Many times the false teachers get the Bible-believing Christians who are not grounded and lead them astray. They deceive their *"hearts."*

When the heart is deceived, it is very hard for the brain to get straightened out. If your heart is falling head-over-heels in love with false teachings, or false doctrines, or false people, it is a very difficult thing to overcome. Notice how the "*hearts*" are deceived. It is "*by good words and fair speeches*." It sounds wonderful and very nice. They deceive the hearts of the simple.

That Greek word for "*simple*" is AKAKOS. It means:

"*without guile or fraud, harmless, free from guilt; fearing no evil from others, distrusting no one.*"

If we are simple in the sense of "*distrusting no one*," we better change our hearts and our minds. Should we not distrust the Devil? Yes, we should. Should we not distrust false teachers? Yes, we should. Should we not distrust any evil thing that comes down the line? Yes, we should. If we are simple, we just accept everything just like a little baby. A little baby cannot tell whether a person is going to kill him, or love him, or hold him, or feed him, or anything else. Little babies are easily led. Pretty soon they begin to know who is helping them and who is hurting them. If we "*distrust no one*," and have no bars or gates against evil, we may be sucked into evil and false doctrine, and swept into all sorts of false teaching.

Romans 16:19

"For your obedience is come abroad unto all *men*. I am glad therefore on your behalf: but yet I would have you wise unto that which is good, and simple concerning evil."
Despite the false teachers pushing at the believers in Rome, Paul commended them. He said, "*your obedience is come abroad unto all men.*" Would it not be wonderful if people could say that this church or this individual in the church is obedient to the Word of God, and that this obedience has traveled all around?

The Need for Obedience

Everyone said of the church in Rome that there were obedient people who obeyed the Word of God. They obeyed the Lord Jesus Christ. They served Him, and not themselves. We do not know how large the church was. It was probably small and met in a home, but their "*obedience*" was spread abroad unto that whole area.

Paul was "*glad*" about this, but he gave them something to be cautious about. He said, "*I would have you wise unto that which is good, and simple concerning evil.*" He wanted them "*wise*" unto the "*good*" and "*simple*" about "*evil.*" He wanted them to know the difference between these two opposites.

There was a similar situation with Adam and Eve in the Garden of Eden. In the garden there was the Tree of the Knowledge of Good and Evil. Adam did not know what good and evil was until he partook of the fruit of that tree. God told them they should not eat of this tree (Genesis 2:17). If they ate of that tree, they would "*surely die*" (Genesis 2:17). Eve was subtly tempted with good words and "*fair speeches*" by the Devil. That is the same type of thing that deceived the hearts of the people there in Rome. Eve was gullible. She took that fruit, ate it, and gave it to Adam. He ate it also (Genesis 3:6). Eve was deceived (1 Timothy 2:14). They did not know evil until they disobeyed God. As soon as they disobeyed God they knew what good and evil was. Good was obeying God and not eating the fruit of the tree, and evil was disobeying God and eating of that tree.

Paul was glad and wants them to be wise about things that are "*good*" and yet be "*simple*" about things that are "*evil.*" The Greek word for "*simple*" here is different from the former word. It is AKERAIOS. It means:

"*unmixed, pure as in wines or metals; of the mind, without a mixture of evil, free from guile, innocent, simple.*"

Do Not Mix With Any Evil

God does not want His born-again Christians to have any mixture of any kind with evil. He wants them to stay away from all kinds of evil and be separated from these evils at all times. This is what God would have us to do.

Romans 16:20

"And the God of peace shall bruise Satan under your feet shortly. The grace of our Lord Jesus Christ *be* with you. Amen." Five times in the New Testament the Lord is called, "*the God of peace.*" The other four places are:

> **Romans 15:33,**
> **Philippians 4:9,**
> **1 Thessalonians 5:23, and**
> **Hebrews 13:20.**

He is a great *"God of Peace."* He can bring peace to the troubled soul. *"The wicked are like the troubled sea, when it cannot rest, whose waters cast up mire and dirt. There is no peace, saith my God, to the wicked"* (Isaiah 57:20-21). The wicked are like those waves that keep going and going on the ocean. When you get out on a small lake, sometimes it is absolutely flat and peaceful. Have you ever seen the ocean flat? Sometimes it has fewer waves, but they just keep coming and coming. There is no rest. Many of the waves are very high and that is how the wicked are. To those who have trusted the Lord Jesus Christ as Redeemer and Saviour, He has said to us, *"Come unto me, all ye that labour and are heavy laden, and I will give you rest"* (Matthew 11:28-29).

Part of His rest is His peace. *"Therefore being justified by faith, we have peace with God through our Lord Jesus Christ"* (Romans 5:1). He is the *"God of peace." "Peace"* has been defined as:

"of Christianity, the tranquil state of a soul assured of its salvation through Christ, and so fearing nothing from God and content with its earthly lot, of whatsoever sort that is."

This *"peace"* comes from the *"God of peace."*

Satan Is Very Active

Then Paul promises the Christians at Rome and says that this *"God of peace shall bruise Satan under your feet shortly."* Apparently Satan was very active in Rome at the time Paul was writing this letter. He is active in Rome today, as we know, with the Vatican and all of the Roman Catholic Churches spread out and built up there. Satan is very active in all of these areas. Paul promised that Satan would be *"bruised"* under their feet shortly.

The Greek word for *"bruise"* is SYNTRIBO. It means:

"break, to break in pieces, shiver; to tread down; to put Satan under foot and (as a conqueror) trample on him; to break down, crush; to tear one's body and shatter one's strength."

That would be the effect when the Lord Jesus Christ would *"bruise"* Satan at Rome then or anywhere now or in the future.

The Meaning of God's Grace

Paul closes this verse with a benediction. *"The grace of our Lord Jesus Christ be with you. Amen."* Every born-again Christian needs God the Father's grace and also the grace of our Lord Jesus Christ. Grace has been defined as *"getting something we do not deserve."* God's *"grace"* is also that which affords joy, pleasure, delight, sweetness, and loveliness. God's grace should attend all true believers in our Saviour.

Romans 16:21

"Timotheus my workfellow, and Lucius, and Jason, and Sosipater, my kinsmen, salute you." Paul lists four people who are with him at Corinth who greet the Christians at Rome. They were probably Jews like Paul was. Timothy was Paul's *"workfellow."* Timothy worked closely with Paul. Timothy's father was a Greek and his mother was a Jew. He was saved by God's grace through personal faith in the Saviour. Timothy was a great friend of Paul. When they needed a church at Ephesus, Paul sent Timothy to do that work and to be the pastor of that church. Ephesus is one of the seven churches mentioned in Revelation 2 and 3. Paul sent Timothy from Corinth to be the pastor of Ephesus. Paul gave direction to Timothy in 1 Timothy and in 2 Timothy as to how to be a good pastor. So, Timothy was a strong and valuable helper of Paul. Paul led Timothy to Christ (1 Timothy 1:18) and he accompanied Paul on one of his several missionary journeys.

Not too much is known for the other three men mentioned in this verse, Lucius, Jason, and Sosipater. Lucius was one of the prophets at Antioch (Acts 13:1). Jason's name is mentioned in four verses of Acts 17 (verses 5, 6, 7, and 9). Sosipater is mentioned only here.

Romans 16:22

"I Tertius, who wrote *this* epistle, salute you in the Lord." I believe the Lord Jesus Christ told the Holy Spirit what to communicate to the human writer. Then Paul, the writer, told Tertius what to write. Tertius apparently was Paul's secretary for this letter. In this sense only, Tertius *"wrote this epistle."* Paul dictated this letter and Tertius copied it down as Paul gave it to him. They did not have typewriters, computers, or fax machines.

Paul's eyes were perhaps weak. He spoke of *"how large a letter"* (Galatians 6:11) he had written. He probably wrote in large letters because it was easier for him to read what he had written. If you cannot see too well and you want to be sure you have spelled everything right you might write in big letters. Because it is believed Paul had eye problems, this might be the reason he asked Tertius to write the letter for him.

Romans 16:23

"Gaius mine host, and of the whole church, saluteth you. Erastus the chamberlain of the city saluteth you, and Quartus a brother." Here are three other men of the seven from Corinth that are greeting the Christians at Rome. Gaius was Paul's *"host."* A *"host"* is a person that entertains somebody, giving them hospitality. Gaius was hospitable to Paul. Paul did not have any home when he went to different cities. He stayed with various people. They did not have any motels or hotels. At this time he stayed with Gaius.

Then he says the *"whole church"* brings greetings to the believers at Rome as well. This is probably a reference to the church at Corinth where Paul was when he wrote this letter. Paul mentions Erastus also. He was the *"chamberlain of the city."* The Greek word for *"chamberlain"* is OIKONOMOS. It is like the word *"dispensation."* OIKOS is *"house"* and NOMOS is *"law."* Literally it is *"the law of the house."* It has various meanings:

> *"the manager of household or of household affairs; esp. a steward, manager, superintendent (whether free-born or as was usually the case, a freed-man or a slave) to whom the head of the house or proprietor has intrusted the management of his affairs, the care of receipts and expenditures, and the duty of dealing out the proper portion to every servant and even to the children not yet of age; the manager of a farm or landed estate, an overseer; the superintendent of the city's finances, the treasurer of a city (or of treasurers or quaestors of kings); metaph. the apostles and other Christian teachers and bishops and overseers."*

A chamberlain of the city was a manager of the whole city. He was the treasurer of the entire city. It was good that he knew the Lord Jesus Christ as his Saviour. This is not true of all city treasurers.

Because *"the love of money is the root of all evil"* (1 Timothy 6:10), sometimes this *"love"* takes hold of people. The Apostle Judas was a treasurer. He had the money-bag and carried what was put in that (John 12:6). I think he coveted that silver. When Judas sold out the Lord Jesus Christ, he received thirty pieces of silver to do it. As a treasurer he was conscious of money and what it could buy. What a way to treat the Lord Jesus Christ Who had never done anything to Judas. It was of the devil to do this deed because at this time the devil put this betrayal into his heart (John 13:2). In our 𝕭𝖎𝖇𝖑𝖊 𝕱𝖔𝖗 𝕿𝖔𝖉𝖆𝖞 𝕭𝖆𝖕𝖙𝖎𝖘𝖙 𝕮𝖍𝖚𝖗𝖈𝖍, we make a financial report each quarter and distribute it to our people so there is no question as to our income and expenditures.

I remember the first church where I was pastor when I left the Naval Chaplain Corp after five years of active duty in the Chaplain corps. I went to a church that had about three hundred fifty members. The treasurer before I came had been charged and was found guilty of theft. I do not know how many thousands of dollars he had stolen from that church, but he knew how to do it and that is what he did. When I became Pastor of that church, one of the things that I insisted on was to have at least two men count the money, put the money into a bag with a lock, and deposit it into the bank that very Sunday morning or evening. We did not let the money sit around. That is just the way we did it so that there could be nobody who could possibly be charged again with stealing the church's money. I know churches are different. Sometimes churches put money in a safe at the church for the morning service and then after the evening service they take it to the bank. But what if someone would break into that church and steal all the money from the morning service?

In addition to others who greeted the believers at Rome was Quartus who was a "*brother*" in Christ.

Romans 16:24

"The grace of our Lord Jesus Christ *be* with you all. Amen." Think about what "*the grace of our Lord Jesus Christ*" means. Do you know "*the grace of our Lord Jesus Christ*"? One of the clearest definitions for our Saviour's "*grace*" is found in 2 Corinthians 8:9:

> "*For ye know the grace of our Lord Jesus Christ, that, though he was rich, yet for your sakes he became poor, that ye through his poverty might be rich.*"

The Lord Jesus Christ was "*rich*" in Heaven, yet He left Heaven's glory and came down to this earth to suffer for my sins, your sins, and the sins of the entire world. He was a gracious Saviour. He was gracious to those who hated Him. He was gracious to those who loved Him. He healed the blind. He cleansed the lepers. He raised the dead. He was a Man of grace, perfect Man and perfect God. He was gracious even to those who crucified Him. "*Then said Jesus, Father, forgive them; for they know not what they do.*" (Luke 23:34).

May Christ's Grace Be Seen in You

When Paul said, *"The grace of our Lord Jesus Christ be with you all,"* he is hoping that His grace will be with them and that they will represent that grace wherever they might be. May our Saviour's grace be upon you who are born-again. May people see that you are blessed of the Lord, and that you have the grace of Christ in your countenance, in your attitudes, and may He be with you all in genuine spiritual power.

You cannot have the grace of the Lord Jesus Christ with you unless you first are one of His. First you have to be saved. After that you can have His grace and the fruit of the Spirit of God upon your life.

Romans 16:25

"Now to him that is of power to stablish you according to my gospel, and the preaching of Jesus Christ, according to the revelation of the mystery, which was kept secret since the world began." Paul's benediction begins by speaking about the character of God. He has the *"power to stablish you."* God wants His dear children to be stablished.

The word *"stablish"* is shortened from *"establish."* The Greek word for this is STEIRIZO. It means:

"to make stable, place firmly, set fast, fix; to strengthen, make firm; to render constant, confirm, one's mind."

God wants His own to be stable, made firm, and constant. He does not want us to be knocked over or pushed around. We often sing the gospel song, "Constantly Abiding." It is a continuing thing. God's power is able to establish us and make us firm.

You may have been a genuine Christian for five years, eight years, ten years, twenty years, or whatever it might be. Are you stablished yet? Are you still loose and on sifting sand? Some people have been Christians for years, but there is no establishment. God has the *"power to stablish"* us. He can make us fixed in our beliefs and doctrines. We do not have to change our doctrines every time some new voice comes along and preaches something else that we do not find in our Bibles. We do not have to accept it. We can tell such people that we believe in the Bible's teachings and are going to stick with the Words of God. You can tell them that you read your Bible, you know your Bible, and God has established you in the Scripture.

Things On Which To Be Established

Here are some of the things every well-taught Christian should be "*established*" on:

He or she should

(1) be a separatist both in personal and ecclesiastical areas.

(2) believe in a pre-tribulation rapture of the saved.

(3) believe in the 1,000 year millennial reign of Christ.

(4) believe in traditional music and oppose Contemporary Christian Music (CCM).

(5) oppose the New Evangelicalism compromise such as that of Evangelist Billy Graham.

(6) oppose the Charismatic movement and speaking in tongues.

(7) appreciate a Bible teacher who preaches the Bible verse by verse.

(8) use and defend the King James Bible.

(9) use and defend the Hebrew, Aramaic, and Greek Words underlying the King James Bible.

(10) oppose hyper-Calvinism.

(11) believe in the preservation of the original Hebrew, Aramaic, and Greek Words underlying the King James Bible

(12) believe in the Dispensationalism approach to the Bible.

(13) read the Bible daily (if possible 85 verses per day to finish the Bible in one year) each year of his Christian life.

(14) oppose the modern Bible versions in English and other languages as well.

(15) oppose the modern-style worship-leader type church services.

(16) oppose the Rick Warren type purpose-driven programs.

All the things that should be "*established*" must be in accordance to three things: (1) according to Paul's "*gospel,*" (2) according to the "*preaching of Jesus Christ,*" and (3) according to the "*revelation of the mystery, which was kept secret since the world began.*"

The preaching according to the "*mystery*" refers to the prophecy concerning Him as revealed in the prophets of the Old Testament. 1 Peter 1:11 speaks about how the prophets spoke of "*the sufferings of Christ and the glory that should be revealed.*" They did not know exactly what was meant, but they wrote about it as the Lord told them. The book of Isaiah was written. The book of Jeremiah was written. The book of Daniel was written. None of these prophets understood the details, but they wrote down what the Lord revealed to them. We can understand it looking back at it. They were prophets who wrote concerning the Lord Jesus Christ. They wrote about His sufferings first of all, and then the glory that should follow.

This "*revelation*" concerning the fullness of the gospel of Christ and all that is involved in it was "*kept secret since the world began.*" The Lord Jesus Christ was to come as a perfect Man, yet perfect God. He would take upon Himself the sins of the world. This was a sacred secret or a "*mystery,*" the details of which were "*kept secret since the world began.*" It says in the book of Galatians that God "*preached before the gospel*" unto Abraham (Galatians 3:8). It says those very words. So apparently God revealed to Abraham at least part of this "*mystery*" concerning our Saviour.

I think I know how Abraham got the gospel preached to him. Abraham was told by God to take his son up to land of Moriah and offer him as a sacrifice (Genesis 22:2). Abraham went up and raised his hand with the knife to slay Isaac. His son was on the altar and God's voice from Heaven said, "*Lay not thine hand upon the lad, neither do thou any thing unto him: for now I know that thou fearest God, seeing thou hast not withheld thy son, thine only son from me*" (Genesis 22:12). He found a ram caught in the thicket and he offered the ram instead of his son (Genesis 22:13). The whole gospel picture was there.

Isaac--Not Offered, Yet Offered

In the book of Hebrews it says that Abraham "*offered up Isaac*" (Hebrews 11:17). Did he offer Isaac? He just had the knife up ready to offer him. As far as God was concerned it was a *fait accompli* as the French would say. It was an accomplished fact. It was as good as done. His faith made him obey the Lord's command.

God told Abraham that he would have sons. He would have children as many as the sands of the sea and of the stars in the Heaven. God promised Abraham that and Abraham believed God. If need be, God would have raised up Isaac from the dead to fulfill that promise. In fact, Paul wrote in Hebrews:

Isaac--Back From the Dead

- Hebrews 11:19

Accounting that God *was* able to raise *him* up, even from the dead; from whence also he received him in a figure.

He believed so firmly that God would fulfill His promise to give Abraham all the seed and all the children throughout the years to come that, even if he did slay him, God would raise him up. Abraham even believed in the resurrection of his son, Isaac, and of God's Son as well.

Romans 16:26

"But now is made manifest, and by the scriptures of the prophets, according to the commandment of the everlasting God, made known to all nations for the obedience of faith:" This *"mystery"* or *"sacred secret"* as some have termed it *"now is made manifest."* It was hidden during the Old Testament period, but now is made manifest. This refers to what the Lord Jesus Christ has done in His sacrificial death, burial, and resurrection. All of this has been made clear in the New Testament *"Scriptures of the prophets."* This probably refers to both the Old Testament prophets in seed form and the New Testament prophets who made things clear for all to see and to understand.

This has all been done *"according to the commandment of the everlasting God."* It was His command and will that the gospel of salvation by genuine faith in His Son should be made manifest. This manifestation was to be *"made known to all nations for the obedience of faith."*

The Lord wants the gospel of His Son to go out to all nations. Remember what the Lord Jesus said before he went up into glory? *"Go ye into all the world, and preach the gospel to every creature"* (Mark 16:15). That is our mission. This gospel is to be *"made known to all nations."* The *"gospel of Christ"* is the *"power of God unto salvation to everyone that believeth"* (Romans 1:16). We must proclaim this gospel of our Saviour.

On the John Ankerberg telecast about the Bible-version issue some time ago, one of his guests was Samuel Gipp. Samuel Gipp is a follower of Peter Ruckman and follows many of Ruckman's errors regarding the King James Bible. One of the men of the six who favor the false Westcott and Hort Greek text and the modern versions asked him a question. He asked what a Russian had to do to know about the Bible. Samuel Gipp, contrary to the will and Word of God, said this Russian would have to learn English. He said that the Russian would have to read the King James Bible in order to know what God said. That is false. Samuel Gipp was saying that the English language and the English King James Bible was the only Bible that should be in existence today. He said we had the Greek of the New Testament, the Hebrew for the Old Testament, and now we have the English. He did not believe that we should take the Word of God and translate it into Russian, Chinese, Japanese, Spanish, and all the other languages of the world. I believe that Gipp's position is unscriptural. I wrote against this position in my book called, *Foes of the King James Bible Refuted.* The book is an answer to the John Ankerberg telecast. It is **BFT #2777** and is available for a gift of **$9.00 + $4 S&H**.

In this verse God says that this gospel is to be *"made known to all nations for the obedience of faith."* All nations cannot possibly learn English in order for them to know the Bible. They must have the Bible accurately translated into their heart language, whatever that might be. That is why we must translate the Words of God into all the languages of the world. To do this we must use the proper Hebrew and Aramaic Words and the proper Greek Words which underlie our King James Bible. We have to have translators who know what they are doing. We have to use the proper translation technique. The Words have to be translated and not just the thoughts and the ideas. The theology must be proper. By all means let all the nations know the fullness and accuracy of what we know in our King James Bible.

Notice the purpose of making the gospel known to all nations. It is not to be *"made known to all nations"* for intellectualism. It is *"for the obedience of faith."* God wants *"all nations"* in the world genuinely to obey the faith of our Lord Jesus Christ. He wants us to obey the faith of our Lord Jesus Christ. It is not just enough to know what is in the Scriptures. We have to know them and obey them.

Concerning the believers at Rome, Paul says *"your obedience is come abroad unto all men"* (Romans 16:19). This *"obedience"* is to be made known to all nations as well.

Romans 16:27

"To God only wise, *be* glory through Jesus Christ for ever. Amen. People might think they are *"wise"* but certainly such wisdom is so minuscule compared to the wisdom of God.

- **1 Corinthians 1:21**

  For after that in the wisdom of God **the world by wisdom knew not God**, it pleased God by the foolishness of preaching to save them that believe.

If these religious leaders had known the *"wisdom "of God "they would not have crucified the Lord of glory"* (1 Corinthians 2:8). Paul wrote, *"For the preaching of the cross is to them that perish foolishness; but unto us which are saved it is the power of God. . . . Where is the wise? where is the scribe? where is the disputer of this world? hath not God made foolish the wisdom of this world?"* (1 Corinthians 1:18, 20). Since that is the case, God simply decided to do something that men might call *"foolish"* in order to confound the wise. He decided to have the gospel of His Son preached in order for people to be saved by genuine faith in the Lord Jesus Christ.

Salvation by genuine faith in the Lord Jesus Christ sounds foolish to the those who consider themselves to be *"wise"* in this world. That is why many *"wise"* men do not accept Christ as their Saviour. They think it is too simple. The Lord Jesus Christ died for the sins of the world and people must repent and change their minds about their sin and change their mind about the Saviour Who took their sins *"in His own body"* (1 Peter 2:24). That might seem a little foolish to some, but it is wisdom with God. Just because it is simple does that mean God could not have made it more difficult? He is the *"only wise"* God. He has plenty of wisdom, but He puts salvation down so that even a little child can understand it, believe it, and receive it. There are other verses which show how God is wise.

- **1 Timothy 1:17**

  Now unto the King eternal, immortal, invisible, **the only wise God**, *be* honour and glory for ever and ever. Amen.

- **Jude 25**

  To **the only wise God our Saviour**, *be* glory and majesty, dominion and power, both now and ever. Amen.

God Is All-Wise

God is called a "*wise*" God. He is so wise that he could never make a mistake. That is omniscience. God knows all things. He is so loving that He never makes a mistake with His own children.

We must glorify this God "*through Jesus Christ,*" His beloved Son "*for ever.*" I hope you who read this letter will obey Paul's last appeal to magnify God the Father through exalting God the Son.

Our All-Wise God

"Lord, I forego all anxious thought,
And cast on Thee my care;
Content that Thou art over all,
And rulest everywhere.

Teach me to listen for Thy voice
When the storm howleth loud;
Help me to look for light from Thee,
Beneath the darkest cloud.

Thy face I seek with earnest prayer,
For Thou art all my stay,
Now let Thy mighty arm appear
And drive my griefs away."

From Spurgeon's *Morning and Evening Devotions*

Index of Words and Phrases

About the Author

The author of this book, Dr. D. A. Waite, received a B.A. (Bachelor of Arts) in classical Greek and Latin from the University of Michigan in 1948, a Th.M. (Master of Theology), with high honors, in New Testament Greek Literature and Exegesis from Dallas Theological Seminary in 1952, an M.A. (Master of Arts) in Speech from Southern Methodist University in 1953, a Th.D. (Doctor of Theology), with honors, in Bible Exposition from Dallas Theological Seminary in 1955, and a Ph.D. in Speech from Purdue University in 1961. He holds both New Jersey and Pennsylvania teacher certificates in Greek and Language Arts.

He has been a teacher in the areas of Greek, Hebrew, Bible, Speech, and English for over thirty-five years in ten schools, including one junior high, one senior high, three Bible institutes, two colleges, two universities, and one seminary. He served his country as a Navy Chaplain for five years on active duty; pastored two churches; was Chairman and Director of the Radio and Audio-Film Commission of the American Council of Christian Churches; since 1971, has been Founder, President, and Director of THE BIBLE FOR TODAY; since 1978, has been President of the DEAN BURGON SOCIETY; has produced over 700 other studies, books, cassettes, or VCR's on various topics; and is heard on both a five-minute daily and thirty-minute weekly radio program IN DEFENSE OF TRADITIONAL BIBLE TEXTS, on radio, shortwave, and streaming on the Internet at BibleForToday.org, 24/7/365. Dr. and Mrs. Waite have been married since 1948; they have four sons, one daughter, and, at present, eight grandchildren, and two great-grandchildren. Since October 4, 1998, he has been the Pastor of The Bible For Today Baptist Church in Collngswood, New Jersey.

Order Blank (p. 1)

Name:_____

Address:_____

City & State:_____Zip:_____

*Credit Card #:*_____*Expires:*_____

Books by Dr. D. A. Waite

[ ] Send *Romans--Preaching Verse by Verse* by Pastor D. A.
   Waite 736 pp. Hardback ($25+$5 S&H) fully indexed
[ ] Send *Fundamentalist Deception on Bible Preservation* by
   Dr.Waite, ($8+$3 S&H), A hardback book, fully indexed
[ ] Send *Defending the King James Bible* by Dr. Waite ($12+$4
   S&H) A hardback book, indexed with study questions.
[ ] Send *Four Reasons for Defending KJB* by DAW ($3+$3)
[ ] Send *The Case for the King James Bible* by DAW ($7
   +$3 S&H) A perfect bound book, 112 pages in length.
[ ] Send *Foes of the King James Bible Refuted* by DAW ($10
   +$4 S&H) A perfect bound book, 164 pages in length.
[ ] Send *Central Seminary Refuted on Bible Versions* by Dr.
   Waite ($10+$3 S&H) A perfect bound book, 184 pages
[ ] Send *Fuzzy Facts From Fundamentalists* by Dr. D. A.
   Waite ($8.00 + $3.00) printed booklet
[ ] Send *Fundamentalist Distortions on Bible Versions* by Dr.
   Waite ($6+$3 S&H) A perfect bound book, 80 pages
[ ] Send *Fundamentalist MIS-INFORMATION on Bible Ver-
   sions* by Dr. Waite ($7+$3 S&H) perfect bound, 136 pages
[ ] Send *Westcott's Denial of Resurrection*, Dr. Waite ($4+$3)
[ ] Send *26 Hours of KJB Seminar* (4 videos*)* by DAW ($50.00*)*
[ ] Send *Theological Heresies of Westcott and Hort* by Dr. D.
   A. Waite, ($7+$3 S&H) A printed booklet.
[ ] Send *Holes in the Holman Christian Standard Bible* by Dr.
   Waite ($3+$2 S&H) A printed booklet, 40 pages
Send or Call Orders to:
THE BIBLE FOR TODAY
900 Park Ave., Collingswood, NJ 08108
Phone: 856-854-4452; FAX:--2464; Orders: 1-800 JOHN 10:9

Order Blank (p. 2)

Name:_____

Address: _____

City & State:_____Zip:_____

Credit Card #:_____Expires:_____

[ ] Send *Contemporary Eng. Version Exposed*, DAW ($3+$2)

[ ] Send *NIV Inclusive Language Exposed* by DAW ($5+$3)

More Books by Dr. D. A. Waite

[ ] Send *Colossians & Philemon--Preaching Verse by Verse* by Pastor D. A. Waite ($12+$5 S&H) hardback, 240 pages.

[ ] Send *Philippians--Preaching Verse by Verse* by Pastor D. A. Waite ($10+$5 S&H) hardback, 176 pages.

[ ] Send *Making Marriage Melodious* by Pastor D. A. Waite ($7+$3 S&H), perfect bound, 112 pages.

[ ] Send *Ephesians--Preaching Verse by Verse* by Pastor D. A. Waite ($12+$5 S&H) hardback, 224 pages.

[ ] Send *Galatians--Preaching Verse By Verse* by Pastor D. A. Waite ($12+$5 S&H) hardback, 216 pages.

[ ] Send *First Peter--Preaching Verse By Verse* by Pastor D. A. Waite ($10+$5 S&H) hardback, 176 pages.

Books By Dr. Jack Moorman

[ ] *Early Manuscripts, Church Fathers, & the Authorized Version* by Dr. Jack Moorman, $18+$5 S&H. Hardback

[ ] Send *Forever Settled--Bible Documents & History Survey* by Dr. Jack Moorman, $20+$4 S&H. Hardback book.

[ ] Send *When the KJB Departs from the So-Called "Majority Text"* by Dr. Jack Moorman, $16 + $4 S&H

[ ] Send *Missing in Modern Bibles--Nestle-Aland & NIV Errors* by Dr. Jack Moorman, $8 + $4 S&H

[ ] Send *The Doctrinal Heart of the Bible--Removed from Modern Versions* by Dr. Jack Moorman, VCR, $15 +$4 S&H

Send or Call Orders to:

THE BIBLE FOR TODAY

900 Park Ave., Collingswood, NJ 08108

Phone: 856-854-4452; FAX:--2464; Orders: 1-800 JOHN 10:9

Order Blank (p. 3)

Name:_____

Address:_____

City & State:_____Zip:_____

Credit Card #:_____Expires:_____

[ ] Send *Modern Bibles--The Dark Secret* by Dr. Jack Moorman, $5 + $2 S&H

More Books By Dr. Jack Moorman

[ ] Send *Samuel P. Tregelles--The Man Who Made the Critical Text Acceptable to Bible Believers* by Dr. Moorman ($2+$1)

[ ] Send *8,000 Differences Between TR & CT* by Dr. Jack Moorman [$54 + $5 S&H] Over 500 large pages of data

Books By or About Dean Burgon

[ ] Send *The Revision Revised* by Dean Burgon ($25 + $4 S&H) A hardback book, 640 pages in length.

[ ] Send *The Last 12 Verses of Mark* by Dean Burgon ($15+$4 S&H) A hardback book 400 pages.

[ ] Send *The Traditional Text* hardback by Burgon ($16 + $4 S&H) A hardback book, 384 pages in length.

[ ] Send *Causes of Corruption* by Burgon ($15 + $4 S&H) A hardback book, 360 pages in length.

[ ] Send *Inspiration and Interpretation*, Dean Burgon ($25+$4 S&H) A hardback book, 610 pages in length.

[ ] Send *Burgon's Warnings on Revision* by DAW ($7+$3 S&H) A perfect bound book, 120 pages in length.

] Send *Westcott & Hort's Greek Text & Theory Refuted by Burgon's Revision Revised--Summarized* by Dr. D. A. Waite ($7.00 + $3 S&H), 120 pages, perfect bound.

[ ] Send *Dean Burgon's Confidence in KJB* by DAW ($3+$3)

[ ] Send *Vindicating Mark 16:9-20* by Dr. Waite ($3+$3 S&H)

[ ] Send *Summary of Traditional Text* by Dr. Waite ($3 +$2)

Send or Call Orders to:
THE BIBLE FOR TODAY
900 Park Ave., Collingswood, NJ 08108
Phone: 856-854-4452; FAX:--2464; Orders: 1-800 JOHN 10:9

Order Blank (p. 4)

Name:_____

Address:_____

City & State:_____Zip:_____

Credit Card #:_____Expires:_____

[ ] Send *Summary of Causes of Corruption*, DAW ($3+$2)

[ ] Send *Summary of Inspiration* by Dr. Waite ($3 + $2 S&H)

Books by D. A. Waite, Jr.

[ ] Send *Readability of A.V. (KJB)* by D. A. Waite, Jr. ($6+$3)

[ ] Send *4,114 Definitions from the Defined King James Bible*
by D. A. Waite, Jr. ($7.00+$3.00 S&H)

[ ] Send *The Doctored New Testament* by D. A. Waite, Jr.
($25+$4 S&H) Greek MSS differences shown, hardback

[ ] Send *Defined King James Bible* lg. prt. leather ($40+$6)

[ ] Send *Defined King James Bible* med. prt. leather ($35+$5)

Newly Published Book

[ ] Send *The LIE That Changed the Modern World* by Dr.
H. D. Williams ($16+$4 S&H) Hardback book

Miscellaneous Authors

[ ] Send *Guide to Textual Criticism* by Edward Miller ($7+$4)
Hardback book

[ ] Send *Scrivener's Greek New Testament Underlying the King
James Bible*, hardback, ($14+$4 S&H)

[ ] Send *Scrivener's Annotated Greek New Testament*, by Dr.
Frederick Scrivener: Hardback--($35+$5 S&H);
Genuine Leather--($45+$5 S&H)

[ ] Send *Why Not the King James Bible?--An Answer to James
White's KJVO Book* by Dr. K. D. DiVietro, $10+$4 S&H

[ ] Send Brochure #1: "*1000 Titles Defending KJB/TR*"(N.C.)

Send or Call Orders to:

THE BIBLE FOR TODAY

900 Park Ave., Collingswood, NJ 08108

Phone: 856-854-4452; FAX:--2464; Orders: 1-800 JOHN 10:9

E-Mail Orders: BFT@BibleForToday.org; Credit Cards OK

Romans--Preaching Verse by Verse